Christian Prophecy

Christian Prophecy

The Post-Biblical Tradition

NIELS CHRISTIAN HVIDT

OXFORD

UNIVERSITY PRESS

2007

OXFORD
UNIVERSITY PRESS

Oxford University Press, Inc., publishes works that further
Oxford University's objective of excellence
in research, scholarship, and education.

Oxford   New York
Auckland   Cape Town   Dar es Salaam   Hong Kong   Karachi
Kuala Lumpur   Madrid   Melbourne   Mexico City   Nairobi
New Delhi   Shanghai   Taipei   Toronto

With offices in
Argentina   Austria   Brazil   Chile   Czech Republic   France   Greece
Guatemala   Hungary   Italy   Japan   Poland   Portugal   Singapore
South Korea   Switzerland   Thailand   Turkey   Ukraine   Vietnam

Copyright © 2007 by Oxford University Press, Inc.

Published by Oxford University Press, Inc.
198 Madison Avenue, New York, New York 10016

www.oup.com

Oxford is a registered trademark of Oxford University Press

Library of Congress Cataloging-in-Publication Data
Hvidt, Niels Christian.
Christian prophecy : the post-biblical tradition / Niels Christian Hvidt.
    p. cm.
Includes bibliographical references and index.
ISBN 978-0-19-531447-2
1. Prophecy—Christianity.   I. Title.
BR115.P8H85 2007
231.7'45—dc22   2006024866

9 8 7 6 5 4 3 2 1

Printed in the United States of America
on acid-free paper

For Elisabeth

Foreword

What is a prophet? A prophet is not a soothsayer; the essential element of the prophet is not the prediction of future events. The prophet is someone who tells the truth on the strength of his contact with God— the truth for today, which also, naturally, sheds light on the future. It is not a question of foretelling the future in detail, but of rendering the truth of God present at this moment in time and of pointing us in the right direction. As far as Israel is concerned, the word of the prophet has a particular function in that faith is essentially understood as hope in Him who will come: a word of faith is always the realization of the faith, especially in its structure of hope, because it leads hope on and keeps it alive. It is equally important to underline that the prophet is not apocalyptic, though he may seem so. Essentially, he does not describe the ultimate realities but helps us to understand and live the faith as hope.

Even if, at a moment in time, the prophet must proclaim the Word of God as if it were a sharp sword, he is not necessarily criticizing organized worship and institutions. His mandate is to counter misunderstanding and abuse of the Word within the institution by rendering God's vital claim ever present. However, it would be wrong to misconstrue the Old Testament as antagonistic dialectics between the prophets and the Law. Given that both come from God, they both have a prophetic function. This is a very important point in my mind because it leads us into the New Testament. At the end of Deuteronomy, Moses is presented as prophet and he too presents himself as such. He tells Israel: "God will send you a prophet like me." What does 'a prophet like me' mean? Again, according to Deuteronomy—and I think this is the decisive point—Moses' particularity lay in the fact that he spoke with God as with a friend. I tend to see the root of the prophetic element in that 'face to face' with God, in "talking with Him as with a friend." Only by virtue of this direct encounter with God may the prophet speak in moments of time.

Revelation attained its goal with Christ because, in those beautiful words of Saint John of the Cross—when God has spoken in person there is nothing more to add. Nothing more about the Logos can be said. He is among us in a complete way and God has nothing greater to give us than Himself, or to say to us than His Word. But this very wholeness of God's giving of himself—that is, that He, the Logos, is present in the flesh—also means that we must continually penetrate this Mystery. And this brings us back to the structure of hope. The coming of Christ is the beginning of an ever-deepening knowledge and of a gradual discovery of what, in the Logos, is being given. Thus, a new way is inaugurated of leading man into the whole truth: as Jesus puts it in the Gospel of John, the Holy Spirit will come down. I believe that the pneumatological Christology of Jesus' leave-taking discourse is very important to our theme, given that Christ explains that his coming in the flesh was just a first step. The real coming will happen when Christ is no longer bound to a place or limited to a body, but when he comes to all of us in the Spirit as the Risen One, so that entering into the truth may also acquire more and more profundity. It seems clear to me that—considering the entire life of the Church, which is the time when Christ comes to us in Spirit and which is determined by this very pneumatological Christology—the prophetic element, as element of hope and appeal, cannot naturally be lacking or allowed to fade away. Through charisms, God reserves for himself the right to intervene directly in the Church to awaken it, warn it, promote it and sanctify it. I believe that this prophetic-charismatic history traverses the whole time of the Church. It is always there especially at the most critical times of transition.

Niels Christian Hvidt has worked for a number of years with the theme of Christian prophecy in the framework of fundamental theology. This doctoral dissertation is the fruit of his research and provides many new insights in this complex but vital theme. The Fathers of the Church knew that Christianity could not be the final stage of salvation, but an intermediary phase between the Incarnation of Christ and his glorious Return. This realization and what it means to the very nature of Christianity needs further elaboration, and Niels Christian Hvidt provides an important contribution hereto.

In the historical part of the work, Hvidt shows that the prophetic call of God through the prophets appears throughout the history of the Church. In his discussion of fundamental theology, Hvidt therefore investigates the purpose and preconditions of Christian prophecy in light of developments in the past 50 years in Revelation theology, which have given new impetus to the discussion of Christian prophecy. In this way he offers a new approach to the actualization of Revelation and to the development of tradition and dogma regarding Revelation. Prophecy proves to be operative in all areas of the actualization of Revelation, especially in the very life of the Church, which sociological investigations show in an interesting way. Prophecy is constantly challenged by false prophecy, which always represented the greatest threat to the true prophetic gift. The criteria that Hvidt presents for discerning prophecy are therefore vital.

With his discussion, Niels Christian Hvidt has trod new theological land and therewith has made important contributions to a theme that needs further thought. I wish this book many attentive readers.

Joseph Card. Ratzinger

Acknowledgments

This book on Christian prophecy is the final outcome of my doctoral dissertation for the Pontifical Gregorian University in Rome, defended in January 2001, as well as my prize dissertation for the University of Copenhagen, submitted in January 1997. It has been reedited in view of a wider readership, as the theme of Christian prophecy has proven to be relevant for people both in and beyond academe.

My sincere thanks go to a number of people who have provided invaluable feedback during my work with this field of research: My 'Doktorvater' in Rome, Prof. Elmar Salman, OSB, Dean of the Faculty of Philosophy at the Pontifical Athenaeum of Sant' Anselmo, Rome, for his always relevant and exquisite feedback, Prof. Peder Nørgaard-Højen, the Divinity School at The University of Copenhagen, for years of friendship and theological exchange, HE Prof. Rino Fisichella, Rector of the Pontifical Lateran University, Rome, who to my knowledge knows more about Christian prophecy than any other scholar working in fundamental theology. A special word of gratitude goes to HH Pope Benedict XVI, whose theology has been a constant source of inspiration and who so kindly offered to write the foreword of the present book while still the Prefect of the Congregation for the Doctrine of Faith.

I wish to thank the many friends and colleagues who have provided theological and / or editorial feedback on this book, especially Prof. Kirsten Busch Nielsen, Prof. Joseph Carola, SJ, Prof. Lawrence Cunningham, Prof. Prospero Grech, OSA, Mrs. Leslie Huzyk,

Fr. Dr. Joseph Iannuzzi, Dr. Zigmas Kungys, Dr. Francesco Lepore, Prof. Bernard McGinn, Prof. Tore Nyberg, Prof. Edward O'Connor, CSC, Prof. Philipp Gabriel Renczes, SJ, Prof. Yvonne Maria Werner, Prof. Jared Wicks, SJ, my wife, Elisabeth Assing Hvidt, mag.art., and my father, Adv. Torsten Hvidt. Finally, a warm word of recognition and gratitude for the always overly competent and pleasant collaboration with Cynthia Read and her staff at Oxford University Press.

This work could not have been written without the generous support of the following Danish foundations that secured my dissertation research in Rome as well as the time needed for editing the dissertation in view of the present publication, especially: Statens Humanistiske Forskningsråd (Danish Humanities Research Foundation), Augustinusfonden, Carlsbergfondet, Ansgarwerk, Det Teologiske Forskningsudvalg (The Theological Research Committee) at The University of Copenhagen, H. Lundbeck, Direktør Aage Louis-Hansens Mindefond (The Danish Institute in Rome), as well as Sigurd Anders Michael Andersens rejselegat, Borgervennen af 1788, Christian Christiansens Legat, Eivind Eckbo's dansk-norske Legat, Frimodt-Heineke Fonden, Familien Hede Nielsens Legat and Sankt Knuds Stiftelse.

Contents

Christian Prophecy

I

Introduction

"Isn't there here a prophet of Yahweh, that we may inquire of Yahweh by him?"[1] These are the words of a king in ancient Israel who in frustration cried out for a prophetic word as he and his people found themselves in threatening political circumstances. Prophecy continued to be a means by which God guided and saved his people throughout the Old Testament, so that their well-being was directly dependent on his prophetic works that kept them on God's track, which they easily lost when the prophets were silent or silenced: "Where there is no vision the people get out of hand."[2]

But what happened with the Incarnation, death, and resurrection of Christ? Did God stop speaking to his people until the day the Son of man will "come with the clouds of heaven?"[3] Or does he continue to guide, build, and aid his church through the works of his servants the prophets just as he did with the people of Israel?

1.1. Thesis and Purpose

Many Christians believe that prophecy died either with the last Old Testament canonical prophet, with John the Baptist, with Jesus, with the last apostle, with the closure of the canon, with the rise of Montanism, or with Islam. The purpose of this work is to show that this conviction is inadequate. It posits the argument that prophecy, as known in ancient Israel, continued in Christianity as an inherent and continuous feature and charism in the life of the church and that prophets have a vital role to play in the new covenant. Although the claim of prophetic revelations always required careful and difficult discernment, the experience and preaching of many a prophetic personality had great and often very positive impact on the life of the church. Despite the challenge of how to discern between prophecy true and false, healthy and unhealthy, the prophetic charism proved to be leading to purified, renewed, and revitalized faith. Through historical evidence and theological discourse, the aim of this work is then to shed light upon the preconditions, nature, and function of prophecy in the Christian church.

The topic of Christian prophecy has proven to be of interest to readers even outside academe. Furthermore, surprisingly little has been written on Christian prophecy from a perspective of systematic theology. Therefore, this book constitutes an edited version of my dissertation aimed at being accessible and relevant to both professional and nonprofessional theologians; it can function as a general introduction to the issue of Christian prophecy, yet readers with particular interests may find resources in sections relevant for their specific needs. The book is written from a primarily Catholic perspective while seeking to be informed by and be a resource for other Christian traditions as well.

Thomas Aquinas is one of many medieval theologians who held Christian prophetic charisms in high esteem and heralded their continuation in the church. Thomas Aquinas mainly saw the purpose of prophecy as addressing the moral conduct of the faithful, and as such, prophecy will continue to have a great role in the life of the church: "The ancient prophets were sent to establish the faith and to amend morals. . . . Today the faith is already established, since the promises have been fulfilled in Christ. But prophecy that aims at amendment of morals has not ceased, nor will it ever cease."[4]

In another passage regarding Christian prophecy, Thomas Aquinas writes:

> The prophets who foretold the coming of Christ could not continue
> further than John, who with his finger pointed to Christ actually
> present. Nevertheless as Jerome says on this passage, "This does not
> mean that there were no more prophets after John. For we read in the
> Acts of the apostles that Agabus and the four maidens, daughters
> of Philip, prophesied." John, too, wrote a prophetic book about the
> end of the Church; and at all times there have not been lacking per-
> sons having the spirit of prophecy, not indeed for the declaration
> of any new doctrine of faith, but for the direction of human acts.[5]

This assessment of St. Thomas Aquinas has been reiterated many times, as in the radio address by Pope John XXIII at the centenary of Lourdes (February 13, 1959):

> The Roman pontiffs, guardians and interpreters of divine Revelation ... have a duty also to recommend to the attention of the faithful (when after mature examination they judge them opportune for the general good) the supernatural lights which God pleased to dispense freely to certain privileged souls, not for the sake of proposing new doctrines but to guide our conduct [non ad novam doctrinam fidei depromendam, sed ad humanorum actuum directionem].[6]

As Thomas Aquinas did, so do a number of contemporary theologians endorse the continuation of Christian prophecy: prophets "form a major line of continuity between Israel, Judaism, and the church, both historically and theologically";[7] "the history of the church is marked through and through by the fact of prophecy";[8] and the prophets "always possess a permanent and irreplaceable significance for the church."[9] As Migaku Sato writes about prophecy in the ancient church: "Without this rebirth of prophecy, there would have been no Jesus movement, no Gospels, and thus no Christianity."[10] Ben Witherington has summarized this well:

> [The prophets] stood as constant reminders that God was not finished with God's people just yet, nor had God left them without a living witness. To a significant degree, both Judaism and Christianity can be called communities of the word, and one form in which the word often came to these communities was through prophets and prophetesses. They reminded them not merely that "in the beginning was the word" but also that God would have the last word.[11]

One of the theologians, to whom we shall return frequently because of his constructive reflections on Christian prophecy, is Karl Rahner. Rahner highlights the significance of revelations in the church and the need for a theology that places them in their right context:

> If there were such phenomena at the establishment of the Old Testament revelation and of the Christian revelation, then the possibility of similar manifestations occurring in subsequent history cannot be denied *a priori*. It is certain *de fide* that there have been genuine revelations and prophecies in former times, especially under the written law. The same is true under the law of grace. To deny that there have been genuine revelations and prophecies since the time of

the primitive Church would not be heretical but would be at least
temerarious and impious.[12]

During the course of this work I shall, however, do more than highlight
prophecy's continuous Christian presence, for the debate on prophecy leads
to profound, often surprising, insights on the nature of Christianity and the
church as such. For instance, some have argued that Christianity is a perfect
state and that salvation simply occurs in the world when people accept its doctrine as the truth. However, reality is more complex. As we shall see, a differentiated approach, present throughout the history of Christian theology, sees
Christianity's positioning in salvation history as an intermediary state between
the first and the second coming of Christ. Thus, in order fully to be itself, the
church is in constant need of the presence, guidance, and instruction of the
ever-living Word in the church who also speaks through his prophets. From
this perspective, the *telos*, or aim and ultimate goal of Christianity, may be just
as significant a light post on its course on the ocean of history as the *arché*, or
starting point. Just as the Old Testament prophets pointed to the fulfillment of
God's promises to Abraham and Moses, so the Christian prophets serve to keep
alive Christ's promise of coming again to fulfill all things. In this way, Old
Testament and Christian prophecy share the similar fundamental structure of
building on and serving to realize a revealed normative salvation economy
while promising its fulfillment in a yet greater economy in the future.[13]

From a phenomenological point of view, Old Testament and Christian
prophecy share many traits. Both Old Testament and authentic Christian
prophetic messages are defined by implying the experience of direct divine
revelation and intervention and not just of rational reflection.[14] The same God
speaks to both Old Testament and Christian prophets, although the Christian
prophet mainly experiences revelations of Christ. Both Old Testament and
Christian prophets are authorized and ordered to forward the revealed words
to the people of God for their edification. Thus, their fundamental traits are
similar, especially in the writings of Luke: "The *functions* accorded to early
Christian prophecy by Luke are wholly within the scope of prophecy as we
know it from the OT and other parallels in religious history."[15]

Nonetheless, the two phenomena have received very different treatment.
While Old Testament prophecy usually kept its proper name—*prophecy*—
Christian prophecy was, as we shall see, at least after the Montanist crisis
degraded to designations such as *private revelations* or *epiphenomena of the
mystical life*, or simply relegated to the broader category of Christian mysticism. However, such terms do not give enough credit to Christ's free choice of
addressing his people for designs of which only he knows the importance. If

the phenomenon is identical in both contexts of the Old Testament and the church, why do we grant them so different theological treatment?

It is possible to discern a number of reasons for this enigma. First, the concern for the radical nature of the Christ-event and its normative testimony in Sacred Scripture caused many to avoid using the term "prophecy" as a designation for revelations occurring after the completion of Sacred Scripture. The same concern led to the widespread teaching of an "end of Revelation with the last apostle" that in turn led to further resistance to the presence of prophecy in Christianity. We shall return to this vital concern later. Second, as Karl Rahner noted, Christendom was from the beginning marked by a Platonic preference for the wordless and imageless faith to the detriment of the more prophetic and kerygmatic spirituality that he actually considers more authentically Christian than the former.[16] Third, Rahner believes the problem arises from what he calls theological jealousy toward the charismatic authority of prophets, an authority no theologian is able to compete with.[17] Fourth, prophecy has always been connected with the possibility of false prophecy. As Tadeusz Czakanski points out, prophecy's most difficult problem is "how to recognize [the] true and unmask the false."[18] While I personally believe that this fourth point may have contributed most to the misappraisal of Christian prophecy, a differentiated investigation shows that none of these reasons constitute sufficient ground for the so different treatment between Old Testament and New Testament prophecy.

With Rahner, we must therefore ask ourselves the question "whether anything God reveals can be 'unimportant.'... If it be said that [Christian] private revelations contain only such things as can be known independently of them from public Revelation (e.g. the possibility and fruitfulness of a new devotion), then the question arises why God reveals these things instead of leaving it to the sagacity of theologians to deduce them."[19] If Christian prophecy is received and functions in much the same way as its Old Testament counterpart, why treat it differently? Why not admit the importance of Christian prophecy and enhance the exploration of its theological value, place, and function in the church? This work is a modest contribution to this purpose of a responsible theological appraisal of Christian prophecy.

1.2. Limitation

One of the problems with the notion of Christian prophecy is that it has been watered down. It has become, with Erich Fascher, a "frame concept without concrete content."[20]

In secular life, the terms *prophecy, prophet,* or *prophetic* are used, for example, for antiglobalization protesters and for visionary politicians who read the signs of the times. In the Christian context, something similar has happened, so that the prophetic category metaphorically is applied to various instances in the church. In Lutheranism, prophecy has been viewed in light of the *Munus propheticum*—the prophetic criticism of Gospel-faithless Christianity—so that the prophet *is* the protestant, the religious rebel, or just the inspired preacher of God's word. Protestant Eugene Boring has characterized this tendency well:

> Modern religious leaders who are suspicious of charismatic phenomena but want to claim the biblical prophets as their heroes can consider the essence of "prophetic" ministry to be championing the cause of the oppressed in the name of social justice, as in Protestant liberalism, or simply identify "prophecy" and "preaching with authority," so that "every real preacher is a prophet," as in some conservative streams of Protestantism.[21]

The term has been applied in a similar direction in Catholic liberation theology, as a theology distinct from universitarian or academic theology.[22] Apart from this application, Catholics have, however, mainly applied the prophetic category to the Spirit's operations in and through the Catholic Magisterium, guaranteeing its infallibility charism or assuring that it mediates God's truth through time. Thus Rahner talks about the general assistance of the Holy Spirit as a prophetic element,[23] just as the anthology of texts on Vatican II *Il Concilio Vaticano II: Carisma e Profezia,* edited by Tommaso Stenico and Francis Arinze, investigates the prophetic novelty of Vatican II.[24] The prophetic category has been applied to the wider context of the church that carries out a prophetic task for the world of forwarding God's word and ministering his salvation. This has been iterated by the Second Vatican Council,[25] and is a view accepted by most denominations, although Hans-Ruedi Weber is puzzled by "the strange lack of ecumenical reflection about the prophetic vocation of the church."[26] Similarly, the anthology *Chiesa e Profezia,* edited by Gianfranco Calabrese, features numerous applications of the prophetic term to the Christian context, without directly treating the prophets in the church such as Birgitta of Vadstena (Bridget of Sweden) and many others who directly preached the revealed words of Christ to the church of their times.[27]

In other situations, the term is used for individuals who acted under the inspiration of the Spirit, consciously or unconsciously. Thus John Conley and Joseph W. Koterski entitle their book on John Paul II *Prophecy and Diplomacy;*[28] and B. Häring calls Francis of Assisi the greatest Christian prophet ever,[29] although he never wrote down revealed messages as did the Old Testament or Christian prophets.

As Eugene Boring has pointed out, even New Testament scholarly works on prophecy are often watered down. Thus he criticizes David Hill's *New Testament Prophecy* for using the vague phrases "pastoral preaching" and "exhortatory teaching" as his working definition of prophecy, which "allows him to designate Paul's sermon in Acts 13, all of Paul's letters, and the Letter to the Hebrews as 'prophecy.'"[30] Walter Houston's 1973 Oxford dissertation uses "creative manipulator of traditions" as his working definition for prophecy. This description leads him to consider Matthew, Mark, and Luke to be prophets.[31]

We should not be surprised by the fluctuations in terminology, for many phenomena come close to Christian prophecy, without deserving that designation in its fullest sense. Thus, one concern in Marianne Schlosser's excellent dissertation on the medieval evaluation of prophecy was to investigate how the Scholastic theologians viewed the relationship between prophecy and "quasi-prophetic" charisms.[32] However, while wider applications of the prophetic category have important contextual validity, they remain *applications* of the term, not full treatments of the original phenomenon itself. This book seeks to investigate Christian prophecy in this immediate and original form. But what exactly is that?

1.3. The Object of the Investigation

In order to be able to investigate prophecy both for its historical development and evaluate it for its theological significance and function, we need to arrive at a working description of Christian prophecy. Such a description can only arise from an analysis of the phenomenon's New Testament identity, since Christian prophecy emerges directly from the function of prophecy in the early church.

In spite of the pessimism of some, most exegetes do agree that it is possible to arrive at a working description of prophecy as it emerges from the New Testament, even though the phenomenon is quite complex. We will return to a more detailed analysis of the essence of New Testament prophecy in section 3.3.1. Since the New Testament setting must be our normative framework, I shall in that section briefly present the different attempts that have been made in modern research to provide a definition of New Testament prophecy. With this description, we are then equipped with the tools needed to move beyond Scripture and search for the phenomenon in the history of the church, even when it is not labeled prophetic.

We may anticipate the debate between the various exegetical opinions: Christian prophecy requires privileged insight in the mysteries of God, and "Divine revelation is a *sine qua non* of prophecy."[33] As Wayne Grudem puts it: "A 'revelation' from the Holy Spirit is necessary for prophecy to occur. If there is no such revelation, there is no prophecy."[34] But for *mystical experience* to become *prophecy* another element is equally constitutive, namely divine commission,[35] which urges the prophet to forward the revealed communication to the people of God, "building them up and giving them encouragement and reassurance" in order to "build up the community."[36] In its essence, then, *the New Testament prophet, whether labeled as such or not, is a Christian who, through experienced revelations, receives a message that he or she is directed to hand on to the church for its edification as part of a firm design in God's will to save, guide, and bless his people.* It is this phenomenon, in the framework of the above limitations, that this work seeks to elaborate theologically. I will not treat the rediscovery of prophecy in the charismatic movement in this book, since this particular form of prophecy requires a treatment of its own that transcends the limitations of the present study.

1.4. Private, Particular, Special, Dependent, or Prophetic Revelations?

The primary vehicles of prophecy, that is, visions, apparitions, and locutions, are often referred to as *private revelations*. This concept is, however, ambiguous for various reasons. First, as Pierre Adnès writes, private revelations almost always contain an intelligible message, while visions and apparitions may stand alone without accompanying messages. A distinction should hence be made between visions, apparitions, and locutions on one hand and on the other hand revelations as such, which always carry a message. Second, the term *private revelation* not only fails to apply to the individual occurrences of visions, apparitions, and locutions, it also does not address the communication of prophetic messages, which are never "private."[37] In fact, prophetic writings such as those of Hildegard of Bingen and Birgitta of Vadstena cannot be said to have been private. In fact, they always aimed at the edification of the church as a whole. It may happen that a person has a message that is intended for the person herself, and this would be the only legitimate application of the term. But here we leave the scene of Christian prophecy that always aims at the edification of the congregation. When dealing with Christian prophecy, the term *private revelation* is therefore of little avail and has, in fact, been the object of increasing critical scrutiny.

Pope Benedict XVI has argued how the term *private revelations* could be understood in the best way; he has said that the designation "private" can be compared to the term "private mass," which is never private in essence:

> In theology, the concept of "private" does not mean regarding only the person involved and no one else. Rather, it is an expression of the degree of importance, as is the case, for example, with "private Mass." That is to say that the "revelations" of Christian mystics and prophets can never aspire to the same level as biblical Revelation; they can only lead to it and they must measure themselves by it. But that does not mean that these types of revelation are not important for the Church in its entirety. Lourdes and Fatima are the proof that they are important. In the final analysis, they are but an appeal to the biblical Revelation and, for this very reason, they are important.[38]

The widespread success of the term *private revelations* seems mainly due to its employment by sixteenth-century Thomists such as Cardinal Cajetan, Melchior Cano, and Domingo Bañez. Their insistence on this terminology could, as we shall see, be partly explained by the fear of the Lutheran Reformation that, although not being built on prophetic revelations as in Montanism, came across as a modern example of an independent movement breaking off from the church and its leadership (see section 2.2).[39]

The Council of Trent (1545–1563), however, did not employ this terminology. It referred to revelations in its discussion on justification and argued that no one could be certain to be among the elect, unless this had been revealed through a "special revelation."[40] The phrase was hereafter used by other Thomistic theologians, especially Andrea Vega, Francisco Suarez, and Juan de Lugo, who inferred from the council's teaching that the content of postapostolic revelations could indeed be believed with *divine faith*.[41]

Another terminological possibility is the phrase *particular* revelations. As Avery Dulles writes, the phrase was "used by some theologians in their presentations at the Council of Trent."[42] René Laurentin uses the term as a general designation to cover both the particular revelations that are truly *private* (such as, for instance, the three secrets that Bernadette of Lourdes received and whose content no one ever came to know)[43] and the *public* particular revelations, addressed to a greater number of people.[44] The danger with such terminology obviously is a confusion of the Deposit of Faith (see section 4.2) with particular revelations, for the term "public" is used both with regard to the public Revelation (Deposit of Faith) and to those particular revelations that are addressed to the entire church. But this danger seems minor, since public Revelation always assumes a singular case, whereas particular revelations assume a plural case.

Avery Dulles believes that the mentioned designations *particular* or *special* revelations, used at the Council of Trent, might be more apt, but duly notes that the term *private revelations* has "wider currency."[45] Augustinus Suh agrees with Laurentin and Dulles, and writes: "Keeping in mind the nature and the functions of posterior revelations for the life of the Church, the term 'special revelations' or 'particular revelations' might perhaps be more pertinent, because the formula 'private revelation' risks to reduce its reach and purpose to the dimension of a single individual."[46] Interestingly, however, these observances have little practical importance, as Suh in spite of his criticism employs the term consistently throughout his book, even in its title, *Le rivelazioni privati nella vita della chiesa*.

Rahner opts for yet a different distinction. He distinguishes between mystical visions (Laurentin's private particular revelations) and prophetic visions (Laurentin's public particular revelations). Rahner's differentiation is taken from the religious sciences (Religionswissenschaft), and according to his own words it is a problematic concept even there.[47] Rahner's careful self-criticism is reinforced by Volken, who considers it not to apply to reality.[48]

Gerald O'Collins proposes a distinction between what he calls "foundational" and "dependent" aspects of revelation and salvation, designating "the divine self-communication 'now' and its absolute climax 'then' in Christ."[49] This distinction could be fruitfully applied to the different aspects of Revelation that are central to the issue of Christian prophecy: "Foundational" Revelation would hence be the establishment of the economy of salvation and its normative testimony in Sacred Scripture. "Dependent" revelation (or revelations) would designate postapostolic particular forms of divine self-disclosure to actualize Revelation in history. The term would make good sense in regard to prophecy, since the authenticity of postapostolic prophetic revelations are always evaluated on the Deposit of Faith (see section 9.2), hence the "dependence" thereof. Second, they can be said to be "dependent" from the foundational Revelation ontologically, as authentic prophetic revelations can but be a postapostolic manifestation of the one Word, incarnate in Christ, but ever alive in the church.

Having reviewed all the different proposals, and keeping in mind that the function of postapostolic revelations is identical to that of Old and New Testament prophecy, at least in its function, I would argue for using the simple but clear term for postapostolic revelations addressed to a greater number of people, namely, *prophetic revelations*. It is this term that is primarily used in this book. This term marks the difference between the postapostolic revelations and the *revelatio publica*. It indicates not only that such revelations are the direct result of divine intervention, but that they actually fulfill the function in the church of communicating an intelligible message to the congregation and that it has a prophetic purpose.

1.5. Motivation

As it shall be clear during the course of this work, prophecy never ceased in the Christian church but has continued to play a vital role, especially in the Catholic tradition. It is hard to consider the Catholic church without the prophetic tradition that has accompanied its entire history. Prophetic visions and divine instructions accompanied the founding of the vast majority of its religious orders. The same accounts for most pilgrimage sites, which usually became what they did after apparitions of Christ, of the Blessed Virgin, or of an angel to a privileged soul.[50] Much Catholic hagiography has eminent prophetic traits, so that individuals such as Gertrude the Great of Helfta (†1302), Birgitta of Vadstena (†1373), Catherine of Siena (†1380), Joan of Arc (†1431), Julian of Norwich (†c.1416), and Margaret Mary Alacoque (†1690) all come across as classic Christian prophets.

The manifestation of prophetic charisms in the church has not decreased; on the contrary theologians such as René Laurentin speak of an "increase" of prophetic manifestations in our time.[51] Since the big Marian revelations of the last century, beginning with La Salette, Lourdes, and Rue du Bac in France, and Fatima in Portugal, Marian apparitions, mostly to children, have become ever more frequent.[52] The Catholic authorities have, only recently, recognized Banneux and Beauraing in Belgium. In the 1960s the Virgin Mary was said to have appeared to four girls in Garabandal, Spain. In Medjugorje, Bosnia-Herzegovina, she has since the summer of 1981 reportedly been appearing to six children. All six claim to continue to receive apparitions. Three experience them daily, whereas the other three only experience an annual apparition. Thirty million believers are said to have visited Medjugorje.[53]

The messages of the Greek Orthodox mystic Vassula Rydén are another interesting example of apparent contemporary Christian prophecy. Mrs. Rydén is reported to have received messages from Jesus and Mary since 1986. These writings have garnered enormous attention and debate, so much so that the Congregation for the Doctrine of Faith (CDF) in 1995 saw itself obliged to issue a "Notification" to Catholic faithful not to consider the authority of her words above that of Sacred Scripture. The initial caution was followed by deepened study of her messages and a written dialogue with her, leading the CDF's prefect at the time, Joseph Ratzinger, to conclude that she had provided "useful clarifications" of the issues formerly raised against her.[54] As a result of this interest, her messages, first published in 1991 with the title *True Life in God*, were translated and published only ten years later in forty different languages. Respected theologians have written over twenty books about her. Since her first public meeting in 1991, believers have invited her to give over seven hundred public lectures in over fifty-eight nations.[55] Modern experiences such as these show that prophecy continues as a vigorous element of contemporary church life.

Modern forms of communication, and the Internet in particular, serve to enhance the way religions communicate and evangelize.[56] Sociologists of religion discern between *religion online* and *online religion,* referring to the way religions express themselves versus religious activity occurring *online.*[57] On the one hand, the Internet offers great opportunities for religious expression and communication (*religion online*). John Paul II was one of many religious leaders who pointed to the internet's great opportunities:

> The Church approaches this new medium with realism and confidence. Like other communications media, [the Internet] is a means, not an end in itself. The Internet can offer magnificent opportunities for evangelization if used with competence and a clear awareness of its strengths and weaknesses. . . . Finally, in these troubled times, let me ask: how can we ensure that this wondrous instrument first conceived in the context of military operations can now serve the cause of peace?[58]

On the other hand, Internet-based religious communication seems to constitute a new form of religiosity (*online religion*). More than most other forms of religious life, *online religion* has a highly individualistic character—the religious navigator may remain hidden and private without participating in communitarian worship, which has been of the highest importance to Abrahamic traditions.

The Internet's impact on Christian prophecy is no less significant. As the anthropologist Paolo Apolito shows, the Internet is a major resource for interest in prophetic charisms, so much so that one can speak of a new form of postmodern spirituality combining charismatic and traditionalist religious trends with modern communication and media opportunities.[59]

Inasmuch as prophecy itself continues to grow, and reports of prophetic messages proliferate through the mass media, the need for serious theological reflection increases as well. Since true prophecy always has been and will be accompanied by its false counterpart, the need for criteria to "test the spirits" is evident. It seems a norm that for every occurrence of prophecy the church deems positive there usually follow multiple related or associated false prophetic occurrences. This multiplies the need for careful discernment exponentially. Such discernment is presented by New Testament authors as a gift of the Spirit. In the words of David Aune, "there is a connection between the gift of prophecy and the gift of 'distinguishing between spirits.' "[60] But even if God provides his grace to facilitate discernment, prophetic messages have primarily been judged in the light of doctrinal investigation of their conformity with Sacred Scripture.

The purpose of this study is not to provide an overview of false prophetic manifestations and their effect on the life of the church, which has been documented elsewhere—although the damaging results of these cannot be underestimated.[61] Rather, my purpose is to evaluate the nature and function of the authentic charism of Christian prophecy. Nevertheless, the criteria for discernment are of the highest importance as a response to the pastoral need for identifying true Christian prophecy. For only with these criteria is the church today able to apply Paul's exhortation to the Thessalonians: "Do not stifle the Spirit or despise the gift of prophecy with contempt; test everything and hold on to what is good."[62] The discernment that Paul speaks about is twofold. Christians are called to be on guard against false prophets and at the same time to make sure they do not judge and ultimately kill the true prophets.[63] It is a serious matter, for on the one side, false prophecy can, as history has shown, create true confusion in the church. On the other side, it must be remembered that rash judgment of the obviously true prophetic gifts ultimately is a judgment and rejection of the Holy Spirit. The *Didache,* one of the oldest nonbiblical manuscripts speaking of prophecy in the ancient church, even equates the rejection of obviously true prophecy with blasphemy against the Holy Spirit, because "to put those who speak in the Spirit to the test means testing the Spirit working within them."[64]

Along the lines of Max Weber's differentiation between institutional and charismatic authority,[65] it is possible to discern today a tendency to differentiate popular and academic approaches to the life of faith. "Popular spirituality" is easily moved and inspired by charismatic phenomena, both true and false, whereas theologians seem less attracted to such occurrences in the church. The dichotomy between popular, often less theologically grounded, charismatic spirituality and academic, often more rational theology easily becomes polarized to the point that the popular circle of believers are a priori suspicious of the "narrow-minded" attitude of theologians, while theologians are contemptuous of the unreflecting faithful because of their attraction to what Rino Fisichella labels "less demanding forms of faith."[66]

The apparent dichotomy between "lay" and "religious" spiritualities[67] is regrettable, for the different "spiritualities," popular and academic, are in reciprocal need and should enrich rather than antagonize each other. Even true divine charisms need theology to appear in their full significance, while good catechesis could prevent many false charismatic developments. Conversely, theology is in need of the prophetic, for, as Joseph Ratzinger says, "the true and proper way from which great theology may again flow is not generated by the rational side of theological work but by a charismatic and prophetic thrust. And it is in this sense, I believe, that prophecy and theology go hand in glove."[68] Fr. Antonio Gentili has summarized the interdependency between the charismatic and the institutional well:

> The institutional and the charismatic mediations are altogether compresent integrating and enriching each other. Without the support and the ratification of the institution, the charismatic mediations would dissolve in tyranny and . . . disorder as we learn from the first pages of Christian history (see 1 Cor v 12 and 14). Likewise, without the support of the Charisms, the institutional mediations encroach in routinary gestation and formal repetitiveness of rites, doctrines and precepts.[69]

Gentili argues that the laity are greatly enriched by charisms in the church. Vatican II has enhanced the awareness of God being free to diffuse his gifts among his people and that the experiences of the laity are important to the life of the church. While it is true that believers at times do follow easy and often false forms of faith, it is also true that history has shown the benefits of charisms in the life of the faithful. God's life is mediated through the church by the ordered means of the Sacraments and the teaching office of the Magisterium, as well as through the noninstitutional, free mediation of the Spirit of God to the lay faithful. Although they serve in different ways to actualize Revelation in the life of the church, both forms of mediation are vital to the well-being of God's people.[70]

This is why Vittorio Messori finds it a tremendous shame that theological and institutional powers in the church often appear to be prejudiced against prophetic gifts among God's people. Vatican II called the faithful to scrutinize and interpret the "signs of the times" in light of the Gospel, yet Messori observes that these very signs "are, on the contrary, removed, even ridiculed, often by the very ones who have been invaded by that Biblical term ('signs of the times') and have made a banner of it for a 'mature' Christianity, as they call it."[71] Messori argues that the theological opposition to God's charisms in the church is such that it is even dangerous for a writer to elaborate these issues, as they constitute too much of a minefield.[72] Yet he is convinced that this danger should be met with courage, as theologians cannot ignore the true and actual context of the people of God in the twenty-first century. Messori reminds us that the spirituality of the laity has its justification and proper place in the church and that revelations are one form in which God builds his church. Agreeing with Fr. Antonio Gentili, Messori even has the "courage to ask whether it might not be the 'obscurantists' who were right; and if it might not be in the presumed 'obscurantism' of the disquieting signs that we would receive from the Mystery the greater light."[73]

Theological elaboration of the prophetic is in this perspective no marginal occupation, but the illumination of a vital function and form in the life of the church that not only thrusts the faithful toward more engaged forms of faith but even catalyzes theological progress. With regard to the actualization of Revelation and the development of dogma, the Second Vatican Council, in the Constitution on Divine Revelation *Dei Verbum,* stressed the collaboration of the pastors of the church and the faithful with their particular experiences of faith:

> This tradition which comes from the Apostles develops in the Church with the help of the Holy Spirit. For there is a growth in the understanding of the realities and the words which have been handed down. This happens through the contemplation and study made by believers, who treasure these things in their hearts (see Luke, 2:19, 51) through a *penetrating understanding of the spiritual realities which they experience,* and through the preaching of those who have received through episcopal succession the sure gift of truth. For as the centuries succeed one another, the Church constantly moves forward toward the fullness of divine truth until the words of God reach their complete fulfillment in her.[74]

Much has been written on the role of the Magisterium in the handing on, actualization, and unfolding of Revelation, as well as on the role of the faithful. However, surprisingly little has been written on the *penetrating understanding of spiritual realities that the Christian prophets experience* and that form the basis for their evangelization.

As we shall see, few theological issues have received such scarce attention as the problem of Christian prophecy, so that Rino Fisichella compares the theological elaboration of Christian prophecy to "wreckage after shipwreck" (see chapter 2 here). Therefore, both pastoral and academic interests motivate the debate on prophecy. We shall return to this need for theological elaboration of the prophetic in chapter 2; nevertheless, it seems appropriate here to summarize with Karl Rahner the motivation for a theological elaboration on Christian prophecy:

> We should be quite precise about the nature of these private revelations posterior to Christ, and which have value for the Church and not just for the recipient; because these revelations should be perfectly

inserted into this final phase of the economy of salvation. We have seen that it is not sufficient to say: private revelations are not addressed to the Church or humanity taken as a whole, and their content is not positively guaranteed by the Church's Magisterium. To content oneself with affirming that the content of these revelations has only an accessory and quasi-insufficient relationship with the Christian public Revelation, would raise the question: Can anything that God reveals be insignificant?

Again, to say that private revelations never contain anything but truths which one could know through the common Revelation—for example, the possibility and utility of a new devotion—this is to pose yet another question: why then does God reveal it, and not rather leave to the intelligence of theologians the concern of making explicit this new aspect of Revelation?[75]

Another dichotomy between different approaches to prophetic gifts can be discerned between the Northern and Southern Hemispheres. This divide is not between professional theology and lay spirituality, but rather between different spiritual *and* theological approaches to faith. Christianity is growing in the developing countries, whereas it is stagnant at best in the industrialized West. As is often said, Christianity is moving from North to South. One of the hallmarks of this growing Christianity, "the future of Christianity," is that it is charismatic.

Already, Karl Rahner has said that the "religious man of tomorrow will be a mystic, someone who has experienced God, or else he will no longer be."[76] Philip Jenkins argues similarly in his book *The Next Christendom* that the future of Christianity lies in the developing world, with a form of Christianity that gives space for experiental and charismatic sides of faith:[77]

Worldwide, Christianity is actually moving toward supernaturalism and neo-orthodoxy, and in many ways toward the ancient world view expressed in the New Testament: a vision of Jesus as the embodiment of divine power, who overcomes the evil forces that inflict calamity and sickness upon the human race. In the global South (the areas that we often think of primarily as the Third World) huge and growing Christian populations—currently 480 million in Latin America, 360 million in Africa, and 313 million in Asia, compared with 260 million in North America—now make up what the Catholic scholar Walbert Buhlmann has called the Third Church, a form of Christianity as distinct as Protestantism or Orthodoxy, and one that is likely to become dominant in the faith. There is increasing tension between what one might call a liberal Northern Reformation and the surging Southern religious revolution.[78]

In this development toward a form of Christianity that the South considers closer to Christianity as the Bible portrays it, we see growing wariness toward what has been termed "Western theological imperialism." The South criticizes this theological imperialism for its distance to the biblical accounts, especially with regard to prophetic charisms and spiritual dynamism in general. For instance, Jenkins quotes a contemporary follower of the African claimed prophet Johane Masowe:

> A literal interpretation of the Bible can be tremendously appealing. To quote a modern-day follower of the African prophet Johane Masowe ... "When we were in these synagogues [the European churches] we used to read about the works of Jesus Christ ... cripples were made to walk and the dead were brought to life ... evil spirits driven out. ... That was what was being done in Jerusalem. We Africans, however, who were being instructed by white people, never did anything like that. ... We were taught to read the Bible, but we ourselves never did what the people in the Bible used to do."[79]

The problem is that the gap between northern and southern religiosity and related theology is deepening: "Across the denominational spectrum, Catholics and Protestants alike preach messages that, to a Westerner, appear simplistically charismatic, visionary, and apocalyptic. In this thought world, prophecy is an everyday reality, while faith healing, exorcism, and dreamvisions are all fundamental parts of religious sensibility."[80]

Christianity in the developing Southern Hemisphere is neither atheological nor antitheological; rather it breeds theology of a different kind with particular characteristics, and among these are constructive reflections on charismatic gifts.[81] Werner Kahl argues that people, including theologians, relate to miracles and charismatic gifts on the basis not primarily of theological reasoning but rather their sociocultural mindset. Similarly, people in biblical times valued alleged charismatic experiences on the basis of their cultural and religious identity. According to Kahl, Christians in the developing world are closer to the New Testament mindset and so relate more easily to the miracle stories of the Bible than Christians in the First World. Kahl believes that Western culture has become distanced from the mindset in which miracles, including prophetic gifts, make sense and can be received fruitfully in the Christian community.[82] Hence, without giving up critical thinking, he calls for Western theology to be wary of "ideological imperialism." African American authors[83] and the Latin American liberation theologians have voiced similar criticism, often highlighting problems connected with Western theological imperialism, and especially with critical biblical exegesis.[84] These authors argue that the danger with such imperialism is that it deepens the divide and makes First World critical research seem unappealing, even dangerous, to Third World theologians, not because of the research methodology itself, but rather because of the naturalistic ideologies that threaten the inherent objectivity of Western theology. The Catholic Church has repeatedly been warning against such inherent dangers of objective biblical research, just as it has pointed out the dangers of its opposite extreme: biblical fundamentalism.[85] An important underlying motivation for this book, then, is the desire to bridge "Northern" and "Southern" traditions by investigating the theological foundations for charisms in the church that exist in classical Christian theology and that will be of the highest importance in "the next Christendom."

1.6. Outline

In chapter 2, we shall deal with the theological elaboration of prophecy, examining possible reasons that the theme has for so long been shrouded in the dark and why, apparently, most theological branches have started bringing it to the fore only now.

If history could prove that there is no such phenomenon as prophecy in the church, then there would be no real issue to investigate theologically. The only way the prophetic category could make any sense would be by applying it analogously to elements in the church with which it would seem to fit. Chapter 3, therefore, investigates the historical development of prophecy and shows that it did not cease but only continued to remodel itself according to the needs of the church as it continued to evolve through time. Having examined the existence of specific Christian prophecy, in chapter 4 we shall investigate different models of Revelation and what image of prophecy they produce. We will then be ready to deal in chapter 5 with the much-debated notion of the "end of Revelation with the last apostle" that often has been used to proclaim the necessary end of prophecy. We will then proceed to see how modern theologians consider the concept more a theological artifice fitted for specific apologetic purposes rather than reflecting the reality of salvation history. With theological and historical research, we shall in chapter 6 see how prophecy can be seen to play a continuous role in Christianity of mediating God's salvation, attained in Christ, to every new generation of the church. This accounts especially for the fruits of prophecy in the inner life of the church, which we will examine in chapter 7. The results of prophecy's interaction with tradition and the development of doctrine are summarized in chapter 8, wherein we shall examine a useful typology of different forms of belief and how Christian prophecy fits within that system. Having thus identified the place and function of prophecy in the church, we will be ready in chapter 9 to identify the criteria needed for discerning true from false prophecy in the church. These criteria are vital to Christian prophecy if it is to continue to have a role in the church.

2

Prophecy and Theology

As the prophetic phenomenon has played a vast role in the church and has caused such problems of discernment, one would expect to find a serious amount of theological literature on Christian prophecy as a whole. But this is not the case. While a historical overview of prophecy will prove prophecy's continuous positive presence in Christianity, a similar positive conclusion could not be given to the theological elaboration of Christian prophecy, as prophecy has been one of the least treated issues of Christian theology. Thus Rino Fisichella observes: "Confronting the subject of prophecy today is rather like looking at wreckage after a shipwreck."[1] Likewise, Karl Rahner noted that prophecy never had been treated properly, which was the reason for his rather short *Visionen und Prophezeiungen*:

> Nevertheless prophecy has it foundation in Scripture, and in practice a great history in the Church (labour as theorists may to prove that we already know without the prophets every-thing that they announce), and yet orthodox theology has never paid any serious attention to the question whether there are prophets even in post-apostolic times, how their spirit can be recognized and discerned, what their role is in the Church, what their relationship to the hierarchy, what the import of their mission for the exterior and interior life of the Church.[2]

Hans Urs von Balthasar finds a tendency in theology of avoiding the issue of prophetic revelations in the church. He is surprised by this hesitation, as prophetic revelations are, after all, defined as God himself speaking to his church:

> Today, theologians put [them] with confidence in the bin, telling the faithful that they are a) often uncertain or simply false, b) that they do not require any kind of recognition, in fact c) that all the essential truths are certainly present in the doctrine of the church. One can therefore simply ask why God provides them continuously, although they hardly need to be heeded by the church.[3]

Fisichella finds this a great shame and proposes different reasons to the theological "blackout" on the prophetic agenda:

> The essential role prophecy seems to discharge in the church's life notwithstanding, prophecy as one of the signs mediating the Christian Revelation has been subjected to distinctly inconsistent treatment: rationalism has deprived it of any supernatural character whatever; the theological manuals, conversely, have overrated its importance, lastly, historical-cultural criticism has limited its entire content to its mere *Sitz im Leben,* hence impeding its openness to theological interpretation and preventing any verification of its effects as they gradually occurred in the context of history.[4]

There are surely many more reasons for the scarce theological elaboration of the important fact of prophecy in the Christian church, and we shall examine a greater number of these during the course of this work. But one problem is of primary interest in this section, as it has to do with theology itself. There is a methodological obstacle to the treatment of prophecy that stems from the way theology has been organized, namely as a scientific discipline with many subdisciplines: it is the problem of theology's diversity.

In the following presentation of the different theological disciplines' approach to prophecy, this generally negative theological reception of prophecy will become evident in systematic detail. Prophecy is like a ball thrown from one theological discipline to the other, as each considers the other more apt to deal with the problem, and so none take prophecy as its own responsibility. Ultimately prophecy usually lands on the desk of the mystical theologians, as prophecy implies visions and other irrational occurrences that mystical theology is supposed to take care of. But this is a pity, since mystical theology alone, for reasons to be presented below, is not able to give a full picture of the dynamism and function of prophecy in the church.

It is true that classical Christian prophecy stems from mystical experiences and that these more than anything else characterize the traits that differentiate prophecy from other charisms in the church. This is why the mystical approach is necessary. But presenting prophecy only as mystical experience puts it in a light of exclusiveness and strangeness that endangers a correct assessment of its function in the church.

Another issue is the disadvantage of letting mystical theology be the only theological discipline that deals with prophecy. The classical Catholic mystical school tends, as Rahner shows, to prefer pure contemplative, wordless mysticism to word-oriented, prophetic spirituality;[5] so mystical theology runs the risk of taking an a priori negative attitude to prophecy. Furthermore, a presentation of the full scope of prophecy requires a thorough ecclesiological outlook, which is not the main concern of mystical theology, which mainly deals with the working of the Spirit in the lives of individuals. From this perspective, prophecy falls short, as its main scope—the edification of the greater community of believers—is ignored. (We shall take a closer look at the way mystical theology approaches prophecy in section 4.1.)

In almost all Christian traditions, theology is separated into different branches and disciplines. In the Catholic context, these are dogmatic theology, fundamental theology, exegesis, canon law, church history, moral theology, and mystical theology. Each and every one of these branches has its particular approach to the issue. The foundation and goal of the different branches is the same, namely their *obiectum formale quo,* the divine Revelation,[6] and from this perspective they aim at making out one homogenous entity. Nevertheless their individual approaches to this common mystery are very different, just as the theological disciplines remain greatly differentiated.

In addition, prophecy is a largely differentiated fact in the church. There are many aspects to consider if the treatment of prophecy is to be full and all-inclusive, and this is why a fair and full evaluation of prophecy depends on a synthetic treatment of all the different disciplines. Normally, such synthetic evaluations rarely emerge. Theologians prefer to remain within their specific fields, and this danger to the unity of theology explains the lack of a united evaluation of prophecy, and constitutes yet one more reason for the depreciation of prophecy in the church. For when prophecy is treated only under the perspective of one particular theological discipline it does not emerge in the fullness of its purpose and nature.

2.1. Dogmatic Theology

Dogmatic Theology deals with the mysteries of faith. Its aim is to investigate the contents of revelation and forward these in order that they become accessible and comprehensible to individual believers. As we shall see, much importance continues to be attributed to the idea of an end of revelation with the last apostle. This maxim appears to be the primary cause of the negative evaluation of prophecy in dogmatic theology. When revelation is ended, what role do the prophetic revelations have to play? Volken has rightly summarized the general negative assessment in dogmatic theology regarding the prophetic revelations: "Do they bring us new doctrines—Yes or No? In the first case they must be rejected a priori: dogma does not admit new doctrines. In the second instance they can only repeat what has already been said: these revelations are therefore superfluous."[7] This negative argument is based on the idea that prophecy should relate to dogma only. We have already seen the shortcomings of this approach, as the primary scope of prophetic revelations is not to forward dogmatic teachings but to edify the church.

The negative attitude of dogmatic theology is ever more sad, since it, more than any other theological discipline, can give a valid evaluation of prophecy; it is dogmatic theology that can truly assess and appreciate prophecy in the church. Since prophetic revelations relate less to the teachings of the church than to *the life of the church*, a fundamental evaluation of prophecy must have a robust ecclesiological foundation, and ecclesiology forms part of dogmatic theology. Furthermore, revelations can be considered as edifying gifts of the Spirit to the church, whereby one enters the realm of pneumatology, also a part of dogmatic theology.

2.2. Fundamental Theology

Fundamental theology aims at presenting the fundamental aspects of re-velation and provides arguments for its credibility;[8] and it is thus within the borders of fundamental theology that we find the discipline of apologetics.

Prophetic revelations often come across as spectacular and supernatural graces that can be categorized as miracles or *wonders*. The wonder traditionally has been considered as a sign of God, of his existence and credibility. In the Gospels, Christ's signs (*terata* or *semeion*) are signs of his divinity and of the fact that he is the full revelation of God. In the same way, wonders that occur by the operation of God in the church are signs of his presence. Therefore, one would expect fundamental theology to treat the revelations in the church from their sign-character.

This indeed was the case with particular regard to the manualist circles of the nineteenth century, although they limited prophecy to the Old Testament, foreshadowing the coming of Christ. And yet, fundamental theology deals surprisingly little with prophecy.[9] To consider prophecy primarily as signs is to limit its function. Prophecy verifies and points to the authenticity of revelation not primarily through its provocative qualities as great wonders of God. Prophecy, in itself, contains words that actualize and express the Word anew. As such, prophecy is essential to the actualization of revelation, less through its provocative power than through its intelligibility. While signs point to the fact that God is alive and present, Christian prophecy does that and much more: it confers by means of an understandable message what God wants to say to the church in a given historical context.

Furthermore, prophecy considered as a mere sign lends much uncertainty to the process of verifying its authenticity. It is more difficult to assess the authenticity of a prophetic revelatory experience than, for instance, medically confirmed miraculous healings. In order for a sign to function as such it must be verifiable, and it is very difficult to verify revelatory experiences.

One of the theologians who has had the most influence in the field of Catholic fundamental theology, Melchior Cano, described the different sources of revelation's expression and actualization in time, the so-called *loci theologici*. He did not place prophetic revelations in any of the *loci* of his theological system. As René Laurentin rightly states, prophetic revelations are found in a theological nonlocus in Cano's system.[10] Thus, fundamental theology alone cannot possibly give a complete picture of prophecy.

However, Rahner points out that fundamental (and mystical) theology can contribute in one very important way to the full evaluation of prophecy by confirming the *possibility* of the occurrence of prophetic revelations:

> Mystical and fundamental theology only add that because God can
> reveal himself (in the strict of sense of verbal revelation) and can give
> the recipient of such revelation, and also other people, adequate as-
> surance of the divine origin of his experience—in the latter case by
> external critera [sic] and in the former by both external and internal
> criteria—therefore private revelations and knowledge of their au-
> thenticity and truth are possible.[11]

Even though fundamental theology has been reticent with regard to prophecy, some important changes have occurred that have been of a great theological asset to Christian prophecy. The research that has been done on Christian prophecy in the field of fundamental theology has merely addressed prophecy from the perspective of "private revelation." Tampere considered the notion of *private revelations* in relation to dogmatic progress in his 1954 Gregorian University dissertation "Revelatio privata: Revelatio privata et prog-ressus dogmaticus."[12] In another dissertation, Panakal studied the revelations from the perspective of the Theresian mystical school while addressing the issue of private revelations.[13] In his book *Les Révélations dans l'Eglise* (1961), Laurent Volken gave what remains one of the best studies on the subject.[14] Karl Rahner published a number of works in the fifties and sixties related to the issues, among which especially his *Visions and Prophecies* (1963) and *The Dynamic Element in the Church* (1964) had an important influence and have been quoted often.[15] René Laurentin, in several publications, continued and further developed this research in its perhaps richest form, criticizing the expression of *private revelations* as well as the theological context in which it belonged, namely the doctrinal understanding of revelation.[16] Yves Congar wrote a small booklet on the question,[17] as did Leo Scheffzcyk, presenting the classic Catholic position and evaluation of alleged prophetic revelations in the church.[18] Augustinus Suh also summarized the approach of fundamental theology to *private revelations* in his book *Le Rivelazioni Private nella Vita della Chiesa*, updating it in the light of postconciliar approaches to revelation.[19] Last but not least we should mention the Congregation for the Doctrine of Faith's Commentary to the publication of the Third Secret of Fatima. The document, signed by Joseph Ratzinger, outlines the classical Catholic position in regard to private revelations. As far as I can see, it must be one of the first magisterial documents to use the term *Christian prophecy* for private revelations, although it does so carefully, putting the word *prophecy* in quotation marks:

> The images described by them are by no means a simple expression of their fantasy, but the result of a real perception of a higher and interior origin. . . . The central element of the image is revealed where it coincides with what is the focal point of Christian "prophecy" itself: the centre is found where the vision becomes a summons and a guide to the will of God.[20]

These and other works are useful in clarifying terms and aiding to position the revelations in the church in the perspective of fundamental theology, but they do not constitute a comprehensive study of private revelations from the perspective of *Christian prophecy*.[21]

2.3. New Developments in Revelation Theology

The nineteenth century witnessed an enormous development in revelation theology, especially concerning the transmission of revelation through history. Especially through the catalyzing events of Vatican II, Catholic revelation theology has grown from a neo-Scholastic proposition into a dynamic communication theory of revelation, highlighting God's self-communication revelation rather than mere true sentences, and not to the exclusion of revelation's cognitive aspects. It is difficult to illustrate this theological change better than contrasting theological dictionaries of the beginning of the twentieth century, such as *Dictionnaire de Théologie Catholique,* with modern ones, such as the 1990–2000 versions of *Lexikon für Theologie und Kirche.* Key issues to our problem such as *Depositum Fidei, Offenbarung, Privatoffenbarung,* and *Tradition* appear very differently from their portrayal in modern dictionaries that not only criticize but even contradict issues of vital interest and theological insistence in the earlier versions. As an illustration, we shall briefly consider the two issues of *Depositum Fidei* and *Privatoffenbarung.*

In his article "Dépot de la foi," Dublanchy employs six columns in the 1939 *Dictionnaire de Théologie Catholique* to celebrate the notion along the lines of a propositional approach to revelation. The Deposit of Faith, Dublanchy writes, consists in all the truths that Christ revealed and confided to the infallible teaching office of the Catholic church, charged with keeping it intact, expounding and defending it according to the needs of changing times. It is consigned in Scripture or transmitted by Christian tradition.[22] For a truth to belong to the Deposit of Faith it must first be pronounced by the Catholic Church's teaching office as revealed and prescribed belief to all the faithful. This is the exclusive task of the Magisterium.

The prophetic revelations, in Dublanchy's article named *private* are mentioned in a pejorative way, as he mainly treats them for what they do *not* aim at, granting them a more-than limited purpose. He therefore asserts that public Revelation has nothing to do with private revelations, and that the latter only have the moral direction of the faithful as their goal: "This public Christian Revelation does obviously not concern the entirely private revelations, occurring during the centuries and having only the moral direction of particular acts as their purpose. The ecclesiastical authorities in their giving a simply negative approval do not modify their strictly private nature in any way."[23]

According to Dublanchy, God employed prophets in the Old Testament to maintain and fortify the Tradition, with a clear mission: "To remain in his people, almost at all the periods of history, the prophet having the divine mission of fighting errors opposed to the unity of God and to his worship and of keeping the full integrity of belief in the only true God and his unique worship."[24]

Apart from the fact that Christianity through Revelation knows of God's Trinitarian nature, nothing prevents Christian prophets from exercising the exact same function as that which Dublanchy ascribes to the Old Testament prophets, and yet he makes no mention of Christian prophets.

Things differ in Wolfgang Beinert's article "Depositum Fidei" in the 1995 edition of the *Lexikon für Theologie und Kirche*. Not only does this dictionary sacrifice a mere one and a half columns to the subject, unlike the six columns in the earlier dictionaries, but also the concept itself is criticized for belonging to a dogmatic approach to Revelation. Beinert considers the concept "Deposit of Faith" legitimate in exegesis, as the term appears in the Pastoral Letters. However, with the communication model of Revelation that Vatican II proposed, Beinert suggests that the concept "Deposit of Faith" comes across as less desirable because Neo-Scholasticism has tainted the notion with a too static character.[25] In outright opposition to Dublanchy's limitation of the Deposit of Faith to the magisterial pronouncements, Beinert writes regarding the *Depositum Fidei* that it can never be brought to full expression:

> Any interpretations, including those of the Magisterium, will necessarily remain inadequate, analogous, and (compared to the beatific vision) within the shortcomings of faith. By this, the ecclesial preaching is concurrently empowered and held back, in detaching itself from particular historical forms of expression of the Deposit of Faith precisely in order to be able to keep it in its purest form as the best presentation of the basic occurrence of Christianity for every contemporary situation.[26]

Gerald O'Collins writes along the same lines in his 1983 *A New Dictionary of Christian Theology*, arguing that Revelation's transmission is not limited to the hierarchy, but that the entire people of God take part in its process. The "Deposit of Faith" has been misused by reducing the church to the "hierarchy," whereas "revelation . . . is not to be reified as if it was merely a set of divinely revealed teachings that should be repeated mechanically till the end of time. Fidelity to the living presence of Christ demands fresh understanding and interpretation as new situations and challenges arise."[27] O'Collins finds it vital that the entire people of God enjoys the "instinct of faith" to preserve faithfully the "Deposit of Faith."

With regard to prophetic revelations, already Karl Rahner's article "Privatoffenbarung" in 1963 signaled a significant evolution from earlier dictionaries, as he confirms the existence and vital function of revelations in the life of the church: "Such private revelations *can* indeed oblige the individual that receives them to divine faith. The preconditions are basically the same as for the public and public Revelation."[28] It is obvious that Rahner links private revelations more closely to the public Revelation (Depositum Fidei), in opposition to Dublanchy's view, which eradicated any possible connection. We shall return to this issue when we explore the different notions of faith in chapter 8.

In the 1999 edition of the eighth volume of the *Lexikon Für Theologie Und Kirche*, Georg Essen continues Rahner's appreciation of private revelations, the naming of which are said to belong to a doctrinal approach to Revelation. He promotes their theological validity and function in the church and calls for serious theological reflection on the issue: "The contemporary theological task consists in reformulating the content of the traditional concept on the basis of a communicatory model of Revelation. Its theological dignity emerges when combined with a theory of the history of tradition [Überlieferungsgeschichte] that highlights the constitutive significance of praxis in the process of continuing faith [Glaubensüberlieferung]."[29]

Essen writes that prophetic revelations play a great role in the actualization and development of tradition: "On the basis of their contextual plausibility, private revelations can be a prophetic testimony that the truth of faith only reaches its fullness in exchange with the historical situation. In this sense, private revelations can lead to a deepened understanding of the Revelation of God in the history of Jesus Christ."[30]

All of these statements point to the powerful development of Revelation theology toward a comprehensive communication theory of Revelation that encumbers revelation's divine truths but equally estimates the efficaciousness of Christ's continuous presence in the history of the church. With this more complete insight follows as a natural result a growing appreciation of the purpose of Christian prophecy, raising the need for theological elaboration, to which this work seeks to contribute. The *Sitz im Leben* of such an elaboration is precisely the formal aspects of Revelation, actualizing God's gift of himself by means of his continuous works of salvation in the life of the church. Christian prophets thus come across as important agents of the actualization of Revelation.

The shift that has occurred is from a rather prepositional to a more dynamic understanding of Revelation that sees Revelation as the communication of God's life-reality to his church, a reality that encompasses cognitive aspects while remaining continuously in need of vivification in order to become a powerful expression of God's image in every new historical context. It is this renewed aspect in Revelation theology that greatly favors the topic of Christian prophecy, as the prophets call God's people to life in him.

2.4. Exegesis

Exegesis shows great interest in the many factors that led to the genesis of Christian prophecy and its function and impact in the early church. Exegesis pays less attention, however, to what happened after the closure of the Bible's earliest book. Furthermore, Laurent Volken argues that an a priori cautious attitude can be discerned in exegesis toward postcanonical prophecy, due to the possible danger that it could undermine the authority of Holy Scripture.[31] And Gerhard Dautzenberg is amazed at how little exegetical attention the problem of Christian prophecy has received, given the fact that Paul lists it second only to the apostles. "[This] great appreciation of prophecy contrasts with the usually meager treatment [of prophecy] in New Testament exegesis."[32] This notwithstanding, exegesis is one of the most important contributors to the understanding of Christian prophecy, in that it highlights what prophecy means in the New Testament. In theory, there should be no difference between prophecy in the New Testament after the resurrection of Christ and consequent prophecy in the church. When Luke in Acts or Paul in his letters speak about prophecy, they are actually speaking about the prophecy of the Christian church, as these writings, from a historical point of view, were composed after the two most important elements to the establishment of the Christian church: the resurrection of Christ and the Descent of the Holy Spirit. As we shall see in the presentation of the historical development of prophecy, much research has been conducted in recent years in this field of exegesis. Thus, Eugene Boring rightly dedicates part 2 of his book *The Continuing Voice of Jesus* to "The Rediscovery of Christian Prophecy."

Two heavyweights of historical criticism, Rudolf Bultmann and Martin Dibelius, both believed that tradition was immensely powerful in the shaping of Holy Scripture, allowing for free inventions of the words of Jesus. As Boring writes, Bultmann had a great problem explaining "how it could be that so many sayings of Jesus were created by the church."[33] To find a solution, Bultmann presented Christian prophecy as the Spirit-inspired forum that gave birth to the sayings of the Risen Christ that tradition later merged with the words of the historical Jesus. In this way, Bultmann "hit upon Christian prophecy as he sought for an explanation for the creativity of the church. Whether this was serendipity or rationalization is still debated."[34] Both Bultmann and Dibelius and many disciples of the *form critical school* follow proposed Christian prophecy as an explanation of tradition's impact on Scripture. However, none of them ever ventured to explore the phenomenon that they held had played such a vital role in the ancient church.

This exploration had to wait half a century, but increased tremendously during the last quarter of the twentieth century, and has multiplied extensively in recent years.[35] Many of the works resemble and complement each other while disagreeing on important points.

One of the bigger debates revolves around Eugene Boring, who puts forward Bultmann's thesis that Christian prophets played a creative role in the formation of the canon. While agreeing that this *could* be the case, Boring points out that it is difficult to give any substantial proof for it. His argument is that sayings of the Risen Christ, pronounced by the mouth of Christian prophets, resembled those of the sayings of the earthly Jesus, and that this was the reason why the two types of sayings could be easily interlaced. Aune,[36] Witherington,[37] and others turn the same argument around to make Boring's thesis improvable: just because the two types of sayings were so similar, it is not possible to identify either of them.

While this extensive exegetical research is indispensable to the present study, it also holds one peculiar potential threat to its theme, namely the presence of postapostolic prophecy and its placement in the theological landscape. Except for a few groundbreaking studies on Christian prophecy appearing at the close of the twentieth century (such as those of Boring and Witherington), most earlier exegetical works heralded the end of prophecy in the early church. As we shall see, this does not apply to the history of the Christian church. Perhaps the exegetes who made the point would have come to a different conclusion had they extended their investigation beyond the ancient church. But such study is not within the range of exegesis.

2.5. Church History

While dogmatic and fundamental theology provide the theoretical elaboration of prophecy, church history is the source of its "empirical" investigation. It is church history that portrays the many prophetic characters of Christendom (and its failures), just as it is church history that can show the way prophecy has been important to the life of the church. Of such works there are many, and yet with Laurentin, Volken, and Fisichella one could wish they would play a more significant role in the theoretic evaluation of prophecy's role in the church.[38] Church history gives ample material to the study of Christian prophecy as it portrays the individuals who emerged as classic prophetic types, as well as the movements they initiated. Few works, however, do so from the perspective of Christian prophecy.

There are exceptions to this rule. One is Ernst Benz's book *Die Vision;* and there is the extensive research of Pius Engelbert, Peter Dinzelbacher, and other scholars on medieval vision literature.[39] To this one may add the research of Pierre Benoit, Hans Urs von Balthasar, Jean-Pierre Torrell, and Marianne Schlosser, who have written extensively on the prophecy treatises of medieval theologians such as Albertus Magnus, Bonaventure, and Thomas Aquinas.[40] Marianna Schlosser's *Lucerna in caliginoso loco* is of particular interest, as it rises above the mere exploration of sources toward a more synthetic reading of these theologians from the perspective of important selected aspects of the prophetic category. Although this research provides new insights, the topic deserves more research. Already in 1954, Hans Urs von Balthasar had written in the first publication of his "Thomas und die Charismatik" that the subject of the book was one of the least investigated themes of Thomas's writings and that he hoped his contribution would soon be "passed by more diligent researchers." The preface to the 1996 edition of Balthasar's work dryly states that Balthasar's wish was not fulfilled: "Unfortunately, his wish has not come true."[41]

2.6. Mystical Theology

Of all the different theological disciplines, mystical theology has treated prophecy most and has had the greatest influence on theology's general approach to prophecy, and mystical theology's surprisingly negative attitude toward prophecy is diffused in the other theological branches. Thus, it is necessary to study at length how mystical theology approaches prophecy. We shall return to this in the discussion of the experiential aspects of revelation (section 4.1). Here it is enough to indicate an important tendency in mystical theology, namely that of being inclined toward a word-less infused mysticism rather than a kerygmatic, prophetic spirituality, and this seems to have influenced a negative theological perspective on Christian prophecy.

2.7. Conclusion

We have seen that all the different branches of theology have a contribution to make to the topic of Christian prophecy. Each discipline is needed in order to give a varied and qualitative picture of it. While Volken in his 1961 book *Les Révélations dans l'Eglise* was very pessimistic about basically all branches of theology on the issue, there is reason today to be more optimistic, as there is growing interest in research related to the phenomenon of prophecy in the church. However, in my view, no theologian has sought to contemplate the prophetic phenomenon by pulling the perspectives of the different theological branches into one synthetic treatment. As a modest attempt in this direction, this work builds on the aforementioned research within the different disciplines, as well as my own research on the subject.[42]

3

Prophecy and History

The study of Jewish and Christian history reveals an image of a God who never ceases sending prophets to address his people. From the times of Abraham, Moses, and the Old Testament prophets who followed him to the times of John the Baptist and the New Testament prophets and prophetic personalities in the nascent church, the charism of prophecy has appeared during history as one of God's prime means of guiding his children to salvation. The purpose of this discussion is *not* to give an exhaustive presentation of the various forms of prophecy throughout history, as such an undertaking exceeds the limits and the scope of this work, but rather to prove one particular point: that the charism of prophecy has been present throughout the entire Jewish and Christian epochs to the present and that prophecy played a vital role in the founding of both the Jewish and the Christian religions. Further, I shall show that although revelation, from a Christian perspective, was fulfilled with Christ, prophecy continues to function as a source of vitality and inspiration to the church.

The New Testament and early church sources present prophecy as an essential and constant feature of the Christian church. Christianity would not fully be Christianity without the voice of the prophets in the church. The Christian God is conceived as the Emmanuel—the "God-with-us"—a God whom Scripture reveals as one who never leaves his people but continues to save them. Hence the prophets are the champions of the "God-with-us," who is powerfully and efficaciously present in his church in every age and cultural setting.

In support of this point, this study seeks to refute the strongly established idea of a historical end to prophecy. Some scholars have contended that prophecy died out in early Judaism, while others claim it ended with the coming of Christ, or with the death of the last apostle, or with the closure of the Christian canon, or with the rise of Montanism. This exposé seeks to show that none of these positions is supported by history. Prophecy has changed immensely throughout history, especially with regard to its status within the institutional church, but prophecy has never ceased.

Since the church grew out of God's covenant with Israel, we will first examine the Old Testament, where prophecy played a prominent role. Prophecy in the Old Testament is a vast phenomenon, and scholars often disagree on its various aspects. Bearing in mind that the scope of this work is to give theological value to the issue of prophecy and focus on its historical continuity, we will only focus on some important traits of prophecy that most scholars agree on and that continue in Christian prophecy, rather than pointing out theological disagreements.

3.1. Prophecy in Ancient Israel

Old Testament prophecy has many parallels in the cultures surrounding ancient Israel. In fact, most ancient oriental religions include the idea of the divine communicating with humans. Yet, unlike the religions surrounding ancient Israel, Old Testament prophecy contains a clear view of the characteristics and tasks of the prophet; thus, prophecy as we know it from the Old Testament is something "distinctively Israelite."[1] In the surrounding religions, ecstatic experiences often are the sole requirement for obtaining the title "prophet." Such experiences are often a part of Old Testament prophecy, but it takes more than visions to become a prophet of Yahweh: God gives the prophet an active role in his plans to lead man to the salvation promised in the covenant.

Revelation. The prophet is someone who, out of his encounter with God, speaks the Word of God to his contemporaries. As Clifford Hill writes, his words are not the result of mere intellectual reasoning but stem from a "divine invasion"[2] or supernatural revelation, often in the form of visions and locutions. "Prophecy is 'received' rather than produced by the human mind"[3] and it is a divine call that constitutes the prophet's mission. This call is deeply personally designed, especially for the prophet who is often prepared for the task in his youth—even before he "came forth out of the womb."[4] The call of the prophet can come unexpectedly or after long periods of prayer, but in any event the prophet's vocation originates in God, not in the will or aspirations of the prophet.

Calling. Most of the Old Testament prophetic books tell of a specific moment in which God called the prophet to his or her mission. This moment becomes a wedge that neatly separates the prophet's life into "before" and "after." For example, the prophet Samuel's vocation begins as a youngster while he is resting in the night.[5] Three times he is awakened by a voice, and believes it is the priest, Eli, who is calling him. When Eli realizes that it is in fact God who is calling Samuel, the priest instructs him to answer the call in readiness, saying, "Speak, Yahweh; for your servant is listening." This yes inaugurates his mission.

Resistance. However, many prophets do not respond to their calls with the same readiness as did Samuel, often because they feel unworthy or incapable of fulfilling the task God calls them to. They see the weight of a mountain in front of them and consider themselves unable to lift it, and so they ask God to choose another. When God tells Moses to confront Pharaoh and to lead Israel out of Egypt, he is too embarrassed to speak. He protests and pleads: "Please, my Lord, I have never been eloquent, even since you have spoken to your servant, for I am slow and hesitant of speech";[6] and he asks God to send his brother, Aaron, instead. The prophet Jeremiah argues that he is too young;[7] Isaiah, that he has unclean lips.[8] In each example God responds to the prophet's objection of unworthiness or incapacity that he will be the one who will supply what is lacking. To Moses' objection that he is not a good orator, Yahweh replies: "Who makes a person dumb or deaf, gives sight or makes blind? Is it not I, Yahweh? Now go, I shall help you speak and instruct you what to say."[9] To Jeremiah Yahweh's answer is similar: "Don't say, I am a child; for to whoever I shall send you, you shall go, and whatever I shall command you, you shall speak. Don't be afraid because of them; for I am with you to deliver you, says Yahweh. Then Yahweh put forth his hand, and touched my mouth; and Yahweh said to me, Behold, I have put my words in your mouth."[10]

For Isaiah, Yahweh's answer provides a powerful image. When Isaiah exclaims that he has unclean lips (that he is not worthy of proclaiming God's prophetic word), a seraph flies to him "holding in its hand a live coal which it had taken from the altar with a pair of tongs." Isaiah tells us that: "With this it touched my mouth and said: 'Look, this has touched your lips, your guilt has been removed and your sin forgiven'."[11]

Unworthiness. This unworthiness or incapacity to carry out the Lord's plans is not merely a hindrance: it is part of God's ways with his servants. Because of his being weak and incapable, the prophet's sole source of strength and capacity must come from God, and the prophet must depend entirely on God for it. Rather than weakening the spirit of prophecy, this gives divine strength to it, as both the message and the courage to proclaim it come from God. Later, Paul will confirm this, saying, "For it is when I am weak that I am strong."[12] Thus the Old Testament prophets clearly share this characteristic: *The prophet's words originate from God, because God makes it possible for the prophet to carry out his mission.* As reluctant as most prophets are to take upon themselves the task God calls them to, God proves to be correspondingly determined, patient, and persistent in motivating the prophet to accept the task He offers.

Under God's Authority. The prophet receives the Word in God's power and authority: he or she is authorized to talk on behalf of God, and thus becomes God's bearer or God's "ambassador." *He is a messenger, rather than being an orator.* By the same authority, he is bound to deliver the instructions he has received in total obedience. Because the prophet does not forward his own opinion but binding words from the Almighty, he *must* deliver it to Yahweh's people, even if the consequences are persecution to the point of death.[13] Enrico Norelli has expressed this point well: "Differently from the priest, who creates a communication between man and God through the initiative of the former, the prophet depends in everything on the initiative of God, who allows, and at the same time orders him, to announce the message."[14]

The Old Testament includes several accounts of prophets who, after having been called to prophetic service, do not want to deliver the Word of God, for they know it will cause trouble. Jonah is perhaps the most famous example of a prophet who does not want to deliver a prophetic message; he actually runs away, first to another village and later to a ship, in order "to get away from Yahweh."[15] He may also be the best example of how determined God is in his appeal to the prophet to carry out the mission God has given him.

Friend of God. Even though the prophet's mission does not originate in himself, the prophet is not a detached servant or a "robot" who carries out divine orders mechanically. He is not disinterested in the message God is giving, not a "medium," who, in a state of trance, speaks words that make no sense to him. Through his contact with God, the prophet becomes one who knows God and understands his mind. God then includes his servant in his plans, and often tells him what he intends to do with his people—"Indeed, Lord Yahweh does nothing without revealing his secrets to his servants the prophets."[16] He becomes *the intimate of God*, and shares in God's joys and sorrows. *He is deeply involved* in the entire work of God. In fact, the prophetic words are often only one part of the massive work that God has called him to share: sometimes the prophet's life and Yahweh's message become so interwoven that the message is incorporated and expressed in the prophet's own existence. For example, the prophet Hosea, after being instructed by Yahweh to do so, marries a whore in order to portray the disloyalty of God's people. Even their children receive names that symbolize Israel's infidelity.

3.1.1. The Development of Old Testament Prophecy

Abraham's call is described through visions. Prophetic manifestations are common in the Old Testament even before Moses. However, Moses is the primary prophet in the Old Testament: only Moses sees God face to face without dying from the power of God's glory. The impact on Moses of God's direct presence is such that he has to wear a veil in order for the people not to be blinded. They are not able to stand in God's direct presence and cannot even sustain its impact on Moses. Thus Moses becomes the archetype of the prophets, so that all later prophets in a certain sense become prophets of the prophet Moses. For instance, Moses' brother is called to be Moses' prophet.[17] Moses' walk with God culminated in his encounters with God on Mount Sinai and the gift of the Law. The Ten Commandments are the final constitution and confirmation of the covenant between Yahweh and the people of Israel, promised by God to Abraham. After Moses, the main task of the prophets becomes keeping the people of Yahweh faithful to the fully constituted covenant. After Moses, the prophets' call to repentance is a specific call to remain faithful to the gift Yahweh gave through Moses—to respond to this gift with faithfulness and love.

At the same time, however, the prophets turn their gaze toward a promised period in history in which God and his people will live a more perfect covenant than the one instituted on Mount Sinai. It is the promised time of the Messiah, whose praises are sung, especially in later Israelite prophecy, through the mouths of Jeremiah and Isaiah. Hence the prophetic call to conversion has two perspectives: the prophet looks back in time, calling the people to remain faithful to the God who confirmed his commitment with his people through the covenant of Moses; at the same time, the prophet looks forward to a covenant much greater than the one given through Moses. Therefore, when the prophets call God's people to "follow the ways of the Lord," it is to safeguard what is already given and to prepare the people to receive something greater. The prophet seeks to keep the people faithful to the covenant while guiding them to the coming of the Messiah, living under the Law, which provides a foretaste of the Kingdom to come. It is noteworthy that the New Testament contains similar prophetic structures, where the prophet looks back to the historic works of God and the importance of faithfulness to God, and forward, to the coming Kingdom and preparation for it.[18]

3.1.2. Types of Old Testament Prophecy

From the time of Samuel until the Babylonian exile, Old Testament scholars discern two types of prophet. The first type is the *seer* (*hozeh* or *ro'eh*); the second is the *nabi'* (plural *nebi'im*). *Hozeh* or *ro'eh* is the oldest designation for "inspired individuals who mediate divine communications."[19] *Nabi'* is the most common designation for "prophet," which originally meant "one who is called" and came to mean "speaker, spokesman (of God)," or "proclaimer." The first group, the *seers*, were contemplative types; their visions were followed by personal reflections, and they were usually independent, going alone wherever the Lord sent them. The *nebi'im*, on the other hand, tended to have ecstatic experiences and went about in groups or gangs. For a long period in Israelite history they constituted a formal institution like the priesthood or the monarchy. The Old Testament tells of the *nebi'im* entering into collective ecstasy with Saul when the prophetic spirit overcame them and they prophesied together.[20] Although these distinctions may be useful, Witherington and others argue that it is a theoretical artifice to discern clinically between the *seers* and the *nebi'im*.[21] Often a prophet might be called with both names. This is the case with Samuel, who is usually portrayed as a seer but occasionally gathered with the *nebi'im* as their leader.[22] Yet there could be disputes between individual *seers* and gangs of *nebi'im*. This was often the case when entire gangs of prophets had been proven false and only the seer who was really sent by God prophesized truthfully. An example of such tension is found in 2 Chronicles 18. Here the kings asked the prophet Micah for advice from God whether or not they should go to war. The false prophets advised the kings to go, prophesying victory. Micah said the opposite, telling the kings that they would lose the battle, making Micah extremely unpopular. However, his prophecy proved to be correct.[23]

Which of the two kinds of prophecy was the most genuine and most pertinent to the so remarkable religion of ancient Israel is a matter of debate. A number of scholars argue that the *nebi'im*, while often truly inspired by God, were influenced by the religious practices of the surrounding religions, especially the Canaanite religion. While the religion of Israel originally was a desert and tribal religion, whose God was not of any specific place but was truly the *God of a people*, the Canaanite religion was an agrarian religion that had gods attached to local religious shrines. Each of these shrines had their spiritual leaders. While fighting against spiritual corruption through foreign influence, there are indications that the *nebi'im* were inspired by the Canaanite religions. Like the Canaanites, the *nebi'im* were often attached to specific shrines and would come together in collective ecstasies, spurred on by music and dance, as when Saul joined in a prophetic rapture. Even if the Bible makes it clear that God could operate within this framework, these prophets are often portrayed as falsely inspired. Thus Clifford Hill is convinced that true Old Testament prophecy does not require ecstatic music or other catalyses of trance, but that God is able to communicate himself to a chosen soul without human strivings.

Furthermore, the problems related to the *nebi'im* shed light on the phenomenon of institutionally ordered prophecy. It would seem that institutionalized prophecy easily succumbs to fraud and subjectivity, leading the prophets to prophesy what the group or the religious leaders desire rather than what God would want. Prophecy as such is a phenomenon of momentous endowment, dependent entirely on the Spirit of God; and, as Joseph Ratzinger points out, only with great difficulty can it be structured institutionally.[24]

The *canonical prophets* emerge late in Israel's history. Among these we find prophets such as Jeremiah and Isaiah who have left a great written legacy. There are different views of the origin of the canonical prophets. Some believe they are the successors of the *nebi'im*, as most of the canonical prophets include accounts of mystical experiences. Others believe they stand in direct line from the *seers*, those who served the Lord individually. But it is a matter of consensus that they did have mystical experiences and were not part of any prophetic institution. Much of their activity was centered on Israel's sorrowful experiences of deportation and captivity in Babylon. Hence some of the writings of the canonical prophets contain prophecies of judgment regarding the impending exile, and others speak about the salvation Yahweh will give to end the exile.

3.2. Prophecy in Early Judaism

The main difference between ancient and early Judean prophecy is that ancient prophecy acquired canonical status, whereas the prophetic traditions of early Judaism did not. Only after Christ did prophecy again—for a limited period of time—bear fruit in writings that obtained permanent sacrosanct status in the Christian canon. This difference in the acceptance of ancient and early Judean prophecy does not mean, however, that prophecy died out in the period after the Babylonian exile, though some scholars hold this to be the case.

3.2.1. On the Cessation of Prophecy in Early Judaism

There are diverging opinions on the development of late Israelite prophecy. Several scholars believe that prophecy ceased after the fifth century before

Christ and reemerged with the coming of Christ.[25] They consider prophecy in the last five centuries before Christ to have been virtually extinct and the prophetic function to be assimilated in the office of Israel's religious leaders.

Phillip Vielhauer pointed out the shortcomings of this view, in spite of its popularity, as Judaism in the Hellenistic period in no way was exempt from prophetic personalities.[26] Rudolf Meyer, although he gives evidence as to why prophecy was threatened in early Judaism, also argues that prophecy never ceased before the Christian era.[27] In recent years, increasing numbers of scholars give evidence for the noncessation of early Judean prophecy. David Aune in particular argues powerfully that prophecy did *not* cease: rather, it underwent some enormous changes during the period of the Second Temple, as did many other areas of Judaism during that period. In order to understand what motivated the theory of an *end to prophecy* in early Judaism, it is useful to consider the sources that sustain it. Benjamin Sommer argues against this reevaluation because he considers the changes too dramatic to allow for a "continuation" of Old Testament prophecy.[28] While I do not want to underestimate the degree of the prophetic mutation, the work of Aune and others of identifying signs of the reemergence of the prophetic in early Judaism is nevertheless relevant to the present study.

The texts that provide evidence of the decline of prophecy are later portions of the Old Testament, the Pseudepigrapha, the Apocrypha, Josephus, and other rabbinical literature. Aune claims that these texts must be evaluated carefully in order to avoid hasty conclusions and; moreover, that they in fact provide no proof that prophecy ceased—making the following arguments:

- Early Judaism exhibited great variety, and the views expressed in particular texts reflect only the opinion of that segment of Judaism which produced those texts.
- Some of the texts are relatively late (the rabbinic texts, for example, do not antedate the second century A.D.).
- Although these texts are often lumped together, they do not all refer either to the phenomena of the low esteem in which prophecy was purportedly held or to its ultimate cessation in Judaism.[29]

A passage from the Talmud frequently cited to prove the cessation of prophecy reads: "Until then, the prophets prophesied by means of the Holy Spirit. From then on, give ear and listen to the words of the sages."[30]

Another text frequently quoted—often without its final sentence—is Tosephta Sotah 13:2: "When the last of the prophets—i.e. Haggai, Zechariah, and Malachi—died, the Holy Spirit ceased in Israel. Despite this they were informed by means of oracles."[31]

With reference to scholarly evidence, Aune states that in both passages "the Holy Spirit" is synonymous with the activity of the canonical prophets prior to the construction of the second temple. The texts, rather than giving evidence to the cessation of prophecy, are rabbinical apologetics. The authors were a group of rabbis who considered themselves the only legitimate interpreters of the Mosaic Law—*a charism they believed to have inherited from the canonical prophets.* Since these "rabbinic sages" did not consider themselves to be carriers of prophetic revelations, but rather of tradition, it is understandable that they would downplay the presence of prophetic activity in their own time. It is also possible, as P. Schäfer shows, that these rabbis were speaking out polemically against a rising presence of Christian prophets.[32] And beyond rabbinical groups, there is considerable evidence for the continuation of the prophetic charism. Thus S. Sandmel writes: "Outside the circle of the rabbinical Sages the view that prophecy had ended simply did not exist."[33]

Other than the two rabbinical texts quoted above, three passages of 1 Maccabees[34] have been used to disprove the presence of prophecy in the period of the New Temple:

> They therefore demolished it [the altar] and deposited the stones in a suitable place on the hill of the Dwelling to await the appearance of a prophet who should give a ruling about them (4,45–46).... A terrible oppression began in Israel; there had been nothing like it since the disappearance of prophecy among them (9,27).... The Jews and priests are happy that Simon should, pending the advent of a genuine prophet, be their ethnarch and high priest for life (14,40).

Aune maintains, however, that these passages, when read carefully, refer to specific types of prophecy that had disappeared by the time of the writer of 1 Maccabees.[35] Hence they cannot be used to disprove the presence of all prophecy.

Furthermore, some rabbinic writings point to the evidence of prophetic charisms and occurrences within their own circles. Aune states: "according to the other rabbinic traditions, famous rabbis claimed the gift of prophecy and/ or the possession of the Spirit of God. The same holds for many of the late Jewish sects, particularly to the Qumran community."[36]

If prophecy did not cease, it did, however, take a new form. A prominent feature of this new type of prophecy is that it often invokes prophets of the Old Testament. As J. Blenkinsopp argues, the Jewish canon was in no way a mere creation of the famous "council" of Jabneh around 90 A.D.: the Jewish canon evolved gradually so that Old Testament prophets attained a sacrosanct status around the time of the construction of the new temple.[37] This explains two things: (1) Authors in early Judaism believe that the voices of the prophets have ceased because they are referring to the *canonical prophets*, who are no more; (2) Judean prophecy has a characteristic feature of looking back to the canonical prophets with the aim of interpreting their writings in a prophetic way, and to implement their teaching in the current situation.

Some scholars hold that the closure and delineation of canon effectuated the end of the prophetic age. But Aune disagrees:

> The Formation of the Old Testament canon ... appears to have had no connection with the view that prophecy had ended in Judaism. Even in the famous passage found in Josephus *Contra Ap.* I. 37–41, where the Jewish historian discussed the boundaries of the Hebrew scriptures, he does not say that prophecy has ceased, only that there is no longer an "exact succession" (*akribé diadochén*) of prophets, i.e. there is no direct relationship between the desultory appearances of various prophets.[38]

Ben Witherington writes along the same lines as Aune. His entire work *Jesus the Seer* is dedicated to examining different cultures in the Near East for the prophetic phenomenon, and he agrees that prophecy changed form and appearance but never ceased. Thus he is able to summaries his research by writing:

> This study of the development of prophecy in the ancient Near East and the eastern end of the Greco-Roman world, especially in Jewish and Christian contexts, has journeyed in many directions and through many texts.... One may certainly talk about the development or diminution of prophecy and its proliferation or marginalization across various periods of time, but one can not talk about its extinction, so far as I can tell, for any considerable time in the period 1600 BC to AD 300.[39]

So if classical prophecy did not cease but evolved into something new, what are these new forms? First of all, just as ancient Jewish prophecy was not one unified entity, likewise prophecy in early Judaism was not a single body. Its different forms resulted in different movements—all of which, however, include an apocalyptic approach to history. Aune distinguishes four major types of early Jewish prophecy: apocalyptic literature; eschatological prophecy; clerical prophecy; and sapiential prophecy. Though these four categories are not neatly separable, I will briefly define the different forms, as they are the immediate forerunners of Christian prophecy.

3.2.2. Apocalyptic Literature

The complex ensemble of writings commonly known as apocalyptic literature show amazing similarity with Old Testament prophecy. An ongoing debate in the study of apocalyptic literature is how much of this literature *is in fact* a continuation of Old Testament prophecy. It is certain that there is continuity and discontinuity between the two traditions. Many apocalyptic writings are the result of (or are expressed in) formulas for revelatory experiences, and many have striking similarity to the experiences and writings of the Old Testament prophets. On the other hand, the apocalyptic writings are heavily influenced by Greco-Roman traditions. This influence includes the widespread use of pseudonymity, the dualistic traits of apocalypses, and the interest in individual, transcendent salvation.

Most Jewish apocalypses were written between 200 B.C. and 100 A.D. The Book of Daniel is the oldest piece of writing in the apocalyptic category, which also includes writings such as 1 Enoch, 2 Enoch, 2 Baruch, and the Apocalypse of Abraham. *The Apocalypse of John* and *Hermas the Shepherd* share numerous traits with this group but still are easily distinguished as Christian apocalypses.

Finally, Aune defines an apocalypse as

> a form of revelatory literature in which the author narrates both the visions he has purportedly experienced and their meaning, usually elicited through a dialogue between the seer and an interpreting angel. The substance of these revelatory visions is the imminent intervention of God into human affairs to bring the present evil world system to an end and to replace it with an ideal one. This transformation is accompanied by the punishment of the wicked and the reward of the righteous.[40]

THE PSEUDONYMOUS CHARACTER OF APOCALYPSES. Although much research has been done on the question of pseudonymity in Jewish apocalyptic literature, the reasons for pseudonymity have not yet been explained in a satisfactory way. It is not clear whether apocalyptic writers used pseudonymity in order to deceive or in good faith. Aune gives four reasons for its use;[41] only the first, which he considers the most probable, is an example of manipulation:

- Pseudonymity was used to secure the acceptance of an apocalypse during a period when the canon was virtually closed and prophetic inspiration had ended.

- Pseudonymity was a means of protecting the real authors of apocalypses from reprisal.
- Apocalyptic visionaries may have had revelatory experiences mediated by those figures to whom they attributed their compositions.
- The apocalyptic seer may have identified himself with a prominent Israelite of the past and written as his representative.

Whatever the reasons were for the use of pseudonymity, it was widespread in the Greco-Roman world and in Jewish apocalyptic literature, but *rarely* in Christian apocalyptic literature. The two Christian apocalypses—the Revelation of John and Hermas the Shepherd—have identified authors. If the first reason for pseudonymity given earlier, namely that prophecy for apologetic reasons was never labeled *prophecy* in the postcanonical period, is correct, then this means that Christian prophets did *not* consider prophetic inspiration to have ended or that prophetic inspiration had been reintroduced through the Christ-event. Prophecy was present, only under another name.

THE SOCIAL SETTING OF APOCALYPSES. Aune's thesis is that Jewish apocalypses were written under pseudonym because the author's true identity would undermine its authority. This might indicate that apocalypses were not written for closed groups, since the author's true identity could not remain secret within such a group. It appears that apocalyptic movements imported external apocalyptic material; although a few communities, such as that of Qumran, did produce their own writings.

Researchers discern two principal religious lines emerging in postexilic Judaism. One was the priestly-theocratic line; the other was the prophetic-eschatological one. Both arose after the fall of the temple, and both were interested in the reconstruction of Israel, but they had very different views regarding what this reconstruction should look like. The priestly-theocratic line, composed mainly of Zadokite priestly elements, had a pragmatic, historical outlook on reconstruction, whereas the prophetic line had a more eschatological perspective. Hanson argues in *The Dawn of Apocalyptic* that the apocalyptic genre emerged in the matrix of the conflict between these two groups.[42] The apocalyptic tradition stems from the prophetic-eschatological line, and many of its eschatological traits are rooted in the desire to have Israel resurrect to full vigor after the destruction of the temple. Even though the apocalyptic tradition can be traced back to one group around the fifth century B.C., it later invaded wide areas of the Jewish social landscape. Thus it is not possible to link apocalyptic literature to specific movements or sects.

Apocalypses such as Daniel seem to derive from scribal circles, probably the Hasidim, who wrote "apocalypses as 'tracts for the times' in various times of oppression."[43] Apocalypses focusing on future deliverance largely appear in the different prophetic traditions as outlets of frustration or as beams of hope that things will change for the better by the power of God.

THE RELATIONSHIP BETWEEN PROPHETIC AND APOCALYPTIC LITERATURE. As mentioned earlier, the relationship between prophecy and apocalyptic writing is uncertain. Most scholars agree that the relationship is ambiguous, exhibiting both continuity and discontinuity. Gerhard von Rad contends that apocalyptic writing emerged from Israelite wisdom, not from prophecy.[44] Aune insists that this view has found little support from other scholars. In Hanson's opinion, Old Testament prophecy gradually merged into apocalyptic writing as an "inner-Jewish development."[45] But this does not mean that apocalyptic writing does not have much in common with the Israelite wisdom tradition, only that its forerunner remains Old Testament prophecy.

One of the main differences between Old Testament prophecy and early Jewish apocalypses is the role of the prophet as opposed to the apocalyptic author. The latter plays a more prominent role than the former in the interpretation of his experience, whereas the inspiration of the Old Testament prophet is more direct.

The increasing emphasis on "prophecy through interpretation" that characterized the sixth century B.C. and the early Second Temple period is often correlated with a growing view of the distance and transcendence of God. God does not reveal his word directly to the apocalyptists, as he did to the Old Testament prophets, but indirectly through visions and scripture, both of which require interpretation.[46]

J. J. Collins sees the main difference between prophetic and apocalyptic writing in the message, especially with regard to the foretelling of future events: according to Collins, Old Testament prophecy is conditional, depending on the response by the faithful to the message of the prophet, while apocalyptic predictions reflect an unconditional verdict transfixed in the predetermination of God.[47]

3.2.3. Eschatological Prophecy

The apocalyptic currents in early Judaism led to several apocalyptic (also called *millenarian*) movements that greatly influenced religious life in the decades preceding Christ. These movements were generally centered around leaders who were often called *prophets* because they were believed to have been called by God to restore the rule of God, much like the Old Testament prophets. For example, the Qumran community centered around "the Teacher of Righteousness," another formed around John the Baptist, and Christianity formed around Jesus Christ; and in spite of individual characteristics, the communities shared many common traits. In fact, until the ill-fated revolt centered around Bar Kosiba in 132–35 A.D., Palestine knew many millenarian movements. Though the Christian theologian may see the movement initiated by Jesus Christ as unique, the secular historian sees Christianity as one among many similar apocalyptic currents in early Judaism.

Scholars divide the charismatic leaders of these movements into two neatly distinguishable groups: messianic deliverers and prophetic deliverers. The messianic deliverers were characterized by their desire to restore the earthly Kingdom of God within human history, whereas the prophetic deliverers sought to lead the People of God toward the eschatological, transcendent realization of God's Kingdom. According to Aune,

> [the] Davidic messiah of popular expectation was conceived as a
> military figure whose primary tasks were the defeat of Israel's ene-
> mies, the purification of Jerusalem and the temple, and the ingath-
> ering of dispersed Israelites as a prelude for a golden age. This
> messianic figure did not function as a prophet, a preacher of re-
> pentance, or a miracle worker.[48]

Many Jewish revolts, beaten down by the Romans before and after the coming of Christ, were led by popular messianic deliverers of this type. Even the "Son of Man" tradition appears to belong to this category.

Although some communities saw the messianic figure as religious, the prophetic deliverers were far more religiously oriented than the messianic. The prophetic deliverers were interested in the eschatological, not the earthly, Kingdom of God. They were believed to be endowed with divine powers to perform miracles, especially gifted in interpretation of the Torah, would call the people to repentance in preparation for the coming Kingdom of Yahweh, and would intercede between man and God.[49] Both John the Baptist and Jesus Christ possessed many traits of the prophetic deliverer, though Jesus has been named a messianic deliverer of the religious type as well.

Both types of apocalyptic deliverer are believed to stand in direct succession from the Old Testament prophets: through their revelatory experiences, through the divine mandate of their mission, and through the aim of their mission. The idea that Old Testament prophecy continued through the eschatological prophets is evident in Mt 3:23–24, where John the Baptist is portrayed as the returned Elijah of Mal 4:5–6: "Behold, I will send you Elijah the prophet before the great and terrible day of the Lord comes. And he will turn the hearts of the fathers to their children and the hearts of children to their fathers, lest I come and smite the land with a curse."

3.2.4. Clerical Prophecy

As prophecy reemerged in early Judean apocalyptic literature, so did it continue in *clerical prophecy*. The New Testament knows of at least one important example of the belief in early Judaism that *by virtue of their office* priests were endowed with prophetic gifts:

> One of them, Caiaphas, the high priest that year, said, "You do not seem to have grasped the situation at all; you fail to see that it is to your advantage that one man should die for the people, rather than that the whole nation should perish." He did not speak in his own person, but as high priest of that year he was prophesying that Jesus was to die for the nation—and not for the nation only, but also to gather together into one the scattered children of God.[50]

Both Josephus, Philo, and the New Testament link prophetic experiences and gifts to the office of priests, especially to the High priests.[51]

The Jewish historian Josephus is perhaps the most interesting example of a priest who by virtue of his office considers himself endowed with prophetic gifts, although he never calls himself a prophet. As Blenkinsopp shows, in numerous passages Josephus writes about prophecies he pronounced that came true.[52] Josephus makes this famous speech to Vespasian after his capture:

> You, Vespasian, think that Josephus is just another captive taken, but I come to you as a messenger [angelos] of greater things.... You are Caesar, Vespasian, and emperor, you and your son here. But bind me more securely and keep me yourself. For you Caesar are master not only of me, but also of the earth and sea and all mankind. I ask the punishment of a closer guard if I have capriciously attributed this to God.[53]

Later on Josephus will write that Vespasian released him when he became emperor as he remembered the prophecy Josephus had pronounced. This prophecy is one out of many predictions, prophetic utterances, and inspired interpretations of dreams and Scripture passages that Josephus claims to have performed. One of his frequently mentioned prophetic gifts is the inspired interpretation of Old Testament prophecies and their application to the present. The similarities both to Daniel and to the Teacher of Righteousness are particularly striking.

3.2.5. Sapiential Prophecy

The last area of Early Judean religion identified with prophecy is the sapiential tradition. Sapiential prophecy has much in common with clerical prophecy, especially in the absence of a distinct eschatological outlook. Where both apocalyptic writing and eschatological prophecy have a strong interest in the future—be it the future of immanent world history or an eschatological future—both clerical and sapiential prophecy are oriented exclusively toward the present. While the charism of prophecy in clerical circles was connected to the gifts inherent in the priesthood, sapiential prophecy derived its inspiration from the "faculty of wisdom."[54] The presence of prophecy in early Judean priesthood was thought to facilitate the proper administration of the priestly office. Sapiential prophecy is primarily concerned with the secrets of the cosmos and the prediction of the future.

Philo of Alexandria is (20 B.C.–A.D. 50) a particularly interesting example of a sage carrying the marks of prophecy. In the Hellenistic diaspora, the notion took hold that divine wisdom could turn any person into a prophet by taking possession of that person.[55] Thus for Philo every wise man is also a prophet.[56] Philo was a Jew, living in the Greek diaspora of Alexandria. Inspired by Plato, he considered the highest knowledge to be the knowledge of Ideas. According to H. A. Wolfson, Philo never called himself a prophet. However, in his writings he interchanged the term "prophecy" with the Platonic word *anamnesis* or "recollection."[57] Examining Philo's writings with this in mind, it becomes clear that Philo considered himself a prophet:

> On other occasions, I have approached my work empty and suddenly become full, the ideas falling in a shower from above and being sown invisibly, so that under the influence of the divine possession, I have been filled with corybantic frenzy and been unconscious of anything, place, persons present, myself, words spoken, lines written. For I obtained language, ideas, an enjoyment of light, keenest vision, pellucid distinctness of objects, such as might be received through the eyes as the result of clearest shewing.[58]

The faculty of inner sight was vital to Philo's conception of prophecy. As Aune shows, Philo's oracular passages are usually marked by an introductory description of his inspired state, followed by the prophetic message itself, or simply the description of his vision.[59]

3.2.6. Conclusion

Prophecy did not cease in the period leading up to Christ, as some scholars have argued, and John the Baptist was not the only prophet after a long time of prophetic silence. On the contrary, prophecy managed continuously to mutate according to new cultural and historical settings. The entire early Judean scene was marked by the prophetic phenomenon, and all its main currents, apocalyptic, eschatological, sapiential, and scribal, were influenced by and gave birth to prophetic phenomena. Although prophecy—mainly out of respect for the canonical prophets—no longer enjoyed the name by which it had been formerly known, the phenomenon itself continued. Prophetic movements on the margins of Jewish life showed a great interest in the apocalyptic traditions. Through its promise that God would win in the end, prophecy could give believers hope and consolation in a time when Greeks and Romans had the upper hand.

The prophetic experiences of the Greco-Roman world now became merged into early Judean prophecy. Although this tradition was more rational than the Jewish tradition, it was nevertheless permeated by the conviction that the divine could and did interfere in the human sphere, and although there were differences between the two prophetic traditions, the merge between Jewish and Greek traditions only enhanced the expectation of and room for prophecy.

3.3. Prophecy in Christianity

Prophetic traits penetrate all the different streams of religious life in Palestine prior to Christ—in apocalyptic, priestly, and sapiential circles—and therefore flow into Christianity as already existing traditions. Old Testament prophecy did not have to be reinterpreted in order to make sense for the people in the time of Jesus and the apostles—it already thrived as a living reality of early Judean religious life.

Thus, Christian prophecy emerges as a mutated continuation of its Old Testament and early Judean counterparts. Charles Talbert summarizes this as a strong conviction in the early church:

> Early Christians understood prophecy within the church as a continuation or renewal of the prophecy of ancient Israel.... When Justin martyr said, "the prophetical gifts remain with us even to the present time" (*Dialogue* 82), he was expressing a widespread Christian belief. References to early Christian prophets and prophecies are extensive.[60]

If prophecy never ceased in early Judaism, it did indeed develop and assume different forms. The coming of Christ marks a watershed moment in the development of prophecy. The Incarnation is the event that had the most drastic historical impact on the development of prophecy, not just theologically, but even historically. At the same time, this event opened a considerable theological dispute since some theologians understood the Christ-event as the necessary closure of prophecy. As we shall see, this position does not reflect the New Testament's image of Christianity.

Studying prophecy in the New Testament and in the early church poses a methodological problem: the Old Testament offers many books of prophetic messages and oracular sayings. This is not the case in the early church since only two compilations of prophetic messages exist: "The Revelation of Saint John" and "Hermas the Shepherd." Therefore, the study of New Testament and early church prophecy must rely mainly on what sources say *about* prophecy and prophets, rather than what prophets actually said themselves. The sources reveal far too few oracles for it to be possible to synthesize these alone into a theology of prophecy.

3.3.1. Toward a Working Definition of Christian Prophecy

As mentioned in the introduction, Christian prophecy emerges directly from the early Christian setting and must, at its core, be identical with that of prophecy emerging from the New Testament writings. Its definition is hence of great importance to our work of identifying the nature and purpose of prophecy in the church.

As the phenomenon of prophecy has undergone so many changes in the different historical periods, reducing it to one agreed formula is next to impracticable, and some theologians find it difficult to believe at all in the feat of defining New Testament prophecy, even when they agree that the phenomenon exists. Thus, while admitting that early Christian writings clearly indicate the presence of "important prophetic components," Gerhard Dautzenberg remains pessimistic in regards to its description, since "the allocation of certain texts or traditions to ancient Christian prophecy...nevertheless proves to be very complicated due to the lack of unequivocal criteria based on New Testament statements about prophecy."[61] However, Dautzenberg's assessments have encountered massive opposition, in particular in W. Grudem's "A Response to Gerhard Dautzenberg."[62] Likewise, David Aune has dedicated great part of his life to the study of New Testament prophecy, and has developed exactly the criteria Dautzenberg is missing.

In spite of the pessimism of exegetes as Dautzenberg, most exegetes writing on the issue agree that a working definition can be reached, and Christopher Forbes is right in stating that it is "gratifying to see recent research reaching a reasonable degree of consensus as to the nature of prophecy."[63] There are many pathways toward identifying the image of Christian prophecy as it emerges from the New Testament. The first may be the etymological approach that investigates what the word meant originally and its derivations therefrom. Fascher followed this etymological approach to the word-group *prophet* in his thorough work: *ΠΡΟΦΕΤΕΣ, Eine sprach- und religionsgeschichtliche Untersuchung*, published in 1927.[64] But here it is important to keep in mind that there is no guarantee that the original meaning of the word *prophet* applied to the same word's usage in New Testament times. A word means what it signifies in a given context, not what it signified originally. As we shall see during the presentation of the development of prophecy in early Judaism, the word meant something entirely different by the time of Jesus than it had at the time of the Old Testament prophets.

Second, it is possible to look at a given context in the body of writings in which all the occurrences of the word *prophet* and its variations are used. This has the advantage of examining a phenomenon in its actual setting and usage. The problem with this approach is that it is exclusive. There is no guarantee that all prophetic phenomena are linked to the word-group *prophet*, so a definition based solely on the distribution of words linked to *prophet* will not give a full picture of the measure of prophecy. There are many reasons why certain prophets will not call themselves prophets, even though they and their followers consider themselves transmitters of God's words. As we shall see later, this applies especially to postcanonical prophecy. History indicates a change in the early church and certainly after Montanism, whereby theologians started addressing the phenomenon of prophecy by other names.

If we are to find the possible continuation of the prophetic tradition in the church, we must be able to identify it through its function, and not solely by its nominal designation. Hence the third, and probably most fruitful, way of defining prophecy is the phenomenological way: investigating its function in a given historical setting, and distinguishing it from other offices in the church.

If, however, there is no initial indication of the meaning of prophecy, it is impossible to arrive at a pragmatic definition. Hence the necessity of beginning our investigation by homing in on those passages of Holy Scripture that do refer to prophecy. Having examined those passages that accentuate and illustrate explicitly the phenomenon of prophecy, it is then possible to describe other related phenomena even though they are not imbued with the prophetic nomenclature.

Following this principle, Johannes Lindblom in his classic characterization of the prophetic class among *homines religiosi* gave the following definition:

> [Prophets] are entirely devoted, soul and body, to the divinity. They are inspired personalities who have the power to receive divine revelations. They act as speakers and preachers who publicly announce

what they have to say. They are compelled by higher powers and kept under divine constraint. The inspiration which they experience has a tendency to pass over into real ecstasy. One further attribute may be added: the special call. A prophet knows that he has never chosen his way himself: he has been chosen by the deity. He points to a particular experience in his life through which it has become clear to him that the deity has a special purpose with him and has designated him to perform a special mission.[65]

Along the same principle, Boring gave his description of prophecy in his valuable presentation entitled "'What Are We Looking For?' Toward a Definition of the Term 'Christian Prophet,'" which he gave at a seminar entitled "Early Christian Prophecy" that was held by the American Society of Biblical Literature (SBL) in 1973. According to Boring, "a prophet is an immediately inspired spokesman for the (or a) deity of a particular community, who receives revelations which he is impelled to deliver to the community."[66] In Boring's view, *the mode and the origin* of the prophetic message is what more than anything else characterizes prophecy. But the prophet is not just a mystic, who seeks the godhead and is in communion with God; the prophet is compelled to deliver his message, and this turns him from being a "mere mystic" to being a prophet. Boring excludes self-induced means of obtaining prophetic messages but does not exclude the usage of already given material in the formation of the prophetic message. He elaborates his definition as follows:

> The prophet presents all that he utters as a prophet as the immediately inspired present address of the deity to his community. This message may well include material taken from tradition and the prophet's own reflection, consciously or unconsciously, with or without reinterpretation, but it is not presented as material which a past authority once said, but as what the deity now says. The same material may be presented by the non-inspired teacher or preacher, but with the formal and functional difference that this claim to immediate inspiration is not made.[67]

In a later publication, Boring continued his understanding of prophecy in the specifically Christian context: "The early Christian prophet was an immediately inspired spokesperson for the risen Jesus, who received intelligible messages that he or she felt impelled to deliver to the Christian community or, as a representative of the community, to the general public."[68]

With this definition, Boring explicitly excludes a number of related phenomena in early Christianity that often are labeled "prophetic." Prophecy in the strict sense of the word does *not* apply to the notion that the spirit-filled community consists of believers who by the indwelling of the Spirit are potential prophets, nor does it apply to the general preaching ministry of the church. God can choose anyone he wants to be a prophet, but in order to be a Christian prophet in the full sense, a moment of divine commission is required. Boring includes in the prophetic category only those who actually function as prophets.

At the same SBL seminar where Boring presented " 'What Are We Looking For?' David Aune delivered his definition of a Christian prophet: "The Christian who functions in the prophetic role (whether regularly, occasionally or temporarily) believes that he receives divine revelations in propositional form which he customarily delivers in oral or written form to Christian individuals and/or groups."[69]

Boring is critical toward Aune's specification that a prophet can deliver his message to individuals, as Boring very firmly holds that the Christian prophet's audience is the community. But if one understands Aune's "individuals" as individual members of that community, Boring's worries prove less compelling.

In response, David Hill does not disagree with any of the aforementioned definitions; he simply finds that they lack "any specific reference to 'call': it is implied by both scholars in their definitions, but, in our view, it requires explicit statement."[70] Hill finds this to be well expressed in the definition of Johannes Lindblom quoted earlier. Furthermore, in response to Boring's main thesis with regard to Christian prophecy, presented in his influential, but disputed, *Sayings of the Risen Jesus,* Hill finds Boring's insistence that "the Christian prophet functions as the 'spokesman for the exalted Jesus' . . . unnecessarily restrictive" and asserts that it "may carry hidden presuppositions about the relation of prophetic words to 'oracles of the risen Lord.' "[71] In this respect Hill finds Aune's definition better.

As his own proposal, Hill gives the following definition of prophecy: "A Christian prophet is a Christian who functions within the church, occasionally or regularly, as a divinely called and divinely inspired speaker who receives intelligible and authoritative revelations or messages which he is impelled to deliver publicly, in oral or written form, to Christian individuals and/or the Christian community."[72]

Aune finds Hill's definition insufficient:

This definition will make it very difficult for Hill to distinguish among a prophet, an apostle, a preacher, and a teacher later on in his study, for he later observes that "the prophet is not the only leader in the church whose speech is inspired by the Spirit"[73] and that it

cannot be assumed that all inspired speech in the early Christian community emanated from prophets: were not 'teachers' and
'evangelists' also inspired by the Spirit?"[74] These statements suggest that Hill is [sic] not trying to use history-of-religion categories to
describe the role for the NT prophet.[75]

While this does not mean that the history-of-religion method employed by Hill
and other scholars is wrong, it illustrates Hill's inconsistent application of it in
his work. In fact, he deviates from this principle in the latter parts of his book,
especially in his chapter on the presumed cessation of prophecy in early Christianity, where he claims that the teachers continued the role that prophets had
played before.[76]

Most scholars agree that it is difficult to distinguish prophetic messages
from other messages in the church. Whereas Aune dedicates most of his book
to identifying and categorizing prophetic and oracular speech in early Christianity, he admits that the oral or written product of a prophet alone is not
enough to make him or her a prophet. Thus, the ultimate characteristic note of
true prophecy is its *mode*, namely an *experienced divine revelation* that lends it
divine commission. As we saw, this is the opinion of Boring as well as Aune,
who concluded his chapter "The Basic Feature of Early Christian Prophetic
Speech" with the statement that "the distinctive feature of prophetic speech was
not so much its *content* or *form*, but its *supernatural origin*. Christian prophetic
speech, then, is Christian discourse presented with divine legitimization."[77]

Much like Aune, Grabbe sees in the revealed mode of prophecy its major
characteristic trait: "the prophet is a mediator who claims to receive messages
directly from a divinity, by various means, and communicates these messages
to recipients."[78] Max Turner, summarizing his view and that of several other
writers concerning Paul's interpretation of prophecy, said that it is "the
reception and subsequent communication of spontaneous, divinely given
apokalypsis … the declaring of a revelatory experience."[79] Witherington re-
affirmed this definition—"divine revelation is a *sine qua non* of prophecy"[80]—
as we saw Grudem do: "If there is no *apokalypsis*, there is no prophecy."[81]
Similarly, Robert Omara, in his Lateran University dissertation, infers from
I Corinthians 14.30 that prophecy involves "a sudden revelation at the
moment—the Greek word is *apocalypsis*, revelation."[82] Larry W. Hurtado believes that this trait is equally important for Old Testament and New Testament prophecy: "as with the Old Testament phenomenon, the essential
character of early Christian prophecy was the claim to be speaking under direct
divine inspiration."[83] "Prophecy is instant speech inspired by the spirit and
spoken *hic et nunc* in the congregation."[84]

Several authors rule out the possibility that prophecy could be the result of mere human endeavors, such as James D. G. Dunn: "For Paul prophecy is a word of revelation. It does not denote the delivery of previously prepared sermon; it is not a word that can be summarised up to order, or a skill that can be learned; it is a spontaneous utterance, a revelation given in words to the prophet to be delivered as it is given."[85]

A prophet has mystical experiences that make out the source of his or her cognition and writing, and from this perspective every prophet is also a mystic. Conversely, not every mystic is a prophet, as being a prophet implies more than having mystical experiences: a mystic becomes a prophet only when he or she also forwards his or her received message to the church for its edification.

Thomas Aquinas wrote about the different applications of the prophetic term. However, he also held that the highest realization of prophecy occurred when the prophet was aware that God was addressing him directly through immediate revelation.

Visions, apparitions, locutions, and other means of divine communications are hence requirements for speaking of prophecy in the strict sense. These have often been summarized under the notion of "private revelations," but as we shall see, the modern dynamic understanding of revelation has emptied out the remains of meaning from this notion, which even within the framework of a doctrinal understanding of revelation never managed to do justice to the importance of God's prophetic appeal to his people: true Christian prophecy is never a private affair of the person who mediates the message.

For this study, which deals with the theological significance of Christian prophecy, it is important to determine how prophecy relates to the prediction of future events. It has been common to consider it a main characteristic of the Old Testament prophets that they predicted Christ's coming or, in a limited way, revealed his truth. If this is a valid definition of prophecy, then it follows logically that there can be no such persons as Christian prophets, since the fullness of revelation was revealed in Christ and his coming would have made the predictions of the Messiah futile. But such limiting definitions of Old Testament prophecy have some serious shortcomings. Old Testament prophets did much more than speak about the Messiah and give a foretaste of his doctrine. Their main task was to speak the words that God inspired them to speak, and most of their words referred to their own generation's conversion and their right observance of the Law of Yahweh. Likewise, Christian prophecy is about much more than prediction. Following his analysis of prophecy in Paul's letter to the Corinthians, Omara concludes that prophecy does not necessarily mean a prediction of the future, for even in the O.T. the prophet was primarily the man who spoke the word of the Lord for the contemporary community—that is, what the community needed most to hear at this moment. Occasionally there were promises or threats about the future, but all these emerged out of a concern for hearing the word of God in the present moment and responding to it.[86]

Summarizing the debate between the various opinions, we may conclude that a Christian prophet, whether labeled as such or not, is a Christian who, through experienced revelations, receives a message that he or she is directed to hand on to the church for its edification as part of a firm design in God's will to save, guide, and bless his people.

3.3.2. Prophecy and John the Baptist

If prophecy diminished in its classical form until the time of Jesus, the Gospel portrays John the Baptist as the one who revives the prophetic tradition. His teaching, his call to repentance, his way of life, even his clothing mark him as a successor to the Old Testament prophets. The New Testament connects him directly with Moses and Elijah—two prophets who prophesied the coming of the Messiah. The similarity with Elijah is important since one of the messianic prophecies states that Elijah must return to prepare the way of the Lord.[87] Like Elijah, John the Baptist wears camel-hair clothing and a leather belt, lives in the desert, and eats locusts.[88] At one point Jesus is interrogated about the Baptist. His reply is interesting, as it gives insights on how the tradition of prophecy stands in relation to John's presence on earth:

> "What did you go out into the desert to see? . . . To see a prophet?"
> "Yes, I tell you, and much more than a prophet: he is the one of whom scripture says: 'Look, I am going to send my messenger in front of you to prepare your way before you.' In truth I tell you, of all the children born to women, there has never been anyone greater than John the Baptist; yet the least in the kingdom of Heaven is greater than he . . . it was towards John that all the prophecies of the prophets and of the Law were leading; and he, if you will believe me, is the Elijah who was to return."[89]

John the Baptist is not merely a prophet who can point to a distant future saying "one day the Redeemer will come." He points directly to Jesus, exclaiming: "Look, there is the lamb of God that takes away the sin of the world."[90]

John the Baptist is the last to proclaim Christ's future coming and the first to point him out in time. He becomes the figure that bridges the period of prophetic promises to the time of fulfillment. This makes him more than a prophet and the greatest of the children born to women. Paradoxically, the least in Christ's Kingdom will be greater than he, as the sacrifice of Christ before the death of John the Baptist had not yet opened the gates of Heaven—John would enter the Kingdom of Heaven after Christ had opened its gates with his blood.

In spite of John the Baptist being called the last prophet, in the sense that he is the last to prophesy the coming of Christ, the charism of prophecy does not end in the church; on the contrary, once the Kingdom is opened, the charism of prophecy can be bestowed upon the faithful more profusely than ever before.

3.3.3. Prophecy and Jesus

The Gospels tell of many people calling Jesus a prophet, and, as Morna D. Hooker writes, that Jesus "was regarded in his own day as a prophet seems beyond doubt."[91] Many scholars have pointed to the scriptural evidence that Jesus was regarded as a prophet, and most works on Christian prophecy contain a chapter on Jesus as prophet.[92] Hooker's exposé focuses on the prophetic *actions* of Jesus. Many of Christ's actions and sayings were prophetic and showed similarities with the actions of the Old Testament prophets, as follows.

1. Jesus expounds the Scriptures in a prophetic way, showing how they are fulfilled in his own person.
2. He speaks in prophetic ways, shedding light on his own times and pronouncing judgment on the decay of Israel with prophecies on what will be the result of the apostasy.
3. He performs prophetic deeds in which miracles play a decisive role.
4. He prophesies about his own death and glorification.
5. He is a visionary in the sense that he is able to read the souls of people and has visions that he himself is able to explain.

Thus his contemporaries call Jesus a prophet. In certain passages he is called *the* prophet, as the fulfillment of Deuteronomy 18:15–18, in which Moses speaks of a "prophet like myself"—a passage that historically was linked to the Messiah. With this evidence, it is not surprising that many exegetes consider the term an appropriate or even the best single designation for Jesus, as does Edward P. Sanders: "I continue to regard 'prophet' as the best single category."[93]

Obviously, the designation of Christ as "prophet" has its limitations, too, because the Incarnation transcends the nature of prophecy. A prophet is a spokesperson of God—someone who speaks the word of God on his behalf—whereas Jesus is more than someone who speaks the word of God on behalf of God, but rather *is* the Word of God. This is why the evangelists never call Jesus a prophet, just as Jesus never compares himself to the prophets, except in one passage where he uses the term analogously to describe the violent death that often befalls the servants of God. To the contrary, Peter's confession does not count Jesus among the prophets, but above them: "You are the Christ, the Son of the living God."[94] Even if the Fathers of the church knew of a *prophetic Christology*, discussion about Jesus as a prophet can only be in the analogous sense, for only terms like *Son* or *Christ* cover his nature.

In Christ, revelation and prophecy attain their synthesis and climax. If, as Karl Rahner writes, any prophetic revelation of the Old Testament can add something to the Deposit of Faith and to the divine fullness and truth of revelation, then revelation has attained its full expression in Christ. It could be concluded that after the coming of Christ there is no more need or room for prophecy, since no revelation can exceed the revelation of God in Christ. Yet the New Testament does not support this conclusion, and portrays a boom in prophetic manifestations and charisms after Pentecost. And this makes sense for several reasons, as follows.

Although Christ as the Word is fully present in the world, the church has to penetrate into the knowledge and fullness of this Word. It can do this only under the guidance of the Spirit, who "will remind [us] of all truth."[95] Thus, the role of prophets after Christ is to lead the church to the truth and fullness of God in Christ, just as it was the role of the Old Testament prophets to lead God's people to remain faithful to the revelation God has conferred on Moses. Just as the Old Testament prophets fought to keep God's people faithful to the covenant, so now the prophets in the New Testament, and in Christ's church, are called to keep believers faithful to the covenant of the New Testament, sealed with the blood of the Lamb.

Moreover, Christ's presence in the world does not come to an end with his death and resurrection—in fact, the opposite is true. After the ascension, prophets see and hear Christ in their revelations. The first of these may be Stephen, prior to his martyrdom: "But Stephen, filled with the Holy Spirit, gazed into heaven and saw the glory of God, and Jesus standing at God's right hand. 'Look! I can see heaven thrown open,' he said, 'and the Son of man standing at the right hand of God.'"[96] In the so-called farewell speeches of Jesus in the Gospel of John, Jesus promises that he will return to his disciples through the Holy Spirit, and states that it is necessary that he go to the Father in order to do this: "It is for your own good that I am going, because unless I go, the Paraclete will not come to you; but if I go, I will send him to you."[97] The Spirit Christ talks about is his own Spirit: "Everything the Father has is mine; that is why I said: all he reveals to you will be taken from what is mine."[98] This is why Jesus can say: "In a short time you will no longer see me, and then a short time later you will see me again."[99] Far from coming to a halt with his death and resurrection, the presence of Christ *augments* in the world, for his presence on earth that was confined to time and space, is now uninhibited in his glorified presence.

The day of Pentecost becomes, as Peter states in his speech on that day, the fulfillment of God's prophecy in Joel: "I shall pour out my Spirit on all humanity. Your sons and daughters shall prophesy, your old people shall dream dreams, and your young people see visions."[100] In fact, the Acts of the Apostles speak of prophets and prophetic gifts in connection with Pentecost and throughout the entire book. It becomes clear that the early church knew of many prophets who served permanently at a given church or traveled from congregation to congregation. As we shall see, Acts names both male and female prophets and connects prophetic experiences to a large number of the events that were crucial to the development of the early church. Thus Saint Paul is converted through a vision of Christ, who asks him: "Saul, Saul, why are you persecuting me?"[101] In fact, his entire apostolate is accompanied by visions and prophetic events. Likewise the decision to spread the Gospel to Gentiles followed Peter's vision of different foods descending from heaven, including those unclean to Jews, signifying that all were called to the banquet of Christ.[102] Prophetic visions accompany key events in the early church and serve as divine confirmations that what is happening is according to the Lord's designs. In the following we shall see that whether prophecy occurs from the lips of office-bearers of the church or from lay persons such as the daughters of Philip, it remains a key element in the development of the church.

3.3.4. *Prophecy and Paul*

As a community leader and author, Paul contributed immensely to the development of the early church. He was the first to preach the Gospel to the Gentiles in the consistent way that he did, working more than others for its spreading in the new areas of the Mediterranean world. He was also the only person in the early church to be designated an apostle in the fullest sense without having been one of the immediate witnesses to and companions of Christ during his earthly ministry. Normally one would be counted an apostle only if one had been a firsthand witness to Christ and commissioned by him face to face to carry out the work of apostle.[103] Since Paul's conversion to Christianity occurred after the death of Christ, how could he possibly be named an apostle? The answer is that he received this commission through his Christ-revelation on the way to Damascus. Paul's experience of Christ appearing to him, causing him to fall to the ground, blinding him and keeping him blind until he decided to give him back his sight did not only lead to his conversion, it confided to him the task of serving Christ in a particular way and finally provided him with the direct face-to-face encounter with the Lord required to be an apostle. Hence, at its very root, Christ authorized, commissioned, and empowered Paul by means of a prophetic manifestation, and prophecy characterizes the beginning of Paul's mission. Moreover, several researchers have seen in Paul's entire apostolic career the character and continuation of Old Testament prophecy. Indeed, Paul's profile provides vital information on the continuation of prophecy in early Christianity. As both Aune[104] and Witherington[105] point out, Paul's writings constitute the oldest surviving source material by a Christian author. Therefore, his letters provide us with precious evidence regarding prophecy in early Christianity. We can examine the main Pauline source material for indications of Paul's prophetic charism, evaluating the direct oracular speech that Paul used for prophetic evidence.

PAUL THE PROPHET. Messiah is a designation that incorporates many charisms and religious tasks, and, as Witherington writes, "no one title or label adequately explains a figure as complex as Jesus."[106] In the same way, the role of apostle is complex and requires many spiritual gifts.[107] Modern scholarly work shows that the boundaries between prophetic and priestly functions in the Old Testament are not as distinct as was once thought; likewise, the boundaries between teachers, prophets, and apostles are far from clear-cut in the New Testament. Nonetheless, Corinthians 12:10 and 12:29, Romans 12:6, and Ephesians 4:11 speak about these different ministries in a way that suggests that it is possible to differentiate them. Though Paul appears to have assimilated several roles, it does not mean that it is impossible to come to an appreciation of Paul as a prophet. Witherington gives several reasons that this is indeed possible:

> (1) Christian prophets, to judge from texts such as 1 Cor 14 or Acts 11:27–30 or Acts 21:10–11, were figures who spoke intelligible, fresh messages that were spontaneously granted to them by God by means of the Holy Spirit. (2) On occasion, God might reveal truths or ideas to these prophetic figures in visions or dreams, and Paul claims to have occasionally had such visions and dreams (see 2 Cor 12:1–10),

but again this is not simply identical with evangelizing Gentiles or speaking in synagogues. (3) Prophets in the OT, while they can be said to be like prosecutors of the covenant lawsuit that Yahweh had against his people, are not, by and large, exegetes or scribes. They are those who deliver a late, pertinent word from God to God's people. (4) In view of the third point, it is not clear that "charismatic" contemporizing or interpreting of Old Testament texts at Qumran or by various New Testament figures should be seen as a prophetic activity. There were other persons filled with the Spirit—teachers, scribes, or sages—who are more likely candidates to have carried out such activities. In short, prophets were apparently distinguishable in function from apostles, scribes, teachers, and evangelists even if there was some occasional overlap between their roles and functions.[108]

So the fact that the charism of the apostle implied various gifts does not rule out the possibility that Paul the apostle was also Paul the prophet.[109] However, differentiating between various charisms is not the only problem in uncovering Paul's specific prophetic traits. Even if Paul's prophetic characteristics are recognized, the question remains: what *kind* of prophet was he? E. E. Ellis argues that if Paul does not speak often of prophecy directly, he makes numerous indirect references to prophecy with the word *spirit-filled* (πνευματικὸ / πνευματικοὶ), as this term implies the prophetic charism.[110] Ellis's research is most useful, but it is not definitive: Paul emerged as a spirit-filled preacher in an era that included many different spirit-filled role models. We saw that the Old Testament prophetic tradition continued in all major early Judean traditions—apocalyptic, eschatological, clerical, and sapiential. And, as it is difficult to discern between the different charisms in the ancient church, likewise prophecy, apocalypses, and wisdom are not contained in hermetically sealed containers, but share traits and interact. Witherington states that "what makes the whole matter devilishly difficult is that Paul lived at a time after the confluence of three great Jewish traditions—prophecy, apocalyptic, and wisdom."[111] But, as he further shows, there is evidence that Paul acted both as apocalyptic and eschatological prophet,[112] and that his usage of different prophetic traditions increased his reputation as a prophet. For Paul, the prophet could incorporate different manifestations of the prophetic phenomenon and still be seen as *one* prophet. And because Paul was able to do this he proved to his followers that he was an instrument of all the Spirit's gifts: he did not rely on tradition alone, but moved as the Spirit moved him. "It is the combination of prophecy and the work of the Spirit that, among other things, made Paul a powerful figure to reckon with."[113]

Little has been written about Paul's spiritual life in the last two decades, with the exception of G. D. Fee's book *God's Empowering Presence*.[114] Witherington believes this is because Paul was "reticent to talk about such things, not least because he is not like many a modern Western individual bent on revealing his innermost thoughts. . . . Such discussions would be seen as antisocial to the ancient mind-set."[115] This does not mean that Paul never speaks about his spiritual experiences, but when he does it is for a specific purpose in his apostolic ministry, not merely to draw attention to himself. In the beginning of the twentieth Century, "precious little was said about Paul as a prophet." If researchers accorded prophetic activity to Paul's ministry, it was compared to Hellenistic mystery religions. However, recent scholarship has sparked a growing "revival of interest in Paul as a prophetic figure" and recognition that "Paul's understanding of prophecy and prophets owes far more to the Jewish tradition than to the Greco-Roman tradition."[116]

In the many new works that have been written about Paul as a prophet, this has been borne out. The research of Aune[117] and Evans[118] has made this especially clear, and K. O. Sandnes's *Paul: One of the Prophets?*[119] is dedicated entirely to portraying Paul as a prophet in line with the Old Testament tradition. The article "Is Paul Also among the Prophets?" by J. M. Myers and E. D. Freed[120] provides seven points in support of the view that Paul exhibits a relationship to Old Testament prophets:

> (a) he has a fondness for them and frequently quotes them (b) Old Testament prophets are called "servants of the Lord" and [as already mentioned] Paul calls himself a "servant of Christ," (c) he speaks favorably of the phenomenon of Christian prophecy, and (d) much of his language has a poetic quality. (e) His call is analogous to Old Testament prophetic calls. (f)He experienced a "wilderness period." (g) He was a visionary. (h) He was an intimate at the council of the Lord. (i) He functioned as an extension of the personality of Christ. (j) His discordant attitude toward ecclesiastical authorities parallels the anticultic attitude of some Old Testament prophets.[121]

All this research has lead David Aune and others to the conclusion that Paul's role of apostle appears to have been a functional equivalent to that of the Old Testament prophets.[122] But, unlike them, he did not gather his oracles into oracular books. "Although prophecy is clearly alive and well in the Pauline churches, Paul's letters do not read like the works of classical prophets." [123]

And Paul never calls himself a prophet. The closest he gets to self-designation as prophet is when he refers to himself as the δοῦλος or servant of Christ.[124] David Hill notes that several Old Testament books refer to the prophets as the "servants of the Lord,"[125] and "almost without exception in these cases the Septuagint renders the word 'servant' ('e̲b̲e̲d̲) by *doulos*."[126] Indeed, Paul's letters provide the reader with a functional image of him as a prophet, and they make it clear that he thought of himself as a prophet. Hill and others believe "it would be . . . difficult if not impossible to deny that Paul may rightly be called a Christian prophet, although nowhere in the New Testament is he given this title."[127]

More than anything else it is Paul's conversion and vocation by means of a revelation on his way to Damascus that attributes to Paul the image of a prophet. It is described both by Luke[128] and by Paul himself, especially in his letter to the Galatians:

> Now I want to make it quite clear to you, brothers, about the gospel that was preached by me, that it was no human message. It was not from any human being that I received it, and I was not taught it, but it came to me through a revelation of Jesus Christ. You have surely heard how I lived in the past, within Judaism, and how there was simply no limit to the way I persecuted the Church of God in my attempts to destroy it; and how, in Judaism, I outstripped most of my Jewish contemporaries in my limitless enthusiasm for the traditions of my ancestors. But when God, who had set me apart from the time when I was in my mother's womb, called me through his grace and chose to reveal his Son in me, so that I should preach him to the gentiles, I was in no hurry to confer with any human being, or to go up to Jerusalem to see those who were already apostles before me. Instead, I went off to Arabia, and later I came back to Damascus. Only after three years did I go up to Jerusalem to meet Cephas.[129]

Like the Old Testament prophets, Paul does not choose his ministry—it is conferred to him by direct divine revelation, despite his former opposition to the will of Christ. It comes when he is persecuting the Christians; at the moment of his prophetic calling he was on his way to hunt down Christians in Damascus. So God chose someone who was indifferent to his gospel and someone who combated it as well. It is precisely this distance between the perfection of the God who calls and the unreadiness and unworthiness of the human who is called that we find the key to the prophetic dynamism in Old Testament prophecy, related earlier: the greater the human wretchedness, the greater God's grace and power that is revealed. It is not surprising that Paul is one of the first to affirm this principle: "But he [the Lord] said to me, my grace is sufficient for you, for my power is made perfect in weakness."[130] "The science of the Cross is also the science of the prophet: what may be foolish in the eyes of man but wise in the eyes of God is also wise in the eyes of the prophet. Paul's ministry does not derive from his having made a decision for Christ, or his having voluntarily changed the course of his life. On the contrary, Paul declares that God made the decision that Paul would witness to the Gentiles before he was born!"[131] In this manner, Paul's conversion experience echoes several of the charismatic vocation accounts of Old Testament prophets, in particular that of Isaiah:

> Yahweh has called me from the womb; from the bowels of my mother has he made mention of my name. . . . Now says Yahweh who formed me from the womb to be his servant, to bring Jacob again to him, and that Israel be gathered to him. . . . He says: "It is too light a thing that you should be my servant to raise up the tribes of Jacob, and to restore the preserved of Israel: I will also give you for a light to the Gentiles, that you may be my salvation to the end of the earth."[132]

Like Isaiah, Paul is called from before his birth, raised to the status of prophet by means of divine intervention, and charged to preach God's salvation to all peoples, including the gentiles. Paul's vocation is also similar to that of Jeremiah: "Before I formed you in the belly I knew you, and before you came forth out of the womb I sanctified you; I have appointed you a prophet to the nations."[133]

Similarly, from Elijah to John the Baptist, many of the prophets lived in the desert. Before his ministry, Paul lived through a "desert period" while he became schooled in the science of prophets. D. Hill points out that Paul's letters are full of references to prophetic experience and divine guidance that recall Old Testament prophets.[134]

Paul's letters testify to revelatory experiences accompanying his entire ministry. In his second letter to the Corinthians, Paul discloses his most famous "visions and revelations from the Lord," when he was "caught up right into the third heaven . . . caught up into Paradise and heard words said that cannot and may not be spoken by any human being."[135] In this state he is informed of secrets and mysteries that could only be experienced by humans by means of prophetic revelation. Some scholars suggest that since Paul writes to the Corinthians of this prophetic experience fourteen years after it occurred,[136] prophecy played no role in his life thereafter. This view finds little support. As Witherington points out, the reason why Paul mentions this event so long after its occurrence is that "to him it was especially notable and outstanding."[137] This view is supported by A. T. Lincoln, who observes that the plural in 2 Corinthians 12.1 ("I will move on to visions and revelations from the Lord") means that Paul "thought about relating more than one such vision or revelation."[138]

In 1 Corinthians 14: "If I come to you speaking in tongues, how shall I benefit you unless I bring you some revelation [ἀποκαλύ'ψει] or knowledge [γνώσει] or prophecy [προφητεία] or teaching [διδαχῆ]" (v. 6). As Aune points out, Paul "apparently regarded himself as able to do all of these"[139] and adds that he has spoken in tongues more than the Corinthians (v. 8). In Galatians 2:2 Paul speaks of his going up to Jerusalem "by revelation" (κατὰ ἀποκάλυψιν), which Aune believes to imply a "dream or vision experience,"[140] and in 2 Corinthians 13:3 he clearly says that Christ speaks through him.

Paul's prophetic calling is not inferred merely from his own writings. The conversion experience that Paul refers to is described in complementary passages of Acts 9, 22, and 26 as a prophetic experience, and Acts 13.1 speaks of the Holy Spirit who calls Barnabas and Paul to their work: "In the church of Antioch the following were prophets and teachers, Barnabas . . . and Saul. One day while they were offering worship to the Lord and keeping a fast, the Holy Spirit said, 'I want Barnabas and Saul set apart for the work to which I have called them.'" In numerous passages, Acts provides an image of Christ guiding and corroborating Paul's ministry by means of revelations and visions[141] and night visions in which angels appeared to him as well.[142]

Although Paul's letters, Acts, and later Christian writings[143] describe Paul as a prophet, there is another way of seeing the prophetic in Paul. David Aune, using form-critical tools, distils a great number of passages from the letters that live up to the criteria for oracular speech without Paul's designating the passages prophetic revelation.[144] Aune believes that the letters could contain more oracular speech, but that "the absence of any sure marks of identification makes their recognition dubious."[145] Using the aforementioned sure prophetic passages to draw conclusions about Paul's prophetic vocation is not without problems, as it is not clear whether Paul is referring his own oracles or those of others in these passages. Yet the usage of the oracles and their frequency implies familiarity with prophetic speech, and thus Aune concludes that Paul is referring to personal oracles as well as oracles pronounced by other prophets.[146] Aune's research confirms what has been said; "all this evidence combines to suggest that Paul was a prophet who experienced many revelatory phenomena, some of which he communicated to others."[147] Since Paul can clearly be described a prophet, it is not surprising that he had some things to say about prophecy's function in the church.

PAUL'S INSTRUCTIONS ON PROPHECY IN THE CHURCH. While Acts treats prophecy mostly in relation to historical events in the early church, Paul's letters treat prophecy more theoretically, with a strong focus on how to incorporate the prophetic charism into the life of the church.[148] When dealing with

the charismatic structure of the church, Paul treats no other charism as carefully as the charism of prophecy.

There are different ways of understanding the term "apostle." It may refer
strictly to the twelve original disciples of Christ. It is also possible to see the
apostles as "distinguished from other types of Christian leaders by virtue of
having received a divine commission for their task, and by the range of spiritual gifts at their disposal."[149]

The tasks of the apostles are to establish the foundations of the Christian
faith and consolidate the testimony of Jesus. On the other hand, the task of
the prophets is to keep this testimony alive, to help the congregation to see its
historical, anamnetic relationship to the earthly Jesus, and to live in the reality
of the resurrected Christ's immediate closeness. If Paul dedicates so much
attention to the presence of prophecy in the church, this must be in part
because prophecy played a pivotal role in the early church. As we have seen,
Paul did indeed consider himself a prophet according to the Old Testament
scheme.[150] But, while Paul's letters give examples of early Christian oracular
and prophetic speech, Paul's primary concern is not prophesying to the
churches, such as in the Apocalypse of John. Rather, he aims to instruct the
young churches—many of which he himself founded—on how to administer
the gifts of the Spirit. Paul tells the faithful to be aware of false prophets.
Thus, he seeks the proper implementation of the prophetic office so that it
may not be corrupted, but rather bear as much fruit as possible. Paul considers
prophecy so important to Christian life that in his first letter to the Corinthians he names prophecy immediately after the charism of apostlehood, and
before the charism of teaching.[151]

Fifty years ago H. Greeven wrote: "Who the prophets are, what they do and
what significance prophecy has for the community—all these questions are
answered for Paul at their clearest in 1 Cor 12:14."[152] According to David Hill,
even though this is an acceptable conclusion, Paul nevertheless speaks about
prophecy in other important passages.[153]

In his letter to the Romans, Paul indicates that prophecy is a charism that
the Spirit gives to certain members of the church, and that it is different from
other gifts given to the faithful: "if it is a gift of prophecy, we should prophesy
as much as our faith tells us."[154] David Hill interprets the word *faith* as "confidence that God's Spirit is speaking in the actual words he is uttering," and Hill
concludes: "What Paul is saying, then, is that the person who exercises the gift
of prophecy should speak only when conscious of his words as inspired, and
presumably only for as long as he is confident that God is speaking through
him."[155]

2 Thessalonians 5:19–21 provides clear guidelines for judging the gift of prophecy: "Do not quench the Spirit, do not despise prophesying [προφετεια] but test everything." What can be inferred from this passage is that there was such a phenomenon as prophecy in the church: in fact, it was so well known that it needed directions for its correct administration—namely, neither to disdain it nor to fail to test its validity.

The most significant passage in Corinthians in which Paul discusses prophecy in the church is 1 Corinthians 12:28–30. In a list of different offices and spiritual gifts within the church, prophecy is listed second, right after the office of apostle. The passage has been interpreted in many different ways, but what is important to note is that prophecy seems to have been an institution in the ancient church, or at least in some churches—an office along with the office of apostle and teacher, and an office that functioned in the liturgical settings of everyday worship.[156] Many other passages support this theory, but just how institutionalized this office was and what the requirements were for fulfilling it are not known definitively. Nonetheless, Rino Fisichella has attempted to point out the differences between the charisms of apostle, prophet, teacher, and evangelist in his approach to this problem:

> Prophets are not apostles; the latter found and direct the community, whereas prophets are believers who accept apostles and their message. Neither are prophets teachers; the latter receive the Lord's word from apostles and prophets. Whereas teachers read and interpret the Scripture, prophets, as people of the Spirit, read all Scriptures in the light of Christ's word. Lastly, prophets are not evangelists, for the latter draw on personal experience of inspired activity to formulate a particular theology, whereas prophets are concerned with the immediate good of the community and with particular conditions arising in individual communities.[157]

Paul's letter to the Corinthians continues by describing the substantial principles that the charisms must serve. As with all other gifts, the charism of prophecy must first serve *Love*. Paul sums this up in his first letter to the Corinthians: "And though I have the power of prophecy, to penetrate all mysteries and knowledge, and though I have all the faith necessary to move mountains—if I am without Love, I am nothing."[158] Only when rooted in divine love is the prophet able to fulfill the purpose of his mission, which is to build up, encourage, and console the church.[159] Furthermore, if love is at the root of prophecy, then prophecy should be sought more than any other gift: "Make love your aim; but be eager, too, for spiritual gifts, and especially for prophesying." Prophecy, unlike other spiritual gifts (such as speaking in tongues), can be comprehended by the faithful and thus has the power to build up the community.[160]

When reading 1 Corinthians 14 it must be kept in mind that Paul speaks about the right handling of prophecy in opposition to the Corinthians' understanding. But what was it exactly that the Corinthians did wrong? Witherington argues that the Corinthians were influenced by an overly Hellenistic approach to the prophetic phenomenon.[161] Though they exhibit the similar fundamental characteristic of speaking for the deity, prophetic traditions differ in East and West. In the eastern Semitic cultures, prophecy was seen as the spontaneous and unsolicited expression of God. Jewish traditions also sought answers from God by means of sacred lot: thus priests used the Urim and Thummim to find divine answers.[162] There is one reference to this manner of divination in the New Testament—namely, when the apostles choose who is to succeed Judas as apostle by means of a lot.[163] Otherwise, the biblical reference to this practice is scarce, and as Omara shows, "'directive' prophecy . . . is conspicuously absent in the New Testament";[164] for Semites saw prophecy as the sovereign God announcing himself when he desired to do so, not when humans needed an answer to a question.[165]

But the latter was by far the most widespread form of prophecy in the Greco-Roman world. The most famous Greek oracle, the Pythia of Delphi, was not far from Corinth. It functioned as a divine "communication central" where people could come to find answers and advice on everyday issues such as: Shall I marry that man? Will I have children? Will this year be a good harvest? The oracle of Delphi had institutionalized this practice: the inquirer came to the oracle and presented his request to the priest, who, in turn, presented it to the Pythia. The reply required interpretation by a priest, so that the obliging priest was often called the prophet as well as the Pythia.[166] But this does not imply that the Pythia's response was incomprehensible. It is possible that the priest's function was simply to provide the oracle with a poetic form.

Although unsolicited oracles, carried out by an inspired diviner who most resembled the Old Testament equivalent, did exist, they were rare in the Greco-Roman world.[167] Witherington believes that the debate between Paul and the Corinthians was exactly on this issue, and that it was especially ordinary domestic questions that "most likely would have been asked of prophets in the Corinthian congregation."[168] Use of prophecy to obtain answers to practical questions came dangerously close to mere divination and, it follows, to reducing God to a mere informer of secrets. Paul insists that in the Judeo-Christian form of prophecy the sovereign God acts spontaneously only when he considers it to be necessary—not when human curiosity demands an answer to a question.

3.3.5. Prophecy and the Acts of the Apostles

Almost every chapter of the Acts of the Apostles speaks about prophets or about people being instructed directly by Christ through revelations. These prophecies play a remarkable role in Acts and accompany the early church during its most decisive moments, so much so that M. T. Kelsey rightly notes that "beginning with what happened at Pentecost, every major event in Acts is marked by a dream, a vision, or the appearance of an angel, and it is usually upon this experience that the coming events are determined."[169] It is enough to recall Peter's deliverance from prison through an angel; Peter's vision of a tablecloth coming down from heaven with the command to eat the "improper" food it contains—a vision that leads to the Gospel proclamation to the heathens; Saul's conversion through a vision of Christ (followed by the vision to Ananias, who is called to receive Saul). Many more could be mentioned.[170] In addition, Aune has done a significant job in identifying and categorizing prophetic utterances in Acts, demonstrating that Acts portrays an early church in which God guides his people intimately through the prophets.[171]

3.3.6. Prophecy and the Apocalypse

The study of the Apocalypse bolsters the conviction that prophecy played a prominent role in the early church. The Apocalypse is the only unified piece of New Testament writing that not only speaks about prophecy but *is* itself a prophetic product of oracles and prophetic visions;[172] *is* itself "a work of Christian prophecy."[173] As Kilian McDonnell and George T. Montague assert, "the Book of Revelation teems with prophetic words and, in fact, is in its entirety an example of early Christian prophecy."[174] Thus, as Richard J. Bauckham asserts, one will only understand the Apocalypse when situating it in "the context of early Christian prophecy."[175] "Moreover, it is a work of Christian prophecy which understands itself to be the culmination of the whole biblical prophetic tradition. Its continuity with Old Testament prophecy is deliberate and impressively comprehensive."[176] The author claims to write down prophecy[177] and calls himself a prophet.[178] He must have worked as a prophet in the early Christian communities, as he has detailed knowledge of "each local situation."[179] Boring believes that the equation of "servant" and "prophet" in 22:9 and 11:18 are programmatic for the entire book, so that the frequent references to "servant" should be seen as a metaphor for "prophet."[180] We saw that this was the case in Paul as well.

These direct indications of the nature of the Book of Apocalypse are enhanced when viewing its form and content. As mentioned earlier, the Revelation of John has particular bearing on our topic, as it is the only concentrated collection of New Testament oracles. The sum of these is a book that tradition rightly has called the Apocalypse, as their frequency and form follows the pattern of early Judean apocalyptic writings as described earlier. And yet, as David Hill[181] and Ben Witherington,[182] among others, have noted, the Book of Revelation is no pure continuation of the apocalyptic tradition but a unique new Christian product, as it incorporates the prophetic into a new synthesis. As we saw, one of the characteristic traits of apocalyptic literature was its pseudonymous character, in which the author does not name himself but speaks of himself in the third person, for instance as a "messenger." Another example of this is clear in the pseudonymous nature of location, where the places in which apocalypses were written had no significance in their final product. Conversely, the author of the Apocalypse clearly names himself, as well as the place he was when he had his visions, namely the island of Patmos. The link between the apocalyptic and prophetic traditions in the Book of Revelation is therefore ambiguous.

E. Schüssler Fiorenza has reflected on this relationship and believes that Christian prophecy was a pure incarnation of the apocalyptic tradition, albeit in new form: "Early Christian prophecy is expressed in apocalyptic form and early Christian apocalyptic is carried on by early Christian prophets."[183] Witherington does not entirely agree with Schüssler Fiorenza's view of the exclusive apocalyptic character of Christian prophecy or that "apocalyptic is the mother genre and prophecy a subset under it," as he believes the relationship between the apocalyptic and prophetic in the Book of Revelation are more complex, but he does agree with her that the Book of Revelation is directly related to an experienced revelation of God: "But this much is absolutely correct—apocalypses like that of John are not purely literary products of tradents. They are generated by prophets and grounded in prophetic experience of an apocalyptic sort."[184]

The main function of the Book of Revelation is the "exhortation and strengthening of communities,"[185] and this distinguishes Christian prophecy from its Greco-Roman counterpart. As mentioned earlier, the Greco-Roman experience is private in character, aiming at personal inspired consultation, whereas Christian prophecy is communal, meant to be read aloud in congregational worship in order to point the church's attention to the presence and promises of the risen Lord. The Book of Revelation, and the entire subsequent Christian prophetic tradition, has as its primary purpose to give Christians perspective. In spite of possible hardships and trials, the prophet is

the one who keeps the promises of the Lord alive, feeding the believers with
the knowledge that in the Risen Christ they have victory, in spite of all
odds.[186]

3.3.7. Prophecy in Q

Research in the Q source has increasingly shown to what extent Q includes
material from Christian prophecy.[187] Q, which stands for *Quelle*, a term given
by the German researchers who first identified it, is an ensemble of Gospel
traditions that underlie Matthew and Luke but of which neither Mark nor John
apparently are aware. The issue of interest for this study is that the Q tradition
is strongly influenced by prophetic spirituality, which becomes clear from
identifying the Q-inspired passages in Luke and Matthew. In this way, the Q
tradition confirms the other indications of prophecy's prominence in the early
church. The Q source is especially replenished with passages where Jesus
speaks in the first person, the so-called I sayings. Rudolf Bultmann and especially Eugene Boring are eager to see in Q the voice of Christian prophets
speaking for the risen Lord rather than the historical testimony of the apostles
and disciples themselves. Thus, Boring lists fifteen passages in Q that he believes originated as prophetic utterances from Christian prophets functioning
in the congregations of the early church rather than in the direct testimony of
the apostles or disciples themselves.[188] James Dunn believes Bultmann and
Boring are "overeager" in their attempts to identify prophetic speech in the
early Christian tradition.[189] Nevertheless, most scholars agree that prophecy
was very important to the "community of Q," which again points to the importance of prophecy in the early church.

3.3.8. Prophecy's Alleged Cessation in Early Christianity

As we have seen, prophecy plays a prominent role in and underlies most
writings of the New Testament. But what happened after the closure of the
canon of Scripture? There is evidence that prophecy decreased gradually even
before the closure of the canon. Thus Friedrich notices that signs of prophecy
and prophets as well as prophetic language decrease in the various layers of
the New Testament the younger they get.[190] But is this descending line on the
graph of early Christendom, which shines through also in the Didache and
Hermas the Shepherd, so perfectly linear that it eventually hits the baseline
and ends completely? Many New Testament scholars clearly arrive at this
conclusion, stating that prophecy not only ceased but died out entirely in the
early church. We shall conduct a deeper inquiry into this claim in the pages to

follow. Only if it proves wrong will it make sense to investigate the theological value of prophecy in the Christian church. To give a qualified evaluation we shall first examine the aforementioned position of most New Testament scholars.

H. A. Guy contends that prophecy not only decreased but died entirely, as the peak of prophecy reached in Christ is unsurpassable. Without specific biblical references, he claims that Jesus himself held prophecy to cease with his coming: "There are hints in the Gospels that Jesus himself regarded the prophetic order as closed, because he saw himself as its culmination."[191] Rather than presenting historical or exegetical evidence as proof for his opinion, Guy's theological preconceptions distil essences of Scripture that are not there. From a theological perspective, claiming that prophecy should cease because Christ was the most perfect prophet is no less than saying that no more women should be born on earth after his Mother, as she was the most perfectly sanctified creature of God.

Ernst Dassmann and Werner H. Schmidt continue the theory of prophecy's early Christian end in their foreword to the anthology *Prophetie und Charisma*, building their arguments along the "end of revelation with the last apostle" theory:

> Status and vocation does not end with the Old Testament, but lives on in the early Christian communities—albeit not for long. In the third century, the community prophets have died out, at least in the main body of the Church.... So far, the swift cessation was explained through the suppression of the stronger institution. When revelation is considered to be ended, teachers (bishops) who keep and expound what was received will be more important than charismatic preachers.[192]

É. Cothenet argues along the same lines. Cothenet's Catholic viewpoint shines through in his assessment that the formation of the institutional church rendered New Testament prophecy unnecessary. He argues that prophets transmit apostolic tradition and that prophecy therefore belongs only to the period of the foundation of the church: when the church had been institutionally structured in a way that safeguarded the historical continuation of the apostolic tradition, prophecy became superfluous. Cothenet thus distinguishes "between the constitutive prophecy of the Church that played a decisive role for the elaboration of Christian tradition and the particular gifts of the Spirit that, along the ages, present themselves in different forms.[193] The natural result of this is the "rapid disparition of prophecy in the Church."[194] To Cothenet, this does not mean that the Spirit stopped manifesting himself after the end of prophecy, but such working of the Spirit no longer occurred in the form of revelations. Cothenet's argument obviously rests on a theological rather than phenomenological appreciation of prophecy, according to which prophecy relates to the *foundation* of the church, and not to its *edification* as in Paul. Cothenet's description of prophecy is in opposition to the view of the vast majority of New Testament scholars and follows the theological interest of safeguarding the institution as a unique charismatic vehicle of the Spirit in actualizing the Deposit of Faith through history. As will become clear in the theological discussion of the function of prophecy, this book does not oppose the idea that the institution plays a normative role in the actualization of revelation, but rather that the entire people of God participate in this actualization, and in a very special way those charged with a prophetic vocation. Cothenet's argument makes sense only if prophecy relates to the *foundation* of the Deposit of Faith alone. But, as mentioned, the function of prophecy is different as God speaks to reactualize revelation and call the faithful to live according to its truth in new historical contexts.

Another Catholic writer, G. Hasenhüttel, shares Cothenet's view that the institution did not squeeze prophecy out of the life of the early church, but that one superseded the other in a Spirit-guided sequence of events. Hasenhüttel and other writers with him argue that the cessation of prophecy was the necessary result of the decline of prophecy. After a presentation of the beginning secularization in the early church, he writes:

> The end of the prophets begins! That which took place in the communities by charismatic authority is now—by sociological necessity—taken over by the appointed ministers of the church [Ordnungsbeamten]. Certainly, this does not diminish the position of the prophets; rather their appreciation grows. However, they lose their purpose [Wirksamkeit] for the life of the community.[195]

Thomas Gillespie, first pastor in different Presbyterian churches and later professor and president of Princeton Theological Seminary, also believes that prophecy and growing institutionalization are related, but he is more reserved with regard to the logical transformation from charismatic to institutional authority in the early church. Following Ernst Käsemann's research, he prefers to speak of the "transmutation" of primitive Spirit-enthusiastic Christianity into "nascent early Catholicism."[196]

Another categorical herald of the idea of prophecy's cessation is David Hill, who dedicates an entire chapter in his *New Testament Prophecy* to the decline of prophecy and bluntly states that Montanism exterminated prophecy: "Although the dogma that there are Christian prophets survived longer than prophecy itself, the repudiation of Montanism marks the effective end of prophecy in the Church."[197]

In the conclusion of the same chapter, he even laments the ill fate of prophecy: "Irenaeus did issue a warning to his contemporaries that true prophecy was being driven out of the church as a consequence of the battle against false prophets (*Adv. Haer.* 3.9.9) but his warning was in vain and the church lost the immensely valuable contribution to its life that comes from genuinely inspired prophetic utterance."[198]

It is not quite clear whether Ben Witherington believes prophecy survived in post-Montanist Christianity or not. In one passage he obviously argues for its survival. He maintains that a major change did occur in the second century A.D. Before this time it was legitimate, he contends, to call Christianity, as a whole, a prophetic movement.[199] This is especially evident in the writings of Luke, who "strives to present Jewish Christian prophecy in a light that shows its continuity with Old Testament prophecy and with the larger prophetic context of the Greco-Roman world."[200] Although prophecy changed and became a more sporadic phenomenon in the centuries to follow, after the death and resurrection of Christ, he argues, it did not die out:

> A variety of reasons ... led to the gradual decline, *though not to the death, of prophecy in early Christianity.* The prophetic movement had gradually become a movement with the occasional prophetic voice and finally, by at least the time of Constantine if not before, changed into an established institutionalized religion. Yet the ongoing living voice of prophecy continued to remind the church that neither God nor God's word had ceased to be active well into the church's history, and it could neither be tamed, domesticated, nor entirely placed under human control.[201]

In another place he continues to reflect on the continuation of prophecy in spite of the detrimental effects of Montanism: "Unfortunately, when this movement was branded by the orthodox church, prophecy itself suffered a decline through guilt by association. It was never entirely eliminated but became a minority voice in a largely non-prophetic movement becoming an institution."[202]

However, in the book's last chapter, "The Progress of Prophecy," he writes:

> In the second century of the Christian era, it appears that some, if not most, of the roles of the prophet were taken over by figures such as the monarchical bishop. As eschatological fervor faded in the second

and third centuries, this became increasingly easy to do, and one must surely see the Montanist movement as a sort of last strong prophetic and eschatological challenge to a church settling down for a long winter's nap.[203]

Here it seems that Witherington opts for the end-theory, but passages quoted earlier contradict this; he seems rather to speak of congregationally ordered forms of prophecy (to the point of institutionalization) that indeed did cease in the early church. One could even posit the argument that when so many New Testament exegetes speak of prophecy's cessation after Montanism, they are really speaking of the end of this specific form of prophecy. Witherington certainly appears to accept the idea that God's Spirit always found new ways of addressing his people even if the changes and heretical experiences of early Christianity did expel prophecy from the structures in which it had functioned earlier.

Among certain evangelicals of the Cessationist school, the end of prophecy after the completion of the canon of Scripture is nevertheless almost a dogma, usually linked with a very literal interpretation of the sufficiency of Sacred Scripture. The influential publications[204] of Benjamin B. Warfield served to corroborate this trend, although it can be traced back to John Calvin's polemic against Catholicism and the radical reformers who, in Calvin's interpretation, enhanced their authority by reference to miracles and revelations.[205]

Richard B. Gaffin expresses well the fundamental concerns that motivate the Cessationist opinion. With Gaffin, the "Cessationists" believe that miracles continued to occur after Christ but that prophecy ended. The reasons for this view are found in their understanding of Holy Scripture, where the Bible is the full and final Word of revelation. Since Christian prophecy comes across as a revealed word of God occurring after the closure of the canon, many Cessationists consider this view to clash with the idea of sufficiency of Scripture. Gaffin provides a further reason for the position that prophecy did not continue in the church: "How can God reveal something that contains error? How can God, who is *infallible*, reveal something that is *fallible*? The answer is simple: He cannot. He does not."[206] Gaffin does not consider the fact that Scripture itself points out criteria to separate the wheat from the chaff and that these should be employed to retain the good and reject the false. Furthermore, his argument rests on one inherent weakness: he presents true and false prophecy as one single product and asks how God can be its author. The answer is: he is not. In its nature, Christian prophecy is defined as authentic words of God. Tautologically, if they are not authentic, they do not constitute Christian prophecy.[207]

This is of little importance to Gaffin, whose primary concern is to limit God's revelation to the Bible. Wayne Grudem apparently shares this understanding of Scripture's sufficiency[208] and intends to address Gaffin's scriptural concerns and its subsequent denial of Christian prophecy. Boring argues that Grudem's work is framed by the "twin concerns of the doctrine of verbal inspiration of Scripture and the importance of the phenomenon of prophecy as a reality in the contemporary church."[209] Grudem believes that the prophets of the Old Testament as well as the writers of the New Testament (the apostles) were verbally inspired, but that this is not the case with the post-biblical prophets or the prophets of today. This is why he dedicated his doctoral dissertation to present an understanding of Christian prophecy that safeguards the verbal inspiration of Scripture but provides a prophetic phenomenology that all should be able to live with, Cessationists and charismatics alike, but that corrects both.[210] He expresses this view clearly in the introduction to *The Gift of Prophecy in the New Testament and Today*, claiming that his "view of prophecy would still include a strong affirmation of the closing of the New Testament canon (so that no new words of equal authority are given today), of the sufficiency of Scripture, and of the supremacy and unique authority of the Bible in guidance" while still seeking to "preserve the continuing use of prophecy as the spontaneous, powerful working of the Holy Spirit."[211]

Given Grudem's evangelically ecclesial context, his concerns are understandable, yet some of his concerns lead to unsatisfactory conclusions for Christian prophecy and its relationship to the canon. Grudem answers the sufficiency school's concerns by stating that prophecy is about more than doctrine, as its function is "bringing things to mind when the church is gathered for worship, giving 'edification, encouragement, and comfort' which speaks directly to the needs of the moment and causes people to realize that 'truly God is among you.' "[212] From this perspective, there is absolutely no difference between pre– and post–New Testament prophecy. Moreover, Grudem's approach to prophecy weakens its function as criterion for the truth of revelation, and this is unnecessary and undesirable. Christian prophecy may be a word of God just as we read of God revealing himself in Sacred Scripture, although it has a different status. Christian prophecy is not revelation on par with the Bible, but this does not mean that it cannot serve as verification of and support for revelation.[213] Postcanonical Christian prophecy can indeed serve to elucidate points of Scripture that are not clear or that Scripture contains in an implicit way only, and as such it can and has indeed played a very important role in the correction and actualization of our understanding of revelation. From this perspective, Scripture cannot be said to be sufficient in the sense of expressing everything God could or would ever have to say. In fact, the Bible itself testifies to words never being able to contain the mystery of God: "Jesus did many other things as well. If every one of them were written down, I suppose that even the whole world would not have room for the books that would be written."[214]

As mentioned earlier, David Aune defies the long-established thesis that prophecy died out in early Judaism. He gives several reasons why it did *not* die out but only underwent a metamorphosis, anchored in the new settings of postexilic and postcanonical Judean life, but he writes that this development ended with Montanism: "Christian prophets and prophecy were in a constant state of change and development from the earliest eschatological prophecy within a millenarian setting of Palestinian Christianity to the final death rattle of prophecy with the rise and rejection of Montanism."[215] Other passages of his book point in the same direction:

> With the institutionalization of Christianity and the rationalization of its authority structures, prophecy became redundant as well as dysfunctional, [and] the earlier role of the prophets as articulators of the norms, values, and decisions of the invisible head of the church was taken over by the visible figures of the teacher, preacher, theologian, and church leader.[216]

Given Aune's insistence on prophecy's survival and continuation in early Judaism, his continuation of the thesis of prophecy's death in early Christianity is a surprise, for the development of prophecy in early Christianity is analogous to its fate in early Judaism, and many of the arguments that Aune provides to dismiss the idea of prophecy's cessation in early Judaism apply directly to the arena of early Christianity. Claiming the extinction of prophecy in the postapostolic age simply contradicts the historical reality of the early church and the history of Christianity in general. Prophecy did not die out in the early church; merely the new framework of postapostolic and postcanonical Christianity meant a profound change to the forms and nomenclature of prophecy.

Likewise, theological arguments such as those of Guy, Cothenet, or the Cessationist school do not necessitate the exclusion of prophecy from Christianity. On the contrary, the purpose of this book is to prove that prophecy did not cease but rather continues to this day and that it contributes positively to the life of the church. Prophecy *did* diminish after the departure of the apostles and certainly received its most violent blow through the church's traumatic experience with Montanism. With many exegetes, we may even state that it died out in the distinct institutional form in which it appears to have existed in the ancient church. However, it did not die out as a phenomenon and function in the church as such. Something else happened as prophecy once more modeled itself after the new needs of new historical horizons.

> Prophecy as it had been known at Corinth, was no longer considered proper for the sanctuary. . . . It did not, however, wholly die. It went instead to the arena with the martyrs, to the desert with the fathers, to the monasteries with Benedict, to the streets with Francis, to the cloisters with Teresa of Avila and John of the Cross, to the heathen with Francis Xavier. . . . And without bearing the name of prophets, charismatics like Joan of Arc and Catherine of Sienna would have a profound influence on the public life of *polis* and Church.[217]

Joseph Ratzinger believes that, although prophecy seems to have constituted an integral part of the institution ("Amt"), it is by inner logical necessity that it could not continue to exist in its institutional form. He believes this to be evident already in the Old Testament:

> Later the college of the prophets [in the early church] dissolved as institution and certainly not by chance since the Old Testament already shows us that the function of the prophet cannot be institutionalized. The criticism of the prophets is not just directed at the priests but also against the institutionalized prophets. This emerges very clearly in the book of the prophet Amos where he speaks out against the prophets of the kingdom of Israel. The prophets often speak out against the "prophets as institution," because the place of prophecy is eminently the place God reserves for Himself to intervene personally and anew each time, taking the initiative. Therefore this space cannot properly subsist in the form of a college institutionalized once again.[218]

Joseph Ratzinger believes that it will exist in two forms in the Christian church: within the institution, "in the apostolic college in the same way as the apostles themselves were prophets, too, in their own way. The second form envisages God who, through charisms, reserves for himself the right to intervene directly in the Church to awaken it, warn it, promote it and sanctify it."[219]

Prophecy is not a feature of the ancient church only, but prophets are, as Rino Fisichella affirms, "always a constituent part of the church" and of great importance to its passage through time.[220] It would be more difficult for the church to develop and bring to fruition its resources without its prophets, be it in the first years after Christ, after the closure of the canon of Scripture, or at the commencement of the Third Millennium. In the following pages we shall look at some of the different modes in which prophecy has continued to influence the development of Christianity. Although prophecy did not die out, the rising influence of ecclesiological institutions and the canon of Scripture did affect how prophecy would function. We shall see that prophecy was just as much an influence on the development of these entities as it was influenced by them.

3.3.9. Prophecy, Institution, and Holy Scripture

As mentioned earlier, the closure of the Old Testament canon enhanced the authority of priests and scribes, so that their ministry to some extent took over that of the prophets. The same thing occurred in early Christianity when functions formerly carried out by congregational prophets were gradually taken over by institutionalized ministries within the church. As Witherington argues, this is clear in the writings of Irenaeus, where "we find the office of the prophet assumed by the monarchical bishop, a new sort of central prophet who makes possible the further marginalization of those prophets at the periphery of Christian communities."[221]

Many theologians, especially Lutheran, see the relationship between prophecy and institution as a clean-cut dialectic where an increase of institution with mathematical predictability signifies the equivalent decrease in prophecy, as expressed by the sociologist R. Lourau: "at the origin of every institution there is always the defeat of prophecy."[222]

G. Friedrich, for instance, sees the final institutionalization following the extinction of Montanism as the primary reason for the alleged extinction of prophecy: "Montanism was the last great flare up of prophecy in the church. When it was resisted and vanquished, the institutional office gained a decisive victory over the *charisma*."[223] Even if this view has merit, it is not exclusive, for events in the early church prove to be much more complex. In fact, the opposite scenario is equally credible. Rather than the institution squeezing the prophetic life out of the church, it appears that the decline of prophecy necessitated the church's institutionalization.

Hans von Campenhausen is one among a growing number of researchers who holds this view. Campenhausen believes that the function of the prophets in the early church was the charismatic transmission of apostolic truth. Since the church soon had problems discerning between true and false prophets, and the amount of prophets in the church had generally decreased, it needed new offices and structures to secure and forward the task that the prophets had carried out. The bearers of this responsibility became the scribes and teachers of the tradition—a process that naturally implied institutionalization:

> To start in every case from a supposed opposition between two separate blocs, the official and the charismatic, is a typical modern misunderstanding. Not only do office-holders possess the Spirit, but the spirituals for their part, to the extent that they rightly belong to the church, derive the power of their teaching from traditional apostolic truth.[224]

From this perspective, the interaction between prophecy and the institution is a complex one, as the institution itself in part is a child of changes in the prophetic tradition, and not its executioner. Just as the relationship between prophecy and ecclesial institutional development in the early Christian period is complex, likewise the interrelation between the prophetic role and the formation of the canon of Scripture is profound and heterogeneous. We shall address this issue in the following section.

3.3.10. Prophecy and the Rise of the Christian Canon

In his article "The Earthly Jesus, the Gospel Genre and Types of Authority," the Danish exegete Geert Hallbäck contributes considerably to the understanding of the complex interaction of factors that led the church from its initial charismatic phase as a "prophetic movement"[225] to its establishment as a world religion.

According to Hallbäck, the main agents in this interactive development are charismatic and historical authority, the danger of false prophecy, institutionalization, and the canon of Scripture.

The first part of Hallbäck's article departs from Werner Kelber's research on the formation of the Christian canon and its impact on early Christianity.[226] Hallbäck maintains "that the gospels reflect a Christological transition from the heavenly Christ, as is represented in the earliest New Testament genres, to the earthly Jesus."[227] The New Testament is not the mother of early Christian faith—quite the opposite: the New Testament is an expression of the faith of the early Church, whose belief chronologically precedes the formation of the canon, and so the New Testament is itself an expression of a particular tradition. The same New Testament will later become the main agent in the formation of Christian tradition.

The New Testament has its *Sitz im Leben* in the transition from oral to written tradition. In the period in which there was no fully defined Christian canon, the church stood in an immediate and direct relationship to Christ, and its Christology was that of the heavenly Christ. Many researchers believe this is reflected in the earliest layers of the New Testament. These testimonies of the earliest Christology are found above all in the oldest Christian literary corpus, the writings of Paul. The Philippian hymn in particular[228] is a direct written copy of an oral confession, one that exhibits all the traits of belief in the heavenly Christ. The same is the case with the hymn in Col 1.15–20, which complements the Philippian hymn. Together they provide a good image of the first Christian's conception of Christ, which Hallbäck summarizes as follows:

> Christ is a pre-existent heavenly figure who was involved in the cre-
> ation event itself. He has descended to earth, where he brings about
> reconciliation between creator and creature through his human
> death. However, he has also risen from the dead and has ascended
> back to heaven, where he was seated as ruler. And it is there that he
> now resides, in the present of the hymn, as the living, cosmic Lord.[229]

Another testimony of the Christology of presence is the aforementioned Q tradition, which most exegetes believe to be a written source that Luke and Matthew used but of which neither Mark nor John show any knowledge. Q greatly reflects the pre-Gospel appreciation of the heavenly Christ. The Q tradition received the prophetic in written form more than any other New Testament material (see section 3.3.7).

Mark, "located on the borderline between orality and literality," reflects this heavenly Christology much more than the other Gospels. "Being the oldest gospel, it must be regarded as the written form of the oral tradition."[230] Form criticism sees in it clear and characteristic signs of orality:

> The episodes are scenic with only a few active individuals; the *dra-
> matis personae* are defined by the actions, and not the reverse; they are
> types rather than characters. The gospel is dependent on repetitions:
> there are series of narratives structured in the same way (healings;
> dialogues; parables; etc.). These are easily recognized and activate the
> reader's conventionalized expectations. . . . The oral Christology is
> characterized by presence; the living and resurrected Christ is present
> in the congregation in his prophetic speech.[231]

Paul, whose letters predate the Gospel of Mark, does not differentiate between the earthly Jesus and the risen Christ. Mark makes this distinction and refers to both, which suggests that Mark wrote on the threshold between the two traditions, so that "the most decisive break in the history of Christianity" is documented in the Gospel of Mark and "entails an entirely new Christological orientation: from the living, heavenly Christ of the oral tradition to the past and earthly Jesus of the written one."[232]

The writing of the Gospels took place during the transition from the first to the second generation of Christians—a shift that saw the departure of the first witnesses, the disciples, and the missionaries who founded the various churches. Their departure left a vacuum of authority and necessitated the emergence of new types of authorities. Hallbäck interprets this transition in the light of Max Weber's typology of authority, which distinguishes between three kinds of authority: the charismatic, the traditional, and the institutional. (We shall return to this in chapter 7.) In Judaism, charismatic authority was carried by the prophets and was linked to the individual through "a special and privileged relationship to the divine."[233] Traditional authority was carried by those who controlled normative tradition, and was realized in the scribal tradition. And Hallbäck defines institutional authority as united to the "possession of an *office* the authority of which depends on already-existing social agreements. Here authority is not attached to the individual, but to the role he performs."[234] In Judaism priests and kings carried this type of authority.

Thus Weber and Hallbäck understand the changes in early Christianity as a transition from charismatic authority via the traditional toward institutional authority. According to Weber, charismatic authority must gradually leave the scene as the new religion is established in the world in order to assume institutional structures. And it is this transition from charismatic to institutional authority that Hallbäck presents as the primary agent of the creation of the Gospel genre.

Hallbäck believes that charismatic authority, which dominated the first Christian period, was carried out by missionaries and prophets:

> This authority was anchored in and guaranteed by the heavenly Christ, who manifested his presence—in the congregations through prophetic speech and other charismatic phenomena. However, this sort of authority encountered a crisis during the transition from the first to the second generation of Christians, as it was then no longer attached to individuals who in and of themselves represented the very beginning of the movement. Of course, prophecy and so forth lived on, but prophecy was ambiguous.[235]

From the beginning, prophecy was connected with its counterpart—false prophecy. The first witnesses had been able to identify false prophecy through their ability to discern spirits as well as their certain knowledge of true Christian doctrine, on which prophets were judged. How would the church now judge the prophets? The answer is: *from the Earthly Jesus.* Only Jesus could provide the necessary framework to judge the authenticity of a prophet. Previously, in a "vertical" way, prophets transmitted the truth they had learnt from the Heavenly Christ. Now this vertical, charismatic authority was replaced by a historical, horizontal authority, strictly based on the Jesus who once lived on earth and whose people must now incorporate that authority. Scholarship suggests that it was this process that spurred the formation of the Gospels.[236]

Hallbäck's analysis is important, as it continues to deconstruct the aforementioned stereotypical and simplistic view of the institution overpowering and exterminating prophecy. In point of fact, it is not possible to determine a precise chronology in the progression of events. Most scholars agree that prophecy played an important role in the early church, and that the problems of how to handle it lead to a change in authority in the early church, even to the formation of the Gospel genre.

The church seems to have gone through this transition in a fruitful way, establishing a new historical and institutional authority while maintaining sufficient space in it to keep the prophetic flame alive. But it was not without difficulty. In his letter to the Thessalonians (considered the oldest letter in the New Testament), Paul calls the faithful to cherish and to hold on to the prophetic charism. In the letter to the Corinthians he encourages the believers to actively seek the gift of prophecy: "Make love your aim; but be eager, too, for spiritual gifts, and especially for prophesying."[237] Evidence of attention to the prophetic charism continues in many important writings that followed the closure of the canon.

Given the foregoing, it is now possible to conclude: many institutional authorities exhibited prophetic traits and carried out a prophetic task. Growing institutionalization does not, per se, extinguish prophecy. Rather, the institution can secure the prophetic charism in at least two ways: first, according to Catholic conviction, the Magisterium is able to realize its task only through the assistance of the Holy Spirit, with prophetic utterance being one such vehicle. By this the institution itself is in its inner fabric intertwined with charismatic authority. Second, through the institution's experience with prophetic charisms of past centuries, it is able accumulate experience and to develop criteria for the assessment of true and false prophecy in the present, which ideally safeguard the prophetic charism; if there were no discernment at all, it would not be possible to discern between the true and the false, and the prophetic gift would be rendered ineffective. Third, instead of the institution quenching prophecy, some would argue that strong institutional identity actually facilitates and safeguards prophecy. If there is no or only little institutional direction, there is no one to take care that false prophecy does not spread like wildfire, and once more, the risk of false prophecy jeopardizes the positive role of true prophetic gifts. Without ecclesial direction, alleged prophetic charisms can easily lead to mass-hysterical reactions. As had happened with the church's frightful experiences with Montanism, experiences with false prophecy and sectarian hysteria can lead to a desire, especially on the part of the clergy, of wanting to close out all charismatic gifts, even those that might be true.

3.3.11. *Prophecy and Early Postapostolic Writings*

Our primary knowledge of postapostolic prophecy is derived from the Didache. There is some uncertainty as to the time of its formation. Many have assessed it to be from the first half of the second century A.D., but as Chadwick contends, it seems more likely to have emerged somewhere between 70 and 110.[238]

The Didache illustrates that prophets were held in high esteem in the communities where it was composed. In it, prophets are called high priests (13:1–7). Only they are worthy of saying the free Eucharistic prayer during liturgy (10:7). The congregation should pay more attention to the prophets than to the poor, and in contrast to the other servants of God in the congregation, the prophet is not obliged to work for his daily food (13:3–4).[239] The Didache firmly warns against judging those who carry the signs of being sent by the Spirit of God, for this might mean blaspheming against the Holy Spirit—the only unforgivable sin.[240] Prophets were held in such high esteem that the author of the Didache admonishes the faithful not to judge the true prophet: "And you shall not tempt any prophet who speaks in the spirit, or judge him; for every sin shall be forgiven, but this sin shall not be forgiven" (13:10) As G. Schöllgen rightly points out, judging the authenticity of prophets is a necessary but particularly tricky business, because prophets "have at their disposal a gift of divine origin, which is, in principle, impervious to human judgment."[241] That is, any person talking against a *true* prophet risks committing the sin against the Holy Spirit, since the true prophet speaks by the power of the Spirit. Herein lies a serious consequence of prophecy to those charged with discernment: the one who speaks against the true prophet speaks against the very Spirit of God. But this does not mean that prophets are not to be tested. The passage that warns against blaspheming the Holy Spirit is immediately followed by the criteria for distinguishing true from false prophecy.

> So the false prophet and the prophet will be recognized by their behavior. No prophet who orders a meal in the Spirit eats of it himself; if he does, he is a false prophet [11:8–9]. You shall not listen

to anyone who says in the Spirit, "Give me money, or something,"
but if he is asking that something be given for others who are
in need, let no one judge him [11:12].[242]

Thus, while it is impermissible to judge the one who speaks through the Holy
Spirit, the faithful are warned not to listen to the prophet who appears to be
false. In other words: all prophets are to be tested—and those prophets who
have been found to speak in the Spirit are not to be judged.

The immense role that the Didache concedes to the prophets could be an
indication that there were many prophets in the congregations. However, it
could also be argued that, perhaps due to a lesser number of prophets than
before, this particular concession to the prophet was conferred in respect to
those prophets who remained. The latter scenario, which is supported by other
sources, seems likely, due to a passage in the Didache that advises the congregations to chose elders and deacons to take over the role of the prophets
(15:1).[243] What is suggested in the Didache becomes evident in the years to
follow: the decline of charismatic prophecy in the early church had begun.

In the Didache, the first criterion for judging prophecy is not the conformity of the prophetic message to the accepted contents of Christian faith
(as in Hermas the Shepherd) but the lifestyle of the prophet. "From their
conduct the false prophet and the true prophet will be known" (11:8). The true
prophet has no interest in money: "Whoever says in spirit: 'Give me money'
or anything like it, do not listen to him" (11:12).

D. Hill[244] and Schöllgen[245] believe that prophets held an exceptional position in the Didache because the charism of prophecy was threatened and
there were fewer prophets in the congregations than before. Hasenhüttel[246]
and Streeter[247] have no unanimous explanation of why this is so, for the
Didache itself gives no clear answer, but the decline of prophecy is evident. In
the Didache it becomes clear that the number of permanent congregational
prophets decreased, so that other offices can now replace the prophetic office.
According to Hasenhüttel, this is the reason why the Didache calls for the
election of "bishops and deacons worthy of the Lord . . . for they also serve you
in the ministry of the prophets and teachers" (15:1).[248] Again, the relationship
between the recession of prophecy and the formation of institutional authority
is corroborated by the Didache. The institutional elements in the church did
not extinguish prophecy; rather, the well-respected charism of prophecy was
gradually replaced due to sociological necessity, for the simple reason that
there were fewer prophets than before.

A third detail confirms that the number of prophets decreased. Both
Hermas the Shepherd and the Didache speak about a prophet, in the singular

form, whereas the New Testament usually mentions prophets, in the plural form. Aune sees this as an indication that in New Testament times prophets usually went about in groups, while in the postapostolic age they were alone, either as singular congregational prophets or as traveling prophets.[249]

3.3.12. Prophecy and Hermas the Shepherd

After the Didache, the most important source on prophecy is Hermas the Shepherd, a writing that often was considered to have canonical status in early Christianity. Thus Irenaeus quotes Hermas as "Scripture" on a par with other biblical quotations.[250] Likewise, the famous Codex Sinaiticus includes Hermas the Shepherd with the other canonical books of Scripture.

Hermas the Shepherd is characterized as a piece of oracular writing, similar to the Apocalypse of John, written between 90 and 130 A.D. While the author receives visions and forwards revelations, he does not call himself a prophet. If the letters of Paul and the Didache speak of prophecy as part of the structure of the congregation, Hermas the Shepherd does not follow this tradition, for he lists only apostles, bishops, teachers, and deacons (3.5.1). Compared to the Didache, prophecy has moved even further away from the structures of the church in this source. And yet the writer knows of persons who are filled with the Divine Spirit and who speak as prophets do. Describing people who act as prophets and play an important role in the church without, however, calling them prophets or including them among the church officers could indicate that prophecy remains in the congregation as such, but is no longer part of the ecclesial structure.

Hermas the Shepherd might represent that moment in church history when the authoritative shift from charismatic to institutional authority took place, without the eradication of prophecy per se. Prophecy continued, but in Hermas it is no longer called by that name.

3.3.13. Prophecy and Montanism

Early sources such as the Didache testify to the difficulties the early church encountered in discerning and administering prophetic experience. Nevertheless, if there were pressures in the ancient church that led to a recession of the prophetic ministry, nothing can compare to the blow the Montanist heresy gave it. As Ben Witherington writes, authentic prophetic charisms suffered tremendously through the church's negative experiences with Montanism.[251]

Montanism emerged around the year 156 in Phrygia and spread rapidly to other parts of the Christianized orient—to France, Italy, and Northern Africa, where it gained one of its most important adepts, Tertullian. Montanus, who portrayed himself as a new prophet, taught that his movement rested on a groundbreaking development in salvation history: Christ's promise to send his Holy Spirit had been fulfilled only in Montanus, who was the mouthpiece of Christ. This full coming of the Holy Spirit in Montanus was the event preceding the second coming of Christ. As Volken demonstrates, the primary reason for the church's rejection of Montanism was its claim that the full revelation had not come with the apostles, not even with Christ, but only with the Holy Spirit's revelations to Montanus.[252]

Montanus gained many followers who possessed great moral and ascetic reputations. D. Hill asserts that one of the reasons for the rapid growth of Montanism was the growing institutionalization of the church, which caused many believers to long for the more radical and ascetic Christianity of an earlier century. Montanism quickly grew wild, and the signs of Montanus's acquaintance with non-Christian cultic practices became more and more evident. When the Montanists appointed Pepuza in Phrygia to be the new Jerusalem, they challenged the authority of all governing ecclesial seats. Furthermore, the Montanists encouraged the faithful to expect new revelations to supersede the commonly accepted biblical canon. As time progressed, the Montanists were not merely critical of the institutional Church on the basis of their newfound revelations, but developed into a community existing mostly outside of the main body of Christendom.

In Montanism, all the potential dangers of prophetic claims suddenly became horribly evident. Up until the Montanist heresy, prophecy, either in its authentic or false form, never rose above the historical, institutional authority in the church. The challenge of Montanism shocked the church and its relationship to prophecy in such a way that it has been said that it has never fully recovered. Montanism presented itself at a time during which many important patristic writings were being composed—a time critical to the formation of the church's theological self-identity. This struggle with Montanism created an a priori aversion toward prophecy that became enshrined in the experience of the early church and its writings.

Montanism was still a threat in the time of Augustine, who wrote of it in the present tense, and it is possible that his experience with prophetic heresy augmented his caution against prophecy.[253] Even though his writings refer to visions he had and that played an important role in his life,[254] his polemics against the Montanists cast a rather negative light on prophecy throughout his writings.

Although Montanism endangered prophecy that was sound and edifying, substantial historical evidence indicates that this event did not itself bring about the end of prophecy. This will be clearer in the following exposé of the sources that collectively point to the continuation of the prophetic charism in the life of the church even after the rise and fall of Montanism.

3.3.14. Prophecy's Continuation Despite Montanism

In spite of the general blow Montanism dealt to prophecy, significant early Christian writers pointed to the continued presence of prophecy in the church. In fact, they exhibited a clear balance when rejecting false phenomena while retaining and appreciating true prophetic phenomena in the church. If theologians rejected Montanism because it claimed to be the final plenitude of revelation, they equally denounced the argument that there were no more prophets after Montanism's three founders, Montanus, Priscilla, and Maximilla, passed from the scene. In fact, as we shall see, these writers held that God could not have been the inspiration behind Montanism, since Christian tradition had established prophecy as a *permanent* trait of the church and the prophecy of Montanism ceased with its founders. Although many argued for the continued presence of prophecy in the church, for the sake of brevity, I shall limit our exposé to Eusebius, Irenaeus, Epiphanius, and Clemens of Alexandria.

For Eusebius, the "authenticity of Christian prophecy was of vital concern... and he was particularly anxious to prove the inefficacy of pagan oracles."[255] Eusebius argued that Montanism was false, because Montanists did not produce any more prophets after the death of Montanus; a fact that contradicts Christian historical experience:

> For if after Quadratus and Ammia in Philadelphia, as they assert, the women with Montanus received the prophetic gift, let them show who among them received it from Montanus and the women. For the apostle thought it necessary that the prophetic gift should continue in all the Church until the final coming. But they cannot show it, though this is the fourteenth year since the death of Maximilla.[256]

In fact, Maximilla had declared: "After me shall be no more prophets, but the end of the world,"[257] and several early church writers opposed Montanists precisely because of this claim that prophecy would end.

In the fourth century, Epiphanius says this against the Montanists: "Since we are called to welcome the charisms and there is a need for charisms in the church, then how is it that after Montanus, Priscilla, and Maximilla they have no more prophets? Has grace lost its vigor? It certainly does not die in the Holy Church."[258]

Irenaeus of Lyon emphatically defended prophecy in the church against the danger of Montanism. He probably had the Alogi, the extreme anti-Montanists, in mind when he wrote of those who suppress authentic prophecy because of the danger of false prophecy:

> Others, in order to suppress the gift of the Spirit which "in latter times, according as it has pleased the Father" has been poured out upon the human race, do not admit this form of the Gospel which is according to St. John and in which the Lord promised that he would send the Paraclete; but they reject both the Gospel and the prophetic Spirit. They are indeed unhappy spirits who, because they do not wish to admit false prophets, would drive out the grace of prophecy even from the Church. In that, they are like to those who, because of a few hypocrites to be found in the Church, refrain from even associating with the Brethren. It goes without saying that these same spirits no longer accept St. Paul. For in his first Epistle to the Corinthians he spoke in detail of the prophetic gifts and he knew men and women who "prophesied" within the Church.... Thus, by their whole attitude they sin against the "Spirit" of God and fall into the "unforgivable" sin.[259]

Like the writer of the Didache, Irenaeus laments that some Christians reject true prophecy because of experiences with false prophecy, and warns that by rejecting prophecy they commit the impermissible "sin against the Holy Spirit."

Cyprian is also a leading figure of episcopal and institutional authority and, like Irenaeus, highly favored the prophetic charism's presence in the church. Even in his work as a bishop he refers positively to revelations that he or people in his entourage received. One of the questions during Cyprian's ministry was whether the church should use water or wine to celebrate the Eucharist. Apart from biblical evidence (which is arguably scarce), Cyprian refers to prophetic experiences that made it clear to him that the use of wine is indeed the Lord's will.[260]

3.3.15. Prophecy in the Monastic Movement and the Founding of Orders

While the nomenclature of prophecy changed, the phenomenon itself proved its vitality in the foundations of monastic orders among the great fathers of the Egyptian desert. In many ways the desert fathers themselves continued the prophetic charism, and rather than seeing the cessation of the prophetic charism after Montanism, one can easily discern its mutated continuation.

The phenomenon of the great desert movement arose partly as a reaction to the growing institutionalization of the church and to its recognition by the state as the official religion of the Roman Empire. The desert fathers did not oppose these events as such: they opposed the lethargy that followed, a lethargy that grew as Christianity changed from being the religion of a radical minority—where the seriousness of religious conviction could literally lead into the lion's mouth—to being generally accepted by all peoples in the Mediterranean world. The reaction to this growing secularization was first manifested by a move into the desert; later, it led to a new phenomenon that would influence Christendom ever thereafter—the development of communal monasticism. At their very root, the monasteries aimed at securing the nascent experience of the Christian mystery in the desert in a socially organized and permanent way. From the beginning, the prophetic cry for holiness and radical abandonment to God was echoed in the voices of the desert fathers and monastic founders; and from the beginning, visions and heavenly directives accompanied the birth and development of these new ecclesiastic orders in both the East and West. This has continued to the present day, so that one can rightly say that among the primary subjects of the prophetic tradition are the founders of the great orders in the church. Benz argues that the founding of orders can be seen as a realization of the reaction of prophetic visionaries against the relaxation of faith: "The fate of their own order and the *ecclesiola in ecclesia* founded by the visionary himself emerges as a type of individuation of this visionary perspective on the fate of the church at large; it is a second main theme of the prophetic vision in the church's primary monastic founders, among whom we find numerous visionaries."[261]

Therefore, the founders of orders echoed the voice of prophets with their call to holiness, and also through the prophetic schema of promise and realization. Here, the primary purpose of prophecy is constituted in being a tool for God in the realization of salvation history. Thus, it is not surprising that the founding of new orders is linked to prophetic experiences, as orders and prophecy share the same purpose: the charismatically intensified actualization and realization of salvation history. Benz is of this opinion, and laments that there has been no historical research done in this prophetic aspect of the founding of new orders:

Even the history of religious life [Ordensgeschichte] occurs in the religious self-awareness of its founders and members through a history led by the schema of promise and fulfillment [Verheissung und Erfüllung], by visions and prophecies. Unfortunately, there is no such history of monastic orders that considers these prophetic and visionary basic attitudes of the orders, especially during the epochs of their constitution. These views have fallen prey to the modern, positivistic view on history, even when writing the history of religious orders.[262]

One of the essential figures in the initiation of Christian monasticism is Pachomius. He founded the coenobite monastic movement that gathered individual monks in the desert under one roof to share their prayers and their faith. Apart from other charismatic experiences, he had two prophetic visions that were of particular importance to the movement he founded. Both visions had to do with the future of the order, and both revealed that many of his disciples and brothers would fall prey to the temptations of the devil. As Benz shows, rather than being downcast by this vision, Pachomius used it in a positive light to conclude that since man is weak he needs strong superiors. This helped him to make the right choice of leaders—"Prophecies of a decline in faith led to measures to counter apostasy."[263] The announced decline is to be "conquered through a holy 'remnant,' a community of greater sanctity."[264]

From the Egyptian desert, the monastic movement spread to the West through the monastic ideals of Benedict, which according to Benz and others, stemmed directly or indirectly from the rule of Pachomius.[265] Benedict's biographer, Gregory the Great, portrays Benedict as a visionary and prophet whom God directed by revelations for the good of his community. The visions and prophecies Benedict received and the miracles he wrought were more than signs of divine election legitimizing the movement he inspired—they guided Benedict through important moments in his life and work. Although doubt has been expressed regarding the accounts' historicity, they nevertheless in any case serve to illustrate importance of prophetic gifts in the lives of saints and monastic communities.

Gregory compares Benedict to the prophets and shows that God gave him similar gifts, enabling him to know hidden realities, and to foretell the future. In several chapters of the *Vita*,[266] Gregory relates that Benedict was a prophet, or possessed the Spirit of prophecy: "Now began the man of God, by the spirit of prophecy, to foretell things to come, and to certify those that were present with him of things that passed far off."[267] One story illustrates Benedict's prophetic gifts particularly well:

> In the time of the Goths, their king informed that the holy man had the gift of prophecy, went toward his Monastery and made some stay a little way off, and gave notice of his coming. To whom answer was made from the Monastery that he might come at his pleasure. The king, being of a treacherous nature, attempted to try whether the man

of God had the spirit of prophecy. There was one of his guards called Riggo, upon whom he caused his own buskins to be put and so commanded him taking on him the king's person to go forward to the man of God, three of his chief pages attending upon him, to wit Vulderic, Ruderic and Blindin, to the end they should wait upon him in the presence of the servant of God, that so, by reason of his attendants and purple robes, he might be taken for the king. When the said Riggo, with his brave apparel and attendance, entered the cloister the man of God sat a little distance off, and seeing him come so nigh as he might hear him, he cried to him, saying: "Put off, son, put off that which thou carriest, for it is not thine." Riggo straightway fell to the ground and was much afraid, for having presumed to delude so holy a man; all his followers likewise fell down astonished, and rising, they durst not approach unto him, but returned to their king, and trembling related unto him how soon they were discovered.[268]

Several chapters speak of God working great miracles through Benedict just as he did with the prophets of old: for example, Gregory tells of Benedict producing money in front of the eyes of a poor man (27) and raising a girl from the dead (26). In the Old Testament, the prophetic word was known to be as informative as it was efficacious—to the point of producing what it pronounced. Conversely, Benedict's disciples were able to perform miracles at his command. And as with Moses, water sprouts from dry rock after Benedict prays and instructs. At a time when Benedict's monastery had no water, the brothers proposed moving the monastery to an area with water, but Benedict went up in the night to pray by a rock, and put three little stones on it. The next day he told his disciples to go dig where he put the stones. They followed his command, and to their surprise water welled forth to supply the monastery ever after.[269]

On another occasion, Benedict ordered his disciple Maurus to save a young monk he had seen drowning in a prophetic vision. The disciple obeyed, ran down to the stream *and out onto the water*, pulled the monk out of the waves by his hair, and saved him. Only afterward did he realize that he had actually walked on water, a miracle he attributed to his master.[270] Benedict's most famous vision is one of the world at large: "as he afterwards related, the whole world, compacted as it were together, was represented to his eyes in one ray of light."[271]

The foundations of other orders were accompanied by prophetic visions that revealed the right structure of the order by which it would become more resistant to the attacks of the devil and to apostasy. Thus, both Francis of Assisi and Don Bosco had visions that concerned future apostasy in the orders they founded and that led them to take action they believed would prevent such apostasy.

St. Dominic, the founder of the Dominican order and an inspiration for Thomas Aquinas, is also described as an example of prophetic inspiration by Joseph Ratzinger.[272] Along the same lines, Richard Woods summarizes the Dominican tradition with the words "mysticism and prophecy" in his book by the same title.[273]

Birgitta of Vadstena (to whom we shall return later) combined most powerfully the charism of prophecy with the foundation of a new religious order. According to Birgitta, Christ himself initiated and realized the founding of her order. As Aaron Anderson writes, several visions announced the founding of "the new vineyard" to Birgitta, the rule of which she received prophetically from Christ: "Now with my own mouth I will give a complete account of its establishment and statutes."[274] This rule is an impressive piece of literature over thirty chapters long.

The prophetic charism continued, not only in the writings of the visionaries of the church; throughout the Middle Ages, great theologians and exegetes were deeply affected by the spirit of prophecy. The church historian Pius Engelbert considers Rupert von Deutz, abbot of the Benedictine Abbey of Saints Mary and Heribert, one of the most unique of medieval thinkers, "his work being an unsurpassably singular voice in the concert of monastic theologians of the twelfth century."[275] Few realize that Rupert von Deutz was also a visionary and mystic, and it is this side of him that Engelbert exposes in his article "Christusmystik in der Autobiographie des Rupert von Deutz." Engelbert's article and Rupert von Deutz's destiny as such are valuable in that they show how important prophetic gifts manifested in the lives and careers of medieval theologians.

As with earlier Israelite and Christian prophets, Rupert received his vocation, both as priest and as charismatic exegete, through visionary experiences. In his early days, he had great doubt regarding his vocation. However, a revelation in 1108 in which a crucifix came to life secured his decision to become a priest. Only thirty days after his ordination, he had another visionary experience in which Christ conferred on him the charism of enlightened interpretation of Sacred Scripture. For Rupert, this divine gift was given to him to build up the congregation and not only for his personal edification. In fact Rupert claimed that the intellectually wise were not as disposed to receive the Holy Spirit's wisdom and enlightenment, which rendered a soul capable of grasping the true meaning of Scripture—and in this regard he was unlike other medieval authors whose knowledge flowed from a typological-allegorical hermeneutic of Scripture. Rupert believed intellectual knowledge to be a hindrance to divine knowledge, as God gives his gifts to the poor. Engelbert summarized this well: "The Wine of spiritual comfort is reserved rather for the mourning, the embittered and suffering: It is to these, the poor, that the sense of the Scriptures, the Law and the Gospel, is disclosed as they read."[276]

The modern distinction between faith and science was foreign to Rupert, who observed the growing "scientification" of theology but "approached it, as did all monks at the time, with a merely defensive spirit."[277] Instead, God's knowledge was sought directly through prayer, and often prophetic gifts were experienced through such prayer.

3.3.16. Prophecy and the Medieval Visionary Genre

As mentioned, after Montanism, prophecy seems to have continued mainly implicitly in the spirituality of confessors and martyrs and in the early monastic movements. There is little source material making explicit mention of prophecy from the early medieval period. There may be several reasons for this. One is that there in general exists less source material from the earlier than from the later medieval period; but that explanation alone does not suffice. First, it seems that the general lack of trust toward prophetic charisms ensuing from the scare of Montanism lasted for a long while. Second, the strength of the established church neither favored nor required the prophetic ministry as much as had been the case in the church's earliest phases of establishment. Third, as Bernard McGinn argues, in the period between 400 and 1100 the view was maintained that prophecy was subsumed in the ministries of the established church, and was understood as "the possession of hermeneutical skill to interpret and preach the mysteries of the Bible."[278] There are records of a few female saints possessing the *spiritus prophetiae*, but their inspirations related to individuals and were never public. One woman named Thiota began preaching in the Rhineland in 847; "pretending 'to know the precise date of the end of the world and other matters known only to God,' she was hauled before a group of bishops and sentenced to a public whipping for both her message and for 'the preaching office she had taken on in an irrational way and dared to claim against church custom.' "[279] McGinn concludes that "the new, predominantly clerical, understanding of prophet meant that there was little or no public role for prophetesses for almost nine hundred years."[280]

All this changed in the middle of the twelfth century in Germany with the emergence of the female visionary literature of Hildegard of Bingen and Elisabeth of Schönau. Church historians such as Ernst Benz, Pius Engelbert, Peter Dinzelbacher, Bernard McGinn, and many others who have examined this literature have concluded that prophecy is lively and abundant in it. Although these historians work from different perspectives, they share the assumption that visionaries received and continued the prophetic charism in the church, and that the majority of these visionaries were women.

In the *Annales Palidenses* Hildegard von Bingen and Elisabeth of Schönau were hailed as being "filled with the spirit of prophecy."[281] The reason for this dramatic change appears to be the church's widely felt failure of living up to the requirements of the Gospel and the need for reform, combined with a conviction that only divine initiative could bring it about. Only through divine intervention could the church be made pure as it needed to be prior to the end of times.[282] The female visionary literature was one of the forms in which calls for reform were realized most astutely. Women actually had an advantage in this call because of their perceived weakness, as Christ always had favored servants who had to rely on his strength to forward his initiatives (on the Pauline "inversion topos" see section 9.3.1). Men were being accused of being too sure of their own strength and therefore not open to the promptings of God's timely initiatives.

German Lutheran church historian Ernst Benz's monolithic opus *Die Vision* (seven hundred pages) is, in his own words, the result of three decades of research.[283] Benz believes that the great visionaries of the church are equivalent to the prophets of Israel in carrying out this call for reform: "The great visionaries of the Christian church have emerged as its great prophets. Their visions have a largely prophetic content. Thereby, all forms of prophecy that emerged through the Old Testament prophets are repeated in the Christian visionaries."[284] Benz sees the Old and New Testament prophetic tradition continued mainly in the visionaries' call for repentance and reform: " 'Repent, for the Kingdom of God is near!' This calling for penance in view of the coming Kingdom of God and the preparation of the way for the coming Lord has remained the central content of Christian prophecy, as is evident in the great visionaries of the Christian church."[285] And according to Benz, this view has caused particular problems in the Christian context, mainly because the church sees itself as the fulfillment of the promised reign of God in the world. The prophetic call for repentance evidently implies that the church has not fully lived up to its task of representing faithfully the reign of God.[286] Benz believes that this idea could not originate with the representatives of the hierarchy, who disdained the charge of apostasy. Therefore, the idea of apostasy could only be attributed to visionary-prophetic experience:

> One could even say that the idea of apostasy, which so contradicts the theological and dogmatic self-awareness of the institutional church

and especially its hierarchy's self-understanding, only emerged from the fact that visionaries dared to propose it on the weight of their powerful visionary experiences. The idea of apostasy is a child of the vision.[287]

If the majority of prophets in the Old Testament were men, from the twelfth century onward the proclamation of the prophetic word of God became more and more a female privilege. These women acquired many titles, but, apart from the title *prophetess*, the most accurate designation might be "secretaries of God,"[288] as they wrote down impressive amounts of messages that they claimed to receive directly from God. Some of these prophetesses carried out a very active role in the society of their time, disseminating their messages widely.

3.3.17. Hildegard of Bingen

Hildegard of Bingen was one of the first mystics to be called a prophet and was recognized as such by her contemporaries. M. Columbus Hart summarizes this in the introduction to her publication of twenty-six visions of Hildegard: "The bearer of a unique and elusive visionary charism, she was also a prophet in the Old Testament tradition—the first in a long line of prophetically and politically active women."[289] As Barbara Newman writes, Hildegard's role developed from that of a rather secluded visionary to that of a public prophet:

> Hildegard saw herself primarily as a prophet and modeled her self-understanding on biblical heroes.... For Hildegard herself, the unfolding of her visionary gift was *the* story of the first half of her life. This development took place in distinct stages, beginning in early childhood and culminating at the midpoint of her life when the seer became a prophet, the timid recluse a commanding leader.[290]

Her visions regarding everything from the constitution of the universe to the healing power of little herbs, as well as her many prophecies regarding the future, have made her one of the best known exponents of Christian prophecy.[291] Due to her holistic view of the world, she has gained a popular hearing in present times and has had a strong influence on movements outside the church such as the New Age. Nevertheless, her thoughts and writings remain deeply and firmly rooted in the Christian tradition.

Hildegard began to receive revelations in childhood, but it was not until 1141 that her public ministry began. She was convinced that she was prophesying because the age initiated with Emperor Henry IV was a perilous time of "womanish lightness" (tempus muliebre). As she writes in her *Physica,* a brief survey of various ages, "therefore, now women are prophesying to the scandal of men, and it will go on like this until the time when justice will arise after the destruction of some churches."[292]

Hildegard was herself deeply convinced of being a prophet. This conviction was embedded in a sophisticated theology of prophecy. Hildegard positioned Christian prophecy firmly in the overarching perspective of salvation history. For instance, in the *Liber divinorum operum,* an entire treatise on prophecy, she writes: "Prophecy began in God's first work, that is, in Adam. It has shone from generation to generation through the different ages of humanity like a light through darkness and it will not cease its sound until the end of the world, sending forth voices of manifold meanings, imbued in divine mysteries with the Spirit's inspiration."[293]

According to Hildegard, Adam and subsequent generations lost this permanent gift of prophecy, but it was bestowed on individuals in order for God to realize his designs of salvation and especially proclaim the coming of Christ, who "illustrates prophecy through himself." However, prophecy does not end with Christ, but continues in the New Testament, in the "spiritual prophecy" of Mary, the Apostles, and their successors, both men and women. Hildegard was equally convinced that this gift of prophecy would be intensified in a more perfect era of prophecy to come before the end.[294]

Hildegard's apocalyptism was unique, featuring five different stages and kingdoms represented by five different animals. However, unlike her contemporary Elisabeth of Schönau, whose otherwise impressive influence was somewhat reduced after she in 1154 predicted the world would end the year after, Hildegard avoided such predictions. Therewith, she did not break with the tradition of not knowing the time of the end that was known only to the Father (Acts 1:7). Although her path was certainly not smooth, at the end of the 1150s she "had achieved a public recognition beyond that given to any woman before her in the history of Latin Christendom." Her prophetic ministry was realized in writing, painting, and musical compositions and corroborated by various preaching trips.

I could mention a great number of female visionary mystics who fit well with the prophetic category: Rose of Viterbo (†1252), Douceline de Digne (†1274), Mechthild of Magdeburg (1207–82), Gertrude the Great of Helfta (†1302), Catherine of Siena (†1380), Joan of Arc (†1431), Julian of Norwich (†1442?), Margaret Mary Alacoque (†1690), and many others. Several women who many have seen as carriers of God-given charisms in the twentieth century (Luisa Piccaretta, Maria Valtorta, and Marthe Robin) lived completely secluded lives, often because of chronic illness. The writings of these women became known mainly through the activities of their confessors, and through the interest of ordinary believers whose lives had been changed for the better by their writings. Many of these prophetesses share in the spirituality of the early Christian martyrs, for they considered their sufferings as participatory in the salvific paschal mission of Christ. (We shall look at them in section 3.3.19.) A primary example is that of Birgitta of Vadstena (also called Bridget of Sweden).[295]

3.3.18. Birgitta of Vadstena

Birgitta of Vadstena, one of the visionary mystics who carried the marks of prophets most clearly, is probably the most notable Scandinavian in the Catholic tradition. In point of fact, in October 1999, Pope John Paul II proclaimed her patron saint of Europe (along with Catherine of Siena and Edith Stein). Of aristocratic descent, Birgitta was born in Finsta in 1303. At an early age, she married Ulf Gudmarsson, with whom she had eight children. Birgitta lived a normal family life until her husband's death in 1344. In the *Motu Proprio* document that accompanied the nomination of Birgitta as patroness of Europe, the pope wrote that through her example he wished to point out the importance of Christian family life to contemporary Europeans. However, Birgitta's role in European affairs did not begin until she started to have revelatory experiences after her husband's death, a total of seven hundred known revelations.[296] As a northern European who traversed by foot a major part of the continent before she settled in Rome, where she lived for twenty-three years until her death in 1373, Birgitta of Vadstena symbolizes the European unity that Pope John Paul II has called for in many sermons and papal documents. Furthermore, since Birgitta lived in the fourteenth century—two hundred years before the Reformation—she is a sign of the unity between northern and southern Europe that existed before the Reformation and, as such, it cannot be said that she was either Lutheran or Catholic. She is not a figure of confessional dispute but a person whose life, activity, and preaching point toward unity, both within and beyond the church in Europe.

Earlier I concluded that a *Christian prophet, whether labeled as such or not, is a Christian who through experienced revelations receives a message that he or she is called to hand on to the church for its edification as part of a firm design in God's will to save, guide, and bless his people.* In many respects, Birgitta of Vadstena enters perfectly into the category of prophecy thus described: first, she had revelatory experiences; second, she had a clear vocation experience; and third, she communicated the contents of her "revelations" to the people of God for their conversion and edification.

Birgitta never called herself a *prophet* or *prophetess*, nor did her heavenly interlocutors refer to her as such.[297] There may be several reasons for this: Birgitta and her confessors might find references to the term too presumptuous in her own writings, or the term *prophet* may have been too closely linked to the Old Testament prophet's foretelling of the coming of Christ.[298] However, already Bishop Alphonse Pecha, who knew Birgitta well, called her "apostola et prophetissa Dei,"[299] and other of her confessors emphasized her prophetic role in the full biblical sense in "speaking out for God, reminding the people of the examples of the past, evaluating the present, and urging all to think of reward and punishment in the future."[300] Pope Gregory XI "honoured Birgitta as a prophet."[301] And, as W. A. Purdy and Bernard McGinn point out, although controversy continued over the content and authenticity of Birgitta's revelations at the councils of Constance and Basel, "Boniface IX's bull of canonization (1390), confirmed by Martin V in 1418, included a general assertion that Birgitta had been granted 'various visions and revelations' and 'the spirit of prophecy,'"[302] implying that her prophetic endowment was of divine origin.

A later pope, John Paul II, in the aforementioned *Motu Proprio* regarding the three patron saints of Europe, speaks of Birgitta's prophetic charism and says that her voice at times "did seem to echo that of the great prophets of old."[303]

Johannes Lindblom dedicates an entire chapter to Birgitta as another example of the continuation of Old Testament prophecy in the Christian tradition, and finishes his elucidation of the convergence between Old Testament prophecy and the spirituality of Birgitta by saying: "among all the representatives of the prophetic type outside Israel, there are few who have so great an affinity with the prophets of the Old Testament as Birgitta of Sweden."[304] The affinities listed by Lindblom are many; as examples in the writings of Birgitta he notes

> revelations of Heaven and Hell and the spheres of spiritual life, of descriptions of sin and exhortations to penitence and amendment of life, of convincing and comforting speeches about God's grace and forgiveness, of visions and ecstasy and other supernormal powers and gifts, of the communication of messages of various kinds, received by religious inspiration and based on revelations from the divine world, of a feeling of being called, overwhelmed, and compelled by God, and of the consciousness of being in God's service and under His special protection.[305]

Many contributors to Bridgettine research have focused on her prophetic role. Thus, to a revelation that speaks about divine punishment, Ingvar Fogelqvist attaches the following commentary: "This revelation is from 1345. A few years following this prophecy, the Black Death hit Sweden."[306] Similarly, Jesus Castellano writes of a prophetic message given to Birgitta: "This appears to be a prophecy of the conversion of new peoples to the Catholic Church."[307]

Important contributions have also been made by Anders Piltz,[308] who sees in Birgitta a reemergence of the prophetic charism:

> She is a prophet in the Old Testament sense, a voice of God's word. In strikingly many cases, the generic characteristics given any one of the Old Testament prophets in any textbook could, with slight modifications, be applied to St. Birgitta as well. She does not only use biblical expressions and metaphors, she has thoroughly assimilated the "narrative strategies" of prophetical discourse. Also, the prophetic warnings are always conditioned by the addressee's willingness to repent.[309]

Claire Sahlin has worked on the spirituality of Birgitta as the reflection of a prophetic charism.[310] Sahlin deals with the prophetic character of the revelations, her prophetic mission, and the discernment by others of the authenticity of her messages. Many more references to Birgitta's role as prophet could be mentioned,[311] but the anthology *Saint Birgitta: Prophetess of New Ages*[312] is of particular importance in this regard. In this work, Roger Ellis calls to mind that figures on the margin are important to the center, which cannot hold without them. Birgitta is a marginal figure in at least three respects: in being a prophet, a widow, and a pilgrim.[313] Tore Nyberg seeks ways of interpreting the importance of Birgitta's prophetic vision for the present age, concluding that she "showed us the way in a prophetic manner."[314] Peter Dinzelbacher opposes I. Cecchetti's thesis that Birgitta's primary role was to lead Christians toward a mystical union with the divine; stating, rather, that she is mainly a prophet and that only secondarily can value can be given to "the elements of mystical union." He believes that Birgitta's charism transcends the limits of mere mysticism and should be found "in that which St. Ambrose presented to her as her existential task: 'to see spiritually, to listen, and to understand, for the purpose of what you have heard in your soul, you can reveal to others according to the will of God.' "[315]

He concludes his characterization of Birgitta by writing:

> The *revelationes* are not a "Book of light, fluent with the divinity," neither an "Ambassador of Divine Mercy," nor a "Book of particular grace" (as well known texts of medieval feminine mysticism are titled). They are, if you allow me this formulation, books of a charismatic theology and witness to divine prophecy, mediated by a woman who by the order of Jesus and Mary wanted to be considered nothing

else than a "channel of the Holy Spirit": a conduit through which the Spirit lets eternal wisdom flow to men.[316]

When dealing with Birgitta's revelations and the general theme of this work, the charism of Christian prophecy, the most crucial issue at stake is the relationship between prophecy and revelation. We saw that the Montanist heresy sought to mislead the Christian church by positing an unmitigated closure to the Deposit of Faith; an argument that has often been translated into the concept of an end of revelation with the last apostle (see chapter 5). However, the complete revelation of Christ needs to be continuously actualized to address new and challenging historical situations. Prophets, as we shall see, have contributed greatly to the concept of a "development of dogma."

Birgitta herself reflected upon the relationship between prophecy and revelation when speaking of the Word as addressing himself again to his people and seeing in her own charism exactly that of the eternal Word being spoken again in his church:

> After this I see a Book on the same lectern, shining like most bright gold. [This] Book, and its Scripture, was not written with ink, but each word in the book was alive and spoke itself, as if a man should say, do this or that, and soon it was done with speaking of the Word.... Also the Word spoke to me and said "The Book that you see on the lectern means that in the Godhead is endless justice and wisdom, to which nothing may be added or lessened. And this is the Book of Life, that is not written as the world's writing, that is and was not, but the scripture of this Book is forever. For in the Godhead is endless being and understanding of all things, present, past and to come, without any variation or changing. And nothing is invisible to it, for it sees all things." That the Word spoke itself means that God is the endless Word, from whom are all words, and in whom things have life and being. And this same Word spoke then visibly when the Word was made man and was conversant among men.

Birgitta is called a prophet of unity even by Protestant theologians. The primate of the Swedish Lutheran Church, Archbishop K. G. Hammar, in a press release issued on the same day on which Pope John Paul II nominated Birgitta as patron saint of Europe, pointed to her great importance for the unity of the Church: "Birgitta belongs to us all.... Even though she lived such a long time ago, she plays a strong ecumenical role today."[317]

Why is this so? In the time of Birgitta, the popes had left Rome and lived in the palaces of Avignon. This posed a real danger to the unity of the church in Europe—a danger that became acute during the "Western Schism" around the turn of the fourteenth century, a period that at one point featured three persons who each claimed to be the legitimate pope, supported by different regions in Europe. To this day no consensus exists as to who was the legitimately elected pope. Had the different factions held to their respective claims, the result could have been a tripartition of the church in Europe a century before the Reformation. It was this danger that Saint Birgitta fought incessantly, calling the popes to return to the tombs of the apostles in Rome with sharp, prophetic words.[318]

Catherine of Siena lived shortly after Birgitta. Like her, she received revelations that when published comprised several volumes. Like Birgitta, Catherine's mystical experience coupled with her social and ecclesial activity had clear prophetic traits.[319] Catherine echoed Birgitta's prophetic insistence in calling the successors of Peter back to Rome. In the *Motu Proprio* document, John Paul II writes that Catherine completed Birgitta's work and witnessed the return of the papacy to Rome. Like Birgitta, Catherine had tremendous influence on the ecclesial scenario of Europe. Inspired by her prophetic visions, she operated broadly and boldly as a negotiator of peace, corresponding with European leaders such as Charles V of France, Charles of Durazzo, Elizabeth of Hungary, Louis the Great of Hungary and Poland, and Giovanna of Naples. Her assistance in the conflict between Florence and the Holy Chair was the main reason for her nomination as the patron saint of Italy.

One cannot complete this short overview of feminine visionary mysticism from the perspective of Christian prophecy without mentioning Joan of Arc. She, like the others, carries the characteristic traits of a Christian prophet. Most notable among these is the fact that her entire prophetic activity stemmed from a dialogue with her heavenly interlocutors and that she sought to act on behalf of these divine instructions in order to carry out a task that was far beyond her own capacities. Thus Mariana Warner, dedicating a chapter to Joan of Arc as prophet, sees in her the continuation of Birgitta's and Catherine's prophetic charisms:

> For instance, seers like Catherine of Siena and Birgitta of Sweden . . .
> made it their business to pronounce on the papal schism. Division . . . was their forcing-ground and their main sustenance. Joan was again identified with this type of prophet, and again the mistake was not of her seeking, was of no interest to her, and placed her in great danger.[320]

Even though there are many male saints and mystics who share traits with these prophetic figures, prophecy, understood in the strict sense of receiving messages directly from God and passing them on to the church, seems to be a primarily feminine privilege. Francis of Assisi, for instance, certainly in an indirect manner can be said to carry out a prophetic task, as he *acted in a prophetic way* and is considered by immense numbers of Christians to have been inspired by the Holy Spirit. Still, his main charism was not to receive and write down teachings from Christ for the benefit of the church as it was for Birgitta of Vadstena and Catherine of Siena. A glance at church history seems to indicate that this task is one that, even up to our own time, has been a privilege given to women alone.

3.3.19. Prophecy and Passion

Prophets have never had an easy time! As Gerhard von Rad pointed out, one of the characteristics of the prophet is that he or she is contradicted, persecuted, and marginalized. The reason the prophets have such a hard time is that they speak God's truth in clear and critical ways, and the truth is never very popular. Since the beginning of Jewish religion, the role of the prophet has been that of calling God's people back to him. According to Nehemiah, this often led to the death of the prophets (9:26). O. Michel maintains that "struggle and conflict, suffering and martyrdom are necessary features of true prophetism."[321] In his view, suffering belongs equally to the fate of the Old Testament and the New Testament prophets.

As David Aune shows, some of the millenarian movements in early Judaism introduced suffering to the features of prophecy in a new way. Suffering was a part of the prophet's vocation as such and had a value in itself.[322] Millenarian movements in that period applied the prophecy of Isaiah[323] regarding the "Suffering Servant" of God to their respective leaders. Christianity adopted this conviction that prophets are bound to suffer because of their God-given ministry. Acts of the Apostles portrays one of the most forceful proclamations of the suffering fate of prophets, uttered by the first Christian martyr, Stephen: "Can you name a single prophet your ancestors never persecuted? They killed those who foretold the coming of the Upright One, and now you have become his betrayers, his murderers."[324]

In various passages, Jesus corroborates the convergence between prophecy and suffering. One of these passages is found in Luke:

> That is why the Wisdom of God said, "I will send them prophets and apostles; some they will slaughter and persecute, so that this generation will have to answer for every prophet's blood that has been shed since the foundation of the world, from the blood of Abel to

the blood of Zechariah, who perished between the altar and the Temple."[325]

However, in Christianity, a new notion evolves around the idea of suffering in which suffering is not only the result of the prophetic exhortations; it has an independent value of its own. Especially Catholic tradition has nurtured the idea that suffering can in some mystical way serve to aid other souls toward salvation in Christ. The importance of Christ's passion is not only that his suffering authenticated his prophetic mission, but that this suffering was the very purpose of his coming. The sufferings of many Christian mystics can be understood as the fullness of their unity with the suffering Christ.

The word *com-passion* itself reflects the idea of suffering with others or for others. Just as the "Suffering Servant" passages in Isaiah's prophecies parallel the sufferings of Christ, other passages exist that call Christian believers to follow Christ's example and mission as God-sent sufferer and sacrifice. Among the more famous passages are the words of Paul in his letter to the Colossians: "It makes me happy to be suffering for you now, and in my own body to make up all the hardships that still have to be undergone by Christ for the sake of his body, the church."[326]

The early Christian martyrs continue this principle of identification with Christ. It was evident to many church fathers that the martyrs suffer for and in Christ, but that also the Logos suffers in the martyrs, just as he did formerly in patriarchs and prophets of the past.[327]

The convergence between the role of martyr and prophet is already clear in the aforementioned martyrdom of Stephen, who just before expiring had a vision of Christ with the promise of his eschatological victory. In the Apocalypse, the unity between prophecy and martyrdom seem to be confirmed once more: "Blessed are those who die in the Lord."[328]

Early Christian history exhibits many examples of the convergence between prophets and martyrs. Famous in this regard is the martyrdom of Felicitas and Perpetua, and the *Acts of the Martyrdom of Sts. Perpetua and Felicitas,* which tells the story of their last days, shows the place of prophecy in the early church in a fascinating way, as it contains a long apology defending the reception of visions and revelations in the time of the new covenant and links prophecy with martyrdom.[329] The time of their visionary experience, especially that of Perpetua, begins at the initiation of their martyrdom. As Peter Brown writes: "Her entry into the prison-house at Carthage was an entry into the world of the Holy Spirit."[330] The accounts of their martyrdom hold five visions that clearly place them in the prophetic category. Famous is the prophecy that they will be victorious—Felicitas and Perpetua themselves were not aware that this referred to their martyrdom, not to their survival. Since there appears to have been a strong link between the roles of martyr and prophet in the early church and there is evidence that the martyrs and confessors assumed part of the prophetic ministry, it is not a surprise that great parts of the writings of later Christian prophets are oriented toward the passion of Christ.

Birgitta of Vadstena is one example of a medieval prophet who often saw Christ in the moments of his passion and who set these sufferings of the Lord as an example of perfect love that Christians should follow. Francis of Assisi and many other stigmatized mystics have equally been spokespersons in support of an active theology of the Cross.

Especially in the past two centuries it is possible to talk about *the suffering prophets* as a specific group within the category of prophecy. Most of these are women. They are characterized as being bedridden most of their lives, usually either due to corporal ailments or mystical sufferings such as stigmatization. Many of them have displayed other mystical features, such as being able to survive for decades on nothing other than the Eucharist. While the church is aware of several examples of such figures, a certain number are of particular interest, in that they incorporate the role of "victim soul" into their prophetic ministry. Some of these bedridden women have produced an impressive amount of writing considering their dire circumstances.

As examples of such suffering prophets we may give Anne Catherine Emmerich (beatified in October 2004), Theresa Neumann, Luisa Piccaretta, and Maria Valtorta; but many others could be named.[331] These could easily be considered spurious women who had ecstatic trances because of their sufferings, but they have truly inspired modern Catholic spirituality and led many to deeper faith. For instance, the writings of Anne Catherine Emmerich, interpreted by the poet Leon Bloy, inspired the conversion of Jacques and Raissa Maritain.[332] Another person who could be added to this category of suffering prophets, but from whom we do not have prophetic writings, is Marthe Robin.[333]

Many of these mystics suffered immensely, to the point that medical doctors were not able to explain how they could endure such sufferings. Meanwhile, they themselves were fully aware of why they suffered. In fact, one of the common features of the category of the suffering prophets is that through their visions they are instructed in the meaningfulness of their sufferings; that Christ presents his Cross as the biggest gift of love he can give a soul and that he also provides the strength to carry it. In reading their writings, it also becomes evident that they have given their full consent to their missions, fully convinced that they would bear fruit in a mystical way.

It is possible to give other motives for their sufferings, but one is particularly interesting. The suffering prophets call to mind the primary dynamism of their ministry, namely that it is not their capability, but their incapacity that makes it fruitful. This feature of prophecy comes across not only as a troublesome barrier in spite of which the prophets are able to carry out their ministry; it is a part of the prophetic role as such. Only if the person is weak and unable to fulfill his or her task by his own power, whereby he turns to God, is he or she fully equipped to be a prophet; for the dynamism of prophecy is such that God acts through the prophet and hence the entire mission, not just the message, originates in God. This weakness of the prophet also comes across as one of the factors that authenticate the prophet's experience and mission. One may safely argue that if the message transcends the wisdom and formation of the prophet and the hardship of the mission exceeds the prophet's strength, so long as the judgment criteria do not indicate the influence of occult powers, only God can be at work through the prophet's weakness. This is a feature that also applies to the last prophetic category that I shall examine in this historical exploration.

3.3.20. Prophecy and Marian Apparitions

In the nineteenth century, the prophetic charism surfaced in yet another forceful way in the form of Marian apparitions. Beginning with the French apparitions of La Salette in 1846, Lourdes in 1858, and Pontmain in 1871, continuing in the twentieth century with Fatima in 1917, Banneux and Beauraing (1932–33), Garabandal (1961–63), and Medjugorje (ongoing from 1981), just to mention a few, a new wave of prophetic messages presented themselves to Christians. These apparitions have created apparition sites that function as centers of pilgrimage and prayer with reports of repeated miraculous healings and other extraordinary experiences. The impact that these many modern pilgrimage sites, which Victor Turner has described as "postindustrial Marian pilgrimage" places,[334] have had on the fruition and development of life in the church in all parts of the world cannot be underestimated.[335] A few things make apparitions a prophetic category of their own. First of all, those who receive the apparitions are mostly children of both genders. This seems a new development, since the Bible rarely speaks of children being prophets or receiving messages,[336] and there are few earlier known historical examples of children having revelations.

Furthermore, apparitions are remarkably different from earlier forms of prophecy, in that they are almost exclusively Marian. In apparitions of the past two centuries, the visionaries mainly see the Mother of Jesus. Sometimes they may see her holding Jesus in her hand, though he would never give messages, and in a few apparitions, such as those of Fatima, an angel occasionally may take the place of Mary. However, the primary heavenly spokesperson is and remains Mary.

As Gottfried Hierzenberger and Otto Nedomansky have shown in their study, Marian apparitions have occurred throughout the entire Christian age.[337] However, they have intensified during the last two centuries as a new current of charismatic Mariology that is in line with, and perhaps even one of the causes of, a general growing Marian awareness in the Catholic Church. It is this growing Marian awareness that functioned as a catalyst for the promulgation of the Dogma of the Immaculate Conception.

The setting around Marian apparitions could be compared to that found around certain prophets of the Old Testament such as Jeremiah. Jeremiah was the prophet, and Baruch wrote down his prophetic utterances. Analogously, Mary could be called the real prophet of apparitions, whereas the children's task is to take her words down and pass them on to the broader church. Something similar is evident in early Judean apocalyptic literature, such as the "Revelation of John," as interpreting angels play important roles in relegating divine instructions.

Partly because of this function of Mary as prophetic spokesperson of Christ, her Son, the title *prophet* or *prophetess* has been attributed to Mary from the ancient church, much rather than the title *priestess*. The reasons for Mary's designation as prophet are multiple, and varying lines of thought by different church fathers contribute to the general Marian prophetic image.

Mary is *prophet* because of her ability to listen to God's Word, receive it, and carry it fruitfully to the world;[338] another interpretation is presented by Origen, who creates a bond between prophecy and virginity, as a "vaticinium virginale" in Mary prior to the birth of her Son. With Ambrose, special emphasis is put on the special prophetic gifts conferred to Mary, equivalent to a quasi habitus that enables her to know heavenly secrets. Finally, some Fathers, especially Maximus of Turin, see her presence and activity at the Wedding in Cana as prophetic, pointing toward her mediating role, evident in Marian apparitions.[339]

DIFFERENCES BETWEEN PROPHECY AND APPARITIONS. Even though apparitions and the prophetic charism share many features, and it is fully justifiable to situate both in the category of prophecy, it is possible to trace out distinct differences between the two as well, as follows. (1) While the "secretary" type of prophecy presents itself as a feminine gift, it is children of both genders who are most often the recipients of Marian apparitions—perhaps with the one significant exception of the apparitions to the young nun Catherine de Labouré at Rue du Bac in Paris in the nineteenth century. (2) The messages of the secretary-type prophets are usually remarkably long, making out many volumes of visions and conversations with Jesus and the Saints. These are often very elaborate and frequently contain penetrating insights into Christian spirituality and other areas of theological significance. Messages derived from apparitions, on the other hand, are normally rather short and the content simple, often including exhortations to live in prayer and in the love of God and neighbor. (3) The occurrence of visions to the secretary-type prophets is not limited to any geographical location; in fact, many of the female prophets traveled extensively, an example being Birgitta of Vadstena. With Marian apparitions, on the other hand, the location is extremely important and usually does not change during the course of the phenomena. As a result, the geographical location in which the apparitions take place becomes an *apparition site*: a place of pilgrimage that benefits the life of the church long after the departure of the visionaries.

THE WORLDWIDE RELEVANCE OF APPARITIONS. Even though the messages of these apparitions are usually rather simple, adapted to the minds of children, not only do they have an impact on the spiritual life of believers but also many apparitions contain messages and prophecies that enter the worldwide scenario of human events and often come true in surprisingly concrete ways. The famous example is the apparitions of Fatima. Here, one of Mary's prophecies focuses on the potential dangers of Russia—something that modern civilization has identified with communism. The messages of Fatima portray austere warnings from the Mother of Jesus, calling the world to conversion and prayer and warning that the world would suffer if it did not heed these admonitions: "If my requests are heeded, Russia will be converted, and there will be peace; if not, she will spread her errors throughout the world, causing wars and persecutions of the Church. The good will be martyred; the Holy Father will have much to suffer; various nations will be annihilated."[340]

This message is an excellent example of Christian prophecy disclosing future events. Such warnings of future chastisements are never unconditional and do not reflect a photographic image of an already programmed occurrence. As in the Old Testament, prophecies of impending dangers are mostly conditional;[341] there is always an "if" that renders the prophetic predictions plastic and open to human intervention. Hence these prophets remind us of the fact that human destiny is always contingent on the choices we make with our own free wills. Thus, the fulfillment of the prophecy is always predicated on the free response to the call for conversion, prayer, and sacrifice from the faithful. A study of the history of Christian prophecy reveals that prophecies of future calamities are *not* the capricious inventions of a malicious God. Rather, they are fatherly warnings about *the very real consequences of evil actions taken by the children of the earth* according to the Old Testament scheme: what comes from the earth will descend on the earth; *you reap what you sow*.

This discussion touches on another issue at the heart of Christian prophecy. The prophet is presented as an important player in the ongoing spiritual battle between good and evil. Even though history shows that prophecy indeed has had an influence on the development of Christian dogma—that is, the relationship between Catherine de Labouré's revelations and the promulgation of the Dogma of the Immaculate Conception—the prophet's main function is not to disclose unknown doctrines. The essentials of Christian faith are persent in Holy Scripture. Hence the task of the prophet is rather to encourage the church to live the Gospel and to guide it through the rough waters of history; pointing out dangers and admonishing the faithful to keep in union with God and his truth.

3.3.21. A Twenty-First-Century Case History: Vassula Rydén

To conclude this exploration of the continued presence of prophecy in the history of the church, I shall present what comes across as one of the most interesting and complicated cases of today, namely the experience and activity of the Greek Orthodox mystic Vassula Rydén. Few other contemporary mystics exhibit the prophetic charism as does Mrs. Rydén, and she certainly is one of the most debated modern mystics. Nevertheless, after an initial critical attitude, the CDF has scrutinized and passed a not unfavorable judgment on the messages transmitted by Mrs. Rydén. Without attempting to evaluate the authenticity of her experience, my aim here is to show what a prophetic experience could look like in practice in our times.[342]

Mrs. Rydén says her conversion began with the stroke of a pen. Vassula, as she is normally called, comes across as an ordinary, rather appealing woman. Up until her conversion, she lived a normal life as the wife of a Western foreign aid official deployed in various third world countries. Her lifestyle differed little from that of many such women expatriates who try to alleviate the tedium of their exile with a social life devoted to tennis, bridge, and receptions. She rarely thought about God, until November 28, 1985, when everything changed. While she was writing a grocery list, she reports to have suddenly experienced a light electrical feeling in her right hand and at the same time an invisible presence. She says she felt led by this presence, and permitting her hand to be guided, she wrote a line in a very different style from her own with the words "I am your guardian Angel and my name is Daniel."[343]

This experience was the beginning of the reported conversations between Vassula and Daniel, from whom she claims to have obtained "a crash-course in Christian doctrine." A few weeks later, she started having visions and locutions from Christ, through which she learned to seek God in prayer. Before this experience, God had rarely crossed her mind. Now she often dedicates six hours a day to prayer and spiritual writing, when she is not traveling to hold conferences about her messages.

Since the beginning of these experiences, Vassula has written down thirteen volumes of conversations with the Father, the Son, and the Holy Spirit, as well as with the Virgin Mary, the Archangel Michael, and especially in the beginning, her guardian angel, Daniel. The books, entitled *True Life in God*, have been translated into over forty languages since 1991 and have become bestsellers. In Brazil, where an estimated half million copies of her books have been translated and distributed by a priest and two nuns in Portugal, running their own printing press at night, Vassula has drawn crowds of as many as thirty thousand people; her meetings have attracted crowds of over four hundred thousand.[344]

Vassula's case is interesting, as it fits well with the image of Christian prophecy that emerged in my earlier discussion of Old and New Testament prophecy (see sections 3.1–3.2): a prophet is a person who receives a message that he or she is ordered by God to forward to the church for its benefit. Vassula did not become "a prophet" through human qualities, as she had no theological training that would equip her for her task; she believes herself that she was chosen exactly because she did not have any merits or assets and that all initiative thereby had to be Christ's. She claims not to have chosen her mission and that it came to her as a surprise, that she would have preferred to stay home with her family, but after Christ had asked her to serve him she could not refuse his request to proclaim his words to his people. And last, Vassula and people who have studied her case believe that God through her message seeks to consolidate his church, especially by bringing it into unity, which is the main theme of her books.[345]

Vassula's experience has thus caused believers of all denominations in the twenty-first century to raise the same old questions that prophets provoked earlier in the life of the church. Does Almighty God reach down to earth and speak to human beings even today? Would he not thereby cheapen his divine works? Would the Creator of all things, the "Inaccessible Light," lower himself, step down from his throne, and speak words in modern English to modern people?

The interest in Vassula Rydén today indicates that many Christians still consider this to be the case. They confirm the uninterrupted Christian conviction that God did not only speak to Abraham and Moses in the time of the Old Testament, but has revealed himself throughout the Christian era to this day. In fact, theologians speak of a proliferation of prophetic manifestations in our times, with Vassula as one of the main examples.[346] Some believe that the third millennium shift has given humanity reasons to reflect on where it is heading; they see this as the reason for the recent proliferation. Others, including Vassula herself, believe Christ speaks because his Creation is endangered in the "great apostasy,"[347] caused mainly by a "spirit of rationalism,"[348] the main "weapon to combat" God's divinity, a subject considered to have been less of an issue in the New Testament period than it is today.[349]

Vassula was born in a desert. Her parents were part of the Greek community in the town of Heliopolis in Egypt, and she was baptized in the Greek Orthodox Church. Early in her life the family moved to Switzerland. Her husband's work brought the couple first to one Third World country after another, then to Switzerland, where they lived for eight years, and finally to Rome in 1998. Vassula has two sons, both of whom have left home, one to work in Sweden, the other in Singapore.

When the revelations began, the family was living in Dhaka, the capital of Bangladesh. "My only responsibilities were the occasional cocktail parties I had to arrange for my husband," Vassula says. "Otherwise I was living a rather placid and privileged life which I filled with tennis and painting, my two favorite occupations. Whenever you wanted to find me, the place to call would be the tennis club, where I spent most of my time." Vassula won the doubles finals of the Bangladesh national championship. In addition, her paintings were becoming well known. She won a competition with a portrait of the last emperor of Ethiopia, Haile Selassie, which was transformed into a postage stamp that was printed in nineteen denominations. "I loved my family, my friends and had no worries, no sorrows, nothing that moved me to reflect deeply about life or about religion," she continues. "I did not speak to my children about God, nor did I speak against him. I was as many people are today—indifferent. Religion was just not important to me. Thus, when I had the first revelation of my Angel, I was totally unprepared. I took the experience with great joy and considered it a pearl that I revealed only to my closest family and friends. They immediately believed me; they knew I was not crazy."[350]

Vassula says she understood that what had happened to her was unique, and she did not know where her angel would lead her. She was unaware that many people in the history of Christendom had visits from God or from angels, but she has come to know Christ as one who keeps a constant watch over his creatures and therefore will keep sending prophets: "Jesus says he has come many times in the history of the church to guide his people and remind them forcefully of what he had already taught," Vassula says. In one message Jesus explains why he is revealing himself through his "Love Hymn":

> The Holy Bible is indeed the truth, the true revelation, but I have not ceased to exist. Look, I am the Word and I am active in Spirit. My advocate is with you all, the Spirit of truth that many tend to forget or ignore, for all that the Spirit tells you is taken from what is mine. He is the reminder of my Word, the inspiration of your mind. This is why my child, I am continually recalling you the same truths. Understand the reasons and why I am constantly stirring you up with the reminder. Accept my Holy Spirit of truth. I come to remind you of my Word, I come to call you to repent before my day comes.[351]

IMPLEMENTATION AND ACTUALIZATION OF REVELATION. Although Vassula's writings in this way are no "new" revelations, they point out many aspects of revelation and of the Christian faith that according to the writings are not implemented properly or at times are even ignored. To believers who never thought about these truths, they could well appear as "new" insights. Furthermore, many passages concern realities in today's world that were not issues in the early church. Many examples could be given, but I shall limit myself to two: the aforementioned damaging effect of rationalism and the "grave sin" of the division of Christians.[352]

Vassula reports to have been instructed over and over again on the danger of rationalism, both to the lives of individual believers and to the church as a whole. The warnings go against an interpretation of faith that reduces faith's transcendent elements to the minimum, thereby leaving little more than an empty technological silhouette, whereas faith was meant to irradiate the dynamic truth and life of God: "It is the spirit of rationalism and of naturalism that led most of you into atheism—this is the spirit that makes you believe you are self-sufficient and that you can achieve *everything* by your own efforts and by your own strength."[353]

Those who serve in the church but follow an overrationalistic interpretation of Christian faith are accused of turning the temple of God into a factory: "You have industrialized my House, this House which should have been a House of prayer!"[354] These are even called apostates:

> They have apostatized from me, yes, they have accustomed their steps to walk with apostasy and have as their guide and traveling companion rationalism, the weapon to combat my divinity. If any man is thirsty for knowledge let him come to me and drink and I shall give him living water; do not go and drink from a man's doctrine which is

coming from his own rationality. That man is putting honor from men before the honor that comes from God.[355]

The main theme of the writings is the unity of the church. The present disunity among Christians is presented not only as a sad fact but as a sin against the will of Christ that annihilates the credibility of Christians. Although the church was always challenged by schisms, the present disunity among Christians is such that it severely damages the body of Christ: "All are the same in my eyes; *I* have never wanted my Body parted, it is *you* who have dismembered me! *You* have decided upon my Body! You lamed me."[356] The instructions on unity are good examples of prophetic exhortations, as they point to aspects of the Christian message of reconciliation that have not been followed. Furthermore, they give instructions on how the called-for goals can be implemented in practice. In the case of the unity of the church, Vassula claims that Christ told her the way back to the initial unity of the church, Christ's "sovereignty," is not mainly through lengthy theological discourses but by means of a simple nondogmatic act, namely the unification of the dates of Easter: "My sovereignty was split in two and from thereon into splinters.... How glorious you were in your earlier days! Come and rebuild my house into One by unifying the dates of Easter."[357] And in another passage:

> I have sent you My Spirit to live in your hearts, this is why the Spirit that lives in you will show you that My Church will be rebuilt inside your hearts and you will acknowledge each other as your brother in your heart. Will I, brother, one more season go through the pain I have been going through year after year? Or will you give Me rest this time? Am I going to drink one more season the cup of your division? Or will you rest my Body and unify, for my sake, the Feast of Easter?[358]

Vassula notes that "Christ promised us that if we unify the dates of Easter, He will do the rest."[359]

POETIC LANGUAGE. Vassula's writings are rich in poetry, metaphors, and parables, similar to the Old Testament Psalms or to the Gospels. In one revelation the Creator speaks about the joy he experiences over Vassula's conversion, portraying her revival through a parable:

> I happened to be taking a walk nearby a river when I saw a driftwood drifting away with the worldly current; I leaned over and picked it out of the stream; I brought it Home with Me and planted it in My Garden of Delights. From a dry piece of wood I made out of you

a Tree; I said: "grow! grow and take root in My garden, in My own property, and from your blossoms exhale a perfume to appease My Justice.... I, Yahweh, will see to it that you prosper; I take pleasure in picking now and then on My way pieces of driftwood. I can give life to anything I pick on My way.[360]

After her initial happiness and joy at meeting God, Vassula entered a period of doubt, but was soon reassured by her interlocutor. She relates:

I had doubts whether if what I was receiving was truly from God. Everything pointed to the fact that it was: After all the revelations had brought me to love him with a fire inside me. Nonetheless there was one big question that led me to my doubts: "Why on earth did he chose me?" I asked Jesus this question many times. He answered me saying, "I choose unworthy souls to form, ones who know little or next to nothing. I will supply you, Vassula, for I am wealthy; with Me you will lack nothing." He had to teach me everything. Sometimes he uses words I don't even know. Once he spoke about this present generation and said: "Fastidious you have become." I did not know what fastidious meant. This happened many times.[361]

As mentioned earlier, one of the hallmarks of the prophet is that he or she has no authority to lean on other than God's, and Vassula and other commentaries have seen this as a reason that the majority of Christian prophets are women and children in their capacity for trusting.[362] A spiritual zero before the revelations began, Vassula believes that God chooses those otherwise incapable of such achievements so as to leave no doubt that it is his power at work. She believes that she was chosen for all that she was not. "Jesus wanted a nothing," she explains, "in order to prove that I have not invented all this and that it comes from Him. He said it in a message: "All you have comes from Me and is My Work and not yours. Without Me, you are unable to even wink your eyes—so abandon yourself to Me."[363]

Before long, Vassula's inner doubts were compounded by outward skepticism. She learned that prophets are usually persecuted for their direct words. Vassula recalls that Jesus from the very beginning made her understand that her path would not be easy and that it would entail suffering and persecution: "You will appear as the loser My Vassula, but have I not appeared as the loser too? I appeared to have failed My Mission; I appeared in the world's eyes as the greatest loser ever."[364]

Some prophetic characters were never recognized as being sent by God, partly because the church saw problematic aspects in their writings and activity. Joan of Arc, who had many revelations and visions, charged with being a witch, was burnt at the stake. Twenty years after her execution she was exonerated, and she was canonized in the twentieth century. Another less violent case parallel to Vassula's happened in the last century. The Polish nun Sister Faustina Kowalska had frequent revelations and communications with Christ that she wrote down in a diary. In 1958, the Vatican CDF banned her writings by placing them on the Index of forbidden books, and she died considered a heretic. Twenty years later the same CDF revoked its decision, due to the intervention of a certain Cardinal Karol Wojtyla. In April 2000, the same man, then known as Pope John Paul II, canonized Sister Faustina in Rome.

PRO ET CONTRA. Vassula's writings and activity have caused similar uproar, with articles and books published in support or disregard of her. In his *Vassula and the CDF,* Edward O'Connor calls Vassula's story one of the more troubling ironies in life today.[365] This affirmation is repeated by René Laurentin in *When God Gives a Sign,* in which he describes the criticism leveled against Vassula as a continuation of the "spirit of the inquisition."[366] In the Catholic Church there are some who accuse her of being a guru of the New Age movement, a witch bent on destroying the Catholic Church, or simply the greatest false prophet today; some just criticize her for not becoming a Roman Catholic. Ironically, members of her own Orthodox community have accused her of being one of the cleverest mouthpieces ever of Catholic propaganda, paid by the pope to turn the Orthodox into Catholics. Others have called her the Antichrist disguised as a woman. The first Catholic book against her was published by Fr. Dermine in Italian in 1995.[367] It was followed by a series of related negative books and articles, classifying Vassula as a false prophet or an adept of the New Age movement.[368]

An even more extensive array of positive articles and books has been published by theologians such as Fr. René Laurentin, Fr. Umaña, Fr. Edward O'Connor, Fr. Ovila Melançon, Jacques Neirynck, and the late Fr. Michael O'Carroll.[369] The late Archbishop Franic of Split, for years the head of the Yugoslav Catholic Bishops' Conference and an expert on mystical phenomena, wrote strongly in favor of Vassula.[370] He expressed the astonishment shared by many theologians and church leaders who cannot understand how a normal woman who never received theological training can write down messages whose beauty and profundity stand out among contemporary spiritual writings.

INVESTIGATION BY THE CDF. In 1996 the CDF issued a *Notification* in which it affirmed that Vassula's messages are "merely the result of private meditations."

The authors of the unsigned *Notification* held that her messages, "in addition to positive aspects . . . [contain] a number of basic elements that must be considered negative in the light of Catholic doctrine."[371] In reaction to this, most newspapers in Switzerland, where she lived at the time, ran headlines such as "Vassula Condemned by the Vatican." This enabled the critics of her experience to refer to the *Notification* as proof that they were right and therewith considered the case "Vassula" closed. As with other prophetic polemics, Vassula's case proved that things are less simple with prophecy. In fact, her traveling activities have only increased since the *Notification*, just as more prominent church leaders have come forward to defend her case, arguing for the conformity of her writings with Catholic faith.[372]

The prefect of the CDF, Joseph Ratzinger, on several occasions mitigated the condemnatory interpretations of the notification, for example, in an interview published in 1999. His words deserve attention, as they reflect some of the difficulties involved with prophecy. The problem is not only that there are true and false prophecy, but that even true prophetic inspiration must pass through the noninfallible filter of human language. The former prefect of the CDF affirms:

> [The] *Notification* is a warning, not a condemnation. From the strictly procedural point of view, no person may be condemned without a trial and without being given the opportunity to air their views first. What we say is that there are many things which are not clear. There are some debatable apocalyptic elements and unclear ecclesiological aspects. Her writings contain many good things but the grain and the chaff appear to be mixed. That is why we invited Catholic faithful to view it all with a prudent eye and to measure it by the yardstick of the constant faith of the church.

> *Is the procedure to clarify the question continuing?*

> Yes, and during the clarification process the faithful must be prudent, maintaining a discerning attitude. There is no doubt that there is an evolution in the writings which does not yet seem to have concluded. We must remember that being able to set oneself up as the word and image of interior contact with God, even in the case of authentic mysticism, always depends on the possibilities of the human soul and its limitations. Unlimited trust should only be placed in the real Word of the revelation that we encounter in the faith transmitted by the church.[373]

From 2000 to 2004 a dialogue followed between Vassula Rydén and the CDF. The CDF's collaborators examined her writings for doctrinal errors. Subsequently, the CDF submitted five questions to her in a letter dated April 4, 2002. The five questions were meant to clarify certain expressions that could be misinterpreted but that were not in themselves heretic according to Catholic doctrine. At the request of Joseph Ratzinger, Vassula's answers were published in the twelfth volume of her writings.[374] As a conclusion to this dialogue, Joseph Ratzinger wrote in a letter to a number of bishops' conferences that Vassula Rydén through the published answers had supplied "useful clarifications regarding her marital situation, as well as some difficulties which in the aforesaid *Notification* were suggested towards her writings and her participation in the sacraments."[375] The *Notification* had charged Catholic bishops with not allowing any space for the writings of Mrs. Rydén in their diocese. Now, on the basis of the "useful clarifications" she has provided, following the dialogue, prayer groups inspired by her writings are allowed, as long as they follow the guidelines of the diocesan bishop.

In spite of this affirmation, some resistance continued by opponents to Mrs. Rydéns writings, insisting that the dialogue did not change a thing. The most radical of these negative interpreters of the dialogue is the secretary general of the Swiss Bishops' Conference, after it received the cardinal's communication. In a letter dated February 23, 2005, he asserts: "The Congregation for the Doctrine of the Faith maintains all its reservations regarding the writings and actions of Mrs. Ryden."[376]

Like any other person claiming to have revelations from God, Vassula Rydén is likely to continue to draw attention from all sides, both from those who trust her authenticity and from those who do not. The attention drawn to her experience, however, is not only due to the fact that she claims to speak with Jesus. Believers attending her meetings have reported experiencing inexplicable phenomena. Medical reports confirm cures of grave illnesses in her presence. Many people have reported the phenomenon of seeing Jesus appear in Vassula's face, and with other prophetic experiences of the past, such alleged miraculous occurrences have buoyed belief that the message originates in God.

To most people in Vassula's neighborhood, she is just a normal modern woman living a normal life. However, when she is on the prophetic podium, she is sure to be a lightning rod of controversy and a "sign that will be opposed."[377] Because her claim is so large, there is very little middle ground between skeptics who can only dismiss or ridicule her and faithful followers who are utterly convinced that they are hearing the voice of the Good Shepherd through her writings.

3.4. Conclusion

The phenomenon of prophecy continued from ancient Israel over early Judaism into the early church and the entire Christian period. Prophecy has always fulfilled an integral role in the church, whether the phenomenon was gratified by the prophetic title or not, disproving the thesis that prophecy ended in early Judaism. What happened was that the phenomenon continued in new forms and among new social groups, but it was not named prophecy, mainly out of respect for the prophets of the Old Testament. The New Testament authors reinvented the prophetic term for John the Baptist—calling him the "last prophet," who, along the lines of Old Testament prophets, foresaw the coming of Christ; for Jesus, although mostly in a metaphorical sense; and for several apostles and important personalities in the nascent Christian church. Luke's writings especially are imbued with prophetic phenomena and nomenclature, whence Kelsey is right in emphasizing the prominence of dreams and visions in the Acts of the Apostles.[378]

Unlike the case of the Old Testament, only one book in the New Testament can be rightly called a collection of oracles, namely the Revelation of John, but Aune has produced criteria by which he is able to identify oracular speech throughout the New Testament. This intriguing research contributes to the assessment of prophecy's influence on the Q source, and is buttressed by Boring's conviction that prophetic words of the risen Christ inspired the tradition of the sayings of the earthly Jesus; likewise, Hallbäck's analysis of how the change in early Christian prophecy played a decisive role in the formation of the New Testament canon has helped toward the understanding of prophecy's impact on the formation of early Christianity. All these points suggest that prophecy played a significant role in the early church, a fact that the New Testament writings themselves support, in particular through Paul's placing prophecy on the second position of the list of offices in the church immediately after the apostolic office.

Many postcanonical writings point to the continued presence of prophecy in the early church, in particular the Didache, which contains instructions on the administration of the prophetic office in the church, and Hermas the Shepherd, which, much like the Revelation of John, comes across as a collection of oracles. However, while these writings together with the New Testament reveal the place of Christian prophecy, they nevertheless point to prophecy's decline, as the earliest writings manifest a greater prophetic presence than the later. The decline of early Christian prophecy may stem from several factors that appear to have been strongly interactive: the decline of vertical prophetic authority in the early church and the danger of false prophecy produced the need for a new type of authority, which was to assume historical forms, namely growing institutionalization and the formation of Sacred Scripture. These in turn decreased the need for prophecy and, according to both Protestant and Catholic theologians, effectuated a beginning conflict between institution and prophecy. While this conflict remains evident, the my historical exploration suggests that prophecy's fate does not stem only from growing institutionalization—rather that the institutional developments were partly due to the decline of prophecy.

Many New Testament scholars have seen the decline of prophecy in terms of a linear descending graph on the chart of the early church, thereby indicating the total extinction of prophecy once the graph hit the null line. The conclusion of my investigations is that this view is incorrect, as prophecy—just as in early Judaism—did not cease in the early church but only continued in new forms that better suited the changed context of Christianity as official religion in the Roman Empire. Although prophecy was no longer an officially institutionalized charism in the church as the office of deacons, priests, and bishops, it continued in various forms: among the martyrs and confessors and the Desert Fathers and founders of the monastic movements; in early mediaeval vision literature, especially in nascent female mysticism, with "secretaries of God"[379] writing down volume upon volume of refined divine dictations about the suffering prophets; and in the simple messages and appeals to prayer and conversion conferred by visionary children at apparition sites such as Lourdes and Fatima. History shows that prophecy has kept mutating but has never failed.

4

Prophecy and Revelation

We have seen that prophecy as a phenomenon in the church never ceased. But as it is hardly possible to use history to infer the theological conclusion that a matter is soundly rooted in Christian theology for the simple reason that it exists within the church; we need to examine the notion of Christian prophecy to determine whether it is theologically valid. Further, if theology agrees that the Christian system can hold such a phenomenon, it also needs to define its nature and function. Such an assessment of prophecy has no other starting point than the Christian concept of revelation; so now we shall look at themes from revelation theology that are important to our subject and explore what consequences they have for the concept of prophecy.[1]

The idea of revelation has been seen from the outset of Christian thinking as arising from the concept of love. One who loves a person desires the other person's openness; openness is required for two persons to communicate and ultimately be united in love. This is what lies in the German expression "Offenbaren," to carry something openly. Revelation means not only knowledge of a person's traits but entrance to an exchange of persons, of fellowship.

Augustine reflects profoundly on the relationship between revelation and love when discussing the theology of the Trinity. The foundation of the Christian idea of revelation is that God is love and that love can never be love without a person to love, hence the dynamic bond between the three persons of the Trinity is love. This dynamism is not only an internal one between the three persons *(ad intra operatio)* but a Trinitarian power that is directed to other creatures *(ad extra operatio)*. The inner-Trinitarian love between the Trinity's three persons cannot be separated from the One God's desire to love others.

In the original relationship between God and man, God and Adam, there was unity, openness. There was no need for particular revelation between God and Adam but continuous openness. In the Fall this union was broken, and Adam had to hide from God, leading God to ask: "What have you done?!" Sin and concealment are inseparable. The consequence of sin is that there is no more "Offen-bar-heit," and this is the lot of fallen man: not so much the distancing from God, the veil, the lack of openness, or the lack of unity, but rather the radical separation that is portrayed in the biblical recounting of the expulsion from Paradise, in which the doors to the place of union with God are shut and guarded by an angel.

Thomas Aquinas expresses in his *De ente et essentia* the relationship between the Creator and the fallen creature. According to the idea of the *analogia entis*, an analogy will always exist between God and man. This analogy is based in man's being created in God's image, which is expressed primarily in man's reason, the direct place of encounter between him and God. For Thomas and the entire Scholastic tradition, reason is seen as the umbilical cord between God and man, and yet reason in itself will never suffice to fully understand and know God. Even if the analogia entis teaching expresses that there is and remains an analogy between God and man, it is far more important to acknowledge in this analogy a greater difference: while man and God can meet, this meeting can occur only on the condition that God never can be completely or fully comprehended.

This continued analogy guarantees the possibility that God can lift the veil that lies between himself and man and communicate himself to man. Although before the Fall there was continued openness, after it revelation was required whereby man might commune with God. And if the continued analogy makes continued revelation possible, God's love makes it necessary.

During the entire history of Israel, the prophets are the champions of continued openness and communication between God and man, his instruments through which he seeks to reestablish the broken unity. It is this revealing activity of God's love that is continued in the vocation of the Christian prophets, whereby Christian prophecy may be seen as the most immediate expression of God's revealing activity. It is immediate because not only is it a *sign* of God's general revealing activity, but it is, in itself, a type of experienced revelation. The prophet is convinced he or she does not speak his or her own words but transmits the words of the One who in reality has spoken. Thus, Christian prophecy is an expression of revelation in a twofold manner:

Prophecy is revealing in its mode, inasmuch the prophet considers his or her experience a form of direct communication from God through which God reveals his truths. Second, *Prophecy is revealing in its scope,* inasmuch as God through the prophet seeks to attain the goal of his activity, namely, to lead man back to his original union with God. In the following I will consider two different aspects of the category of revelation: revelation as experience and revelation as a concept to be reflected on. When talking of the experiential aspect, I consider revelation as an experienced reality, of a concrete occurrence within history that, through the prophet, results in a revealed message. When I speak of the reflective aspect, I take a general look at the motives of individual revelations and of the intention of God's self-disclosure.

4.1. Revelation as Concept of Experience

Since classical prophecy addresses the reception and proclamation of revelations, we must consider these revelations from psychological and phenomenological perspectives. As we shall later encounter, the function of prophecy, in Catholic thinking, has many similarities to that of the church's Magisterium, inasmuch as both serve to forward and actualize the truths of revelation. A fundamental difference lies, however, in the *way* this actualization occurs. From here on, I shall use "truths" in the plural to convey an "effect" of revelation and not revelation itself. In other words, it may be wise to keep distinct, though not separate, revelation's *activity* (the *causa efficiens* of God's self-disclosure, or dynamic uncreated power) that produces external results and internal activity in the soul of the human creature that enables the soul to correspond to revelation's *truths* (the knowledge or the *causa finalis* of God's activity).

The Magisterium forwards and actualizes the truths of revelation as a heritage from the apostles. The workings of the Magisterium in its root must be a charism; if it shall serve the ever-living Logos, it must do so in a charismatic way, echoing the dynamism of the Logos itself. It is from this that the Magisterium's task of safeguarding and presenting revelation for every new generation emerges as a historic progression.

The prophetic ministry, on the other hand, comes across as a receptive actualization of the Deposit of Faith. The prophet experiences his or her words and gives them to the church as words of God. Inasmuch as God's Logos is the source that actualizes both the Incarnation and prophetic inspiration, it is not primarily a historical heritage that is transmitted, but an immediate participation in the fullness of the Logos. Inasmuch as God's Logos operates and is present in the Incarnation and in the prophetic inspiration, albeit in different forms, the true prophet's proclamation expresses nothing else than and takes from nothing else than the fullness of the Logos—expresses nothing apart from nor adds anything to the substance of the fullness of the revelation of the Logos. Hence, the prophet says nothing that is radically new about the salvation in Christ, but, through his or her immediate experience of this fullness, expresses it anew for his or her own context. The unexpected often flows from the wisdom of the Logos through the prophets, thus providing freshness, nutrition, and water to the already planted vineyard of the Word, the church, that the Magisterium must look after with already appointed care.

In theory it is possible to look at prophecy without taking into consideration the experiential dimensions by focusing solely on its *function*. Examples of this are found in Rino Fisichella's article "Prophecy" in *Dictionary of Fundamental Theology*,[2] and P. Mariotti's article "Contestation prophétique" in *Dictionnaire de la vie Chrétienne*.[3] Likewise, *Dictionnaire de la Spiritualité* does not pay much attention to the experiential aspects of prophecy, and the reason for this omission is not due to an approach focusing on the *function* of prophecy only, but to one that limits itself to examining the Magisterium and its prophetic vocation.

When prophecy is presented as a dynamic actualization of revelation, the experiential aspects are treated thoroughly, as, for instance, in Karl Rahner's *Visions and Prophecies*[4] and Johannes Lindblom's *Prophecy in Ancient Israel*[5] and *Gesichte und Offenbarungen*.[6] Rahner maintains that in order to present prophecy fully, it is essential to present its experiential aspects.[7] We saw that New Testament exegetes saw experienced revelation as constitutive of prophecy (see section 3.3.1). Considered as an experiential concept, revelation means cognition that results from a supernatural encounter with the divine that is not accessible to the human creature under normal circumstances. As Hasenhüttel has shown, it is mainly this aspect that characterizes prophecy as *phenomenon*:

> Prophecy counts as the greatest of all charisms (1 Cor 14:1). What does this concept that is so foreign to us today signify? What lends it this significance? Is it not so that in our minds the prophets emerge only in Old Testament times? All others that call themselves prophets in the church are often considered false prophets, *Schwärmer,* or simply fortunetellers. However, none of this is evidently meant with the word.[8]

Moreover, Max Seckler presents the provocative aspects of the category of revelation, namely, its being a supernatural means of cognition whose form of immediate revelation is strange to our world of today:

> In today's world of life, work and thought, revelations and revelation are mainly fringe topics with an exotic air and dubious validity

that are often confronted with incomprehension and disinterest, even distrust and rejection.[9] . . . Already the unusual circumstances and forms of experience that can be connected with them appear to be as doubtful in worth as they are tenuous.[10]

Throughout the Middle Ages and all the way up to the beginning of the twentieth century, this charismatic approach to revelation was predominant, if not exclusive. The clash between these two aspects of the revelation category (revelation as experience and revelation as concept to be reflected on) may be what creates the greatest theological uneasiness concerning the phenomenon of prophecy, as the prophecy is so intimately linked with revelation's experiential aspects. Volken is convinced that this clash is the main reason why prophets have been met with such resistance. Thus opposition to the prophet becomes a mechanism to safeguard the faithful from breaches of faith in the ongoing and dynamic development of the phenomenon of prophecy, but often stifles the prophet, preventing him or her from pronouncing a word even before it is spoken. As a result, the prophet is put in a category of his or her own to which little attention is given. It is as sure as the law of gravity that the receiver of prophetic revelations will be ridiculed.[11]

But the difficulties around the experiential aspects of revelation give rise to more than ridicule of the prophet. There is great theological incertitude with regard to the relationship between divine inspiration and its human expression. In a given prophetic revelation, which is the part of God and which is the part of man? Is a revelation only the human interpretation of the Spirit's inspiration or is every single word conveyed directly to the prophet's ear? In other words, in a given prophetic revelation, what percentage is from God, and what is from the prophet?

The insecurity about the experiential aspects of revelation is evident in the academic presentations of known prophetic figures. Let us consider, for example, the scientific elaboration of the writings of Birgitta of Vadstena. Ingvar Fogelqvist speaks repeatedly in his *Apostasy and Reform in the Revelations of St. Birgitta* of God's inspiration in her writings. It is clear that he considers her to be endowed with a prophetic charism, for he voices the opinion that Birgitta on several occasions pronounced prophecies that proved to be true. Regarding a revelation of chastisement, Fogelqvist comments: "This revelation is from 1345. A few years following this prophecy, the Black Death hit Sweden. . . . The Black Death is probably also referred to in VIII 57 A and VI 113.5."[12]

At the same time, one of the constitutive elements of Fogelqvist's scientific work is precisely to prove analogies between Birgitta and Thomas Aquinas, and between Birgitta and Benedict of Nursia. When Fogelqvist explains the purpose of these comparisons, he makes it explicitly clear that the purpose is *not* to prove that Birgitta depends on these writers, but rather that they have parallel thoughts: "My aim is not to establish any influences, but merely to let these references illustrate and clarify Birgitta's views."[13] In this way he avoids the critical question of to what extent Birgitta's spirituality is an expression of interiorized tradition and to what extent of directly revealed knowledge. The revelatory aspects of Birgitta's writing remain intact, and it is up to the reader to decide what is of God and what is of Birgitta.

Other interpreters of Birgitta are less delicate, for example, Sven Stolpe, for whom Birgitta's so-called revelations are nothing more than a particular medieval genre.[14] When Birgitta says "Thus says the Lord," she merely endeavors to flavor her words with divine authority. Many other researchers have expressed the same opinion. The revelatory genre is a powerful one that the prophetic characters employed to express themselves where other speech found no open ear. This technique is ascribed in particular to medieval women. They are said to have had no other way of being heard than to express themselves in revelatory terms. Kari Børresen, as many authors, presents this as the reason why the majority of medieval mystics are women:

> The . . . conflict between ecclesiastical androcentricity and charismatic gynecocentricity is particularly manifest in the lives and writings of religious women. . . . Medieval women's history, hagiography, and written works amply demonstrate their proficient exploitation of this religious outlet for female assertion. Considered creationally powerless, mulieres sanctae invoke divinely inspired revelations in order to affirm their God-given empowerment.[15]

The same argument has been proposed by P. Dinzelbacher, E. Gössmann[16] and Claire Sahlin, who writes:

> Often, as in the case of medieval women, revelations and visions have provided women with one of the only avenues for expressing religious insights and calling for moral reform. While women traditionally have been excluded from the priesthood, they have frequently assumed religious leadership through prophecy. Convinced that God spoke directly through them, prophetic women have boldly condemned moral evil and called for repentance.[17]

Sahlin, more than others, abstains from passing judgment on whether prophetic speech was a convenient genre in some women's strategy of exercising influence, or whether there was no strategy behind it and women prophets, rather, felt compelled by God to speak, so that the cause of the female prophetic preaching was not the lack of other means of female influence but rather the intuition of God's desire to work through instruments where he would be the only authority. In either case, the question is intimately linked with the intricate relationship between divine and human influence in a given prophetic message, which is no secondary issue, as the authenticity of the prophet depends directly on the extent to which his or her revelations truly coincide with God-given inspiration. Insofar as authentic supernatural inspiration in some form or other is constitutive of Christian prophecy, prophetic revelations must tautologically originate in God, or they will be no revelations at all; hence the inseparable blending of prophetic authenticity and the convergence between divine inspiration and human expression.

There is yet another, more simplistic way of addressing authenticity. If, for instance, a message presented as a revelation bears good fruit, one may still call it "authentic," as good fruit is one of the primary criteria for authentic prophecy. According to Volken, God can avail himself even of nonrevealed messages, provided that the believer adheres to this message with a pure and good will. But here the word "authentic" appears in its broad application, which can easily be abused. Let us consider the prophet who presents a message as "revealed" when, in reality, it is the mere product of his or her imagination or even of sinister inspirations. He or she would appear to be a liar if it was known that his or her message was the fruit of his or her own invention, and not of God's inspiration. In this case the message would not be considered "authentic."

As we shall see (see section 8), one of the challenging questions posed is what is it that the church actually confirms? Does it only approve the orthodoxy of the message, or does the approbation hint directly at the "divine authorship"? Since the judgment process does not limit itself to the orthodoxy of the message but also examines the prophet's spiritual life and the possible signs that accompany the revelation, it follows that the judgment must hint at more than the mere message. But it is unclear as to what this *more* consists in. The question of the authenticity of a given prophetic message is thus intimately linked to the relationship between divine inspiration and human experience and the expression of inspiration. It is this issue we shall turn to in the following.

4.1.1. Inspiration and Experience

A prophetic message makes sense only if it is expressed in an understandable language. Only in this way can it play a role in the church. Its power lies less in being a supernatural sign than in the promulgation of its understandable message. According to Paul, prophetic speech excels tongues, inasmuch as it is capable of being understood by all and, by this means, is able to edify the church, whereas tongues only edify the person who possesses this gift. The intelligibility is rooted in its being useful not only to the community, but in the divine pedagogy. According to the "law of divine adaptation" proposed by Volken, prophetic messages always occurred in the preferred language of the prophet.[18] Thus, the intelligibility of prophecy is constitutive to the entire concept of prophecy, and prophecy is no prophecy at all if it is not understandable.

On the question of revelation there has long been a tendency for theologians and psychologists to communicate with difficulty. Some theologians have highlighted the supernatural origin of revelations to the point of ending up with rather fundamentalist positions that leave little space and importance for the human mechanisms in the revelatory process: the revelation is from God, hence there is no more to be said about this question. Psychologists, on the other side, often focus only on what happens in the human psyche in the revelatory moment, since, as Marc Oraison shows, they are able only with difficulty to operate with the idea of a divine origin of any message formulated in human terms.[19] Preferring to try to prove that various aspects of revelatory experiences have analogies in clinical psychology, they tend to deny divine intervention. When this tendency is strengthened by a rationalistic view of the world that excludes divine interaction with the natural order, it is not surprising to find an a priori resistance to the idea of divinely inspired spiritual experiences.

Today there are various tendencies toward enhanced communication between the two lines. Psychologists have accepted the fact that religious experiences, simply because they have parallels in clinical psychiatry, need not be pathologic themselves. As Antoine Vergote illustrates, human beings can have many vision-like experiences that do not derive from psychological defects.[20] Thus dreams are a form of hallucinations that, far from being pathological, actually have health-regulative effects on the human person. In his presentation of the development of psychiatry, Philippe Loron proposes that today it is legitimate to research into the relationship between soul and body, which is one of his own spheres of interest.[21] As a psychiatrist, Marc Oraison is able only with great difficulty to see divine activity in an ecstatic mental state that calls to mind hallucinatory experiences: "All that I can say, and that corresponds to a possible apprehension, is that we are talking about a hallucinatory phenomenon. The remainder escapes to me completely, and I think that it escapes me not only as a medical doctor, but also as a theologian."[22] At the same time, he does not deny that God can employ such mental states in divine communications: "Nothing enables us to solve the question whether [God's]

mystery appears in this manner."[23] Jean Dierkens writes that apparitions normally are treated in two ways: as within the boundaries of either religious
or psychopathologic phenomena. This is wrong, he writes, as "each of these
attitudes is reductionist and creates obstacles to the serene study of this phenomenon."[24] If apparitions are treated as true divine communications, theologians hardly ever venture to investigate the mechanisms by which they occur
in the mind of the prophet. If, on the other hand, theologians, for theological
reasons, conclude that a given apparition is not from God, or from the devil, it is
seen as the imagery of a deficient psyche, whereby the case is transferred to the
realm of psychological pathology. Moreover, to treat apparitions with the psychological approach only fails to do justice to the phenomenon as well, as
psychology has few other ways to explain religious experiences than that they
diverge from the normal state, which often enters in the realm of the pathological. Therefore, Dierkens justifiably calls for a new, "neutral terrain" on which
to approach the fact of religious experience that objectively examines the phenomenon for what it is and leaves aside a priori judgments on their origin.[25]

These conclusions and new positions have been aided by modern medical
examinations of visionaries during ecstasy. Indeed scientists have made interesting examinations, as in the case of the six young visionaries at the
Bosnian pilgrimage site of Medjugorje during their ecstasies.[26]

Today, on the other hand, theologians are not afraid of admitting that God
may avail himself of psychological mechanisms when wishing to communicate himself to the world. In fact, the thesis has been abandoned according to
which a natural explanation excludes a supernatural cause. That God is the
direct and effective cause of a revelation does not indicate an abolition of those
laws of the human psyche. On the contrary, a vision that admits a true and
divinely inspired process into the human mind no longer appears foreign to
the psychiatrist, who may still regard it phenomenologically as a classical
hallucination or dream.

A medical doctor who examined the visionaries at the apparition site
Beauraing in Belgium, approved by the Catholic Church, identified their experiences precisely as pathological hallucinations, since the visions of the children coincided with what he knew as pathological hallucinations. According to
Vergote, his aggressive accusations ironically turned out to be one of the primary incitements leading the ecclesial authorities to investigate the apparitions.[27]

Along the lines of classical Incarnation theology, it makes most sense
today to maintain that God in no way necessarily suspends the natural faculties of the human psyche but much rather avails himself of the created
when communicating with humans. Psychiatrists may describe the processes

in the mind during visionary experiences, while the theologian contributes
with his or her views on the origin, function, and meaning of these communications. The two may thus be complementary rather than contrary. As Adnès
writes, hallucinations and visions could follow the same mind-mechanisms
while having completely different causes: "Il s'en suit que le mécanisme psychologique de certaines visions pourrait être identifié à celui des hallucinations
sensorielles."[28] And Gabriel de Sainte-Marie-Madeleine assures the reader that
this fact should not be shocking:

> Let no one be scandalized by this: it is not a question of identifying
> visions and hallucinations, but to point out that, in the two phe-
> nomena, the representation of the sense object can be the working
> of the same psychological mechanism; however, the driving causes of
> this mechanism remain completely different. While in hallucinations
> they are morbid tendencies, in visions it is grace at work.[29]

C. S. Lewis observes: "The very same phenomenon which is sometimes not
only natural but even pathological is at other times ... the organ of the Holy
Ghost."[30] Whereas pathological hallucination derives from an unbalanced
psyche, divine revelation or vision stems from a divine inspiration. Where the
point of encounter between the divine and the human is found remains a
mystery.

Many mystics are also *mystical writers,* in the sense that they write or
speak about their own mystical experiences. Many of them describe how they
experience the divine inspiration with different force, sometimes stronger,
sometimes weaker. Anders Piltz writes of Birgitta of Vadstena's revelatory
experiences and describes how she has sometimes received her messages
word for word, whereas at other times she has only experienced the essence of
the message and has had to give words to it herself.[31]

In spite of the many contributions to the theory of the relationship between divine inspiration and human experience, many questions remain unanswered. This is not only because we find ourselves in front of a mystery that
modern science is far from able to explain. Even the believer, who has many
criteria of discernment that enable him to assess the authenticity of a given
prophetic revelation, has to ultimately make an assent of faith if the message
is to bear any fruit. Instead of limiting myself to the manifold questions concerning the processes in revelatory experiences—wondering what percent is
of God what percent is of man—it is more expedient to shift attention from
the revelatory process to its final product. The written product of an objectively
authentic revelation can indeed be seen from an incarnational perspective.
Just as Christ cannot be limited to certain human and divine percentages, so

objectively true revelation cannot be confined to certain human and/or divine percentages. In point of fact, in true revelation both the divine and the human synergetically and symbiotically coincide.

4.1.2. Visions, Apparitions, Locutions

Divine communication is experienced through numerous modes, and mystical terminology in particular presents many different modalities of the divine disclosure of hidden realities. Although prophets have experienced the word of God through infused knowledge, without the addition of revealed images or an audible voice, the prevalent forms of prophetic experience in most religions, including Christianity, are those of *visions, apparitions,* or *locutions.* As they are of such importance to the appreciation of Christian prophecy, I shall now take a closer look at them.

Pierre Adnès gives a general definition of visions, which is also applicable to apparitions and locutions. According to his definition, visions are sensorial or mental manifestations of realities that are not normally visible and are difficult to grasp (*insaisissables*) to humans.[32] Laurentin offers an approach to discerning between visions and apparitions according to which visions are a "subjective perception" and apparitions "an objective manifestation." Although he considers this distinction quite simple, as every "perception," including the natural, encompasses both subjective and objective elements, he considers it valid for the general evaluations of visions and apparitions.[33]

Apparitions are first and foremost of a tangible and sensorial nature. The visionary sees apparition objects as three-dimensional material objects similar to ordinary physical objects, the only difference being that the objects are visible only to the visionary.[34] The seer of apparitions is usually in a state of trance and maintains that he or she has seen the apparition with his or her own eyes. The objects of apparitions normally appear in the natural, physical surroundings of the visionary. When a visionary for instance sees an angel, he or she is usually later able to indicate where exactly the angel was standing. When there are several visionaries present, they enter the state of trance at the same moment, while their reactions, especially eye movements, are mostly synchronized, suggesting simultaneous responses to the same object. On the basis of these observed facts, most analysts are inclined to generalize apparitions as experiences of objective realities that merely are not accessible to all.

The angel's manifestation to Peter, leading him out of prison, falls into the category of apparitions, since he, with his own eyes, saw the angel leading him out of a concrete place in which he found himself; likewise his late reaction of coming to himself indicates a state other than the normal state of consciousness. Similarly, the Marian manifestations that have increased in recent centuries are usually defined as apparitions. Hence the experiences of the visionaries in places like Fatima, Lourdes, Pontmain, Banneux, Beauraing, Garabandal, and Medjugorje all share the traits just described.[35]

The concept of *vision*, on the other hand, is more often used for revelations that occur through the imagery of the human cognitive faculty, which places it in the realm of subjective experiences. The visionaries are usually being transported away from their normal surroundings, and the change of backdrop is characteristic for the vision genre.[36] Visions may occur while awake, often during ecstasy,[37] or while asleep, whence arise what is referred to as *dream visions*. Dream visions differ from normal dreams in their clarity, which lets the visionary remember them in particular detail.[38] Locutions, auditions, or inner words (*paroles intérieures*) are inspired communications connected to the hearing faculties of the mystic, who hears something that normally is not discernible to the senses.[39] Locutions often accompany apparitions and visions, enhancing their intelligibility. Most classic prophetic revelations occur through a combination of locutions and visions or apparitions.

As we shall see (section 4.1.3), theology since Augustine has ordered visions hierarchically as corporal, imaginary, and intellectual. The corporal visions are those whose object appears as a physical reality, among other objects of reality, as in the majority of cases of apparitions. The imaginary visions occur in the imagination of the visionary and hence cover the majority of visions, as described earlier. The intellectual vision is the highest in Augustine's hierarchy, communicated directly to the intellect without the support of images from material reality.

4.1.3. Theology of Apprehensio and Consequences for Christian Prophecy

Dogmatic theology looks at revelations from the perspective of their importance to the life of the community. Mystical theology, however, considers them from the perspective of their importance in the spiritual life of the individual believer. Dogmatic theology investigates them from the perspective of their *purpose*; mystical theology from the perspective of their *modus*.

Mystical theology deals with the spiritual development of believers and considers prophetic revelations from the perspective of how they occur in the psyche and what role they play with regard to spiritual progress, without taking into consideration their *prophetic scope*, which is to edify the community. Everything in mystical theology points to the soul's union with God, the *unio mystica*. And here prophecy is not in its right element. Prophecy can make out an important call to conversion and to seek this union, but the message in itself does not equal the sanctifying grace that actually leads to and secures the spiritual union between God and soul. It is insufficient to look at prophecy from the perspective of this one goal of spiritual union, since its scope is beyond the individual's spiritual growth.

As we shall see, mystical theology tends to prefer wordless, infused contemplation to intelligible and prophetic spirituality. Rahner criticizes this tendency sharply: "Indeed, it can be said with but little exaggeration that the history of mystical theology is a history of the theological devaluation of the prophetic element in favour of non-prophetic, 'pure,' infused contemplation."[40]

Thus, there is a clear tendency to dichotomize between intelligible, prophetic spirituality and the spirituality of wordless, infused grace. This dichotomy became evident in the first theological treatises on the theme of vision, and must be understood in the light of what Balthasar rightly laments, namely, that Christian mysticism has lost its ecclesiological outlook. For Balthasar this tendency of Christendom goes back to the Montanist crisis: "This substantially social aspect of all Christian mysticism was lost to a large extent in the theological and spiritual tradition since the Montanist crisis and must absolutely be recovered again."[41]

One major problem in the discussion of visions is, as shown by Pierre Adnès, that the concept of vision has an enormous range, which has led to much confusion.

> A vision is the manifestation in the senses or the mind of realities held
> to be naturally invisible and imperceptible to man in the circum-
> stances currently given. In fact, the term *visions* embraces a universe of
> very varied phenomena of knowledge, which one cannot easily bring
> back to a common denominator except by the impression that they
> give of coming from somewhere else, from beyond the subject, who
> does not have the sense of producing them and cooperating actively in
> the process, but receives them free, like a gift, an unexpected favor.[42]

Augustine was the first to treat the concept of vision, and his approach to the theme has colored theological elaborations of the subject ever since.

4.1.4. Aurelius Augustinus

One of Augustine's great interests was the philosophy of cognition, of how man obtains knowledge. In order to explore this question he dealt extensively with the concept of vision and visions. As Courcelle argues, these played a great role in his writings,[43] but they receive special attention in two important works: *Contra Adimantum* from the year 394 and even more so *De Genesi ad litteram*—a larger work whose twelfth book, written in 414, is dedicated entirely to the question. In *Contra Adimantum* Augustine primarily explores various visions in the Bible, whereas in the latter work he treats the concept of vision in connection with his cognitive theories. Even though Augustine's concept of *vision* is very different from how mystical theology treats the visionary category, his thoughts have influenced mystical theology profoundly.

Augustine's teaching, especially his triple categorization of visions, is echoed in the writings of Gregory the Great and later in Isidor of Sevilla,[44] from whom it was passed on to medieval theologians such as Thomas Aquinas.[45] This tripartition of visions has been one of the ever-returning classics of spiritual theology, and was, for instance, used in the writings of Birgitta of Vadstena. As Johannes Lindblom shows in *Prophecy in Ancient Israel,* the tripartition of visions played an important role for Birgitta of Vadstena. He synthesizes the teachings of which Birgitta was inspired in the following way:

> In the corporeal revelation the visionary believes that he sees and
> hears by means of the natural senses, with all the characteristics of
> ordinary sensation. In the imaginative revelation the visionary sees
> with "the eye of the soul," while the natural senses are put out of
> function. The intellectual revelations are the influx into the mind of
> thoughts and ideas of a more or less theoretical nature.[46]

Augustine deals with visions in an all-inclusive cognitive theory that Pierre Adnès recapitulates as "knowledge taken in all its dimensions: sensitive, imaginative and intellectual, moral and pathological, profane and mystical, intramundane and celestial. The three kinds of visions mark the advance of the soul from the body all the way to the realm of knowledge."[47]

Augustine's teaching perpetuates a Neoplatonic theory proposed by the philosopher Porphyry, who separates visions into the three groups of corporal, imaginary, and intellectual. As Adnès shows, Augustine's preference for the intellectual vision is in line with the assessment that pure, nonmaterial reality stands above the physical reality, which is nothing but a reflection of the ideas the *rationes aeternae.* The highest knowledge is thus obtained by contemplating the ideas by means of divine illumination that renders them accessible to man.[48]

The first group covers those visions in which a person sees something that no one else can see but that the visionary sees with his or her physical eyes. The object of the vision is seen as a physical, three-dimensional entity. In Augustine's terminology, these are the visions seen with the eyes of the body, and they are the *corporal visions.*

The visions in the second group constitute the majority of visions; Augustine calls them *spiritual,* but the tradition mostly renders them by the term *imaginary.* These are visions realized through mechanisms of the human psyche that are made up of images that the soul has acquired through contact with the physical reality.[49] Even if the objects of the visions are not the immediate result of sense contact with reality, the visions are reflections of the physical world.

The two aforementioned categories are both in their ways related to the senses, either by means of immediate contact with reality as in the first group, or through the treasury of imagination filled by sense contact with reality as in the second group. The bodily visions can be called *direct corporal visions* and the imaginary visions can be described as *indirect corporal visions,* but both are derived from reality.

The *intellectual* visions do not relate to the senses in any way at all, being immediately God-given cognition, directly communicated to the intellect. As such, they are unsullied by the interference of the senses, which limited in their discernment of the spiritual as they are bound to the material realities.

Peter Dinzelbacher has summarized the teaching on this tripartition of visions well:

> The "Visio corporalis" is our everyday experience by the sensory organs, which we share with the animals. The "Visio spriritalis" refers to the images of the imagination, be it those of fantasy or those of memory. Our dreams belong in this category. The "visio intellectualis" is the rational cognition of abstract realities, like love or justice.[50]

Augustine himself explained his theory with a parable about a person contemplating the commandment to love your neighbor as yourself.[51] The letters of the text are seen by corporal perception, the absent neighbor's image by spiritual (imaginary) perception, and the abstract idea, *love,* by intellectual perception.[52] The three groups of visions are interrelated. The visions in the highest group can exist or be of significance without the support from the corporal and imaginary visions in order to make sense; not so with respect to the corporal or imaginary visions. The corporal or imaginary visions, on the other hand, make no sense and have no meaning if they are not accompanied by the inner illumination informing the soul of their true meaning, they can lead astray without the convincing guidance of the intellectual vision, which is considered infallible: "intellectualis autem visio non fallitur."[53]

This short presentation of Augustine's system shows that it already contains the foundations for a dichotomization of visible (corporal vision) or mentally visible (imaginary vision) on the one side and the invisible (intellectual vision) on the other, and this dichotomization of the concept of vision has had repercussions on the treatment of prophecy. As we shall see in comparing Augustine and John of the Cross, Augustine does not advance this dichotomization to the point of opposition, but his system contains the foundations of such confrontation.

C. Butler argues in *Western Mysticism* that although Augustine's terminology is susceptible to Platonism, he actually speaks about truly mystical experience. Therefore we should not be surprised if many writers of mystical theology took him for one of their main authoritative teachers in the spiritual life.[54] At the same time there remains a difference between Augustine's system and the way it is employed in mystical theology. Augustine applies the term *vision* in a broader sense than do mainstream mystical theologians, who use it to refer to an experience that is not accessible under normal circumstances: "In the mainly religious language, which alone interests us here, a vision is a manifestation in the senses or the mind regarding realities considered naturally invisible and imperceptible to man in the currently given circumstances."[55] Augustine, on the other hand, speaks in broad terms of the cognition of physical and spiritual reality.

One can then rightly ask, how is it possible that the thoughts of Augustine in spite of these differences have won such popularity in mysticism? Apart from the mere authority of Augustine's name, the answer must lie in his vision theories, which cover reality and correspond to his system, as follows. (1) We experience through the senses. (2) We think and dream in categories derived from sense experience. (3) We do experience certain emotions and realities such as love, loneliness, power, that we do not connect directly with physical reality. Augustine's terminology is applicable simply because it fits with reality. Furthermore, Augustine's usage of the word *vision* is so broad that it can be applied loosely to other models of visions.

4.1.5. *Thomas Aquinas*

Thomas Aquinas refers explicitly to Augustine's teaching in visions and transmits it faithfully.[56] He treats visions frequently, especially in his prophecy treatise. According to Thomas, imaginary visions can be produced in two ways: either through images that God imprints directly in the mind of the visionary, or by means of the visionary's imagination obtained through his or her precedent impressions through the senses. Needless to say, God can rearrange them in a particular way in order to produce the revelatory experience.[57] In the same manner, Thomas distinguishes between intellectual visions that are directly infused into the mind of the prophet and those that, albeit being inspired by God, reemploy intellectual perceptions of the person that he or she could well have obtained through the senses.[58] Like Augustine, Thomas places the intellectual vision at the top of the hierarchy, as it confers to the prophet the purest knowledge of the very substance of a given matter. In fact, the intellectual vision comes close to the state of heaven, where the truth is contemplated in the essence of God.[59] Thomas insists that most visions are not actually "real" images of the object of the vision (for instance of Christ or the Virgin Mary) but are reflections of the object produced in the mind of the visionary. Only in such rare cases as Christ's appearance to Paul on his way to Damascus does Thomas consider the vision to be one of Christ's actual presence, even though Paul's companions did not see anything but light.

Thomas Aquinas's teaching on visions and prophecy in general can lead in two directions: toward communitarian and toward individualistic theories of prophecy's purpose. The first direction can be pursued because Thomas positions the prophecy treatise in his *Summa* between his teaching on *virtues* and on *religious life*. In this way he goes from individual spirituality over prophecy to communitarian life. Furthermore, Thomas is faithful to Augustine's teaching not only in the tripartition of visions but also in keeping the prophetic discussion in a cognitive perspective.[60] Marianne Schlosser's *Lucerna in caliginoso loco* is a fine example of a communitarian reception of Thomas's teaching on prophecy. She applies his teaching to the wider context of the church, investigating whether it is possible to talk of "quasi-prophetic charisms, such as the priesthood or teaching."[61]

The second direction has nevertheless been the predominant understanding of Thomas's teaching on vision and prophecy. It is based on the fact that the content of Thomas's prophecy discussion, not its position, is mainly individualistic. Thomas's theology is thereby continuing in the heritage of Greek thinking and the teaching on prophecy of Maimonides. Balthasar argues that Thomas continues an old *skepticism* toward charismatic spirituality, to which the Messalianic heresy had contributed. Thomas's concern about retaining

the inner unit of *dona* and higher, internal charismata remains an authentic concern, in spite of all Messalianic errors, a concern that did not receive enough attention in later Scholasticism with its sharp distinctions. The striking power of Messalianism faded, without the necessity of a sharp statement by the church; the completely anticharismatic mysticism of Dionysios gained victory in the East, whereas Augustine's mysticism of love and the sober asceticism of Benedict prevailed in the West.[62]

Thus, it may well have been because Thomas did not want to enter the debate with this general Scholastic depreciation of charismatic spiritualities that most of his concrete examples of prophecy are taken from the Old Testament. The Old Testament prophet "constitutes the focal occurrence, the *analogatum princes,* and other cases point toward him."[63]

His approach to the prophetic phenomenon is phenomenological rather than functional and ecclesiological. He thus dedicates many lines to discussions of questions such as whether prophecy becomes a habitus (an ability that becomes part of the visionary's own system) or a continuous free gift of the spirit, rather than discussing its relationship to the revelation in Christ. The reasons for Thomas's individualistic approach to the prophetic category are rooted in the understanding of the concept of revelation that was predominant in his times. As mentioned, the notion of revelation remained one of experience much more than of reflection all the way until the beginning of the twentieth century (see section 4.1.1). Therefore, when treating the question of prophecy, which in Thomas's time was inseparably linked to that of revelation, Thomas naturally gave priority to the question of *how* prophetic experiences occurred rather than what their function in the church should be.

4.1.6. *John of the Cross and Teresa of Avila*

A great part of mystical theology builds on the writings of John of the Cross and Teresa of Avila—both *doctores* in the Catholic Church. John of the Cross and Teresa of Avila were contemporaries and good friends; they were even canonized at the same ceremony. It is difficult to define the extent of their mutual theological dependency, but in spite of their belonging to the same order and being friends, they often went their own individual ways, deploying great variation of spiritual thought. Large parts of the writings of John of the Cross are in the form of poetry, reflecting the style of the biblical Song of Songs. Poetry as a prime tool for expressing the inexpressible, especially God's union with the soul, functions in John of the Cross's spirituality as an expression of the goal of mysticism, combined with considerations of how the believer reaches this unity. John of the Cross's perhaps most important work, *The Ascent of Mount Carmel,* is exactly such a combination of poetry and concrete instructions on how the believer reaches the summit of Mount Carmel, synonymous with the soul's union with God.

Teresa's spirituality has the same fundamental goal but is more practical in its orientation. The sources of her writings spring from her own experience of the mystical way, as she writes of her daily life in the monastery. On the basis of these experiences, which often serve as examples, she gives believers instructions on how to walk. Her best known work, the *Vida*, is actually an autobiography.

JOHN OF THE CROSS. The works of John of the Cross follow by and large the Augustinian tradition. Moreover, John of the Cross is inspired by Pseudo-Dionysius and the trend in mystical theology that followed his preference for word-less, contemplative mysticism over the more kerygmatic mentioned above.[64] This trend is significant in Christianity, so that Karl Rahner rightly speaks of a general preference for the word-less mystical tradition rather than for the more kerygmatic, prophetic spirituality that he actually considers more Christian than the former. The distinction actually mirrors a fundamental dichotomy between Greek, mainly Platonist ontology that dwells with God's absolute, immovable being and the passionate, personal God of Judaism, who first and foremost appears in the prophets. John D. Caputo has in his work on Jacques Derrida articulated this dichotomy well:

> That very finite Hellenistic creature called "God" is a being cut to fit the narrow needs of Greek ontology, of Parmenides and Plato, who were scandalized by time and motion and change, and of Aristotle, who did the best he could to make the name of matter and motion respectable among the Greeks. But from a biblical point of view, this highly Hellenic *theos* was an imperfect—may I say a pathetic, or better an *a*pathetic?—way to think of God. It had nothing to do with Yahweh who was easily moved to anger and jealousy, who was a God of tears and compassion, who suffered with his suffering people, who was moved by their sighs and lamentations, who was angered by their meanness of mind and had a well-known and much respected temper.[65]

Although there are important differences, as pointed out by Andrew Louth, between John of the Cross and Dionysius,[66] the preference for the wordless and nonprophetic spirituality is nevertheless visible in many areas of the writings of John of the Cross, for example in *The Dark Night of the Soul*.[67] One finds next to no accounts of actual visions in the writings of John of the Cross. This notwithstanding, he writes extensively on how to deal with visions. Just as in Augustine's system, the visionary genre covers more than just seeing something hidden. When speaking of the soul's comprehension, seeing and understanding are synonymous.[68] As Adnès writes, to John of the Cross, any cognition, in spite of its object, is a vision of the truth.[69] John does not use the Augustinian term *vision* but the term *apprehensio*, and it is this I will employ in presenting his system. In Latin *apprehensio* means to grasp something, and this is central to John's spirituality. In the end it is to reach, to grasp, and to be one with God. All other "apprehensions" are subordinate to this highest goal of spirituality.

John's tripartition reminds us in many ways of that of Augustine, but there are some notable differences. His first group contains the *natural apprehensions*. This group covers the cognition we gain through physical reality, be it directly through the senses or indirectly through the images formed in the mind, "à l'intérieur par l'imagination."[70]

The second group covers the *supernatural imaginary apprehensions*. These consist in images as well, derived directly from the senses (2.16.11) or through mental activity (2.16.3). Both are, however, the result of supernatural intervention, be it by God or the devil.

The two first groups of Augustine's system appear *in each of the two first groups of John's system.* In Augustine's system the first group consists in corporal visions, the second of imaginary visions. John's first group may contain both corporal and imaginary apprehensions, but here they are natural. His second group may likewise contain corporal and imaginary apprehensions, but here they are supernatural (see the table below).

John's third group is the *supernatural spiritual apprehensions*. This group shares major traits with Augustine's third group. Just as in the second, the apprehensions in the third group stem from supernatural intervention. They are called spiritual because they occur without any intervention of the senses, be it of the exterior or "interior" senses.[71] They are visions or revelations communicated directly to the mind without any form or image. Whereas the mind in the two lower groups is *active* in the apprehension process, it is *passively* receptive in the spiritual apprehensions, resting in their reception. While apprehensions of the two lower groups are submitted to the infiltration of human realities, the spiritual apprehensions are purely spiritual, without any material, human infiltration. *What is received is received in its purest form.*

The spiritual supernatural apprehensions can deal with created substances, with creatures, or with God himself, and thus John's third level contains *a partition in the partition.* The spiritual supernatural apprehensions are split in those that concern Creation and those that concern God directly.

The difference between Augustine and most writers on visions that he inspired, including Teresa of Avila on one side and John of the Cross on the other, is that Augustine does *not* separate natural from supernatural apprehensions as John does; in fact the distinction between natural and supernatural is not present in Augustine's thought in the way we know it today. In the two first groups, Augustine separates *corporal* from *imaginary* visions, whereas

John separates *natural* from *supernatural* apprehensions. The reason for this difference lies in varying interests. Augustine contemplates the apprehensions from the question of how man obtains knowledge in a broad theory of cognition, whereas John is mainly interested in the cognition of and ultimately union with God. John's cognitional goal is one of cognition in general, not exclusively spiritual, and this is why John makes a division between natural and supernatural.

For Augustine there is no such sharp dichotomy. There are different grades in the hierarchy, but no opposition between the different groups as with John. Augustine seeks simply to explain the moment of cognition without grading the apprehensions, while John appraises some and dismisses others. The reason for this difference is again their varying goals. With John there is opposition between the corporal and the spiritual. This is why the corporal visions are assessed very negatively. Not only do they range lower in hierarchy than in Augustine's system, but they present a danger to spiritual development, inasmuch as the soul who has a corporal vision, be it from God or the devil, risks remaining content with this vision, never reaching the ultimate apprehensions—the intellectual vision or union with God. A. Bord recapitulates John's thought well: "The other [apprehensions]—supernatural imaginary or supernatural spiritual but concerning creatures—are unable to allow the union of the heart with the divine substance; rather, they are an obstacle; one should therefore be detached from them."[72] There is little affinity between spiritual and corporal substances in John's system (2.11.3).

This tendency toward an opposition in John's system between corporal and spiritual may well constitute the main reason for the negative evaluation of visions and revelations, hence prophecy, in mystical theology. No other theologian has had such influence on mystical theology regarding the evaluation of revelations as John has; no other has had such authority. He has been quoted repeatedly in writings limiting the scope of revelations. From mystical theology, this evaluation has spread to theology as a whole, contributing to its generally negative assessment of prophecy. Thus it is necessary to resurface his evaluation so as to understand it, investigate it, and determine whether or not it is acceptable. Is the devaluation of the lower groups of apprehensions always valid? Is it true that all other apprehensions than the highest logically impede the *unio mystica*? With regard to our subject in particular, one fundamental question arises: can revelations that truly arise from God be cast aside as unimportant or even dangerous?

John sharply denunciates apparitions several times in his work. Taken out of context, some of his statements could even appear heretical, echoing the reproach of the Old Testament prophets: why do you not listen, when the Lord is speaking? The following quotations are an example of how sharply he rejects any kind of revelation, be it of God or the devil:

> Regardless of the cause of these apprehensions [if from God or the devil] it is always good for people to reject them with closed eyes.[73]

> But when there is a question of imaginative visions or other supernatural communications apprehensible by the senses and independent of one's free will, I affirm that at whatever time or season they occur (in the state of perfection or one less perfect) individuals must have no desire to admit them even though they come from God.[74]

According to John even the visions of saints should be ignored:

> In conclusion, individuals must not fix the eyes of their souls on that rind of the figure and object supernaturally accorded to the exterior senses, such as locutions and words to the sense of hearing; visions of saints and beautifully resplendent lights to the sense of sight, fragrance to the senses of smell; delicious and sweet tastes to the palate; and other delights, usually derived from the spirit, to the sense of touch, as is more commonly the case with spiritual persons. Neither must they place their eyes on interior imaginative visions. They must instead renounce all these things.[75]

Such pronouncements would, if separated from their context, appear disrespectful to the gifts of God, who never reveals himself without a purpose. If Paul when he had his vision of Christ on the way to Damascus had denied the vision, it would have been to deny Christ himself. Auguste Saudreau has thus reflected on the seriousness of denying what appears to be a true message of God to his church. Saudreau refers to, among others, Juan de Lugo, who argues that the believer who is convinced of the authenticity of a revelation has a duty to believe and obey its contents, since "the reasons to believe can be so great that all prudent doubt is made impossible; the one who then would refuse to believe and to obey would lack respect and submission to God and would fall into grave sin."[76]

John of the Cross writes as he does because of his particular context and his vocation as spiritual director. Because his context is such a particular one, his writings cannot be applied broadly to theology, especially to an ecclesiologically valid outlook on prophecy, but this is exactly what happened when it came to theology's approach to prophecy.

John of the Cross devalues prophetic visions and revelations as heavily as he does for the following reasons.

(1) Initially it must be emphasized that John of the Cross does not negate the meaning of visions in all his writings. They can have a positive and corroborating scope when they manage to lift the soul to higher forms of apprehensions.[77]

(2) For John, visions are never goals in themselves but can be of benefit in certain situations, when they are thoroughly tested by the spiritual director.[78]

(3) While Augustine, and most theologians following him, considered visions in relation to cognition, John considers visions only from the perspective of how they relate to unity with God. There is a clear shift from cognition to personal experience, from insight to union of beings. In this context the intellectual vision is the only acceptable goal, not only because it gives the highest divine insight, but because it gives the purest and highest *apprehension* of God, that is, unity with God.

(4) John admonishes the pilgrim not to become caught up in a search for God that ranges on a level lower than God himself. The only appropriate way of understanding John is in view of his considering all lower levels of apprehensions dangerous if they make the pilgrim stop on his way to the top of the Mount Carmel, halting at the lower levels. An image often used by Carmelite writers to illustrate this point is that of the pilgrim on his way toward union with God: along the way there are many beautiful flowers, true divine graces encouraging the pilgrim toward this higher goal.[79]

These flowers could be visions or revelations that help to make the way sweeter and clearer, but if the pilgrim stops along the roadside, contemplating these flowers for their own beauty and losing the vigor of continuing toward the real goal, then these flowers are no longer graces but obstacles. God's graces are turned into temptations.

(5) Revelations can be of great danger to persons who seek the supernatural for reasons of curiosity or sensationalism. For such persons, visions and other graces become dangers, since they can lead them to contemplate the gifts instead of God, the giver of the gifts.[80] At another point John becomes even more explicit: "And so the devil rejoices greatly when a soul desires to receive revelations, and when he sees it inclined to them, for he has then a great occasion and opportunity to insinuate errors and, in so far as he is able, to derogate from faith."[81] Also Rahner, who otherwise is critical toward the Carmelite "imageless" mysticism, warns against allowing God's graces be one's focus instead of the God to whom they are intended to lead; although he writes in favor of prophetic revelations, he warns against allowing them to become goals in themselves.[82]

In order rightly to understand John, it may be useful to quote Auguste Saudreau, who recapitulates the motives for John's devaluation of revelations as follows.

> Saint John of the Cross strongly protested against the excess of credulity and importance that some people at times lend to visions and revelations, even if they might be true, because he observed in this matter, as he declared, a lack of discretion that was harmful to many hearts. It seems there had been, at that time, great abuses in the Order of Carmel, and the Saint had to remind of the foundations and point out the dangers of illusions.[83]

(6)(a) John gives two further reasons why the pilgrim should reject the corporal and imaginary visions, even the ones that originate in God. First, John reflects on God's spiritual motion in the soul. This motion is manifest in different ways, either in images or in pure spiritual enlightenment or insight. If the soul rejects the images, only the spiritual light remains, and this is the goal of the spiritual pilgrimage.

(6)(b) Second, the soul, seeking God, should reject revelatory experiences in order to avoid exhaustion by having to discern if the visions are authentic or not (*Ascent* 2.17.7).

(7) In one particular context, John says that everything is already revealed with Christ, and that there is henceforth no more reason for revelations: "In giving us his Son, his only Word (for he possesses no other), he spoke everything to us at once in this sole Word—and he has no more to say" (2.22.3). This pronouncement appears to have been written in a particular and polemic setting, for in another passage he does indeed speak of visions of Christ, but only says that they are difficult to comprehend. Even though this does not imply a general appreciation of visions, it does contradict the statement that Christ would have nothing to say whatsoever.

(8) John maintains that visions, including the authentic ones, are very difficult to understand and easy to misinterpret. He gives many biblical examples of why believers have misunderstood and misinterpreted God's true prophetic messages, and in this regard he says: "Although . . . God's visions and locutions are true and certain in themselves, they are not always so for us. The first reason is that our manner of understanding them is defective, and the second is that their basic causes are sometimes variable."[84] "In this and many other ways souls are misled by understanding God's locutions and revelations according to the letter, according to the outer rind. As has been explained, God's chief objective in conferring these revelations is to express and impart the spirit that is enclosed within the outer rind. This spirit is

difficult to understand and richer and more plentiful, very extraordinary and far beyond the boundaries of the letter."[85] It is likely that John in his role as spiritual director came across believers who mis- or overinterpreted prophecies, thereby losing their way, and that his general resistance to revelations and prophecies stems from the desire to overcome these human errors.

(9) A very important reason for the general devaluation of revelations rests in John's understanding of the very nature and origin of revelations. In John's thought, visions are not the direct manifestation of a clear plan of God's providence and continued salvation. This may be the one most important reason that he evaluates revelations so negatively. His assessment of the source of revelations and visions is entirely different from the biblical presentation of prophecy as God's operative salvation. Paul portrays prophecy as God's salvific activity through the Spirit, building the community. Prophetic messages are important acts of God, resting in a firm decision of God, whose saving and creative love in the end is the origin and dynamism of prophecy.

For John things are different. Revelations are the "epiphenomena" of mystical life. Rahner summarizes this assessment of prophetic experience well: People who approach visions from this a priori negative perspective consider them to belong to the category of "pseudo-mysticism."[86] Visions are mishaps of spiritual activity, undesired and undesirable side effects of the contact of weak humans with Almighty God:

> Just as ecstasy, the suspension of the activity of the senses, is only a concomitant phenomenon, a result of the central mystical process, which indeed disappears at the highest degree of perfect mystical development, and is even considered a certain weakness in the nature of the mystic, who cannot contain the abundance of God's mystical self communication, so the imaginative vision, which presupposes such infused contemplation, is only the radiation and reflex of contemplation in the sphere of the senses, the Incarnation of the mystical process of the spirit.[87]

Likewise, according to Pierre Adnès, John considers visions to be a "failure of the body which cannot support the soul's contact with God."[88] Obviously, there is a significant difference between this view of true prophetic gifts and the biblical-classical assessment of prophecy, where true prophetic experience is the result of direct intentions and actions of God aimed at the guidance of his church.

(10) As mentioned, John views visions from the perspective of their importance to the individual who seeks loving union with God, without giving much attention to the importance of revelations for the congregation. This is

in line with his general spirituality, which many authors consider too individualistic and not oriented to the wider context of the church. Lucien-Marie de Saint-Joseph has in his article on John of the Cross in *Dictionnaire de la Spiritualité* summarized this critique well:

> John of the Cross does not transcend the problems of individuals. He is reproached for not having focused on the mystery of the church and on God's intention with the world. This is correct. To this one can answer that one should not transfer our current concerns to him, which probably will not be the same tomorrow. Furthermore, the authors of his time do not seem either to have had the communitarian or ecclesial sense that so rightly is dear to us today.[89]

Since John's outlook is precisely the individual's journey with God, one may then understand why he wrote the following: "A person should renounce them and endeavor to avoid them. The only reason to admit and value them would be the profit and good effect the genuine ones bring to the soul. But admitting them is unnecessary to obtain this good effect; for the sake of progress, rather, one should always deny them."[90]

This quotation may serve as an example of the nonecclesiological outlook, placing the discussion in an entirely different context from the normal *Sitz im Leben* of prophecy.

(11) Like the Reformers and other personalities of his times, John has a general negative attitude toward the usage of images in spiritual life. Images (including everything that aims at expressing the spiritual in human ways) belong to the initial stages of spiritual life. "Great, therefore, is the error of many spiritual persons who have practiced approaching God by means of images and forms and meditations, as befits beginners."[91] Herein lies another reason for the devaluation of prophecy, since the building function of prophecy, according to Paul, lies precisely in its intelligibility.[92] Without intelligibility, no building; without "images" there can be no spiritual edification of importance to the congregation. A spirituality that is to be true spirituality for the entire congregation *must* be prophetic, *must* be intelligible, or it will not be constructive for the congregation at all. And this brings us back to what was said earlier, namely, that John's focus is the individual's union with God rather than the community. This is why there is little room for prophecy in John's thought.

(12) Finally we must remember that John of the Cross was under strong persecution and was put in prison by his confreres. One of the main accusations brought against him was that his thoughts led to *illuminism* and that he caused people to lose touch with reality. He had to defend himself and his

writings against such accusations, and this polemical position explains, as Laurentin and others argue, many of his very sharp expressions.[93]

These points may shed light on the motives for John's devaluation of revelations. They are not meant to criticize his thoughts but merely to serve as observation. John's focus cannot lead to a fruitful appreciation of the edifying scope of prophecy. In his approach, prophetic revelations may well come from God, but they have little purpose and may be disturbing factors in what was his primary objective. The goal of his entire spirituality, in recognition of which the Catholic Church appointed him *doctor*, is the individual's mystical union with God. In this context prophetic revelations fall short.

TERESA OF AVILA. Teresa of Avila is the second great authority of mystical theology. She has contributed to the fact that the term *vision* has obtained the significance it has in normal religious terminology, as her influence is great in the area of mystical theology that deals with visions.[94] Teresa's background is different from those of both Augustine and John of the Cross. Augustine's theory of vision could be characterized as a primarily philosophical, cognitive system; that of John of the Cross as one of individual spirituality with certain philosophical underpinnings. Teresa's, on the other hand, can be described as practical philosophy with next to no philosophical reflections. Visions have a great place in her spirituality and appear often in her writings.[95]

Teresa uses the term *vision* according to its popular usage of seeing something that cannot be seen under normal conditions. When Teresa speaks of visions, they are always supernatural. Augustine made no distinction between natural and supernatural. To him, all apprehensions were recognitions of the ideas that precede material realities. When the apprehensions are intellectual, they permit immediate contemplation of the ideas themselves. When the apprehensions are imaginary, the ideas are beheld indirectly through the images, already contained in the mind. When the apprehensions are of material realities, even this form of apprehension leads the soul closer to the eternal ideas, since the material is nothing but a reflection of the ideas. In this way, one can rightly say, all types of apprehensions for Augustine ultimately are above the realm of matter, in the sense that every apprehension of reality leads to cognition of the ideas. For Teresa, on the other hand, visions are simply supernatural, when they give insight into what is not normally discernible. Natural objects are generally and immediately accessible, whereas the objects of visions are accessible only to the mystic to whom God gives the grace of supernatural sight. With Teresa we have a much more practical, concrete approach to reality and the process of discernment and experience.

Teresa continues the known tripartition of the vision genre. First in her system we find the visions that are seen with the eye of the body ("que se ven con los ojos corporales"), which Teresa claims never to have seen.[96] Next are the visions that are seen with the eyes of the soul ("con los ojos del alma"), which she, according to the classical Catholic school, calls imaginary visions ("visión imaginaria"). Finally there are the visions that are *not seen* ("que no se ven") because they are inherently meaningful and need no visual expression. In her earlier writings, (and among others in her autobiography) she never calls these *intellectual* visions. She employs this terminology only in the *Moradas*, but even here she confesses not to understand why they are called *intellectual*.[97] Teresa seems through her confessors or by other means to have become acquainted with the Augustinian tradition and terminology, but does not seem to share all its aspects. This is confirmed by the fact that she uses the same terminology as Augustine and John of the Cross but in a different way.

Just as her employment of the term itself is different, even her hierarchical assessment of the visions is different from that of the others. In her system there is no hierarchical classification of the visions. According to Adnès, "her own visions defy any rigid classification. With [Teresa], the phenomena are combined and amalgamated."[98] Even if she uses the known terminology, the visions she describes in her works are difficult to place in an hierarchical and ordered system.

As mentioned, she claims never to have had any corporal visions, so I can leave them out of this presentation; they have no place in her spirituality, and we must focus on the imaginary and intellectual visions. To Teresa, visions are primarily of an intellectual kind, giving immediate insight into the mysteries of God. Sometimes it happens that God lets an imaginary vision accompany the intellectual one in order to vest it in human forms to make it more tangible and accessible to normal man: "Then sometimes an imaginative vision is added to accompany, surround and humanize them."[99] The intellectual visions form the basic insight. The imaginary visions are graces that help in a fuller way to understand what in actual fact it is that God wants to communicate to the soul.

The classical prophetic revelation, where human imagery plays an important role in the process of divine communication, in Teresa's system appears as a combination of imaginary and intellectual vision. With Teresa there is no depreciation of the imaginary vision compared to the intellectual, as with John. The imaginary vision with its human imagery is a grace that helps man more easily to comprehend the divine.

Like John, Teresa is careful that visions never become goals in themselves. The wise pilgrim on the way of prayer will initially reject any kind of vision. In this way, if it is from the devil, it will do no harm. If it is from God, the resistance will result in improved spirituality—the more the true graces are resisted, the stronger they get. The initial resistance to the visions breeds spiritual progress, since it is an expression of humility and absence of self-interests. The resistance to any desire of *wanting* visions forms the right foundation to receive true divine visions, since they will occur without the interference of human ambition.

If there are few accounts in his writings of visions that John experienced himself, every second page in Teresa's books speaks of such experiences. In the entire life of Teresa, visions played a great role, especially when she was about to make important decisions. Christ often revealed himself to her in order to give her direct practical instructions. Here we find ourselves on the home ground of prophecy. Revelations were given Teresa in order to guide her and those close to her particular historical situations. As Volken writes, it is impossible to conceive of Teresa's great work without the divine instructions through which she claims to have been guided during her entire ministry: "And anyone who wished to deny, for example, the divine origin of all the revelations made to St. Teresa of Avila, especially during the period when she was founding her convents, could not explain her life."[100] Whereas the revelations in John's writings appear as mishaps and undesired side effects of the spiritual life, they stem directly from divine providence in the Theresian books. Revelations are given to facilitate the apprehension of divine truth and to guide the faithful throughout history. Even if Teresa along with John forms the inspirational fabric of most mystical thought that followed, Teresa comes closest to giving word to mainstream prophetic theology.

COMPARISON BETWEEN JOHN OF THE CROSS AND TERESA OF AVILA. For the sake of clarity, John's and Teresa's spirituality may be illustrated for comparison in the following table.

John of the Cross	Teresa of Avila
Tripartition of visions; more complex than Augustine's and Teresa's systematization.	Tripartition of visions.
The term *vision* is understood as *apprehensio*—not just understanding, but grasping, achieving.	Vision is understood as experience and comprehension.
Vision (apprehensio) is understood as an ontological reality in the *unio mystica*.	Vision is understood as intelligible communication.

(continued)

John of the Cross	Teresa of Avila
The vision's ultimate goal is to grasp God in the beatific vision—an ontological union in the ultimate apprehension.	The vision's goal is to lead the individual on the way of faith to a closer relationship with God. The vision is not identical with the ontological, mystical union with God but may be one of the many means that lead to that goal.
Most supernatural visions—even those that come from God—are temptations that should be avoided.	Supernatural visions are means of divine providence and pedagogy. Through their human expression they help man to understand the divine.
Visions are *epiphenomena* of the soul's contact with God.	Visions and revelations stem from God's intentions of guidance and salvation.

4.1.7. Conclusion

Even though revelations play a great role in Teresa's spirituality, they are–just as in John's thought–rarely put into the larger ecclesiological context. This is why the full scope of prophetic revelations that aim at the encouragement of the entire congregation cannot be fully appreciated in Teresa's authorship. Something is lacking before we can speak of true prophetic mysticism. Teresa's revelations remain what Rahner calls *mystical revelations*. As already mentioned, Teresa's mysticism has clear prophetic traits: It is very clear and intelligible and aimed the church's practical guidance. What is lacking is for these intelligible and practically oriented revelations to be communicated to larger parts of the church or even the entire church, like the revelations of Birgitta of Vadstena. Many writers have argued that Teresa's ministry is impacted by the individualistic movement of the sixteenth century that colored all later Christian mysticism. Most probably this is why prophecy is never assessed fully by and in mystical theology, as prophecy is simply not in its right context there. André Derville is one who highlights this trend of mystical theology. The mystical writers do not look at visions from a systematic angle but are interested "primarily in spiritual direction and discernment, much less in speculative mystical theology."[101] Hence mystical theology is able to treat certain elements of the spiritual life that touch upon the prophetic charism, but it is not apt at treating Christian prophecy as such.

Classical prophetic revelations can never in themselves compensate for the divine union. They cannot even confer divine grace; they only call the contemplative to be open to the grace of God. Since mystical theology primarily aims at the ineffable and imageless union with God, it is almost a natural consequence that revelations receive no particular attention or are rejected, as with John. It is a shame that revelations are seen as spiritual occurrences without taking their prophetic purpose into consideration, since Christian revelations mainly function as a service to the community and are prophetic.

John of the Cross and Teresa of Avila, the two most important authorities on mysticism, as already mentioned, differ in their evaluation of revelations. Furthermore, their prevailing negative attitude toward prophecy is anything but all-pervasive, as becomes clear through deeper investigations.[102] At the same time, however, one should never expect a full and adequate evaluation of prophetic revelations from the realm of mystical theology. With Rahner, interest is almost only in questions regarding "the psychology of such phenomena and hence the authenticity of the revelations and the truth of their content."[103] An investigation of Christian prophetic revelations can in no way be limited to this horizon, since they point beyond the individual's spiritual life to the common good of the congregation, and here we are in need of a symbiosis between mystical theology and ecclesiology, which is not very common.

4.2. Revelation as Concept of Reflection

Throughout the history of theology, revelation has predominantly been a concept of experience. When Scholastic theologians, for instance, spoke about revelation they mainly meant the reception of prophetic revelations. It was not until around the middle of the nineteenth century that theologians began approaching the idea of revelation as a concept of reflection. From this approach, revelation is understood as the ensemble of truth toward which the Christian faith is directed, otherwise known as the Deposit of Faith. This concept was known from the early church. As the Second Vatican Council's constitution on revelation, *Dei Verbum,* reassumes, it is constituted by sacred tradition and sacred Scripture. It is entrusted to the church in such a way that the Magisterium is not superior to it but is its servant, so that it only teaches what has been handed on to it, drawing "from this one deposit of faith everything which it presents for belief as divinely revealed."[104]

To avoid anticipating the discussion of the relationship between prophecy and revelation, I shall briefly consider the relationship between the *reflective concept of revelation* and the *experiential concept of the many prophetic revelations.* While the individually experienced prophetic revelations contribute to the explication of revelation's truth, it does not follow that the sum of all individual prophetic revelations produces the fullness of revelation. On the contrary, such individual revelations are but incomplete expressions of the fullness of the revelation of Jesus Christ, and prophetic revelations are one of many different means through which man has access to and enters the reality of faith. The aim of such prophetic revelations is not only to contribute to the *explication of the* knowledge of the truth promulgated by Christ and the apostles, but to lead Creation to the full participation in the vivid reality of this truth, realized only in the eschaton, when God will fulfill all in Christ (see chapter 5).

The Christian prophets secure the individual and *fragmentary* disclosures of the truth of God. Their motion stems from God's universally salvific will, the goal of which is the realization of revelation in the union of God and man. Even if the Christ-event is a full and objectively unsurpassable revelation of God, it does not change Creation's need to help realize this truth and put it into practice. Hence prophets serve to help realize the full openness and oneness between God and creation, and their evangelization may be seen only as an implementation of what was achieved in Christ, and an integral part of the same Christ-event that will become universal in the eschatological future. As will become clear later on, the realization of revelation therefore is not a mere anamnetic operation, looking back in time, but a movement, no less, toward a future reality; the implementation of the truth of Christ receives its power both from the Christ-event in the past and from the eschaton (see section 6.2.3). As we shall see, it is in building the church that prophecy serves the purpose of implementing the salvation of Christ until its final fulfillment in the eschaton.

In order to arrive at a diversified apprehension of the complex category of revelation I will in what follows examine various models of revelation. We shall then be able to better perceive the ways of understanding revelation as a concept of experience and a concept of reflection.

4.3. Models of Revelation

In order to distil and contemplate different aspects of the concept of revelation, it proves advantageous to specify them in different models. Such models shed light on different areas of the category of revelation without them necessarily contradicting each other. Thus, Max Seckler in *Handbuch der Fundamentaltheologie* presents three different models, each of which has dominated not only different historical periods that provide different aspects of revelation but also the historical development of the concept of revelations. Likewise, Avery Dulles in his somewhat later *Models of Revelation* presents five different models that coincide on various levels with Seckler's three models. On the basis of Seckler's and Dulles's work, I will examine the models of revelation that are of interest, investigating how they relate to the concept of prophecy, in all six models of revelation. The first model, the *epiphanic* model of revelation, has been designated the one most represented in the biblical writings, although they are very diverse. The second one, the *dogmatic* or *instructive* model *(instruktionstheoretische)*, which is rooted in Greek thought, has dominated Catholic theology from the Middle Ages to the Second Vatican Council. The third model sees revelation as the self-communication of God and is often called the *personalistic* model of revelation. In Catholic theology this model emerged around the Second Vatican Council, largely inspired by Protestant theology where it for long has been the dominant model. The fourth model, the *historical* model of revelation, shares many traits with the personalistic model and has been proposed in particular by Wolfhart Pannenberg. The fifth, the *dialectic* model, has found most resonance in Protestant thinking, and has been proposed in particular by Karl Barth, Rudolf Bultmann, and Emil Brunner. The sixth and last model I shall consider is the *ontological* model, which looks at revelation as inner experience. While this model is particularly important in Orthodox thinking, it is also present in the Catholic tradition, mainly in the area of mystical theology.

The different models designate tendencies: They have never been isolated from each other, and they interrelate naturally. The models have almost always existed simultaneously, accentuating different elements of the category of revelation. The individual models become problematic only when they are isolated and proposed as all-encompassing realities, for they then dismiss other important aspects of revelation.

This presentation of the different models of revelation will form the background for my later presentation of prophecy, insofar as each approach to revelation accentuates different aspects of prophecy. Just as the presentation of the different models of revelation does not aim to oppose differences in the understanding of revelation, the aim of the presentation of prophecy is not to present conflicting views on the subject, but to point to the different characteristics of the concept of prophecy. It would be simplistic to radically contrast different models, and would, in turn, obstruct the purpose of this work, which is to lead to a comprehensive understanding of prophecy based on a multifaceted portrait of revelation.

4.3.1. The Epiphanic Understanding of Revelation

The Bible is not a revealed book, but an *inspired* book. In the words of Max Seckler, it is "das Grundbuch der Offenbarung im christlichen Sinn,"[105] or in the words of Avery Dulles, the "Document of revelation."[106] It does not contain one systematized doctrine of revelation but is, as already mentioned, rich in perspectives. With Werner Bulst, revelation in the Bible combines both *die Tatoffenbarung* (God's actions in history), *die Schauoffenbarung* (theofanies), and *die Wortoffenbarung*.[107]

From the experiential perspective, it contains what Joseph Schumacher calls "the most different forms of revelation such as the appearing, the uncovering, the announcing and the speaking of God."[108] But, in spite of the manifold nature of revelatory experiences, Seckler can summarize revelation in the Bible as that which it is not: it is not merely the "communication of knowledge, but rather God's concern [Zuwendung] for man."[109] Seckler does not rule out the cognitive aspect of revelation, as revelation is also about the works and deeds of God, but this is revelation only in a derivative sense.

While the expression ἀποκάλυψις (generally translated "revelation") appears in the New Testament, it is not the Bible's common denominator for the category of revelation. This concept imbued the idea of revelation with a predominant sense of disclosure of something otherwise hidden and unapproachable. According to Seckler, this is not the approach of the Bible, in which revelation is not something unusual. God's revelation is not primarily something mystical, mythic, strange, and distanced. There is affinity between God and the world in which he acts, and the people of God maintain a general "attitude of expectation and a praxis of experience" of God's self-disclosure, an expectation that God does intervene and make himself manifest in human categories.[110]

This is the manner in which one may classify the many revelatory events in the Bible as God's activity, manifestation or epiphany. By this, revelation does not merely signify "God's showing himself, that is, an epiphanic event of mythical and mystical character, but rather the announcement of the relationship of dialogue between the saving God and the perished man that occurs in the word."[111] The concepts φανέρωσις and ἐπιφάνεια are key biblical concepts. Both are revelatory terms that nonetheless designate more than Christ's epiphany[112] and his return.[113] Designating biblical revelation as epiphanic does not necessarily signify epiphany and theophany. God acts in history, and it is this very activity of his that is epiphanic.

Still, there remains a distinctive yet close relationship between God's general epiphanic activity and theophanies, in which this action at times may emerge concretely. Especially in the Old Testament, such theophanies are closely related to God's activity, as is evident through the ancient prophets. Theophanies are also evident in the New Testament, in particular in the Acts of the Apostles, where they abound. In point of fact, the Christ-event changed prophetic revelations in such a way that the theophanies thereafter were replaced by *christophanies*. In line with Schumacher, Seckler summarizes the biblical concept of revelation as not only "uncovering or disclosing hidden

things, but rather a creative act of God that is new and brings true reconciliation and true salvation; and [this concept] is comprehensively applicable on
the entire historical being and action of God."[114]

God calls to belief in *the one who is*, rather than the one whose existence is
obscure and hidden, and in his prophetic manifestations the main emphasis
is on who he is and what he does, rather than what he says. God's revelation
understood as God's activity with man emerges in the "revelation" of God's
life,[115] God's love,[116] God's grace,[117] and in particular in the revelation of God's
son.[118] "In his holy being, the living God brings himself as creative, guiding,
judging, and redeeming power *at each moment in time as concrete present reality
to be 'revealed' and 'experienced.'* "[119] This is why divine revelation and salvation, in a certain sense, are identical in the biblical world. God acts in revelation, and his activity is always his will of salvation at work, so that God's
action and salvation coincide.

As we shall see in my presentation of the concept of prophecy, this is the
foremost goal of prophecy, namely being a divine tool in the fulfillment and
realization of God's salvation in history. The task of the prophet is to guide on
behalf of God, and this is why the prophet plays a primary role in the epiphanic model of revelation. Many of the biblical multifaceted approaches to
revelation resurface in the more distinct models presented by Avery Dulles.

4.3.2. Doctrinal Understanding of Revelation

Even if the biblical epiphanic understanding of revelation continued to play a
role throughout the history of Christian theology, Hellenistic and Gnostic
thought soon managed to introduce the roots of a more intellectual or doctrinal understanding of revelation.

According to Greek philosophy, man obtains true knowledge through the
contemplation of the eternal ideas, an idea that is elucidated by Plato's cave-
image. In Plato's cave, man sits with his back to reality, contemplating, on the
back wall of the cave, the images—the shadows–of the true reality outside the
cave. As shown in Augustine's idea of vision (section 4.1.4), a synthesis is
produced between the biblical concept of revelation and the Hellenistic theory
of cognition. In short, Augustine's theory represents a Christian reinterpretation of the Hellenistic cognition theory; in other words, there is a great prox-
imity between Christian vision, revelation, and cognition and the Greek *vision*
of ideas, whence emerges the foundation for the doctrinal understanding of
revelation.

Through revelation, man participates in and attains knowledge of the
truth. This view interprets revelation as the goal of thought, which changes the

understanding not only of revelation but of salvation in a very profound manner. Salvation is to reason the ultimate good, and revelation may likewise be considered the *gaudium de veritate*, the joy of the truth. Man participates in God's salvation because, through cognition, he partakes in the divine truth, whereby his knowledge or revelation of truth not only becomes the vehicle of salvation, but its goal and salvation itself. Whereas salvation emerges in the epiphanic model as that which God did for and through man, salvation in the doctrinal approach emerges as the fulfillment of the intellect and the joy of the truth. Yet such an understanding dangerously limits itself to cognition, and fails to place salvation within the proper relationship between God and his people.

The doctrinal understanding of revelation became predominant in the Middle Ages when many theologians saw faith as a supernatural gift that requires revelation: revelation is not only that which is conferred through Scripture but a unified, divine activity. Thus the medieval thinkers did not exclusively designate revelation as Scripture; they understood the history of revelation as one continuous, cognitive pedagogy. When posited in this casuistry, revelation becomes the "foundation as well as the object of revelation."[120] Revelation is both the dynamism in which faith has its root and the content of faith itself.

The ontological philosophy of cognition, predominant in Scholastic thinking, shines through in the understanding of revelation such that it retains an ontological aspect, namely, allowing revelation to remain in part the revelation of God's *being*, and not only his *doctrine*. In the medieval approach, God gives both outer, instructive revelation and inner revelation through the enlightenment of grace. This twofold form introduces man to the entire truth.

The death of Thomas Aquinas is emblematic in this regard for the complex Scholastic understanding of revelation. When he was dying his complaint was not that he had not finished the *Summa*, but how futile everything is compared to the knowledge of God himself. In point of fact, it was the conquest of this knowledge that he, in his last moments, conferred to his disciples. Thus, the medieval understanding of revelation is much more complex than the mere understanding of God's doctrine. In Seckler's words, it remains a "language and truth event with many dimensions,"[121] secured by its strong ontological elements.

Nominalism lost this ontology and hence surfaced and underwent all the dangers that had threatened Scholastic thinking. In Nominalism, the ontological and dynamic elements of revelation are reduced, whereby their place in the salvific activity of God's revelation becomes inconsequential. To the Scholastics, revelation could elucidate great mysteries while allowing them to remain mysteries. Conversely, Nominalism, to a certain extent, reduced mysteries to being the secrets of reason that revelation serves to uncover, while limiting faith to the acceptance of revealed true sentences. This is where the latent downsides of the doctrinal model of revelation become evident: God reveals a supernatural doctrine, and faith consists in the adherence to its content.

One of the major disadvantages of this model in its extreme form is the conscious distinction between revelation and salvation history. God instructs man *about* salvation, hence the distinction. According to this casuistry, revelation informs man about salvation, but revelation is not salvation, for revelation is not God's *action,* it is his divine *information.*

However, Emil Brunner, P. Althaus, and others criticize this aspect of the doctrinal model, in which revelation becomes "ein Es," a thing, a mere doctrine. For Brunner, the danger with such an understanding, which he primarily finds present in Catholic thinking, is that revelation may become an object, which the church can employ to rule over the masses. Brunner's criticism is interesting, as it points to an important danger relevant to prophecy: when revelation becomes a doctrine that can be monopolized and ruled on, the prophetic is driven out. There is no place for renewal, and prophecy and revelation are in conflict, for prophecy seeks the living application of the truth and not the rigid conservation of its expression.

Even if Brunner's criticism is a most adequate warning to keep one from reducing revelation to mere intellectual cognition, the question must be raised whether the "Catholic" understanding of revelation that he criticizes is truly compatible with the Catholic position. In short, Catholic revelation theology is more complex than the simplified image Brunner provides. Yet in order to evaluate it in a more detailed manner, we must turn to the two Vatican councils that, in different ways, dealt with this issue.

4.3.3. Vatican I

Vatican I was the first Council that addressed the concept of revelation. It did so, however, polemically, in opposing the criticism of revelation. Even if it is true that this Council tended to focus on the doctrinal aspects of revelation, it must also be noted that it did not deal in a systematic and exhaustive way with revelation as a whole, since such a treatment first came at Vatican II.[122] However, Vatican I treated the themes that rationalism questioned, and the focus of this treatise was predicated largely on the premises of rationalism as a reaction to its claims. Rationalism criticized the idea that revelation was necessary for the full cognition of the truth, claiming the autonomy of reason.

In opposition to rationalism's claim for the self-sufficiency of reason, the Council emphasized that God provides the knowledge reason cannot obtain by itself. Revelation is what God has revealed ("divinitus revelata" [DS 3011]). God's activity, letting man share in the divine blessings ("ad participanda scilicet bona divina" [DS 3005]) as well as in the inner help of the Holy Spirit [DS 3009], or God's helping grace ("Dei aspirante et adiuvante gratia" [DS 3008]), is not explicitly related to his revelation or revealing activity. Revelation is, on the other hand, a means of obtaining knowledge (DS 3027) and a source of knowledge (DS 3005, 3015). Here, *revelation and information are synonymous.* Revelation confers the doctrine of faith ("fidei doctrina" [DS 3020]), revealed doctrine ("doctrinae revelatae" [DS 3042]), or revealed truth [DS 3032], as well as "divine truths" [DS 3015, 3041]. It would appear there is here a "distinction" between God's activity and revelation.

As the Council has been used as an example of a doctrinal understanding of revelation, as in Josef Schmitz's contribution in *Handbuch der Fundamentaltheologie,*[123] it must be remembered that the Council's aim is not to provide a comprehensive and synthetic presentation of the Catholic understanding of revelation but to respond to the challenges of rationalism on certain aspects of revelation. It cannot be evaluated correctly without this in mind.

This becomes even clearer when taking a closer look at the documents themselves. In spite of all the formulations that call to mind the doctrinal understanding of revelation, there are clear traits of a personalistic understanding of revelation: in God's wisdom and love he has deigned to reveal himself and the eternal decrees of his will.[124] Man's answer to revelation is not limited to reason's acceptance of the revealed truths but implies the will's submission to the God who reveals himself ("plenum revelanti Deo intellectus et voluntatis obsequium fide praestare tenemur" [DS 3008]). Thereby, revelation is not limited to intelligible cognition but comes across as a personal encounter between God and man.

In the reply to the challenges of growing, Vatican I remained within the framework of the relationship between reason and revelation. Thereby the discussion remained largely within the framework of a doctrinal understanding of revelation, and this was criticized. But this forced, particular attention to one aspect of revelation did not rule out from Catholic theology revelation's other aspects. And here is where some critics missed the mark. Regarding Brunner's criticism, it must be said that Catholic theology never proposed an exclusively doctrinal understanding of revelation, and this is important in order to assess rightly prophecy's place within the Catholic context. If Catholic theology proposed a purely doctrinal *understanding* of revelation where revelation and salvation were separated, there would not be much place for prophecy stemming from God's salvific *activity* in history, hence, its foremost place in the historic model, which contains many *doctrinal* aspects. The fact that Catholic thinking maintains both aspects of revelation means that prophecy has a peculiar position here.

The doctrinal elements provide a general, negative attitude toward prophecy that is rejected precisely with the argument that prophets have no more to say after the full revelation in Christ and for this reason they are unnecessary. However, the idea of a development of dogma, and the permanence of the historical understanding of revelation, secures an integral place for prophecy within the context of revelation. With regard to Vatican I's teaching of the handing down of revelation in tradition, the Council confirms the full constitution of revelation with the last apostle, and it is only after this stage that revelation is handed on. In this context, tradition itself is named revelation, which is interesting, as this in theory leaves room for the role of the prophet in the distillation of revelation. We shall return to this theme later.

Prophets have always been known by their action, passionately calling the faithful to conversion and repentance. It is obvious that there are many doctrinal "instructions" in any prophetic call, since the prophet can only call the people of God away from a wrong way by portraying the right one. However, a radical doctrinal approach to revelation leaves little space for prophecy, and one of the reasons for the gradual diminishment of prophecy's role in the church may be the gradual shift from an epiphanic approach to revelation to a more propositional and doctrinal approach. Seckler believes this process to have started already in the first centuries after Christ, during which period the prophetic vocation and form of the church shifted in the direction of a more institutional expression of Christianity.

4.3.4. Personalistic Understanding of Revelation

The personalistic model presents revelation as God's activity in history, as in the historical model, but with less attention to the mere disclosure of doctrine. *God reveals himself.* He does so not just because he has something to say, but because his love moves him to seek communication and union with man. The personalistic model can be designated one of communication and participation.[125] According to this model, God's revealing activity results from his salvific will. Hence there are many similarities between the epiphanic and personalistic models, inasmuch as both focus on God's action. The difference between the two is slight; according to the epiphanic model, revelation is what God *does*, whereas according to the personalistic model, it is how God *shows himself to be.*

In the epiphanic model, revelation was salvation in the sense that God manifests himself as the one who saves through salvific activity; God reveals himself as Savior. The same might be said of the personalistic model, with this one difference: salvation is not simply what God *does* but what God *is*: God is himself salvation. In the epiphanic model, faith is directed toward God who does great deeds, not the least being the Incarnation. In the personalistic model, faith is to a higher extent directed toward God himself, with confidence not only in his deeds but in his own person. In this case, salvation is realized in a relationship of trust in and dependence on the God who shows himself in Christ and gives himself to the world as salvation. In the personalistic model, revelation and salvation are identical, as God reveals himself as the God who himself is salvation, expressed ultimately in Christ's death on the Cross, securing union between the history of salvation and revelation. We saw that revelation according to a pure doctrinal approach is salvation to the extent in which man participates in the knowledge of revealed truth: salvation coincides with knowledge of the truth. Here in the personalistic model, salvation is formed by God's personal deed and giving of self. Salvation rests on Christ's activity but is realized anew in the faith relationship between God and every believer.

The personalistic aspect of the category of revelation has thrived in Protestant theology. In the Catholic context it is best expressed in the Second Vatican Constitution *Dei Verbum*. Several preparatory documents preceded *Dei Verbum;* they were rejected because critics considered them a redundancy of Vatican I's understanding of revelation with insufficient complementarity. The Council fathers wanted to provide a *corrigendum* to Catholic mainstream theology and its too high focus on the propositional approach to revelation. A more nuanced and combined understanding had been reached, very much under the influence of evangelical theology, that points to a personalistic approach to Catholic revelation theology. As Seckler writes, a consensus in understanding had been reached already at the World Conferences for Faith and Church in Edinburgh and Montreal.[126]

Unlike Vatican I, Vatican II's *Dei Verbum* is not a polemic declaration, but rather one of an ecumenical understanding to revelation. It is interesting to see the coherence between the World Conferences and Vatican II. The Council combines and secures the different aspects of revelation, which, according to Dulles,[127] secure the understanding that revelation no longer provides an obstruction to unity. One of the few Protestants who criticized *Dei Verbum* is Karl Barth, who considered the confirmations of the relationship between revelation and its expression as "ein Schwächenanfall" of the Council.[128] The two Vatican councils do not contrast with each other, as they are simply written on the basis of different motives. Vatican I presented the doctrine of revelation in contrast with rationalism and presented only those aspects of revelation that had become "endangered species." Contrary to Vatican I, which did not intend to present a comprehensive Catholic view of the category of revelation, Vatican II's *Dei Verbum* constitutes the most complete Catholic treatment of revelation theology.

4.3.5. *History as Revelation*

The presentations of the three aforementioned models provide a view of the development of the concept of revelation. As we have seen, both the epiphanic and the personalistic models featured an understanding of revelation whereby God acts in a personal way during history. The main emphasis in the epiphanic model is on God's *action*, whereas in the personalistic model it is on the *communication* of his very self. Since much has been said earlier concerning the historical aspects of revelation, I will now analyze some of these aspects of an understanding of revelation that are of particular importance to my subject of prophecy. G. Ernest Wright authored many books on Old Testament theology and was the leading figure behind the "biblical theology movement" that sought to reconcile historical critical exegesis with a more traditional hermeneutic of the Bible as *Word of God*, thereby seeking to avoid its often evident inherent relativism; Wright summarizes his view of the historical understanding of revelation by saying: "We know God is like this, because it is what we infer from what he has done."[129] According to this understanding, the Bible testifies to revelation not mainly because it says what God has said but because it shows what God has done.

Oscar Cullmann proposes a historical understanding of revelation that focuses on salvation history, whereby God's revealing work is grounded in his universal salvation will. The prophets play an important role, as they are the ones who interpret God's action so that it clearly comes across to the people of God as salvation.[130] Thus Cullmann speaks of revelation in an equivocal way, designating it partly God's activity and partly the enlightenment God confers on the prophet to let him or her perceive and present a given historical event as a disclosure of God's revealing activity. Prophecy has great importance as the concrete emanation of God's indirect revelatory activity, but it can only be seen as revelation through the prophet's interpretation. In this way, Cullmann affirms that the Bible is no mere book of history but rather "revealed prophecy concerning history."[131] If revelation was *only* God's general presence in history, then there would be no need for prophecy. But Cullmann does more than safeguard prophecy's importance, as he sees the prophet as the one who, in a particular historical setting, reveals God's action in history at large. Hence both Wright's and Cullmann's theologies are clearly marked by a double understanding of revelation history, partly as God's action in history at large and partly in the prophet's interpretation of history.

In his *Revelation as History*, Wolfhart Pannenberg opposes this bipartite understanding of revelation. He believes that God's salvation, eminently fulfilled in the Incarnation, does not apply to a particular part of history but *is part* of history and hence important for its universal implications. Revelation is not to be found only in one particular historical timeframe, but rather in the sum of history as such. W. Pannenberg therefore disagrees with Cullmann's thesis that revelation needs interpretation to appear exactly as revelation. Avery Dulles summarizes his idea as follows: "According to Pannenberg the events are self-interpreting: they bear their meaning intrinsically in themselves, and have no need to be elucidated by a supplementary prophetic disclosure." When the events "are taken seriously for what they are" he writes, "and in the historical context to which they belong, then they speak their own language, the language of facts."[132] Revelation never occurs directly through theophanies or prophetic revelations. This is why classical prophecy has little place or function in Pannenberg's system, and this is simply because he does not allow particular revelations to occupy a particular role with regard to revelation—all revelation occurs indirectly through history at large. Even God's self-revelation in Holy Scripture is always indirect. God is revealed through his activity in history, not through revealed words. This does not mean that all that happens in universal history is an expression of God's action. If this were the case, the Holocaust would have revealed God as an evil God. Pannenberg does not want to universalize the entirety of history as God's action, but merely to emphasize that the scene of God's action is the *one* and universal history in which his action would often be to stop events that are evil. Even if prophecy might still find a place in Pannenberg's system as the particular realization of God's action, it remains a compromised prophecy, inasmuch as revelation is never direct–thus contradicting the understanding of prophecy that this book presents, namely, God's particular intervention in history.

4.3.6. The Dialectic Understanding of Revelation

Dialectic theology has many representatives, of whom Karl Barth, Rudolf Bultmann, and Emil Brunner are the most important. They often have contradicting opinions and motives but may nevertheless be treated as one. For dialectic theology, revelation mainly consists in man's encounter with the living God. Revelation is realized where the Word of God is preached and is received exactly *as* the Word of God. This does not comprehend an ontologically synchronized encounter in time and nature between God and man, since

God is considered totally different from man, and revelation occurs in spite of the infinite distance between God and man. According to Barth, revelation in the Bible means "the self-unveiling, imparted to men, of the God who by nature cannot be unveiled to men. . . . It is the *Deus revelatus,* who is the *Deus absconditus.*"[133] The platform where the meeting between God and man occurs is faith, which again is considered an integral part of revelation itself. It is from this perspective that Barth can say that faith and revelation are correlatives.[134]

All three authors agree that the Bible and church evangelization never in themselves constitute revelation, but that they can become God's Word and revelation to the extent that God chooses to talk through his chosen witnesses. For Brunner, the Bible furthermore becomes the Word of God in the moment of revelation in which the "I" becomes contemporary with Christ.[135]

Revelation always occurs in spite of the odds through human faith. In fact, Kierkegaard's influence, particularly on Barth, shines through in the strong emphasis he places on the premise that revelation always contains a leap of faith. As mentioned, revelation that is neither ever-immediate nor follows from a convergence between God and man can only occur through faith—an issue that, according to Kierkegaard, is discussed in the question of whether the contemporary disciple of Christ has any advantage over the disciples of all later ages.[136] For Kierkegaard, the answer is no, since the first disciples had to decide and make a leap of faith just like all later disciples if they truly wished to be disciples.

This important insight of Kierkegaard has often been taken as an opposite to the mystical understanding of faith, as it has been seen to rule out the direct ontological and charismatic meeting between God and man, which is a precondition for the classical understanding of prophecy; prophecy is one form of mediated religion that is not close to dialectic theology, which emphasizes the absolute divide between God and man, necessitating the absolute leap of faith that does not rest on reason and arguments—certainly not the arguments derived from a prophet's mystical experiences. Prophecy is, however, of even less use from the perspective of revelation as inner experience, which we shall now examine.

4.3.7. Revelation as Inner Experience

All the Christian traditions that highlight God's continued presence and activity in the world in some way or another connect revelation with the immediate experience of God. This is especially true with respect to the Orthodox Church, for which revelation is fully realized when the individual believer *grasps* its content, ultimately God himself, through grace. Thus the purpose of theology is not to dissect and map the content of revelation as an object of human reason, but, according to Vladimir Lossky, "a new mode of thought where thought does not include, does not seize, but finds itself included and seized."[137]

In the West, the concept of revelation as inner experience has found several important exponents in twentieth-century liberal theologians such as Friedrich Schleiermacher, Albert Ritschl, and Wilhelm Herrmann. According to Herrmann, for example, revelation consists more than anything else in the inner fellowship with God that has been awakened by the Image (*Bild*) of Jesus in the New Testament. Christ may be the image of God, but revelation is not in itself that image, it is rather the relationship with God that is nourished by that image. The Swedish Lutheran Nathan Söderblom was another exponent of such thought who saw the great advantage of creating a more respectful platform for the meeting with believers of other faiths. Söderblom believed that all religions provide the basis for an authentic meeting with the divine. Divisions thrive where revelation is made equal with doctrine, and this is why Söderblom preferred the notion of revelation as inner experience to any other revelation concept; it fit with his pan-Christian engagement.

Evelyn Underhill also heralds the experiential rather than propositional aspects of revelation: "So we may say that the particular mental image which the mystic forms of his objective, the traditional theology he accepts, is not essential. . . . We cannot honestly say that there is any wide difference between the Brahman, Sufi, or Christian mystic at their best."[138]

Where some theologians have preferred to isolate revelation's experience from other aspects, others have incorporated them into comprehensive theologies. One example is Karl Rahner, for whom revelation has an authoritative and binding expression that he calls "predicamental revelation," which is at the same time always in need of that which his system terms "transcendental revelation."[139] Rahner links the idea of revelation closely to the works of grace in the life of the individual, whereby enlightening grace and revelation are inherently correlative. Similar ideas are found in the writings of Joseph Ratzinger,[140] Hans Urs von Balthasar, and others. Furthermore, ecumenical documents such as those of the conferences in Montreal and Edinburgh have the same differentiated approach to revelation, where revelation is conceived as God's activity through the Holy Spirit that gives life to the Body of Christ, the church.[141]

The "pure" version of this model that opposes revelation as experience to revelation as revealed teaching leaves little room for prophecy. Prophecy is powerfully linked with experiences of the Word of God, which fulfils its purpose solely in the prophetic admonition to implement it. Prophecy as such does, however, fit well into systems of thought of Karl Rahner and Joseph Ratzinger that combine the experiential and historical approaches to revelation.

4.3.8. Conclusion

As mentioned, the different aspects of revelation never appear isolated from one another. The Fathers of the church and medieval theologians right up to the Tridentine Council applied the term *revelation* in many different senses. As mentioned earlier, Karl Rahner and several other modern theologians look at the category of revelation in varying ways, allowing different simultaneous models. Rahner's distinction between the *predicamental revelation* as the authoritative expression of truth and the *transcendental revelation* as its dynamic continuation in the church points to different realities that are not directly correlative but are, at the same time, inseparable aspects of the revelation category.

Different theologians, such as Joseph Schumacher, have criticized this use of terminology, which they believe creates confusion, whereas the opposite opinion could be just as easily defended. Admittedly, confusion is inevitable when the realities pertaining to the category of revelation assume different nomenclatures, especially when it is not possible to differentiate neatly between the different revelatory ways that God seeks to introduce Creation into the life of God.

Happily, one may conceive of revelation's different aspects as the multicolored rays that protrude when a regular beam of light is filtered through a prism. Thus it is not possible to isolate different aspects without upsetting the category of revelation. If, for instance, one isolates the intelligible aspects of revelation in order to present revelation solely as doctrine without keeping in mind its dynamic continuation in the life of the church, then faith, whose object revelation is, truly becomes the "Es-Glaube" of Emil Brunner's criticism. Conversely, if one sees revelation solely as God giving himself as an inner experience while leaving no room for its normative expression, revelation then becomes arbitrary, relative, and nonverifiable. If keeping the different aspects together under one perspective is important to the category of revelation, it is equally essential for a complete and valid understanding of prophecy.

4.4. The Concept of Prophecy Based on Revelation Models

Having now addressed those issues of revelation that directly or indirectly concern prophecy, I shall now look specifically at the category of prophecy.

First, I shall reassess how the different aspects of revelation are organically linked to different views on prophecy. Thereafter, I shall look at specific aspects of prophecy, which, for the sake of clarity, will be distilled into different models. Much like the concept of revelation, prophecy has different aspects that can never be seen as elements that are independent of each other. The different aspects are as branches of the same trunk, which is God's revealing activity.

In the light of the *epiphanic model* of revelation, prophets express God's manifestation and activity. God reveals himself and communicates with his people in order to help them in varying historical contexts. In other words, revelation maintains intelligible aspects that never remain finite goals in themselves but are vehicles of truth.

This is somewhat different in the *doctrinal model,* whereby a prophet primarily is a divinely inspired teacher who foresees essential events of salvation history, especially the coming of Christ. To theologians of the doctrinal school, Old Testament prophets would continue to reveal new aspects of the truth and nature of God and thereby add to the Deposit of Faith.[142] Since this is complete with the last apostle, many of these theologians ignore or even deny the idea of postapostolic prophecy. The argument is often simplistic: prophecy relates to the cognition and instruction of truth and to the augmentation of the Deposit of Faith. This was fulfilled with the last apostle. Hence there is next to no place for prophecy after the postapostolic age. Joseph Ratzinger believes this to constitute a double misunderstanding (see section 6.2.3).

The effects of the doctrinal approach lead to a strong insistence on the predictive elements of prophecy, and several medieval and especially neo-Scholastic theologians such as Pesch and Tromp investigated the *argumentum propheticum.* They still linked prophecy with inspired information, but conceived it more and more as the sure disclosure of the future. With great care and attention, these theologians sought out all the Old Testament passages they believed to foretell the coming of Christ. They showed less interest in what the prophets *did,* but greatly stressed what they taught and foretold. Although the term *prophecy* found many applications in the Middle Ages,[143] its interpretation as the foretelling of the future played such an important role in that period that several prophetic personalities were influenced by it. Birgitta of Vadstena, for instance, although she continuously received revelations, did not consider herself a prophet, partly because she had few prophecies that dealt with future events.[144] According to Birgitta's instruction, it was not enough to receive divine revelations and preach them to the world in order to be a prophet. The revelations had to deal with the future, and this was why she sought the true prophets among the writings of the Old Testament. This very well reflects the idea and problematic result of the doctrinal understanding of revelation.

In light of the *personalistic model* of revelation, where revelation primarily is seen as the communication of God's very person, the prophet's foremost function is to reveal God as he shows himself with all his divine characteristics that make out the foundation for and partly the content of the union between God and his creatures. The prophet is to preach not only the divine secrets and truths but God himself, his person and love for man, and the ultimate task of the prophet is to enable God and man to meet. Through prophecy, God wills to reestablish his union with Creation, and in this perspective, prophecy is communicative in two ways: the prophet announces the Creator's affection and desire for union with Creation. At the same time, he calls fallen man to conversion and to return to a true life in God. The prophet's words are always both edifying and admonishing, sweet and bitter.

Much has already been said on prophecy's position according to the *dialectic model* of revelation. It leaves limited space to prophecy, at least prophecy understood as revelation. If a dialectic understanding could be paired with a historical understanding of revelation, it would leave plenty of room for prophecy. Karl Barth must be said in many ways to have acted prophetically, not the least in his fight against Nazism. But for prophecy in the narrowest biblical form (proclamation of experienced revelation) there is little space in this understanding, as revelation is mainly conceived as occurring where the Word is received in faith.

In the model of revelation as inner experience, prophecy stems from the fullness and reality of the Logos with the purpose of expressing this reality to the faithful. Prophecy is the proclamation of that divine life with the purpose of implementing that very life of God in creation; hence the prophet easily appears as a divinely inspired teacher. Having himself or herself savored the sweetness of God, the prophet through his or her activity and writing seeks to introduce the faithful to that same life, calling readers to think not just of the message but of themselves, through contemplation, so as to attain that transcendent relationship with God. History shows that numerous prophets, through their preaching and writing, have led to renewed spirituality and often to the foundation of new orders seeking to realize the true life in God here on earth through prayer and charity.

4.5. Models of Prophecy

Having seen how the concept of prophecy is shaped by the different aspects of revelation, I shall now distil and examine various models of prophecy. As with the category of revelation, prophecy does not allow individual aspects to be dissected and presented as the one true definition of prophecy, much less place them in opposition with each other, even though some have attempted to do this.

4.5.1. Prophecy's Edification as Phenomenological Autocriterion

I have already portrayed prophecy as a charism that stems from a particular experience of the Word of God, but with God's purpose of edifying the congregation (see section 3.3.1). The prophet is called to make the reality of revelation accessible and real for his or her contemporaries and to warn and divert the people of God from ways that are in opposition to God's truth. This will be further clarified in chapter 5. This principle of prophecy's edification is the primary phenomenological criterion and hermeneutic key for the assessment of prophecy in all of its aspects, before and after Christ. This becomes most evident in the Incarnation, where God's saving and edifying activity reaches its climax in Christ's death on the Cross, precondition of and entrance to the union between God and Creation. The edifying character of prophecy is the common denominator that relates all the different aspects of prophecy to each other. Just as with the category of revelation, we can see prophecy as a tree, where the trunk is the edifying function that carries the different aspects of prophecy as branches. To use the another image, the different aspects of prophecy are like the differently colored rays that have been produced by a prism, spreading of the main beam of prophecy, as it were–the edification of the people of God, occurring from the divine love and will of salvation.

This primary phenomenological criterion leads to a second criterion. If prophecy is to edify the congregation, it must relate to the present age. Even if prophecy may often deal with the future or provide inspired interpretations of past events, its goal is always the present. Hence we encounter prophecy only if it is relevant and edifying to the *now* of the church.

As we saw in my discussion of the historical development of prophecy, Paul worked intensively with the subject of prophecy in his letters. If he, in the First Letter to the Corinthians, prefers prophecy to other charisms, it is because of its superior capacity of edifying and building up the community. No one understands tongues, but "someone who prophesies speaks to other people, building them up and giving them encouragement and reassurance."[145] Hence a third phenomenological criterion follows from the first, namely the intelligibility of the prophetic message. In contrast to certain types of New Age channeling, where mediums write down messages from "the other world" in often nonunderstandable languages, the Christian prophet always communicates what the people understand.

4.5.2. Prophecy as Encouragement

As mentioned, Rino Fisichella is one of the theologians who has worked most extensively with the theological argument of Christian prophecy, and he has extended the idea of edification to new areas. He draws a distinct line between Old and New Testament prophecy, emphasizing the radical new that happened with the Christ-event. "In New Testament prophecy," Fisichella says, "any kind of *fear, judgment,* and *condemnation* has completely disappeared. Instead, the prophet is the one who infuses courage and brings a message of salvation."[146] The resurrection of Christ is the one event that changed everything and that lets prophecy appear in an entirely different light. Where the Old Testament prophets often could be rough and carry words of criticism and judgment of sin, New Testament prophecy bears no trace of such hardness and is known to be only edifying. Words of warning or judgment may appear in conjunction with prophetic messages, but such moments should be labeled *apocalyptic,* and not *prophetic.*[147]

Rino Fisichella thus brings the principle of prophecy's edification to its most consistent reach. Without disagreeing with the basic concern with highlighting prophecy's edifying function, it seems useful to emphasize the purpose of the warning aspects of prophecy. For the question arises of where we place the New Testament prophetic characters who were severe and rebuking toward the nonconverted? John the Baptist could be called the last Old Testament prophet in the sense of being the last to foretell the coming of Christ (see section 3.3.2); he was also slaughtered before the renewing death and resurrection of Christ. But there are other clearly New Testament prophets who are just as strict in the condemnation of sin as John the Baptist. One example may be Peter's very prophetic acts toward Ananias and his wife, perhaps the strongest of all prophetic accounts in the New Testament. Nevertheless, the event is edifying in its context, as the community sees how concrete God's presence is and is built up in the fear of God.[148] Likewise, the Apocalypse contains many words of prophetic judgment on those who were not fervent in their faith: "I know about your activities: how you are neither cold nor hot. I wish you were one or the other, but since you are neither hot nor cold, but only lukewarm, I will spit you out of my mouth."[149] It is a difficult passage to accept; however, it is followed by the reassurance of its grounding in Christ's salvific love: "I reprove and train those whom I love."[150] As George Eldon Ladd writes, "if the Laodiceans will anoint their eyes with the eye-salve Christ provides and are thereby enabled to recognize their blind, impoverished state, it will not be too late to replace complacency with zeal, and thereby repent."[151]

Finally, a detailed look at Christ himself, the prophet par excellence, and the ways he fought to build God's Kingdom reminds us again how, from the beginning to the end of his earthly existence, the Word and image of God acted and even foretold the future in very authoritative and strict ways. One example may be the purification of the temple that reminds one of the Old Testament prophets' judgment of the decline of religious observance among the people of God. Another example may be Jesus' hard prophecies, such as the one on the destruction of Jerusalem and the unkind judgment of those who did not believe in him.

In the same way, the life of the church is full of recognized prophetic figures such as Catherine of Siena, Birgitta of Vadstena, and so forth who were immensely critical when criticism was needed to truly change things, speaking words of judgment on lifestyles and ecclesial practices that they saw as opposed to the truth of the faith that was so strongly impressed within their minds. Fogelqvist[152] and Dinzelbacher[153] present a timely illustration of some of Birgitta's visions of warning, in which Christ describes what will happen to individuals because of their sin if they do not convert. Whereas the apparitions of Lourdes were full of hope and encouragement, more recent Marian apparitions such as those of Fatima express great sorrow over and warnings against the dangers of the church, dangers that at times are accompanied by visions of Hell or Purgatory that present the warnings in even more serious light.[154]

Identifying *edification* too closely with *encouragement* could be at a high cost, as the two are distinct. If prophecy is reduced from edification to encouragement, Christian prophecy is deprived of important vehicles of divine charity and providence. A father who observes his child unknowingly do things that lead to his destruction would be an unloving father if he failed to correct the child with any possible means. Sometimes one word of rebuke bears more fruit than a thousand words of encouragement.

4.5.3. Prophecy as Correction

A significant number of earlier theological elaborations on the subject, Lutheran and Catholic alike, point in a somewhat different direction from Fisichella's approach. In the Catholic *Dictionnaire de la vie Chrétienne* an entire article is dedicated to the question of the "contestation prophétique." P. Mariotti writes that prophecy has received little theological attention and that it is impossible to say much about prophecy other than that, for the sake of truth, prophecy is always sharp and corrective (prophecy is *contestant*) and that through its clarity and sharpness it will be met by resistance (prophecy is *contestée*). Prophecy is contestant and will be contested.

The notion of prophecy as being critical has had its greatest success in Protestant theology. To the reformers, their opposition to certain practices of the church of their times was a preeminently *prophetic* mission, seeking to oppose derailed practices.[155] This mission constituted a sharing in Christ's prophetic ministry, the *munus propheticum Christi*—that is, it was part of his threefold ministry (*munus triplex Christi: munus sacerdotale, munus regale,* and *munus propheticum,* Christ's sacerdotal, kingly, and prophetic ministries). Protestants do highlight the importance of the entire church's prophetic role vis-à-vis the world,[156] but tend more readily to see prophecy realized in individuals guided by Christ from within the church criticizing lapsed office bearers.[157] Many of Luther's contemporaries and later followers considered him a prophet; thus, for instance, five years before the two fell into conflict over the Lord's Supper, Zwingli had labeled Luther a contemporary "Elijah, the eschatological prophet who was to proclaim the Word of the Lord in the last times."[158] To Luther, the purpose was not to establish a new church but to correct those religious traditions and theologies that were in opposition to the Gospel. To the reformers, the criticism unintentionally ended up with the establishment of the Lutheran community, whereby the critical element can almost be seen as constitutive of the reformed churches, an element that still shines through in the name "Protestant."

The prophetic opposition within the church perpetuated large areas of Protestant thinking and research and has been raised by the sociologist Max Weber to a matter of sociological "natural law," making charism and institution two necessary opponents. Prophecy is a corrective factor to the extent that institution and prophecy at times become opposite entities. This is visible especially in exegesis, where Lutheran treatises on prophecy in the ancient church are much more inclined than the Catholic to blame the growing institution for the decline of prophecy.

Catholic theologians, on the other hand, tend more often to point out how the Magisterium in union with the entire people of God carries out Christ's prophetic task,[159] and have traditionally been more reticent to propose the corrective factors of prophecy whereby some Christians correct other Christians. We saw Rino Fisichella's position as on example thereof (see section 4.5.2), while Cothenet was another (see section 3.3.8). This is especially the case when prophecy is directed not only against the laity but, as in the case of Birgitta of Vadstena, also against the authorities of the church. Although Birgitta sharply criticized the office bearers, she cannot be said to be antihierarchical. Likewise, modern Catholic scholars find it important to point out that prophecy is not per se antihierarchical.[160] While the view of prophecy as inspired correction has been widespread in the Lutheran context, there are nevertheless more and more Catholic theologians who forward the same opinion. Thus, Karl Rahner, Johannes Feiner, Georg Hasenhüttel, and Norbert Greinacher recognize the fact that prophecy and institution have been in conflict. Rahner, for instance, believes that prophecy and the prophetic revelations have received so little theological attention precisely because of the problematic relationship between prophecy and institution. To Rahner, the problematic relationship rests on jealousy between prophecy and institution, as the "direct line to heaven" provides prophecy with an authority with which the institution's historically based authority is unable to compete.[161]

Johannes Feiner writes that the institution, in spite of its general infallibility, because of the sinfulness of man, is imbued with the risk of a "collusion and neglect of individual statements in the kerugma and misunderstandings in the experience of faith."[162] Even though Feiner unfortunately does not associate prophecy and its importance with the tradition of revelation, he says in a footnote on prophecy that God's eschatological word of revelation has been confided to the church, but "naturally, this does not mean that God would not avail himself of New Testament prophecy in order time and again to call the church and especially its leaders to deepen the awareness of revelation."[163]

G. Hasenhüttel distinguishes himself from the majority of Catholic theologians by adopting the mainly Lutheran thesis that prophecy ceased in the ancient church as a result of its growing institutionalization (see section 3.3.8). When the church institutionalizes, the prophetic element diminishes, he argues.[164]

Inspired by Hans Küng, Norbert Greinacher writes that the church in order to be faithful to its mission, apart from the apostolic succession, must have a prophetic succession.[165] He believes that this prophetic dimension in today's church is held by progressive personalities, activist groups, and movements who work for the reform of church and society.

It must be observed that most Catholic theologians who discuss the difficult relation between prophecy and institution never question authoritative doctrinal pronouncements. Likewise, traditional Catholic prophecy never questions the divine foundation and authority of the institution, as prophetic criticism aims at the bearers of the institutional posts, not their office; the very fact that the institution has a charismatic dimension charges the ministers with an ever greater responsibility. Ingvar Fogelqvist clearly shows how Birgitta of Vadstena safeguards the divine necessity and task of the institution while being very stern with ministers who fail to fulfill their tasks.[166]

As Auguste Saudreau[167] and Augustinus Suh[168] indicate, history has often needed a prophetic voice to draw forth from the Deposit of Faith important aspects that have been ignored or have never been formulated. This was the case in particular with the Sacred Heart tradition that emerged from the prophetic revelations of Gertrude the Great and Margaret Mary Alacoque. The latter in particular lived at a time of Jansenism, when prophetic correction was greatly needed. For various reasons the image of God had devolved into that of a great judge, causing the faithful to avoid approaching the altar to receive the Eucharist, and to approach Christ himself primarily through the Virgin Mary. As Michael O'Carroll shows, the need for correction was met through the revelations of Margaret Mary Alacoque. They focused on the infinite love of Christ, expressed symbolically through the tradition of the Sacred Heart.[169] Other examples are the dogma of Mary's Assumption into heaven, inspired by the revelations of the French nun Catherine de Labouré, and the Feast of the Eucharist, inspired by the revelations of St. Juliana, the Cistercian prioress of the monastery of Mont-Cornillon (see section 6.3.4).[170]

Even theologians like Rahner who admit possible tensions between independent prophets and the institution illustrate the importance of the charismatic dimension of the Magisterium: "To that extent, therefore, ecclesiastical office and ministry is charismatic in character, if we understand by charismatic, what is in contradistinction to what is purely institutional, administered by men, subject to calculation, expressible in laws and rules."[171]

Protestant theologians place less emphasis on the dimension of the institution. The *Confessio Augustana* does portray ministry as participation in the sacrificial office of Christ and hence, in line with the ecumenical document it intended to be, comes close to a Catholic understanding of ministry.[172] Nevertheless, the majority of Lutheran interpreters infer from Luther's insistence on the *priesthood of all believers* that ministry is a mainly practical invention that does not belong to the essence of the church.[173] A person is ordained a priest as leader of the congregation so that order and not disorder may reign in the church. When the entire congregation knows who the official priest of the congregation is, there is then less danger of someone taking the reins out of personal ambition, seeking to impose himself as leader of the church. In the same way the ministry of the bishop is assessed by Peder Nørgaard-Højen as a *bene esse ecclesiae*, and never an *esse ecclesiae*.[174] This is why the ministers of the church are always in need of direction—in order to remain on the right path; and they do so through the prophetic impulse that often is expressed through reform movements or prophetic personalities. Somewhat tendentiously, it could be said that the prophetic charism to many Catholic theologians is an integral part of the Magisterium, while Protestant theologians tend rather to consider it an extrainstitutional corrective factor.

With the understanding of ministry and institution comes ecclesiology. Catholic theology often tends toward what could be called an *ontological ecclesiology*, in which the Holy Spirit is thought to be so present that there is no need for clear prophetic correction. *The church is autocorrective:* It is like an organism that through its immune defense system will always adapt to the changing times and dangers in order to evolve into new cultural forms of the same immutable Body of Christ. Prophecy may oppose the church, but it remains a voice *of* the church *for* its benefit. The general infallibility, anchored in Christ's words "the gates of Hell shall have no power over it [the church]," [175] is guaranteed by the Holy Spirit's presence in the church. This is why Catholic theology sees prophecy as an inseparable and integral part of the church, rooted in its very nature. This does not mean that individual persons cannot act in prophetic ways, but rather that they never attack the church in its foundation. The prophets of the church illustrate one of its autocorrective factors through which the church keeps adapting to the times and, by this means, purify it of what is not of God. The general infallibility of the church is always concentrated in the Magisterium. [176] Extrainstitutional prophecy can provide inspiration and positive new orientation, but it can never equal guaranteed truth, and cannot boast of a charism of infallibility like the Magisterium. [177] Protestant theology contradicts this connection of ministry and infallibility, and today in Lutheran-Catholic circles the primary ecumenical difficulties are centered on the questions of ministry and ecclesiology.

To the Protestant theologian, the infallibility of the church is not an inseparable part of the being of the church. In order to be infallible, the church is continuously in need of prophets when things go wrong. Paul Althaus expresses this orientation well:

> The promise of the spirit to the church means the following: God will never abandon the church to die by itself through its own sin and weakness. Rather, somewhere in the Church, the spirit of God lets truth and life break through anew for the entire church, somewhere he arouses prophets and reformers. This is the Protestant notion of the Spirit's direction and the "infallibility" of the church. [178]

The Catholic theologian does not necessarily deny prophecy outside of the institution, *inasmuch as* it carries no similar sort of infallibility. Traditional Catholic theology sees the Magisterium as being imbued with *negative infallibility*, that is, the charism of infallibility prevents the church from making wrong authoritative doctrinal expressions—"inerrancy in what is formally taught and defined as ultimate truth." [179] Catholic theology sees the infallibility of the church as concentrated in a special way in the Magisterium. But this does not rule out the fruitful interplay of prophecy and institution. Thus, it does make sense today to speak of a prophetic correction not just of the members of the church but also of its leaders. The negative infallibility of the Magisterium means that the faithful can find authoritative, infallible, true doctrinal expressions in ecumenical councils or papal doctrinal statements *ex cathedra*. The Magisterium is, on the other hand, never imbued with the guarantee of an all-encompassing *positive expression* of the Christian truth, and has never claimed to possess it. This is where prophecy carries out an important role, as it can help to explore and bring forth new aspects of the truth that later in theory could be proposed as such *ex cathedra* by the pope. Prophecy contributes to the full positive adherence to the truth, as it is the entire church, and not just its ministers, who make out the full positive infallibility, given Christ's guarantee that "the gates of Hell will not overcome it"[180] and it will not perish. From this perspective, Scripture and tradition, Magisterium and people of God *together* carry the truth to the world. In Catholic theology there has been a tendency to underestimate the importance of the entire people of God in communicating the fullness of faith to the world. As a result of historical factors, especially the church's confrontation with rationalism and liberalism in the nineteenth century, a one-sided focus on the infallibility of the Magisterium has diminished the awareness of the "contribution of the noninstitutional carriers, the laity and the charismatic, prophetic personalities in handing on revelation [offenbarungsvermittelnde Funktion]."[181] Much of this was addressed during Vatican II.

This discussion on the relationship between prophecy and institution holds important ecumenical perspectives. Lutheran theology primarily sees prophecy as the factor that corrects the Magisterium from without. Catholic theology, on the other hand, sees prophecy as an ontological part of the church, intensified in the Magisterium, lending the institution an integral autocorrective profile. An ecumenical discussion of the internal and external prophetic elements of ministry could throw new light on old theological discussions.

To conclude, the corrective element can never be without its corrective factors. If prophecy is defined as the edification of the church, it must be both corrective and encouraging. Without its encouraging aspects, the corrective function of prophecy would be pure judgment and the prophetic words only the expression of God's anger, not the expression of the love that Christianity attributes to God as his primary trait. If, on the other hand, prophecy only encourages and does not purify that which grows wild and false, then the good that the prophet's encouraging words would have produced would soon be suffocated. If prophecy is to be edifying, it must be both encouraging and corrective.

4.5.4. Prophecy as Divine Direction or Imperative

Karl Rahner and Laurent Volken may be the two theologians who have contributed most to the right understanding of prophetic revelations in the church in the past century. In their view, prophecy cannot be anything fundamentally new in relation to that which Scripture and tradition profess as the truth: *"They do not reveal an 'accidental' supplement to public revelation or simply be identical with it."*[182] This does not mean, however, that prophecy is a superfluous expression, but rather that prophecy has a scope distinct from that of providing doctrinal novelties. Famous in this regard is Rahner's theory that prophetic revelations constitute imperatives on the actions of the faithful:

> Private revelations are essentially imperatives showing how Christianity should act in a concrete historical situation: no new assertions but new commands. What they affirm is already known from faith and theology. Yet they are not superfluous, are not mere heavenly refresher courses in public revelation or a Socratic method used by God in order to lead us to the knowledge of what in principle could be learnt without this help. Because what God wishes to be done in certain given circumstances cannot be logically and unequivocally deduced from the general principles of dogma and morals, even with the help of an analysis of the given situation.[183]

Theology may provide various paradigms on how the church can better orient itself in a concrete historical setting, but theology cannot always indicate which of the proposed solutions is the best. And this is precisely where Rahner believes prophecy is essential. In the multitude of theories and ideas indicating different directions, Rahner asks why Christians should not seek to follow the voice of Christ, who still speaks today:

> Among the many possibilities [of choices] equally good in principle, should not the Christian's choice be made with the help of lights other than theoretical principles? Why could these lights not be that very enlightenment and that word of the Lord which we call—too carelessly perhaps and with a certain disdain—"private revelations," and which we consider as a luxury left to certain pious souls? Then it is that the theology and the psychology of these revelations—each as indispensable as the other to a true discernment of spirits—will take on all their practical significance.[184]

Laurent Volken follows a similar train of thought. He affirms that the task of prophecy is not to add something new to the Deposit of Faith. The prophetic revelations in reality say the same thing as the revelation, expressing it anew, without, however, being its mere repetition.

> The definition does not raise a question of doctrine but of practical direction. Certainly doctrine is not excluded from the aim of revelations. However, by comparison with their aim revelations are only a means of achieving an end ... "an edification";[185] that is the most venerable and most traditional term by which to designate the aim of revelations. . . . The call to conversion, also, is the strongest expression of the I of particular revelations.[186]

The aim of prophecy is to secure the fidelity of the people of God to revelation, deriving from it the right orientation for the people of God. What distinguishes prophetic revelations from the *revelatio publica* is that the latter is the general norm of faith and hence has universal and perpetual significance, whereas the *prophetic revelations* relate to the concrete historical context that becomes its *Sitz im Leben:* "It is precisely this 'particular situation' which especially characterizes the aim of a particular revelation, and this aim distinguishes it from public revelation."[187]

Again we see the conviction that prophecy is edifying, and this because it has a concrete historical context as its goal. Prophecy does not present a general thesis or doctrinal idea, but proposes God's truth for a particular moment in time, as prophecy is not itself without the particular historical context. On the contrary, its aim is precisely to shed light on aspects of the Deposit of Faith that in the times of the prophets were either neglected or undeveloped. While always edifying in the present context of the prophet, prophecy may nonetheless shed light on events of the past, present and future.

4.5.5. Prophecy Shedding Light on the Past

Prophecy in the Old Testament, in the New Testament, and in the Christian church refers to important historical events of the past. The Old Testament prophets called the people of God to live according to the law of Sinai, rendering it accessible and important. Thus the prophet points to the mighty works of Yahweh with the intention that the people of God may live up to its election in a way that is worthy of his mighty works. *The prophets shed light on the past in order to renew the present age.*

In addition, prophets in the present have sometimes referred to prophecies of the past and explained how they were being fulfilled in the present. Thus, the New Testament presents Jesus' interpretation of Isaiah's text on the "Anointed One of the Lord" as a prophetic interpretation of a former prophecy, namely the prophecy of the coming of the Messiah.[188] Peter's talk on Pentecost, which Luke presents as truly inspired by the Spirit of God, likewise refers to a former prophecy, namely that of Joel on the outpouring of the Holy Spirit. Here again, the purpose of Peter's reference to the ancient text is to elucidate that which occurs in the present.[189]

The same applies to the prophetic contemplation of Christ's passion. In the prophetic tradition of the church, especially in classical mysticism, the contemplation of Christ and his sufferings occupies a very central role. Once more we may consider Birgitta of Vadstena, in whose writings Fogelqvist finds innumerable meditations on the passion of Christ.[190] The prophetic attention to the former event, here the sufferings of Jesus, again has a purpose in the present, for the contemplation of Jesus' passion as the preeminent expression of his love serves to awaken repentance and love in the believer and thereby edify the believer's spiritual life.

4.5.6. Prophecy Shedding Light on the Present

Prophecy can function as the revelation of important, hidden factors of the present. The Old Testament prophetic call to repentance is such an inspired indication of the sins of the people who do not take apostasy seriously that it emerges as a sign of divine authority. Prophetic discourse on the present can also serve to disclose secrets. The account of Jesus' meeting with the Samaritan woman by the well is of particular interest in this regard. Jesus reveals that she has lived with five men, whereupon she exclaims: "Lord, I see you are a prophet."[191] Once again, the prophetic manifestation serves as edification. Jesus' prophetic words convince the woman of his authority and of the truth of what he says, and as a result she and "many Samaritans of that town believed in him on the strength of the woman's words of testimony, [since] 'he told me everything I have done.' "[192]

Also in the life of the church, prophecy has been the element that interprets the signs of the times, whereby the church receives new direction. Earlier I spoke of prophecy as correction and that part of its purpose has been to shed light on that which, in the present age, does not conform to the truth of the Gospel.[193]

4.5.7. Prophecy Shedding Light on the Future

In the popular understanding, prophecy is often defined as the foretelling of future events. This is an understanding that has often overshadowed the edifying aspects of prophecy, since prophecy regarded as mere future-telling serves few other purposes than to satisfy one's curiosity. In the right understanding of the prophetic phenomenon, prophecy can indeed relate to the future, but always in relation to and in the context of the present.

PROPHECY AS PURE INFORMATION ABOUT FUTURE EVENTS. For long periods, in the Middle Ages and all the way to the present, prophecy has been defined only in relation to predicting the future. This understanding of prophecy received its most systematic expression in the classical manualist treatises *De revelatione*. Christian Pesch gave it its most famous expression: "Profeteia est certa predictio futuri eventus qui ex principiis naturalibus praesciri non potest" (prophecy is a prediction with certainty of a future event that is not predictable by means of human and natural knowledge).[194] Referring to Birgitta's *Sermo Angelicus* 9, Anders Piltz argues that Birgitta was so influenced by this predictive notion of prophecy that she did not consider herself a prophet, since few of her prophetic revelations dealt with the future.[195] In the manualist tradition, the reductionist and mechanistic approach to prophecy became evident, as it only sought to identify the fulfillment of the Old Testament prophecies in the Christ-event.[196] As this definition was paired with a propositional/doctrinal approach to revelation, prophecy's purpose devolved to mere prediction.

This understanding of prophecy may be the farthest notion from the correct assessment of prophecy, since it hardly serves the present and seeks to inform the intellect of future events that reason alone cannot determine. The only way this approach can edify the faithful is by illuminating the intellect, which occurs in the famous *gaudium de veritate*, where salvation and knowledge of truth are identical (see section 4.3.2). But as mentioned earlier, this understanding of salvation and revelation is incomplete and has little life-transforming momentum.

This does not mean, however, that the preview-aspects of prophecy have no edifying effects at all. On the contrary, it is a historical fact that most known Christian prophets preached words to their contemporaries concerning the future. The future-oriented aspects of prophecy can, therefore, be edifying within the framework of a personalistic and historical approaches to revelation, just as future prophecy can provide a healthy outlook on the present. Prophecies of the future either relate to events within the history of this world, or they deal with the eschatological future, that is, with events that will occur when world history ends. These future prophecies can be interpreted as serving several edifying purposes in helping believers to attain to a full spiritual life. Future prophecies help the people of God to live in the knowledge of the world's transiency, the knowledge that what belongs to this world is ephemeral and that history has an end, both the history of the individual believer and humankind as such. Furthermore, having an inspired estimate of developments in the future may help the church make good decisions at the present moment. According to Rahner, it helps the faithful to introduce the reality of God into the present even before the eschaton: "There will always be men in the Church with charismatic gifts, who will look into the future like the prophets of old and warn us to make the right decisions in the present."[197]

PROPHECIES OF JUDGMENT. When prophecies of future events deal with the history of this world and not only with what will happen in the hereafter, they refer to future catastrophes. Such prophecies are often called prophecies of judgment or warning. They occur in the Old Testament and in the New Testament (in particular in the Apocalypse of John) as well as in the life of the church. It is very important, however, to identify what is meant by the expression *prophecies of judgment*. This type of prophecy never depicts a God who intends to harm his people. Rather, its scope is to throw light on the natural result of the chosen people's conduct; hence an impressive number of judgment prophecies are, as many authors have indicated, conditional. As Witherington writes, prophets are not judges, but "crisis intervention specialists," and the more the crisis grows, the more need there is "for reflection on Israel's future, and thus the need for prophecy."[198] The book of Jonah may be the most flagrant example of the salvation-beyond-judgment character of chastisement prophecies. To the great regret of Jonah, who risked his life proclaiming the prophetic warning, God decided to withdraw his promised punishment, since the people converted because of Jonah's words.[199] In this way the prophecies of warning, rather than revealing a revenging God, reveal a Yahweh who, out of love, discloses what will happen if the people do not repent.

Just as Israel knew of the prediction of future chastisements, so recognized Christian saints and prophets foretold catastrophes. As in the Old Testament, some of them did not come to pass due to the conversion of the faithful. The most famous and extreme example is that of Vincent Ferrer, later canonized by the Catholic Church. In his last twenty-one years (1398–1419) Ferrer preached far and wide that the end of the world was close at hand. In this period his biographies report that he performed over three thousand miracles, which leads hagiographers to the conclusion that his prophecies pleased the Lord, who thus confirmed their validity by signs and wonders. Ferrer's predictions did not come to pass, and his biographies explain this by affirming that his prophecies were conditional and managed to save the people. The biography written by P. H. O. Fages, O.P., says: "The preaching of Jonah saved Nineveh; the preaching of Vincent Ferrer saved the universe."[200]

In a more recent context, Ovila Melançon interprets the prophecy of judgment by saying that it is never absolute but always depends on circumstances. This is so because the prophetic prediction never describes a neatly and immutably programmed series of events. Prophecy is rather an inspired insight into a contemporary cause-and-effect relationship between the sins of the people and the consequential bad effect. It is this that can change, since the prophetic revelation, according to Melançon, "only reproduces from divine prescience the knowledge of the relationship between the causes and their effects, and the causes can change."[201] When sin and evil works are diminished, the chastisement is diminished. And this is where the authentic prophecy of judgment has its edifying role. The prophecy of judgment never prophesies chastisement as an end in itself, but as a means to avoid chastisement, often with the indications of *how* to avoid it. Its purpose is to lead the people away from the dangerous results of apostasy.

The aforementioned aspects of future prophecies serve for the edification of the contemporary age. The *fulfillment* of the prophecy occurs in the future, but its edifying function lies in the present, aiming at the spiritual healing and conversion of the faithful. However, future prophecies can also be of a nature that edifies the faithful not at the moment when the prophecy is pronounced, but when it seems to be fulfilled. From this perspective, we can name two more types of future prophecy: future prophecies as divine providence and the a posteriori future prophecy.

PROPHECY AS DIVINE PROVIDENCE. The prophetic announcement of future events can have an assuring effect on the faithful at the moment when the prophecy is announced. This may be the case even when the announcement aims at worrying events. The believer who is aware of the divine announcement of an event can rest assured that God, in spite of the seriousness of the situation, has foreseen it and hence will also provide a solution. This kind of future prophecy has its most important expression in the Gospel of John where Jesus reveals: "I have told you this now, before it happens, so that when it does happen, you may believe."[202] Christ instructs the disciples to be calm on behalf of the words he has uttered and to have faith in him when they are fulfilled.

A POSTERIORI FUTURE PROPHECY. Another kind of future prophecy is the a posteriori future prophecy. Prophecies of the future never disclose details with the precision of a surgeon; they are never a priori, never given in all detail in advance. Only when the event comes to pass is the prophecy fulfilled, and then it becomes clear what the prophetic message hinted at and intended. Prophecies are to be interpreted anamnetically, *post factum*. From this perspective, the prophetic message, expressed in the past, may help to shed edifying light on the present age, helping to understand it and the causes of its present course. This is how the prophecies of the coming Messiah work in the New Testament, aiming at elucidating through the ancient texts what happens in the present with the coming of Christ.

God through prophecy always introduces his people to important events, that are to happen in the church, as in Amos: "No indeed, Lord Yahweh does nothing without revealing his secret to his servants the prophets."[203] This fact is almost as a law of nature, rooted in the unity between Christ and his church, which he desires to take part in his plan of salvation.

4.5.8. Conclusion

In all the various models or aspects of prophecy we have seen that it always serves the edification of the church. Thus Christian prophecy clearly stands out from the various forms of fortunetelling and other esoteric practices by never serving futile curiosity or the desire of knowing things, otherwise secret, for the sole satisfaction of knowing the secret. Although the various aspects of prophecy have been opposed, each of them highlights the basic purpose of prophecy, namely the edification of the community. Prophecy always aims at the practical edification of the present age, seeking to call the faithful to conversion and a life worthy of their belief, and in this sense, it helps to actualize the reality of faith. This means that there is a close relationship between prophecy and tradition. I will address this relationship at greater length in the next chapter. Prophecy serves the true and ever-living reality of the Word, of which tradition ideally should be the expression and realization.

5

Prophecy and the End
of Revelation

We have now examined different approaches to revelation and how
they affect the notion of prophecy. We have also seen different general
approaches to the concept of prophecy, showing how they need not
oppose each other but rather emphasize different aspects. So far,
however, we have not raised one of the main questions of this book:
how does it make sense at all from a theological perspective to speak of
prophecy in the World of Christendom? Does the Christian system
allow such a phenomenon? And if so, what are the theological preconditions of such a phenomenon?

Christianity is markedly different from all other world religions
in proclaiming the Incarnation of the only begotten Son of God, Jesus
Christ. The fullness and perfection of God's manifestation in Christ
is such that it necessarily places prophecy in a different light from
that of most other religious beliefs that expect prophets to complete
God's general manifestation in history. Christianity's belief in the
totality and perfection of God's revelation in Christ has led to the
idea that nothing greater could ever occur in this world, often expressed through the notion of an "end of revelation with the last
apostle." It is this idea and principle of Christian thinking that I
will treat in order to elucidate its influence and effects within the
framework of Christian prophecy. If the "end" idea were taken *literally,* it would signify the end of revelation in its different forms after
the last apostle and hence no more prophecy, and this is, in fact, how
the notion has been employed.

As demonstrated earlier, John of the Cross proposed the idea that there is no more revelation after Christ:

> But in this era of grace, now that the faith is established through Christ and the Gospel law made manifest, there is no reason for inquiring of him in this way, or expecting him to answer as before. In giving us his Son, his only Word (for he possesses no other), he spoke everything to us at once in this sole Word—and he has no more to say.[1]

Martin Luther called for the same principle, as it was vital for him to secure Scripture as revelation's sole authoritative testimony. All that is important is enclosed here, Luther affirms, maintaining that one should not listen to prophecies, for they only lead one astray. Luther gives several examples of false prophecies and miraculous works. He writes:

> Therefore let us faithfully adhere to this revelation or proclamation of the Holy Spirit. He alone must tell us what we are to know; He will make prophets of us and will show us what the future has in store for Christendom, how Christ will reign until the end and preserve His Christendom, and how He will finally destroy the rule of the Antichrist and his lord, the devil. This prophecy is more certain to us than all signs and wonders, for it will survive the devil's most spiteful opposition.[2]

Moreover, in our times theologians apply the fullness of God's revelation in Christ as the primary argument for rejecting contemporary prophetic claims (see section 3.3.8).

In addition, some contemporary writers advance the idea that since we now have the Bible, we do not need prophecy. For instance, Floyd Barackman, writing about the gifts of the Holy Spirit, identifies some gifts that both were needed in the ancient church and are needed today and others that were only needed then. One of the gifts that are not needed today is the gift of prophecy:

> This gift enabled a person under divine inspiration to speak or to write God's words (Deut. 18:18; Heb. 1:1; 2 Peter 1:21).... Before the NT Scriptures were written and widely distributed, God made known His will and direction to the local churches through people with this prophetic gift (Acts 13:1–2; cp. Eph. 2:20). However, today there is no need for prophecy since the New Testament gives us all the divine revelation we need for Christian life and ministry at this time (2 Tim. 3:16–17; cp. Rev. 22:18–19).[3]

The end-argument has been used throughout the centuries to repudiate alleged prophetic revelations. A recent example is that of the late head of the

Greek Orthodox Church in Switzerland, Metropolitan Damaskinos, who, prior to
the scheduled January 1996 meeting in Geneva with Vassula Rydén, denounced
the same meeting through an official communiqué that contained the following statement:

> At least in the eyes of all those who are regarded as the authentic
> carriers and continuators of the tradition of the Orthodox Church,
> Mrs. Vassula Rydén opposes this Church's through the centu-
> ries, an oral and written conscience according to which the Divine
> revelation was once and for all completed with the Apostles.[4]

As mentioned earlier, Vassula Rydén is known as one of few modern Orthodox writers to allow to the successor of Peter a vital role in safeguarding the
unity of the church. It is this position that the metropolitan opposes, affirming
that it is contrary to Orthodox doctrine, which alone is the true expression of
revelation as transmitted by the apostles.

Since this idea of an end of revelation with the last apostle has been proposed and so often and insistently used to repudiate prophecy, especially in less
academic forums, a review of this idea will help to better articulate its meaning and purpose. Indeed the application of this idea in the aforementioned
antiprophetic way hampers vital Christian principles.

The purpose of this discussion is not merely to disarm one of the most
important weapons against Christian prophecy and the object of this book.
There are other interests at stake. First, treating the end-issue will prove that
it *does* make theological sense to accept Christian prophecy as a vital, *almost
inherent/constitutive*, feature of the Christian religion. Second, it will positively
serve to elucidate the status and task of prophecy in the church: how prophecy
is important *in keeping the tradition of the ever-living Logos alive*, interpreting the
Signs of the Times in God's light. And third, it will shed new light on the category of revelation, opposing some of the negative residues of neo-Scholastic
doctrinal tendencies. The treatment of the maxim of the apostolic end of revelation is like a hinge on which turn all other subsequent issues that regard
revelation and its actualization through prophecy; it serves as an archimedic
point that removes from obscurity topics that are important to prophecy.

5.1. Historical Overview of the "Apostolic End of Revelation"

The idea of an *end of revelation with the last apostle* is no new concept. It has
roots in certain patristic writings, and was echoed in various meanings and in-
tensity throughout the history of theology. However, paired with the portrayed

propositional approach to revelation, it received its most systematical expressions in the Catholic disputes with modernist theology that considered revelation an inherently open and undefined process, whence it influenced some Catholic theologians all the way up to the Second Vatican Council; it entered Catholic thinking and often lost its orthodox orientation, to such an extent that the term "end" became a far more radical and far-reaching concept than originally intended. By this means the idea of revelation's end became one of the primary reasons for theological concerns regarding the notion of Christian prophecy.

The Second Vatican Council's constitution *Dei Verbum*, along with theologians such as Joseph Ratzinger, Karl Rahner, and Hans Urs von Balthasar, somewhat differentiated the approach to revelation, thus avoiding the downfalls of the mere propositional approach and safeguarding its legitimate motives. While safeguarding the main concerns inherent to the end-notion, Vatican II contains many passages that clearly indicate that revelation refers to God's communication of his own self to the church, that is, Christ's continuous gift to the church of his own self in the Holy Spirit and through the Eucharist. At the same time the Council manages to maintain the cognitive aspects of revelation.

In order to fully appreciate the origins and developments of the idea of "the apostolic end of revelation," a historic overview of this term will be useful.[5] Here it will become clear that the origins of the term and its meaning, often identified with the literal end to God's revealing activity, initially had a quite different significance from what they have often come to signify today. The nineteenth-century use of the word "end" in actual fact is a very unfortunate rendering of the Latin *compleo*, which does not mean *end* but *complete*. One cannot underestimate the value of this distinction in terms, whose far-reaching effects have influenced theology to this day. We shall look at the emergence and development of this term and notion and see what it signified during the centuries. The historical treatment of the concept will shed light on prophecy's place in relation to the actualization of the revelation in Christ. This treatment will enable us to draw conclusions about the relationship between revelation and prophecy, which is the only valid approach that arrives at a comprehensive synthesis of the purpose of prophecy in the church.

5.1.1. Early Church

The church Fathers of the first two centuries knew nothing of an *end* of revelation and wrote only little on its *completion*. They were more interested in highlighting the fact that Christ had promised he would come again, and they awaited Creation's full participation in the fullness of God revealed in Christ.

The Fathers made no sharp distinction between themselves and the apostles, and they did not clearly separate between apostolic and postapostolic heritage. *Hence, in its origin, the transition from the normative constitution of the apostolic heritage to its tradition was subtle.*

This does not mean that they showed no interest in the criteria of true revelation. Clement of Rome, Ignatius of Antioch, pseudo-Barnabas, and Polycarp of Smyrna saw a difference between themselves and the apostles. These authors regarded the apostles as the immediate and therefore particularly authoritative witnesses of Christ and of the Gospel, and this heritage had to be kept pure. At this moment in history, the Deposit of Faith had not yet received its authoritative expression in Holy Scripture, as the Christian canon was only formed in the middle of the second century; only after the Council of Nicaea in 325 did theologians begin using the concept "canon." Even so, the aforementioned patristic authors heralded an authoritative and universally valid truth, inherited from the apostles, which, in its substance, equals the fullness of God revealed in Christ although received normatively in the testimony of the apostles. Hence there was from the beginning a close relationship between the revelation in Christ and its authoritative apostolic testimony.

Even though there is a fundamental difference between Christ and the apostles, the Fathers nevertheless highlight the testimony of the apostles as being inherently related to the Christ-event itself, and this because they were the authoritative witnesses of Christ, whose revelation of the truth would have been fruitless without them. Hermas the Shepherd, which we examined earlier (see section 3.3.12), continues this tradition and speaks of the believers who faithfully keep the proclamation of the apostles. He is not just interested in any given Christ-tradition, but in the specific preaching of the apostles.[6]

Justin so closely relates Christ and the apostolic testimony that he was able to say that Christians receive the teaching of Christ and the apostles, thus presenting their teachings as a synthetic whole that comprises the constitutive elements of the true faith.[7]

As Dulles shows, these are the basic opinions that continued echoing through the thought of the ancient church, especially when threatened by heresies that sought to place other sources of revelation alongside those of Christ and his first witnesses.[8] As shown earlier (see chapter 3), it was in this period of church history that the complex transition occurred from charismatic, vertical authority to more historic, horizontal authority. It was by the threat of heresies that the church moved to historically founded authoritative traditions whose purity the institution was to safeguard, and this led subsequent Christian thinkers to reflect even more on the normativity of the apostolic testimony of Christ.

In Irenaeus's writings we find a very complete teaching of the divine revelation and its tradition, which, according to G. Blum, became programmatic for all subsequent understanding of revelation and ecclesiology.[9] And since Irenaeus had especial influence on Catholic revelation theology, more needs to be said of his teaching and ideas. Irenaeus consolidated the idea of Christ being the fullness of God's revelation, seeing Christ's teaching as complete, since he as the Word revealed God's truth completely.[10] The revelation in Christ cannot be outdone, for there can be no more complete revelation of God than the Incarnation of the Word. Schumacher summarizes Irenaeus's thought as follows: "The novelty of the Incarnation consists in the eternal Word's salvific visibility, which cannot be transcended and which through its becoming man in this world has brought the fullness of all revelation."[11]

It is this fullness of revelation that the faithful meet in the *traditio apostolorum*.[12] The Gospel is given through the apostolic proclamation occurring in Holy Scripture and the παράδοσις of the apostles.[13] Thus Irenaeus strongly connects the divine fullness of Christ with its expression through apostolic witnessing, and sees the church as heir and carrier of the apostolic heritage.

Irenaeus expresses an understanding of revelation that is far removed from the mere propositional approach to revelation. The apostolic heritage cannot be reduced to the level of doctrine but is rather seen as a living and dynamic reality that reflects and expounds God's fullness. And yet Irenaeus is able to affirm that the fullness of revelation is expressed in the proclamation of the church. The main corpus of the canon was confirmed later but existed already at the time of Irenaeus. However, with *proclamation of the church* he suggests the living teaching of the church, originating with the apostles and transcending the mere word of Scripture.[14] Therefore, there must be something *more* than the written or orally repeated words of the apostles that secures the unity between the Deposit of Faith and its actualization in the church, and Irenaeus identifies it as the succession of bishops from the apostles.[15]

Irenaeus's teaching contains all the key elements of later Catholic revelation theology and ecclesiology. He never affirms that the reality received by the apostles is confined to or ended in limited pronouncements, as it expounds the limitless fullness of God. Their tradition and teaching is *normative* but not *ended*. It is a guideline for the church to discern between true and false teaching, but not a limited corpus of facts. This is where Irenaeus, without directly mentioning prophecy, sheds light on its place in the church: the apostolic heritage is given to the church as to a treasury. The apostles' teaching is normative for the proclamation of the church, which, in turn, discovers its roots in the historical succession of bishops that guarantees the apostolic heritage. But this guarantee does not reduce the apostolic heritage to predefined doctrine; it confirms the dynamic reality or mystery of Christ's presence in the church. Even though Irenaeus presents the episcopal succession as a guarantee for the right teaching of the church, it always remains in need of prophetic inspiration in order to realize the life of the Logos in the world. Hence the guarantee that Irenaeus presents can be named a *prophetic guarantee* that rests on God's continued activity and care for the church throughout history.

Irenaeus confers special authority on those churches that historically stem directly from one of the apostles,[16] and this is where Irenaeus touches on yet another primordial Catholic principle: the most important of the apostolic churches is the one of Rome, founded by Peter and Paul.[17] In this way, Irenaeus manages to combine clearly defined and concrete historical persons and geographical places with completely nonconcrete realities such as the dynamic presence of God's truth in the church. He combines and intertwines vertical and horizontal, and builds, from charismatic and historical bricks, the mystery of the church. The church depends on the episcopal, apostolic succession in order to secure and announce the apostolic teaching through the ages, and the genuine form of handing down revelation depends on a historical reality, namely the unbroken historical continuity of the bishops. But this is not enough, as the church also depends on Christ's continuous immediate presence, lest the apostolic heritage devolve into a mere repetition of correct teachings, and so that it may evolve into a dynamic and relevant actualization of the life of God to peoples of all places and all ages.

According to Schumacher, most Fathers after Justin and Irenaeus continued their thoughts,[18] affirming that (1) Christ is the absolute revelation of God, (2) the apostolic testimony is the normative propagation of Christ's truth, and (3) the church is the continuation and home of this dynamic heritage until the end of times. It is this tripartition that is at the heart at a balanced understanding of prophecy's place and function in the church, for the idea of the fulfillment of revelation in Christ and its continuation and actualization is both historical and transcendent, just as prophecy itself is. Justin and Irenaeus shed light on a very important fact of Christian prophecy: prophecy must be prophecy *of* and *for* the church at the same time, since the actualization of revelation, which is the purpose of prophecy, belongs not only to the task but also to the nature of the church. At this stage of the history of theology, no one talks of an end of revelation. Revelation is fully realized with Christ, and the apostolic testimony thereof is the norm of the church's teaching; but no church Father writes that it stops or ends after Christ.

On the contrary—as Peter Stockmeier has shown in reference to Portmann—the Cappadocian fathers, Gregory of Nyssa, Basil, and Gregory of Nazianz clearly testify that revelation *continues* to the Parousia.[19] Even though the apostles' teaching is normative, God continues to reveal himself in order to lead the church into the fullness of revelation. The teaching of these three fathers is very important to my topic: revelation has reached the climax in Christ and has been normatively witnessed by the apostles, but *continues* until the second coming of Christ. Stockmeier argues convincingly that revelation in the entire patristic period is not a finished process but a continuous possibility.[20]

Schumacher, whose aim it is to secure the idea of an end of revelation, interprets this pivotal patristic teaching by affirming that the Fathers profess the end of revelation implicitly in their teaching:

> The conclusion of public, generally obligating Revealing is not put in doubt by the fathers.... If the witnesses of the tradition do not expressly profess the conclusion and sufficiency of the revelation in Christ, they nevertheless do so indirectly by means of the contentwise completeness of the Deposit of Faith. It is not a question to them that the "revelations" do not transcend the revelation in Christ.[21]

Interpreting the term *end* as *fulfillment* justifies Schumacher's interpretation. The question is, however, whether applying the term *end* to the Fathers—a term the Fathers never used—is indeed adequate. The fact is that, while safeguarding the normativity of the apostolic testimony, the Fathers positively professed the continuation of revelation after Christ. Revelation remained from the New Testament all the way up to the Council of Trent an ambiguous concept of plural meanings. Schumacher is aware of this:

> The border between private revelations, first proclamation, the public, generally obliging revelation, the reception of revelation through faith, its subsequent elucidation and deepening through the workings of the Holy Spirit, or more simply the divine enlightenment that cooperates in each act of cognition, even purely natural cognition, is not drawn clearly. Each "effort in the life of the church toward truth and sanctity" could be conceived of as revelation.[22]

Joseph Ratzinger shows how early church and medieval theologians spoke of the Holy Spirit's continued realization of God's truth in history *as revelation* because they conceived of revelation on the basis of its formal aspects rather than its material.[23]

The thought of a fulfillment of revelation also grew in its different varieties through the conflict with heresies and cultures that threatened the normativity of the apostolic teaching. Thus Augustine, for instance, had to deal with the Montanist threat to ulterior revealed doctrine by offering the response that what Christ revealed through the prophets, himself, and the apostles was sufficient.[24] With questions of doubt regarding the interpretation of the apostolic heritage, the faithful should orient themselves according to the entire church's teaching.[25] Like Irenaeus, Augustine ascribes particular doctrinal authority to the Roman church.[26]

5.1.2. The Middle Ages

Joachim of Fiore proposed a tripartition of history that medieval theologians considered threatening to the normativity of the apostolic testimony.[27] Each of these three epochs is connected to each of the three persons of the Trinity. The first period is that of the Father, covering the old covenant. The second is that of the Son, extending from the Incarnation to a nondefined point in the history of the church, which Birgitta of Vadstena later believed herself to stand at the end of. The third period is that of the Holy Spirit, extending to the second coming of Christ. In this third period, revelation does not occur through images, words, or Sacraments but directly through an "intelligentia spiritualis," and man lives in a permanent and immediate revelation in God that, however, is no *new* revelation since it stems from the Incarnation. It may be on the grounds of this precision that the church never condemned Joachim's teaching. Only the spirituals and the *fraticelli* unfortunately interpreted the immediate experience of God in the third period as a revelation that transcends the revelation in Christ, and against these the church reacted insistently. One of the theological authorities who reacted against the spirituals was Thomas Aquinas. He stressed the time-limits of the fulfillment of the Deposit of Faith in his dispute with the spirituals. The Deposit of Faith is fulfilled in Christ, whereas the apostles' testimony of Christ is imbued with particular authority, and their faith is the norm for all later Christian faith.[28] Thomas considers revelation not only to be materially achieved but also sufficiently witnessed in Holy Scripture, whereby nothing can be said of God that Scripture does not contain explicitly or implicitly. He makes this statement while discussing the origin of the Holy Spirit:

> We ought not to say about God anything which is not found in Holy Scripture either explicitly or implicitly. But although we do not find it verbally expressed in Holy Scripture that the Holy Ghost proceeds from the Son, still we do find it in the sense of Scripture, especially where the Son says, speaking of the Holy Ghost, "He will glorify Me, because He shall receive of Mine" (Jn 16:14).[29]

Thus Thomas claims that the promulgation of new dogmas must always have a horizontal and historical origin, being well anchored in Scripture. It is this sufficiency of Scripture that the majority of theologians follow all the way to the Tridentine Council.

This does not mean, however, that new doctrinal formulations and achievements cannot have a vertical and charismatic *point de départ*, for there may be unclear points of doctrine with regard to Scripture's implicit content. Hence, while maintaining the sufficiency of Scripture, Thomas Aquinas acknowledges the need for a hermeneutic element of verification besides that of Scripture to determine whether a given doctrine belongs to the Deposit of Faith. Even though there are different proposals in the writings of Thomas and his contemporaries as to the nature of this extrascriptural principle, it is interesting to see how they often refer to prophetic revelations when determining whether a given doctrine is implicitly contained in Scripture or not. Thomas, Bonaventure, and other pre-Tridentine theologians often referred to sources of revelation outside of Sacred Scripture when discerning the truth of disputed *questiones* or doctrines. One could argue that among these sources there could be prophetic revelations, occurring after the death of the last apostle and after the closure of the Bible–a theory that, as we shall see, was taken up by theologians who followed this thread, especially William of Ockham and Gabriel Biel.

For instance, whether images could be the object of veneration or not is one of the most famous examples of questions that both Thomas[30] and Bonaventure[31] sought to answer by referring to traditions not explicitly found in Sacred Scripture. Another is whether or not the Holy Spirit proceeds both from the Father and from the Son, just as the question of the sacrament of confirmation was seen to have a poor basis in Scripture.[32]

Even though both Thomas and Bonaventure accepted sources beyond Sacred Scripture when determining the truth of revelation, they disagreed on one particular point. Thomas referred all doctrine to Christ, in contrast to Bonaventure, which becomes evident in the way they evaluated the institution of the sacrament of confirmation. Thomas believed this sacrament to have been instituted by Christ himself during his stay on earth, whereas Bonaventure believed it to proceed from Pentecost and hence was instituted by the Holy Spirit. Both use prophetic revelations as proof of the validity of the sacrament of confirmation; Thomas ascribes its institution to Christ, whereas Bonaventure ascribes it to the Holy Spirit.[33]

Bonaventure wrote that revelation continues after Christ. He believed that the formulations of new dogmas require a *revelatio* that, even if these dogmas may have roots in Scripture, are truly new creations and not just the interpretation or explication of something already existing. Bonaventure stresses the vertical element of the church's recognition of truth while maintaining the horizontal through the reference to Scripture. The knowledge that a new dogma expresses has its foundation in Scripture and is deepened ("profectum vel incrementum") through reason, but reaches its completion through revelation ("consummationem a revelatione").[34]

As Schumacher shows, many other medieval theologians follow Bonaventure's approach to revelation.[35] Sharpening the issue again toward the question of prophecy's place in the Christian context, one must ask what Bonaventure means by *revelatio*. Is he talking of a new revelation that materially exceeds the revelation in Christ or is it rather an inspired deepening of the knowledge of and entrance into the reality of the Incarnation? Everything points to the latter interpretation. Bonaventure and the majority of other medieval theologians are influenced by Augustine's illumination theory, claiming that cognition stems from a revelatory introduction to the eternal ideas (rationes aeternae). It is this process of participation in the mystery of faith that Bonaventure describes in his *Itinerarium mentis in Deum (Itin.)*, portraying the mystical way of gradual cognition of God, and Bonaventure refers to this as *revelatio*.[36]

It may be useful to summarize how the Fathers and medieval theologians contribute to the understanding of our topic. They used the term *revelatio* to refer to many different realities, united under the common denominator of the *disclosing of God's truth*. But these varying aspects separate into two groups: Christ's revelation of God and his salvation, and the actualization and realization of this salvation throughout history until the end of times. *From an objective point of view* the two must have the same essence, as there is but one God, and Christ revealed the same glory of God that the believer is introduced to through the workings of the Spirit. In this way the two aspects or forms are identical in essence but different in realization. The revelation in Christ and its transmission through the apostles is constitutive and normative. However, as Joseph Ratzinger argues,[37] Bonaventure and with him so many other medieval theologians present a dynamic approach to tradition, considering it to be more than the mere repetition of existing dogmatic formulations. Tradition and the ongoing process of cognition through history imply and cannot be conceived without the continued revelatory activity of the Holy Spirit. Even if new dogmas are rooted in the complete revelation of Christ, normatively witnessed in Holy Scripture that forms the explicit or implicit cognitive foundation of the new dogma, this still does not occur without God's revealing activity in history. *The foundation of revelation and its realization are too closely related not to call both revelation.* Thus, the idea of *revelation's apostolic end* constitutes a perspective that is too narrowly defined in order to be compatible with medieval theology.

Thomas, Bonaventure, and with them the majority of medieval theologians taught that Scripture implicitly contains all that had to be known about salvation. There were, however, also those who believed in a possible later revelation, transcending Holy Scripture *and tradition*. William of Ockham and Gabriel Biel proposed such a view. In addition to Scripture and tradition as sources for revelation, Ockham names the possibility of later "revelatio vel inspiratio nova divina."[38] Although he does not present historical evidence that further revelation could have functioned as evidence in the argumentation against heresies, he does not consider it impossible that God would grant such revelation. He believes that the doctrine of transubstantiation possibly originates in such a new revelation, since Scripture makes no mention thereof, the Fathers of the church followed a different theological thread, and the doctrine of coexistence would have been more logical.[39]

Ockham is aware that faith in new revelations opens the door to random subjectivity; this is why he demands that the truth of such revelations should be measured against Scripture and the experience of the church.[40] In addition, Gabriel Biel accepts those truths that flow from revelations that God gives to his faithful.[41] Paradoxically, Ockham and Biel in some parts of their writings affirm the sufficiency of the apostolic testimony, be it oral or written, yet in other parts, they highlight the significance of postapostolic revelations. Pierre-Réginald Cren believes that they do so in order to secure the freedom and omnipotence of God. Thus, Ockham writes that "God, if he so wishes, is able to reveal or inspire many new catholic truths."[42]

Likewise, Heinrich Totting von Oyta wrote on "sources, from which the truth of faith flows and of which no Christian should be doubting," as truths that were known through postapostolic revelations and inspirations. These, he affirms, would also be possible in the future.[43]

Even Jean Gerson taught the possibility of postapostolic revelation. Next to Scripture and tradition, he introduced a third locus of truths—the "veritates specialiter aliquibus revelatae."[44] However, only those who received the revelations are obliged to believe in the truth they express, unless miracles, Sacred Scripture, or the conviction of the church affirms them as part of God's truth.[45] He does not consider these to transcend Scripture and tradition, but still his distinction is interesting insofar as he admits that prophetic revelations constitute the source of knowledge of aspects of revelation not explicitly contained in Scripture or in tradition. In this way he connects prophetic revelations and revelation's historical cognition and realization more intimately than many other theologians do.

The examination of the perspectives of the church Fathers and medieval theologians on revelation does not result in one uniform theory. On the contrary, it serves to distinguish the various aspects of the category of revelation that are often left uncoordinated and identified as synonymous, whereas they in actual fact embrace different aspects of the category of revelation. As it has become clear, these theologians actually *never* speak of an end of revelation. They consider Christ to be the summit of revelation, and all later revelatory occurrences never exceed the revelation realized in the Incarnation. However, the important issue is to assess where the transmission of that revelation takes place in the life of the church. The apostles are seen as the normative testimonies of this revelation, but the theologians I have discussed here are very open to the possibility of new prophetic revelation that brings forth aspects of God's truth that have not been actualized or realized historically before.

5.1.3. *The Council of Trent*

The Council of Trent confirmed the plenitude of God's manifestation in Christ but never called it *revelatio*. Just as theologians before the Council never speak of revelation's end, the Council Fathers sought in their polemics against the reformers to assess the formal principle of revelation, that is, the normative criteria of revelation's doctrinal content, contained in Scripture (*libris scriptis*) and in unwritten traditions (*sine scripto traditionibus*).[46] The Council obviously opposes the reformers' *sola-scriptura* principle and affirms the apostolic tradition through the church as the normative teaching principle besides Scripture. Luther used *Scripture alone* as proof for his interpretation of the Christian faith and especially to reject many of the postbiblical traditions that he dismissed as nonbiblical, and it is precisely this argument that the Council sought to refute. Scripture and tradition stem from the proclamation of Christ and from the apostolic witness *as well as* from the revelations that the Holy Spirit conferred directly on the apostles ("ab ipsis Apostolis Spiritu Sancto dictante"). This sentence is very important to our issue, as it proposes an idea of tradition according to which the constitutive completion of the Deposit of Faith occurs not only through Christ speaking to the apostles but also, transcending both, through a direct revelation to the apostles through the Holy Spirit. If Christ lays the foundation of the Deposit of Faith, the apostles receive revelations that the church hands down through history. By this means, the apostles are not only witnesses to Christ, but they themselves transmit to the church the constitutive revelation through the Holy Spirit. Whereas Christ had mainly been seen as the revealer and the apostles as the witnesses of this revelation, the Tridentine Council confirmed another tradition that sees not only Christ but also the apostles as the normative revealers of God's truth that the church is to forward through time. In point of fact, not one of the Council documents speaks of an end of revelation.

Hence the Council of Trent is very important to the theology of revelation, as it opened up important issues to be discussed by the theologians to follow. The most important of these may be the question of Scripture's sufficiency. The initial documents regarding the question of Scripture and tradition use the terms "partim in scriptura, partim in traditione" (partly in Scripture, partly in tradition), clearly indicating Scripture and tradition as two independent sources of revelation. This wording was changed in the final document to the more open but also ambiguous "et in scriptura, et in traditione" (both in Scripture and in tradition).[47] The first version affirmed positively that revelation has two separate sources and that each in principle could produce independent insights into doctrine, whereas the second version leaves this question open, stating only that both sources serve the one truth.[48]

Second, the Council defined a constitutive element of revelation beyond Christ through direct revelations by the Holy Ghost to the apostles. This made it necessary to assess whether this ulterior constitutive revelation continues or has an end, and here lies the foundation for the later affirmation of an "end of revelation."[49] If it is possible that the constitutive revelation has a moment of fulfillment beyond Christ, then it is vital to determine *when* this possibility ends in order to avoid evolutionism.

It is easy to discern reactions to issues raised by the reformers in the time following the Tridentine Council. Luther had rejected tradition as a source of revelation next to Scripture. Even if Vatican I left the question of Scripture's sufficiency open (by the aforementioned "et . . . et"), the post-Tridentine Catholic theologians developed the concept of revelation's two sources. A number of Catholic theologians in the twentieth century,[50] especially Joseph Geiselmann,[51] criticized this tendency and argued that it was not well rooted in the documents of the Council. Others have proposed the opposite view and considered the post-Tridentine theologians correct in their interpretation of Trent.[52] Whichever the correct interpretation may be, the notion was nevertheless so prevalent in the time after the Council of Trent that it became incumbent upon post-Tridentine theologians to define certain expressions of this source of revelation running parallel to Scripture and to point out what did indeed belong to revelation and what did not. The conviction of tradition's true revelatory capacity is of no use if it is not clear what it contains.

Earlier I observed that some pre-Tridentine theologians were convinced that God provided prophetic revelations to illuminate theologians on doctrinal issues that did not occur explicitly in Scripture. After the Council this changed, and theologians generally ceased to consider prophetic revelations as criteria for revelation. One such theologian was Melchior Cano.

5.1.4. *Melchior Cano*

Melchior Cano's work *De locis theologicis* is for several reasons of primary importance to the subject of Christian prophecy. This is due primarily to the fact that this work is "the premier methodological treatise of modern Catholic theology"[53] and has thus influenced later Catholic thought immensely.[54] Cano's work is of importance also because, second, his theological activity mainly assesses the guidelines whereby the church and theologians may recognize and verify what is true apostolic teaching, and, third, because he denies prophetic revelations a place in the process of revelation.

Cano works with the question of how the church comes to the knowledge of true revelation. He sees revelation actualized in different *loci*, which are "the 'domiciles' of all those elements with which one carries on theological argumentation."[55]

Cano's first two loci are Scripture and tradition. He understands tradition as "the complex of those apostolic traditions coming from Christ or the Holy Spirit's instruction of the apostles, which have proved to belong to the perennial doctrinal patrimony."[56] Following the Council of Trent, he understands these as a source of unwritten traditions ("sine scripto traditionibus"), existing next to Scripture as the expression of revelation. The instances that serve to interpret, protect, and actualize these two main sources of God's self-attestation may be found in the following five *loci*. They are:

The common faith of all believers
Synods and councils
The Roman church and its shepherds
The Fathers of the church
The Scholastic theologians

Cano adds three additional loci to the five "main dwelling places of theological evidence."[57] He calls the following three loci "annexes," although they have their own particular contribution to make:

Natural reason
The work of philosophers
The teaching one can draw from the course of history

With these three ulterior loci, Cano has actually completed his own system. But when inquiring about our specific topic, one could rightly ask, what has become of prophecy? What happened to the prophetic revelations that medieval theologians assessed as important signs of the theological truths and that thus comprise genuine loci theologici? The answer appears to be: nowhere! Cano's writings thus constitute one of the most complete and systematic disregardings of prophetic revelation's role in the actualization of revelation in all of its aspects. Cano does not count prophetic revelations among any of the five loci, much less among the annexed loci. In Laurentin's words, prophetic revelations are to Cano "a theological nonlocus."[58] One can argue that although Cano does not list prophetic revelations as a locus theologicus, it could be indirectly incorporated in the notion of the people of God, as it is usually here that God employs his liberty to diffuse charisms and graces. Cano makes it very clear, however, that this is not what he means when he clearly affirms that prophetic revelations, in his vocabulary named *private*, play no role with regards to revelation's actualization: "fides de qua hic sermo fit, non est privata virtus, sed communis . . . quo circa privatæ revelationes, cuiusmodicunque et quorumcunque illæ sint, ad fidem catholicam non spectant, nec ad fundamentum et principia ecclesiasticæ doctrinæ quæ vera germanaque Theologia est."[59]

Because of Cano's insistence that prophetic revelations are merely private, it is not strange that he denies the significance for faith of prophets like Birgitta of Vadstena, even when recognized by the church: "It matters little whether or not one believes in St. Birgitta's revelations or those of other saints; these things have nothing to do with faith."[60]

In "Die ekklesiologische Bedeutung des Systems der 'Loci Theologici,'" Max Seckler investigates Cano and his theological system from a new perspective.[61] In light of a dynamic understanding of revelation, Seckler argues that in fact Cano did *not* propose a mere doctrinal approach to revelation. Seckler demonstrates how Cano understands each proposed locus not as a fossilized expression of Christ's truth, or as a mere instance that actualizes revelation by the mere reception of the message of the apostles. Seckler asserts that Cano considered the loci to be dynamic expressions of God's transcendent truth that can never be pinned down to finished sentences or ecclesial structures. Hence they are in constant need of the inspiration of God in order truly to be what they are—loci theologici.

While these considerations provide an interesting new perspective of Cano, they do not answer the question why prophecy occupies no place in his theological system, given the importance prophecy plays in the actualization of revelation. Rather, Seckler's results enhance this mystery! If it is true that Cano's system has prophetic features, it should have made it all the more easy and natural for him to incorporate the prophetic in his thought, but this did not happen.

As mentioned earlier, even though the Reformation was no directly prophetic phenomenon, it caused the post-Reformation Catholic theology, and

Cano in particular, to limit as much as possible any instance that might develop into movements in the church, such as the Reformation. Since prophecy has always been marked precisely as the inspired and dynamic interpretation and implementation of the Christian truth in the church, it is no wonder that Cano and others with him fought prophecy methodologically.

Instead of emphasizing prophecy's place within the church, Seckler's findings show how damaging Cano's system was to Christian prophecy. If the permanent loci listed by Cano were mere historical traditions and horizontal realizations of revelation, then there would be dire need for specific prophecy. But instead Cano incorporates the prophetic charism in the permanent, easily controllable loci of the church, and this renders classical prophetic revelations unnecessary. If the prophetic charism is bound up in the permanent structures of the church, then there is no need for free individual prophecy. After Cano, little is written on the positive connection between prophetic revelations and matters of doctrine. The idea that the knowledge of revelation can be inspired by prophetic revelations is generally abandoned.

As we have seen, the Fathers of the church and the majority of medieval theologians knew and professed the notion of the fulfillment of revelation in Christ. The Tridentine Council strengthened the foundation of the idea of an apostolic end of revelation by holding that revelation occurred through Christ *as well as* through the apostles by means of direct revelation from the Holy Spirit; if revelation continued after Christ, it had to be reiterated when it ended! Nevertheless, until Melchior Cano, prophecy had at the same time continued to play an important role with regard to the cognition of the Deposit of Faith. In point of fact, the Council of Trent states that it is impossible to know whether one is saved by any other means than *special revelations*.[62] Even this understanding of prophecy's importance to tradition was questioned with Cano, and this assessment influenced theology immensely henceforth.

This notwithstanding, the explicit shift from the nomenclature "fulfillment" to the "end" of revelation did not occur in the history of theology until the end of the nineteenth century. The most important motives for this shift appear to be the renewed danger to the normativity of the apostolic testimony, this time brought about through rationalism. Earlier in history, such attacks had been fought against by pointing to the fulfillment of God's revelation in Christ and its normative apostolic testimony. Now more powerful weapons were needed, and the counterattack was revelation's "end"! A change in the understanding of revelation took place, in which the propositional approach began to dominate theological landscape. This led the "end of revelation"–idea to its radical consequences.

5.1.5. The Threat to the Normativity of Revelation

The new rationalistic and evolutionist ideas of revelation emerging with the Enlightenment provided perhaps the most important threat to revelation's fulfillment with Christ and the apostles. Modernism continued this tradition, leading to an evolutionist view of dogma according to which new formulations not only explicate nonexposed aspects of tradition, but create something substantially new, which Schumacher expresses as a "negation of the end of revelation, if it is possible at all here to speak of revelation. In this view, dogmas disappear and entirely new ones appear in their place."[63] Alfred Loisy was one of the main fathers of modernism. Contending that Christianity has no immutable essence, he considered its truth to be evolving, relative, and progressive. René Latourelle summarizes Loisy's understanding of revelation as follows: "To sum up, for Loisy, revelation is not a doctrine offered to our faith or an unchanging deposit of truths, but rather an intuitive and experimental perception, always in development (always becoming), of our relationship with God. Revelation, like dogma and theology, always evolves; it is always becoming."[64] But theology opposed evolutionary revelation theories like these by powerfully employing the notion of revelation's fulfillment with Christ and the apostles. And it was only at this point that the term *end* emerged. Of particular interest is the decree *Lamentabili sane exitu* by "the Holy Office", today's Vatican "Congregation for the Doctrine of Faith". Stressing the completion of revelation, this decree addresses many modernist issues, rejecting in particular thoughts that Alfred Firmin Loisy proposed in *L'Évangile et l'Église* (1902)[65] and *Autour d'un Petit Livre* (1903).[66] Thus the twenty-first thesis of the decree reads: "Revelatio, obiectum fidei catholicae constituens, non fuit cum Apostolis completa." [67] The decree contains several similar expressions. Obviously, *completa* need not be understood as *ended,* but rather as *complete,* and in this sense the decree changed nothing from earlier discourse on revelation's climax and fulfillment with Christ and his apostles. Still, Schumacher believes that this sentence determined twentieth-century explicit and little-nuanced teaching on the *end of revelation.*[68] This was fuelled by the changed understanding of revelation mentioned earlier (see 4.3.2). As a result, revelation theology turned ever more propositional, viewing revelation more as true sentences than as God's historical activity. Only in the context of nineteenth-century doctrinal approaches to revelation did the nomenclature change from the aforementioned *complete* ("Lamentabili sane exitu") to the problematic *ended.* This change in revelation theology was accompanied by a new understanding of the very concept of *revelation.* Where the term designated both revelation's material fulfillment in Christ *and* revelation's formal actualization, explication, and reception in the life of the church, the material aspects of revelation now became predominant. As Schumacher demonstrates, German dogmatic works especially began using this terminology to secure revelation's fulfillment.[69] He demonstrates that this change began gradually and snowballed to the point where it had become a dominant term. Most of the works were rather careful, though, to explain what the concept means, namely that revelation is fulfilled only materially and that Christ still manifests himself during history, and that formally revelation must always be received anew. Hence this terminology was a new, many would say more radical, way of expressing the old thought that Christ's revelation of God is perfect, and that the apostolic testimony is the norm of faith and of how this faith can or cannot mature through time.[70] One of the theologians who worked most intensely with the idea of *revelation's end* was J. M. Scheeben, a representative of neo-Scholastic theology. He continued the tradition from the Council of Trent, while focusing on the material aspects of revelation, and contending that God conferred his revelation directly to the apostles not only through his Incarnation in Christ, but by the power of the Holy Spirit: "Divine revelation is, although destined for all humans in all places and times, nevertheless not accessible to all; in Christ and the apostles it is *ended [abgeschlossen]*."[71]

Having affirmed the normative constitution of revelation with the last apostle, the question now is whether its formal testimony in Scripture and tradition is exhaustive, and Scheeben's answer to this question is *no!* As we saw, revelations obtained no place in Cano's loci. Scheeben, however, is open to their admission when assessing prophetic revelations and the means by which constitutive revelation finds its formal expression. God continues addressing himself to people, but no longer in a constitutive manner. From an *objective* point of view, God's later revelations add nothing, although from a *subjective* standard, they may very well explicate unexposed aspects of the Deposit of Faith. This may include issues that have already been proposed as "Offenbarungsgut," or it may be something new, as opposed to what has already been formulated. This is where Scheeben addresses prophetic revelations: they can bring forth aspects of revelation that the church has never proclaimed. While these divine revelations may be tremendously important, they do not have universal value, leading merely "with moral and historical certainty to more or less general acknowledgment."[72] Only if the Magisterium receives the new idea, expressed through the prophetic revelation, and officially proclaims it as part of the Deposit of Faith will it become *official* in its character. In this way, private revelation can help to bring forth important new aspects of public revelation. Scheeben believes this is the case with new spiritual traditions such as that of the Sacred Heart and the feast of Corpus Christi.[73] Later on, we shall reaffirm this assessment when adding other examples, such as the tradition of the divine mercy, initiated through the revelations of Saint Faustina Kowalska, who was canonized in April 2000, as well as such new doctrinal formulations as the immaculate conception and Mary's Assumption into Heaven.

It is interesting to note that Scheeben, who does call prophetic revelations "private," in contrast to the Deposit of Faith, allows prophecy to play a great role in the actualization of revelation. Normally, theologians like Cano are very reluctant to affirm a link between prophecy and dogma, and the term *private* has been used as a weapon against prophecy. But although Scheeben so readily employed the distinction between public and private, he puts great emphasis on the importance of *private* revelations, ascribing to them the inspiration for the formulation of new dogmas.

5.1.6. *Vatican Council II*

Last in the presentation of the emergence and development of the notion of an "apostolic end of revelation" we shall look at the Second Vatican Council, which treated revelation theology profoundly in the constitution *Dei Verbum*. As Rahner shows, the Council did *not* reflect on a historical, apostolic *end* of revelation at all.[74] The making of *Dei Verbum* entailed an intense debate on terminology that ended with Vatican II's Doctrinal Commission refusing, twice in fact, to include in the final document any reference to revelation being "closed" with the apostles.[75] Rather, the Council affirmed revelation's fulfillment in Christ: "Jesus Christus ... opus salutare *consummat*"; and elsewhere: "Ipse ... revelationem *complendo perficit*." All three terms—*consummo* (to bring about, accomplish, complete), *compleo* (complete, fulfil), and *perficio* (bring to completion)—point to revelation's fulfillment or perfection rather than to its end. Christ's revelation of God is so perfect that it cannot be matched until the end of times ("Œconomia ergo christiana ... numquam praeteribit"). The constitution states that the apostles received revelation from Christ *and* the Holy Spirit, hence proposing the idea that the constitutive revelation continues after Christ; and there are no explicit indications as to *when* this should end. As Schumacher indicates, in theory it is possible to interpret the constitution to *imply* an end to revelation after the apostles, in virtue of article 9, which discerns between the ministry of the apostles and that of the bishops. This designation marks a distinction between the "constitution of the deposit through the apostles and its interpretation through the authority of the Teaching Office." [76] But again, this does not indicate an actual end to revelation, but an end to revelation's constitution in the church.

The reason the Council does not employ the term "end" may come from the growing concern in Catholic theology by the mid–twentieth century about the misinterpretation of revelation as doctrine only. As stated earlier, the notion of an *end* of revelation may be correctly understood only within the framework of the propositional understanding of revelation, which emphasizes revelation's apostolic constitution over its subsequent transmission. The growing historical and personalistic appreciation of revelation that was visible in the documents of Vatican II highlighting God's communication of himself to the church complicated the "end" idea even more. After all, it is evident that God continues to give himself to humankind, even though revelation may have reached its zenith in Christ and in the normative testimony that is contained in Scripture and in tradition. This diversified notion comes through clearly in the final document, especially in chapters 8, 21, and 25—that is, that revelation has reached its expressive summit in Jesus, but one that constitutes an ever-present actuality.

5.1.7. *Conclusion*

As mentioned earlier, the church Fathers and medieval theologians employed the term *revelatio* in different ways, indicating primarily the supernatural cognition of divine mysteries and man's growing knowledge of and union with God. They stressed revelation's formal realization in the life of the church rather than its material fulfillment in Christ, which explains the multiplicity of their terminology. When viewed in the patristic and medieval context, prophecy occupies a very important role in the life of the church, making it one of the most direct ways by which God realizes revelation and leads the church into the fullness of Christ's life.

Only after the Reformation that shocked the established church was revelation theology restricted in many of its expressions, as if to avoid future developments of the reformers' doctrine. Melchior Cano's preoccupation with limiting the actualization of revelation to controllable sources (loci) is the primary example of this tendency, which effectuated a situation in which prophecy and prophetic revelations were, if not eradicated, assigned a minuscule place in the church's recognition of the truth. It was not until Vatican II that this restriction was revisited and removed, as it were, thereby stressing once again the role of the laity as well as the importance of charismatic, prophetic impulses in the church.

5.2. The Unfruitfulness of the Term "End"

Joseph Schumacher's book *Der apostolische Abschluss der Offenbarung Gottes* is the most important work investigating this question. He devotes 325 pages to the argument that the notion "end" should indeed be maintained. He goes about proving his point through an exhaustive process of clear and precise definitions on what "end" means and, more important, what "end" does not mean, thus clarifying the misuse of the term and its potential future misusages:

> The term "end" gives indeed support to a linguistic misunderstanding in which revelation is understood primarily as teachings. If one speaks of the abundance or the completion of revelation, then the danger of restricting revelation to its word dimension is less compelling.[77]

Others have placed the maxim of the apostolic end of revelation in a more critical light than does Schumacher, who provides it with little more than a bearable interpretation. The most important critics are Karl Rahner, Joseph Ratzinger, and Hans Urs von Balthasar.

For Rahner, the notion causes serious problems, mainly by colliding with modern man, who more and more understands himself as having "existence in history...that is limitless [and] open." Instead of referring to an end of revelation, he refers to "the irreversible and victorious self-promise of God to the world in the Christ-event...which does not close but opens itself into an eternal future."[78] Christ reveals himself in order to establish an open relationship between God and man, initiating the powerful opening of a vital process, not its closure:

> Furthermore, the "conclusion" of revelation ("since the death of the Apostles") must not be misunderstood so as to signify that God thereafter, differently from before, assumes a rejecting and silent relationship to individual and collective history. This "conclusion" means that the Christ-event cannot be overruled and that it has lasting and normative character, and that the same Christ-event continues to drive new proofs of the Spirit into the church.[79]

Hans Urs von Balthasar writes along the same lines as Rahner. Christ is the fulfillment of God's glory, and this plenitude has no end:

> One would do better to avoid the word "conclusion," as not an adequate term for Christianity. The reached abundance is not a conclusion, much rather [is] a beginning. [It is] the beginning of the infinite working [Auswirkung] of the abundance of Christ into the abundance of the church, the growth of church and world into the abundance of Christ and God, as the letter to the Ephesians describes it.[80]

Balthasar affirms that the Holy Spirit continues working through the Christian prophets,[81] and, like Paul, he sees the apostles along with the prophets as the foundations of the church.[82]

To Joseph Ratzinger, it is clear that Christ is the plenitude of revelation and that this full revelation is conferred in all times. Yet Ratzinger also believes that talking of an end of revelation is unfruitful. Christ is not only a figure of the past but a power of the present, as "the one who is to come." Insistence on the "end of revelation" causes the faithful to misunderstand true Christianity, considering it an account of something that happened 2000 years ago, thus ignoring what can rightly be said to be the basis of Christianity, namely that God continues his revealing activity in the church.[83] The Fathers spoke much more of God's continued revelatory activity in the church than of revelation's fulfillment in Christ, even though they never entirely dismissed it. Likewise, Ratzinger mentions medieval theologians on whom the Holy Spirit conferred revelations "through which the Church penetrates perceptions to which it formerly had no access."[84] Joseph Ratzinger points to a distinction and difference between the Incarnation and later revelatory actions. This notwithstanding, many theologians interpret prophetic revelation merely as revelation's actualization. Ratzinger nonetheless contends that early church and medieval theologians considered God's revelation in Christ and his continued revelatory guidance of Christianity to be much too closely linked to constitute separate realities. He sees Scripture and tradition as lasting norms for the explication of revelation, but these cannot signify a "closing and closed quantity of fixed revelatory sentences . . . but rather constitute a formative norm for the always remaining ongoing history of faith."[85]

Moreover, René Laurentin, who has written extensively on prophecy from the perspective of apparitions in the church, has criticized the notion of the end of revelation. Much like the aforementioned authors, Laurentin places the "end" notion in the context of a narrow-minded, orthodox, and dogmatic understanding of revelation that fails to see Christ as the Risen One. God's revelation consists not only in true statements, "independent, speculative information, but also [in] the expression of this gift: the Agapè, that is, the God-Love, who gives himself to man in order to be all in all."[86] This gift of God is directed not only toward man's intelligence, but to the praxis of faith, "not as though all was done, but rather that much still has to occur."[87] Revelation today is understood far less speculatively and more practically and existentially. Instead of referring to true statements, Laurentin hence prefers to refer to a "'light' that 'makes truth' in lives. The biblical revelation itself comes across, not like the communication of images and radically new concepts, but as an enlightenment that transfigures the cultural circumstances and gives them a new meaning in reference to the saving God."[88]

In other words, although from a theological perspective revelation reached its zenith and ultimate fulfillment in Christ, on the phenomenological and psychological level it is identical with the prophetic tradition of Israel: "The process of revelation is the same for biblical prophecy and the particular revelations of today."[89]

Laurentin rightly points out that one milestone has been set, namely the New Testament canon, but even here, theologians are more hesitant with regard to the end-idea, as modern exegesis shows that parts of Scripture were written after the death of the last apostle. This is one more reason why Laurentin considers theology to have recently reached a greater balance. Laurentin's may be considered the most profound, balanced yet innovative, conclusions, as he manages to formulate the idea of a continued revelation without touching on the unique character of what was given in Christ:

> More profoundly, the notion is strongly represented of a radica gorge and qualitative change between the apostolic and later times. The lights in the beginning, and later the transmission of formulas resulting from these lights. This change in degrees does not correspond to the intentions of God: an ascending intention, which goes from the death of Christ (his human end on Calvary) and from his discrete resurrection to the eschatology of God, all in all.
>
> The current situation must thus be characterized as continuing revelation, similar to continuing Creation, because the revealing act of God, like the creative act, is not a momentary act. The Holy Spirit diffuses the same lights in his church and in the hearts of the faithful; the difference lies in the nature of the initial foundational gift: a gracious gift of inspiration, above all, which constitutes the Word of God in Sacred Scripture, but Scripture actually remains Word of God through the same essential light of God.[90]

The authors mentioned here are but a few of those who have questioned and continue questioning the validity of the use of the term "end of revelation," as today more than ever it is important to point to the continued activity of God in this world and in history, which have witnessed his absence and apparent "death" through events like the Holocaust. The church has an obligation to present God as being continuously present through history.

The nomenclature "end of revelation" not only fails to convey the interminability of God's continued activity in salvation history, but among the very theologians who support this notion, there is, as we shall see, great incertitude as to when this "end" should have occurred and why it is "apostolic."

5.3. Three Ends?

As it is, there appear to be three possibilities as to *when* revelation may have ended: (1) with the cessation of Christ's physical presence on earth; (2) with the death of the last apostle; and (3) with the closure of the Bible's last book. I shall examine each of these and show how far the experts diverge on this important issue.

5.3.1. The End of Revelation with the End of Christ's Physical Presence on Earth

Some academics interpret the concept *apostle* in the sense of it being only those who were authorized witnesses of Christ. According to this view, the only difference between the apostles and all subsequent believers lies in the former enjoying the privilege of being contemporaries of Jesus. Johannes Feiner writes that these have not received revelations that transcend the revelation in Christ. "Does the process of revelation continue in the proper sense after the Ascension of Christ, so that the event of revelation would be not be concluded with the end of the visible presence of Christ?" Feiner asks, and replies with a no: "To us, the view seems more justified and consistent that we should not be speaking of an actual contentwise addition to the event of Christ's visible (pre- and post-Pasqual) revelation, so that the end of the actual event of revelation rather coincides with the end of the visible presence of Christ."[91]

Karl Rahner is of the same conviction as Feiner: "While textbook theology usually says that revelation was closed with the death of the last apostle, it would be better and more exact to say that revelation is closed with the achievement of the death of Jesus, crucified and risen."[92]

This does not mean that the Holy Spirit cannot be active in a particular way in the apostolic age, rather that his activity does not imply revelation that would in no way be given in the Christ-event.[93] According to Feiner, the particular activity of the Holy Spirit in the apostolic age aims not at bringing anything substantially new to revelation, but constitutes "divine assistance for the clearer and more pondered unfolding of God's word of revelation that has been spoken out sufficiently with the appearance of the Resurrected."[94]

Feiner's views are interesting but raise new problems, especially on the difference between the pre- and postapostolic ages. Does the special activity of the Holy Spirit, helping to illuminate the apostles on the true reality of the Christ-event, not apply equally to the postapostolic age? Are Christians after the apostles no longer in need of the Spirit's assistance in this regard, in-asmuch as they, unlike the apostles who were ocular and auricular witnesses of Christ, did not behold him face to face? Is Feiner not perhaps speaking of the actualization of revelation that will last until the end of time? In point of fact, Feiner affirms this: "Thus, the function of the Holy Spirit should be understood—even in the postapostolic time—as opening the faithful to the inexhaustible dimensions of revelation."[95]

Hence, rather than speaking of a constitutive difference between the pre- and postapostolic times, Feiner indicates a *gradual difference* between the two. It is clear that such a notion leaves little room for an *apostolic* end of revelation, as there is no constitutive difference between the time of the apostles and the time of the institutional church that follows. Feiner arrives at this interpre-tation in order to demonstrate in no uncertain terms that there is *no* substan-tial difference between the activity of the Holy Spirit that helped to illuminate the apostles on the true reality of the Christ-event and the activity of the Holy Spirit that helps all the faithful who follow the apostles. He argues that many of the ecclesial statements proposing the "end of revelation" can be inter-preted as indicating no *essential* difference between the two periods of the apostles' and the church's participation in the mystery of Christ through the Holy Spirit. Hence Feiner interprets the Tridentine Council's "Spiritu Sancto dictante" reference to tradition as an indication of the Holy Spirit's revelation to the apostles, which he considers no new revelation at all but the intro-duction to "a deeper and more pondered understanding of the Christ-event through a special direction and illumination by the Holy Spirit, as it cor-responds to the establishment [Eingründung] of revelation in the normative ancient church."[96] The aim of the prophets is to confer the particular enlight-enment of the Holy Spirit to the church. And it is precisely this function that ascribes to them the office of servants of the same task that the Council ascribes to the apostles. With Feiner's interpretation of the Council of Trent it is therefore impossible to speak of an end of revelation during the time of the apostles. On the contrary, the opposite may be concluded with respect to proph-ecy, namely that prophets are there to continue the mission of the apostles, albeit in a less normative way.

When Feiner sounds this distinctive note, it is with the purpose of high-lighting the unique character of the revelation of Christ. Speaking of an *ap-ostolic end* of revelation implies including the apostles in the process of constitutive revelation. Feiner fears that this could make God's revelation in Christ appear partial, needing completion through the Holy Spirit's enlightenment to the apostles *after* Christ's ascension. Even if one acknowledges that the apostles received revelations, these cannot *transcend* God's revelation in Christ but only render it understandable, as "this subsequent revelatory activity of the Spirit is subordinate to the substance of the revelation that itself occurred in the Christ event; in fact, it serves its very seizure and unfolding." [97]

5.3.2. The End of Revelation with the Death of the Last Apostle

Other theologians insist that revelation was complete only with the last apostle. Duns Scotus was, as evidenced earlier, one example of this.[98] Heinrich Fries is another. If Feiner's primary interest was to mark the difference between the time of Christ and all subsequent periods, Fries wishes to highlight the difference between the apostles and their successors. Fries agrees with Gottlieb Söhngen, who believes that the apostles themselves stand "within the process of revelation." The apostles are themselves "recipients of and witnesses to revelation and thereby with Christ the first initiation of a tradition [Überlieferung] whose carriers and witnesses would be those who only came after the apostles.... The apostles are in a unique way with Christ; and according to his own desire, Christ is not without the apostles."[99]

Fries concludes that the apostles are not only the specially authorized witnesses to what they saw in Christ, but that they themselves take part in the genesis of that revelation that all later times receive as the Deposit of Faith. By virtue of his theology, Fries is able to affirm the maxim that revelation, fulfilled in Christ, ends with the apostles. Fries writes that it is not possible to indicate a fixed point in time where revelation ended, as the end refers to an issue, not an event. *End* indicates a "basic distinction between revelation and tradition [Überlieferung], of initiation and following, of source and flow, of normative constitution and continuation, of the setting and following of standards [Maßgebendem und Maßnehmendem]."[100]

Although they may be reconciled to some extent, Feiner's and Fries's positions appear to be in outright opposition. Both affirm that Christ is the full revelation of God while holding that there must be a difference between the time of the apostles and of the later church. Both operate with two distinctions, the former between Christ and the apostles and the latter between the apostles and all times to follow until the final coming of Christ. The difference between the two lies in their emphasis on one event over another. Feiner sees Christ as revelation's source with the apostles forming part of the stream that flows from this source, whereas Fries includes the apostles themselves as an integral part of this source.

5.3.3. The End of Revelation with the Closure of Holy Scripture

Things are further complicated by the fact that theologians approaching and following the Second Vatican Council have shown ever-growing inclinations to introduce yet a third distinction. Until Vatican II, most Catholic exegesis traced each New Testament writing directly back to the apostles, inasmuch as the biblical books were written either by an apostle or by some of the apostles' close collaborators, such as Peter's interpreter, Mark, or Paul's traveling companion, Luke. New results from exegesis question this assessment, casting doubt on the sure connection between all New Testament writings and the apostles. Joseph Schumacher is one such theologian for whom it is vital to count Scripture among the "constitutive elements of the church and thus of revelation"[101] while maintaining that Scripture is not materially equal with the fullness of God, but is its normative expression. Hence he expands the revelation-event from the period of the last apostle's death—which had previously been understood as having occurred in the year 100—to the general "apostolic age," thereby conferring on revelation a more elastic timeframe that embraces the redaction of the last biblical writing. According to Schumacher, theologians from the time of the Council of Trent to the Second Vatican Council considered the last apostle to have died around the year 100, and in so doing, assessed this year as the approximate "end" of revelation.[102] Wanting to include Scripture in this period, Schumacher expands it to be "roughly the time of the ancient church. It is limited by the emergence of the last New Testament writing, the second letter of Peter, and thereby reaches approximately into the middle of the second century."[103] Schumacher's deliberations, or at least his indication that the closure of sacred Scripture occurred in the second century, face the exegetical objection that the closure or completion of the sacred canon occurred from the mid–second to the mid–fourth century.[104] As is well known, the Lutheran reformers denied the full canonical status of certain Old Testament books that were present in the Greek version of the Old Testament (the *Septuaginta*) but not in the Hebrew version. As such, Schumacher's thesis can be identified with regard to its content, that is, revelation is complete with the books of the biblical canon, but it will be painful to designate its historical completion.

5.4. Conclusion

As we have seen, there are three main positions as to *when* revelation should be ended, and these were proposed by Johannes Feiner, Heinrich Fries, and Joseph Schumacher.

Feiner places major emphasis on the fullness and unsurpassable character of God's revelation in Christ. In so doing, he places the distinction between Christ and the apostles.

Fries refers to a period that is constituted and normatively given for all times to follow. He envisions the apostles not only as witnesses of Christ's revelation but also as bearers of revelation. He creates the distinction between the apostles and the times to follow, which is the time of the church.

For Schumacher it is not enough that the apostles possessed normative faith, as this faith needed an expression to help the church live. Hence he includes Scripture in the process of revelation (Offenbarungsvorgang), even though it is not itself revelation. By this means, Schumacher places the end of revelation at the completion of the last canonical writing, somewhere in the second century A.D., *after* the death of the last apostle.

While each of the three positions aims at securing vital aspects of revelation and its transmission, the multiplication of locations of revelation's "end" nevertheless leads one to question the notion seriously. Influential theologians can arrive at varying conclusions as to the significance of revelation's end, and this is exemplified in Johannes Feiner's and Heinrich Fries's diverging interpretations of the same work, *Mysterium Salutis*. Hence one may well argue that the whole notion of revelation's "end" should be either ignored and dismissed, or qualified in such a way that the doctrine that was revealed, complete and materially fulfilled in Christ and in the normative testimony of the apostles in the form of Scripture, has yet to be fully explicated, actualized, and completed in the church.

As we have seen, Ratzinger, Rahner, and von Balthasar favor the dismissal of the notion of revelation's end as the most appropriate option. To each of these it is of primary importance to safeguard those vital points that the notion intends to secure, namely revelation's material fulfillment in Christ and its normative transmission through the apostles in the form of Scripture. And yet the dynamic presentation of God as The-One-Who-Is (the Hebrew meaning of Yahweh) and as ever-present and active in history seems more needed in today's secularized world than ever before.

To avoid further confusion, the clear-cut distinction needs to be made between revelation's material and formal aspects, while affirming that *both* are part and parcel of revelation. Ratzinger indicates that these two aspects of revelation are revelation in *actu primo* and in *actu secundo,* and both belong to the category of revelation as the one event of revelation that continues to occur in every new context ("Ereignis der Offenbarung, dass sich immer neu ereignet").[105] Only by ascribing the dynamic actualization of revelation's reality to the *ensemble* of divine revelation, which the historic and personalistic approaches to revelation ensure, is theology able to adjust to the world's needs for the presence of God. And only this approach to revelation secures a rediscovery and fruitful appreciation of prophecy in the church. Even though it thus seems best not to use the term "end," the three propositions may actually elucidate the issues we are discussing and help to position prophecy properly.

As we have seen, the maxim of the apostolic end of revelation has been used with three meanings: first to indicate revelation's fulfillment in Christ, second to indicate revelation's fulfillment with the last apostle, and third with the redaction of Scripture's last book. I shall here explore these three instances and see whether or not it makes sense to speak of an end of revelation. This differentiation will help to place Christian prophecy in its right context, and further position it in its legitimate context.

First, when talking of revelation's *material* fulfillment in Christ, it is a mistake to talk about an "end." God acts in all times as the God who reveals himself. The risen Christ is a living and active presence. Christ is therefore not the end of revelation but its ultimate historical fulfillment, which the church renders accessible through the sacraments and the grace of the Holy Spirit. It therefore appears vital to speak of the *fulfillment* and not the *end* of God's revelation in Christ. The term *end* may be used to indicate the sole fact that God's revelation in the Incarnation had a historical end, but even here it would seem problematic to talk about an *end,* as the fullness of the *Logos* continues in and is fundamental to the nature of the church.

Second, the nomenclature has been used to refer to the time period during which God's revelation in Christ was fully received by the apostles through the illumination of the Holy Spirit. Revelation is witnessed in but transcends Scripture, given that it is more than a collection of correct propositions, rather is the living relationship between Christ and his body, the church. In this context, revelation's *end* must indicate the normative and constitutive relationship between Christ's revelation of God and the apostles' inspired reception thereof. No one after the apostles has experienced God's revelation in its constitutive phase as they did, that is, in the material and substantive revelation that, as Aquinas states, does not ever change, and was expressed in the apostles' writings and kerugma in a formal and normative manner, although it could be explicated further in tradition. This was the reason for the second distinction.

The first distinction serves to indicate the difference between revelation's material completion in Christ and its formal expression in the faith of the apostles. The second indicates that the church needs the apostles' full reception of the constitutive revelation in order to pass it on fully to the faithful, so that the two moments appear as one constitutive revelation. In this sense, the second distinction almost vanishes in light of the importance of the first, for the church receives revelation in the unity of its material completion in Christ and its formal completion in the apostles. Thus, the Deposit of Faith is constituted both through God's revelation in Christ and its reception by the apostles, and it is this fullness of revelation that, after the apostles, is no longer constituted but continued. It is only within this context that the classic dogmatic works use the word *end* also in its Latin form: "revelatio cessavit or clausa est." A timely example is found in the writings of J. Perrone, a representative of the neo-Scholastic Roman school, who writes: "Exploratum quippe est ecclesiam dogmata sua non cedere, aut de novo proferre, cum apostolorum obitu omnis in ea cessavit revelatio, quae ad fidei depositum spectet."[106]

E. Doronzo writes along the same lines: "Post mortem autem ultimi apostoli (adeoque circa finem saec. 1, cum mortuus est Joannes) clausa est publica revelatio, quae sola est obiectum fidei."[107]

Third, the nomenclature "end of revelation" was used as a third distinction to indicate the closure of Sacred Scripture as the normative expression of Christ's revelation of God. Yet new times will constitute new challenges to faith and put revelation in a new light, necessitating the activity of the Logos to guide anew. Here it makes no sense to speak of an end to revelation. Scripture must be the primary criterion for true Christian doctrine, yet not all is explicitly expressed in the Bible.

The notion "revelation's end" has been used to discard prophecy and prophetic revelations as unimportant, as they add nothing new, and thus are superfluous. At the basis of such a pronouncement seems to lie the idea that the church has already expressed everything of revelation, as in a secret book that encloses all divine truths and constitutes God's entire revelatory activity. This approach leaves little room for the church's continued growth and renewed explication and appreciation of God's truth, and must therefore be abandoned. Thus the expression "revelation's apostolic end" cannot exclude prophecy. On the contrary, the discussion of the concept of tradition shows that prophecy is an indispensable part of revelation's actualization in history.

As we have seen, it would be better to speak of revelation's *completion*. And, as Richard P. McBrien writes, even as such, the term only means that "the Christ-event, which is definite and normative self-communication of God by which all other communications are to be measured and tested, has already happened."[108]

The two aspects of revelation, the material and the formal, are both important and inherent parts of the category of revelation, and when keeping both aspects of God's revelation together, it is *not* possible to reduce this to a one-period occurrence. Evaluating prophecy necessitates the indication of a clear distinction between the material and formal aspects—which is what I shall aim at next.

6

Prophecy and Tradition

Summarizing what we have seen so far, we may evaluate the relationship between prophecy and tradition from the foundational maxim that Christ is the full and perfect expression of the reality of revelation, for the fullness and the truth of God. All later works of God, including his subsequent revelations, are necessarily less complete than his revelation in Christ, though this does not signify that from a *material* point of view they have no relation to the Christ-event; given the oneness of God, they must basically express the same reality. The revelations that precede and those that follow are equally less perfect than the Incarnation, but at the same time they originate in the same mystery. Hence, *from a material point of view,* it makes little sense to speak of a growth of revelation that should have ended with Christ, as prophetic revelations before and after Christ originate in the same reality of God's word. And this has significant implications for the quality of Christian revelation, inasmuch as they express the *same ultimate content* whether they occur before or after Christ! Both point to Christ and what he reveals, yet the first anticipates his revelation and the latter recalls it. The former prepares its way, and the latter unfolds its inexhaustible meaning.

The revelation in Christ thus becomes a maximum in God's revelation in time that no revelations before or after can match; only the final coming of Christ will transcend this, allowing all of Creation to participate in the full life of the Trinity. This is the limit and the place of prophecy from a material perspective. The material object of tradition is the fullness and truth of Christ. If a prophetic revelation is a true revelation of Christ, it must from a material perspective have the same source and object as tradition, namely Christ, and it must continue his mission.

The second aspect, which we must consider in order to clarify the transmission and actualization of revelation during history, is the formal aspect. In order to be accessible to man, revelation must have an expression and a form before it can be received by and bear fruit for the faithful. Even though Christ is the full revelation of God, this would have little historical importance without its formal transmission and reception by humans. Revelation is not only revelation *of* something or someone, it is revelation *to* someone. Theologians also call this formal level of revelation revelation *in actu secundo*. From the formal perspective there must be a continued growth in the knowledge and implementation of revelation's truth. This growth begins with man's first questions about existence, is intensified through God's revelations to the Old Testament prophets, and reaches a perfect realization in Christ, but continues nevertheless after his ascension until judgment day.

The locus of this transmission is the complex entity called tradition, making up much more than the product of pious traditions and dogmas in the church. The church is made up of more than the number of its believers by virtue of the Holy Spirit's internal activity. It is the Holy Spirit's activity that explicates and actualizes Christ's revealed truth in history through the use of the church's various traditions and doctrinal expressions, whereby it makes *tradition* Christ's continued presence.

Thus, in recent approaches to revelation, theologians such as Henri de Lubac, Hans Urs von Balthasar, Karl Rahner, Joseph Ratzinger, and others[1] talk of tradition as the reality that in the dynamism of the Spirit transcends the sum of the individual traditions. Here, tradition is seen as the expression of the reality of the Word that the Word itself actualizes in and through the church. Hence tradition is seen less as the formulation and expression of the doctrine of faith, and more as the life of faith that the Holy Spirit realizes in the church. Tradition and traditions are related, and yet it appears one must distinguish between the two, as they cover different realities. Tradition with a capital *T* could be synonymous with the transmission of revelation and cover the reality of God's revelation as such. In Scripture and the ratified traditions, the faithful discern the norm for what Tradition truly hints at, as witnesses of Tradition.

Tradition has a historical starting point, and it is evident that the traditions as historic realization of the expressible aspects of revelation belong to Tradition. However, the true transmission of revelation powerfully transcends the sum of the traditions, as Tradition's ontological and transcendent aspects as well as prophecy continuously accompany Scripture and the many traditions. Revelation's transmission in history is not only the transmission of a historical event, not only a description of what the Word did, but a continuous expression of what the Word *does* and *who the Word is*. With Pottmeyer, Tradition is the "ongoing self-transmission of the word of God in the Holy Spirit."[2] The Holy Spirit produces the continuous offer and life of salvation that wells forth from Christ's revelation. Both God's revelation in Christ and its continuous unfolding, realization, and actualization are *inherent* to the category of revelation in the modern understanding. In the foregoing presentation, we saw that the starting point of God's revelation is his universal will of salvation (see chapter 4). Precisely because revelation gives rise to Tradition, God's continuous, saving activity is vital to the proper understanding of Tradition. God's salvific activity, moreover, is rendered continuous through the truly prophetic element and continued prophetic revelations. In this sense, *Tradition must be prophetic in order to be Tradition.* In order to be a true transmission of the mystery of the Word—rendering it—it must contain both horizontal and vertical elements; horizontal because it originates in a full salvific event in history, which is the event of Christ; vertical because the revealing activity of the Holy Spirit must continuously renew the church in order that Tradition may be a timely and plentiful expression of revelation. Tradition is not a mechanical repetition of the first witnesses of Christ's revelation of God, but an ongoing expression of the same revelation. It is precisely this ongoing expression that reveals prophecy as an integral element of Tradition. When understood in this way, Tradition has many theological implications, especially with respect to the understanding of the church and of Christendom as such that emerge not as perfect and final-divine stages, but as a foretaste of what is to come in the fulfillment of all things in *the World to Come*.

6.1. The Unicity of Christ and the Holy Spirit—The Unicity of the Economy of Salvation

The danger of pointing too coarsely to the completeness of God's work in the incarnate Christ endangers the unicity of Christ's salvific action in his Incarnation and passion as well as in his subsequent saving presence and activity in his Spirit. Various theological currents have bred the idea of an economy of the Holy Spirit that transcends the scope of the activity of Christ, crucified and risen. In an attempt to safeguard against such currents, several documents of the Catholic Church's Magisterium have pointed to the unicity of all aspects of God's salvation in Christ. Three documents deserve particular mention: (1) the Second Vatican Council's constitution on revelation, *Dei Verbum*,

(2) John Paul II's encyclical letter *Redemptoris Missio*, and (3) the CDF's document *Dominus Iesus*.

In *Redemptoris Missio*, John Paul II writes that there are different "participated forms of mediation of different kinds and degrees." One could easily allocate the prophets to this category of *participated forms of mediation*, inasmuch as prophets share in a particular way in the ongoing self-communication of the Word. The encyclical nevertheless points out that "they acquire meaning and value only from Christ's own mediation, and they cannot be understood as parallel or complementary to his."[3] All forms of mediations are subordinate to that of Christ because included in his action. But precisely as such, they are of highest value.

Another important document to highlight the unicity of the salvific activity of Christ is the CDF's document *Dominus Iesus*. Although it could have gotten better reception, especially among non-Catholic Christians, it has historical value in its clear assessment of the unicity of God's salvific ongoing work in Christ.

According to the document, published in 2002, Christ (and indeed the entire Holy Trinity) is present and active in all the stages of salvation, both in the Creation of world and man, in the paschal mystery, and in the Spirit's operation of actualizing Christ's gift until the eschaton. The document mentions that the Second Vatican Council "closely links the mystery of Christ from its very beginnings with that of the Spirit."[4] "The entire work of building the Church by Jesus Christ the Head, in the course of the centuries, is seen as an action which he does in communion with his Spirit."[5]

The work of Christ and the work of the Spirit are rooted in the same mystery of God's salvific plan for mankind:

> Hence, the connection is clear between the salvific mystery of the Incarnate Word and that of the Spirit, who actualizes the salvific efficacy of the Son. . . . Thus, the recent Magisterium of the Church has firmly and clearly recalled the truth of a single divine economy. . . . The action of the Spirit is not outside or parallel to the action of Christ. There is only one salvific economy of the One and Triune God, realized in the mystery of the Incarnation, death, and resurrection of the Son of God, actualized with the cooperation of the Holy Spirit, and extended in its salvific value to all humanity and to the entire universe: "No one, therefore, can enter into communion with God except through Christ, by the working of the Holy Spirit."[6]

According to mainstream Catholic theology, Christ's giving himself to man in order to draw man back to himself does not end with his physical presence on earth, but continues until the eschaton. While there is a logical distinction between the foundation of the Deposit of Faith and its actualization in Christ's Spirit, it is equally important to highlight the unicity of God's salvific action in Christ.

6.2. Christianity as Preliminary Stage of Salvation

Following this fundamental consideration, I shall in the subsequent passages examine the general prophetic charism of Tradition and how Christianity constitutes a preliminary stage that leads to its final fulfillment at the second coming of Christ. This I shall do by looking at reflections on the issues at hand by Philipp Gabriel Renczes, Hans Urs von Balthasar, Joseph Ratzinger, and John Zizioulas, who from their respective perspectives have again contributed new insights into the nature of Christianity and the church on the way to its eschatological fulfillment. They all oppose the widespread opinion that Christianity is the fulfillment of God's purpose, asserting that in reality it is an intermediary stage between what Christ did at his first coming and what he will do at his second coming. Christianity is and remains God's "already-but-not-yet-fully."

Philipp Gabriel Renczes argues from the writings of Maximus the Confessor that the fundamental structure of the Christianity is directed not by the beginning but by the end. This applies especially to the sanctification and salvation of the individual. Balthasar shares this view and broadens it to the ecclesiological realm by looking at the end not mainly of the individual but of the church as a whole, while Joseph Ratzinger provides further conclusions to this structure of Christianity as such and to its continuous need for becoming what it potentially is, a need that cannot be fulfilled without Christian prophets. Along with this eschatological outlook on Christianity I will also examine the origin of the fullness of revelation in Tradition. Here we shall look at an ancient theory, received and reproposed by the Orthodox theologian Metropolitan John (Zizioulas) of Pergamon, who believes not only that Tradition draws its dynamic power from the fullness of the Christ-event two thousand years ago, but that it remains in the present, in the eternal now as it were, in the dynamism of the eschaton, which is made available through participation in the Eucharist in the glory of the Kingdom to come.

On the basis of this appreciation of Christianity as a nonclosed and nonstatic reality—the people of God journeying toward its telos—we shall be ready to examine the different instances through which God actualizes and realizes revelation in history, the different loci. We will see how prophecy relates to all of these, partly because they by their very structure are charismatic expressions of God's action and truth, and partly because prophetic revelations were powerful vehicles of God's direct intervention, which has availed itself of the loci, agents of actualization, during the entire history of the church.

Important currents of Christian theology have seen a radical difference between Judaism and Christianity. These theologians saw the Incarnation and Jesus' redemptive death on the Cross to be such a complete and final salvific event as to be considered the ultimate peak of Redemption. This position, in turn, led them to various conclusions: while Judaism was a preliminary state, Christianity was complete. While Judaism was constantly imbued with a radical structure of hope anticipating the coming Messiah, Christianity would always look backwards to Christ Incarnate as the Messiah who now had come. And while Judaism constantly needed prophets to keep the hope in the coming salvation alive; Christianity no longer needs prophets, for the hope of the coming Messiah has been exchanged for an already fulfilled salvation. As Wayne Grudem shows, this opinion is particularly diffused among Protestant theologians of the Cessationist School.[7] Richard B. Gaffin is one who gives word to this view (see section 3.3.8), but there are many who follow his opinion; even Catholic theologians are among them.

This view has encountered serious theological opposition in recent years; many qualified publications have sought to modify it. Many factors have led to these corrective approaches, mainly new developments in revelation theology, which, as we saw, consider God's revelatory activity not merely as a revelation of propositions that require little more than being handed down from one generation to the next, but as God's salvation in which the church shares through the redemptive work of Christ. This sharing in the redemptive work of Christ is not a mere *anamnesis* of Christ's passion; it is more significantly a continuous ontological participation in the reality of the Word of God. If this is so, it is no wonder that prophecy as articulation of the Word has played such a role in Christianity.

6.2.1. Maximus the Confessor

Maximus the Confessor, one of the later church Fathers, is experiencing a renaissance in recent years. In his 1999 Sorbonne and Institute Catholique Dissertation, *L'agir de Dieu et la liberté de l'homme*,[8] Philipp Gabriel Renczes provides a valuable presentation of his theology. Renczes writes of Maximus's synthetic approaches to the often difficult theology of grace, in particular with respect to the interaction of God's grace and man's action. Renczes shows that, while insisting on the importance of man's origin, Maximus is more interested in his end or final destiny in God. Because of the fall, man can no longer know his origin, only his end in God:

> Man embedded in movement [κίνησις] directed by a principle [ἀρχή], and an end [τέλος], no longer has access, according to the Confessor, on the level of his knowledge with what ontologically constitutes the initiation of his openness to God [ἀρχή], i.e. to his origin as an efficient cause, insofar as the human condition, impregnated by the "fault of Adam," perceives its origin as being irremediably lost, leaving him from then on the possibility of finding it only in his end![9]

Maximus himself distinguishes between searching and re-searching: "searching naturally refers to the order of the origin [προς τὴν ἀρχήν] and the researching of the order of the end [πρὸς τὸ τέλος]:"[10] "For after the transgression [the sin of Adam], the end is no longer evident from the origin [τοὺς τῆς ἀρχῆς λόγους], but rather the origin from the, nor does anybody seek anymore the reasons of the origin, but one seeks the reasons that bring those who are driven toward the end [τοὺς πρὸς τὸ τέλος τοὺς κινουμένους ἀπάγοντας]."[11]

This event of man's moving toward his goal occurs in his divinization, in which God becomes himself in man. In reference to time, it occurs eminently after man's death but also already now during his earthly life, by the works of the Holy Spirit, through which God is continuously united to man. This union is possible through the mystery of the ontological unicity of the within ("en-deçà") and the beyond ("au-delà") of man's existence. We will encounter in the writings of Balthasar and Zizioulas this relationship between man's earthly and eschatological life, which is not one in which the eschatological life begins simply at the terminus of earthly life; both occur simultaneously in the present through man's participation in God, and no human life can be conceived without the spark of God's divine life, as " deification is ensured by the inherent purpose in this which characterizes the human condition in all ways, directing its movement toward God, the fulfillment of all action."[12]

In this way, man is in his innermost being oriented toward his fulfillment, which does not simply equate the reception and implementation of his origin, but which more significantly occurs through man's anticipation of and participation in the divine life that Christ conquered and made accessible to man through his death and resurrection, and that he will completely fulfil in the eschaton. Likewise, the Fathers of the church understood Creation's fulfillment in Christ's return as a more perfect state than the original, paradisiacal state, since the world had merited Christ as its Savior (the "felix culpa"). In this way, the fate of every individual is analogous to that of Creation as such.

6.2.2. Hans Urs von Balthasar on Christianity and Eschatology

Hans Urs von Balthasar laments the lack of serious theological reflection on the vital eschatological hopes of Christianity. Balthasar observes that the theological issue of eschatology has been so watered down that it lost the radical hope of creation's ultimate fulfillment. In its lapsed reinterpretation, eschatology has been taken to mean the general period of Christian salvation announced and initiated with the Christ-event. Thus eschatology could even broadly signify Creation, on the basis that God created the world with a preconceived plan of salvation for it. God does indeed have a plan of salvation, and in this sense the entire history of humankind emerges as one of salvation history. It is this history of God with man that has been called the eschatological realm, as it implies God's leading creation toward its goal of progressively resembling the eschatological Kingdom of God. While Balthasar does not directly oppose such views on eschatology, he nevertheless considers them to be metaphorical applications within the eschatological category. As a counterbalance to such broad applications, Balthasar ventures to present eschatology as it was conceived by the Fathers of the church in its strict sense, and as it should be conceived by Christians that wish to keep the radical hope of God's ultimate salvific action alive. Without referring to Maximus, on whom Balthasar has written, he agrees with Maximus's conviction that man's end is more important than his origin, although the two are ontologically related:

> "Omega" can only be understood from the "alpha," the two are one in the salvific plans of God, eschatology is the conclusion [Mündung] of protology and not representable without it . . . [so that] the last distance carries within itself the entire road, its preconditions and ordinances, yes precisely in its conclusion reveals the sense that it held from the beginning.[13]

Along the lines of classical eschatology, Balthasar presents the two ways by which creatures enter the eschatological realm. One entrance occurs in relation to the individual, also called the first judgment, which follows a person's death. The second occurs with the general—also called the final—judgment, which occurs at the end of history, when "the Son of Man will come on the clouds of Heaven." Balthasar reflects at length on the difference between these two kinds of judgment, on the role and features of the judge and the person being judged, and on the nature and blessed state of the eschatological life. But of Balthasar's eschatological reflections the most important to our theme are those on the fate of Creation as such, on what it is now and on what it shall be. Already now, Balthasar writes, Creation lives in the eternal and limitless life of the eschaton: "In this simple, albeit often difficult preference for the divine will...do we see the realization already in this mortal life of what will be the center of eternal life, and this in a much more central way than what is reachable through individual feats of contemplation or experiences of union with God."[14]

The shift from this world to the eschaton is not one of linear sequence, where one continues at the "end of the time of history," but reigns in a dimension that is "incommensurable with this one."[15] This world and the *World to Come* are ontologically linked in the mystery of the church that unifies "definitiveness and preliminarity"[16] and where chronological time is less important than God's time or, in other words, the eternal now, as Christ swallowed up time in his death. There is a direct ontological link between God's life in the church today and the life in the World to Come, whereby the church's divine life today does not come from mere reception of a perfect doctrine but from the church's participation in the eschaton that the church foretastes already now. Whence Balthasar affirms that

> The new Aeon does not proceed chronologically from the old, but
> rather protrudes from it in a right angle. And that existence in tran-
> sition is not, as in the religions of nostalgia for the absolute, an
> escape from time...but rather existence within the existence
> of Christ, who, as no other, assumed responsibility for all tem-
> poralness and prevailed until the paschal mystery.[17]

The Christian church exists after the death of Christ but anticipates and shares the glory of his second coming; it reigns in the "turn of the Aeon between Holy Friday and Easter."[18] Joseph Ratzinger agrees with these outlooks on Christianity.

6.2.3. Joseph Ratzinger on Christianity's Hope of the Kingdom to Come

In spite of often being accused of being merely a traditionalist theologian, Joseph Ratzinger in various publications has displayed an appreciation of Christianity that, while retaining revelation's cognitive aspects, portrays Christianity as awaiting the Spirit's ongoing activities and Christ's final redemptive works in his second coming. Like Balthasar, Ratzinger laments the lack of serious theological reflections on eschatology. In my interview with him in 1999, Ratzinger provided crystal-clear expression to this outlook on the church. His interpretation on the nature of Christianity and leads to conclusions on the role of prophets that deserve particular attention. Ratzinger clearly rejects the idea that prophecy should have ended with the fulfillment of revelation:

> There is a thesis whereby the fulfillment of revelation marked the end of all prophecy. I think this thesis harbors a double misunderstanding. First of all, it harbors the idea that the prophet, who is essentially associated with the dimension of hope, has no further function for no other reason than Christ is now with us so that hope has given way to presence. This is an error, because Christ came in the flesh and then rose again "in the Holy Spirit." This new presence of Christ in history, in the sacrament, in the Word, in the life of the church, in the heart of every man is the expression and beginning of the definitive advent of Christ who "fills all things."[19] This means that Christianity always tends towards the Lord who comes, in an interior movement. This still happens now though in a different way because Christ is already here. However, Christianity always carries a structure of hope within it. . . . The New Testament has a different structure of hope within it but it is still always a radical structure of hope.[20]

Ratzinger refers to the Eucharist as the primary place in which this eschatological dimension is realized, as it represents the whole church going toward the Lord who comes.

PROPHETS AS SERVANTS OF HOPE. This openness of Christianity moving toward the Lord's second advent indicates that the church will always grow in the fullness of Christ. Ratzinger affirms:

> The coming of Christ is the beginning of an ever-deepening knowledge and of a gradual discovery of what, in the Logos, is being given. Thus, a new way is inaugurated of leading man into the whole truth, as Jesus puts it in the Gospel of John when he says that the Holy Spirit will come down.[21] I believe that the pneumatological Christology of Jesus' leave-taking discourse is very important to our theme given that Christ explains that his coming in the flesh was just a first step. The real coming will happen when Christ is no longer bound to a place or to a body locally limited but when he comes to all of us in the Spirit as the Risen One, so that entering into the truth may also acquire more and more profundity.[22]

Because this is so, Ratzinger believes Christianity to be constantly imbued with a general prophetic spirit that not only allows but needs the works of concrete prophets as those who point to and carry out the hope-dimension of

Christianity: "It seems clear to me that—considering that the time of the church, that is, the time when Christ comes to us in Spirit is determined by this very pneumatological Christology—the prophetic element, as element of hope and appeal, cannot naturally be lacking or allowed to fade away."[23] Radicalizing the difference between the old and the new covenants is an error that the Fathers of the church carefully avoided:

> They proposed a tripartite schema, "umbra, imago, veritas," in which the New Testament is the *imago*. Thus, the Old and New Testaments are not set in opposition to one another as shadow and reality but, within the triad of shadow, image and reality, the expectation of the definitive fulfillment is kept alive and the time of the New Testament, the time of the church is seen as an ulterior plane, a more elevated one but still on the pathway of the promise. This is a point which to date, it seems to me, has not been given sufficient consideration. The Fathers of the church stressed with force the intermediate nature of the New Testament in which not all the promises have been fulfilled yet. Christ came in the flesh, but the church still awaits his full revelation in glory.[24]

Ratzinger believes that the "unfinished state of Christianity" is a theological issue that has been seriously underdeveloped with surprisingly grave results, leading to not only theological misgivings but also erroneous ideologies and political utopias that have pestered the world:

> It is of extreme importance to specify in which sense Christianity is the fulfillment of the promise and in which sense it is not. I believe that there is a close tie between the current crisis of faith and the insufficient clarification of this question. There are three inherent dangers here. The first is that the promises of the Old Testament and the expectation of the salvation of men are seen only in an immanent way in the sense of new and better structures, of perfect effectiveness. Conceived in this way, Christianity proves to be just a defeat. From this basic perspective, there has been an attempt to replace Christianity with ideologies of faith in progress and then with ideologies of hope which are just variations of Marxism. The second danger is to see Christianity as something solely associated with the afterlife, something purely spiritual and individualistic thus negating the totality of the human reality. The third danger, particularly menacing at times of crisis and historical turning points, is to take refuge in infatuations with things apocalyptic. In opposition to all of this, it is

increasingly urgent that the authentic structure of promise and fulfillment inherent in the Christian faith is presented in a comprehensible and liveable way.[25]

With these fundamental conclusions on the nature of Christianity, Ratzinger is then able to explain how he conceives the working of concrete historical prophets: "The prophets are the ones who bring out Christianity's dimension of hope. They are the channels of access to what must still come to pass and, therefore, allowing us to go beyond time to attain what is essential and definitive. This eschatological character, this thrust to go beyond time, is certainly part of the prophetic spirituality.[26]

6.2.4. John Zizioulas on Charismatic Apostolic Continuation

Much like Ratzinger and Balthasar, Zizioulas proposes a Christian economy of salvation that continues after the groundbreaking Christ-event. The Christian life is not realized only through an anamnetic movement backward in time; rather Zizioulas revivifies an ancient Eastern tradition according to which Christianity reigns in the power of the eschaton, in the World to Come that is continuously expressed, realized, and made accessible in the Eucharist. Zizioulas perceives this to be the biblical view:

> As all Biblical scholars know the anamnesis of which the Bible speaks, above all in relation to the Eucharist, is not only an anamnesis of the past but also, if not mainly, the remembrance of the future, of the last days of the eschatological state of the church and the world.[27]

Zizioulas poignantly proposed this view during a lecture at the 1995 conference "Apostolic Succession and Continuity" at the Centro pro Unione in Rome. The aim of the conference was to examine from an ecumenical viewpoint the problems that theologians from different traditions face when trying to come to grips with the complex issue of apostolic continuity: how the church realizes the reality to which the apostles were primary witnesses and how the church continues in time. This issue, which Zizioulas rightly calls "thorny and divisive," remains one of the most challenging of all ecumenical questions. And yet, Zizioulas believes that because the ancient church reveals a "diversity of approaches" to the problem, a homogeneous presentation of these approaches may be a way of solving the issue.[28]

Delving into the diversity of ancient church approaches to the problem not only aids ecumenical advancement, it sheds light on the complex nature of

Christianity itself. It does so by demonstrating that the church realizes salvation by simultaneously looking back to the faith and the teaching of the apostles in a historical, horizontal way, and by receiving it directly from the Word
himself through an ontological participation in the eschatological Kingdom.[29]

HISTORICAL CONTINUATION. The first approach to the apostolic continuation
is linear, as it highlights the historical succession of faith from the apostles. It
is the concept that by far has most influence in theology:

> In speaking of continuity and succession we normally have in mind a
> linear historical sequence coming to us from the past to the pres-
> ent and involving the psychology of a retrospective anamnesis. This is
> in line with our typical cultural formation influenced as it is by
> Greek, especially Platonic, thought in which remembrance or "an-
> amnesis" cannot but refer to the past.[30]

The apostles are "regarded as *missionaries* sent by Christ to preach the Gospel,
ordain ministers and establish churches."[31] This means that the church historically derives from the work and tradition of the apostles, and this gave
birth to the concept of apostolic succession according to the following schema:
"God sends Christ ⇒ Christ sends the apostles ⇒ the apostles transmit the
Gospel and establish churches and ministries."[32] Scripture echoes this linear
view in several passages.[33]

The linear approach continues after the apostles in the early church, where
1 Clement (written 95 A.D.) says that the apostles established "επισκόπους και
διακόνοες" in the various cities[34] and later explains why: "Our apostles knew
through our Lord Jesus Christ that there would be quarrels concerning the
ministry of *episkopé*. For this reason they . . . established the aforementioned
[ministers] and made provisions that when these die other worthy men should
succeed their ministry."[35]

This concept builds on the driving force of historic continuity: "Historicity, dispersion and mission constitute the fundamental ecclesiological presuppositions of this conception of apostolic succession."[36] For our theme of
Christian prophecy it is very important to understand the philosophy that
underpins this view. Zizioulas writes that it grows out of the Jewish concept of
shaliach, which is one of *vicariousness* or *representation*.[37] As K. H. Rengstorff
and G. Dix have shown, it contains the "plenipotential," which Zizioulas summarizes as "someone invested with authority to represent someone fully and
in all matters."[38] The bishops in the church represent the apostles and thereby
are able authoritatively to make present and confer to the faithful the faith
reality that the apostles attained during their life with Christ.

Cyprian amplified this tradition decisively, in particular through his insistence that the church is based on the *cathedra Petri*. Against Fr. Afanassieff, Zizioulas argues that Cyprian does not propose a universalistic ecclesiology, since he "understands the '*cathedra Petri*' not in relation to the universal church but to *every local church headed by a bishop*."[39] Nevertheless, Cyprian identifies the bishop "fully and exclusively with the office of the apostle."[40] Cyprian says this explicitly: "Apostolus id est episcopus."[41] With this, apostolic continuity and succession became a matter of forwarding a historical tradition, handed down from one generation to the next, and from bishop to bishop in a linear historical movement; this understanding eventually became widely accepted, especially in the West and in Orthodox academic theology.[42]

If this linear concept of succession of the reality of faith were exclusive in the ancient church, then the prophet would indeed be ill fated in Christianity. For if the successors of the apostles, the bishops in union around Peter, the pope, were able to fully and explicitly transmit the apostolic tradition to their subordinates such that it might be fully and explicitly lived, then there would indeed be no more need for prophets. After all, if one were to affirm that the prophets continued to fulfill and explicate the tradition that the apostles already transmitted, it would present a continuous challenge to the hierarchy's unique authority and transmission of divine doctrine and life. But, as we shall see in the following, in point of fact, this historical-horizontal concept of continuing and realizing the Christian life anew was *not* unique in the Bible or in the ancient church.

SYNTHESIS OF HORIZONTAL AND CHARISMATIC APOSTOLIC AUTHORITY. Already Hippolytus and Irenaeus present a more diversified view of apostolic continuity where they synthesize the view of linear succession of authority from the apostles with a Christ-based *shaliach*, a "*Christological* view of succession, *i.e.* with the belief that succession perpetuates and affirms also the presence of Christ as head of the community, especially in its Eucharistic form."[43] Even though Hippolytus's *Apostolic Tradition* dates back to the beginning of the third century, Harnack has shown that it builds on traditions and ecclesiologies from the middle of the second century.[44] As Zizioulas shows, this document reveals that "Hippolytus—and the church of his time— perceives the bishop simultaneously as *alter Christus* and *alter apostolus*." This is visible in the prayer of ordination to the episcopate, contained in the *Apostolic Tradition*, where God is asked to do the following: "(a) give the ordained bishop the 'princely Spirit' which according to Psalm 51,14 was given to Christ, thus making him an 'image of Christ' or one acting in *persona*

Christi, and (b) 'the authority You [God] gave to the apostles,' i.e. making him *alter apostolus*."[45]

The bishop succeeds Christ as the one who offers the Eucharist, "while his capacity as *apostolus* relates to his power to 'bind and lose' sinners and teach the people."[46]

Battling against the Gnostics, who claimed a secret source of divine teaching, Irenaeus is particularly known for insisting that the church obtains its authority through historical succession from the apostles. However, it is wrong to conceive Irenaeus solely as a spokesman for mere horizontal authority: although the true doctrine that Irenaeus proposes goes back to the apostles, it remains the expression of a present, ontological relationship with the resurrected Christ. The continuous realization of this union between inherited faith and its lived realization occurs in the Eucharist. This is why Irenaeus is able to say: "Our opinion (γνώμη) i.e. faith or doctrine agrees with our Eucharist and our Eucharist agrees with our faith."[47] Irenaeus combines apostolic Tradition as the linear representation of Christ-given authority with the concept of charismatic reactualization of the Christ-reality through the Eucharist.

CHARISMATIC APOSTOLIC AUTHORITY. The insistence on direct Christ-given authority in the vertical realization of the Christian faith progressively augments as we turn our gaze toward the East, in particular toward Ignatius of Antioch. Zizioulas observes the "interesting fact that in all historical and dogmatic studies on apostolic succession reference to Ignatius of Antioch is avoided."[48] One could think this to be due to the fact that he does not express himself on the matter, but the contrary proves to be the case. Ignatius has much to say on apostolic succession, in particular, that does not "fit our classical view of succession" as known in the West.[49] If the author of 1 Clement and Cyprian were spokesmen of a horizontal succession of authority from the apostles only, and Hippolytus and Irenaeus spokesmen of a synthesis between horizontal and vertical authority, then Ignatius is a spokesman mainly of the Christological *shaliach* and its consequent vertical understanding of authority. In fact, Ignatius does not connect the bishop with the office of the apostles. Instead he proposes a Eucharistic view of the church and is thus, according to Bernhard Körner, of "groundbreaking importance to the development of theology." To Ignatius, the "continuity of the church is not realized through *historical* continuity...but through the gathering of the faithful for the celebration of the Eucharist."[50] The Eucharist is the place in which the Christian faith is actualized and empowered anew. It is an empowerment that the church receives not only by imitating the Eucharistic celebration of Christ, but by a direct participation in the Eschatological reality it signifies. Indeed Ignatius sees the image of the eschatological community in the Eucharistic gathering as a remembrance of the future! Zizioulas reflects well on this apparent paradox by referring to his own Orthodox tradition:

> This means that for him [Ignatius] the church's continuity passes through the experience of the eschata and not through the retrospective reference to the past. This is a continuity involving a *remembrance of the future* such as the Liturgy of St. John Chrysostom that we celebrate in the Orthodox Church has in mind when it says in the Anaphora that we remember not only Christ's death, resurrection etc., but also "His second coming." It sounds, of course, very strange to "remember" something that has not yet taken place. Just as it is strange to speak of succession and continuity to us not from the past but from the future, the eschaton. And yet this is what a Eucharistic view of the church involves. Ignatius' ecclesiology is of this kind.[51]

This view of continuity or realization of the Christ-reality implies a different understanding of the apostolic ministry from the one known from 1 Clement and the subsequent horizontal concept of Tradition. This view does not see the apostles as those *individuals* spread throughout the world to preach and ordain followers; "they form a *college* surrounding Christ in His eschatological function. Their function is to "sit on the twelve thrones judging the twelve tribes of Israel"[52] and this they can do only in the context of the *gathered* people of God and under the headship of Christ. . . . It is a succession of *communities* and not of individuals."[53]

This does not mean that the bishop occupies a role of little importance; on the contrary, he is primarily the representative of Christ, not of the apostles. This Christological *shaliach* is evident in most Orthodox churches in the symbol of the bishop's seat. Usually it has the form of a greatly ornamented chair with a canopy and an icon of Christ the King. When the bishop is not present, the seat is empty, but this does not mean that it has no symbolic value. In fact, when the bishop is present he represents Christ directly, whereas when he is absent, it is the empty seat that represents Christ in his community.[54]

Ignatius is not alone in his teaching, as it is continued in other Syro-Palestinian sources, for instance the third-century Syriac *Didascalia Apostolorum,* in which, "the church is an eschatological community in which the apostolic ministry is exercised by the apostles headed by Christ in the presence of the community."[55]

The Christological *shaliach* is continued in yet another Syriac source of the fourth century, the so-called Pseudo-Clementine literature. Zizioulas shows in detail how this literature continues the collegial view of Tradition that portrays Christ along with his apostles gathered around him ruling in glory over his pilgrim church on earth. Zizioulas insists that this portrayal signifies that the apostolic traditions do not come from Peter only but from James, "and finally by the bishop of every local church" as a continuity of *communities*.[56] Zizioulas draws the following theological conclusions from this scheme of succession:

> Each local church in its Eucharistic structure is the image of the *New Jerusalem* coming down from heaven (see Apocalypse), i.e. a repetition and a copy of Jerusalem as the point on which the dispersed people of God were expected to gather in the last days. The outlook is *eschatological* and not historical [with the community as] the image of the community of the New Jerusalem of the last days.[57]

The excessive Western emphasis on the historical, horizontal realization of revelation led to a number of erroneous practices in the life of the church, all of which were the result of "the loss of the Christo-centric and eschatological approach to apostolic continuity."[58] Zizioulas presents a number of such mishaps that should be replaced with a synthesis of the two approaches "more or less in the sense in which we find it in St. Hippolytus of Rome and in the New Testament itself":[59]

> It became sufficient to speak of a continuous chain of Episcopal ordinations in order to establish apostolic succession, as if it were a matter of some sort of mechanical activity. It became also a matter of transmission of power and authority from one individual to another. It also led to an understanding of the apostolic college as something standing outside and above the communities of the church and transmitting prerogatives of a self-perpetuating cast.[60]

Furthermore, Christianity was considered an accomplished fact that only needed to reiterate what was given in the apostolic times in order to carry out its mission in the world. By perceiving the reality of the word by looking only backward in time, some western theologians put aside the fact that the church lives through the continuous power of the Word, whose servants are the prophets. This endangered pneumatological Christology that sees the Word as the one who continues to address his people in every new historical context. In order to be a full and ever-active representation of the Word incarnate, the church needs both the horizontal and the vertical forms of anamnesis, which Zizioulas justifiably calls for in his binomial synthesis:

> The church is an entity that receives and re-receives what her history transmits to her (παράδοσις), but this transmission is never a purely

historical affair; it takes place *sacramentally* or, if you prefer, *eucharistically*, i.e. it is experienced as a gift coming from the last days, from what God has promised and prepared for us in His Kingdom. This passage of the historical tradition through the eschaton is what the Holy Spirit does in apostolic succession, since the Spirit brings about the last days into history (see Acts 2:17), wherever He blows. Apostolic Tradition ceases to be a gift of the Spirit if it is simply a matter of historical continuity.[61]

The church actualizes a message that has historical roots but that participates ontologically in the eternal life of God that the blessed share with him, in which the church participates during history until the eschaton. It is only this synthesized historical and charismatic actualization that we can rightly define as "revelation" or the Deposit of Faith.

6.2.5. Conclusion

We have thus far carefully examined all the various contexts of the category of revelation in order to determine whether or not it makes sense to speak of an end of revelation. While being open to any given outcome, the result of this investigation is consistently clear: it does not make sense to speak of an end of revelation from the perspective of contemporary revelation theology, unless the terminology is qualified by a number of decisive limitations; the price for employing the notion today seems indeed higher than its benefits.

From the material perspective, a prophetic revelation occurring after the resurrection and ascension of Christ must be just as much an expression of God's reality as prophetic revelations in ancient Israel. Materially, Christ is the climax of revelation but not its end. From the formal perspective, things are more complex, although the results of our investigations are the same: revelation has been expressed eminently in Christ, of whom the apostles were particularly graced witnesses. Their normative testimony in Holy Scripture remains the required, "negative" norm, *norma normans*, for all later expressions of revelation, so that any word pronounced to express God's truth that clearly contradicts Scripture must be rejected as a faulty actualization and expression of revelation. While Scripture enjoys this normative status, it is by far *not* God's only means of self-communication, as he keeps expounding, explicating, and actualizing not just his true doctrine but *himself* to every new generation, with the aim of being received as Savior once again. This leads us to the conclusion that it is not only allowed, but, for the sake of highlighting all aspects of God's continued revelatory and salvific action until the eschaton, the most fruitful of available options to speak of a *continuation* of revelation. Only by using this terminology do we sufficiently highlight the inherent link between revelation's unique and complete establishment in Christ and its dynamic unfolding and actualization until the eschaton. It is only when one clearly acknowledges this that God's oneness and continuous dynamism in time will receive full merit.

From a material point of view, these prophetic manifestations of the Word do not transcend God's ultimate self-expression in Christ. On the formal level they may, however, at times appear as truly "new revelations" when pointing to truths explicitly or implicitly contained in Scripture that the church has neglected.

If these fundamental considerations are true, we must then ask ourselves why so many generations of theologians have heralded the quasi dogma of revelation's historical end. Why was it so important? Part of the answer is as reported earlier, namely that the theologians who invented the idea found themselves in a dispute with relativistic philosophies that threatened the normativity of Scripture-based church teaching, hence needed a timeframe in order to indicate when the normative treasure over which the church presided was filled up and deposited, as in a treasure chest. However, this explanation still leaves many questions unanswered. The contribution of the aforementioned scholars enables us to peer into the contemporary theological gallery that has, in large part, dissipated the old winds of the end-idea and its consequential clouds of dust, in order to release a pneumatic theology whose foundation is built on Scripture and Tradition. Christ *was* the climax of revelation, and *something* was given and constituted with him and the apostles. Today the question is: *what?*

As Gerald O'Collins and others argue, this *something* cannot be the concept of the Deposit of Faith interpreted in the neo-Scholastic tradition. The church did not merely receive a collection of true sentences. Rahner supports the notion when understood correctly; he portrays it as a deposit, the filling or constitution of which occurred through the gradual contribution of the Old Testament prophets and the ultimate contribution of Christ. Rahner has such veneration for this principle that he is in need of finding a function for prophecy that is totally eclipsed from the context of the public revelation, both materially and formally. This notion of the Deposit of Faith features the idea of a continuous growth of revelation with every successive Old Testament prophetic word until Christ, when the summit is reached, the Deposit-reservoir is full, revelation is ended, and growing revelation has become continued revelation. The church reigns in the dynamism of Christ, the Word himself, who is its head. Its life-giving secret is not a doctrinal possession that is static and immobile. Its life-giving secret is its ontological union with Christ, with the Word with which it is constantly and continuously synchronizing. Given the foregoing, one cannot affirm that the prophets served only in the laying of the foundation of the church, filling up the treasure that became in Christ its secret principle of being. Because the principle of the church's being is the ever-living Word and prophet par excellence himself, prophecy necessarily becomes enormously important to Christianity, *even more important than it was to Israel.* In Christ prophecy becomes an immediate and continuous means of rephrasing the Word through which the church exists.

Revelation thus comes across as the very life and truth of God himself. It was complete in seminal form, but not constituted or fulfilled in a perfectly explicit or actualized way with the apostles; God's people continue to grow in its fullness. To my view it makes sense to assess the constitution of three instances that are perfect and immutable entities, guaranteed in the will of God, as follows.

(1) *A perfect economy of Salvation.* Christ fulfilled the law and thereby was able to extend to his people a new law of grace that works salvation for those who believe in him. This economy is fully constituted with Christ. Nothing needs to be added to it, and it will not be overruled by a new economy until the return of Christ, when it will be realized in all Creation. Although it is fully constituted, it nevertheless needs to be fully explicated and actualized through the faith of believers in every new generation, and in this sense the collabo-ration, the "coredemptive mission" of every believer in every new generation is required, aiding in "filling up what is lacking in the afflictions of Christ on behalf of his body, which is the church."[62] It is in this context of the con-tinuous explication and actualization of the Salvation wrought in Christ that the prophets have the most excellent part to play.

(2) *Scripture.* While scripture may contain grammatical errors and dif-ferent versions of the sacred texts and may not have been written in the finest Greek of its times, God has nonetheless *chosen* to express his truth norma-tively therein. In this way, Scripture becomes the normative testimony of revelation, but it is not to be equated with the reality of revelation itself, which is God's life in his church. Referring to Ricoeur,[63] Elmar Salmann has sum-marized well the extent and limitation of Scripture and how it relates to the Word:

> One would have to say more exactly that the text of Sacred Scrip-ture is the actualization [Niederschlag] of a never fully comprehen-sible word event and of the initiation of a history of interpretation and application, whereby precisely the particular traits of the different

text forms in their indissoluble contradiction (narration and prophecy, cult and wisdom texts, legend and parabola) let these become the open reference to the always larger Verbum and the always more appropriate reception.[64]

(3) *The church.* The church, like Christ, is the mystical fusion of history and transcendence, of human frailty and divine grace. It is the realm in which the economy of salvation that Scripture expresses normatively is continuously realized and extended to Creation until the fulfillment of all things. The entire people of God are the inhabitants of this area, and they are those who live and realize revelation during the course of history. The Magisterium plays a particular role in intensifying and authoritatively expressing aspects of revelation, but this does not prevent God from employing prophecy, calling individual members of his people, to address the church with a message that actualizes and revitalizes his life.

This confirms the conclusion of my examination of the historical development of prophecy (chapter 3): just as there is no historical evidence that indicates a radical change in prophecy's function phenomenologically from the old to the new covenant, so there are no theological reasons that require the function of Christian prophecy to be any different from that of its old covenant counterpart. True, there are differences: while the Old Testament prophet is most likely to speak in the name of Yahweh, the Christian prophet mostly speaks in the name of Christ (when not in the name of the Father, the Holy Spirit, or the Holy Trinity). While the old covenant collected God's people in a covenant, Christ in his new covenant collected his people in the church, which as his Body is the continuation of his own presence on earth. But if the functional definition of prophecy is *God calling and guiding his people directly through means of revelations to live in his truth and receive his life again*, then prophecy is and remains an uninterrupted means of God's guidance throughout the entire history of his salvation.

6.3. Prophetic Implementation of Revelation

Following the conclusions predicated on the aforementioned investigations, one must deduce that although Christ did constitute the church to be his own body and continued presence on earth, this does not change its need for growing into what it potentially is, namely the realization and realizer of his truth. Revelation still needs to be mediated and actualized in every new historical context.

In what follows I shall examine those instances, or loci, that actualize revelation in time. I will show how the prophetic impulse is vital to each one of these loci in order to truly reflect the truth they serve, and give concrete historical examples of how prophecy influenced their development and function. I will moreover call to mind that prophecy inspired the Bible's formation and interpretation and how it related to and inspired the Magisterium together with its theologians. I will show how prophecy influenced the development of dogma, the understanding of the sacraments, the rise and diffusion of spiritual traditions and places of worship. And last, we shall enter the realm of sociology in order to delve into the interaction of prophecy and the general religious life of the faithful. Although the charism of prophecy is realized in various forms, I shall in what follows continue to focus on those forms that have been identified as the most important, namely visions, apparitions, and locutions.

In spite of the importance prophecy had in the actualization of revelation, it is surprising how few works there are that deal with this issue. While searching the literature for insights on Christian prophecy, more often than not one encounters incomplete (to the point of faulty) presentations on the issue, such as is found in Melchior Cano's *De locis theologicis. Mysterium Salutis* is a prime modern example that may serve to illustrate this point. *Mysterium Salutis* employs 286 pages[65] to portray the different instances that serve as revelation's sources throughout history. Interestingly, in *none* of these pages, either in the text or in the footnotes, is reference made to the importance of Christian prophecy in the transmission of revelation, except in one very cautious footnote in the chapter on the handing down of revelation: "One ought probably to count private revelations in the continuation of revelation [Überlieferung der Offenbarung]."[66] The same applies to the works of Joseph Schumacher. In his 336-page work *Der apostolische Abschluss der Offenbarung*, it is surprising that he devotes only a four-page "Exkurs" to the issue of private revelations.[67] Now, the inevitable question arises, how can this strange exclusion of prophecy be explained if not by either the theologian's inability to discern ongoing prophetic revelations in light of Scripture and Tradition, or a theological sentiment of jealousy toward prophecy's authority that Rahner points out?[68] The fact is that prophetic revelations continued through the entire Christian history and played an immense role in reactualizing and reexpressing revelation with greater explication. In the following sections, we shall see how.

6.3.1. Prophecy and Scripture

Scripture as the permanent authoritative testimony to revelation is the criterion for God's truth and serves, as such, as the primary measuring rod for evaluating prophecy in the church. In this sense, Scripture has supreme power over prophecy, which can never oppose it. This does not mean, however that prophecy had no influence on Scripture; on the contrary. As mentioned in section 3.3.9, entire books in Scripture are collections of prophetic oracles, and only God knows how much the prophetic spirit was present when the authors of the various parts of Scripture lifted their pens to write. And though Scripture is the norm for Tradition, it is itself part and parcel of Tradition, inasmuch as it is a literary product of the early church. With Hallbäck and Kelber we encountered the manner by which the decline of the earliest Christian prophecy influenced and was one reason for the editing of the New Testament in its shift from oral to written tradition (see section 3.3.10). We saw how much the Q source, reflecting the theology of a genuinely prophetic tradition, influenced the final Gospel products (see section 3.3.7). And with Boring we encountered Bultmann's thesis that demonstrated how Christian prophets played an overwhelmingly important role in forwarding words of the historical Jesus in the light of their own experience of the risen Christ (see section 2.4). Although Witherington and others emphasize the difficulty in proving this thesis, the aforementioned scholars overwhelmingly favor the conclusion that the Scripture-creative role of Christian prophets of the Old Testament and New Testament greatly influenced the formation of the canon.

Prophecy has influenced not only the formation of Scripture but its continuous hermeneutic as well. With Ellis and Boring we evaluated the idea that one of the functions of New Testament Christian prophecy is inspired exegesis (see section 2.4). As evidenced in the writings of Engelbert (see section 3.3.15), this function continued in the life of the church, to such an extent that many Christian prophets elucidated obscure parts of Scripture, to the point that the prophetic revelations could even be of inspiration when determining the correct interpretation of Scripture. Needless to say, these prophetic insights into Scripture, of which I have given but an infinitesimal view, have never attained in the Catholic context the hermeneutic authority of the Magisterium.

6.3.2. Prophecy and the Magisterium

Catholic theology ascribes to the Magisterium, formed by the bishops in union with the pope, a particular role in transmitting revelation. In the ordinary Magisterium the general infallibility of the church is considered to be concentrated in a way that lends it special authority, charging it with the task of interpreting Scripture, of keeping the church's true teaching, and of safeguarding during history the treasure it received from Christ and the apostles. In order that the safeguarding task may not evolve into its suppressing opposite, the

Magisterium depends on a direct prophetic influx that Rahner refers to as the assistance of the Holy Spirit.[69] It must be imbued with a "negative" prophetic dimension, assuring that the Magisterium's task of safeguarding does not degenerate into error, while maintaining also a "positive" prophetic dimension, assuring in the Holy Spirit that the Magisterium continues to forward the eternal truths it received in order that they are rendered accessible to every new historical context. The ministry of Peter and the ecumenical councils play a particular role in this regard. Papal pronouncements *ex cathedra* and officially ratified council promulgations are considered to be imbued with a particular grace avoiding the profession of wrong doctrines, also known as papal infallibility. The Magisterium never professes the faith of the church in isolation from the people of God—it does so *on behalf of the people,* expressing the faith of the entire church as expression of the truth of Christ. And indeed it is important to highlight that the infallibility of the church has three realizations: "the church's general infallibility (the *sensus fidelium),* the infallibility of the bishops (together with the bishop of Rome) both in general councils and in their ordinary Magisterium, and the infallibility of the pope without the bishops."[70] In the third instance, Alistair McGrath is referring to those instances where the pope has presented *ex cathedra* an authoritative dogmatic expression; yet it should be remembered that even this action is never done without the participation of the authority of other bishops and that it has only happened twice in history (1854 and 1950).

Countless papal documents have pointed out the importance of prophecy and prophetic revelations in the life of the church.[71] What is perhaps more interesting is that countless prophets have presented divine instructions, messages, and encouragements to the leaders of the church: "That revelations were intended for members of the hierarchy is a fact."[72] History knows many examples even of popes whose actions were inspired by the messages of often simple believers.

Famous in this regard are the words and actions of Birgitta of Vadstena and Catherine of Siena, who both insisted that the popes return from their exile in Avignon to Rome, and in so doing carried out their prophetic vocation by admonishing the leaders of the church to change in order to secure its unity.[73] Although he honored Birgitta as a prophet,[74] Gregory XI declined the prophetic warnings of Christ that were presented to him through her, and it took the later warnings of Catherine of Siena to realize the Avignon-to-Rome papal transfer. But according to Saudreau, even Catherine's words would not have touched the pope's heart and would not have "triumphed over the oppositions of the prelates of the pontifical Court, who showed incredulity toward her mission," had it not been for the undeniable sign that, according to former prophetic patterns, in 1376 accompanied and corroborated her revealed words. As a proof that Catherine was indeed sent by God, she told the pope that Christ had unveiled to her a vow he had made and that was known only by him.[75]

In 1582, a young girl, named Orsola Benincasa, presented herself before Pope Gregory XIII and told him the Lord had sent her to ask the church to work harder toward its reform. First, no one believed her, and the Pope had her examined by cardinals, by theologians, and by Philipp Neri in particular. Neri spent seven months examining her and eventually came to the conclusion that this simple girl was truly sent by God with an important message to his church. The pope accepted Neri's conclusion and decided to further the reform of the church, a reform that was carried out in the years that followed.

Furthermore, two important consecrations of the human race, one to the Sacred Heart of Jesus and another to the Immaculate Heart of Mary, were not only directly inspired, but *urgently requested* by Jesus and Mary through various prophets, as follows.

On May 25, 1899, Leo XIII announced in his encyclical "Annum sacrum" that he expected a great event to have lasting fruits in the life not only of God's people but for the entire human race: the consecration of mankind to the Sacred Heart of Jesus. In the same encyclical we read a somewhat enigmatic sentence in which the pope presents one of the motives that lead him to the solemn act of consecration, which he called "The greatest act of my pontificate": "There is one further reason that urges us to realize our design; we do not want it to pass by unnoticed. It is personal in nature but just as important: God, the author of all Good has saved us by healing us recently from a dangerous disease."[76] This sentence in the encyclical only makes sense if one knows the story behind it.

On June 10, 1898, the superior of the monastery of the Good Pastor in Porto (Portugal), Mary of the Divine Heart Droste zu Vischering, wrote a letter to the pope, telling him that the Lord wanted his vicar to consecrate the entire world to the Divine Heart. The pope initially did not believe her and took no action. But on January 6, she wrote another letter in accordance with her spiritual director, telling the pope that he should not only venture toward the consecration of mankind to the Sacred Heart but also recommended increased devotion to it by encouraging pastors and the faithful to observe the first Fridays of the month in its honor. The following words are reported in her letter: "Last summer, Your Holiness suffered an illness that caused your children to worry, given your advanced age. The Lord gave me the sweet consolation that he would prolong the days of Your Holiness in order that you may realize the consecration of the entire world to his divine Heart."[77]

Volken shows that this moved the pope's heart.[78] Although the act of consecration caused theologians certain difficulties, especially with regard to the possibility of consecrating even non-Christians to Christ, it took place, as did other requests of Christ through the same superior.

The second act of consecration occurred on December 8, 1942, twenty-five years after the Virgin Mary of Fatima had asked that the world be consecrated to her Immaculate Heart. On July 7, 1952, the consecration was renewed, this time with particular attention to Russia: "As we have consecrated some years ago the human race to the Immaculate Heart of the Virgin Mary of God, so we now consecrate to the same Immaculate Heart in particular all the peoples of Russia."[79] In order to discern a strong link between this act and Fatima, it is enough to recall the content of the Fatima apparitions and their strong insistence on the consecration of Russia to Mary's heart. On October 9, 2000, in the presence of the original statue of Our Lady of Fatima, 1,450 of the world's 4,500 Catholic bishops gathered in Rome for the special jubilee celebration for the bishops, at which Pope John Paul II once again consecrated the world to Mary's Immaculate heart. In a press release the president of the jubilee committee, Mons. Crescenzio Sepe, made it clear that the reason why the consecration occurred in the presence of the original Madonna of Fatima was precisely to link this consecration in the year 2000 to the apparitions of Fatima, in which the Virgin's request was expressed.[80]

More examples can be given in this regard, but I limit myself to the foregoing, as it sufficiently shows just how much prophets have inspired the course of Christian history by moving the hearts and actions not only of the laity of God but of the church's hierarchy as well.

6.3.3. Prophecy and Theology

Theologians play a vital role in transmitting revelation. As Basil Studer wrote, they support the Magisterium's task of interpreting and actualizing revelation in "hervorragender Weise" through their "engen Verbindung mit dem kirchlichen Lehramt," while employing ever-new scientific methods.[81] As with the Magisterium so, too, theology, if it is to be true living theology, needs the influx of prophecy. Joseph Ratzinger illustrates this point well:

> While one proceeds with the mind only, nothing new will ever
> happen. Increasingly more definite systems may well be construed,
> increasingly subtle questions raised but the true and proper way from
> which great theology may again flow is not generated by the ratio-
> nal side of theological work but by a charismatic and prophetic thrust.

And it is in this sense, I believe, that prophecy and theology go hand in glove.[82]

As examples of this fruitful collaboration, Joseph Ratzinger proposes the the theological-prophetic companionships of Augustine and Athanasius, of Thomas Aquinas and Dominic, of Bonaventure and Francis of Assisi, and of Hans Urs von Balthasar and Adrienne von Speyr. Theology as a scientific discipline is not prophetic, but "but may only truly become living theology under the thrust and illumination of a prophetic impulse."[83]

The collaboration of Balthasar and von Speyr is a particularly striking example of this point. Balthasar, one of the most widely published and respected innovators of modern Catholic theology, wrote shortly prior to his death that his theology and the lay movement he helped to found was derived *directly* from von Speyr's experience: "[I want] to prevent any attempt being made after my death to separate my work from that of Adrienne von Speyr. [This] is not in the least possible, either theologically or in regard to the secular institute now underway."[84]

6.3.4. Prophecy and Development of Dogma

The relationship and interaction between Christian prophetic revelations and ongoing growth in the church's cognition of the truth of the Triune God is one of the more complex issues in the contemporary discussion of prophecy's role in Christendom. The interaction between prophecy and dogma is reciprocal, in that prophetic language is inspired by doctrine, just as prophetic paranesis is largely directed to the implementation of Christian truth. Ernst Benz reflects upon this prophetic-dogmatic interaction well:

> On the whole there is such a close relationship between vision and dogma that one can say that the history of Christian visions in their overall process are a type of picture book of the history of dogma; likewise one can say that the visions of a given epoch in the history of the church constitute a characteristic picture book of the specific dogmatic viewpoints of this specific period, as long as these visionaries do not play their revelations out against the teaching of the church and thereby initiate a new epoch of dogmatic creativity.[85]

I have already questioned the prevailing thesis that the church's prophetic revelations have nothing to do with the Deposit of Faith and concluded that although they add nothing to the material fullness of God's revelation in Christ, they are among the main catalysts in the continuous historical unfolding of revelation and "growth into the full truth." Even though the teaching office may have the last word in proclaiming this deepened knowledge through authoritative doctrinal proclamations, no theological argument writes of prophecy as an instance that helps to draw forth issues that, at least explicitly, were not proposed before as part of Christian truth. I shall now briefly examine this theological assessment that enjoys historical evidence.

As mentioned earlier, pronouncements by the Magisterium are thought to summarize, concentrate, and proclaim truths that are the heritage of the entire church, the *sensus fidelium*. Historically, ideas growing out of the writings of Christian prophets often spread first among the faithful before they become part of the general faith of the church and then, sometimes, attain official expression through the Magisterium. To the Catholic theologian, a prophetic revelation can never in itself express a new dogma. As Rahner shows, the revelation may express a not-yet-realized truth that, however, becomes dogma when it is promulgated as such by the Magisterium.[86] The prophetic revelation may be an inspired hypothesis for theologians to work on, which provides them with an important insight that, in turn, causes them to consider new aspects of revelation and investigate their basis into Scripture and Tradition. This hermeneutic verification of new possible insights in Christian truth is, according to Rahner, one of theology's main tasks: "The problem of dogmatic development actually consists in the task of showing the identity of the later 'unfolded' faith expression with what was given in the apostolic revelation realized in Christ."[87]

Volken agrees with Rahner and equally considers the message of prophetic revelations as a working hypothesis for theology. Volken portrays the relationship between prophetic revelations and development of dogma by means of a parable: a boy receives a violin from his uncle and becomes a famous violinist. The gift of the uncle was not the violinist's career in itself but an important incitement to its initiation. Likewise, prophetic revelations can lead to new dogmatic understanding without the revelation equally being the dogma itself. Other examples could be given of how prophecy both inspires and confirms dogmatic developments, but I shall limit the investigation to the Dogma of the Immaculate Conception of Mary.

CATALYZING NEW IDEAS. The promulgation of the immaculate conception is closely linked with various accounts of miracles and prophetic messages dispensed in its support. In a text attributed to Anselm of Canterbury, a story is told of the Abbot of Helsin who around 1070 undertook a mission for William the Conqueror to the king of Denmark. While he was on his way back, a violent storm threatened his life. He invoked the Virgin Mary. A vision

followed in which a messenger told him that if he wanted to see his home-
land again he should promise faithfully to celebrate the feast of the conception
of Christ's mother.[88] A number of similar occurrences continued to increase
the awareness of the dogma, and these manifestations reached their climax at
the Rue du Bac in Paris in the apparitions to Catherine Labouré, with the
request that a medal be struck and its devotion spread: "By means of the
Miraculous Medal, devotion to the Immaculate Conception was universally
spread . . . the doctors of the Church were stimulated by the very fact to consider this belief more attentively."[89] From there it continued growing as a
theological issue toward the proclamation of the dogma, and although Pope
Gregory XVI was cautious, the secretary of state, Cardinal Lambruschini,
"stepped from behind the anonymity of a public servant" and published a
book in which he argued that such a dogmatic definition was much desired
and referred directly to the Miraculous Medal.[90]

In recent years, such an ever-growing interest has spread among the
faithful in the Catholic church for the idea of Mary as Mediatrix, Coredemptrix,
and Advocate, which many would like to see it confirmed in the form of an ex
cathedra papal dogmatic pronouncement. Some furiously reject the idea as
"paganism."[91] Others, although they might agree with the idea, do not wish to
see it defined, as they believe dogmas divide and may jeopardize ecumenical
progress. Thus, the Pontifical International Marian Academy appointed a
commission consisting of fifteen Catholic mariologists as well as an Anglican,
a Lutheran, and three Orthodox to look at the issue. The commission's verdict
was that "any doctrinal elevation of Mary would be contrary to the direction established by Vatican II and would be distasteful to Protestants and the Eastern
Orthodox."[92] Nevertheless, interest in the possible dogma continues to grow.

The idea of Mary as Coredemptrix is old and can be discerned in Bonaventure.[93] It emerges forcefully in the revelations to Birgitta of Vadstena.[94] It
discovers its roots in the teaching that every believer participates in Christ's
work of redemption, thus "filling up what is lacking in the afflictions of Christ
on behalf of his body, which is the church,"[95] and the Virgin Mary occupies a
special role in this regard. Paul Maria Sigl has shown that all the elements of
prophetic inspiration and interaction with dogma are present in this new
development: the idea finds its roots in Scripture, and has been continuously
proclaimed by great leaders and theologians of the Christian church.[96] Because
this development has never been sufficiently explicated in the Catholic Church,
it needed an extraordinary, visionary impulse to place it at the very fore of
Christian prophecy, where it might best occasion dogmatic recognition. Sigl
shows how this prophetic surge was realized through the apparitions of Our
Lady of All Nations to Ida Peerdeman in Amsterdam.[97]

Her apparitions began on March 25, 1945. Already in 1951, the local bishop of Haarlem, Mons. Huibers, approved a particular prayer associated with the apparitions, while the two bishops Mons. Bomers and Mons. Punt approved of the title "Lady of All Nations." Although they gave no authoritative judgment on the authenticity of the apparitions, they nonetheless left every believer free to decide on their veracity. With this, the apparitions obtained the freedom needed to be received by the faithful. Sigl shows how the apparitions have raised awareness and knowledge of this development and that they might very well be the primary urge necessary to make it dogma. As with other prophetic messages, those of Amsterdam were said to be accompanied by divine signs that influenced the confirmation of their authenticity. One such sign was Ida Peerdeman having foreseen the gathering of Vatican II.[98]

Given the foregoing, if this new development should become dogma, it will provide us with a contemporary example of prophecy's influence on dogmatic development, but even if not, one cannot deny the powerful interaction between the two.

INSPIRING AND CONFIRMING DOGMATIC DEVELOPMENT. As Volken, Laurentin, and Suh all argue, prophetic revelations often serve to confirm the validity and importance of new dogmatic developments. Numerous theologians maintain that apparitions of the Virgin Mary are confirmations that indeed bolster dogmatic pronouncements, and this is evidenced in the Virgin's apparitions to Bernadette of Lourdes. In the Lourdes apparitions, which occurred only four years after the proclamation of the dogma of the Immaculate Conception, the Virgin presented herself, saying: "I am the Immaculate Conception." In the encyclical *Fulgens corona*, Pius XII expressed the widespread opinion that Lourdes confirmed the dogma: "Moreover, it seems that the Blessed Virgin Mary herself wished to confirm by some special sign the definition, which the Vicar of her Divine Son on earth had pronounced amidst the applause of the whole Church."[99]

6.3.5. Prophecy and Development of Pious Traditions

The spiritual life of the people is where revelation is realized in practice. Numerous new devotional practices were inspired by prophetic revelations. Tradition ascribes the origin of a number of chaplet-based prayer forms to prophetic revelations: the chaplet of St. Michael (revelations to Sister Antonia d'Astonac in 1751),[100] the Crown of the Infant Jesus of Prague (revelations to the venerable Margaret of the Blessed Sacrament, d. 1648),[101] the chaplet of Divine Mercy (revelations to Sr. Faustina Kowalska, d. 1938),[102] the chaplet of the Holy Wounds of Christ (revelations to Sr. Mary Martha Chambon, early twentieth century),[103] a chaplet emphasizing Jesus' kingship (revelations to two anonymous American women, late twentieth century),[104] and other chaplet prayer practices have been inspired by prophetic revelations.[105]

Another prime example is the Sacred Heart tradition. Although this tradition has roots in Scripture and early church teaching, and although Gertrude the Great had important messages on the importance and love of the heart of Christ, this tradition was supremely introduced and confirmed by church authorities only after the revelations to Margaret Mary Alacoque. In her time, faith in Christ's mercy had so diminished that the faithful hardly dared to approach the altar, hence renewed trust in his charity was greatly needed. The devotion to the Sacred Heart of Jesus as symbol of his tender love became the answer to this need. According to Rahner, Margaret Mary's revelations were "a historical occasion" for the church to accept the devotion to the Sacred Heart that first was greatly opposed.[106] Pope XI expressed himself on the advantageousness of the devotion to the Sacred heart while expressing the importance of the Margaret Mary's apparitions to its realization: "Our Lord himself made manifest to the most innocent disciple of his Heart, Saint Margaret Mary, how much he, moved less by his right than by his immense charity towards us, desired that men should pay him this homage of devotion."[107] The spirituality stemming from the revelations of Margaret Mary has led believers ever since to have Fridays set as days of special devotion to the Sacred Heart of Jesus.[108]

A number of other devotional practices with origin in prophetic revelations should be mentioned: the Scapular of the Most Blessed Trinity (revelations to John of Matha, 1160–1213), founder of the Order of the Most Holy Trinity, Trinitarians),[109] the Black Scapular (according to tradition from revelations to seven noblemen of Florence, later canonized, early thirteenth century),[110] the praying of Three Hail Marys (revelations to Mechtilde of Helfta, d. 1298),[111] Via Matris, the Way of the Mother (revelations to the founders of the Servants of Mary, thirteenth Century),[112] the Fifteen Tortures of Christ (revelations of Blessed Mary Magdalene Martinengo, 1687–1737),[113] the Green Scapular (revelations of Daughter of Charity sister Justine Bisqueyburu, nineteenth century),[114] the Golden Arrow (revelations to Sister Marie de Saint-Pierre, 1843),[115] the Rosary Novena (revelations to Fortuna Agrellie, 1880s),[116] the First Person of the Holy Trinity (revelations to Sister Eugenia Elizabetta Ravasio, 1907–90),[117] First Saturday (attendance at Mass the first Saturday of the month in reparation of the sins of the world, revelations to the children of Fatima, 1917),[118] the Holy Face Medal (revelations to Sister Maria Pierina of the Daughters of the Immaculate Conception, 1940s),[119] Our Lady of

All Nations (revelations to Ida Peerdeman, twentieth Century),[120] Jesus, King of All Nations, with specific chaplet and other joint devotion forms (revelations to two American women wishing to remain anonymous, contemporary).[121] Similar development can be attributed to the apparitions of Christ to Faustina Kowalska on God's divine mercy (see 6.3.6). One should mention also the popular devotion to Mary as she has been seen in specific forms by visionaries all over the world, mostly with related pilgrimage sites and specific devotional depictions of Our Lady too many to mention (i.e., Our Lady of Lourdes, our Lady of Fatima, Our Lady of Guadalupe, etc.). As already mentioned (see chapter 3), numerous religious orders that furthered specific devotional traditions were initiated through prophetic directions from Christ or the Virgin Mary.[122] In this way, prophecy helped to further a tradition in the church that has always served as an oasis of revelation in the midst of the busy world, assuring spiritual thresholds—limens, in anthropological terms—providing connection with the world of the Spirit. I shall return to this theme in chapter 7.

6.3.6. Prophecy, Liturgy, and Sacraments

As Alois Stenzel shows, the actualization of revelation finds its most living expression through the liturgy, the place where God's people, through the sacraments in particular, are brought into his immediate presence. The liturgy is that forum in which the church, more than in any other way, becomes itself and truly lives as church,[123] as an icon of the eschatological life of the people of God. As Alois Stenzel writes, the liturgy is the "proper place of the edification of the community," and as prophecy serves this purpose in particular, it is understandable that Paul in his letters, especially to the Corinthians, affirms that the prophets ideally should talk one by one *during* the liturgy.[124]

Numerous liturgical feasts were instituted on direct instructions of Christ through prophecy. The revelations to St. Juliana of Mont-Cornillon and the subsequent institution of the feast of Corpus Christi are important examples thereof, as they pointed both to the importance of the sacrament of the Eucharist and asked for a feast for its commemoration. In 1208, Juliana had visions at the age of sixteen. She died in 1258. Only six years later, Urban IV, who had met her in Liège in 1246 and who knew her revelations, issued the bull that instituted the feast known as "demandée par le Seigneur."[125] In 1312, the Council of Vienna confirmed this decree, and in 1316 Urban IV prescribed that the feast become solemn.

Recently, the interaction between prophecy and papal decisions on liturgical developments has come into focus for the church once more. In the beginning of the twentieth century, Sister Faustina Kowalska, whom Pope John Paul II canonized in 2000, received numerous prophetic messages, mainly from Christ, in which he reveals his ardent desires that his children believe more in his mercy. To catalyze this, he asked that a feast be instituted in honor and memory of his mercy on the Sunday following Easter. Pope John Paul II, who, as a bishop, had brought her Index-banned revelations back to honor, instituted in the year 2000 the feast requested by his Polish compatriot and thereby carried out the request of the revelations he had confirmed by canonizing her.

It is important to call to mind also what we saw in chapter 3, namely that prophetic revelations inspired the initiation and development of monastic communities and how these in turn inspired the development of the church (see section 3.3.15). Likewise, we saw how prophetic revelations were linked to the formation of numerous pilgrimage sites and especially Marian shrines (see section 3.3.20).

6.3.7. Conclusion

We have now seen that all the partial loci that serve to actualize and implement revelation in time are both prophetic in nature and have always interacted with prophetic revelations in the life of the church. Prophetic developments in the ancient church spurred the formation of Holy Scripture and influenced its content greatly. Moreover, throughout the history of the church, prophets have played a great role in shedding light on important passages of Scripture that were once obscured or ignored. And prophets called the people of God to live according to these truths.

Like all other loci of revelation, the Magisterium needs the prophetic influx in order to carry out its proper role of expressing the Christian truth. History has proven that this influx has been realized in many ways, in particular by the general assistance of the Holy Spirit, who works mysteriously through the carriers of institutional offices. Prophetic personalities have constantly inspired the actions of church leaders, and ideas born from true prophetic revelations were eventually received and confirmed by the Magisterium. Although theology as a scientific discipline may not be prophetic in structure, history has proven that truly great and enlightening theology has always emerged through a direct prophetic impulse. In fact, as Ratzinger recalls, many of the church's greatest theologians collaborated closely with people whom they considered to be imbued with the prophetic gift.

Closely related to this is the interaction of prophecy and new dogmatic developments. Although a prophetic revelation as a contingent historical fact does not create dogma in the strict sense, inspired truths that individuals such as Catherine Labouré have forwarded to the church under prophetic inspiration have often been the spark that has ignited new dogmatic insights and promulgations in the church. Likewise, the prophetic revelations to Bernadette of Lourdes also served to confirm and corroborate further dogmatic developments. Nevertheless, the same prophetic revelations served a much wider purpose than the expression of dogmatic truths: They were often the direct cause of new pious traditions in the church through which the faithful found more timely ways of practicing their faith, and they have given rise to the vast majority of pilgrimage sites that have played an immense role in both Catholic and Orthodox salvation history.

All loci are prophetic in nature and were influenced by prophetic revelations; all serve as windows or rooms for revelation, channels of God's grace and signs of his truth. However, all these loci realize their function only when the people of God actually *live* God's life. In the following chapter I shall explore how prophecy has played its biggest role in the life of the church in advancing precisely this inner dynamism of God's life among his people.

7

Prophecy and Sociology of Religion

As Löhrer affirms in his reference to Augustine, the church emerges as the general instance that realizes revelation in time ("Sakrament der ganzen Heilswirklichkeit Christi").[1] The church's teaching office plays a particular role in this regard, but it is the entire people of God who live and transmit God's revelation. Vatican II brought this general task of the people of God—which neo-Scholasticism had underestimated—back to the attention of mainstream Catholic theology. The concept *sensus fidelium,* so appreciated by Scheeben,[2] covers this collective faith in the entire people of God. Every Christian, having been introduced to Christ's mission of revealing God's Kingdom by baptism, shares in his prophetic vocation. All believers are called to be prophets and priests for Christ.

Fisichella interprets this general prophetic vocation of the people of God by drawing a distinction between the Old Testament and the New Testament. In the new covenant, Joel's prophecy that "your sons and daughters shall prophecy"[3] has been fulfilled and applies to the entire people of God such that all, at least potentially, "are in the condition of being able to prophecy."[4] All are called to be prophets, wherefore limited, Old Testament prophecy has been extended to the entire people of God. This thought could lead and has indeed led to the Christian denial of specific prophecy, with its traits of particular vocation and visionary experiences. After all, when all Christians are prophets why allow a specific prophecy with a particular vocation and empowerment? The same principle applies to the priesthood: just as a strong affirmation of the general priesthood of all believers can lead to the widespread denial of a *specific ministry*, as in important areas of Lutheran thought, so the insistence on the general prophetic vocation of every believer can lead to the dismissal of the specific prophetic vocation in the church.

This, however, is not Fisichella's purpose. Acknowledging that the prophetic potential of every believer does not eliminate, but rather enables specific prophecy, he points to the classical examples of prophets in the church, such as Catherine of Siena and Birgitta of Vadstena.

Prophetic revelations have served throughout the church's history to call people back to true life in God, as did God through his prophets of the Old Testament. As mentioned, from a functional, phenomenological point of view, there is *no* difference between the two covenants in this regard, although especially apropos of the Sacraments the new covenant may provide more means of grace. As Suh has shown,[5] prophecy calls Christians to take their faith seriously and let it permeate all aspects of their lives. Prophecy calls people to pray and to ultimately live the life of grace in the mysterious fusion of God's gift with man's effort. However, even though prophets always preached repentance, prophecy is able to help realize God's life in the church far more powerfully than through mere moral exhortation, as it is able through its inner dynamism to move the faithful to live more closely to the mystery of their faith, which is what we will investigate in this chapter.

Prophetic claims like those of Montanus and Mohammed often produced new movements that began as marginalized bodies within the church before their "new" revelation drove them out of Christendom and into new religious societies with independent institutions, sacred writings, and creeds. We saw that the fear inferred from such experiences produced by post-Montanist and especially post-Islamic Christian prophecy, as well as its scarce theological elaboration, may well have been the main initial factors that led to a devaluation of the nomenclature regarding prophecy. It is likely that theologians and church leaders could easily have inferred from such negative experiences, which continued after Montanus and Mohammed, that all prophetic activity and proclamation of revelations is dangerous to the unity of the church, and that prophecy by its very nature, whether true or false, marginalizes people from the church, although this was rejected by Irenaeus and other church Fathers (see section 3.3.14). But is this reaction to the dangers sometimes associated with prophecy justifiable?

History says no, and we have seen that prophecy did inspire all the various instances of revelation's actualization in history. But to arrive at an answer that transcends mere historical evidence and that explains *why* true Christian

prophecy does not lead people away from the church's core, one needs to turn
to religious anthropology and sociology; it is by this means that we arrive at an
in-depth analysis of the phenomena surrounding a person who claims to have
messages from God. The fruits of such research lead to interesting answers:
true Christian prophecy does *not* lead believers to the margins of Christendom
but leads them to what religious anthropologists term the "limen," that is, the
threshold of the very core of religious society. Instead of being centrifugal, the
prophetic thrust is centripetal. Through the prophet's experience of the Word
of God, believers are led to the mystery of that very same Word that the true
prophet experiences. Sociology affirms this function of prophecy: it receives
and forwards a historically realized mystery: That the Word of God became
flesh in Christ. But it does not stop it's the mere historical repetition of the
Word, but seeks to lead the faithful to an authentic encounter with the reality of
this Word. This theme enhances the common thread of the past chapters: the
prophet's task of leading the church through the valley of the dynamism between the past and future fulfillment of God's Word. As a result of this experience, believers seek to gather or organize themselves in structures that may
initially appear further away from mainstream Christianity but that they consider to be a more genuine response of their time, as they more effectively
reveal how to live the mystery of that Word in the light of the "signs of the
times." History proves that these new movements and structures often renewed
and later became what we today define as mainstream Christendom that opposed the antistructures that eventually ended up reneging the church's past.
This places prophecy in the fascinating dialectic of structure, antistructure, and
restructurization—a dialectic on which prophecy proves to have a great impact.

7.1. Alessandro Toniolo's Reception of Victor Turner

Victor Turner is one of the best known anthropologists, famous for his research in initiation rites within indigenous religions. But can such rites, which
appear to be very different from the practice of mainstream Christianity, have
anything to say to Christian theology? The answer seems to be affirmative;
Turner's research proves to have tremendous resonance in the Christian
context. Although his work only applies in the full sense to indigenous religions without sacred scriptures, Turner believes the term "initiation rite" can
be fruitfully applied to "processes, phenomena, and persons in large-scale
complex societies" such as the Christian church, although "its use must in the
main be metaphorical."[6] Christian scholars' reception of Turner's research
has proved that he is right. Not only does he himself apply the results of

his indigenous-religion research to major historical religious bodies such as Christianity, but many other researchers have done so as well.

One such researcher is the Italian religious anthropologist Alessandro Toniolo of the Liturgical Institute of Padova. Toniolo has combined Turner's research with that of Mircea Eliade and others and applied it to different aspects of Christendom. The outcome is vital new insights and subsequent publications on classical Christian themes: Christian religious initiation,[7] the sociological function of the catecumenate,[8] as well as the (mainly) post–Vatican II phenomena of new ecclesial movements.[9] Applying the term *liminal* in the metaphorical sense to the Christian context sheds light on certain aspects of religion that theology is unable to appreciate and extract fully.

The preceding insights on prophecy's sociological impetus permit me now to examine how sociologists define a given movement within a larger structure. In fact, it is such movements within larger structures that tend to implement in their time the notion of the ideal or golden age, with which some associate prophecy. I will describe the effects of these movements and show that when they are indeed driven by the prophetic expression that connects them with the "ideal state," they are led not away from, but toward, the core of the church. Also worthy of mention is the way anthropologists consider the prophetic to lead the faithful not only through movements, but in other multiple ways. In point of fact, the limen here proves to be an important factor, as it is incorporated in different permanent "oases" such as monasteries and pilgrimage sites, where believers seek the central mystery of their faith, drawn toward the center of the religious body to which they belong.

7.2. The *Communitas* as Antistructure

Victor Turner opposes the idea that a community or a group of people can exist by their own power, otherwise known as a *fait total*—an organism that rests chiefly in its own creed and culture. He affirms that groups of people sharing the same approach to a creed always do so *in dialectic with other groups* that they positively relate to or oppose. Turner elucidates this insight as follows: "In the ritual celebration, the community, even if it be only a 'symbolic' or 'juridical' community rather than a spontaneous group, discovers that 'the social structure' is nothing but an artifact, a 'lie,' noble or ignoble, 'an artificial social construction of the truth.' The true reality is the antistructure."[10]

This puts the notion "antistructure" in a more positive light. Turner calls this antistructure *communitas*, the Latin equivalent for *community*, as the term "antistructure" carries the notion of existing only to oppose other groups, which is no more Turner's definition of *communitas* than it is his definition of "antistructure:"

> I have used the term "antistructure," but I would like to make clear that the "anti" is here only used strategically and does not imply a radical negativity. . . . When I speak of antistructure, therefore, I really mean something positive, a generative center. I do not seek the eradication of matter by form, as some of my French-inspired colleagues have tried to do in recent years, but suppose a matter from which forms may be "unpacked," as men seek to know and communicate.[11]

Therefore, different *communitates* may exist side by side, marked as one group with features quite distinct from other groups, but not necessarily in opposition to them. In this way it may be said that the church is made up of a multitude of little communities that nonetheless relate to each other and form one body. In like manner, movements such as the Franciscans not only began as antistructures, but continue their own particular charism that marks them as independent structures within the general body of the Catholic Church.

These groups are convinced of having attained a refreshed and more dynamic apprehension of the Christian mystery, and this conviction not only leads them to relate more existentially to the objects of their faith than they did before, it leads them to relate more closely to those people with whom they share the same conviction. Hence the inner social dynamism of the communitas becomes the motive force of the close relationship of the people in it, gathered around the same ideal. It is precisely this social dynamism that Martin Buber sees as the strength of the communitas, as it gives rise to the close relationship between individuals where they no longer simply find themselves side by side in a predefined structure, but where they actually *relate* to one another:

> Community is the being no longer side by side (and one might add, above and below) but *with* one another of a multitude of persons. And this multitude, though it moves towards one goal, yet experiences everywhere a turning to, a dynamic facing of, the others, a flowing from *I* to *Thou*. Community is where community happens.[12]

By this means, a movement does not come across as a menace to the unity of the church, for it redefines and actualizes the true content of faith through the unity of the people who are consciously aware that they are united for the sake not of the structure, but of the common experience of the mystery of divine life that they have discovered through faith in God. Even though there are usually tensions between existing structures and new movements, and despite the fact that history has known of movements that separated from the church, history has also shown that movements' collective experience of the Christian mystery ideally do not mutilate the church, but renew it to vibrate in its inner dynamism and hence progressively strengthen the church through newly created structures from within that are better suited to face new historical challenges.

Christianity knows of many such movements that have appeared in opposition to existing structures—without which, however, such movements could not have initially existed. Christianity itself began with one such structure. Toniolo shows that early Christianity knows of two such stages.[13] One was the period of foundation, during which the movements around John the Baptist and around Jesus himself were the most important. It is noteworthy that Jesus himself reveals to the disciples that they are different from the people gathered in the existing structures:

> If the world hates you, you must realize that it hated me before
> it hated you. If you belonged to the world, the world would love
> you as its own; but because you do not belong to the world, be-
> cause my choice of you has drawn you out of the world, that
> is why the world hates you.[14]

In a classic Catholic understanding, Jesus' words refer to the "spirit" of the world, and not specifically to the church's "social structures." Prophets always worked on the moral reform of the church, rather than suggesting structural changes, which does not mean that this moral reform could not have structural *consequences*. An important, albeit rather evident, almost "tautological," aspect of Catholic hagiography is that saints such as St. Francis of Assisi or St. Birgitta of Vadstena sought reform from *within* the church, and most of them sought the church's blessing or approval, despite the possible initial opposition, to underscore one of the hallmarks of such divinely inspired structures, namely the virtue of docility exemplified in desiring or seeking to remain "within" the church. St. Clare is a prime example: she struggled for the church's blessing on her new Franciscan structure or order, literally to the point of death. In point of fact, it was not until moments preceding her death, as she lay on her deathbed, that the letter arrived from the Holy See recognizing her structure; the same occurred with Birgitta of Vadstena, who waited until her death in Rome for the approval of her order. And although the church may not immediately give its blessing, this does not deter the prophet from his or her mission, or dissuade him or her from desiring or seeking the church's eventual blessing.

The second stage Toniolo suggests is the apostolic age after the ascension of Jesus. The Acts of the Apostles provides many examples of how the group was united and shared all that it possessed:

> And all who shared the faith owned everything in common; they sold their goods and possessions and distributed the proceeds among themselves according to what each one needed.[15] ... The whole group of believers was united, heart and soul; no one claimed private ownership of any possessions, as everything they owned was held in common.[16]

Christian history knows many more examples of such movements, as those around the great Desert Fathers, the monastic movements in the middle of the first Christian millennium, and the rise of the Christian mendicant orders such as the Franciscans and the Dominicans, to mention a few. Since Vatican II the number of such movements has multiplied, and this may be one of the main novelties of Catholic Christendom in the twentieth century.

The interesting thing in all this is that prophets or prophet-like mystics initiated the great majority of these movements. The names John the Baptist, Jesus, Francis of Assisi, and Ignatius of Loyola are just a few highlights on the list, which keeps growing with the rise of new communities and religious orders. Modern ecclesial movements such as Opus Dei, the Neocatechumenate, or the Focolari each have their particular leaders whom the faithful often consider to be imbued with prophetic gifts and charismatic leadership. Even silent suffering prophets such as Marthe Robin have enormously influenced the rise of new communities. She founded the Foyers de Charité and greatly influenced communities such as the Beatitude (formerly known as Lion de Juda), L'Émanuelle, and The Little Sisters of the Lamb.[17] Prophets just have enormous power to raise the religious horizon over the petrifaction of existing thought and spirituality. To illustrate this point Turner refers to Bergson,

> who saw in the words and writings of prophets and great artists the creation of an "open morality," which was itself and expression of what he called the *élan vital*, or evolutionary "life-force." Prophets and artists tend to be liminal and marginal people, "edgemen," who strive with a passionate sincerity to rid themselves of the clichés associated with status incumbency and role-playing and to enter into vital relations with other men in fact or imagination. In their productions we may catch glimpses of that unused evolutionary potential in mankind which has not yet been externalized and fixed in structure.[18]

Aldo Natale Terrin has also described the importance of such prophets to the rise of new groups within the church:

> The function of the charismatic leader is important because it re-assumes the fundamental ethical moment of communitas, inasmuch as the members in such contingency do not feel themselves ruled over, in the sense that they succeed in the concurrence of acts of utmost dependency—seen as pure forms of initiation [oblavità]—with acts of absolute freedom. On the other side, the charismatic leader presents himself with tangible signs of authority: prophecy, revelation, visions that corroborate his function and creates around him an aura of mystery. In this context, the entire communitas refers to the leader, finding in him its driving center, the force with which to defend itself outwardly and have inward cohesion.[19]

Referring to Turner, who calls the prophetic founders of new ecclesial movements "outsiders," Toniolo contends that they are not people who lead the faithful away from the divine mystery. While they may oppose existing structures, this is not their main aim. Toniolo describes the placement of such founders as follows. They are

> in the particular state of being external to the social structure but at the same time exercising a particular role to this social structure. The fundamental characteristic of the *outsiders* is that of being in a particular anomalous situation compared to normal social forms of life, but at the same time to be considered only a different way of living a particular situation of the same system.[20]

Most of the prophets we have examined have had main functions that extended beyond the founding of new movements within the church. For instance, Birgitta of Vadstena's primary task was that of communicating revelations to the people of her time and battling for the unity of the church. This notwithstanding, she also founded the Bridgettine order, which in many ways opposed some of the traditions of her time while seeking to renew others profoundly.

There is one characteristic trait that all communitates have in common and that according to Toniolo greatly applies to the Christian context. It is the paradigm of the nostalgia for a golden age in which the divine mystery found its most pure and powerful realization, the *nostalgia for the origin*. Mircea Eliade wrote extensively on this paradigm, from which Toniolo distils five characteristic aspects that apply to Christianity; for the purpose of my theme I shall summarize these in three: first, *the necessity of destruction for the re-creation of perfection*, second, *the surety of a new beginning and the eschatological tension*, and third, *the pursuit of the heart of faith* (Eliade's "Regressus ad uterum"). Following Toniolo's elaborations on the thoughts of Eliade, I shall briefly explore these three aspects here.

7.3. The Necessity of Destruction for the Re-creation of Perfection

At the basis of the nostalgia for the origin lies an unprovable and widely accepted postulate, summarized by Eliade: "In general, there is a belief in the possibility of recovering the absolute 'beginning'—which implies the symbolic destruction and abolition of the old world. Hence the end is implied in the beginning and vice versa."[21] "It is a paradise that has been lost, it is a period of beatitude that can no longer be found, it is deeply ecstatic and ineffably fascinating moment that must be restored, but at times is not found to emerge from the historical reality or from oneself."[22]

This is a feature that the vast majority of religions share but that each realizes in different ways. It is often expressed in ideas of the cyclic nature of a cosmic year, linked to the change of seasons, with the basic paradigm emerging in a variety of contexts. Eliade concludes that religions indeed share an important common feature, namely, that perfection lies in the beginning: "The idea that perfection was at the beginning appears to be quite old. In any case, it is extremely widespread. Then too, it is an idea capable of being indefinitely reinterpreted and incorporated into an endless variety of religious conceptions."[23]

Eastern thinking carries the myth of a cycle that ends with a complete dissolution, the *pralaya,* and that attains its radical climax in the *mahapralaya,* the "great dissolution" at the end of the thousandth cycle that is characterized by the "deterioration, annihilation, and re-creation of the universe."[24] It is on the basis of such accounts that Eliade concludes that the paradigm of the origin contains a radical demand for the destruction of the existing order before it is possible to arrive at the golden age: *"For something genuinely new to begin, the vestiges and ruins of the old cycle must be completely destroyed.* In other words, to obtain an *absolute* beginning, the end of a World must be total."[25]

With Toniolo, I believe the Christian context to be somewhat different. Christian prophecy has both similarities and dissimilarities with the paradigm described by Mircea Eliade. The strong insistence on the total destruction of the existing order that is needed in order to arrive at the origin does not fully apply to the messages of Christian prophets. The proof of this assessment lies beyond the limits of this study, as it would require a comprehensive, comparative analysis of the writings of several important Christian prophets, and such work lies in the future. It suffices here to acknowledge that Christian prophets often presented powerful apocalyptic images of the ages to come, marked by chastisement and purification of sin. It is noteworthy that prophets' sole aim was not to tear down *all* existing structures in order to arrive at the origin. Rather, the catastrophes they predicted were ordered to the purification of the people. *Rather than tearing down, they sought to build up through purification.* Birgitta of Vadstena is one fine example of a Christian prophet who did not call for the demolition of the existing hierarchical institution, whose legitimacy she never questioned. Rather, her prophetic call was to the carriers of institutional offices to fulfil their vocation with the required moral standard.

Conversely, the Judeo-Christian tradition has a great corpus of apocalyptic material. Although it holds the Apocalypse of John in the highest esteem, it also esteems such apocryphal writings as the ascension of Isaiah, the martyrdom of Isaiah, the Apocalypse of Peter, the fifth and the sixth book of Esdra, and the Odes of Solomon. To these are added the writings of many Christian seers that have heralded the purification of a present evil generation with the promise of a future paradisiacal age. One may witness such a message of promise in writings that span from Joachim of Fiore to Birgitta of Vadstena, and in our days from the Marian apparitions to the writings of Vassula Rydén. The research of Eliade indicates that this recurring message does not serve to predict the future but to help believers in the present to transcend and to cross over into the realm of what he calls the mythic, that is, the vibrant dynamism of religion, which theologians may well define as the reality of the Word or the Deposit of Faith. The aim of their message would therefore be that of leading the faithful, not to another historical stage, but to a life of faith closer to the paradisiacal mystery of God's truth realized in the present. Eliade's teaching coincides with what I have said earlier, namely that the predictions of future chastisements and catastrophes do not express independent goals that seek to satisfy the human curiosity for external future events, but express one and the same goal, aimed at the reconstruction of the present. Rather than breaking with concrete historical orders or institutional structures, prophetic apocalypticism seeks to lead the faithful beyond the mere historical reality into the transcendent realm of God. Its aim is to implement God's life in the church. Eliade summarizes this point:

> For centuries the same religious idea recurs again and again: this world—the World of History—is unjust, abominable, demonic; fortunately, it is already decaying, the catastrophes have begun, this old world is cracking everywhere; very soon it will be annihilated, the

powers of darkness will be conquered once and for all, the "good will triumph, Paradise will be regained."[26]

7.4. The Surety of a New Beginning and the Eschatological Tension

Destruction is never destruction for its own sake or punishment per se but a means for a new beginning. This is evident in the idea of destruction, according to Toniolo, inasmuch as "it is associated to the theme of the beginnings and can be in no other way inherently in the paradigm of the nostalgia of the origins."[27] Destruction and purification are required for a new beginning. This historical period is seen as the *golden age*, usually a period of poverty that nonetheless excelled in virtue and spiritual plenitude. Most Christian reform movements have looked back at the early church as a period in time that incarnated the divine in an ideal manner. Their aim can be assessed as combat with structures and developments that are obstructing this golden age from emerging in the present. As Toniolo shows, one can cite many other examples of historical periods that Catholic reformers and prophets have looked at as divine manifestations within a golden age.

Not only does the Christian realm utilize the myth of the origin, but among the humanistic sciences, psychoanalysis does so as well. It does not build on a mythic structure, nor does it accept the Christian notion of a paradise and a fall. However, Eliade holds that a comparison can be established between psychoanalysis and the myth of the origin, and that this comparison is "based on the fact that Freud discovered the decisive role of the 'primordial and paradisiac time' of earliest childhood, the bliss before the break (= weaning), that is before time becomes, for each individual, a 'living time.'"[28]

7.5. The Pursuit of the Heart of Faith

Now, the interesting point in our theme is that the notion of a golden age does not get locked into a concrete historic period that it seeks to realize through a simplistic reiteration. Prophecy does more than reiterate in the present a past historical period; rather it transcends history. The regressus ad uterum transcends the mere realm of history and embraces what is defined as the mythic. And this accentuates the present theological study on revelation and prophecy, inasmuch as God's dynamic activity in the world not only transcends history, it lies before, above, and ahead of the church (see section 6.2, on the preliminary nature of Christianity). Mircea Eliade shows how the paradigm of the origin builds on the cosmogenesis by means of the recountings of the creation of the universe, best exemplified in Genesis, the Biblical creation account and the Enuma Elis, its Babylonian counterpart. Eliade affirms that the myths of the origin employ the cosmogenesis, but that the two are not identical—the myths of the origin "extend and complete the cosmogonic myth; they tell how the world has been modified, enriched or impoverished."[29] The future reign is mostly seen as a recuperation of what happened in the cosmogenesis, which religious rites serve to symbolize: "The recapitulation is simultaneously a commemoration and a ritual reactualization through songs and dance of the essential mythical events that occurred after creation."[30]

The constellation between the cosmogenetic myth and the myth of the origin becomes especially clear in times of crisis. By comparing the present with the myth of the origin, what deviated and was lost and hence has to be healed is made evident. In the words of Toniolo, the myth of the cosmogenesis operates within the myth of the origin *as an embolism,* so that the former gives power and efficiency to the latter. By utilizing the myth of the cosmogenesis, the myth of the origin not only suggests a reproduction of a historic period, but it truly re-creates the present in the dynamism of the cosmogenesis. In this way, he writes: "It is not a simple reparation, a patch, but a true and real *recreation.* It is not a recovery from the disease or an overcoming of the critical situation, but a return to the origins, a restoration of the perfection of the beginnings."[31]

It is in this way that the prophecy is able to implement the divine origin in history not merely by reconstructing a historical period but by transcending history itself: "the cosmogonic myth as well as the mythical story serve to overcome history, which is contingent and ruins the original beauty and hence must be cancelled. Furthermore, it leads us to forget the origins with its incrustation that must be removed in order to make the vase shine in its chromatic clarity [pregnanza]."[32]

According to Eliade, the idea of the golden age builds on the myth of a prehistoric ideal stage: "The idea implicit in this belief is that *it is the first manifestation of a thing that is significant and valid,* not its successive epiphanies. Similarly, the child is taught not what its father and grandfather did but what was done for the first time by the Ancestors, in mythical Times."[33]

Prophecy seeks to realize an ideal or "mythic state" that lies not only at the origin of the universe but beyond it, in the realm of the divine itself. Hence prophecy draws on the cosmogenetic myth by means of the myth of the origin in order to propel a future rebirth in the power of God's reality. The prophetic retrospection in time usually discerns a concrete ideal stage in history, while nevertheless peering back into a state prior to or beyond history that becomes the *real* dynamism of the prophetic message, and not a mere portrait of the golden historical example. In the same way, the prophet looks ahead in time and seeks concretely to implement in the present the future state that he or she envisions, while simultaneously raising his or her eyes above the historical horizon in order to peer into the eschaton, into the realm of God, to which the church is ultimately heading. By this means, prophecy utilizes the nostalgia of the origin in a vibrant dynamism between past and future (see section 6.2.3).

According to Toniolo, the harmful effects of the time between the golden age and the present that defiled the faithful and led them to forget their origins can be overcome in three different ways:

> by apparitions or visions that exceed memory and history, because in this way the memory of the origins is clear, intentional from God; by restoring the initial order and pulling down whichever interpretation might have arisen in the intermediate moment; by searching in oneself, in one's own spirit, in one's own soul, in one's own mind for the sense of things; by liberating oneself of mortality; by honing the spirit, thus entering in direct contact with who or with what can reveal the intimate and deep sense of reality.[34]

For our theme of prophecy, the first form is the most important, as it helps to explain why the prophet is so important in religious society. Through charismatic gifts, he or she can provide the "perfect memory, that can emerge only through an inner way or through divine revelation."[35] This quality gives the prophet immense influence:

> We should not be astonished, therefore, if from time to time it happens that researchers, be they theologians, philosophers, or scientists, remain fascinated by the one who is called to have the perfect memory through revelations or visions. The knowledge of the origin of things and their history confers a magical dominion on the same. The one who is able to remember disposes over a magical-religious force more precious than any other form of knowledge.[36]

The prophet possesses insight in the pure prehistoric stage, the realm of the Creator, that can be attained only through perfect memory by means of prophetic revelations, and this re-creation is that of a stage within history that always possesses eschatological undertones *transcending history*, whereby the prophets lead the church beyond the historical to exist in the dynamism of the Creator and ultimately be united with him there.

7.6. The Prophetic Is in the Liminal

Having examined the sociological notion of communitas as well as the paradigm regressus ad uterum, we are now ready to turn again to Victor Turner,
who, through his research on initiation rites, provides valuable insights into
the way prophecy sparks the nostalgia of the origin, and into where this spark
takes the communitas. To illustrate these two distinct movements, Turner
distinguishes between two different types of groups, namely marginal and
liminal. One group moves away from the religious core, whereas the other
moves toward it. Turner borrows the term *limen* "from van Gennep's formulation of the processual structure of ritual in *Les Rites de passage*—[which] occurs
in the middle phase of the rites of passage which mark changes in an individual's or a group's social status and/or cultural or psychological state in many
societies past and present."[37]

The rites of passage are not limited to indigenous religions. According to
von Gennep and Turner, they occur frequently in all religious and social
structures when there is a passage from one state to another. They are characterized by three phases that Turner defines as follows.

> The first phase (of separation) comprises symbolic behavior sig-
> nifying the detachment of the individual or group either from
> an earlier fixed point in the social structure, from a set of cul-
> tural conditions (a "state"), or from both. During the intervening
> "liminal" period, the characteristics of the ritual subject (the "pas-
> senger") are ambiguous; he passes through a cultural realm that
> has few or none of the attributes of the past or coming state. In
> the third phase (reaggregation or reincorporation), the passage is
> consummated.[38]

The limen is hence the prime locus at which an individual or group, having
left an existing stage and structural integration, goes through a passage stage,
before entering the fuller reintegration of the same structure, as shown in the
diagram. From this a description emerges of a communitas as a group of people
in the limen phase, united around the same experience of their fundamental
belief. As Turner writes, "the spontaneity and immediacy of *communitas*—as
opposed to the jural-political character of structure—can seldom be maintained
for very long." Either the individuals of the group are reintegrated into the
structure of their origin or the *communitas* itself "develops a structure, in which
free relationships between individuals become converted into norm-governed
relationships between social personae."[39]

The limen is characterized by different elements: first, the individual or group exists apart from and does things differently from normal society, with the aim of fuller reintegration into the same after the liminal phase. "The classifications on which order normally depends are annulled or obscured—other symbols designate temporary antinomic liberation from behavioral norms and cognitive rules."[40] Secondly, the relationship with group leaders is unique in both requiring submission and allowing extreme freedom: "This aspect of danger requiring control is reflected in the paradox that in liminality extreme authority of elders over juniors often coexists with scenes and episodes indicative of the utmost behavioral freedom and speculative license."[41]

Both liminal and marginal groups are those that, in line with the foregoing description of the communitas, are clearly distinguished from the rest of the structure in which they originate. According to Toniolo, both groups have lost their character of universality, as they seek to enclose themselves in clearly identifiable groups. "In an industrialized society it is the marginality as well as the liminality that find anti-structure in the sacred and that have what is necessary to construct a place, a fort, a city in order to confine themselves."[42]

The main difference between the two is the counterposition between transitory and permanent state, and the two differ in the way they relate to the structure of their origin. The marginal groups are in their very nature already a foreign element to their original structure, closing themselves off from it with no intentions of reunion. The one who lives on the outskirts of society in marginal structures "in order to re-enter in the so-called normal social structure [is] in need of a process of reeducation."[43] The liminal groups are, on the other hand, not external to their origin, although they may oppose it in one way or another—they were always part of the origin and sooner or later prove that they continue as such by becoming even more vibrant reflections of their origin than the structures from which they derived. "Who instead has lived in liminality is considered entirely initiated in the social structure that he or she will be integrated in."[44] To this end, the liminal groups aim at short periods of separation before reentering the original structure, and the swiftness of this transitory stage becomes evident in the way the groups are structured, with few elements that aim at securing permanent independent survival, whereas the opposite is the case with the marginal groups: "*Liminality* tends towards momentary forms of separation for the full social integration of the person, while marginality configures itself as a permanent antistructure."[45] The liminal groups form preliminary structures aimed at becoming part of a greater structure, whereas the marginal groups become total structures. According to Erving Goffman, one of the characteristic traits of marginal groups is how closed they are, through "the impediment to the social exchange and the escape toward the external world, often concretely founded in the same physical structures of the institution."[46]As Toniolo writes, this means for the marginal groups that "the exclusion mechanisms cannot be overcome and they have no purpose except that of permanently identifying the individual as structurally inferior." The individuals in the liminal groups, on the other hand, knowing that the liminal stage is transitory, "seek to acquire full social identification, and therefore the state of structural inferiority is finalized and functional at the postliminal moment."[47]

The best way of portraying the difference is by looking at the meanings of their names: *margin* refers to that which is on the periphery of society; *limen* means *threshold*. Toniolo exemplifies the two by means of a metaphor:

> Who is on the threshold of a house knows to assume a very precise waiting position: the limiting place is necessary for the passage into the house. Who instead is at the margins of a room or of a house finds himself in the position of a person who is aware of occupying a *status* and exercising roles of inferiority that are already characterized and determined by that person.[48]

Thus, as we saw, the limen is, contrary to the margin, a transitory phase that is structured not to last. People in the liminal groups, given their transitory nature, eventually seek full, even fuller, integration with the group they originally belonged to, whereas the marginal groups have such strong exclusion mechanisms that they become permanent antistructures.

With this we have arrived at a very important delineation of two phenomena that may appear identical at first sight but that have totally different momenta and goals. The marginal seeks to exit the institution and build an independent structure that is apt at remaining self-sufficient. The liminal, on the other hand, never creates such structures, as its aim is not to distance itself from the main structure but to become a renewed part of it. Thus, the liminal is for Toniolo an "antistructure within the structure itself, wanted and determined by the structure, an antistructure of the structure and for the structure."[49] With this we have overcome the often simplistic and inaccurate pattern of structure and antistructure, as the limen becomes a function that does not aim at destroying the existing structure but is like the leaven that renews the structure by becoming a part of it in a new way.[50] Turner summarizes liminality by saying that it "may perhaps be regarded as the Nay to all positive structural assertions, but [serves] in some sense [as] the source of them all, and, more than that, as a realm of pure possibility whence novel configurations of ideas and relations may arise."[51]

The limen is a dynamism that drives the antistructural communitas to the restructuralization that again makes the communitas a part of the complex society from which it originates. Turner expresses this dialectic well:

> We thus encounter the paradox that the *experience* of communitas becomes the *memory* of communitas, with the result that communitas itself in striving to replicate itself historically develops a social structure, in which initially free and innovative relationships between individuals are converted into norm-governed relationships between social *personae*. . . . Yet when this communitas or *comitas* is institutionalized, the new-found idiosyncratic is legislated into yet another set of universalistic roles and statuses, whose incumbents must subordinate individuality to a rule.[52]

The question now is how is the limen effective? The answer is that its effectiveness derives from its ability to lead the faithful into the *statu nascente* and thereby provide them with the primordial experience of that which is the inner mystery and dynamism of the structure itself. One of the most important differences between margin and limen is that the margin draws on a reality or doctrine that is different than that of the structure's origin, whereas the liminal is oriented toward and exists through a reality that is the structure's soul and from which it draws its life and energy. The limen exists in the power of that reality just as it serves its continuous reactualization, whereas the margin can only oppose and expel it, since the marginal is different in substance from the reality of its origin, just as water and oil are of different substances that can only separate. This provides some interesting reflections on true and false prophecy. According to the scenario described here, prophecy gives birth to the limen as a room in which the faithful are led to experience the inner mystery of their faith; and it is this very mystery, the Word, that finds expression and room to act through the true prophet. The voice of a false prophet, on the contrary, can only lead away from the church, as it does not express the Word of the origin and hence cannot chant the hymn of the church, but must compose a tune different from the one chanted by the Christian Word.

7.7. Wider Application of the Limen Paradigm to the Christian Context

The limen enables actual groups to pass deeper into the church, but as a phenomenon as such it transcends the sociological borders of distinct groups within the church. This is where the conclusions of my earlier explorations of revelation and prophecy flow together with those provided by sociology into the full picture of the dynamics of prophecy and revelation. For the limen proves to be a phenomenon that is not limited to only movements and their possible prophets, but relates to the very nature of the Christian religion as an inherent part of its being. Liminality is more than antistructure to the social system. It is able to generate "myths, symbols, rituals, philosophical systems, and works of art... [inciting] men to action as well as to thought."[53]

According to Turner, liminality is distinguished from mere structure by its creativity: "Structure tends to be pragmatic and this-worldly; while communitas is often speculative and generates imagery and philosophical ideas."[54]

There is an inherent dialectic between structure and limen and between structure and communitas. Not only can the two exist side by side, but they interact and are both necessary for upholding living ambiences of faith: "There is a dialectic here, for the immediacy of communitas gives way to the mediacy of structure, while, in *rites de passage,* men are released from structure into communitas only to return to structure revitalized by their experience of communitas. What is certain is that no society can function adequately without this dialectic."[55]

This is because liminality enables the church to mutate so that it continues to realize its basic elements and truths in the changing contexts of history. Turner believes this to be the main function of liminality: "But to my mind it is the analysis of culture into factors and their free or 'ludic' recombination in any and every possible pattern, however weird, that is of the essence of liminality, liminality par excellence."[56]

Since this is so, it is vital that there be a healthy balance between liminality and structure. On the one hand, Turner writes that "exaggeration of structure may well lead to pathological manifestations of communitas outside or against 'the law' "[57]—since the experience of the statu nascente is needed in all religious structures. The dangerous outlet for the need for limen would then be *margin,* with the danger of individuals leaving the church for marginal groups and sects. Toniolo agrees with Turner. If the church gives no space for the limen to unfold, the communitas "loses the typical characteristics of spontaneity and self-management, forcing the anti-structure to emerge in marginal forms that, in order to defend themselves, in their turn will have to become institutions."[58]

On the other hand, Turner writes, "exaggeration of communitas, in certain religious or political movements of the leveling type, may be speedily followed by despotism, overbureaucratization, or other modes of structural rigidification.... Communitas cannot stand alone if the material and organizational needs of human beings are to be adequately met."[59]

The limen as a sociological phenomenon exists in numerous different forms and ways. It appears in rituals, in the dynamisms of groups, but also in the very inner dynamics of the church, so that the limen for Toniolo becomes "not only the moment that brings the religious forms back to the statu nascente, but even the space that is capable of creating new forms that further the continuous adaptation of religiosity to the changes of cultural systems."[60] This is why Toniolo agrees with Turner's insistence that no religious structures can function without the limen: "Even the great forms of institutionalized religion, including the Catholic Church, must possess an element of liminality."[61]

The faithful need to be continuously connected with and reintroduced to the mystery of their faith, securing that creativity that is given "on one side from the individual's encounter with the original integral nucleus and on the other from the successive reelaboration produced in the moment of adaptation necessary for the reintroduction into the social structure."[62] Without the limen, the archaic makes no sense and comes across as obsolete.

As Toniolo writes, this explains why the church needs the limen as a means of presenting inherited traditions in their original inner dynamism. The prophetic lies in the limen, which carries the faithful to the statu nascente, "the moment of encounter between past and present, between the origins, the tradition, and the mutation."[63] Liminality is not foreign to structure, as it "belongs to the very structure itself that wants to mutate, as the other side of the medal." This is why the church's institutional forms must "seek to understand the liminal situations, distinguishing them with pastoral discernment from the marginal situations, in order to be urged toward a continuous renewal."[64]

7.8. Conclusion

The church must recognize and realize the dynamism of liminality, the dynamism of prophecy, if it is to vibrate in the dynamism of the Word, incarnate at the beginning of its history and continuously the mystery of its being *through which* and *toward which* it moves in history until the eschaton. The church cannot continue to reflect its inner mystery without limen, and one of the primary vehicles of limen is prophecy.

This provides some very interesting conclusions to my topic of prophecy. The results from the sociological investigation of prophecy's effects become a stream that flows together with the other streams of revelation theology and prophecy, treated in the preceding chapters: prophecy serves the realization and reactualization of the fundamentals of faith that have found many concrete historical realizations in "golden ages" of Christendom. Prophets point back to these realizations and call the faithful to live by faith as in the days of old. But by doing so they do not so much point to the historical exemplary realization of the Kingdom as to the Kingdom itself, and this Kingdom, *the very reality of God*, lies before, above, and ahead of the present historical age, as it transcends history. It is not a mere matter of restoration.[65] The prophets are the servants of the church, through which the transcendent Kingdom of God continues concretely and powerfully to realize itself in time. It is the power of this dynamic presence of God's world within the world of humans that enables believers constantly to be drawn toward the World to Come although they live in the world of now.

8

Prophecy's Status and Types of Faith

We have now seen that prophecy played a great role in the actualization of revelation. Prophecy influences all the loci theologici, as well as the pulsating dynamisms of religious society. Thus it is my view that prophecy has played a far greater role than is usually appreciated, and having passed the second millennium, all indications are that prophecy does not lose its influence and importance—on the contrary. The great question following this rediscovery of prophecy's importance is now what becomes of prophecy's status in the church. It obviously has a great role to play, and some people converted through prophecy may be inclined to give it more importance than the Bible or church teaching. And if such importance is misplaced, it is also a misunderstanding of the nature of prophecy, for Sacred Scripture and the authority of the church remain those in which revelation is expressed in a unique, authoritative way. Still, as we have seen, this does not mean that Scripture and church teaching contain all of revelation explicitly. On the contrary, prophecy must be situated somewhere between the normative status of Scripture and church teaching and no status at all. The question is how to explore this middle ground between the two extremes. To answer this question we may find assistance from a surprising front.

Neo-Scholastic Catholic theology operated with a system of different *types of faith*, classified according to their object, whereby faith in objects of fundamental importance, such as the resurrection of Christ, differed from faith in contingent historical objects, such as the possible antiquity of a piece of furniture. This *typology of faith*, which historically dates back to Scholasticism and embraced problematic prepositional approaches to revelation, is being used less today, even though *Mysterium Salutis* still referred to it frequently.[1] In spite of its being less used today, it nevertheless proves tremendously useful in clarifying prophecy's position and status in the church, without compromising itself with the criticism of the propositional approach to revelation that bore this system.[2]

The typology of faith affirms that believers adhere to objects of faith that form part of the Deposit of Faith, conceived as the truths that Christ conferred on the church to be kept and defended faithfully, with *fides divina,* or divine faith, since its objects are the fundamental divine truths contained in Scripture and tradition. If these objects of faith are also proposed authoritatively by the Magisterium *as being part of the Deposit of Faith,* they are then met with a *fides catholica,* also called *fides ecclesiae.* These truths are those recognized by the whole church, even when they are not explicitly part of Sacred Scripture.

This position has been affirmed by the CDF in its *responsio* to John Paul II's *Ordinatio Sacerdotalis,*[3] as well as in the papal apostolic letter *Ad Tuendam Fidem*[4] and in the CDF's *Doctrinal Commentary*[5] accompanying it, where it reads:

> These doctrines [to be believed by all Catholic Christians] are contained in the word of God, written or handed down, and defined with a solemn judgment as divinely revealed truths either by the Roman pontiff when he speaks "ex cathedra" or by the college of bishops gathered in council, or infallibly proposed for belief by the ordinary and universal Magisterium. These doctrines require the assent of theological faith by all members of the faithful. Thus, whoever obstinately places them in doubt or denies them falls under the censure of heresy, as indicated by the respective canons of the codes of canon law.[6]

Because the objects of fides divina ultimately are God's truths, they are authoritative and universal. Through the Magisterium's infallibility, they are seen as the common goods of faith that Catholics are bound to adhere to in order to truly consider themselves part of the one Catholic church.

Next to these objects of faith, whether ratified or not by the Magisterium, are those objects that do not form part of the Deposit of Faith but that the church, nevertheless, guarantees as infallible truths, as they are closely related to the Deposit of Faith objects. Frantz Diekamp expresses well the conviction that these objects are to be the faith of all Catholics:

> If the church passes an infallible judgment upon a truth that, albeit not contained in the sources of Revelation, nevertheless is inherently linked with a teaching of Revelation, then this truth (in the more justified opinion) must be accepted by all Christians *fide ecclesiastica*, because the infallible church has determined (defined) it. And this faith is at the same time a *fides mediate divina*, because God himself guarantees the infallibility of the church as a formal truth of Revelation.[7]

Those objects of faith that are neither part of the Deposit of Faith nor are proposed by the church as fides ecclesiastica phenomena are believed with *fides humana*. This form of faith addresses those faith objects that may be important in the life of the church but that are not vital to the economy of salvation. Since the foundations of salvation were fulfilled with Christ, the objects of fides divina and catholica are limited to the constitutive period of the Deposit of Faith, that is, to the death of the last apostle. All events that occur in the church after this period are according to the classical position believed with fides humana.

The interesting question that arises from our theme is with what faith should a believer believe in a Christian prophetic revelation? The question is no less complex than it is important, for it concerns not only the individual's belief in prophetic revelations but also the position and status of revelations in the church, since fides humana objects of faith range much lower than fides divina ones.

The problem boils down to the following example: a prophetic revelation occurs after the death of the last apostle. To some theologians this means that it occurs after the closure of the Deposit of Faith and that believers can therefore believe in it only with fides humana. But things do not end here. The issue must be confronted with another perspective: if a prophetic revelation is truly from God, how can it express anything else than the one life and truth of the one God? And if this is the same one truth and divine Deposit of Faith with which the church has been entrusted, how can it not be believed with fides divina? From my research in this field a consistent truth emerges: Writers have often disagreed on this point, because they have misinterpreted one another's presentations while failing to make the important distinction between the mere *historical occurrence* of a prophetic revelation and the *doctrinal truth* it expresses. Obviously, we are talking of two *aspects* of prophetic revelations that do not necessarily oppose one another on the same issue. And yet they have been interpreted as opposing aspects.

If we first consider the mere occurrence of a prophetic revelation, that is, the conviction that God has revealed himself to this or that person, it then seems difficult to acknowledge such a revelation with faith other than that of fides humana. And this for the following reasons: the revelatory occurrence takes place after the constitutive period of the Deposit of Faith. Furthermore, there are no elements in this occurrence that could become the object of divine faith, inasmuch as the event itself is an occurrence after the complete foundation of revelation. The only exception would be the revelatory process in the visionary's soul, seen as an emanation of God's glory and truthfulness, thus connected with the Deposit of Faith. However, this process is very complex and open to many contingent factors. It is the individual believer who must decide with personal conviction if a given oracle is from God. I here recall the aforementioned examination of the Carmelite school, which—in line with its spiritual father, John of the Cross—is rather negative toward prophetic revelations as one expression of this opinion (see section 4.1.6). This school gives most weight to historical occurrence of the revelation, that is they do not emphasis what is being said as much as the fact that a person claims to have received a revelation. And this claim cannot be believed with fides divina as the revelation experience of the visionary occurs after the constitutive period.

Second, we must address the problem from the perspective of the prophetic message itself, ignoring how or when it occurred. In order to do so we must consider two issues. If what has been expressed in the revelation is identical with already ratified church doctrine then it is a logical necessity that the prophetic revelation must be met with fides divina *and* fides catholica, as the church has already proclaimed it part of the Deposit of Faith. If, on the other hand, a prophetic revelation expresses an issue not yet ratified by the Magisterium but that could well belong to the Deposit of Faith, can a believer convinced of the authenticity of the revelation believe in the message with fides divina?

In order to provide a response to this query, we must first address another question: are there issues of doctrine that belong to the fides divina objects that are not also fides catholica objects? In other words, are there objects of divine faith that the church has not yet professed as such? It should be noted that this question does not seek to determine whether revealed truths become divine truths before or after they have been proclaimed as such by the church. After all, it is not the Magisterium that invents the truth by proclaiming it. Rather, the Magisterium proclaims and ratifies that which it discerns as already being the faith of the church and gives authoritative witness to this truth through its proclamation. The church believed some truths, such as the Assumption, for centuries before they were ratified by an ex cathedra proclamation.

The question can be asked differently: is the objective truth (the objects of fides divina) not already the truth of the entire church and hence part of the objects of fides catholica even before it has been proclaimed authoritatively by the church? The church is Christ's body on earth; he is the church in union with the faithful. Since he ultimately is the material content of the Deposit of Faith, how can his complete truth not also be the truth of all the church, even before it has been recognized and proclaimed as such by the Magisterium? This is one of the key questions to be addressed when dealing with the prophetic revelations and their status in the church.

Frantz Diekamp supports the view that fides divina truths indeed are part of the fides catholica objects prior to their ratification:

> If the propositio Ecclesiae is missing, then the individual Christian who by study of Sacred Scripture or a private revelation has come to the conviction that God has revealed a particular teaching is obliged by the fides immediate divina, because God holds the truth of such a teaching according to the firm conviction of the concerned person.[8]

Rahner supports this view: "Whether there can be fides divina (in the sense of faith in public, general Revelation, not private revelations), which is not also in some way fides catholica is disputed. The view seems to be more correct that each (theological) faith is bound in some way or another to the community of the church."[9]

In other words, truth claims can be believed as part of the Deposit of Faith and hence fides divina even before they have been proposed by the church. From this follows his conclusion on how the person who has the revelation can believe in it:

> The adherence of faith flows naturally from the fact that it is a Divine word.... In the present case, we would not have to distinguish anymore between a general obligation and an individual obligation in the public revelation and in private revelation. The distinction would be only in this: that in the second case, private revelation, the guarding of what was revealed would not be confided to the official Church. Consequently, if the public faith, which is possible and under certain conditions even obligatory, in the content of a private revelation, was not Catholic faith, it would however always be possible and obligatory as divine faith.

Since theologians in general admit that the immediate recipient of private revelations can adhere to the communications of God with Divine faith, "fide divina," and even ought to if there is sufficient certitude about the authenticity of the recipient's experience, we cannot see why that experience would not be worthy of Divine faith for others who have acquired the same certitude about the reality of the revelation—a certitude that in principle is not impossible to acquire.[10]

Pierre Adnès supports Rahner's and Diekamp's positions but also provides a terminological distinction to avoid misunderstandings. Adnès proposes that those revealed truths that believers consider part of the Deposit of Faith before their institutional ratification can be believed as such with a *foi théologale*. When it comes to prophetic revelation it is possible for those believers who with good reasons consider it authentic to believe in the truth it expresses with this *foi théologale*. Adnès considers the difference between the *fides catholica* and the *foi théologale* to be of form rather than of substance (accidental): "In the first case (fides catholica) the revelation is proposed by the Church, in the second (theological faith) by God in a direct way. But the reason for the assent is the same in both instances: the authority of the revealing God."[11]

The conclusion of these insights is as follows: since the prophetic revelations that we investigate for their function and status in the church occur *after* the constitutive period, it is not possible to believe in their mere occurrence as a divine truth in line with other truths such as the Incarnation of Christ. The belief in the revelation's *fact* must be a matter of personal conviction based on criteria that support it. At times, divine signs such as miracles may sustain the conviction, but this does not move it two thousand years back in time to the constitutive period of the Deposit of Faith. Thereby, belief in the fact of a given prophetic revelation remains a *fides humana*. Conversely, a person who is convinced of the divine origin of a prophetic revelation can and must believe in its message *fide divina*, as he or she is convinced it originates in and expresses the same truth as the Deposit of Faith.

8.1. The Consequence of Ecclesial Approbation for Prophecy's Status

I have discussed the nature of faith in revelations on the basis of how they relate to the Deposit of Faith. In the Catholic Church there is, however, another element that determines how the faithful believe in prophetic revelations, and this is the approbation that the Magisterium may give them. To provide a full picture of the status of church revelations, we therefore need to discuss the implications of their institutional approbation.

As we shall see, up to the fifteenth century, the church had no official rules for judging prophetic revelations. When they were produced, the question arose as to which should be the character of the ecclesial judgment and whether the church should propose the judgment as infallible so that the faithful would have the church's guarantee on the revelation's authenticity.

This question was first treated during the Lateran Council in 1516. The text of the Council deals primarily with how bishops should relate to prophetic revelations. First of all, the Council prescribes that revelations should be forbidden until recognized by the church.[12] Second, it calls to limit the same recognition.[13] In principle the Magisterium should examine the revelations ("ex nunc Apostolicae Sedis examini reservatae"), but if it is urgent the local bishop can intervene and ask for a proper investigation. The local bishop's active role grew with the years, so that it today it is he who normally performs the investigation of a given prophecy occurring in his diocese unless its attraction spreads beyond his territorial jurisdiction, on which case the CDF intervenes. With regard to the character and quality of the judgment, the document laid the ground for all later evaluations on the issue, as the council declared that the judgment is but a permission ("licentiam concedere possint").

The Council of Trent repeated this assessment by treating revelations together with miracles. That Council confirms the Lateran Council's eleventh session stating that the approbation of prophetic revelations can be nothing more than a mere permission to believe them, and that the church does not guarantee their authenticity. The short statements of the Lateran and Tridentine Councils are the *only conciliar promulgations* indicating the nature of the church's judgment of revelations. They are interesting, as none of the believers could adhere to revelations with fides divina.

Individual authorities in the church nevertheless gave restrictive guidelines later. The most important of such negative assessments by a church official on prophetic revelations is found in the important work of Prospero Lambertini *Doctrina de servorum Dei beatificatione et canonizatione in synopsim redacta*.[14] This work was first published 1734–38, before Lambertini was elected pope as Benedict XIV (1740–58), hence it does not carry the authority of papal pronouncements. Rather than being a positive assessment of revelations' meaning and place in the life of the church, the document provides a *negative* assessment of them, indicating the "nots" of Christian prophecy. Lambertini's text has had enormous influence on how theologians evaluate the issue. There is a substantial difference between the pronouncements of the two council documents and that of Lambertini. The two councils only described the way the church should judge revelations, qualifying the judgment as a nonguarantee. Lambertini repeats this evaluation but draws the conclusion that *because* the church cannot guarantee a prophetic revelation, the faithful can only adhere to it with fides humana.[15] This means that Lambertini produces a necessary connection between the ecclesial lack of guarantee and the faith of the believer: the church does *not* guarantee the authenticity of a prophetic revelation; *therefore* a believer can *not* believe in it with fides divina!

Even though many theologians follow Lambertini's connection between the *church's judgment* and the *faith of the believers*,[16] the majority limit their investigations to the character of the church's judgment, and do not assess the consequent faith of believers. Very few theologians draw necessary conclusions that are the same as Lambertini's from the absence of institutional guarantee with regard to how people should believe in revelations. On the contrary, many theologians have questioned this connection. Rahner, Diekamp, and Adnès, whom I discussed earlier, are but three examples. Focusing on the revelation's message, they argued that it is possible for a believer to adhere to a prophetic revelation with fides divina even though the church does not guarantee its authenticity. With them, it is possible to disagree with Lambertini. To this day there are no official church documents that impede believers from believing in revelations with more than fides humana, as the church only positively claims that the faithful are permitted to believe in revelations. There are no indications on how they could and should believe in them. Only one document could be interpreted in this way: a publication from the *Congregation of Rites* from February 6, 1875. It confirms that belief in approved revelations is not prescribed but only permitted ("permissa") as object of pious faith ("pie credenda") with an assent "tantum fide humana."

The (linguistic) question is now whether the *tantum* means that it is possible to believe in a revelation *only* with fides humana, that is, fides divina is excluded with regard to prophetic revelations. The wording of the document could well be interpreted as permitting belief in a revelation with fides humana, but that nothing prevents the faithful from believing in it with fides divina. Pope Pius X's pronouncements point in the same direction. The faithful are not obliged, but are allowed to believe in the approved revelation.[17] Thus Pierre Adnès summarizes the classical thesis: "When there is approval, it is usually an approval in the broad sense. The Magisterium intervenes on a prudential basis to allow the spreading of accounts of revelations where nothing is found that is reprehensible or inappropriate. One therefore is not obliged to believe in it. This is evident even in magisterial declarations."[18]

As H. Holstein writes with regard to the judgment of the Lourdes revelations, the church's approval of revelations is generally considered a sort of *nihil obstat* that indicates that their message is orthodox;[19] believers are permitted to believe in them, and there is no danger related to faith in what they express.

8.2. Between Fides Humana and Fides Divina

A number of theologians have criticized the unequivocal statement that the church merely *permits* belief in revelations and does not encourage the faithful to acknowledge them, especially when they have had an impact on church life, as is the case with the revelations to Margaret Mary Alacoque and Bernadette of Lourdes. At times, popes and ecclesial authorities spoke of these revelations in ways so positive that they appear to be than mere permissions. These apparitions have become such an important part of the heritage of the church that theologians are not satisfied with the idea that they should strictly and unequivocally belong to the realm of the fides humana, the realm of mere opinion. After all, since their author is God, these theologians would say, they are of value to all of the faithful. Moreover, most of these apparitions do not demand an official institutional guarantee for their authenticity before believers could adhere to them with fides divina. What the theologians examine here is the terrain between the objects of mere fides humana and those of fides divina.

Elaborating on this intermediary terrain, Yves Congar already in 1927 had published a text in which he treated the issue of prophetic revelations and their judgment by the church. He observed that the church's pronouncements often transcended mere permissions, especially with regard to Lourdes. Congar sought to solve the problem by remaining within the framework of the classical thesis. The church only calls for a fides humana, but he considers this pure human faith that could also more simply be called *opinion* to be strengthened by the believer's respect for the church's judgments, including those judgments that do not claim infallibility. Thus he manages to arrive at a form of faith that officially is not more than fides humana but that nevertheless enjoys a greater weight than individual opinion:

It seems ... that one can qualify the adhesion necessary here as an act
of human faith, ruled by obedience that in turn is obliged by
the virtues of piety and "observance.". ... This adhesion of human
faith is not given here on the basis of a critical credibility study, but

for the very reason of obedience due to the ecclesiastical authority within the limits of its competence.[20]

It is not ecclesial or logical but *pious reasons* that cause the believer to give his assent to the ecclesial approbation of revelations.

Much like Congar, Eugenio Valentini asks for a reassessment of the right approach to approved revelations if neither the fides humana nor the fides divina are appropriate. Where Congar stayed within the confines of a fides humana intensified by the pious respect for the church, Valentini ascribes revelations to a third category, to that of *faits dogmatiques*. The faith objects of this category are known from the canonization of saints. The act of canonization is an act of judgment of an object of faith that historically belongs to the time *after* the constitutive period and that does not pertain to the Deposit of Faith. As a logical result, one would expect that the church would not be in a position of guaranteeing the status of the authenticity of canonizations, due to its lacking link to the Deposit of Faith. Surprisingly, this is *not* the case. Although Eric Kemp wrote that canonists and theologians in the Catholic Church tended to disagree so that canonists were against the notion and theologians were for it, still it has been the practice of the church to propose canonizations as infallible acts and judgments of the Magisterium.[21] The canonization of saints belongs to the so-called faits dogmatiques, which are objects of faith that *albeit not belonging to the Deposit of Faith are nonetheless sustained by the infallible guarantee of the church.*

It is to this category that Valentini seeks to ascribe the church-approved prophetic revelations, which is most understandable, as the *criteria* for judging revelations and canonizations are similar (see below). Valentini claims that the prophetic revelation, although human in its form and function, must still be characterized as a divine fact by virtue of its divine origin:

> The human fact that has become a dogmatic fact is virtually revealed by its necessary connection with the church's infallible presentation. The divine fact of the private revelation could (on this ground) become a dogmatic fact and therefore enter in the domain of public revelation by its proven historical link with the authentic presentation of Revelation by the church in its universal magisterium, under certain conditions that the church would need to define.

> Le fait humain devenu fait dogmatique est virtuellement révélé par sa nécessaire connexion avec la présentation infaillible de la Révélation de l'Église. Le fait divin de la révélation privée pourrait (à ce titre) devenir fait dogmatique, et pour cela, entrer dans la révélation

publique par sa connexion historiquement prouvée avec la présentation authentique de la Révélation de la part de l'Église dans son
magistère ordinaire universel, sous certaines conditions qu'il con-
viendrait à l'Église de fixer.[22]

Valentini's approach appears the most interesting of all, as it seeks to link the
divine origin of true prophetic revelations to the Deposit of Faith; and his
approach cannot be dismissed, as it is established on the premise that both
designate the same truth of God. He affirms that the inspired nature of true
revelations necessarily implies an inner ontological relation to the public revelation or the Deposit of Faith if they are to express the same truth. It is this
ontological connection that Valentini tries to honor.

Like Valentini, F. Roy seeks to arrive at an evaluation of the faith by which
believers, on the basis of ecclesial approbations, adhere to recognized revelations. Roy believes that the approved revelations must lead to a *foi ecclesiale,*
as the church, when judging true revelations, judges what belongs to its very
being, "that which it alone can know: its being, its way of operating."[23]

The Franciscan priest Carlo Balic, former president of the Pontifical International Marian Academy (PAMI) and adviser to the Holy See, went yet
further. At the Marian congress celebrating the centenary of the Lourdes revelations, he presented his opinion that the Lourdes revelations were of such importance to the church that their approbation might be backed by the church's
infallibility charism and that the faithful might adhere to them *fides divina:*

> One could ask the question if in this case there would not be infal-
> lible approbation and if one should not ascribe to the apparitions of
> Lourdes an assent of *foi théologale* [synonym for *fides divina*] rather
> than an act of mere human faith. . . . The fact and message of Lourdes
> should not, as commonly held, be the object of free assent or rejec-
> tion. It must be said that he who rejects it is certainly imprudent.[24]

The questions concerning the place of prophetic revelations in regard to the
Deposit of Faith have never been addressed in a satisfactory manner. For the
faithful adhering to revelations strictly with *fides humana,* they range low on
the scale of truth within the church. Although this may render their character
less dangerous, and avoid theological arguments such as "Well, in this and that
revelation, God says so and so, hence . . . ," theologians need not feel threatened
by the prophetic revelations, as they range below the true objects of theological
discussion. The question of prophetic revelations is not so simple that it is
enough to ascribe them to the objects of *fides humana.* Like Rahner, many
others have asked "whether anything God reveals can be 'unimportant.'"[25]

Prophetic revelations originate in God, yet they occur after the historical realization in Christ and the authoritative reception by the apostles of the Deposit
of Faith. The relationship of true revelations with the living reality of the Deposit of Faith is much too close dynamically to reject them as mere contingent
historical occurrences. Hence it is indeed possible to place the status of true
Christian prophecy somewhere between the *fides humana* and the *fides divina*
objects of faith.

This assessment of the place of prophetic revelation within the church is
corroborated by the criteria the church uses when canonizing a person, and it
is bolstered when comparing such criteria with those the church uses for judging prophecy. In both cases the criteria are the same: true doctrine and healthy
psychology of the candidate to sainthood or prophet as well as positive fruits of
their apostolate, in particular miracles. Furthermore, in both cases the judgment rests on contingent historical evidence. With the exception of empirically
verified miracles, evidence for judgment is inferred from believers who witnessed the preaching and activity of both. With this the criteria prove to be
identical not merely in their content but also in the quality of their sources, as
both depend on the authenticity of the given testimony.

Now, surprisingly, the *results* of these similar investigations and criteria
are not identical but opposite: As mentioned earlier, the predominant Catholic opinion has been that the church, when canonizing a saint, does so with
the charism of infallibility. When it judges a prophetic revelation, however, it
presents the judgment as a mere permission. At the root of this difference
Laurentin sees the jealousy that Rahner[26] illustrates, and adds:

> The difference in value between canonizations and the recognitions
> of apparitions does not concern the criteria of discernment, but
> rather political problems of government. One of the congenital con-
> cerns of any instance of power is to control the influences that are
> likely to raise popular movements and to threaten authority. Thus
> one supported the "pure, unutterable, and imageless" contempla-
> tive mysticism that favors incommunicable experiences, and deval-
> uated prophecy . . . because of its spontaneous repercussion in the
> life of the church.[27]

8.3. Conclusion

The occurrence of prophetic revelations is a postapostolic historical event, the
mere facticity of which cannot be adhered to with *fides divine*. On the other

hand, given that true Christian prophecy is a direct operation and expression of the Word, its liaison with revelation is far too intimate for it to be considered a human fact only, to be received with fides humana. If a prophetic revelation is authentic, it is the same divine Word that once again expresses himself through the mouth of the Christian prophet and, as such, flows forth from the same source of revelation that gushed forth in the Incarnation. Exactly which label will be conferred on prophecy from this fundamental consideration may be secondary. But it is of primary importance to the argument of this work to point out that *true* Christian prophecy unites the human and the divine, divine inspiration and human expression and hence remains a vehicle that continues to express and guide to fruition the Word of God in every new age. As such, its function and status in the church cannot be emphasized enough. And it is precisely this function and status that enables Christians to properly discern and judge when prophecy is true and when it is not.

9

Prophecy and Truth

We have seen that prophecy has played a decisive role in the life of the church and that, albeit not ranging on the same normative level as Scripture and church teaching, it has a great role and status in the actualization of revelation. The emergence of new dogmas and religious communities has often been inspired and embellished by experiences of prophetically gifted persons.

Prophecy, however, has never gone without opposition, and the words of Jesus, "a prophet is never welcome in his home country," apply to the entirety of Christian history. The main reason for this paradox is the risk of *false prophecy*, a danger that is truly the "Achilles' heel" of prophecy. For as Tadeusz Czakanski rightly points out, the greatest problem with prophecy "pastorally . . . [is] how to recognize [the] true and unmask the false."[1] As Morton Kelsey illustrates, it is not strange that the church has problems with the spiritual, simply because so many people claim to have spiritual experience.[2] In a 1974 survey run by *Psychology Today*, questioning forty thousand Americans, 60 percent claimed to have had spiritual experiences. In a later survey, 82 percent of Americans said they believed that God is "everywhere and in everyone" and that people therefore should be able to experience miracles.[3]

This reveals a strong need for the discernment of prophetic impulses in the church, whereby prophecy might be fruitfully received in the life of the church. Without this process of "testing the spirits," prophecy will remain an unopened book in the story of Christian history, simply because it is not possible to separate the wheat from the chaff. As James Dunn writes on Paul's teaching on discernment, "his recognition of the 'problem of false prophecy,' and his encounter with the 'false apostles' at Corinth must have made him aware, if it was not already obvious to him, that there are religious experiences and religious experiences, and some can provide a basis for life and authority, while others are at best little more than an exercise in self-delusion."[4] The vital function and status of prophecy delineated above will have no practical realization if the faithful are not able to judge between true and false prophecy. And this introduces the present chapter, wherein I examine the criteria necessary for discerning the authenticity of Christian prophets. Much research exists on the discernment of true and false prophecy in the Bible[5] and in the Christian church.[6]

9.1. The Accuracy of Human Experience

The idea of Christian Prophecy is closely related to human experience. And although human experience usually is closely related to the object that is being experienced, there are many different levels of experience. Some are closely related to their objects. Science, for instance, builds on experiences that can be verified empirically, and the experience reflects its object accurately. If empirical evidence proves the opposite, the experience is deemed imprecise or simply inauthentic. Other experiences are less closely linked to their objects. There may be many links between the object and the subject who has the experience, and these links may render the experience *less accurate*. Some experiences may be altogether wrong in the sense that they do not at all mirror their object. With certain types of experiences the relationship between subject and object is very complex. Love for a person, for instance, is a human experience closely related to the loved one, but at the same time it is related to the mind and soul of the person in love. *There is a strong interdependence between the object and the subject who has the experience of love, although the relation is complex.*

Prophetic experience is of such a complex type. It holds many irrational and subjective elements. In order for divine inspiration to bear fruit it must be adapted to the human system that has the experience, and it is not possible empirically to verify it. What can be monitored is the effect of the experience— or, using biblical language, *the prophets shall be judged from their fruits.*[7]

Almost all criteria used to judge the authenticity of the prophets relate to the fruits of the experience. The Catholic Church has used such criteria in a systematic way since the sixteenth century, although they have biblical origin. The fruits of the experience are studied under three different aspects: the content of the revelations, the personality of the prophet, and the effects of the revelations in religious life. The first two points are the so-called intrinsic criteria, and the third point covers the extrinsic criterion.

9.2. Intrinsic Criteria Relating to the Doctrinal Content of Revelations

When judging the doctrinal content of the prophetic message, the basic rule is that nothing may oppose Gospel teaching. Prophecy may be defined as the divinely inspired actualization of the Deposit of Faith—of the revelation in Christ. God is one and cannot contradict himself. Since in the Catholic context Scripture and tradition range as authoritative expressions of the revelation in Christ, the church allows no inconsistencies between this body of teaching and the prophetic message. With principal elements of Christian doctrine the teaching authorities will immediately reject any prophecy disowning fundamental Christian truths. If, for instance, an alleged prophecy claims that Christ was really not the son of God but only an inspired preacher, the entire body of prophecies pronounced by that person will be rejected as unauthentic, even though it may contain many good elements.

This does not mean that the judgment of prophecy is straightforward and simple, for just as there are many ways of interpreting and expounding the Bible, there are many ways of interpreting the message of a prophet. Therefore, judging a prophet's doctrine always relates to different hermeneutic problems.

First of all, any prophetic message is expressed in the language of a *specific historical context*, just as any book in the Bible is held in the language and imagery of its time. Divine inspiration cannot be extended in the human category without the "law of Divine Adaptation" that Laurent Volken writes about.[8] One may find substantial similarities between prophetic messages of the Middle Ages, such as Birgitta of Vadstena or Catherine of Siena, and those of this century, such as Saint Faustina Kowalska or Vassula Rydén, and yet the language and imagery may be very different. Contemporary analytic philosophy has proven that one group of people may express a reality in terms that would not cover the same reality in language games of another language group.

Finding the core of prophetic messages thus is a delicate hermeneutical endeavor that must avoid being stranded on the limitations of form of speech with specific language games.

Second, prophecy normally is expressed in metaphorical language, similar to that of the biblical Canticle of Canticles. To take these texts in their literal sense is to create problems that could be avoided by a penetrating and lyric reading of the text. This applies to the prophetic texts just as it applies to the Bible. Individual passages may appear to be directly opposed to the main body of the text if they are separated from their context. Rejection of a prophetic message thus can only result from a reading of the text in which the reader has entered the imagery and cultural setting of the text, not from a rigid external measuring with standards of measurement that do not apply to what is being measured. A gardener cannot check a garden for weeds by monitoring it from a tower commanding a wide view. He has to enter the garden, following its paths, making sure he does not mistake flowers for weeds.

If during the reading of the text elements are found that clearly contradict Scripture and church doctrine, then the whole message can be discarded, and thus the doctrinal evaluation of a prophetic message can serve positively to reject a message. However, the contrary usually cannot serve as ultimate proof that the message is truly from God: any theologian would be able to produce a "clean" text holding no words that oppose Scripture or church teaching, but this does not indicate that the text is a divine revelation from God.

As a general rule, this means that the doctrinal evaluation can only serve as an active ("positive") criterion to reject a message. Apart from this it may serve as a required ("negative") criterion for judgment, in the sense that pure doctrine only is one out of many necessary requirements on the road to a final positive judgment.

Laurent Volken maintains that there is one important exception to this rule. In some cases the message of the revelation may serve as an active criterion with positive value for discernment. This is when the text not only is "correct" and free from mistakes but also is marked by "a depth and doctrinal balance which surpasses the capacity of the subject who is presenting it, and when it is, furthermore, simple and original."[9] In other words, one may take the purity and quality of the prophetic message as an *active criterion*—a positive sign—when it transcends the capacity and the spiritual training of the prophet. In the history of prophecy it is rare that believers were inspired only by the fact that the prophet's message would be without theological mistakes. Believers see the voice of God in a prophetic message if their faith is stimulated and edified positively by the *spiritual wealth and divine beauty* found in most church-approved prophetic messages.

9.3. Intrinsic Criteria Relating to the Person Receiving
      the Revelations

The message of a prophetic experience is unique in being a symbiosis of divine inspiration and human expression. Divine inspiration always passes through the "filter" of the person who receives the prophecy, and therefore the person receiving the revelation becomes an important object of study when judging the authenticity of the experience. The examination of the person is performed on the basis of the physiology, psychology, and spiritual life of the person.

9.3.1. Physiology of the Person

Even though many physiological factors may supply evidence to the judgment, two merit particular attention: the person's age and the person's gender. In the history of prophecy two avenues remain the principal means of divine communication—the *apparition* and the *vision*. The recipients of apparitions—visions with short and simple messages—are mostly children of both genders, whereas the recipients of lengthy prophetic messages through visions are mainly found among women above the age of puberty (see sections 3.3.16 and 3.3.18).

It may be surprising how often children have been the recipients of apparitions. As we saw, many known Catholic pilgrimage sites stem from the apparitions of Jesus or Mary to one or several children. This accounts for La Salette and Lourdes in France, Fatima in Portugal, and Banneux and Beauraing in Belgium. It equally applies to Garabandal in Spain (apparitions in the 1960s) and Medjugorje (1982 onward), two sites that are visited by multitudes of pilgrims but of which the church has not yet given final judgment. The only apparition site of similar popularity where the visionary was *not* a child is Rue du Bac in Paris. Here the visionary was a young nun, Catherine Labouré.

Religious anthropologists and psychologists have tried to provide an explanation for the multitude of child visionaries. They consider children to be more open to the nonexplainable world than are adults, as they are not yet equipped with the rationalistic barriers of the learned. Growing with the instinct of always assimilating new facets of reality, children are particularly receptive to types of experience beyond the category labeled "ordinary."

As for the gender of the visionaries, it is a fact of church history that women have dominated the prophetic scene to the point that literary historians such as Peter Dinzelbacher have labeled the body of texts written by or about these women "female mysticism" (*Frauenmystik*). Especially after the sixth century women outnumber male visionaries.[10] There have only been few male classical Christian prophetic visionaries, with Blessed Henry Suso as a primary example.[11]

A few centuries ago it was considered *a negative criterion* if an alleged visionary was a woman. Thus, for instance, E. Amorth, influenced by Gravina and Gerson, in his evaluation of prophecy held that because women are weak, unstable, and light creatures ("Mulier est res imbecillis et mobilis et levis") "revelations of women, if other proofs do not contend in their favor, are very probably false, and these probably false revelations should in practice be considered as absolutely false."[12] Today this is an abandoned position that does, however, reflect how much theologians have been puzzled by the overwhelming majority of female prophets.

The reasons for the predominance of female visionaries are almost identical to those given to explain the large number of child visionaries. Many Christian mystics such as Teresa of Avila themselves believe that women generally more readily become attached to and trust God than men—and God reveals himself to those near to him, a position that was confirmed by Gregory XV in Teresa's canonization bull.[13]

Theologians have sought another explanation that would account for the large number of child visionaries as well: according to the Bible God prefers to reveal himself to those who are humble and pure of heart. They are a sign of the humility and the simplicity that according to Christ's words in the Gospel is the key for entering the heavenly Kingdom.[14] This argument, often called the "inversion topos,"[15] has scriptural basis in Mt 19:30: "But many who are first will be last, and last will be first." Paul built on this in various letters. As McGinn writes, it is ironical that the same Paul who has been accused so often of misogyny provided the strongest scriptural backing for the conviction that God would prefer women to be prophets in the chuch.[16] Paul affirmed that in Christ, "there is no longer Jew or Greek, there is no longer slave or free, there is no longer male and female, for all of you are one in Christ Jesus" (Gal 3:28) and that God's evaluations of power do not coincide with those of men, as he "chose what is weak in the world to shame the strong" (see 1 Cor 1:24–29) and thus he can say about himself that "it is when I am weak that I am strong" (2 Cor 12:2). This "inversion topos" became especially predominant in the time of the revival of female prophetic mysticism in the middle of the twelfth century. As McGinn writes, "this Pauline 'inversion topos' was given new life when individual women and their clerical advisers, admirers, and propagandists argued that God could act in a miraculous way through women to right what sinful men had failed to do—to reform the church in preparation for the final conflict between good and evil."[17]

A number of historians and sociologists consider the visionary genre to have been the only way for a woman in the Middle Ages to give words to her thoughts. In other words, women had visions because what they said otherwise would not have had an impact (see section 4.1). Others seek an argument grounded rather in divine justice, namely that God might favor women with prophetic charisms rather than men because only men can become priests in the Orthodox and Catholic traditions. God compensates for this by letting the majority of prophets be women.[18]

9.3.2. Psychology of the Person

Most visionaries have been simple and normal people. An exalted or unstable mind would constitute a negative criterion, since the subjectivity and fantasies of the person could create spiritual *fata morgana*. Most known prophetic personalities have been down to earth but with openness to the spiritual that does not block the reception of spiritual experiences.

On the other hand, they were not all overwhelmingly spiritual, and this is an important aspect to keep in mind in verifying an alleged prophetic charism. A prophetic vocation may occur after long periods of prayer, but that does not alter the nature of the charism as a free gift of God. Very often the divine gift has surprised and overwhelmed the recipient of the gift. It seems that charisms in most cases do not follow upon an extensive life of prayer but rather anticipate and initiate a fruitful spiritual life. This, for instance, could be said of the contemporary much-debated mystic Vassula Rydén. She did not practice her faith before the revelations began, but they led to her full conversion. She now prays six hours a day.

In the New Age jungle things are exactly the opposite. New Age messengers are not called prophets but "media." They are individuals who become famous because of paranormal capacities that surfaced from early childhood. They usually have a vivid imagination combined with a hypersensitivity to the numinous. They are imbued with parapsychological abilities such as clairvoyance, and a New Age messenger has to possess "natural supernatural capacities." In the Christian context, conversely, such capacities by themselves are signs of false prophecy, so that Volken is right in stating that "constitutional instability, hyper-sensitiveness and excessive impressionability in themselves constitute negative (unfavorable) criteria for discernment."[19] It is a classic measure of church discipline that "the existence of psi xxx demands a reevaluation of phenomena previously accepted as supernatural proof of divine origin of a vision."[20]

9.3.3. Spiritual Life of the Person

The prophetic message is always part of a larger *ensemble* of divine grace. It may be the main catalyst in this ample movement of grace, but when eclipsed by the grace from which it flows, the message itself becomes fruitless. The visionary and those who profit from the message share in this flow of grace. Therefore, when judging the authenticity of a prophetic message, the church looks not only at the message but also at the signs of which the message is part.

Some theologians have argued that only a person who is well advanced in the spiritual life can forward a genuine prophetic message. K. Hock is a spokesman of such a position: "If a soul has not yet arrived at the mystical engagement, if it did not yet enjoy in ecstasy the mystical union of love at least passingly, then all visions and revelations that it comes up with should be considered as deceptions."[21]

This idea is not accepted today, simply because it does not apply to the reality of spiritual life. As mentioned earlier, spiritual experiences often take the visionary by surprise. Here it is enough to think of the many apparitions in which the visionaries where children. Another example is Saint Gertrude, who clearly states that she was converted through a vision on January 27, 1281.[22]

As a general rule, virtue is not a precondition to the reception of prophetic gifts, simply because prophecy is a free gift of the Spirit and one that is supposed to bear fruit in conversion and spiritual growth. If there were already full merit on behalf of the visionary, the gift of prophecy would not be a free gift but the reward of merit. And if there were already advanced spiritual life, prophecy would achieve only little, since the fruit it was supposed to achieve already had been achieved. God chooses what from a natural point of view is weak in order that he may be the one who is strong. He does not depend on innate supernatural abilities to give birth to a "supernatural communication." *The prophetic grace remains a grace.*

When all has been said, three spiritual qualities remain as good indications of a true revelation: humility, obedience, and strength. Jean Gerson places the virtue of *humility* at the top of the list. The humble person seeks not his own glory but rather his diminution. By this he is in a good position to receive without adding of his own. Humility does not seek itself and does not have interests, and therefore one finds sincerity where there is humility.[23]

The second virtue is *obedience.* Where humility is a precondition to receive authentic divine communications, obedience grows forth as a response to the revelation. L. Volken shows Teresa of Avila as such an example. Teresa' confessor told her at a certain point not to respond to an apparition. Next, when she saw Christ in the vision, she told him: "I am sorry, I am not allowed to speak with you!" And Christ in the vision was happy with her obedience.[24] One can read something similar in the diary of Sr. Faustina Kowalska.[25]

The third virtue is *strength*. As history shows, almost all prophets meet resistance. L. Volken portrays the problem accurately, deeming it as sure as the law of gravity: "A revelation places its subject—prophet or visionary—in an exceptional situation and thereby necessarily in opposition to ordinary ways of life and normal attitudes that as certain as the law of gravity will seek to reduce all other situations that might transcend it."[26]

When God gives a person a prophetic vocation he also provides the individual with the necessary strength to fulfil that vocation. This applies to all visionaries, but becomes acute when the visionaries are children, as abnormal strength is especially evident with children who are more sensitive to threats. Bernadette of Lourdes is one example of a child that would not shrink from the prison-threats that she should cease to see the Virgin Mary, a command she dismissed, as reported by L. Cros in his presentation of the apparitions of Lourdes.[27] The same thing may be said of the children of Medjugorje and their families, who resisted the threats of officials of the Communist regime that the children would be sent to mental hospitals and their parents to prison.[28]

9.4. Extrinsic Criteria

So far we have been looking only at criteria relating to the message of the prophecy as well as to the character of the person having the prophetic experience. These criteria focus on the immediate characteristics of the prophecy. As mentioned earlier, one must remember that the experience of the prophet is nonetheless always a part of a larger ensemble *of* edifying operations of the Spirit—prophecy is never on the stage alone, that is without the orchestra of grace backing its performance of the divine designs. If, therefore, the prophecy is truly from God, it must also have edifying fruits in the community. An evaluation of a given prophecy must focus on the fruits of the experience and ministry of the prophets. The two aforementioned criteria range as *negative criteria*—necessary requirements for a positive judgment. The extrinsic criteria, however, to a much higher degree count as positive criteria for the overall evaluation. Usually these are what finally lead to a positive judgment, especially if among the fruits there are miracles. Miracles have been considered the strongest incentives leading the church to a positive judgment of a prophetic revelation. This applies equally to the approbation of prophecies and the canonization of saints.

The principal reason why the *accompanying signs* and especially the miracles count as such significant criteria is that they are more tangible than the others. The prophet's message or personal profile is a matter of interpretation, but the especially well documented healing miracles are more easily discernible than other types of miracles, the "objectivity" of which are accessible only to the person who received the grace. A miracle is objectively a *fact*, albeit of course with subjective interpretations. It is an almost fixed rule that the Catholic Church, when venturing to approve an apparition site such as Lourdes or Medjugorje, appoints commissions to register and evaluate given miracles, which are primarily spontaneous healings.[29] In most approved apparition sites numbers of such miracles have been medically attested, and the miracles function as signs of the reality to which they relate.

When a person seeks to judge a prophecy, he or she should always base the judgment on the aforementioned criteria. To the majority of the Catholic faithful, however, the most important of all criteria is one that does not relate internally to the prophecy, and this is the final judgment of the church.

9.5. How the Church Approves a Prophetic Revelation

As mentioned earlier, since the Fifth Lateran Council, the judgment of prophecy has been the responsibility of the highest authorities of the church, a responsibility that usually belongs to the local bishop in whose diocese the prophetic message is being conveyed. Local bishops have approved the apparitions in Lourdes and Pontmain (France), in Fatima (Portugal), in Banneux and Beauraing (Belgium), in Akita, Japan, and in Betania, Venezuela (approved by Bishop Ricardo, November 21, 1987).[30]

The document approving the apparitions of Betania serves as a good example of a positive pronouncement. It holds the classical points of an approval. First, it evaluates positively the claim that the Virgin has appeared, and second, it approves and defines the location of the apparitions as a sanctuary of pilgrimage and prayer:

> Having studied the apparitions of the Virgin Mary at Finca Betania and having prayed assiduously to God for spiritual discernment, I declare that in my judgment the aforementioned apparitions are authentic and are supernatural in character. I therefore officially approve that the place where they occurred be considered a sacred place.

May it become a place of pilgrimage, a place of prayer, reflection, and cult.[31]

This is an example of *direct positive evaluation*. Positive evaluation can, however, also result *indirectly* from a prophetic personality being canonized. Here the words the person conveyed as words of God are implicitly approved when the person is proclaimed a saint. If a person claims to have received divine revelations and this appears not to be the case, the canonization process usually is halted. Often the recognition of prophetic messages precedes canonization. This was the case with the Polish nun Sister Faustina Kowalska of Krakow. Initially the book of Sister Faustina's revelations was banned, placed on the Index. The Congregation for the Doctrine of Faith also published a so-called notification warning the faithful against the messages. Thirty years later, Bishop Wojtyla, later pope John Paul II, obtained the withdrawal of this document as the first step toward canonizing Sister Faustina. Here again it was a necessary precondition that the prophetic messages of the later saint were cleared of any doubt.

9.6. How the Church Rejects a Prophetic Revelation

Just as with positive approbation, it is usually the local bishop who rejects a prophetic message. As a matter of fact most apparition sites, including those later approved, were initially looked on with incredulity by local authorities. This was the case for Lourdes and Fatima, for example. In the second half of the twentieth century Garabandal (1960s) and Medjugorje (beginning in 1981) were the best known apparition sites. Between 1981 and 1996 an estimated twenty million pilgrims visited Medjugorje, making it one of the most visited pilgrimage sites of the end of the century. Both in Garabandal and in Medjugorje the local bishops have reacted negatively. In both cases, the bishops appointed a commission to judge the alleged apparitions, leading to a negative conclusion. Laurentin quotes the bishops' description of the apparitions as "not of divine origin."[32] However, Rome did not simply accept the results of the commissions. In the case of Medjugorje the prefect of the CDF, Joseph Ratzinger, dissolved the episcopal commission, enjoining the Yugoslav National Episcopal Council to appoint a new one.[33]

Bishops both approve and reject prophetic revelations. As mentioned, when the church ventures to approve a prophecy, it usually does so either through the local bishop or indirectly through the canonization of the prophet, in which case the responsibility rests with the Congregation of Rites. When the church rejects a prophecy it does so again through the bishop or through the intervention of the CDF. The Congregation of Rites has mainly had a positive function, confirming and proclaiming the heroic virtues in a human soul. The charge of the CDF has been mainly the opposite. Its main task is to keep the Catholic faith pure of heresy, and the CDF constitutes the Vatican organ that historically has rejected prophetic messages that have spread beyond the range of any local bishop or that have simply not been linked to a specific geographic location. The diffusion of Birgitta's writings is one example of how prophetic messages can attract an audience that exceeds a geographical or historical frame. It is enough to read the documentation of the canonization of Birgitta, published by Boniface XI, to see how widely her revelations spread and carried fruit in the church.

In the case of Birgitta, the revelations had such an impact that church authorities found it necessary to question parts of her writings *even after she was canonized.* Influenced by Joachim of Fiore, Birgitta assumed a tripartition of history.[34] The first period was that of the Father and was to last from the creation of the world to the Incarnation. The second period would last from the Incarnation to the period of the Holy Spirit, which in turn would last to the end of times. Birgitta thought and taught that her generation found itself at the threshold of this last period, and this worried some. Thus, for example, Master Mattias broke with her apparently because he was afraid her ideas would lead people astray. This may serve as an example of how a possible negative approbation often rests not on doctrinal but on disciplinary grounds.

The *Acta Apostolicis Sedis* hold some classical examples of negative judgment: in the case of Loublande, "the occurrences cannot be proven."[35] In the case of Heroldsbach, "they do not appear to be supernatural."[36] In the case of Ezquioga, "they show no sign of supernatural origin whatsoever."[37] These examples reflect a crescendo of gravity: in the first case the revelations cannot be proven, in the second case evidence indicates that they are false, and in the third case it is strongly underlined that they are void of supernatural qualities.

Some statistics from the International Marian Research Institute in Dayton, Ohio, may be helpful in showing ecclesial intervention with Christian prophecy:

A statistical analysis of the Marian apparition directory reveals the following results. During the twentieth century, there have been 386 cases of Marian apparitions. The Church has made "no decision" about the supernatural character regarding 299 of the 386 cases. The Church has made a "negative decision" about the supernatural character in 79 of the 386 cases. Out of the 386 apparitions, the Church has decided that "yes" there is a supernatural character only in 8 cases: Fatima (Portugal), Beauraing (Belgium), Banneux (Belgium), Akita (Japan), Syracuse (Italy), Zeitoun (Egypt), Manila (Philippines) (according to some sources), and Betania (Venezuela). Local bishops have approved of the faith expression at the sites where these 8 apparitions occurred. Besides the 8 approved apparitions, there have been 11 (out of the 386 apparitions) which have not been approved with a "supernatural character," but which have received a "yes" to indicate the local bishop's "approval of faith expression (prayer and devotion) at the site."[38]

9.7. The Nature of the Church's Judgment

The church's judgment of prophetic revelations is a relatively new phenomenon. The procedures for the judgment of prophecy and even the formal canonization of saints as known in contemporary Catholicism only date back to the late Middle Ages. As mentioned earlier, holy humans were considered saints simply by their reputation for a life reflecting the marks of sainthood, and popes could canonize saints even without the formal procedures known today.[39] The Eastern churches mirror this tradition to this day. One of the most important medieval mystics, Hildegard of Bingen, has not been canonized in the modern Catholic sense, although her contemporaries, including popes and emperors, considered her one of the greatest prophets of the ages.[40] It remains a mystery why she was not, but part of the reason may have been that the official procedures for canonization were only being formalized during that time, namely by Pope Gregory IX.[41]

During fourteenth century, the Roman church enhanced its official rules for judging prophets, in part because the death of Birgitta of Vadstena in 1373 increased the need for such official judgment. Birgitta was quite a personality, who was not afraid of proclaiming her visions and prophecies to people of all classes, including the highest church authorities. She lived in a moment of turmoil in Europe. The popes resided in Avignon, far away from Peter's Rome. This threat to the unity of the church, climaxing at the turn of the fourteenth century, when there were two and then even three popes at the same time, seriously challenged the stability of the Western church.[42] It could have led to a tripartition of the West even then in the fourteenth century. Ingvar Fogelqvist sees in Birgitta's battle to bring the popes back to Rome "a fundamental feature of her mission for unity and reform in the church, as well as for the peace of Christendom."[43] In her admonitions to the pope in France she was very direct:

> Birgitta mentions that severe temporal punishments will visit him should he remain in France. Urban V will receive a blow so violent as to make his teeth chatter, his sight will become dim and dusky, and all his limbs will tremble; the fire of the Holy Spirit will recede from him, and the faithful will weary of praying for him; he will be forced to account before God for what he has done as pope.[44]

Words like these partially explain why the church needed a proper investigation of Birgitta's mission, and her revelations "provoked a debate, the most important and most solemn debate which had taken place in the Church on the subject of particular revelations. The most prominent theologians were to display their competence in the course of it."[45] Despite her renown for miracles and pious life, she had gained many enemies. Church leaders at the Council of Basel decided to investigate her revelations, and this process produced the basic principles of judgment that have been applied ever since. The two main characters in this process were Jean Gerson and John of Torquemada. Gerson's work *De probatione Spirituum* was rather critical toward Birgitta. Along with his general great caution about false revelations—"no one fought them more than Jean Gerson"[46]—he believed no more destructive and unhealthy desire exists than that for revelations: "Vix est altera pestis vel efficacior ad nocendum et insanabilior."[47] Torquemada was more positive toward Birgitta and, in the end, managed to convince the Council of the authenticity of her experience.

When the Catholic Church evaluates a prophetic revelation, it is never with the seal of infallibility, and it is therefore not binding. The positive ecclesial evaluation of a prophetic revelation is nothing but a *permission* to believe that God has spoken, whereas the negative pronouncement is usually a strong advice not to accept its heavenly origin. This is why the institutional pronouncement is *one among other criteria*.

This is the truth in theory. In practice, things are different. Normal Catholics take the ecclesial pronouncement for more than permission or advice. There are other motivations than infallibility that lead believers to listen to the Magisterium and adhere to its pronouncement. We saw that Yves Congar defined this motivation as the general respect for the church and considered unreflected disregard of the pronouncements of the church to be imprudent.

Equally so, however, is the position that it is wrong to believe in a prophetic revelation until the church has spoken. As history shows this often might mean waiting for centuries. This position seems to be widespread due to the fact that judging a prophetic revelation entails a good piece of work studying the revelation, and many believers do not want to make that effort. Second, belief in a given prophecy can be risky due to the danger of false prophecy mentioned earlier. A believer who has been inspired by a given prophecy would feel shaken if it proved to be false. And yet, waiting for the official pronouncement does not appear to be a responsible standpoint for believers: there are good rules and criteria that can be used when judging prophecy. They are varied and concrete and ought to lead to a valid judgment. The rules are there to be applied and used.

Furthermore, the church only ventures to judge a given prophecy when sufficient numbers of believers show interest in it. *If all Christians should wait for the judgment of the church, it would never start investigating.* Most experts agree that any true prophetic revelation has an edifying and guiding scope. The message of the prophet primarily concerns his or her contemporaries and to a lesser degree later generations, although believers use prayers of prophets such as Birgitta to this day. Since the church can ill afford such blunders and the judgment machinery is heavy, a pronouncement usually follows decades after the close of the prophet's activities. If all were to choose to wait, the faithful might miss the helping hand of the Shepherd, and the approach of the Holy Spirit would not produce as much fruit as it could have done. Thus a wise approach to prophecy before its eventual ecclesial evaluation seems to be one of cautious openness, avoiding constructing one's life on the prophecy, but equally allowing it to bear fruit when the criteria seem to prove its authenticity.

Often prudence becomes the excuse for awaiting the official judgment of the church. Here it is necessary to reflect a moment on the concept of prudence. There is such a thing as distorted prudence—false caution that in reality becomes *imprudence.* For instance, extreme prudence is no longer care, but rigid resistance to the renewing activity of the Holy Spirit. If Paul in defining prophecy as God's edification and guidance is implying that prophecy is a warning, then distorted prudence proves to be imprudence as it closes to the warnings of the Spirit. There are two forms of prudence—one is passive and static; another is active and dynamic. The passive prudence is solely protective and preserving, leading in the end to the "extinction of the Spirit."[48] The dynamic prudence, on the other hand, is that which actively seeks to give heed to the voice of the Spirit, while carefully applying the criteria of discernment in order to reject what comes across as false and welcome what proves to be true.

Thus, although the judgment of the church may justifiably hold primacy over all other criteria, the importance of individual discernment cannot be emphasized enough. This was stressed at the Second Vatican Council, which

can rightly be called the council of the laity. As Laurentin writes, this is because Vatican II has pointed to the importance of the discernment of all members of the church: "Today, the Second Vatican Council, which revalorized the
people of God, its initiative, its participation, its joint responsibility, is a invi-
tation to carry out discernment in a collective, educational, and pastoral way.
May this same people be involved as much as possible with the exercise of discernment and critical judgment."[49]

Hill believes the main reason for the poor role of prophecy in the church is
that the "ability to discern and repudiate the false seems not to have been
balanced by ability to discern and retain the true."[50] Already Irenaeus warned
not to reject the true prophets due to the mere existence of false ones.[51] This
warning seems no less timely today than in his time.

9.8. Conclusion

Prophecy has an incredible force. As Karl Rahner has indicated, the authority
of prophets is almost unbeatable.[52] Even though a prophet clearly speaking by
the inspiration of the Holy Spirit may say the same words as a given good
priest, great numbers of believers prefer listening to the words of the prophet,
as they want to hear as directly as possible "the voice of the Shepherd." Karl
Rahner believes that the unbeatable prophetic authority has created a general
spirit of jealousy on behalf of priests and theologians, and that this is the
reason why prophets have always been persecuted, and subsequently the reason why so surprisingly little research has been done on the theological theme
of prophecy.[53] This jealousy may also explain why there are so many theological misconceptions of prophecy, such as the famous but truly erroneous
position that prophecy ended with the completion (achèvement) of revelation
with the last apostle.

What Rahner points out is undoubtedly true, but it does not change the
fact that the church still has reason to be careful with the danger of false
prophecy. Since prophecy is so powerful, it is normal that the church would be
more careful with possible false teachings proposed by prophets than by "normal" theologians. What Rahner does provide, however, is a healthy reminder
not to let the combined jealousy and fear of false prophecy evolve into an a
priori negative attitude toward any prophetic manifestation.

The criteria I have presented here function in two ways. They are not just
negative criteria used to cast aside all that might come across as false prophecy.
They have a positive function as well, no less important than the negative one:
they help us to recognize and receive the gifts and works of the Spirit of God.

The former prefect of the CDF, Joseph Ratzinger, speaks of this double function of the church's engagement in the discernment of prophecy. While defending the general, careful attitude of the CDF toward mystical claims, he admonishes the church to be careful not to "kill the prophets."[54]

No prophecy can have an influence on the life of the church unless individual believers or the church, as such, first have evaluated whether or not the prophecy is true. This fact contains a dilemma: prophetic messages often contain critical words to those with responsibilities in the church, that is, to the same church that holds the charge of judging the prophecy. The church that prophetic messages call to conversion and a true life in God is the same church that has the power to reject prophetic messages. One could ask if this makes the church disqualified in judging prophecy. Some people have held this to be the case; how can the church be objective in its judgment of prophets who are critical toward the church? The answer is found in the following description of the church's *modus operandi*: it is the ecclesial authorities who have the competence and the responsibility to judge every kind of message in the church, including those labeled *prophetic*, just as it is the ministry of justice in the secular society that has the charge and authority to judge the administration of justice, including the ministry of justice itself! Such is the nature of this dialectic. It is like a natural law in the structure of the church that cannot be changed. However, the church must be constantly aware of the dangers it contains, namely of refuting a priori prophetic messages that criticize how ecclesial offices are administered, as in the writings of Birgitta of Vadstena. This ecclesial "law of nature" charges the church and especially its leaders with the double responsibility of maintaining a healthy balance between rejection and positive reception of prophetic messages in the spirit of the oldest and perhaps most important New Testament passage on prophecy: "Do not stifle the Spirit or despise the gift of prophecy with contempt; *test everything and hold on to what is good*."[55]

IO

General Conclusion

The phenomenon I have investigated for its meaningful presence in Christianity is controversial. As Christ came to be a sign that would be spoken against,[1] so the charisms he has bestowed on his people have often been signs and objects of contradiction. Prophets are easily associated with religious fanatics who, in an ecstatic spirit, preach doom and gloom to people attracted by sensational spirituality. Even those with prophetic traits who after their death have been recognized as saints have often been ousted during their lifetimes for their words of correction, pointing to aspects of the Gospel that were neglected. And yet St. Paul speaks of the ministry of prophets, naming them next after the apostles, showing their fruitful purpose and calling believers "to be eager for spiritual gifts, and especially for prophesying."[2]

Historical, exegetical, and theological arguments have been adduced for the extinction of prophecy variously with the last Old Testament canonical prophets, with John the Baptist, with Jesus, with the death of the last apostle, with the closure of the biblical canon, or with the rise of Montanism. My conclusions are that none of these arguments hold water, since what they do is argue for the cessation of *one form of prophecy*, but not the prophetic phenomenon itself. Prophecy never died, but rather proved its dynamism by mutating according to the preconditions of new historical developments.

The inspirations that prophetic personalities have proclaimed to the world as the Word of God have often been called *private revelations* due to the concern with differentiating them from *public revelation,* which they may help articulate and actualize, but never expand or overrule. However, while the term *private revelations* supports this concern, its disadvantages outweigh its advantages because it has such damaging effects on the right understanding of the relation between prophecy and revelation. Christ's prophetic gifts are never private, but the "manifestation of the Spirit is given for the common good,"[3] and "everyone who prophesies speaks to men for their strengthening, encouragement and comfort...[and] edifies the church."[4] While other alternatives exist that embody the same concern of not overruling public revelation, such as *special, particular,* or *dependent revelations,* I found that the term *prophetic revelations* would be preferable. The term *prophetic revelations* indicates the purpose of prophecy, that is, that of realizing the continuous salvific dynamism inherent to revelation. Thus, exploring Christian prophecy as a theme for systematic theology helps envisage revelation as more than a past occurrence. Rather, inherent to revelation is the eternal Word's continuous salvific operation that actualizes and realizes what was given in Christ's Incarnation for the edification of the church. Therewith, prophecy becomes an integral part of revelation as one of the forms in which the Word of God continues to unfold and give itself to the people of God.

Prophecy appears to have been in some form part of the very structure of the early church, with both permanent and itinerant prophets being supported by the community. However, especially after the first witnesses to Jesus had passed away, the discernment between true and false prophecy constituted an increasing difficulty. This raised the need for firm, historically grounded loci of revelation, so that the faithful were not constantly depending on the difficult discernment between true and false words from the heavenly Christ, but could rely on the testimony of the earthly Jesus through the formation of canon and the structural establishment of the church. Moreover, the teaching of the historical Jesus in this way could become the standard for judging the authenticity of continuous manifestations of the heavenly Christ. Thus, the view of prophecy as the mere victim of growing institution and finalized canon falls short, since prophecy itself was part of the dialectic that led to the formation of both.

The experiences with Montanism and Islam, which came across as two prophetic heresies, led to ever greater marginalization of prophecy and arguably indeed to the cessation of one *form* of Christian prophecy, namely the congregationally integrated function of prophetic speech in the early church and its liturgy.

However, the prophetic phenomenon itself continued to be manifest in new ways through the history of the church. Thus, forms of prophecy can be seen with the early Christian martyrs and confessors, with the Desert Fathers, and with the initiators of both Eastern and Western monastic movements. It reemerged powerfully in the medieval period, especially in the form of female visionary mysticism and, especially since the nineteenth Century, in Marian apparitions. Thus, in crucial periods in the history of the church, mostly women with a prophetic profile, such as Birgitta of Vadstena, Catherine of Siena, and Joan of Arc, stood up much like the Old Testament prophets and called the people of God to live in accordance with his Word. Marian apparitions—and the pilgrimage places that have been established where they occurred—have led to spiritual renewal, as did the devotional practices that stemmed from many prophetic messages. Thus, Christian prophecy has been fruitfully present throughout the entire history of the church, and possible prophetic charisms can be discerned in the present day, with ongoing apparitions in pilgrimage sites with millions of visitors, such as Medjugorje in Bosnia-Herzegovina.

Given prophecy's impressive historical impact, one would expect intense concern for its theological elaboration. However, at least in systematic theology, Christian prophecy has received limited theological attention, so that Rino Fisichella is right when he notes that "confronting the subject of prophecy is rather like looking at wreckage after a shipwreck."[5] The foundations that indeed exist in Scripture for a theology of prophecy have never been developed into a comprehensive theological synthesis. Five primary reasons may be given for this fact, as follows.

(1) As many authors have noted, the integration of prophetic graces in the life of the church has never been easy, for handling prophetic gifts in ecclesial life implies difficult acts of discernment that when handled badly can cause spiritual harm. Although we saw that criteria do exist that aid pastors and faithful alike in their efforts to "test the spirits to see whether they are from God,"[6] there is a great need for prudence so that the harmful effects of false prophecy may be limited, but equally that the fruits of God's authentic gifts can be harvested for the benefit of the church.

(2) As Rahner, Balthasar, and others have pointed out, it is possible to discern in theology, and in mystical theology in particular, an often a priori preference for a Dionysian-like wordless and purely contemplative spirituality over the more kerygmatic spirituality to which prophecy belongs, since its constitutive element is God's Word revealing himself again to remind believers of his truth through one or several persons that he has called in a particular manner. Prophecy implies extraordinary forms of experience that are not easily reconciled and accommodated within the more rigorous structures of theology and the organized religious life of the church.

(3) The elaboration of prophecy entails a methodological complexity: prophecy is a multifaceted topic the investigation of which requires coping

with several theological disciplines. It entails systematic theology: what part does the prophet play in the life of the church, and what is the relationship between prophecy and institution? What are the preconditions of prophecy on the basis of a theology of revelation? In order to contemplate the practical impact of the prophets, a theology of prophecy must look at the history of the church. Since a theology of Christian prophecy must be consistent with the picture of prophecy given by the New Testament, it must imply exegesis. And finally, it requires looking at the problem of the experiential aspects of prophecy, whereby one enters the realm of mystical theology. In most systems of theology, there are rather strict boundaries between the different disciplines, and these boundaries, which naturally raise obstacles for the unity of theology, also cause difficulty for the problem of prophecy.

(4) Certain concepts in the theology of revelation have raised problems for a theology of Christian prophecy. In the early church and the Middle Ages, the idea of revelation was ambiguous and multifaceted, and there was plenty of room for the integration of the charism of prophecy within the theology of revelation. The concept of revelation covered both the Incarnation of Christ and his Spirit's ongoing activity unfolding and actualizing the salvation he wrought. Thus, prophecy served as an important function as signs of the truth of revelation and at times indeed served in the discernment of its right interpretation. Thus, it was very much a locus theologicus.

Nevertheless, several movements in the history of the church, not the least the Reformation, enhanced the reticence toward prophetic manifestations, bolstered by tendencies that equally worked against prophecy: the role of the laity decreased; the preference grew for a religious life that flowed from the initiatives of ecclesial ministers; and the notion of revelation as a deposit of doctrinal teaching became dominant well into the twentieth century. Prophecy and the prophetic revelations were less and less an integral part of the doctrine of revelation. In this process one particular example emerged of a theological system in which prophecy was moved to the periphery, namely Francisco Melchior Cano's *De locis theologiae* of 1563, considered "the premier methodological treatise of modern Catholic theology"[7] and for centuries a normative work. As such, the impact of Cano's work on the relationship between theology and prophecy cannot be underestimated.

Cano presented a hierarchical system of different theological loci. These loci constitute the sources for the church's knowledge of revelation. For instance Scripture is presented as the primary locus. Art, conversely, is placed in one of the last loci. One could ask, now, where the prophetic revelations would be found in Cano's system, and one would expect them to be placed somewhere in between, given their historical role in the actualization of revelation. This, however, is not the case. The prophetic revelations appear in none of the theological loci, not even in the additional loci. They are placed outside the theological loci in what can only be named non–loci theologiae and by this lose all relevance to theology. They no longer function as criteria for discerning the truth.

(5) The maxim of the *end of revelation with the last apostle* has been interpreted in such different ways that one might doubt that it had to do with the same theological problem. There has been great confusion and lack of clarity on the matter, which can be exemplified by the fact that in the first volume of *Mysterium Salutis* one finds two opposite interpretations of the same concept. In relation to prophecy, the maxim has nevertheless been used with one meaning: when Christ is the full and final revelation of God in history, how then can there still be a need for Christian prophecy? Before answering this question one must turn to the underlying assumptions of the theological mindset in which it was raised. For at the root of this question lies an apprehension of revelation that comes very close to the doctrinal model of revelation, according to which God reveals himself only to instruct the church.

In order better to understand the idea of the apostolic end of revelation, the distinction between revelation's *material* and *formal* aspects proves to be helpful. From the *material* point of view, Christ is the full divine self-revelation, in whom God communicates himself to the world as man. No prophetic revelation can ever say anything more complete about God than what God in Christ has revealed himself to be. But this full revelation in Christ would have no meaning in history were it not for the *formal* aspects of revelation. Revelation must have a formal, expressive side, or else it could be neither transmitted nor communicated, and thus could not be received in the life of faith. Belief in revelation presupposes its formal expression.

Even if there are still problems to be solved concerning the mutual relationship of Scripture and tradition, it is clear that the formal aspects of revelation are realized in both. It appears most fruitful to view Scripture as the norm and criterion of what can be said and—in particular—of what can *not* be said about revelation. The reality of the Word, on the other hand, even though it is presented in Scripture, is historically actualized in tradition, and it is in tradition that the salvation that we read about in Scripture becomes actualized in every new period of time. In this regard tradition clearly encompasses a prophetic element. It is in the frame of this general prophetic dimension of tradition that the specific prophetic revelations play a part in actualizing the Deposit of Faith. It is surprising to discover how many examples in history support these considerations. The classical prophetic messages have had enormous impact on the itinerary of the church in history and thus have played a very important part in the actualization of revelation.

This process of actualizing revelation through prophecy can with great advantage be viewed from the perspective of different models of revelation. According to the personalistic and historical understanding of revelation, most prevalent today, it makes no sense to speak of an *end of revelation*, unless one accepts a deistic basis. Christ will, as the head of the church, continue to guide it through history, and in this guidance, prophecy serves the edification of the church and the actualization of revelation in all its aspects. One aspect of revelation's implementation has been virtually uncovered, however, and this is prophecy's effect on the inner life of the church. While it is true that false prophecy has led to sectarian groups that eventually left the church, true prophecy cannot be said to lead believers away from the core-mystery of the church. Rather, the sociology of religion has shown how prophetic mani-festations inspire the faithful to a more intimate and immediate experience of the reality of Christ's Word for them in their time. Although this experience of interchange on the threshold between historical structures and their tran-scendent origin for a period may lead believers to gather in structures that are new and sometimes unorthodox compared to the structures of their prove-nance, these transient states will eventually lead to new structures considered more apt to realize God's life in their time. Rather than being a principle that propels believers out of the church true prophetic charisms are hence among the main agents in the church's continuous process of vital "autogenesis" according to the "genetic code" of Christ's Kingdom.

There has been a tendency, in the history of the theology of prophecy, to view it primarily as a foretelling of future events. C. Pesch provides the best summary of this tendency: prophecy is "certa predictio futuri eventus qui ex principiis naturalibus praesciri non potest."[8] The notion of prophecy as the foretelling of the future was so predominant in the Middle Ages that Birgitta of Vadstena, one of the most important Christian prophetic figures, never dared to speak of herself as a prophet. She only had a very few revelations dealing with future events. This reductionist approach to prophecy became especially evident in the manualist tradition, as it only sought to identify the fulfillment of the Old Testament prophecies in the Christ-event. The idea of prophecy as foretelling the future has persisted to this day and is no less present in popular language. One often hears words like "He was a real prophet! He predicted that this or that party would win the elections. It was a real prophetic statement!"

Christian prophecy, however, has little to do with the mere prediction of future events, as its energy is never thrust toward the future. *It always aims at the present.* Were this not so, prophecy could not be edifying to the church at the time of the prophet, which, as we saw, is the main criterion of authentic Christian prophecy. The word *prophecy* itself seems to come from the Greek προφημι which conveys the meaning to *speak forth* rather than *foretelling.*

It is true that prophecy often regards the future. It may also deal with the past. But regardless of whether a given prophecy deals with something pertaining to the past or to the future, it is always of relevance to the present. In this way, prophecy can be edifying regardless of the time that is the focus or scene of a given prophecy, in the following ways.

Prophets look back in time. The prophet may look on former mighty works of God, and thus edify the people of God in admiration and trust. The Old Testament prophets recalled the mighty works of God when he led Israel out of Egypt. Jesus, the supreme Christian prophet, looked back on the words of Isaiah regarding the anointing of the Lord, and explained it in the light of his coming upon Earth. The Christian prophets themselves, normally speaking in Christ's name, usually look back on his work and life in order to praise the salvific actions of divine charity. Prophets like Birgitta of Vadstena and many with her encourage believers to contemplate the passion of Christ as a means to enter into communion with his love.

Prophets look at the present. They denounce and mourn over the sins of the people of God and that the people has become so blinded that it no longer recognizes their corrupt state They may also point to dangerous challenges of new periods, for instance the threat of Communism, as in one message of Fatima.

Prophets look at the future. Here the view of the prophet may imply warnings of impending trials. One can rightly ask what the foretelling of future catastrophes has to do with the edification of the church. It does not appear very uplifting to be told that the world is heading toward disaster, as has been part of the message of many prophetic revelations. Here, it may be worthwhile, once again, to focus on Birgitta of Vadstena. When she proclaimed warnings of future chastisements, it was always with the goal of bringing the church to conversion through the warning. The warning of a future disaster is hardly ever a message of unconditional punishment on behalf of God, but should rather be viewed as the portrait of a natural relationship between apostasy and its effects: disaster will follow if man continues self-destructive, evil ways, which are not in accordance with the divine will. Thus, even the foretelling of future catastrophes may be viewed as an expression of divine providence rather than condemnation, since the church through the prophet is warned of the natural effect of its apostasy. The future depicted, however, is not simply that of doom and gloom. Prophets always looked at the future as the realm of fulfilled promises, and prophecy has been throughout Christian history a means of keeping hope in the promises of faith alive. The people of God are edified in knowing that God's guidance has not left them in the present age of suffering, but that Christ will return to fulfill the promises of his first coming.

In the twentieth century, and especially with the Second Vatican Council, developments have emerged that aid a fruitful apprehension of prophecy in the church. Initially the *personalistic aspects of revelation* were recovered. A good example of this rediscovery is found in the writings of Pope Benedict XVI, who, as a young professor, worked extensively with the theology of revelation in the writings of Bonaventure. We have seen many examples of how the dynamic apprehension of revelation is found throughout the writings of the pope. Further, the Second Vatican Council focused on the importance of the laity by stressing the prophetic and priestly vocation of every believer. These tendencies prepared the ground for a fruitful apprehension of prophecy, by pointing out its theological preconditions and establishing the negative boundaries of Christian prophecy. In spite of this change regarding the preconditions, however, a positive theology of prophecy cannot be said to have been developed. And yet, the features of Christian prophecy may be a fruitful inspiration to the theology of revelation as they point out that God is involved in the salvation of his children to such an extent that he not only sends his son to earth to pay the necessary ransom for salvation to occur but through his son continues to draw people to himself.

As is evident in the farewell discourses in the Gospel of John, Christ is the mediator of God's salvation to such an extent that he not alone provides the necessary preconditions for God's children to embrace salvation through the sacrifice of his Cross. Christ himself is so deeply involved in the realization of this salvation through his church and its sacraments, through his Spirit, and through his prophets until it is fulfilled in the eschaton that we may rightly say that we may view the *actualizing aspect* of his mediation to be as important as its foundation through the Cross. *Potential foundation* would be of little worth without *continuous historical actualization*. If a theology of revelation intends to reflect the reality of Christ's salvation it must equally highlight revelation's past foundation and its subsequent actualization in a corresponding view of Christological *shaliach* from the past as well as from the future. Hence a theology of revelation that sees prophecy as a mere sign of the truth of revelation comes across as incomplete. Conversely, deepened reflections on the notion of Christian prophecy may help complete the mediating role of Christ—two thousand years ago in his Incarnation and today in his Spirit.

As such, prophecy is more than a sign of revelation, but is itself a *form* and integral part of revelation: it is "good for the disciples that Christ goes," not only to redeem them through his Cross but so that he may come in the Spirit and draw all men to himself:

> Now I am going to him who sent me, yet none of you asks me, "Where are you going?" Because I have said these things, you are filled with grief. But I tell you the truth: It is for your good that I am going away. Unless I go away, the Counselor will not come to you; but if I go, I will send him to you.... I have much more to say to you, more than you can now bear. But when he, the Spirit of truth, comes, he will guide you into all truth. He will not speak on his own; he will speak only what he hears, and he will tell you what is yet to come. He will bring glory to me by taking from what is mine and making it known to you. All that belongs to the Father is mine. That is why I said the Spirit will take from what is mine and make it known to you.[9]

Notes

CHAPTER I

1. 2 Kgs 3:11. All biblical references are from *The New Jerusalem Bible* (Garden City: Doubleday, 1985).

2. Prv 29:18.

3. Mk 14:62; see Dn 7:13 and Ps 110:1.

4. Simon Tugwell, ed., *Albert and Thomas: Selected Writings* (New York: Paulist Press, 1988), commentary on the Gospel of Matthew, chap. 11.

5. Thomas Aquinas, *Summa Theologica*, II-II q. 174, a.6, ad3, cited from Thomas Aquinas, *Summa Theologica*, available from http://eresources .library.nd.edu/databases/aquinas.

6. Domenico Bertetto, *Acta Mariana Joannis PP. XXIII* (Zurich: PAS-Verlag, 1964), 56. Ref. to Thomas Aquinas, *Summa Theologica*, II-II q. 174, a.6, ad3.

7. Eugene Boring, *The Continuing Voice of Jesus: Christian Prophecy and the Gospel Tradition* (Louisville: John Knox Press, 1991), 16–17.

8. Rino Fisichella, "Prophecy," in *Dictionary of Fundamental Theology*, ed. René Latourelle and Rino Fisichella (New York: Crossroad, 1995), 788.

9. Ibid., 795.

10. Migaku Sato, *Q und Prophetie: Studien zur Gattungs- und Traditionsgeschichte der Quelle Q* (Tübingen: Mohr, 1988), 411.

11. Ben Witherington, *Jesus the Seer: The Progress of Prophecy* (Peabody: Hendrickson, 1999), 404.

12. Karl Rahner, "Les Révélations Privées: Quelques Remarques Theologiques," *Revue d'Ascétique et Mystique* 25 (1949): 16. English version: *Private Revelations: Some Theological Observations*, CatholicCulture.org, available from www.catholicculture.org/docs/doc_view.cfm?recnum=202.

13. I shall deal with this issue in section 6.2.

14. "As with the Old Testament phenomenon, the essential character of early Christian prophecy was the claim to be speaking under direct divine inspiration." Larry W. Hurtado, *Lord Jesus Christ: Devotion to Jesus in Earliest Christianity* (Grand Rapids: Eerdmans, 2003), 150. See section 3.3.1.

15. James Dunn, *Jesus and the Spirit: A Study of the Religious and Charismatic Experience of Jesus and the First Christians as Reflected in the New Testament* (Grand Rapids: Eerdmans, 1997), 172–73.

16. Karl Rahner, *Visions and Prophecies* (London: Burns and Oats, 1963), 20.

17. Karl Rahner, *Visionen und Prophezeiungen*, 2nd ed. (Freiburg: Herder, 1958), 21.

18. Tadeusz Czakanski, "The Christian Prophets and the Charism of Prophecy in the New Testament and the Origins of the Church" (Ph.D. diss., Rome: Università Lateranense, 1987), 189.

19. Rahner, *Visions and Prophecies*, 25–26.

20. "Ein Rahmenwort ohne konkreten Inhalt"; Erich Fascher, *Prophetes: Eine sprach- und religionsgeschichtliche Untersuchung* (Giessen: Töpelmann, 1927), 51.

21. Eugene Boring, *The Continuing Voice of Jesus: Christian Prophecy and the Gospel Tradition* (Louisville: John Knox Press, 1991), 35. Ref. to John W. McGarvey, *Short Essays in Biblical Criticism, Reprinted from the Christian Standard, 1893–1904* (Cincinnati: Standard, 1910), 118.

22. Gustavo Gutiérrez, *Teología de la Liberación: Perspectivas* (Salamanca: Ediciones Sígueme, 1972); Francois Malley, "*Las Casas* et les Théologies de la Libération," *La Vie Spirituelle* 139 (1985): 58. See the discussion of the use of the prophetic category in liberation theology in José Luis Espinel, *Profetismo Cristiano: Una Espiritualidad Evangélica* (Salamanca: Editorial San Esteban, 1990), 169–79.

23. Karl Rahner, *The Dynamic Element in the Church* (Freiburg: Herder, 1964), 40.

24. Tommaso Stenico and Francis A. Arinze, *Il Concilio Vaticano II: Carisma e Profezia* (Vatican City: Libreria Editrice Vaticana, 1997).

25. Paul VI, *Dogmatic Constitution on the Church: Lumen Gentium* (Boston: St. Paul Editions, 1965), 35.

26. Hans-Ruedi Weber, "Prophecy in the Ecumenical Movement," in *Prophetic Vocation in the New Testament and Today 45*, edited by J. Panagopoulos (Leiden: Brill, 1977), 218.

27. Gianfranco Calabrese, ed., *Chiesa e Profezia* (Rome: Edizioni dehoniane, 1996).

28. John J. Conley and Joseph W. Koterski, *Prophecy and Diplomacy: The Moral Doctrine of John Paul II: A Jesuit Symposium* (Bronx: Fordham University Press, 1999).

29. Bernhard Häring, "Prophètes," in *Dictionnaire de la vie Chrétienne* (Paris: 1983), 912.

30. Boring, *The Continuing Voice of Jesus*, 35–36.

31. Walter Houston, "New Testament Prophecy and the Gospel Tradition" (Ph.D. diss., Mansfield College, Oxford University, 1973), 282.

32. Marianne Schlosser, *Lucerna in caliginoso loco: Aspekte des Prophetie-Begriffes in der scholastischen Theologie* (Paderborn: Schöningh, 2000), 10.

33. Witherington, *Jesus the Seer*, 3.

34. Wayne A. Grudem, *The Gift of Prophecy in the New Testament and Today* (Westchester: Crossway Books, 2000), 116.

35. Boring, *The Continuing Voice of Jesus*, 38.

36. 1 Cor 14:3–4.

37. Christian Meyer, "Von der 'Privatoffenbarung' zur öffentlichen Lehrbefugnis: Legitimationsstufen des Prophetentums bei Rupert von Deutz, Hildegard von Bingen, und Elisabeth von Schönau," in *Das Öffentliche und Private in der Vormoderne*, edited by Peter von Moos and Gert Melville (Köln: Böhlau, 1998).

38. Joseph Ratzinger, "Das Problem der Christlichen Prophetie: Niels Christian Hvidt im Gespräch mit Joseph Kardinal Ratzinger," *Communio* 2 (1999): 186–87.

39. Avery Robert Dulles, *The Assurance of Things Hoped For: A Theology of Christian Faith* (Oxford: Oxford University Press, 1994), 199.

40. Avery Dulles refers to session 6, chap. 12, in Denzinger, Heinrich, and Schönmetzer, *Enchiridion symbolorum, definitionum et declarationum de rebus fidei et morum*. 33rd ed. Barcinone: Herder, 1965 1540; canons 14–16, DS 1564–66.

41. We shall return to this question in section 8.

42. Dulles, *The Assurance of Things Hoped For*, 199.

43. Richard P. McBrien, *The HarperCollins Encyclopedia of Catholicism* (San Francisco: HarperSanFrancisco, 1995), 80.

44. René Laurentin, "Fonction et Statut des Apparitions," in *Vraies et Fausses Apparitions dans l'Église: Exposés*, edited by Bernard Billet (Paris: Bellarmin, 1976), 163.

45. Dulles, *The Assurance of Things Hoped For*, 198.

46. "Tenendo conto della natura e delle funzioni delle rivelazioni posteriori per la vita della Chiesa, i termini 'rivelazione speciale' o 'rivelazione particolare' sarebbero forse più pertinenti, perché la formula 'rivelazione privata' rischia di ridurre la sua portata e la sua finalità alla dimensione di un singolo individuo." Augustinus Suh, *Le Rivelazioni Private nella Vita della Chiesa* (Bologna: Dehoniane, 2000), 32.

47. Rahner, *Visions and Prophecies*, 17.

48. Laurent Volken, "Um die theologische Bedeutung der Privatoffenbarungen: Zu einem Buch von Karl Rahner," *Freiburger Zeitschrift für Philosophie und Theologie* 6 (1959): 436.

49. Gerald O'Collins, *Fundamental Theology* (New York: Paulist Press, 1981), 102.

50. Auguste Saudreau, *L'État Mystique, sa Nature, ses Phases et les Faits Extraordinaires de la Vie Spririutelle*, 2nd ed. (Paris, 1921), 216–22.

51. René Laurentin, *The Apparitions of the Blessed Virgin Mary Today* (Dublin: Veritas, 1990), 1.

52. See Yves Chiron, *Enquête sur les Apparitions de la Vierge* (Paris: Perrin-Mame, 1995); Mark Garvey, *Searching for Mary: An Exploration of Marian Apparitions across the U.S.* (New York: Plume, 1998); Joseph Goubert, *Apparitions et Messages de la Sainte Vierge, de 1830 à nos Jours* (Paris: La Colombe, 1954); Peter Heintz, *A Guide to*

Apparitions of Our Blessed Virgin Mary (Sacramento: Gabriel Press, 1995); Gottfried Hierzenberger and Otto Nedomansky, *Erscheinungen und Botschaften der Gottesmutter Maria: Vollständige Dokumentation durch zwei Jahrtausende* (Augsburg: Bechtermünz Verlag, 1993); Laurentin, *The Apparitions of the Blessed Virgin Mary Today;* Catherine Odell, *Those Who Saw Her: Apparitions of Mary*, rev. ed. (Huntington: Our Sunday Visitor, 1995); Sandra Zimdars-Swartz, *Encountering Mary: From La Salette to Medjugorje* (Princeton: Princeton University Press, 1991). For a detailed bibliography on Marian apparitions, separated in different world regions: David C. Van Meter, *A Marian Bibliography*, available from http://members.aol.com/UticaCW/Mar-bibl .html. For internet-based overviews of Marian apparitions, kept updated for possible church evaluation, see David C. Van Meter, *Apparitions*, available from http:// members.aol.com/UticaCW/Mary-App.html. For a directory of several hundred resources online, see the page kept by the International Marian Research Institute in Dayton on twentieth-century apparitions, J. C. Tierney and Michael P. Duricy, *Marian Apparitions of the Twentieth Century*, available from http://www.udayton.edu/mary/ resources/aprtable.html.

53. In 1981–97 alone, twenty-two million people made pilgrimage to Medjugorie; see Vjekoslav Perica, *Balkan Idols: Religion and Nationalism in Yugoslav States* (Oxford: Oxford University Press, 2002), 276.

54. Joseph Ratzinger, "Letter Regarding Mrs. Vassula Rydén," in *True Life in God: Clarifications with the Congregation for the Doctrine of Faith* (Amsterdam: True Life in God Association, Netherlands, 2004), 9, available from http://www.tlig.org/ downloads/en/cdf.pdf.

55. See www.tlig.org for further information.

56. See Brenda E. Brasher, *Give Me That Online Religion* (San Francisco: Jossey-Bass, 2001); Gary Bunt, *The Good Web Guide: World Religions* (London: Good Web Guide, 2001); Gary Bunt, *Virtually Islamic: Computer-Mediated Communication and Cyber Islamic Environments* (Cardiff: University of Wales Press, 2000); Lorne L. Dawson and Douglas E. Cowan, eds., *Religion Online: Finding Faith on the Internet* (New York: Routledge, 2004); Michael Evans, *Jesus, Fads, and the Media: The Passion and Popular Culture* (Philadelphia: Mason Crest, 2006); George N. Lundskow, ed., *Religious Innovation in a Global Age: Essays on the Construction of Spirituality* (Jefferson: McFarland, 2005); Sophia Marriage and Jolyon P. Mitchell, eds., *Mediating Religion: Conversations in Media, Religion and Culture* (London: Clark, 2003), especially pt. 6; Andrew T. Stull, *Religion on the Internet 1999–2000: A Prentice Hall Guide* (Upper Saddle River, N.J.: Prentice Hall, 2000); Stephan Van Erp, Hille Haker, and Erik Borgman, eds., *Cyberspace-Cyberethics-Cybertheology* (London: SCM Press, 2005); Jeffrey P. Zaleski, *The Soul of Cyberspace: How New Technology Is Changing Our Spiritual Lives* (San Francisco: HarperEdge, 1997).

57. "I understand the categories of religion online and online religion to entail two distinctions. These are: (1) the provision of information about religion versus the opportunity for participation in religious activity; and (2) primary reference to offline, preexisting religious traditions versus primary reference to religious activities taking place online." Glenn Young, "Reading and Praying Online: The Continuity of

Religion Online and Online Religion in Internet Christianity," in *Religion Online: Finding Faith on the Internet*, edited by Lorne L. Dawson and Douglas E. Cowan (New York: Routledge, 2004), 93. The distinction is also used in Christopher Helland, "Online Religion/Religion Online and Virtual Communitas," in *Religion on the Internet: Research Prospects and Promises*, edited by J. K. Hadden and Douglas E. Cowan (London: JAI Press, 2000).

58. John Paul II, *Message of the Holy Father for the Thirty-sixth World Communications Day. Theme: Internet: A New Forum for Proclaiming the Gospel*, available from www.vatican.va/holy_father/john_paul_ii/messages/communications/documents/hf_jp-ii_mes_20020122_world-communications-day_en.html.

59. Paolo Apolito, *The Internet and the Madonna: Religious Visionary Experience on the Web* (Chicago: University of Chicago Press, 2005). See also Jessy C. Pagliaroli, "Kodak Catholicism: Miraculous Photography and Its Significance at a Post-conciliar Marian Apparition Site in Canada," *Canadian Catholic Historical Association* 70 (2004): 71–93.

60. David Edward Aune, *Prophecy in Early Christianity and the Ancient Mediterranean World* (Grand Rapids: Eerdmans, 1983), 220.

61. See for instance Bernard Billet, ed., *Vraies et Fausses Apparitions dans l'Église*, 2nd ed. (Paris: Bellarmin, 1976); Joaquim Bouflet, *Faussaires de Dieu* (Paris: Presses de la Renaissance, 2000).

62. 1 Thes 5:19–21.

63. Lk 13:34 and Mt 23:37–39.

64. 11:11—see commentary in Kurt Niederwimmer and Harold W. Attridge, *The Didache: A Commentary* (Minneapolis: Fortress Press, 1998), 178.

65. See chapter 7 here.

66. "Forme meno impegnative per la fede"; Rino Fisichella, "Prefazione," in *Le Rivelazioni Private nella Vita della Chiesa*, Augustinus Suh (Bologna: Dehoniane, 2000), 8.

67. Antonio Gentili, *Profezie per il Terzo Millennio* (Milan: Àncora Editrice, 2000), 13–20.

68. Joseph Ratzinger, "Christianity Always Carries within It a Structure of Hope: The Problem of Christian Prophecy," *30 Days*, January 1999.

69. "Le mediazioni istituzionali e quelle carismatiche sono del tutto compresenti e si integrano e arricchiscono a vicenda. Senza il supporto e la ratifica dell'istituzione, le mediazioni carismatiche si risolverebbero in arbitrio e . . . disordine, come apprendiamo dalle prime pagine della storia cristiana (1. Cor. 12 e 14). Analogamente, senza l'apporto dei carismi, le mediazioni istituzionali si chiudono in una gestione routinaria e in una ripetitività formale di riti, dottrine e precetti." Gentili, *Profezie per il Terzo Millennio*, 234.

70. "Le seconde rimandano all'insieme di doni che lo Spirito Santo suscita nei credenti e che offre alla Chiesa per il suo pieno sviluppo la sua trascendente bellezza." Ibid.

71. "Sono invece rimossi, quando non ridicolizzati, spesso proprio da chi più si è invaghito di quella espressione evangelica ("segni dei tempi") e ne ha fatto una

bandiera per un cristianesimo "adulto" come lo chiamano." Vittorio Messori, "Presentazione," in Gentili, *Profezie per il Terzo Millennio,* 9.

72. Ibid., 10.

73. "Coraggio di chiedersi se per caso non abbiano ragione gli 'oscurantisti'; e se nel presunto "oscurantismo" dei segnali inquietanti che sembrano giungerci dal Mistero non ci sia forse da attingere la luce maggiore." Ibid., 9.

74. Paul VI, *Dogmatic Constitution on Divine revelation Dei Verbum,* available from www.vatican.va/archive/hist_councils/ii_vatican_council/documents/vat-ii_const_1965II18_dei-verbum_en.html. Author's emphasis.

75. Rahner, "Les Révélations Privées."

76. Karl Rahner and Paul Imhof, *Schriften zur Theologie* (Einsiedeln: Benziger, 2001), 5:22. In English: Karl Rahner, *Theological Investigations* (Baltimore: Helicon Press, 2001), 5:22.

77. Philip Jenkins, *The Next Christendom: The Rise of Global Christianity* (New York: Oxford University Press, 2002). See also the shorter summary of his argument in Philip Jenkins, "The Next Christianity," *Atlantic Monthly* 290, no. 3 (2002): 53–68.

78. Jenkins, "The Next Christianity," 54.

79. Ibid., 62. Jenkins's quotation is from Elizabeth Allo Isichei, *A History of Christianity in Africa: From Antiquity to the Present* (Grand Rapids: Eerdmans, 1995).

80. Philip Jenkins, "After the Next Christendom," *International Bulletin of Missionary Research* 28, no. 1 (2004): 21.

81. For an overview of some of the characteristics of charismatic theology, see Mark Cartledge, "Charismatic Theology: Approaches and Themes," *Journal of Beliefs and Values* 25, no. 2 (2004).

82. Werner Kahl, "Überlegungen zu einer Interkulturellen Verständigung über Neutestamentliche Wunder," *Zeitschrift für Missionswissenschaft und Religionswissenschaft* 82, no. 2 (1998): 98–107.

83. Kahl refers to Brian K. Blount, *Cultural Interpretation: Reorienting New Testament Criticism* (Minneapolis: Fortress Press, 1995), and A. K. M. Adam, *What Is Postmodern Biblical Criticism?* (Minneapolis: Fortress Press, 1995), 45–60. To this should be added A. K. M. Adam, *Postmodern Interpretations of the Bible: A Reader* (St. Louis: Chalice Press, 2001), a valuable resource of texts on the issue.

84. Thomas Schmeller, *Das Recht der Anderen: Befreiungstheologische Lektüre des Neuen Testaments in Lateinamerika* (Münster: Aschendorff, 1994). See also Stefan Alkier, *Wunder und Wirklichkeit in den Briefen des Apostels Paulus: Ein Beitrag zu einem Wunderverständnis jenseits von Entmythologisierung und Rehistorisierung* (Tübingen: Mohr, 2001).

85. See for instance Pontifical Biblical Commission and Congregation for the Doctrine of Faith, *The Interpretation of the Bible in the Church* (Vatican City: Libreria Editrice Vaticana, 1993); Catholic Church, Pontifical Biblical Commission, *Instruction Concerning the Historical Truth of the Gospels,* edited by Benjamin N. Wambacq available from http://catholic-resources.org.

CHAPTER 2

1. Rino Fisichella, "Prophecy," in *Dictionary of Fundamental Theology*, edited by René Latourelle and Rino Fisichella (New York: Crossroad, 1995), 788.

2. Karl Rahner, *Visions and Prophecies* (London: Burns and Oats, 1963), 21.

3. "Oggi i teologi [le] mettono con disinvoltura dentro il cassetto, spiegando ai fedeli che esse sono: a) spesso incerte o semplicemente false, b) non obbligano nessuno al riconoscimento, difatti c) tutte le verità essenziali sono presenti certamente nella dottrina di fede della chiesa. Ci si può allora domandare semplicemente perché Dio accondiscenda continuamente nonostante ciò a tali operazioni che non devono essere ascoltate o quasi dalla chiesa." Hans Urs von Balthasar, "La vita, la Missione Teologica e l'opera di Adrienne von Speyr," *Mistica oggettiva*, no. 35 (1989): 35.

4. Fisichella, "Prophecy," 788.

5. Karl Rahner, *Visionen und Prophezeiungen*, 2nd ed. (Freiburg: Herder, 1958), 5.

6. Franz Diekamp, *Katholische Dogmatik nach den Grundsätzen des heiligen Thomas* (Münster Westfalen: Aschendorff, 1958), 10.

7. Laurent Volken, *Visions, Revelations and the Church* (New York: Kenedy, 1963), 214.

8. Rino Fisichella, *La Rivelazione: Evento e Credibilità: Saggio di Teologia Fondamentale* (Bologna: Edizioni Dehoniane Bologna, 1985), 344–46.

9. Fisichella, "Prophecy," 788; Volken, *Visions, Revelations and the Church*, 214.

10. "Non-lieu théologique"; Laurentin, "Fonction et Statut des Apparitions," 166.

11. Rahner, *Visions and Prophecies*, 19.

12. G. Tampere, "Revelatio privata: Revelatio privata et progressus dogmaticus" (Ph.D. diss., Gregorian University, 1954).

13. Justin Panakal, *Intimacy with God: Praying with St. Teresa of Avila* (Rome: Pontifical Institute, 1993; reprint, 1997).

14. Laurent Volken, *Les Révélations dans l'Église* (Mulhouse: Salvator, 1961). In English: Volken, *Visions, Revelations and the Church*.

15. For some of Rahner's works on prophetic revelations in the church see Karl Rahner, "Der Tod Jesu und die Abgeschlossenheit der Offenbarung," in *Pluralisme et Oecuménisme en Recherches Théologiques: Mélanges offerts au R.P. Dockx OP*, edited by Yves Congar and R. P. Hoeckmann (Gembloux: Duculot, 1976); Rahner, *The Dynamic Element in the Church* (Freiburg: Herder, 1964); Rahner, "Les Révélations Privées: Quelques Remarques Theologiques," *Revue d'Ascétique et Mystique* 25 (1949); Rahner, "Privatoffenbarung," in *Herders Theologisches Taschenlexikon* (Freiburg: Herder 1975; Rahner, *Saggi di Cristologia e di Mariologia*, 2nd ed. (Cinisello Balsamo: Edizioni San Paolo, 1967); Rahner, "Über Privatoffenbarungen," *Münchener katholische Kirchenzeitung* 40, no. 49 (1947); and Rahner, *Visions and Prophecies*; Karl Rahner and Joseph Ratzinger, *Revelation and Tradition* (Freiburg: Herder, 1966).

16. I.e. René Laurentin, *The Apparitions of the Blessed Virgin Mary Today* (Dublin: Veritas, 1990); Laurentin, "Fonction et Statut des Apparitions"; Laurentin, *Le Apparizioni della Vergine si Moltiplicano* (Casale Monferrato: Piemme, 1989); and Laurentin, *When God Gives a Sign* (Independence: Trinitas, 1993). See also the various relevant

chapters in the Festschrift for René Laurentin: Charles Augrain and Theodore A. Koehler, eds., *Kecharitoméne: Mélanges Rene Laurentin* (Paris: Desclee, 1990).

17. Yves Congar, "La Crédibilité des Révelations Privées," *Supplément de la Vie Spirituelle* 53 (1937).

18. Leo Scheffczyk, *Die theologischen Grundlagen von Erscheinungen und Prophezeiungen* (Leutesdorf: Johannes-Verlag, 1982).

19. Augustinus Suh, *Le Rivelazioni Private nella Vita della Chiesa* (Bologna: Dehoniane, 2000).

20. Pontifical Biblical Commission and Congregation for the Doctrine of Faith, "Theological Commentary" in *The Message of Fatima* (Vatican City: Libreria Editrice Vaticana, 2000),

21. One could mention many more contributions to the question that point to the function of prophetic revelations from a perspective of fundamental theology: Pierre Adnès, "Révélations Privées," in *Dictionnaire de Spiritualité Ascétique et Mystique: Doctrine et Histoire*, edited by M. Viller et al. (Paris: Beauchesne, 1987); Pietro Cantoni, "Lo 'Status' Teologico del Messaggio di Fatima," *Cristianità* 313 (2002); E. Dhanis, "Sguardo su Fatima e bilancio di una discussione," *La Civiltà Cattolica* 104, no. 2 (1953), in particular 397; Georg Essen, "Privatoffenbarungen," in *Lexikon für Theologie und Kirche*, edited by Michael Buchberger et al. (Freiburg: Herder 1999); Rino Fisichella, *Gesù di Nazaret: Profezia del Padre* (Milan: Paoline, 2000); Fisichella, "La profezia come segno della credibilità della Rivelazione," in *Gesù Rivelatore*, edited by Rino Fisichella (Casale Monferrato: Piemme, 1988); Fisichella, "Prefazione," in *Le Rivelazioni Private nella Vita della Chiesa*, edited by Augustinus Suh (Bologna: Dehoniane, 2000); and Fisichella, "Prophecy," in *Dictionary of Fundamental Theology*, edited by René Latourelle and Rino Fisichella (New York: Crossroad, 1995); Jean Galot, "Le Apparizioni Private nella Vita della Chiesa," *Civiltà Cattolica* 136, no. 2 (1985); Giandomenico Mucci, "Le Apparizioni. Teologia e Discernimento," *Civiltà Cattolica*, no. 4 (1989); Giandomenico Mucci, *Rivelazioni Private e Apparizioni* (Rome: Civiltà Cattolica, 2000); Christoph von Schönborn, *Offenbarung und Privatoffenbarung*, *Katechesen 1999/2000*, available from www.kirchenweb.at/schoenborn/; Eugenio Valentini, "Rivelazioni Private e Fatti Dogmatici," *Maria et Ecclesia* (1962); Laurent Volken, "Um die theologische Bedeutung der Privatoffenbarungen: Zu einem Buch von Karl Rahner," *Freiburger Zeitschrift für Philosophie und Theologie* 6 (1959).

22. E. Dublanchy, "Dépot de la Foi," in *Dictionnaire de Théologie Catholique* (Paris, 1951), 526.

23. "De cette révélation chrétienne publique ne relèvent évidemment point les révélations entièrement privées, faîte au cours des siècles et ayant uniquement pour objet la direction morale d'actes particuliers.... L'autorité ecclésiastique en leur donnant une approbation simplement négative ne modifie aucunement leur nature strictement privée." Ibid., 527.

24. "Pour maintenir dans son peuple, presque à toutes les périodes de son histoire, des prophètes ayant la divine mission de combattre les erreurs opposées à l'unité de Dieu et à son culte, et de garder dans toute son intégrité la croyance au seul vrai Dieu et son culte unique." Ibid., 531.

25. "[Wegen] seines früher hervorgehobenen statischen Charakters als wenig geeignet." Wolfgang Beinert, "Depositum Fidei," in *Lexikon für Theologie und Kirche*, edited by Michael Buchberger et al. (Freiburg: Herder, 1995), 101.

26. "Jede Auslegung, auch die des Lehramts, bleibt notwendig unangemessen, auf Analogien angewiesen und in der (im Vergleich zum Schauen der Heilswirklichkeit auszusagenden) Mangelhaftigkeit des Glaubens. Damit ist die kirchliche Verkündigung aber zugleich ermächtigt und angehalten, sich von bestimmten historischen Darstellungsformen des Depositum Fidei zu lösen, gerade um es unverfälscht zu bewahren als für die je gegenwärtige Situation am besten geeignete Präsentierung des christlichen Grundereignisses." Ibid.

27. Gerald O'Collins, "The Deposit of Faith," in *A New Dictionary of Christian Theology*, edited by Alan Richardson and John Bowden (London: SCM Press, 1983), 152–53.

28. "Solche Privatoffenbarungen *kann* den Einzelnen, der sie selbst empfängt, unter bestimmten Voraussetzungen durchaus zu göttlichem Glauben verpflichten. Die Voraussetzungen dafür sind grundsätzlich die gleichen wie bei der allgemeinen und öffentlichen Offenbarung." Karl Rahner, "Privatoffenbarung," in *Lexikon für Theologie und Kirche*, edited by Josef Höfer, Michael Buchberger, and Karl Rahner (Freiburg: Herder, 1963), 8:772.

29. "Die gegenwärtige theologische Aufgabe besteht darin, den mit dem traditionellen Begriff angezeigten Sachverhalt auf der Grundlegung des kommunikationstheoretischen Offenbarungsmodells zu reformulieren. Seine theologische Dignität erhellt sich, wenn er eingebunden wird in eine Theorie der Überlieferungsgeschichte, die die konstitutive Bedeutung der Praxis im Prozess der Glaubensüberlieferung herausstellt." Essen, "Privatoffenbarungen," 604.

30. "Privatoffenbarungen können aufgrund ihrer situativen Plausibilität ein prophetisches Zeugnis dafür sein, dass erst im Wechsel der geschichtlichen Situation die Glaubenswahrheit zur Fülle ihrer Bedeutung gelangt. Insofern können Privatoffenbarungen zu einem vertieften Verständnis der Selbstoffenbarung Gottes in der Geschichte Jesu Christi führen." Ibid.

31. Laurent Volken, *Visions, Revelations and the Church* (New York: Kenedy, 1963), 215.

32. "[Diese] hohe Schätzung der Prophetie [steht in] einem eigenartigen Mißverhältnis zu den üblicherweise kargen Auskünften neutestamentlicher Exegese." Gerhard Dautzenberg, "Prophetie bei Paulus," in *Prophetie und Charisma*, edited by Ingo Baldermann, Ernst Dassmann, and Ottmar Fuchs (Neukirchen-Vluyn: Neukirchener Verlag, 1999), 55.

33. Eugene Boring, *The Continuing Voice of Jesus: Christian Prophecy and the Gospel Tradition* (Louisville: Westminster, 1991), 20.

34. Ibid. See discussion in para. 8.2.

35. Among the most significant contributions to the exploration of New Testament prophecy we find David Edward Aune, *Prophecy in Early Christianity and the Ancient Mediterranean World* (Grand Rapids: Eerdmans, 1983); Aune, *Revelation 1–5* (Nashville: Nelson, 1997); Aune, *Revelation 6–16* (Nashville: Nelson, 1998); Aune,

Revelation 17–22 (Nashville: Nelson, 1998); Ingo Baldermann, Ernst Dassmann, and Ottmar Fuchs, eds., *Prophetie und Charisma* (Neukirchen-Vluyn: Neukirchener Verlag, 1999); Enzo Bianchi, ed., *La Profezia* (Bologna: 2000); Boring, *The Continuing Voice of Jesus*; *Sayings of the Risen Jesus: Christian Prophecy in the Synoptic Tradition* (Cambridge: Cambridge University Press, 1982); and Boring, "What Are We Looking For? Toward a Definition of the Term 'Christian Prophet,'" *Society of Biblical Literature, 1973 Seminar Papers* 2 (1973); Edouard Cothenet, "Les prophètes chrétiens comme exégètes charismatiques de l'Écriture," in *Prophetic Vocation in the New Testament and Today*, edited by J. Panagopoulos (Leiden: Brill, 1977); and Cothenet, "Prophétisme dans le Nouveau Testament," in *Dictionnaire de la Bible: Supplement*, edited by Louis Pirot (Paris: Letouzey et Ané, 1972); Sidney D. Crane, "The Gift of Prophecy in the New Testament: An Inductive Study in the Exercise and Meaning of the Prophetic" (Ph.D. diss., Princeton University, 1962); Theodore M. Crone, *Early Christian Prophecy: A Study of Its Origin and Function* (Baltimore: St. Mary's University Press, 1973); Tadeusz Czakanski, "The Christian Prophets and the Charism of Prophecy in the New Testament and the Origins of the Church" (Ph.D. diss., Rome: Università Lateranense, 1987); Gerhard Dautzenberg, "Prophetie bei Paulus," in *Prophetie und Charisma*, edited by Ingo Baldermann, Ernst Dassmann, and Ottmar Fuchs (Neukirchen-Vluyn: Neukirchener Verlag, 1999); Gerhard Dautzenberg, *Urchristliche Prophetie: Ihre Erforschung, ihre Voraussetzungen im Judentum und ihre Struktur im ersten Korintherbrief* (Stuttgart: Kohlhammer, 1975); James Dunn, *Jesus and the Spirit: A Study of the Religious and Charismatic Experience of Jesus and the First Christians as Reflected in the New Testament* (Grand Rapids: Eerdmans, 1997); E. Earle Ellis, *Prophecy and Hermeneutic in Early Christianity: New Testament Essays* (Tübingen: Mohr, 1978); José Luis Espinel, *Profetismo Cristiano: Una Espiritualidad Evangélica* (Salamanca: Editorial San Esteban, 1990); Craig A. Evans, "Paul as Prophet," in *Dictionary of Paul and His Letters*, edited by Gerald F. Hawthorne, Ralph P. Martin, and Daniel G. Reid (Downers Grove: Intervarsity Press, 1993); Erich Fascher, *Prophetes: Eine sprach- und religions geschichtliche Untersuchung* (Giessen: Töpelmann, 1927); Rino Fisichella, *Gesù di Nazaret: Profezia del Padre* (Milan: Paoline, 2000); Rino and Fisichella, "Prophecy"; Gerhard Friedrich, "Prophets and Prophecies in the New Testament," in *Theological Dictionary of the New Testament* (Grand Rapids: 1969); Thomas W. Gillespie, *The First Theologians: A Study in Early Christian Prophecy* (Grand Rapids: Eerdmans, 1994); Heinrich Greeven, Greeven, "Propheten, Lehrer, Vorsteher bei Paulus: zur Frage der "Ämter" im Urchristentum," *Zeitschrift für die neutestamentliche Wissenschaft und die Kunde des Urchristentums* 44, nos. 1–2 (1952–53); Norbert Greinacher, "Apostel, Propheten und Lehrer: Damals und Heute," *Theologische Quartalsschrift* 171 (1991); Wayne A. Grudem, *The Gift of Prophecy in the New Testament and Today* (Westchester: Crossway Books, 2000); and Grudem, "A Response to Gerhard Dautzenberg," *Biblische Zeitschrift* 28 (1978); Harold A. Guy, *New Testament Prophecy: Its Origin and Significance* (London: Epworth Press, 1947); Bernhard Häring, "Prophètes," in *Dictionnaire de la vie Chrétienne* (Paris, 1983); Adolf von Harnack, *Die Mission und Ausbreitung des Christentums in den ersten drei Jahrhunderten*, 4th ed., 4 vols., vol. 1 (Leipzig: VMA-Verlag, 1924); Clifford Hill, *Prophecy Past and Present: An Exploration of* the Prophetic Ministry in the Bible and the Church Today (Guildford: Eagle, 1995); David Hill, New Testament Prophecy (Atlanta: John Knox Press, 1979); Hill, "On the Evidence for the Creative Role of Christian Prophets," New Testament Studies 20 (1973); Hill, "Prophecy and Prophets in the Revelation," New Testament Studies 18 (1971); Walter Houston, "New Testament Prophecy and the Gospel Tradition" (Ph.D. diss., Mansfield College, Oxford University, 1973); Heinrich Kraft, "Vom Ende der urchristlichen Prophetie," in Panagopoulos, Prophetic Vocation in the New Testament and Today; Robert Omara, "Spiritual Gifts in the Church: A Study of 1 Corinthians 12:1–11" (Ph.D. diss., Lateran University, 1997); Panagopoulos, Prophetic Vocation in the New Testament and Today; Karl Olav Sandnes, Paul, One of the Prophets? A Contribution to the Apostle's Self-Understanding (Tübingen: Mohr, 1991); Migaku Sato, Q und Prophetie: Studien zur Gattungs- und Traditionsgeschichte der Quelle Q (Tübingen: Mohr, 1988); Elisabeth Schüssler Fiorenza, The Book of Revelation: Justice and Judgment (Philadelphia: Fortress Press, 1985); Benjamin D. Sommer, "Did Prophecy Cease? Evaluating a Reevaluation," Journal of Biblical Literature 115 (1996); Ben Witherington, Jesus the Seer: The Progress of Prophecy (Peabody: Hendrickson, 1999).

36. Aune, Prophecy in Early Christianity, 240f.

37. Witherington, Jesus the Seer, 320f.

38. Fisichella, "Prophecy," 788; Volken, Visions, Revelations and the Church, 217–18.

39. Ernst Benz, Die Vision: Erfahrungsformen und Bilderwelt (Stuttgart: Klett, 1969); Peter Dinzelbacher, Mittelalterliche Visionsliteratur: Eine Anthologie (Darmstadt: Wissenschaftliche Buchgesellschaft, 1989); Dinzelbacher, "Revelationes" (Turnhout: Brepols, 1991); Dinzelbacher, "Saint Bridget and Mysticism of Her Time," in Saint Bridget: Prophetess of New Ages. Proceedings of the International Study Meeting, Rome, October 3–7, 1991, edited by Tore Nyberg (Rome: Casa Generalizia Suore Santa Brigida, 1993); Dinzelbacher, Vision und Visionsliteratur im Mittelalter (Stuttgart: Hiersemann, 1981); and Peter Dinzelbacher and Dieter R. Bauer, eds., Frauenmystik im Mittelalter (Ostfildern bei Stuttgart: Schwabenverlag, 1985); Pius Engelbert, "Christusmystik in der Autobiographie des Rupert von Deutz," in Mysterium Christi: Symbolgegenwart und theologische Bedeutung (Festschrift für Basil Studer), edited by M. Löhrer and E. Salmann (Rome: Pontificio Ateneo S. Anselmo, 1995).

40. Hans Urs von Balthasar, Thomas und die Charismatik: Kommentar zu Thomas von Aquin, Summa Theologica Quaestiones II-II.171–182 (Einsiedeln: Johannes Verlag, 1996); Pierre Benoit and Paul Synave, Prophecy and Inspiration: A Commentary on the Summa Theologica II-II Questions 171–178 (New York: Desclee, 1961); Marianne Schlosser, Lucerna in caliginoso loco: Aspekte des Prophetie-Begriffes in der scholastischen Theologie (Paderborn: Schöningh, 2000); Jean-Pierre Torrell, Recherches sur la Théorie de la Prophétie au Moyen Âge, XIIe–XIVe Siècles: Études et Textes (Fribourg: Éditions Universitaires Fribourg Suisse, 1992).

41. Balthasar, Thomas und die Charismatik, XI.

42. See Niels Christian Hvidt, "Profeti og Åbenbaring" (Prize diss., University of Copenhagen, 1997). "Christian Prophecy and Birgitta of Vadstena," Birgittiana 16

(2003); Hvidt, "Christian Prophecy: Actualizing Revelation," in *Pax in virtute*, edited by Francesco Lepore and Donato D'Agostino (Rome: Libreria Editrice Vaticana, 2003); Hvidt, "De l'Ancien Testament à l'Eglise," in *La Voix des Prophètes* (Paris: Famille Chrétienne, 2000); "Les Critères de Discernement," in *La Voix des Prophètes* (Paris: Famille Chrétienne, 2000); Hvidt, "Prophecy and Revelation: A Theological Survey on the Problem of Christian Prophecy," *Studia Theologica* 52, no. 2 (1998); and Hvidt, "Så siger Herren!" *Teol-information* (Winter 1998).

CHAPTER 3

1. Henry Jackson Flanders, David A. Smith, and Robert W. Crapps, *People of the Covenant: An Introduction to the Hebrew Bible*, 4th ed. (Oxford: Oxford University Press, 1996), 330.
2. Clifford Hill, *Prophecy Past and Present: An Exploration of the Prophetic Ministry in the Bible and the Church Today* (Guildford: Eagle, 1995), 32.
3. Ibid., 13.
4. Jer 1:5.
5. 1 Sm 3:1-18.
6. Ex 4:10.
7. Jer 1:6.
8. Is 6:5.
9. Ex 4:10–12.
10. Jer 1:7–9.
11. Is 6:6–7.
12. 2 Cor 12:2.
13. See Dt 18:15–22; 4:21–22; Is 52:13–53:12; Jer 37–40.
14. "Diversamente dal sacerdote, che crea una comunicazione tra l'uomo e Dio muovendo dall'iniziativa del primo, il profeta dipende in tutto dall'iniziativa di Dio. che gli permette, e al tempo stesso gli impone, di annunziare il proprio messaggio." Enrico Norelli, "I Profeti nella Comunità Cristiana," in *La Profezia*, edited by Enzo Bianchi (Bologna: Dehoniane, 2000), 148.
15. Jon 1:3.
16. Am 3:7.
17. Ex 7:1-2.
18. I shall return to this in section 4.5.5.
19. David Edward Aune, *Prophecy in Early Christianity and the Ancient Mediterranean World* (Grand Rapids: Eerdmans, 1983), 83.
20. 1 Sm 10:5-13.
21. Ben Witherington, *Jesus the Seer: The Progress of Prophecy* (Peabody: Hendrickson, 1999), 41.
22. 1 Sm 9:18-19.
23. 2 Chr 18:12-13.
24. Joseph Ratzinger, "Das Problem der Christlichen Prophetie: Niels Christian Hvidt im Gespräch mit Joseph Kardinal Ratzinger," *Communio* 2 (1999): 181. English

translation is Ratzinger, "Christianity Always Carries within It a Structure of Hope: The Problem of Christian Prophecy," *30Days*, January 1999.

25. See discussion in Klaus Koch, "Propheten/Prophetie II," in *Theologische Realenzyklopädie*, edited by Gerhard Möller and Gerhard Krause (Berlin: de Gruyter, 1997), 494, and Rudolf Meyer, "Prophecy and Prophets in the Judaism of the Hellenistic-Roman Period," in *Theological Dictionary of the New Testament*, edited by Gerhard Kittel, Gerhard Friedrich, and Geoffrey William Bromiley (Grand Rapids: Eerdmans, 1969).

26. Ref. in Aune, *Prophecy in Early Christianity*, 103.

27. Meyer, "Prophecy and Prophets in the Judaism of the Hellenistic-Roman Period," 828.

28. Benjamin D. Sommer, "Did Prophecy Cease? Evaluating a Reevaluation," *Journal of Biblical Literature* 115 (1996).

29. Aune, *Prophecy in Early Christianity*, 103.

30. Seder 'Olam Rabbah 30, quoted in ibid., 104.

31. Tosephta Sotah 13:2, quoted in ibid., 103.

32. Peter Schäfer, *Die Vorstellung vom heiligen Geist in der rabbinischen Literatur* (Munich: Kösel-Verlag, 1972), 144–46.

33. Samuel Sandmel, *Judaism and Christian Beginnings* (Oxford: Oxford University Press, 1978), 174.

34. 4:45b–46; 9:27; 14:41.

35. Aune, *Prophecy in Early Christianity*, 105.

36. Ibid.

37. Joseph Blenkinsopp, *Prophecy and Canon: A Contribution to the Study of Jewish Origins* (Notre Dame: University of Notre Dame Press, 1977), 3.

38. Aune, *Prophecy in Early Christianity*, 106.

39. Witherington, *Jesus the Seer*, 381.

40. Aune, *Prophecy in Early Christianity*, 108.

41. Ibid., 109.

42. Paul D. Hanson, *The Dawn of Apocalyptic: The Historical and Sociological Roots of Jewish Apocalyptic Eschatology*, rev. ed. (Philadelphia: Fortress Press, 1979), 20.

43. Aune, *Prophecy in Early Christianity*, 111.

44. Gerhard von Rad, *Old Testament Theology*, 2 vols. (Louisville: Westminster John Knox, 2001), 2:301–8.

45. Hanson, *The Dawn of Apocalyptic*, 27–29.

46. Aune, *Prophecy in Early Christianity*, 113.

47. John Joseph Collins, *The Apocalyptic Vision of the Book of Daniel* (Missoula: Scholars Press, 1977), 75–76.

48. Aune, *Prophecy in Early Christianity*, 123.

49. See the prophet Jeremiah in 2 Mc 15:14.

50. Jn 11:49–52.

51. Aune, *Prophecy in Early Christianity*, 138.

52. Blenkinsopp, *Prophecy and Canon*, 239–62.

53. Translated by and quoted in Aune, *Prophecy in Early Christianity*, 140.

54. Ibid., 144.

55. Meyer, "Prophecy and Prophets in the Judaism of the Hellenistic-Roman Period," 821.

56. Klaus Koch, "Propheten/Prophetie II," 495.

57. Harry Austryn Wolfson, *Philo: Foundations of Religious Philosophy in Judaism, Christianity, and Islam* (Cambridge: Harvard University Press, 1947), 10.

58. Quoted in Aune, *Prophecy in Early Christianity*, 147.

59. Ibid., 147–52.

60. Charles H. Talbert, *Reading Corinthians: A Literary and Theological Commentary on 1 and 2 Corinthians* (New York: Crossroad, 1987), 112. There are extensive references to early church sources on the continuation of prophecy in Talbert's presentation.

61. "Bedeutenden prophetischen Komponente"; "die Zuordnung bestimmter Texte oder Traditionen zur urchristlichen Prophetie . . . sich indes mangels eindeutiger, aus den neutestamentlichen Aussagen über Prophetie entwickelter Kriterien als äußerst schwierig [erweist]." Dautzenberg, *Urchristliche Prophetie*, 129 and 147.

62. Wayne A. Grudem, "A Response to Gerhard Dautzenberg," *Biblische Zeitschrift* 28 (1978).

63. Christopher Forbes, *Prophecy and Inspired Speech in Early Christianity and Its Hellenistic Environment* (Tübingen: Mohr, 1995), 219.

64. Erich Fascher, *Prophetes: Eine sprach- und religionsgeschichtliche Untersuchung* (Giessen: Töpelmann, 1927).

65. Johannes Lindblom, *Prophecy in Ancient Israel* (Oxford: Blackwell, 1962), 6.

66. Eugene Boring, "What Are We Looking For? Toward a Definition of the Term 'Christian Prophet,'" *Society of Biblical Literature, 1973 Seminar Papers* 2 (1973): 147.

67. Ibid.: 149.

68. Eugene Boring, *The Continuing Voice of Jesus: Christian Prophecy and the Gospel Tradition* (Louisville: Westminster, 1991), 38.

69. David Hill, *New Testament Prophecy* (Atlanta: John Knox Press, 1979), 7.

70. Ibid., 7.

71. Ibid., 7.

72. Ibid., 5.

73. Aune, *Prophecy in Early Christianity*, 129, refers to Hill, *New Testament Prophecy*.

74. Ibid., 167.

75. Aune, *Prophecy in Early Christianity*, 338.

76. Hill, *New Testament Prophecy*, 167.

77. Aune, *Prophecy in Early Christianity*, 338.

78. Lester L. Grabbe, *Priests, Prophets, Diviners, Sages: A Socio-Historical Study of Religious Specialists in Ancient Israel* (Valley Forge: Trinity Press International, 1995), 83.

79. Max Turner, "Spiritual Gifts Then and Now," *Vox Evangelica* 15 (1985): 10–11. See also Max Turner, *The Holy Spirit and Spiritual Gifts: In the New Testament Church and Today*, rev. ed. (Peabody: Hendrickson, 1998).

80. Witherington, *Jesus the Seer*, 3.

81. Wayne A. Grudem, *The Gift of Prophecy in the New Testament and Today* (Westchester: Crossway Books, 2000), 143.

82. Robert Omara, "Spiritual Gifts in the Church: A Study of 1 Corinthians 12:1–11" (Ph.D. diss., Lateran University, 1997), 96.

83. Larry W. Hurtado, *Lord Jesus Christ: Devotion to Jesus in Earliest Christianity* (Grand Rapids: Eerdmans, 2003), 150.

84. J. Reiling, "Holy Spirit," in *Dictionary of Deities and Demons in the Bible*, edited by Karel Van Der Toorn, Pieter W. Van Der Horst, and Bob Becking (Grand Rapids: Eerdmans, 1999), 422.

85. Max Turner, *The Holy Spirit and Spiritual Gifts: In the New Testament Church and Today*, rev. ed. (Peabody: Hendrickson, 1998), 228.

86. Omara, "Spiritual Gifts in the Church," 96.

87. Mal 3:23.

88. 2 Kgs 1:8.

89. Mt 11:7–14.

90. Jn 1:29.

91. Morna Dorothy Hooker, *The Signs of a Prophet: The Prophetic Actions of Jesus* (Harrisburg: Trinity Press International, 1997), 15.

92. For instance, chap. 6 in Aune, *Prophecy in Early Christianity*, chap. 2 in Hill, *New Testament Prophecy*, chap. 8 in Witherington, *Jesus the Seer*, chap. 6 in Rino Fisichella, *Gesù di Nazaret: Profezia del Padre* (Milan: Paoline, 2000), and chap. 2 in José Luis Espinel, *Profetismo Cristiano: Una Espiritualidad Evangélica* (Salamanca: Editorial San Esteban, 1990). See also Bart D. Ehrman, *Jesus: Apocalyptic Prophet of the New Millennium* (Oxford: Oxford University Press, 1999). Ferdinand Hahn presents Jesus as an eschatological prophet in *The Titles of Jesus in Christology: Their History in Early Christianity* (London: Lutterworth, 1969), 399. For a terminological presentation of the ways the term "prophet" is applied to Jesus, see Markus Öhler, "Jesus as Prophet: Remarks on Terminology," in *Jesus, Mark and Q: The Teaching of Jesus and Its Earliest Records*, edited by Michael Labahn and Andreas Schmidt (Sheffield: Sheffield Academic Press, 2001).

93. E. P. Sanders, *The Historical Figure of Jesus* (London: Penguin Press, 1993), 153. Sanders writes in opposition to Morton Smith, who considered the term "magician" most fitting for Jesus—see Morton Smith, *Jesus the Magician* (San Francisco: Harper and Row, 1981). Quoted in Öhler, "Jesus as Prophet," 131.

94. Mt 16:16.

95. Jn 14:26.

96. Acts 7:55.

97. Jn 16:7.

98. Jn 16:14.

99. Jn 16:16.

100. Jl 2:28/3:1.

101. Acts 9:4.

102. Acts 10:3–33.

103. Aune, *Prophecy in Early Christianity*, 202.

104. Ibid., 248.

105. Witherington, *Jesus the Seer*, 301.

106. Ibid., 246.

107. Ibid., 311.

108. Ibid., 309–10.

109. Traugott Holtz, "Zum Selbstverständnis des Apostels Paulus," *Theologische Literaturzeitung* 91 (1966). See also Ernst Lohmeyer, *Grundlagen paulinischer Theologie* (Tübingen: Mohr, 1929), 200–208.

110. E. Earle Ellis, *Prophecy and Hermeneutic in Early Christianity: New Testament Essays* (Tübingen: Mohr, 1978), 23f.

111. Witherington, *Jesus the Seer*, 311.

112. Ibid., 314–15.

113. Ibid., 315.

114. Gordon D. Fee, *God's Empowering Presence: The Holy Spirit in the Letters of Paul* (Peabody: Hendrickson, 1994).

115. Witherington, *Jesus the Seer*, 304.

116. Ibid., 307–8.

117. Aune, *Prophecy in Early Christianity*, 195–262.

118. Craig A. Evans, "Paul as Prophet," in *Dictionary of Paul and His Letters*, edited by Gerald F. Hawthorne, Ralph P. Martin, and Daniel G. Reid (Downers Grove: Intervarsity Press, 1993), 763–65.

119. Karl Olav Sandnes, *Paul, One of the Prophets? A Contribution to the Apostle's Self-Understanding* (Tübingen: Mohr, 1991).

120. Jacob M. Myers and Edwin D. Freed, "Is Paul Also Among the Prophets?" *Interpretation* 20 (1966): 422.

121. Recapitulated in Aune, *Prophecy in Early Christianity*, 422.

122. Ibid., 202 and 48.

123. Witherington, *Jesus the Seer*, 328.

124. Rom 1:1; Gal 1:10; Phlm 1:1.

125. 2 Kgs 9:7, 17:13, 23, etc.; Ezr 9:11; Jer 7:25; 25:4, 26:5, 29:19, etc.; Zec 1:6.

126. Hill, *New Testament Prophecy*, 111.

127. Ibid.

128. Acts 9.

129. Gal 1:11–24.

130. 2 Cor 12.

131. Witherington, *Jesus the Seer*, 302.

132. Is 49:1–6.

133. Jer 1:5.

134. Hill, *New Testament Prophecy*, 111.

135. 2 Cor 12:1–6.

136. 2 Cor 12:1.

137. Witherington, *Jesus the Seer*, 304.

138. Ref. in ibid.

139. Aune, *Prophecy in Early Christianity*, 249.

140. Ibid.

141. Acts 18:9–11; 20:22–23; 21:4, 10–11; 22:17–22; 23:1.

142. Acts 16:9–10; 27:23.

143. For example, Hippolytus, *Ref. vviii.* 20.1.

144. Thus Aune is able to discern oracular sayings in the following passages of Paul's writings: 2 Cor 12:9; 1 Cor 15:51–52; Rom 11:25–26; 1 Thes 4:16–17a; 1 Cor 12:3; 1 Cor 14:37–38; Gal 5:21; 1 Thes 3:4; 1 Thes 4:2–6; 2 Thes 3:6, 10, 12. Aune, *Prophecy in Early Christianity*, 249–61.

145. Ibid., 261.

146. Ibid., 248f.

147. Ibid., 249.

148. See Hill, *New Testament Prophecy*, 110, and Gotthold Hasenhüttel, *Charisma: Ordnungsprinzip der Kirche* (Freiburg: Herder, 1969), 190f.

149. Aune, *Prophecy in Early Christianity*, 202.

150. Holtz, "Zum Selbstverständnis des Apostels Paulus." See also Lohmeyer, *Grundlagen paulinischer Theologie*, 200–208.

151. 1 Cor 12:28.

152. Heinrich Greeven, "Propheten, Lehrer, Vorsteher bei Paulus: Zur Frage der 'Ämter' im Urchristentum," *Zeitschrift für die neutestamentliche Wissenschaft und die Kunde des Urchristentums* 44, nos. 1–2 (1952–53): 3, quoted in Hill, *New Testament Prophecy*, 118.

153. Hill, *New Testament Prophecy*, 118.

154. Rom 12:6.

155. Hill, *New Testament Prophecy*, 119.

156. Karen L. King, "Prophetic Power and Women's Authority: The Case of the *Gospel of Mary (Magdalene)*," in *Women Preachers and Prophets through Two Millennia of Christianity*, edited by Pamela J. Walker and Beverly Mayne Kienzle (Berkeley: University of California Press, 1998), 22.

157. Rino Fisichella, "Prophecy," in *Dictionary of Fundamental Theology*, edited by René Latourelle and Rino Fisichella (New York: Crossroad, 1995), 794.

158. 1 Cor 13:2.

159. 1 Cor 14:3.

160. 1 Cor 14:1–4.

161. Witherington, *Jesus the Seer*, 316f.

162. Aune, *Prophecy in Early Christianity*, 82–83.

163. Acts 1:26.

164. Omara, "Spiritual Gifts in the Church," 96.

165. David Edward Aune, *Prophecy in Early Christianity*, 25.

166. Witherington, *Jesus the Seer*, 319.

167. Aune, *Prophecy in Early Christianity*, 36.

168. Witherington, *Jesus the Seer*, 320.

169. Morton T. Kelsey, *God, Dreams, and Revelation: A Christian Interpretation of Dreams*, rev. and expanded ed. (Minneapolis: Augsburg, 1991), 90.

170. Hill, *New Testament Prophecy*, 94f.

171. Aune, *Prophecy in Early Christianity*, 262f.

172. See "Revelation as Christian Prophecy," in Richard Bauckham, *The Theology of the Book of Revelation* (Cambridge: Cambridge University Press, 1993). Elisabeth Schüssler Fiorenza has written extensively on the Book of Revelation from a perspective of Christian prophecy; see Elisabeth Schüssler Fiorenza, "Apokalypsis and Propheteia: The Book of Revelation in the Context of Early Christian Prophecy," in *L'Apocalopyse Johannique et l'Apocalyptique dans le Nouveau Testament*, edited by J. Lambrecht (Louvain: Duculot, 1980); and *The Book of Revelation*. The reference work on the revelation of John remains David Aune's three-volume commentary *Revelation 1–5* (Nashville: Nelson, 1997); *Revelation 6–16* (Nashville: Nelson, 1998); and Aune, *Revelation 17–22* (Nashville: Nelson, 1998).

173. Jerome Crowe, *From Jerusalem to Antioch: The Gospel Across Cultures* (Collegeville: Liturgical Press, 1997), 58.

174. Kilian McDonnell and George T. Montague, *Christian Initiation and Baptism in the Holy Spirit: Evidence from the First Eight Centuries* (Collegeville: Liturgical Press, 1991), 74.

175. Richard Bauckham, *The Theology of the Book of Revelation* (Cambridge: Cambridge University Press, 1993), 2.

176. Ibid., 144.

177. Rv 1:3; 22:7, 10, 18–19.

178. Rv 22:9.

179. Bauckham, *The Theology of the Book of Revelation*, 2.

180. Eugene Boring, *Sayings of the Risen Jesus: Christian Prophecy in the Synoptic Tradition* (Cambridge: Cambridge University Press, 1982), 79.

181. Hill, *New Testament Prophecy*, 76f.

182. Witherington, *Jesus the Seer*, 361.

183. Schüssler Fiorenza, *The Book of Revelation*, 149.

184. Witherington, *Jesus the Seer*, 360.

185. Ibid.

186. Aune, *Prophecy in Early Christianity*, 278.

187. Boring, *The Continuing Voice of Jesus*, 191; Richard Alan Edwards, *A Theology of Q: Eschatology, Prophecy, and Wisdom* (Philadelphia: Fortress Press, 1976); Burton L. Mack, *The Lost Gospel: The Book of Q and Christian Origins* (San Francisco: HarperCollins, 1994); Migaku Sato, *Q und Prophetie: Studien zur Gattungs- und Traditionsgeschichte der Quelle Q* (Tübingen: Mohr, 1988). See also the relevant sections in the books of the Documenta Q series, e.g. Christoph Heil, ed., *Q 12:8-12: Confessing or Denying* (Louvain: Peeters, 1997); and *Q 22:28, 30: You Will Judge the Twelve Tribes of Israel* (Louvain: Peeters, 1998); Werner H. Kelber, *The Oral and the Written Gospel: The Hermeneutics of Speaking and Writing in the Synoptic Tradition, Mark, Paul, and Q* (Philadelphia: Fortress Press, 1983).

188. Boring, *Sayings of the Risen Jesus*, 179–80.

189. James D. G. Dunn, *Jesus Remembered* (Grand Rapids: Eerdmans, 2003), 188.

190. Gerhard Friedrich, "Prophets and Prophecies in the New Testament," in *Theological Dictionary of the New Testament*, 861. Friedrich's arguments are congruent with Ernst Käsemann, "An Apologia for Primitive Christian Eschatology," in *Essays on New Testament Themes* (Naperville: Allenson, 1964), 188.

191. Harold A. Guy, *New Testament Prophecy: Its Origin and Significance* (London: Epworth Press, 1947), 153.

192. "Stand und Berufung sind mit dem Alten Testament nicht zu Ende gegangen, sondern leben in den frühchristlichen Gemeinden weiter—allerdings nicht lange. Im 3. Jahrhundert sind die Gemeindepropheten zumindest in der Großkirche ausgestorben.... Als Grund für das schnelle Aussterben wurde bisher meist die Unterdrückung durch das erstarkende Amt angegeben. Wenn die Offenbarung als abgeschlossen gilt, werden Lehrer (Bischöfe), die das Empfangene bewahren und auslegen, wichtiger als charimatische Verkünder." Ingo Baldermann, Ernst Dassmann, and Ottmar Fuchs, eds., *Prophetie und Charisma* (Neukirchen-Vluyn: Neukirchener Verlag, 1999), IV.

193. "Entre la prophétie constitutive de l'Eglise, qui a joué un rôle décisif pour l'élaboration de la tradition chrétienne, et les dons particuliers de l'Esprit, qui, selon les âges, se présentent sous des formes diverses." Edouard Cothenet, "Prophétisme dans le Nouveau Testament," in *Dictionnaire de la Bible. Supplement*, edited by Louis Pirot (Paris: Letouzey et Ané, 1972), 1335.

194. "Disparition rapide de la prophétie dans l'Eglise." Ibid.

195. "Das Ende der Propheten beginnt! Was aus charismatischer Vollmacht in der Gemeinde geschehen ist, wird jetzt aus soziologischer Notwendigkeit von den Ordnungsbeamten übernommen. Gewiß, die Stellung der Propheten wird deshalb nicht geringer, sondern ihre Wertschätzung wächst noch. Aber für das Gemeindeleben verlieren sie ihre Wirksamkeit." Gotthold Hasenhüttel, *Charisma: Ordnungsprinzip der Kirche* (Freiburg: Herder, 1969), 196.

196. Thomas W. Gillespie, *The First Theologians: A Study in Early Christian Prophecy* (Grand Rapids: Eerdmans, 1994), 1.

197. Hill, *New Testament Prophecy*, 191.

198. Ibid., 192. The reference in Hill to *Adversus haeresis* (hereafter *Adv. Haer.*) is incorrect; should probably be to 3.11.9.

199. Witherington, *Jesus the Seer*, 328f.

200. Ibid., 340.

201. Ibid., 397, my emphasis.

202. Ibid., 396. Witherington devotes an entire chapter to the rise of Montanism and how it led to the decline of prophecy in the church; Witherington, *Jesus the Seer*, 384f.

203. Witherington, *Jesus the Seer*, 403.

204. Benjamin Breckinridge Warfield, *Miracles, Yesterday and Today, True and False* (Grand Rapids: Eerdmans, 1953). Many have sought to diminish Warfield's influence by pointing to the shortcomings of his arguments, both biblical and (mainly) historical, see Jon Ruthven, "Answering the Cessationists' Case against Continuing Spiritual Gifts," *Pneuma Review 3, no. 2*, available from

www.pneumafoundation.com/resources/articles/answer02.pdf; "On the Cessation of the Charismata: The Protestant Polemic of Benjamin B. Warfield," *Pneuma* 12 (1990); and Ruthven, *On the Cessation of the Charismata: The Protestant Polemic on Postbiblical Miracles* (Sheffield: Sheffield Academic Press, 1993); Gary-Steven Shogren, "Christian Prophecy and Canon in the Second Century: A Response to Benjamin B. Warfield," *Journal of the Evangelical Theological Society* 40 (1997).

205. Kenneth L. Gentry, *The Charismatic Gift of Prophecy: A Reformed Response to Wayne Grudem* (Lakeland: Whitefield Seminary Press, 1986); James I. Packer, *A Quest for Godliness: The Puritan Vision of the Christian Life* (Wheaton: Crossway Books, 1990), 86; Robert L. Reymond, *"What about Continuing Revelations and Miracles in the Presbyterian Church Today?" A Study of the Doctrine of the Sufficiency of Scripture* (Nutley: Presbyterian and Reformed, 1977); Ruthven, "On the Cessation of the Charismata," 192.

206. Richard B. Gaffin Jr., "A Cessationist View," in *Are Miraculous Gifts for Today? Four Views*, edited by Wayne A. Grudem (Grand Rapids: Zondervan, 1996), 207.

207. See my discussion of the criteria for discerning true from false prophecy in chapter 9.

208. Grudem, *The Gift of Prophecy in the New Testament and Today*, 15.

209. Boring, *The Continuing Voice of Jesus*, 36.

210. Grudem, *The Gift of Prophecy in the New Testament and Today*, 14–15.

211. Ibid., 15.

212. Ibid., ref. to 1 Cor 14:25.

213. Rino Fisichella, "La profezia come segno della credibilità della Rivelazione," in *Gesù Rivelatore*, edited by Rino Fisichella (Casale Monferrato: Piemme, 1988).

214. Jn 21:25.

215. Aune, *Prophecy in Early Christianity*, 195.

216. Ibid., 338.

217. George T. Montague, *The Spirit and His Gifts: The Biblical Background of Spirit-Baptism, Tongue-Speaking, and Prophecy* (New York: Paulist Press, 1974), 46.

218. Ratzinger, "Das Problem der Christlichen Prophetie," 181.

219. Ibid.

220. Fisichella, "Prophecy," 795.

221. Witherington, *Jesus the Seer*, 350.

222. "A l'origine de toute institution il y a toujours la défaite du prophétisme." René Lourau, quoted in Bruno Chenu, *L'Urgence Prophétique: Dieu au Défi de l'Histoire*, 2nd ed. (Paris: Bayard, 1997), 121.

223. Gerhard Friedrich, "Prophets and Prophecies in the New Testament," in *Theological Dictionary of the New Testament*, 861.

224. Hans von Campenhausen, *Ecclesiastical Authority and Spiritual Power in the Church of the First Three Centuries*, translated by John Austin Baker (London: Black, 1969), 178.

225. Witherington, *Jesus the Seer*, 397.

226. Kelber, *The Oral and the Written Gospel*.

227. Geert Hallbäck, "The Earthly Jesus, the Gospel Genre and Types of Authority," in *The New Testament in its Hellenistic Context*, edited by Gunnlaugur A. Jonsson (Reykjavik: Gudfraedistofnun—Skalholtsutgafan, 1996), 135.

228. Phlm 2:6–11.

229. Geert Hallbäck, "The Earthly Jesus, the Gospel Genre and Types of Authority," 138.

230. Ibid., 140.

231. Ibid., 141.

232. Ibid., 142.

233. Ibid., 143.

234. Ibid., 143.

235. Ibid., 144.

236. Bart D. Ehrman, *The New Testament: A Historical Introduction to the Early Christian Writings*, 3rd ed. (Oxford: Oxford University Press, 2004), 302.

237. 1 Cor 14:1.

238. Henry Chadwick, *The Early Church* (Harmondsworth: Penguin, 1967), 46f.

239. Kurt Niederwimmer and Harold W. Attridge, *The Didache: A Commentary* (Minneapolis: Fortress Press, 1998), 191.

240. Mk 3:23.

241. Georg Schöllgen, "The Didache as a Church Order: An Examination of the Purpose for the Composition of the Didache and its Consequences for its Interpretation," in *The Didache in modern research*, edited by Jonathan A. Draper (Leiden: Brill, 1996), 54.

242. Kurt Niederwimmer and Harold W. Attridge, *The Didache: A Commentary* (Minneapolis: Fortress Press, 1998), 178.

243. Ibid., 200.

244. Hill, *New Testament Prophecy*, 187f.

245. Georg Schöllgen, "The Didache as a Church Order: An Examination of the Purpose for the Composition of the Didache and Its Consequences for Its Interpretation," in Draper, *The Didache in Modern Research*, 54.

246. Gotthold Hasenhüttel, *Charisma: Ordnungsprinzip der Kirche* (Freiburg: Herder, 1969), 196.

247. Burnett Hillman Streeter, *The Primitive Church, Studied with Special Reference to the Origins of the Christian Ministry* (London: Macmillan, 1929), 149–50.

248. Hasenhüttel, *Charisma*, 196.

249. Aune, *Prophecy in Early Christianity*, 196.

250. *Adv. Haer.* 4.20.

251. Witherington, *Jesus the Seer*, 396.

252. Laurent Volken, *Visions, Revelations and the Church* (New York: Kenedy, 1963), 54.

253. Augustine, *De Agone* 28.30.

254. Laurent Volken, "Um die theologische Bedeutung der Privatoffenbarungen: Zu einem Buch von Karl Rahner," *Freiburger Zeitschrift für Philosophie und Theologie* 6 (1959): 140.

255. Eusebius, *Life of Constantine*, translated by Averil Cameron and Stuart G. Hall (Oxford: Oxford University Press, 1999), 186 (commentary).

256. Eusebius, *Historia Ecclesiastica*, available from www.ccel.org/fathers2/NPNF2-01/Npnf2-01-10.htm#TopOfPage.

257. Quoted in Eric Robertson Dodds, *Pagan and Christian in an Age of Anxiety: Some Aspects of Religious Experience from Marcus Aurelius to Constantine* (Cambridge: Cambridge University Press, 1991), 66.

258. Pierre Champagne de Labriolle, *Les Sources de l'Histoire du Montanisme: Textes Grecs, Latins, Syriaques* (Fribourg: Ernest Leroux, 1913), 115–16.

259. *Adv. Haer.* 2.49.3. Quoted in Volken, *Visions, Revelations and the Church*, 57.

260. Ref. in Volken, *Visions, Revelations and the Church*, 63–67.

261. "Als eine Art Individuation dieser Blickrichtung der Vision auf das Schicksal der allgemeinen Kirche erscheint dann das Schicksal des eigenen Ordens und der von dem Visionär selbst geschaffenen ecclesiola in ecclesia als ein zweites Hauptthema der prophetischen Vision bei den großen Ordensstiftern der Kirche, unter denen sich zahlreiche Visionäre finden." Ernst Benz, *Die Vision: Erfahrungsformen und Bilderwelt* (Stuttgart: Klett, 1969), 132.

262. "Auch die Ordengeschichte spielt sich in dem religiösen Selbstbewußtsein ihrer Gründer und ihrer Mitglieder als eine durch das Schema von Verheißung und Erfüllung bestimmte, durch Visionen und Prophetien gelenkte Geschichte ab. Leider gibt es keine Geschichte der Mönchsorden, die auf diese prophetische und visionäre Grundhaltung der Orden vor allem während ihrer Gründungsepochen geachtet hätte. Diese Gesichtspunkte sind selbst innerhalb der Ordensgeschichtsschreibung der modernen positivistischen Geschichtsbetrachtung zum Opfer gefallen." Ibid., 136–37.

263. "Die Prophetie des Verfalls führt zu einer Maßnahme, die dem Verfall entgegenwirken soll." Ibid., 138.

264. "Überwindung durch einen heiligen 'Rest,' eine Gemeinde von höherer Heiligkeit." Ibid., 140.

265. Ibid., 139.

266. Chaps. 12, 14, 15, 17, 21, and 27.

267. Yves Chiron, *Enquête sur les Apparitions de la Vierge* (Paris: Perrin-Mame, 1995), chap. 12.

268. Gregory, *Life and Miracles of St. Benedict* (Collegeville: St. John's University Press, 1995), chap. 14.

269. Ibid., 5.

270. Ibid., 7.

271. Ibid., 35.

272. Ratzinger, "Das Problem der Christlichen Prophetie," 183.

273. Richard Woods, *Mysticism and Prophecy: The Dominican Tradition* (London: Darton, Longman and Todd, 1998).

274. Aron Andersson, *Boken om Birgitta, Helgon och Profet* (Vadstena: Birgittasystrarna i Rom, 1977), 50.

275. "Sein Werk als unüberholbar eigenständige Stimme im Konzert monastischer Theologen des 12. Jahrhunderts." Pius Engelbert, "Christusmystik in der

Autobiographie des Rupert von Deutz," in *Mysterium Christi: Symbolgegenwart und theologische Bedeutung (Festschrift für Basil Studer)*, edited by M. Löhrer and E. Salmann (Rome: Pontificio Ateneo S. Anselmo, 1995), 284.

276. "Der Wein des geistlichen Trostes sei vielmehr für die Trauernden, Verbitterten und Leidenden bestimmt: Ihnen, den Armen, werde der Sinn der Schriften, des Gesetzes und des Evangeliums, lesend erschlossen." Ibid., 273.

277. "Verhielt sich zu ihm . . . wie alle Mönche damals, rein defensiv." Ibid., 283.

278. Bernard McGinn, "'Trumpets of the Mysteries of God': Prophetesses in Late Medieval Christianity," in *Propheten und Prophezeiungen/Prophets and Prophecies*, edited by Tilo Schabert and Matthias Riedl (Würzburg: Königshausen und Neumann, 2005), 126.

279. Ibid. Ref. from *Annales Fuldenses* (847), 365.

280. McGinn, "Trumpets of the Mysteries of God," 126.

281. *Annales Palidenses* (1158), 90.

282. McGinn, "Trumpets of the Mysteries of God," 127. Ref. to Kathryn Kerby-Fulton, *Reformist Apocalypticism and Piers Plowman* (Cambridge: Cambridge University Press, 1990); Bernard McGinn, "Apocalypticism and Church Reform (1100–1500)," in *The Encyclopedia of Apocalypticism*, edited by Bernard McGinn, John Joseph Collins, and Stephen J. Stein (New York: Continuum, 1998). See also Ingvar Fogelqvist, *Apostasy and Reform in the Revelations of St. Birgitta* (Stockholm: Almqvist & Wiksell International, 1993).

283. Benz, *Die Vision*, 5.

284. "Die großen Visionäre der christlichen Kirche sind als ihre großen Propheten hervorgetreten. Ihre Visionen haben zum großen Teil einen prophetischen Inhalt. Dabei wiederholen sich bei den christlichen Visionären alle Formen der Prophetie, die schon bei den alttestamentlichen Propheten hervortraten." Ibid., 131.

285. "Tut Buße, denn das Reich Gottes ist nahe herbeigekommen!" Diese Forderung, im Hinblick auf das nahe Kommen des Gottesreiches Buße zu tun und dem kommenden Herrn einen Weg zu bereiten, ist der zentrale Inhalt der christlichen Prophetie geblieben, wie sie sich in den großen Visionären der christlichen Kirche äußert." Ibid., 131.

286. "Die institutionelle christliche Kirche versteht sich ja ihrerseits, als die Erfüllung der Verheißung vom Kommen des Gottesreiches, als das gegenwärtige Gottesreich, als die irdische Repräsentation des Gottesreiches. Wenn an diese Kirche der prophetische Ruf zur Buße gerichtet wird, so ist damit vorausgesetzt, daß die gegenwärtige Kirche offenbar die ihr aufgetragene geschichtliche Sendung, Repräsentantin des Gottesreiches zu sein, nicht erfüllt hat." Ibid., 132.

287. "Man kann sogar sagen, daß die Idee des Verfalls, die dem theologischen und dogmatischen Selbstbewußtsein der institutionellen Kirche so sehr widerspricht und vor allem dem Selbstbewußtsein ihrer Hierarchie so sehr zuwider ist, sich in dem Bewußtsein der Kirche selbst erst auf Grund der Tatsache durchgesetzt hat, daß Visionäre unter dem überwältigenden Eindruck ihrer visionären Erfahrung diesen Gedanken auszusprechen wagten. Die Verfallsidee ist ein Kind der Vision." Ibid., 132.

288. Diane Watt, *Secretaries of God: Women Prophets in Late Medieval and Early Modern England* (Woodbridge: Brewer, 1997).

289. Hildegard, Columba Hart, and Jane Bishop, *Scivias* (New York: Paulist Press, 1990), 9.

290. Barbara Newman, "Hildegard and Her Hagiographers: The Remaking of Female Sainthood," in *Gendered Voices: Medieval Saints and Their Interpreters*, edited by Catherine M. Mooney (Philadelphia: University of Pennsylvania Press, 1999), 19. See also Anne H. King-Lenzmeier, *Hildegard of Bingen: An Integrated Vision* (Collegeville: Liturgical Press, 2001), especially the chapter "From Mystical Vision to Prophetic Witness."

291. On Hildegard as prophetess, see McGinn, "Trumpets of the Mysteries of God." Ref. to K. Kerby-Fulton, "Prophet and Reformer: Smoke in the Vineyard," in *Voice of the Living Light: Hildegard of Bingen and Her World*, edited by Barbara Newman (Berkeley: University of California Press, 1998); Bernard McGinn, " 'To the Scandal of Men, Women Are Prophesying.' Female Seers of the High Middle Ages," in *Fearful Hope: Approaching the New Millennium*, edited by Christopher Kleinhenz and Fannie LeMoine (Madison: University of Wisconsin Press, 1999); Christel Meier-Staubach, "Ildegarde di Bingen: Profezia ed esistenza letteraria," in *Lo Statuto della Profezia nel Medioevo*, edited by G. L. Potestà and R. Rusconi (Bologna: Dehoniane, 1996).

292. McGinn, " 'To the Scandal of Men, Women Are Prophesying,' " 128.

293. Ibid., 129. Ref to *Liber divinorum operum*, 355. The entire second vision of book 3 constitutes a treatise on the nature and function of prophecy.

294. McGinn, "Trumpets of the Mysteries of God," 129.

295. In the *Oxford Dictionary of the Christian Church*, Birgitta is listed under both names. Birgitta is the Scandinavian version of Bridget. Birgitta is normally used for the Swedish saint, Bridget for the Irish saint.

296. McGinn, "Trumpets of the Mysteries of God," 131.

297. Ibid.

298. Claire L. Sahlin, *Birgitta of Sweden and the Voice of Prophecy* (Woodbridge: Boydell Press, 2001), 35–36. Ref. to Anders Piltz, "Inspiration, vision, profetia: Birgitta och teorierna om uppenbarelserna," in *Heliga Birgitta: Budskabet och förebilden. Föredrag vid jubileumssymposiet i Vadstena 3.-7. oktober 1991*, edited by Alf Härdelin and Mereth Lindgren (Stockholm: Almqvist & Wiksel, 1993), 68.

299. Peter Dinzelbacher, "Saint Bridget and Mysticism of Her Time," in *Saint Bridget: Prophetess of New Ages. Proceedings of the International Study Meeting, Rome, October 3–7, 1991* (Rome: Casa Generalizia Suore Santa Brigida, 1993), 371, ref. to *Acta et processus* 372.

300. Albert Ryle Kezel, ed., *Birgitta of Sweden: Life and Selected Revelations* (New York: Paulist Press, 1990), 243, note 58; Patricia Ranft, *Women and the Religious Life in Premodern Europe* (New York: St. Martin's Press, 1996), 89f.

301. Anne B. Baldwin, *Catherine of Siena: A Biography* (Huntington: Our Sunday Visitor, 1987), 112.

302. McGinn, "Trumpets of the Mysteries of God,"131; W. A. Purdy, "St. Birgitta, Her Times and Ours," in *Brigida: Una Santa Svedese. Birgitta: A Swedish Saint* (Rome: Bulzoni Editore, 1973), 89. Because of the Great Schism, Birgitta had to be canonized three times.

303. John Paul II, *Apostolic Letter, Issued Motu Proprio, Proclaiming Saint Bridget of Sweden, Saint Catherine of Siena and Saint Teresa Benedicta of the Cross Co-patronesses of Europe,* available from http://www.vatican.va/holy_father/john_paul_ii/motu_proprio/documents/hf_jp-ii_motu-proprio_01101999_co-patronesses-europe_en.html.

304. Lindblom, *Prophecy in Ancient Israel,* 26.

305. Ibid., 19.

306. Fogelqvist, *Apostasy and Reform in the Revelations of St. Birgitta,* 112.

307. Jesús Castellano Cervera, "The Church in the Life and in the Thought of Saint Bridget," in *Saint Bridget: Prophetess of New Ages,* 259.

308. Piltz, "Inspiration, Vision, Profetia"; "Uppenbarelserna och uppenbarelsen. Birgittas förhållande til Bibeln," in *Birgitta, hendes Værk og hendes Klostre i Norden,* edited by Tore Nyberg (Odense: Odense University Press, 1991).

309. Piltz, "Uppenbarelserna och uppenbarelsen: Birgittas förhållande til Bibeln," 447.

310. Sahlin, *Birgitta of Sweden and the Voice of Prophecy*; Sahlin, "Gender and Prophetic Authority in Birgitta of Sweden's Revelations," in *Gender and Text in the Later Middle Ages,* edited by Jane Chance (Gainesville: University Press of Florida, 1996); Sahlin, "Preaching and Prophesying: The Public Proclamation of Birgitta of Sweden's Revelations," in *Performance and Transformation: New Approaches to Late Medieaval Spirituality,* edited by Mary A. Suydam and Joanna E. Ziegler (New York: St. Martin's Press, 1999); Claire L. Sahlin, "The Prophetess as Preacher: Birgitta of Sweden and the Voice of Prophecy," *Medieval Sermon Studies* 40 (1997).

311. See for instance Barbara Newman, *God and the Goddesses: Vision, Poetry, and Belief in the Middle Ages* (Philadelphia: University of Pennsylvania Press, 2003), 276f.

312. Tore Nyberg, ed., *Saint Bridget: Prophetess of New Ages.*

313. Roger Ellis, "The Swedish Woman, the Widow, the Pilgrim and the Prophetess: Images of St. Bridget in the Canonization Sermon of Pope Boniface IX," in *Saint Bridget: Prophetess of New Ages,* 119.

314. Tore Nyberg, "St. Bridget's Charism and Prophecy for Our Time," in *Saint Bridget: Prophetess of New Ages,* 404–16.

315. Peter Dinzelbacher, "Saint Bridget and Mysticism of Her Time," 371. Ref. to the *Revelationes* 3,5.

316. Ref. to 3,30—*Petrus et Petrus,* "Vita" 188.

317. Lotten Andersson, *Europe's Patron Saint Brings Separated Churches Together,* available from www.svenskakyrkan.se/tcrot/press/eng/99/Heliga_Birgitta.htm.

318. Alban Butler, ed., *Butler's Lives of the Saints,* concise ed. (San Francisco: Harper and Row, 1985), 224; Richard P. McBrien, *The HarperCollins Encyclopedia of Catholicism* (San Francisco: HarperSanFrancisco, 1995), 196; Gerald O'Collins and

Mario Farrugia, *Catholicism: The Story of Catholic Christianity* (Oxford: Oxford University Press, 2003), 72.

319. Anne B. Baldwin, *Catherine of Siena: A Biography* (Huntington: Our Sunday Visitor, 1987), 112; Steven Fanning, *Mystics of the Christian Tradition* (London: Routledge, 2001), 128; Marlene LeGates, *In Their Time: A History of Feminism in Western Society* (New York: Routledge, 2001), 38 and 46–47.

320. Marina Warner, *Joan of Arc: The Image of Female Heroism* (New York: Knopf, 1981), 92.

321. Otto Michel, *Prophet und Märtyrer* (Gütersloh: 1932), 10.

322. Aune, *Prophecy in Early Christianity*, 126.

323. Is 40–55.

324. Acts 7:52.

325. Lk 11:49–51.

326. Col 1:24.

327. Paul L. Gavrilyuk, *The Suffering of the Impassible God: The Dialectics of Carmelite Studies of Patristic Thought* (Oxford: Oxford University Press, 2004), 73.

328. Rv 14:13, see also Rv 20:4.

329. Volken, *Visions, Revelations and the Church*, 59–63.

330. Peter Robert Lamont Brown, *The Body and Society: Men, Women, and Sexual Renunciation in Early Christianity* (New York: Columbia University Press, 1988), 74.

331. Many of these are described in Johannes Maria Höcht, *Träger der Wundmale Christi: Eine Geschichte der bedeutendsten Stigmatisierten von Franziskus bis zur Gegenwart* (Wiesbaden: Credo-Verlag, 1952).

332. Roberta C. Bondi and Linda Kulzer, *Benedict in the World: Portraits of Monastic Oblates* (Collegeville: Liturgical Press, 2002), 144–45. The concept of coredemptive suffering became of great importance to Maritain. See deliberations in Eduardo J. Echeverria, "The Gospel of Redemptive Suffering: Reflections on John Paul II's *Salvifici Doloris*," in *Christian Faith and the Problem of Evil*, edited by Peter Van Inwagen (Grand Rapids: Eerdmans, 2004).

333. Raymond Peyret, *Marthe Robin: The Cross and the Joy* (New York: Alba House, 1983).

334. Victor Witter Turner and Edith L. B. Turner, *Image and Pilgrimage in Christian Culture: Anthropological Perspectives* (New York: Columbia University Press, 1978), 203–30.

335. See Mary Carruthers, *The Craft of Thought: Meditation, Rhetoric, and the Making of Images, 400–1200* (Cambridge: Cambridge University Press, 1998), 198; Suzanne K. Kaufman, *Consuming Visions: Mass Culture and the Lourdes Shrine* (Ithaca: Cornell University Press, 2005), 2 and 92; Richard Madsen, *China's Catholics: Tragedy and Hope in an Emerging Civil Society* (Berkeley: University of California Press, 1998), 91; Rosemary Mahoney, *The Singular Pilgrim: Travels on Sacred Ground* (Boston: Houghton Mifflin, 2003), 61; Angela K. Martin and Sandra Kryst, "Encountering Mary: Ritualization and Place Contagion in Postmodernity," in *Places through the Body*, edited by Heidi Nast and Steve Pile (London: Routledge, 1998); James Martin, *Awake My Soul: Catholics on Traditional Devotions* (Chicago: Loyola Press, 2004), 109;

John F. O'Grady, *Catholic Beliefs and Traditions: Ancient and Ever New* (New York: Paulist Press, 2001), 179–206; Catherine Odell, *Those Who Saw Her: Apparitions of Mary*, rev. ed. (Huntington: Our Sunday Visitor, 1995), 44.

336. Some exceptions would be the calling of the young Samuel (1 Sm 3), Jl 2:28 cited in Acts 2:17.

337. Gottfried Hierzenberger and Otto Nedomansky, *Erscheinungen und Botschaften der Gottesmutter Maria: Vollständige Dokumentation durch zwei Jahrtausende* (Augsburg: Bechtermünz Verlag, 1993).

338. The thought is present in Irenaeus, *Adv. haer.* 3.10.2; 4.55.2), Eusebius (*Eclogae propheticae* 4.5), Cyril of Alexandria (*Isaia* 1 or 5) and is the basis for Joseph Ratzinger's depiction of Mary as archetype of prophets in "Das Problem der Christlichen Prophetie: Niels Christian Hvidt im Gespräch mit Joseph Kardinal Ratzinger," *Communio* 2 (1999): 182.

339. See the presentation of Patristic assessments of Mary as prophetess in Leo Scheffczyk, "Prophetin (Prophetissa)," in *Marienlexikon*, edited by Remigius Bäumer and Leo Scheffczyk (St. Ottilien: EOS Verlag, 1988).

340. Pontifical Biblical Commission and, Congregation for the Doctrine of Faith, *The Message of Fatima* (Vatican City: Libreria Editrice Vaticana, 2000), 16.

341. Some examples can be found in Gn 2:16–17; Dt 28:1,15; 30:15–18; 31:28–29; Jon 3:1–10; 4:1–2.

342. This explication builds on my "Vassula: A Contemporary Christian Prophet?" *Scriptorium* 5 (1998), enhanced with personal interviews with Mrs. Rydén, who with her diplomat husband happened to move to Rome during the completion of this study.

343. The beginnings of Vassula's experience are also described in Vassula Rydén, *True Life in God*, Vol. 1 (Independence, Mo.: Trinitas, 1991–2003), XXf.

344. Vassula was invited by Bishop Teodoro Bacani to speak to an audience of four hundred thousand at an event arranged by the El Shaddai community in the Philippines on November 26, 2005. On several occasions there have been over one hundred thousand attendees at her addresses in India. C. J. John, *Report of Vassula Rydén's Meetings in India, Sri Lanka, and Bangladesh 2002, TLIG Forum*, available from www.tlig.info/forum/forum507.html.

345. Michael O'Carroll, *Vassula of the Sacred Heart's Passion* (Belfast: J.M.J., 1993), 105f.

346. René Laurentin, *The Apparitions of the Blessed Virgin Mary Today* (Dublin: Veritas, 1990), 1.

347. "I come to find no love, no faith and no hope, My House lies in ruin, reduced into rubbles by Rationalism, Disobedience and Vanity, My glorious pastures of the past are now barren, because of the Great Apostasy which penetrated into My sanctuary." October 10, 1989.

348. July 6, 1990.

349. "They have apostatized from Me, yes, they have accustomed their steps to walk with apostasy and have as their guide and traveling companion rationalism, the weapon to combat My Divinity." July 6, 1990.

350. Personal interview with Mrs. Rydén, January 2003.

351. Rydén, *True Life in God*, 3:116–17.

352. Ibid., 11:26f.

353. Ibid., 4:163.

354. Ibid., 4:163.

355. Ibid., 4:43.

356. Ibid., 2:11.

357. Ibid., 8:194.

358. Ibid., October 14, 1991.

359. Ibid., 8:46f.

360. Ibid., 5:37.

361. Personal interview with Mrs. Rydén, January 2003.

362. Rydén, *True Life in God*, 3:99. See further discussion in section 9.3.1 here.

363. Ibid., 3:24–25.

364. Ibid., 4:49.

365. Edward O'Connor, *Vassula and the CDF* (Independence: Trinitas, 1998), 9f.

366. René Laurentin, *When God Gives a Sign* (Independence: Trinitas, 1993), 69f.

367. François-Marie Dermine, *Vassula Ryden: Indagine Critica* (Turin: Edizioni Elle Di Ci, Leumann, 1995). Fr. Dermine's opinion was voiced in his later *Mistici, Veggenti e Medium* (Vatican City: Libreria Editrice Vaticana, 2002).

368. For a comprehensive list of articles and books see http://mypage.bluewin .ch/cafarus/tligbooks.htm.

369. Laurentin, *When God Gives a Sign*; Ovila Melançon, *Jesus Appelle sa Messagère* (Paris: de Guibert, 1994); Fernando Umaña Montoya, *Vassula: Un Charisme Oecuménique pour notre Temps* (Hauteville: Éditions du Parvis, 1995); O'Carroll, *Vassula of the Sacred Heart's Passion*; O'Connor, *Vassula and the CDF*. For a more comprehensive list of books in favor of Mrs. Rydén, see www.vassula.org/bgr_theo.htm.

370. Michael Dore, *Rome et Vassula* (Hauteville: Parvis, 1996), 30f.

371. Quoted in O'Connor, *Vassula and the CDF*, 12.

372. Dore, *Rome et Vassula*. O'Connor, *Vassula and the CDF*, 9f.

373. Ratzinger, "Das Problem der Christlichen Prophetie," 188.

374. Rydén, *True Life in God*, 12: xvii–lii.

375. Joseph Ratzinger, "Letter Regarding Mrs. Vassula Rydén," in *True Life in God: Clarifications with the Congregation for the Doctrine of Faith* (Amsterdam: True Life in God Association, Netherlands, 2004), 9, available from http://www.tlig.org/ downloads/en/cdf.pdf.

376. Abbé Agnell Rickenmann, *Letter of February Twenty-Third*, in *The Catholic Church's Position Regarding TLIG*, edited by Maria Laura Pio, available from http:// mypage.bluewin.ch/cafarus/tligchurchposition.htm.

377. Lk 2:34.

378. Kelsey, *God, Dreams, and Revelation*, 90.

379. This term is also part of the title of an excellent book on female visionary mysticism as prophecy: Watt, *Secretaries of God*.

CHAPTER 4

1. On the sources for this section see note 46.

2. Rino Fisichella, "Prophecy," in *Dictionary of Fundamental Theology*, edited by René Latourelle and Rino Fisichella (New York: Crossroad, 1995).

3. P. Mariotti, "Contestation Prophétique," in *Dictionnaire de la Vie Chrétienne* (Paris: 1983).

4. Karl Rahner, *Visions and Prophecies* (London: Burns and Oats, 1963).

5. Johannes Lindblom, *Prophecy in Ancient Israel* (Oxford: Blackwell, 1962).

6. Johannes Lindblom, *Gesichte und Offenbarungen. Vorstellungen von göttlichen Weisungen und übernatürlichen Erscheinungen im ältesten Christentum* (Lund: Gleerup, 1968).

7. See discussion in Rahner, *Visions and Prophecies* (London: Burns & Oats, 1963), 31f.

8. "Die Prophetie gilt als das größte unter den Charismen (1 Cor. 14,1). Was wird unter diesem für uns heute so fremden Begriff verstanden? Was gibt ihm diese Bedeutsamkeit? Für uns nehmen doch die Propheten nur in alttestamentlicher Zeit Gestalt an. Alle anderen, die sich in der Kirche Propheten nennen, gelten vielfach als Pseudopropheten, als Schwärmer oder ganz einfach als Wahrsager. Nichts davon ist aber offensichtlich hier gemeint." Gotthold Hasenhüttel, *Charisma: Ordnungsprinzip der Kirche* (Freiburg: Herder, 1969), 185.

9. "In der heutigen Lebens-, Arbeits- und Denkwelt sind Offenbarungen und Offenbarung fast nur noch ein Randthema mit exotischem Anstrich und dubioser Valenz, dem vielfach Unverständnis und Desinteresse, ja Mißtrauen und Ablehnung entgegenschlagen." "Schon die außergewöhnlichen Umstände und Erfahrungsformen, die mit ihnen verbunden sein können, erscheinen ebenso bedenkenswert wie bedenklich." Walter Kern, Hermann Josef Pottmeyer, and Max Seckler, eds., *Handbuch der Fundamentaltheologie* (Freiburg: Herder, 1985), 11.

10. "Schon die außergewöhnlichen Umstände und Erfahrungsformen, die mit ihnen verbunden sein können, erscheinen ebenso bedenkenswert wie bedenklich." Max Seckler, "Der Begriff der Offenbarung," in Kern et al., *Handbuch der Fundamentaltheologie*, 60.

11. (Shortcomings in published English translation.) Laurent Volken, *Les Révélations dans l'Église* (Mulhouse: Salvator, 1961), 169.

12. Ingvar Fogelqvist, *Apostasy and Reform in the Revelations of St. Birgitta* (Stockholm: Almqvist & Wiksell International, 1993), 112.

13. Ibid., 13.

14. Sven Stolpe, *Birgitta i Rom*, 5th ed. (Stockholm: Askild & Kärnekull, 1980), 13.

15. Kari Elisabeth Børresen, "Birgitta's Godlanguage: Exemplary Intention, Inapplicable Content," in *Birgitta, hendes værk og hendes klostre i Norden*, edited by Tore Nyberg (Odense: Odense University Press, 1991), 21–22.

16. Peter Dinzelbacher and Dieter R Bauer, eds., *Religiöse Frauenbewegungen und mystische Frömmigkeit im Mittelalter* (Vienna: Böhlau, 1988); Elisabeth Gössmann, *Hildegard von Bingen: Versuche einer Annäherung* (Munich: Iudicium Verlag, 1995).

17. Claire L. Sahlin, *Birgitta of Sweden and the Voice of Prophecy* (Woodbridge: Boydell Press, 2001), 227.

18. Laurent Volken, *Visions, Revelations and the Church* (New York: Kenedy, 1963), 153.

19. Marc Oraison, "Le Point de Vue du Médecin Psychiatre Clinicien sur les Apparitions," in *Vraies et Fausses Apparitions dans l'Église*, edited by Bernard Billet (Paris: Lethielleux, 1976), 139f.

20. Antoine Vergote, "Visions et Apparitions, Approche Psychologique," *Revue Théologique de Louvain* 22 (1991): 220f.

21. Philippe Loron, *J'Ai Vu Écrire Vassula: Analyse Scientifique de la Vraie Vie en Dieu* (Paris: de Guibert, 1994), 136–49.

22. "Tout ce que je peux dire, et qui correspond a une appréhension possible, c'est qu'il s'agit d'un phénomène hallucinatoire. Le reste m'échappe totalement, et je pense que cela m'échappe non seulement en tant que médecin, mais aussi en tant que théologien." Oraison, "Le Point de Vue du Médecin Psychiatre Clinicien sur les Apparitions," 144.

23. "Rien ne nous permet de trancher la question de savoir si le mystère se révèle de cette manière." Ibid.

24. "Chacune de ces attitudes est réductrice et crée des entraves à l'étude sereine de ce phénomène." Alain Dierkens, *Apparitions et Miracles* (Brussels: Editions de l'Universite de Bruxelles, 1991), 7.

25. Ibid., 9.

26. Different research by Professors J. Yvon Saint-Arnaud, Henri Joyeaux, Dr. Frigerio, Michael W. Petrides and others (Michael W. Petrides, "Discernment and Scientific Study of the Visionairies in Medjugorje," *Catholic Transcript*, September 10, 1993.)

27. Antoine Vergote, "Visions et Apparitions, Approche Psychologique," *Revue Théologique de Louvain* 22 (1991): 208.

28. Pierre Adnès, "Visions," in *Dictionnaire de Spiritualité Ascétique et Mystique: Doctrine et Histoire*, edited by M. Viller et al. (Paris: Beauchesne, 1993), 999.

29. "Qu'on ne s'en scandalise point: il ne s'agit pas d'identifier visions et hal-lucinations, mais de faire remarquer que, dans les deux phénomènes, la présentation de l'objet sensible peut être l'œuvre du même mécanisme psychologique; les causes motrices de ce mécanisme restent toutefois complètement différentes. Tandis que dans l'hallucination ce sont des dispositions morbides, dans les visions c'est la grâce opérante." Gabriel de Sainte-Marie-Madeleine, *Visions et Vie Mystique* (Paris, 1955), 60.

30. C. S. Lewis, *Transposition, and Other Addresses* (London: Bles, 1949), 10.

31. Anders Piltz, "Inspiration, vision, profetia: Birgitta och teorierna om up-penbarelserna," in *Heliga Birgitta: Budskabet och förebilden. Föredrag vid jubi-leumssymposiet i Vadstena 3.-7. Oktober 1991*, edited by Alf Härdelin and Mereth Lindgren (Stockholm: Almqvist & Wiksel: 1993), 82.

32. Adnès, "Visions," 949.

33. René Laurentin, "Fonction et Statut des Apparitions," in *Vraies et Fausses Apparitions dans l'Église: Exposés*, edited by Bernard Billet (Paris: Bellarmin, 1976), 156.

34. Joseph de Tonquédec, "Apparitions," in Viller et al., *Dictionnaire de Spiritualité Ascétique et Mystique*, 802.

35. Judith M. Albright, *Our Lady at Garabandal* (Milford: Faith Pub., 1992); Riccardo Caniato and Vincenzo Sansonetti, *Maria, Alba del Terzo Millennio: Il Dono di Medjugorje*, 6th ed. (Milan: Ares, 2002); Yves Chiron, *Enquête sur les Apparitions de la Vierge* (Paris: Perrin-Mame, 1995); Louis Joseph Kerkhofs, *Notre-Dame de Banneux: Études et Documents*, 2nd ed. (Tournai: Casterman, 1954); Daria Klanac, *Medjugorje: Réponses aux Objections* (Paris: Sarment, 2001); René Laurentin, *La Vierge Apparaît-Elle à Medjugorje?* 5th ed. (Paris: de Guibert, 2002); Arthur Monin, *Notre-Dame de Beauraing: Origines et Développements de Son Culte*, 2nd ed. (Bruges: Desclée de Brouwer, 1952); René Rutten, *Histoire Critique des Apparitions de Banneux* Namur, Belgium: Mouvement Eucharistique et Missionnaire, 1985); Francisco Sánchez-Ventura y Pascual, *The Apparitions of Garabandal* (Pasadena: St. Michael's Garabandal Center, 1997); Jacques Serre and Béatrice Caux, *Garabandal: Apparitions Prophétiques de Marie* (Paris: de Guibert, 1999); Fernand Toussaint and Camille J. Joset, *Beauraing: 1932–1982* (Paris: Desclée De Brouwer, 1981); Wayne Weible, *The Final Harvest: Medjugorje at the End of the Century* (Brewster: Paraclete Press, 1999).

36. Peter Dinzelbacher, *Mittelalterliche Visionsliteratur: Eine Anthologie* (Darmstadt: Wissenschaftliche Buchgesellschaft, 1989), 90.

37. Lindblom, *Prophecy in Ancient Israel*, 28f.

38. Peter Dinzelbacher, *"Revelationes"* (Turnhout: Brepols, 1991), 18.

39. André Dervilles, "Paroles Intérieures," in Viller et al., *Dictionnaire de Spiritualité Ascétique et Mystique*, 255.

40. Rahner, *Visions and Prophecies*, 20.

41. "Dieser wesentlich soziale Aspekt aller christlichen Mystik ist in der theologischen und spirituellen Tradition seit der montanistischen Krise weitgehend verlorengegangen und muß unbedingt wieder hervorgeholt werden." Hans Urs von Balthasar, *Thomas und die Charismatik: Kommentar zu Thomas von Aquin, Summa Theologica Quaestiones II II 171–182* (Einsiedeln: Johannes Verlag, 1996), 313. Fur further references on the matter see Paul Mommaers, *The Riddle of Christian Mystical Experience: The Role of the Humanity of Jesus* (Louvain: Peeters Press, 2003), esp. chap. 1, "The Image and the Idol."

42. "Une vision est la manifestation sensible ou mentale de réalités tenues pour naturellement invisibles et insaisissables à l'homme dans les circonstances actuellement données. En fait, le terme de visions embrasse un ensemble de phénomènes de connaissance très variés, qu'on ne peut facilement ramener à un commun dénominateur si ce n'est pas par l'impression qu'ils donnent de venir d'ailleurs, d'un au-delà du sujet, lequel n'a pas le sentiment de les produire et d'y coopérer activement, mais de les recevoir gratuitement, comme un don, une faveur inattendue." Adnès, "Visions," 950.

43. Pierre Courcelle, *Les Confessions de Saint Augustin dans la Tradition Littéraire* (Paris: Études Augustiniennes, 1963), 130–31.

44. *Etymologiarum*, book 7, chapter 8, nr. 37 sq. PL., 82, 286–287.

45. Ia.q.93.6.4m; 2a.2ae.q174.1.3m; q.175.3.4m, and many others.

46. Lindblom, *Prophecy in Ancient Israel*, 36.

47. "La connaissance prise en toutes ses dimensions: sensible, imaginative et intellectuelle, morale et pathologique, profane et mystique, intramondaine et céleste. Les trois genres de visions marquent le cheminement de l'âme du corporel jusqu'à l'intelligible." Adnès, "Visions," 950.

48. Ibid., 966–67.

49. *De Gen. ad lit.* XII.

50. "Die 'Visio corporalis' ist unsere alltägliche Erfahrung durch die Sinnesorgane, die wir mit den Tieren gemeinsam haben. Die 'Visio spriritalis' bezieht sich auf die Bilder der Imagination, sei es die der Phantasie, sei es die des Gedächtnisses. Unsere Träume gehören in diese Kategorie. Die 'visio intellectualis' ist die verstandesmäßige Erkenntnis von Abstracta, wie Liebe oder Gerechtigkeit." Peter Dinzelbacher, *Vision und Visionsliteratur im Mittelalter* (Stuttgart: Hiersemann, 1981), 82.

51. Lv 19:18.

52. *De Gen. ad lit.* XII, 6–9 and 15–20, ref. in Edward Cuthbert Butler, *Western Mysticism: The Teaching of Augustine, Gregory and Bernard on Contemplation and Contemplative Life*, 3rd ed. (London: Constable, 1967), 36.

53. *De Gen. ad lit.* XII, 14.29.

54. Butler, "Mysticism or Platonism," in *Western Mysticism*, 40f.

55. "Dans le langage surtout religieux, qui seul intéresse ici, une vision est la manifestation sensible ou mentale de réalités tenues pour naturellement invisibles et insaisissables à l'homme dans les circonstances actuelles données." Adnès, "Visions," 949.

56. $II^a \ 2^{ab,}$ q, 174, a. 1, ad 3; cf. q. 175, a. 3, ad 4.

57. II, 2, q. 173, a. 2.

58. II, 2, q. 173, a. 2, ad 2 and 3.

59. II, 2, q. 174, a. 2, seeAdnès, "Visions," 978.

60. Balthasar, *Thomas und die Charismatik*, 286f.

61. "Quasi-prophetischen Charismen, etwa dem geistlichen Amt oder der Lehre." Marianne Schlosser, *Lucerna in caliginoso loco: Aspekte des Prophetie-Begriffes in der scholastischen Theologie* (Paderborn: Schöningh, 2000), 10.

62. "Die innere Einheit von dona und höheren, innerlichen charismata festzuhalten, bleibt, über alle messalianischen Irrtümer hinaus, ein echtes Anliegen, das in der späteren Scholastik mit ihren scharfen Unterscheidungen kaum genügend Berücksichtigung fand. Die Stoßkraft des Messalianismus erlahmte, ohne daß eine scharfe Stellungnahme der Kirche nötig geworden wäre; die ganz anticharismatische Mystik des Areopagiten trug im Osten den Sieg davon, im Westen die Liebestheologie Augustins und die nüchterne Aszetik Benedikts." Balthasar, *Thomas und die Charismatik*, 275.

63. "Ist der Zentralfall, das *analogatum princeps*, die andern Fälle werden auf ihn hin ausgerichtet." Ibid., 302.

64. Pseudo-Dionysius et al., *Pseudo-Dionysius: The Complete Works*, translated by Colm Luibheid (New York: Paulist Press, 1987), 30; Janet P. Williams, "Pseudo-Dionysius and Maximus the Confessor," in *The First Christian Theologians: An*

Introduction to Theology in the Early Church, edited by G. R. Evans (Malden: Blackwell, 2004), 187.

65. John D. Caputo, *The Prayers and Tears of Jacques Derrida: Religion without Religion* (Bloomington: Indiana University Press, 1997).

66. Andrew Louth, *The Origins of the Christian Mystical Tradition from Plato to Denys* (Oxford: Oxford University Press, 1981), 182.

67. Evelyn Underhill, *The Essentials of Mysticism and Other Essays* (London: Dent, 1920), 354.

68. John of the Cross, *The Collected Works of Saint John of the Cross*, translated by Kieran Kavanaugh and Otilio Rodriguez (Washington, D.C: Institute of Carmelite Studies, 1991), *Ascent* II, 21.

69. Adnès, "Visions," 983.

70. Ibid.

71. John of the Cross, *The Collected Works of Saint John of the Cross*, *Ascent* II, 2, 2 and II, 12, 3.

72. "Les autres [appréhensions]—surnaturelles imaginaires ou surnaturelles spirituelles mais concernant les créatures—sont incapables de permettre l'union de l'âme avec la substance divine; elles sont plutôt un obstacle; il faut donc s'en détacher." André Bord, ed., *Mémoire et Espérance chez Jean de la Croix* (Paris: Beauchesne, 1971), 86–88.

73. John of the Cross, *The Collected Works of Saint John of the Cross*, *Ascent* II, 11, 8.

74. Ibid., *Ascent* II, 17, 7.

75. Ibid., *Ascent* II, 17, 9.

76. "Les motifs de croire peuvent être tels que tout doute prudent soit rendu impossible; celui qui alors refuserait de croire et d'obéir manquerait de respect et de soumission à Dieu et pécherait gravement." Auguste Saudreau, *L'État Mystique, sa Nature, ses Phases et les Faits Extraordinaires de la Vie Spririruelle*, 2nd ed. (Paris, 1921), 223–32. With ref. to Lugo, *De virt. Fid. Div. D.* 1 sec. 11, n. 229.

77. John of the Cross, *The Collected Works of Saint John of the Cross*, *Ascent* II,17,3.

78. Ibid., *Ascent* II,22,15 and II,11,13.

79. Robert A. Herrera, *Silent Music: The Life, Work, and Thought of St. John of the Cross* (Grand Rapids: Eerdmans, 2004), 93f.

80. John of the Cross, *The Collected Works of Saint John of the Cross*, *Ascent* II,16,10f.

81. Ibid., II,11,12.

82. Karl Rahner, *Visionen und Prophezeiungen*, 2nd ed. (Freiburg: Herder, 1958), 87.

83. "Saint Jean de la Croix s'est élevé fortement contre l'excès de la crédulité et contre le trop d'importance que l'on donne parfois aux visions et aux révélations, alors même qu'elles sont véritables, parce qu'il a constaté sur ce point, comme il le déclare, un manque de discrétion qui a été nuisible à beaucoup d'âmes. Il y avait eu, paraît-il, à cette époque, dans l'ordre du Carmel, de grands abus et le Saint dut rappeler les principes et montrer les dangers d'illusions. " Saudreau, *L'État Mystique*, 237.

84. John of the Cross, *The Collected Works of Saint John of the Cross*, trans. Kieran Kavanaugh and Otilio Rodriguez (Washington, D.C: Publications, 1991), *Ascent* II,19,1.

85. Ibid., II,19,5.

86. Rahner, *Visions and Prophecies*, 9. In the German original, Rahner uses the peculiar word "Aftermystik"; Rahner, *Visionen und Prophezeiungen*, 10.

87. Rahner, *Visions and Prophecies*, 57.

88. "Une défaillance du corps qui ne peut soutenir le contact de l'âme avec Dieu." Adnès, "Visions," 983. Adnès builds his conclusions on *Ascent of the Mount Carmel* II, 11,6; 16,10–11; III, 13,3; II, 32, 3, *Dark Night of the Soul* II, 1,2 as well as *Spiritual Canticle* 14,12; 26,11.

89. "Jean de la Croix ne sort pas du problème individuel. On lui reproche de ne pas avoir fait état du mystère de l'Église et du dessein de Dieu sur le monde. C'est exact. A cela on peut répondre qu'il ne faut pas lui prêter nos préoccupations actuelles, qui vraisemblablement ne seront plus les mêmes demain. Ensuite les auteurs de son temps ne semblent pas avoir eu non plus le sens communautaire ou ecclésial qui nous est cher, avec raison." Lucien-Marie de Saint-Joseph, "Jean de la Croix," 428.

90. John of the Cross, *The Collected Works of Saint John of the Cross*, *Ascent* II, 16, 10.

91. Ibid., *Ascent* II, 12, 6.

92. 1 Cor 14:18–19.

93. Laurentin, "Fonction et Statut des Apparitions," 159. See also Melquiades Andrés Martín, *La Teología Española en el Siglo XVI* (Madrid: La Editorial Católica, 1976), 1:423–25 and 2:227–59.

94. Adnès, "Visions," 989.

95. For more on the importance of visions in Teresa's life, see Adnès's continued presentation. Ibid., 981f., with reference to the following: Gabriel de Sainte-Marie-Madeleine, *Visions et Vie Mystique* (Paris: 1955); and M. Martin del Blanco, *Visiones místicas en Santa Teresa de Jesús* (Comillas: Universidad Pontificia: 1969).

96. *Vida* 29.4; 30.4. An English edition is Teresa of Avila, *The Collected Works of St. Teresa of Avila*, translated by Kieran Kavanaugh and Otilio Rodriguez, 5 vols. (Washington, D.C.: Institute of Carmelite Studies, 1976).

97. *Moradas* VI, c. 8, n. 2.

98. "Ses propres visions sont rebelles à toute classification rigide. Chez elle, les phénomènes se conjuguent et se fusionnent." Adnès, "Visions," 981.

99. "Puis parfois vient s'y ajouter pour les accompagner, les entourer et les humaniser une vision imaginative." Ibid., ref. to Teresa's *Vida* 28.9.

100. Volken, *Visions, Revelations and the Church*, 156.

101. "Surtout à la direction spirituelle et au discernement, beaucoup moins à la théologie spirituelle spéculative." André Dervilles, "Paroles Intérieures," in Viller et al., *Dictionnaire de Spiritualité Ascétique et Mystique*, 255.

102. See for instance: Pierre Adnès, "Révélations Privées," in Viller et al., *Dictionnaire de Spiritualité Ascétique et Mystique;* and "Visions"; Dervilles, "Paroles Intérieures"; Giandomenico Mucci, "Le Apparizioni: Teologia e Discernimento,"

Civiltà Cattolica, no. 4 (1989); Karl Rahner, "Les Révélations Privées. Quelques Remarques Theologiques," *Revue d'Ascétique et Mystique* 25 (1949); and *Visions and Prophecies*; Saudreau, *L'État Mystique*, 178–90 and 209–67; Augustinus Suh, *Le Rivelazioni Private nella Vita della Chiesa* (Bologna: Dehoniane, 2000); and many other favorable publications.

103. Rahner, *Visions and Prophecies*, 19.

104. Paul VI, "Dogmatic Constitution on Divine revelation Dei Verbum," in *Documents from Vatican II*, available from www.vatican.va/archive/hist_councils/ii_vatican_council/documents/vat-ii_const_19651118_dei-verbum_en.html.

105. Seckler, "Der Begriff der Offenbarung," 62.

106. Avery Robert Dulles, *Models of Revelation* (Garden City: Doubleday, 1983), 193f.

107. Werner Bulst, *Offenbarung: Biblischer und theologischer Begriff*, 1st ed. (Düsseldorf: Patmos-Verlag, 1960), chap. 6. English version: *Revelation* (New York: Sheed and Ward, 1965), chap. 6.

108. "Die verschiedensten Offenbarungsformen des Erscheinens, des Enthüllens, des Kundtuns und des Sprechen Gottes." Joseph Schumacher, *Der apostolische Abschluss der Offenbarung Gottes* (Freiburg: Herder, 1979), 317.

109. "Mitteilung von Wissen, sondern Zuwendung Gottes zum Menschen." Max Seckler, "Der Begriff der Offenbarung," in *Handbuch der Fundamentaltheologie*, edited by Walter Kern, Hermann Josef Pottmeyer, and Max Seckler (Freiburg: Herder, 1985), 62.

110. "Erwartungshaltung und Erfahrungspraxis." Ibid.

111. "Sichzeigen Gottes, ein Epiphanieereignis mythischer oder mystischer Prägung, sondern Kundgabe des im Wort ergehenden dialogischen Verhältnisses zwischen rettendem Gott und verlorenem Menschen." Michael Schmaus, *Handbuch der Dogmengeschichte* (Freiburg: Herder, 1956), 26.

112. 1 Tm 3:16.

113. Col 3:4; 1 Pt 5:4; 1 Jn 2:28.

114. "Ein Enthüllen oder Erschließen von Verborgenem, sondern ein schöpferisches Tun Gottes, das neu ist und reale Versöhnung und reales Heil stiftet; und [dieser Begriff] ist umfassend auf das ganze geschichtliche Sein und Tun Gottes anwendbar." Seckler, "Der Begriff der Offenbarung," 65.

115. 1 Jn 1:2.

116. 1 Ti 3:4; 1 Jn 4:9.

117. Ti 2:11.

118. 1 Tm 3:16; Heb 9:26; 1 Pt 1:20; 1 Jn 3:5 and 3:8.

119. "Der lebendige Gott bringt sich in seinem heiligen Sein als schöpferische, führende, richtende und erlösende Macht *je und je als konkret gegenwärtige Wirklichkeit* zur "Erscheinung" und zur "Erfahrung."" Seckler, "Der Begriff der Offenbarung," 63.

120. "Ermöglichungsgrund wie auch der Gegenstand des christlichen Glaubens." Ibid., 65.

121. "Ein vieldimensionales Sprach- und Wahrheitsgeschehen." Ibid.

122. Kern et al., *Handbuch der Fundamentaltheologie*, 12f.

123. Josef Schmitz, "Das Christentum als Offenbarungsreligion im kirchlichen Bekenntnis," in Kern et al., *Handbuch der Fundamentaltheologie*, 19f.

124. *"Se ipsum ac aeterna voluntatis suae decreta humano generi revelare."* Heinrich Denzinger and Adolf Schönmetzer, *Enchiridion symbolorum, definitionum et declarationum de rebus fidei et morum*, 33rd ed. (Barcinone: Herder, 1965), 3004.

125. See Norbert Copray, *Kommunikation und Offenbarung: Philosophische und theologische Auseinandersetzungen auf dem Weg zu einer Fundamentaltheorie der menschlichen Kommunikation* (Düsseldorf: Patmos, 1983), 132f; René Latourelle, *Théologie de la Révélation* (Bruxelles: Desclee de Brouwer, 1969), 235–44; Henri de Lubac, *Credo: Gestalt und Lebendigkeit unseres Glaubensbekenntnisses* (Einsiedeln: Johannes, 1975), 13f.

126. Schmitz, "Das Christentum als Offenbarungsreligion im kirchlichen Bekenntnis," 27.

127. Dulles, *Models of Revelation*, 204.

128. Karl Barth, *Ad Limina Apostolorum* (Zurich: EVZ-Verlag, 1967), 52.

129. George Ernest Wright, *God Who Acts: Biblical Theology as Recital* (London: SCM Press, 1952), 86.

130. Oscar Cullmann, *Salvation in History* (New York: Harper and Row, 1967), 90.

131. Ibid., 98.

132. Avery Robert Dulles, *Models of Revelation* (Garden City: Doubleday, 1983), 59, ref. to Wolfhart Pannenberg, *Revelation as History* (New York: Macmillan, 1968), 135–39.

133. Karl Barth, *Church Dogmatics*, translated by Geoffrey William Bromiley, 2nd ed. (Edinburgh: Clark, 1975), 320.

134. Ibid.

135. Paul King Jewett, *Emil Brunner's Concept of Revelation* (London: Clarke, 1954), 135.

136. See the distinction between "The case of the Contemporary disciple" (title of chap. 4) and "The Disciple at Second Hand" (title of chap. 5) in Søren Kierkegaard, *Philosophical Fragments, Johannes Climacus* (Princeton: Princeton University Press, 1985).

137. Vladimir Lossky, *Orthodox Theology* (Crestwood: St. Vladimir's Press, 1958), 14.

138. Underhill, *The Essentials of Mysticism and Other Essays*, 4.

139. See Karl Rahner and Joseph Ratzinger, *Revelation and Tradition* (Freiburg: Herder, 1966), especially 21f.

140. Joseph Ratzinger, "Offenbarung—Schrift—Überlieferung: Ein Text des hl. Bonaventura," *Trierer Theologische Zeitschrift* 67 (1958): 40f.

141. See for instance Günther Gassmann, ed., *Documentary History of Faith and Order, 1963–1993* (Geneva: World Council of Churches, 1993), 10f (n. 42f).

142. See Rahner's discussion of the difference between prophecy prior to and after Christ in Rahner, "Les Révélations Privées," paragraphs. 2–3. English version: "Private revelations: Some Theological Observations," *CatholicCulture.org*, available from http://www.catholicculture.org/docs/doc_view.cfm?recnum=202.

143. Claire L. Sahlin, *Birgitta of Sweden and the Voice of Prophecy* (Woodbridge: Boydell Press, 2001), 36.

144. Piltz, "Inspiration, Vision, Profetia," 68. See section 3.3.16 below.

145. 1 Cor 14:3.

146. Fisichella, "Prophecy," 795.

147. Rino Fisichella, *Gesù di Nazaret: Profezia del Padre* (Milan: Paoline, 2000), general conclusion.

148. Acts 5:11.

149. Rv 3:15–16.

150. Rv 3:19.

151. George Eldon Ladd, *A Commentary on the Revelation of John* (Grand Rapids: Eerdmans, 1972), 67.

152. Fogelqvist, *Apostasy and Reform in the Revelations of St. Birgitta*, 112.

153. Peter Dinzelbacher, *Vision und Visionsliteratur im Mittelalter* (Stuttgart: Hiersemann, 1981), 168.

154. Kristy Nabhan-Warren, *The Virgin of el Barrio: Marian Apparitions, Catholic Evangelizing, and Mexican American Activism* (New York: New York University Press, 2005), 95.

155. See discussion in Rocco Buttiglione, *Karol Wojtyla: The Thought of the Man Who Became Pope John Paul II* (Grand Rapids: Eerdmans, 1997), 219.

156. See for instance Friedrich Wilhelm Graf, "Vom Munus Propheticum Christi zum prophetischen Wachteramt der Kirche: Erwägungen zum Verhaltnis von Christologie und Ekklesiologie," *Zeitschrift für evangelische Ethik* 32, no. 2 (1988); and Geoffrey William Bromiley et al., eds., *The Encyclopedia of Christianity* (Grand Rapids: Eerdmans, 2003), 3:820.

157. See Emil Brunner on OT prophecy: "The claim very much predominates, and therefore the prophetic messages is above all the declaration of judgment, not good news—god-spel, eu-angelion—because human disobedience calls God's grace in question." Brunner, *Dogmatics: The Christian Doctrine of the Church, Faith and the Consummation*, 3 vols. (Cambridge: James Clarke, 2001), 3:157, on Luther as prophet, see Robert Kolb, *Martin Luther as Prophet, Teacher, Hero: Images of the Reformer, 1520–1620* (Grand Rapids: Baker Books, 1999).

158. Donald K. McKim, *The Cambridge Companion to Martin Luther* (Cambridge: Cambridge University Press, 2003), 211.

159. John Paul II, *Sources of Renewal: The Implementation of the Second Vatican Council* (San Francisco: Harper and Row, 1980), 245; Paul VI, *Dogmatic Constitution on the Church: Lumen Gentium* (Boston: St. Paul Editions, 1965), 12 and 35. For liberation theology, see Gustavo Gutiérrez, *Teología de la Liberación: Perspectivas* (Salamanca: Ediciones Sígueme, 1972), 37.

160. "Que no es antijerárquico ni está fuera de la institución." José Luis Espinel, *Profetismo Cristiano: Una Espiritualidad Evangélica* (Salamanca: Editorial San Esteban, 1990), 181.

161. Rahner, "Les Révélations Privées," 507; Karl Rahner, *Visionen und Prophezeiungen*, 2nd ed. (Freiburg: Herder, 1958), 22.

162. "Verdunkelung und Vernachlässigung von Einzelaussagen in der Verkündigung und Mißverständnisse in der Glaubenserkenntis" Johannes Feiner, "Die
Vergegenwärtigung der Offenbarung durch die Kirche," in *Die Grundlagen heilsgeschichtlicher Dogmatik*, edited by Johannes Feiner and Magnus Löhrer (Einsiedeln:
Benziger, 1965), 513.

163. "Dies bedeutet natürlich nicht, daß Gott sich nicht auch des neutestamentlichen Prophetismus bediene, um die Kirche und gerade auch das Amt immer
wieder zur Besinnung auf die ergangenen Offenbarung zu rufen." Ibid.

164. Hasenhüttel, *Charisma*, 196.

165. Norbert Greinacher, "Apostel, Propheten und Lehrer: Damals und Heute,"
Theologische Quartalsschrift 171 (1991): 196.

166. Fogelqvist, *Apostasy and Reform in the Revelations of St. Birgitta*, 194.

167. Saudreau, *L'État Mystique*, 209f.

168. Suh, *Le Rivelazioni Private nella Vita della Chiesa*, 194f.

169. Michael O'Carroll, *Vassula of the Sacred Heart's Passion* (Belfast: J.M.J.,
1993), 63f.

170. Saudreau, *L'État Mystique*, 219f.

171. Karl Rahner, *The Dynamic Element in the Church* (Freiburg: Herder,
1964), 44.

172. Ola Tjørhom, *Visible Church, Visible Unity: Ecumenical Ecclesiology and "The
Great Tradition of the Church"* (Collegeville: Liturgical Press, 2004), 3f, 12f.

173. Thomas F. O'Meara, *Theology of Ministry*, rev. ed. (New York: Paulist Press,
1999), 112f; Tjørhom, *Visible Church, Visible Unity*, 14.

174. Peder Nørgaard-Højen, "Einig in der Rechtfertigungslehre," *Ökumenische
Rundschau* 1 (1996): 6f.

175. Mt 16:18.

176. Magnus Löhrer, "Träger der Vermittlung," in Feiner and Löhrer, *Die
Grundlagen heilsgeschichtlicher Dogmatik*, 555f.

177. Feiner, "Offenbarung und Kirche der Offenbarung," 517.

178. " Die Verheißung des Geistes an die Kirche besagt aber dieses: Nie wird
Gott die Kirche ganz an sich selbst, an ihrer eigenen Sünde und Ohnmacht, sterben
lassen, sondern irgendwo in der Kirche läß t der Geist Gottes die Wahrheit und
das Leben neu durchbrechen für die ganze Kirche, irgendwo erweckt er Propheten
und Reformatoren. Das ist der evangelische Begriff der Geistesleitung und der
'Unfehlbarkeit' der Kirche." Paul Althaus, *Die christliche Wahrheit: Lehrbuch
der Dogmatik*, 5th ed. (Gütersloh: Gütersloher Verlagshaus Gerd Mohn, 1959), 526.

179. "Irrtumsfreiheit in dem, was formell letztverbindlich gelehrt oder definiert
wird." Basil Studer, "Träger der Vermittlung," in Feiner and Löhrer, *Die Grundlagen
heilsgeschichtlicher Dogmatik*, 560.

180. Mt 16:18.

181. "Offenbarungsvermittelnde Funktion der nichtamtlichen Träger, der Laien
und der charismatischen, prophetischen Persönlichkeiten." Feiner, "Offenbarung
und Kirche der Offenbarung," 535.

182. Rahner, *Visions and Prophecies*, 26.

183. Ibid.

184. Rahner, *Private Revelations*.

185. 1 Cor 14:3–4.

186. Volken, *Visions, Revelations and the Church*, 219.

187. Ibid., 220.

188. Luke 4:16f.

189. Acts 2:37f.

190. Fogelqvist, *Apostasy and Reform in the Revelations of St. Birgitta*, 135f.

191. Jn 4:19.

192. Jn 4:39.

193. 1 Cor 14:24.

194. Christian Pesch, "De Legato Divino," in *Compendium Theologiae dogmaticae* (Freiburg: Herder, 1913), 54.

195. Piltz, "Inspiration, Vision, Profetia," 68. This was not the only medieval interpretation of prophecy; see Sahlin, *Birgitta of Sweden and the Voice of Prophecy*, 36, n. 5. Sahlin refers to Diane Watt, *Secretaries of God: Women Prophets in Late Medieval and Early Modern England* (Woodbridge: Brewer, 1997), 19–27.

196. Rino Fisichella, *Gesù di Nazaret: Profezia del Padre* (Milan: Paoline, 2000), 258.

197. Rahner, *Visions and Prophecies*, 102.

198. Witherington, *Jesus the Seer*, 141.

199. Jon 3–4.

200. "La prédication de Jonas a sauvé Nineve; la prédication de Vincent Ferrier a sauvé l'univers." Quoted in Ovila Melançon, *Jesus Appelle sa Messagère* (Paris: de Guibert, 1994), 32.

201. "Ne reproduit de la prescience divine que la connaissance du rapport entre les causes et leurs effets, et les causes peuvent changer." Ibid., 31.

202. Jn 14:29.

203. Am 3:7

CHAPTER 5

1. *Ascent* II, XXII, 3, John of the Cross, *The Collected Works of Saint John of the Cross*, 230.

2. Martin Luther, *Works*, edited by Jaroslav Jan Pelikan and Daniel E. Poellot, 55 vols. (Saint Louis: Concordia, 1961), 24:371. Original: "Darumb lasst uns bleiben treu dieser Offenbarung oder Verkündigung des heiligen Geists, der es allein soll sagen, was wir wissen sollen, und uns zu Propheten machen und zeigen, was da künftig ist in der Christenheit, wie Christus bis ans Ende regieren und seine Christenheit erhalten und endlich des Endschrifts und seines Herren, des Teuffels, Regiment endlich zerstören wird. Diese Weissagung ist uns gewisser denn alle Zeichen und Wunder, denn diese soll bestehen, ob sich gleich der Teuffel noch so feindlich

dawider sperret." Martin Luther, *Dr. Martin Luthers Werke*, 67 vols. (Erlangen: Heyder, 1912), 46:65.

3. Floyd H. Barackman, *Practical Christian Theology: Examining the Great Doctrines of the Faith*, 4th ed. (Grand Rapids: Kregel, 2001), 218.

4. "Mme. Vassula Ryden se heurte, au moins aux yeux de tous ceux qui sont considérés comme les porteurs et continuateurs authentiques de la tradition de l'Église orthodoxe, à la conscience de cette Église à travers les siècles, une conscience aussi bien orale qu'écrite et selon laquelle la Révélation Divine a été une fois pour toutes achevée avec les Apôtres." Métropolite Damaskinos, "Intervention du Métropolite Damaskinos," *Choisir* 2 (1996): 14.

5. The presentation is indebted to Georg Günter Blum, *Offenbarung und Überlieferung: Die dogmatische Konstitution Dei Verbum des II. Vaticanums im Lichte altkirchlicher und moderner Theologie* (Göttingen: Vandenhoeck und Ruprecht, 1971); Yves Congar, *Tradition and Traditions: An Historical and a Theological Essay*, translated by Michael Naseby and Thomas Rainborough (New York: Macmillan, 1967); Avery Robert Dulles, *Models of Revelation* (Garden City: Doubleday, 1983); Karl Gabriel and Dietrich Wiederkehr, *Wie geschieht Tradition? Überlieferung im Lebensprozess der Kirche* (Freiburg: Herder, 1991); Joseph Schumacher, *Der apostolische Abschluss der Offenbarung Gottes* (Freiburg: Herder, 1979).

6. *Visio* I, 3,4. *Simil* VIII, 6,3; IX; XVI, 4,5, i.e. An English translation is Bart D. Ehrman, *The Apostolic Fathers* (Cambridge: Harvard University Press, 2003).

7. *Apologia* I, 4.13.45; 10.12.17.21.27.46.61.66; 2.4; *Dialogus* 48.133. An English translation is Justin Martyr, *Writings of Justin Martyr* (New Advent, 1885); available from www.newadvent.org/fathers/.

8. Avery Robert Dulles, *Models of Revelation* (Garden City: Doubleday, 1983), 36f.

9. Georg Günter Blum, *Offenbarung und Überlieferung: Die dogmatische Konstitution Dei Verbum des II. Vaticanums im Lichte altkirchlicher und moderner Theologie* (Göttingen: Vandenhoeck und Ruprecht, 1971), 86f.

10. *Adv. haer.* 4.6.3.

11. "Die Neuheit der Inkarnation besteht in der nicht mehr zu überbietenden heilsmächtigen Sichtbarkeit des ewigen Wortes, das durch seine Menschwerdung dieser Welt die Fülle aller Offenbarung gebracht hat." Joseph Schumacher, *Der apostolische Abschluss der Offenbarung Gottes* (Freiburg: Herder, 1979), 85, ref. to Blum, *Offenbarung und Überlieferung*, 39f, and Irenaeus, *Adv. haer.* 2.6.1; 4.14.2; 3.16.6; 5.18.3 (an English edition of Irenaeus's writings is *St. Irenaeus of Lyons Against the Heresies*, translated by Dominic J. Unger ([New York: Paulist Press, 1992]).

12. *Adv. haer.* III. 24.1.

13. *Adv. haer.* III11.1; 12.6; 15.1; IV35.4.

14. *Adv. haer.* II, 28.2; III1-4.

15. *Adv. haer.* III,2.1.

16. *Adv. haer.* III,3.1; III,4.1.

17. *Adv. haer.* 3. 3.2.

18. Schumacher, *Der apostolische Abschluss der Offenbarung Gottes*, 87f.

19. Peter Stockmeier, "Offenbarung in der Kirche," in *Die Offenbarung, Von der Schrift bis zum Ausgang der Scholastik: Handbuch der Dogmengeschichte*, edited by M. Seybold (Freiburg: Herder, 1971), 73.

20. Ibid., 36f and 86f.

21. "Der Abschluß der öffentlichen, allgemein verpflichtenden Offenbarung ist bei den Vätern keine Frage. . . . Wenn die Zeugen der Tradition nicht ausdrücklich den Abschluß und die Vollgenügsamkeit der in Christus ergangenen Offenbarung bekennen, tun sie es indirekt in der Überzeugung von der inhaltlichen Vollständigkeit des Glaubensgutes. Es ist für sie keine Frage, daß die 'Offenbarungen' nicht über die Christusoffenbarung hinausführen." Schumacher, *Der apostolische Abschluss der Offenbarung Gottes*, 89.

22. "Die Grenze zwischen Privatoffenbarungen, erstmaliger Kundgabe, der öffentlichen, allgemein verpflichtenden Offenbarung, der Annahme der Offenbarung im glauben, dem nachträglichen Wirken des Heiligen Geistes zu ihrer Erhellung und Vertiefung oder einfacher göttlicher Erleuchtung, die bei jeder Erkenntnis, auch bei der rein natürlichen, mitwirkt, [wird] nicht klar gezogen. Jedes 'auf Wahrheit und Heiligkeit gerichtete Streben im Leben der Kirche' konnte man als Offenbarung verstehen." Ibid., 90–91, ref. to Karl Rahner and Karl Lehmann, "Geschichtlichkeit der Vermittlung," in *Die Grundlagen heilsgeschichtlicher Dogmatik* (Einsiedeln: Benziger, 1965), 737.

23. Joseph Ratzinger, "Ein Versuch zur Frage des Traditionsbegriffs," in *Offenbarung und Überlieferung*, edited by Karl Rahner and Joseph Ratzinger (Freiburg: Herder, 1965), 67, quoted in Schumacher, *Der apostolische Abschluss der Offenbarung Gottes*, 91.

24. *De Civitate Dei* 11.3.

25. *De doctrina christiana* 2.42.63; 3.2.2.

26. "In qua semper apostolicae cathedrae viguit principatur." *Ep.* 42 n. 7.

27. Fogelqvist, *Apostasy and Reform in the Revelations of St. Birgitta*, 32.

28. Georg Söll, *Dogma und Dogmenentwicklung* (Freiburg: Herder, 1971), 113f.

29. *STh.* 1q.36a.2ad1.

30. "Further, it seems that nothing should be done in the Divine worship that is not instituted by God; wherefore the Apostle (1 Cor 11:23) when about to lay down the doctrine of the sacrifice of the Church, says: 'I have received of the Lord that which also I delivered unto you.' But Scripture does not lay down anything concerning the adoration of images. Therefore Christ's image is not to be adored with the adoration of 'latria. 'Thomas Aquinas, *Summa Theologiae* (STh.) III, q 25 a 3 obj 4: "The Apostles, led by the inward instinct of the Holy Ghost, handed down to the churches certain instructions which they did not put in writing, but which have been ordained, in accordance with the observance of the Church as practiced by the faithful as time went on. Wherefore the Apostle says (2 Thes 2:14): 'Stand fast; and hold the traditions which you have learned, whether by word'—that is by word of mouth—'or by our epistle'—that is by word put into writing. Among these traditions is the worship of Christ's image. Wherefore it is said that Blessed Luke painted the image of Christ, which is in Rome." Thomas Aquinas, *STh.* III q. 25 a. 3 ad 4.

31. III *Sentences Commentary (Sent.)*, dist. 9 a. 1 q 2ad 6.

32. Thomas Aquinas, *STh* I q. 36 a. 2 ad 1; IV *Sent.*, dist. 7 a. 1 q. 1 ad 1. Bonaventure, IV *Sent.*, dist. 7 a. 1 q. 1 ad 1; *STh.* III q. 64. a. 2 ad 2. Duns Scotus, *Opus Oxoniense* IV, dist. 7 q 1 n. 3.

33. Josef Finkenzeller, *Offenbarung und Theologie nach der Lehre des Johannes Duns Skotus: Eine historische und systematische Untersuchung* (Münster: Aschendorff, 1961), 72.

34. I *Sent. dist.* 11 a. un. q. 1.

35. Schumacher, *Der apostolische Abschluss der Offenbarung Gottes*, 96.

36. Bonaventure, *Itinerarium mentis in Deum*, edited by Philotheus Boehner and translated by Zachary Hayes, rev. and expanded ed. (Saint Bonaventure: Franciscan Institute Publications, Saint Bonaventure University, 2002), 7, 4.

37. Joseph Ratzinger, "Besprechungen zu W. Schachten, *Intellectus Verbi, Die Erkenntnis im Mitvollzug des Wortes nach Bonaventura*," *Theologische Revue* 75 (1975).

38. *Dialogus* I l. 2 c. 25, quoted in Schumacher, *Der apostolische Abschluss der Offenbarung Gottes*, 100, with ref. to Finkenzeller, *Offenbarung und Theologie nach der Lehre des Johannes Duns Skotus*, 70 and 76.

39. Schumacher, *Der apostolische Abschluss der Offenbarung Gottes*, 101., ref. to Josef Finkenzeller, *Offenbarung und Theologie nach der Lehre des Johannes Duns Skotus: Eine historische und systematische Untersuchung* (Münster: Aschendorff, 1961), 70.

40. Finkenzeller, *Offenbarung und Theologie nach der Lehre des Johannes Duns Skotus*, 70; Schumacher, *Der apostolische Abschluss der Offenbarung Gottes*, 100-101.

41. "His veritatibus que aliis fidelibus a deo revelate esse sufficienter ostenduntur." IV *Sent. Dist.* 13, q. 2D. III; *Sent. Dist.* 37, q. un C.

42. (*Dialogus* I l. 2 c. 25): "Posset Deus, si sibi placeret, multas veritates catholicas noviter revelare vel inspirare."

43. "Quellen, aus denen die Glaubenswahrheiten fließen, an denen kein Christ zweifeln darf." Schumacher, *Der apostolische Abschluss der Offenbarung Gottes*, 101, ref. to Finkenzeller, *Offenbarung und Theologie nach der Lehre des Johannes Duns Skotus,*79.

44. Ref. in Schumacher, *Der apostolische Abschluss der Offenbarung Gottes*, 101.

45. Schumacher refers to Finkenzeller, *Offenbarung und Theologie nach der Lehre des Johannes Duns Skotus*, 70f; Paul de Vooght, *Les Sources de la Doctrine Chrétienne d'après les Théologiens du XIVe Siècle et Début du XV* (Bruges: Desclée De Brouwer, 1954), 214 and 47.

46. "Hanc veritatem et disciplinam contineri in libris scriptis et sine scripto traditionibus, quae ab ipsius Christi ore ab Apostolis acceptae, aut ab ipsis Apostolis Spiritu Sancto dictante quasi per manus traditae ad nos usque pervenerunt." Heinrich Denzinger and Adolf Schönmetzer, *Enchiridion symbolorum, definitionum et declarationum de rebus fidei et morum*, 33rd ed. (Barcinone: Herder, 1965), 1501, hereafter DS.

47. Joseph Rupert Geiselmann, "Das Konzil von Trient über das Verhältnis der Heiligen Schrift und der nichtgeschriebenen Tradition," in *Die Mündliche Überlieferung: Beiträge zum Begriff der Tradition*, edited by Josef Rupert Geiselmann et al. (Munich: Max Heuber, 1957), 163.

48. The Second Vatican Council has in the constitution on revelation *Dei Verbum* somewhat confirmed the two-source theory: "It is not from Sacred Scripture alone that the Church draws her certainty about everything which has been revealed. Therefore both sacred tradition and Sacred Scripture are to be accepted and venerated with the same sense of loyalty and reverence." Paul VI, "Dogmatic Constitution on Divine revelation Dei Verbum," in *Documents from Vatican II.* Available from www.vatican.va/archive/hist_councils/ii_vatican_council/documents/vat-ii_const_19651118_dei-verbum_en.html.

49. Schumacher, *Der apostolische Abschluss der Offenbarung Gottes,* 103f.

50. See overview of literature in Finkenzeller, *Offenbarung und Theologie nach der Lehre des Johannes Duns Skotus,* 61.

51. Geiselmann, "Das Konzil von Trient,"163.

52. Heinrich Lennerz, "Scriptura sola?" *Gregoriana* 40 (1959); and "Sine scripto traditiones," *Gregoriana* 40 (1959).

53. Jared Wicks, "Loci Theologici," in *Dictionary of Fundamental Theology,* edited by René Latourelle and Rino Fisichella (New York: Crossroad, 1995), 606.

54. "Bahnbrechender Bedeutung für die Entwicklung der Theologie"; Bernhard Körner, "Melchior Cano," in *Lexikon für Theologie und Kirche,* edited by Michael Buchberger et al. (Freiburg: 1994), 918.

55. Wicks, "Loci Theologici," 606.

56. Ibid.

57. Ibid.

58. "Un non-lieu théologique." René Laurentin, "Fonction et Statut des Apparitions," in *Vraies et Fausses Apparitions dans l'Église: Exposés,* edited by Bernard Billet (Paris: Bellarmin, 1976), 166.

59. *De locis theologicis,* Book XII, Ch. 3, conclusion 3. Editions of Cano's work include *Opera* (Rome: 1890); Bernhard Körner, *Melchior Cano, De locis theologicis: Ein Beitrag zur theologischen Erkenntnislehre* (Graz: Styria Medienservice Verlag Ulrich Moser, 1994).

60. Cano, *De locis theologicis,* Book XII, Ch. 3.

61. Max Seckler, "Die ekklesiologische Bedeutung des Systems der 'Loci theo-logici,'" in *Weisheit Gottes, Weisheit der Welt: Festschrift für Joseph Kardinal Ratzinger zum 60. Geburtstag,* edited by Walter Baier (St. Ottilien: EOS Verlag, 1987).

62. "Nisi ex speciali revelatione." Decree on Justification, chapter XII

63. "Eine Negierung des Abschlusses der Offenbarung, sofern man hier über-haupt noch von Offenbarung reden kann. In dieser Sicht kommen und verschwinden Dogmen und treten völlig neue an ihre Stelle" Schumacher, *Der apostolische Abschluss der Offenbarung Gottes,* 115.

64. René Latourelle, *Theology of Revelation, Including a Commentary on the Constitution "Dei verbum" of Vatican II,* 2nd ed. (Staten Island: Alba House, 1967), 276.

65. Alfred Firmin Loisy, *L'Évangile et l'Église* (Paris: A. Picard et fils, 1902); English translation: *The Gospel and the Church* (Philadelphia: Fortress Press, 1976).

66. Alfred Firmin Loisy, *Autour d'un Petit Livre* (Paris: A. Picard et fils, 1903).

67. DS 3421.

68. Schumacher, *Der apostolische Abschluss der Offenbarung Gottes*, 117.

69. Ibid., 121.

70. Ibid., 135.

71. "Die göttliche Offenbarung ist, obgleich für alle Menschen aller Orten und Zeiten bestimmt, so doch nicht allen unmittelbar zuteil geworden; in Christus resp. den Aposteln ist sie *abgeschlossen*." Matthias Joseph Scheeben, *Handbuch der katholischen Dogmatik*, vol. 1 (Freiburg: Herder, 1878), no. 56, my emphasis. This and following ref. to Scheeben in Schumacher, *Der apostolische Abschluss der Offenbarung Gottes*, 124–25.

72. "Mit moralischer und historischer Gewissheit zu einer mehr oder minder allgemeinen Anerkennung." Scheeben, *Handbuch der katholischen Dogmatik*, vol. 1, no. 52.

73. Ibid., no. 53.

74. Karl Rahner, "Der Tod Jesu und die Abgeschlossenheit der Offenbarung," in *Pluralisme et Oecuménisme en Recherches Théologiques: Mélanges offerts au R. P. Dockx OP*, ed. Yves Congar and R. P. Hoeckmann (Gembloux: Duculot, 1976), 263.

75. Jared Wicks, "*Dei Verbum* Developing: Vatican II's revelation Doctrine 1963–1964," in *The Convergence of Theology: A Festschrift Honoring Gerald O'Collins, S.J.*, edited by Stephen T. Davis and Daniel Kendall (New York: Paulist Press, 2001), esp. 118; Jared Wicks, *La Divina Rivelazione e la sua Trasmissione. Manuale di Studio*, 2nd ed. (Rome: Pontificia Università Gregoriana, 1996), 75.

76. "Konstituierung des Depositums durch die Apostel und seiner Interpretation durch die Autorität des Lehramtes." Schumacher, *Der apostolische Abschluss der Offenbarung Gottes*, 139.

77. "Der Terminus 'Abschluß' leistet in der Tat einem satzhaften Mißverständnis Vorschub, in dem Offenbarung primär als Lehre verstanden wird. Spricht man von der Fülle oder der Vollendung der Offenbarung, so besteht weniger die Gefahr, die Offenbarung auf die Wortoffenbarung einzuengen." Ibid., 229.

78. "Existenz in Geschichte ... die nach vorne unbegrenzt offen ist"; "der irreversiblen und sieghaften Selbstzusage Gottes an die Welt im Christusereignis ... die nicht ab-, sondern aufschließt in eine unendliche Zukunft." Rahner, "Der Tod Jesu und die Abgeschlossenheit der Offenbarung," 264 and 66.

79. "Überdies darf die 'Abgeschlossenheit' der Offenbarung ('seit dem Tod der Apostel') nicht dahin mißverstanden werden, als habe seitdem Gott, anders als früher, ein abweisend-schweigendes Verhältnis zur individuellen und kollektiven Geschichte. Diese 'Abgeschlossenheit' bedeutet die Unüberholbarkeit und den bleibend normativen Charakter des Christusereignisses, das bleibend neue Erweise des Geistes in der Kirche treibt." Karl Rahner, "Privatoffenbarung," in *Herders Theologisches Taschenlexikon* (Freiburg: Herder 1975), 81.

80. "Man wird aber hier das Wort 'Abschluß,' als ein dem Christentum nicht adäquates, besser vermeiden. Die erreichte Fülle ist kein Abschluß, viel eher ein Anfang. Der Anfang der unendlichen Auswirkung der Fülle Christi in die Fülle der Kirche hinein, des Wachstums von Kirche und Welt in die Fülle Christi und Gottes

hinein, wie der Epheserbrief es beschreibt." Hans Urs von Balthasar, *Verbum caro* (Einsiedeln: Johannes Verlag, 1960), 27.

81. John 16: 13.

82. Eph 2:20; 3:5; 4:11.

83. Joseph Ratzinger, "Das Problem der Christlichen Prophetie: Niels Christian Hvidt im Gespräch mit Joseph Kardinal Ratzinger," *Communio* 2 (1999): 18.

84. "...durch welche die Kirche in Erkenntnisse eindringe, die ihr früher verschlossen [waren]." Ibid.

85. "...eine abschließende und abgeschlossene Quantität von feststehenden Offenbarungssätzen... sondern bildet eine gestaltgebende Norm für die unerläßlich bleibende weitergehende Geschichte des Glaubens." Ibid.

86. "...une information spéculative, donnée en soi, que l'expression de ce don: l'Agapè, c'est-à-dire le Dieu-Amour, qui se donne à l'homme pour être tout en tous." Laurentin, "Fonction et Statut des Apparitions," 160.

87. "...pas comme tout fait mais à faire." Ibid., 161.

88. "'...Lumière' qui 'fait la vérité' dans les vies. La Révélation biblique elle-même se présente, non comme la communication d'images et de concepts radicalement nouveaux, mais comme un éclairage qui transfigure les données culturelles et leur donne un sens nouveau, en référence au Dieu-Sauveur." Ibid., 161.

89. "Le processus de la Révélation est commun au prophétisme biblique et aux révélations particulières d'aujourd'hui." Ibid., 161.

90. "Plus profondément, on révise une conception selon laquelle il y aurait eu chute radicale, changement qualitatif entre les temps apostoliques et les temps ultérieurs. A l'origine, les lumières, et dans la suite, la transmission des formules issues de ces lumières. Pareille dégradation ne répond pas au dessin de Dieu: Un dessein ascendant, qui va de la mort du Christ (de son échec humain au calvaire) et de sa discrète résurrection, à l'eschatologie du Dieu tout en tous.

"La situation actuelle doit donc être caractérisée comme révélation continuée, analogue à la création continuée, car l'acte révélateur de Dieu, comme l'acte créateur, n'est pas un acte passager. Le Saint-Esprit diffuse les mêmes lumières dans son Église et dans le cœur des croyants; la différence tient à la modalité fondatrice du don fait à l'origine: charisme d'inspiration, avant tout, qui constitue la Parole de Dieu dans l'Écriture, mais l'Écriture reste Parole de Dieu en vérité par la même lumière essentielle de Dieu." Ibid., 163.

91. "Geht der Offenbarungsvorgang nach der Himmelfahrt Christi im eigentlichen Sinn weiter, so daß das Offenbarungsgeschehen selbst mit dem Ende der sichtbaren Gegenwart Christi noch nicht abgeschlossen wäre?" "Uns scheint die Auffassung besser begründet und konsequenter, dass von einer weiteren Offenbarung im eigentlichen Sinn als inhaltlicher Ergänzung der im sichtbaren (vorösterlichen und nachösterlichen) Christus geschehenen Offenbarung nicht gesprochen werden sollte, dass also das Ende des eigentlichen Offenbarungsereignisses mit dem Ende der sichtbaren Gegenwart Christ zusammenfällt." Feiner, "Die Vergegenwärtigung der Offenbarung durch die Kirche," 526.

92. Quoted in Gerald O'Collins, *Retrieving Fundamental Theology: The Three Styles of Contemporary Theology* (New York: Paulist Press, 1993), 95.

93. "Mit dem Christusgeschehen noch in keiner Weise gegebenen Offenbarung." Feiner, "Die Vergegenwärtigung der Offenbarung durch die Kirche," 526.

94. "Göttlichen Beistand zur ausdrücklicheren und reflexeren Erfassung und Entfaltung des mit den Erscheinungen des Auferstandenen zu Ende gesprochenen Offenbarungswortes Gottes." Ibid., 526.

95. "Die Funktion des Heiligen Geistes—auch in der nachapostolischen Zeit—ist also aufzufassen als die der Öffnung der Glaubenden zu den nie voll ausmeßbaren Dimensionen der Offenbarung hin." Ibid., 526.

96. "Ein tieferes und reflexeres Erfassen des Christusgeschehens unter einer besonderen Leitung und Erleuchtung des Heiligen Geistes, wie sie der Eingründung der Offenbarung in die normative Urkirche entspricht." Ibid., 527.

97. "Diese nachfolgende Geist-Offenbarung der Substanz der im Christusereignis selbst geschehenen Offenbarung untergeordnet ist und ihrer Erfassung und Entfaltung dient." Ibid.

98. *Opus Oxoniense* IV, dist. 5 q 1 n 6; IV, dist. 11 q 1. 3 n. 15; IV, dist. 2 q 1.

99. "Innerhalb des Offenbarungsvorgangs"; "Offenbarungsempfänger und Offenbarungszeuge und so mit Christus dem Uranfang und Ursprung einer Überlieferung, deren Träger und Zeugen erst die werden, die nach dem Apostel kommen.... Die Apostel sind in einmaliger Weise mit Christus; und Christus ist—nach seinem eigenen Willen—nicht da ohne die Apostel." Ref. in Heinrich Fries, "Die Offenbarung," in Feiner and Löhrer, *Die Grundlagen heilsgeschichtlicher Dogmatik*, 228.

100. It is "eine sachliche Bestimmung"; "Grundunterscheidung von Offenbarung und Überlieferung, von Ursprung und Nachfolge, von Quelle und Strom, von normierender Konstituierung und Fortdauer, von Maßgebendem und Maßnehmendem." Ibid.

101. "Constitutiva der Kirche und damit zur Offenbarung." Schumacher, *Der apostolische Abschluss der Offenbarung Gottes*, 324.

102. Ibid., 135.

103. "Grob gesagt die Zeit der Urkirche. Sie wird begrenzt durch die Entstehung der letzten neutestamentlichen Schrift, des 2. Petrusbriefes, und reicht damit ungefähr bis in die Mitte des 2. Jahrhunderts." Ibid., 324.

104. Wolfhart Pannenberg and Theodor Schneider, *Verbindliches Zeugnis* (Freiburg: Herder, 1992), 128–55, 377–79.

105. Reassumed in Schumacher, *Der apostolische Abschluss der Offenbarung Gottes*, 144–46. Ref. to Joseph Ratzinger, *Das Problem der Dogmengeschichte in der Sicht der katholischen Theologie* (Kölnand Opladen: Westdeutscher Verlag, 1966).

106. Juan Perrone, *Praelectiones theologicae*, vol. 21 (1866), ref. in Schumacher, *Der apostolische Abschluss der Offenbarung Gottes*, 394.

107. Emmanuel Doronzo, *Theologia Dogmatica* (Washington, D.C: Catholic University of America, 1966), 499.

108. Richard P. McBrien, *Catholicism* (San Francisco: HarperSanFrancisco, 1994), 268.

CHAPTER 6

1. Among important classical contributions to the theology of tradition and the development of dogma are: Yves Congar, *Tradition and Traditions: An Historical and a Theological Essay*, translated by Michael Naseby and Thomas Rainborough (New York: Macmillan, 1967); Paul VI, "Dogmatic Constitution on Divine Revelation Dei Verbum," in *Documents from Vatican II*, available from www.vatican.va/archive/hist_councils/ii_vatican_council/documents/vat-ii_const_19651118_dei-verbum_en.html; Karl Rahner and Joseph Ratzinger, *Revelation and Tradition* (Freiburg: Herder,1966); Joseph Ratzinger, "Ein Versuch zur Frage des Traditionsbegriffs," in *Offenbarung und Überlieferung*, edited by Karl Rahner and Joseph Ratzinger (Freiburg: Herder, 1965). For a good recent overview of the different applications of the word "tradition," see John E. Thiel, *Senses of Tradition: Continuity and Development in Catholic faith* (Oxford: Oxford University Press, 2000). For Hans Urs von Balthsar's approach, see Steffen Losel, "Unapocalyptic Theology: History and Eschatology in Balthasar's Theo-Drama," *Modern Theology* 17, no. 2 (2001): 221. For a Lutheran appreciation of the notion of development of dogma, see Michael Root, "The Development of Doctrine: A Lutheran Understanding and Its Ecumenical Application," *Ecclesiology* 2, no. 1 (2005).

2. Hermann J. Pottmeyer, "Tradition," in *Dictionary of Fundamental Theology*, edited by René Latourelle and Rino Fisichella (New York: Crossroad, 1995), 1123.

3. John Paul II, *Encyclical Letter Redemptoris Missio of the Supreme Pontiff John Paul II on the Permanent Validity of the Church's Missionary Mandate* (Washington, D.C.: United States Catholic Conference, 1990), 5.

4. Ref. to Paul VI, *Dogmatic Constitution on the Church: Lumen Gentium* (Boston: St. Paul Editions, 1965), 3–4.

5. Ref to ibid., 7. See Irenaeus, who wrote that it is in the church "that communion with Christ has been deposited, that is to say: the Holy Spirit" (*Adversus haereses* III, 24, 1: *SC* 211, 472).

6. Ref. to John Paul II, *Encyclical Letter Redemptoris Missio on the Permanent Validity of the Church's Missionary Mandate*, 5.

7. Wayne A. Grudem, *The Gift of Prophecy in the New Testament and Today* (Westchester: Crossway Books, 2000), 228f.

8. Philipp Gabriel Renczes, *Agir de Dieu et Liberté de l'Homme: Recherches Sur l'Anthropologie Théologique de Saint Maxime le Confesseur* (Paris: Cerf, 2003).

9. "L'homme en tant qu'inscrit dans un mouvement (κίνησις) orienté par un principe (ἀρχή) et une fin (τέλος) n'a plus accès, selon le Confesseur, au plan de sa connaissance, à ce qui constitue ontologiquement le principe de son ouverture à Dieu (ἀρχή), c'est-à-dire à son origine en tant que *cause efficiente*, dans la mesure où la condition humaine, imprégnée par la "faute d'Adam" perçoit son origine comme étant irrémédiablement perdue, ne lui laissant désormais la possibilité de la retrouver que dans sa *fin!*" Ibid., 199.

10. "le *chercher* est naturellement de l'ordre du principe (προς τὴν ἀρχήν) et le *re-chercher* de l'ordre de la fin (πρὸς τὸ τέλος)." Ibid., 200.

11. "Car après la transgression [le péché d'Adam], la fin ne se montre plus à partir du principe, mais le principe à partir de la fin ni personne ne cherche plus les raisons du principe (τοὺς τῆς ἀρχῆς λόγους) mais on recherche les raisons qui amènent ceux qui se meuvent vers la fin (τοὺς πρὸς τὸ τέλος τοὺς κινουμένους ἀπάγοντας). Maximus *Thal.* 59, ref. in ibid., 200.

12. "La divinisation est assuré par la finalité inhérente à celle-ci qui caractérise de toutes les façons la condition humaine, orientant son mouvement vers Dieu, l'accomplissement de tout agir." Ibid., 202.

13. "'Omega' ist nur vom 'Alpha' her verständlich, beide sind im Heilsratschluß Gottes eins, Eschatologie ist die Mündung der Protologie und ohne diese nicht darstellbar... [so daß] die letzte Wegstrecke innerlich den ganzen durchlaufenen Weg, dessen Bedingungen und Gesetze in sich schließt, ja ihn gerade im Münden erst in seinem von Anfang an gemeinten Sinn zur Erscheinung bringt." Hans Urs von Balthasar, *Pneuma und Institution* (Einsiedeln: Johannes Verlag, 1967), 410.

14. "In diesem Schlichten, wenn auch oft sehr schwierigen Vorziehen des göttlichen Willens... vollzieht sich schon im sterblichen Leben das Zentrale, was das Wesen des ewigen sein wird, und zwar viel zentraler, als dies etwa durch eigenmächtigen Versenkungsübungen... und vermeintliche Einigungserfahrungen mit Gott erreichbar ist." Ibid., 427.

15. "Zu Ende gelaufenen Geschichtszeit"; "einer dieser gegenüber inkommensurablen Dimension." Ibid., 445.

16. "Endgültigkeit und Vorläufigkeit." Ibid., 446.

17. "Der Neue Äon nicht chronologisch an den Alten anschließt, sondern, ihm inkommensurabel, wie im rechten Winkel daraus entspringt. Und daß die Existenz im Übergang nicht, wie in den Religionen der Sehnsucht nach dem Absoluten, eine Flucht aus der Zeit ist... sondern Existenz innerhalb der Existenz Christi, der wie kein anderer die Verantwortung für die gesamte Zeitlichkeit auf sich genommen und bis zum Paschamysterium durchgestanden hat." Ibid., 451.

18. "Äonenwende zwischen Karfreitag und Ostern." Ibid., 452.

19. Eph. 2:20; 4:11.

20. Joseph Ratzinger, "Christianity Always Carries within It a Structure of Hope: The Problem of Christian Prophecy," *Thirty Days*, January 1999, 75.

21. John 16:13.

22. Ratzinger, "Christianity Always Carries within It a Structure of Hope," 75.

23. Ibid., 75–76.

24. Ibid., 81.

25. Ibid.

26. Ibid.

27. Metropolitan John of Pergamon Zizioulas, "Apostolic Continuity of the Church and Apostolic Succession in the First Five Centuries," *Louvain Studies* 21 (1996): 164.

28. Ibid., 152.

29. Ibid., 153.

30. Ibid., 164.

31. Ibid., 153.

32. Ibid., 154.

33. See for instance Jn 20:21; Lk 10,16; Mt 28:18–20; Rom 10:13–17; 2 Tm 2:2, and Tt 1:5.

34. 42.2–4. Translated and quoted in Zizioulas, "Apostolic Continuity of the Church and Apostolic Succession in the First Five Centuries," 154.

35. 44.1–2. Translated by and quoted in ibid., 154.

36. Ibid., 154.

37. Ibid., 154.

38. Ibid., 155.

39. Ibid., 156–57., ref. to Cyprian's *Epistle* 69 (66) 5; 43 (40) 5; and *De ecclesiae unitate* 4.

40. Ibid.:, 157.

41. *Epistle* 3.3.

42. Zizioulas, "Apostolic Continuity of the Church and Apostolic Succession in the First Five Centuries," 157.

43. Ibid., 156.

44. Adolf von Harnack, *Die Mission und Ausbreitung des Christentums in den ersten drei Jahrhunderten*, 4th ed., 4 vols. (Leipzig: VMA-Verlag, 1924), 1:225.

45. Zizioulas, "Apostolic Continuity of the Church and Apostolic Succession in the First Five Centuries," 155.

46. Ibid., 156.

47. *Adv. Haer.* 4.18.5; an English translation is *St. Irenaeus of Lyons Against the Heresies*, translated by Dominic J. Unger (New York: Paulist Press, 1992).

48. Zizioulas, "Apostolic Continuity of the Church and Apostolic Succession in the First Five Centuries," 158.

49. Ibid.

50. Ibid.

51. Ibid., 159.

52. Mt 19:28.

53. Zizioulas, "Apostolic Continuity of the Church and Apostolic Succession in the First Five Centuries," 159.

54. Tobin Siebers, ed., *Religion and the Authority of the Past* (Ann Arbor: University of Michigan Press, 1993), 175.

55. Zizioulas, "Apostolic Continuity of the Church and Apostolic Succession in the First Five Centuries," 159.

56. Ibid., 161.

57. Ibid.

58. Ibid., 165.

59. Ibid.

60. Ibid.

61. Ibid., 167.

62. Col 1:24; see Bernard Ruffin, *Padre Pio: The True Story*, rev. and expanded ed. (Huntington: Our Sunday Visitor, 1991), 78.

63. Paul Ricoeur, *Dal Testo all'Azione* (Milan: Jaca Book, 1994), 115f.

64. "Genauer wird man sagen müssen, daß der Text der Schrift Niederschlag eines nie ganz faßbaren Wortereignisses und Auslöser einer Geschichte von Auslegung und Applikation ist, wobei gerade die Eigenart der verschiedenen Text-formen (Erzählung und Prophetie, Kult- und Weisheitstexte, Legende und Parabel) in ihrem unaufhebbaren Widerspruch diese zum offenen Verweis auf das je größere Verbum und die je gemäßere Rezeption hin werden lassen." Elmar Salmann, *Der geteilte Logos: Zum offenen Prozess von neuzeitlichem Denken und Theologie* (Rome: Edizioni Abbazia S. Paolo, 1992), 177.

65. Magnus Löhrer and Johannes Feiner, *Die Grundlagen heilsgeschichtlicher Dogmatik* (Einsiedeln: Benziger, 1965), 497–787.

66. "Man müßte wohl die Privatoffenbarungen zu der Überlieferung der Offenbarung mitrechnen." Ibid., 665.

67. Joseph Schumacher, *Der apostolische Abschluss der Offenbarung Gottes* (Freiburg: Herder, 1979), 73–77.

68. Karl Rahner, "Les Révélations Privées: Quelques Remarques Theologiques," *Revue d'Ascétique et Mystique* 25 (1949): 507; Karl Rahner, *Visionen und Prophezeiungen,* 2nd ed. (Freiburg: Herder, 1958), 20.

69. Karl Rahner, *The Dynamic Element in the Church* (Freiburg: Herder, 1964), 42f.

70. Alister E. McGrath, *The Blackwell Encyclopedia of Modern Christian Thought,* (Oxford: Blackwell, 1999), 23. See also Richard R. Gaillardetz, *By What Authority? A Primer on Scripture, the Magisterium, and the Sense of the Faithful* (Collegeville: Liturgical Press, 2003); and *Teaching with Authority: A Theology of the Magisterium in the church* (Collegeville: Liturgical Press, 1997), 184.

71. Augustinus Suh, *Le Rivelazioni Private nella Vita della Chiesa* (Bologna: Dehoniane, 2000), 168f.

72. Laurent Volken, *Visions, Revelations and the Church* (New York: Kenedy, 1963), 245.

73. Joseph Ratzinger, "Christianity Always Carries within it a Structure of Hope: The Problem of Christian Prophecy," *Thirty 30Days,* January 1999, 78.

74. Anne B. Baldwin, *Catherine of Siena: A Biography* (Huntington: Our Sunday Visitor, 1987), 112.

75. "Triomphé des oppositions des prélats de la Cour pontificale, qui se montraient incrédules à sa mission." Auguste Saudreau, *L'État Mystique, sa Nature, ses Phases et les Faits Extraordinaires de la Vie Sprirituelle,* 2nd ed. (Paris: 1921), 220.

76. Leo XIII, *Encyclical "Annum Sacrum" of Twenty-fifth May 1899* (Rome, 1900), 71.

77. Louis Chasle, *Schwester Maria vom göttlichem Herzen Droste zu Vischering* (Freiburg: Herder, 1929), 367.

78. Volken, *Visions, Revelations and the Church,* 247.

79. Acta Apostolicae Sedis. Vaticanis: Typis Polyglottis (hereafter AAS) 44 (1952) 511.

80. Zenit, "Pope Consecrates Third Millenium to Our Lady of Fatima," in *Vatican Dossier*, available from http://zenit.org/english/archive/0003/ZE000322 .html#item5.

81. Basil Studer, "Träger der Vermittlung," in Feiner and Löhrer, *Die Grundlagen heilsgeschichtlicher Dogmatik*, 602.

82. Ratzinger, "Christianity Always Carries within it a Structure of Hope," 78.

83. Ibid.

84. Quoted in Edward T. Oakes and David Moss, *The Cambridge Companion to Hans Urs von Balthasar* (Cambridge: Cambridge University Press, 2004), 5.

85. "Aufs Ganze gesehen besteht ein so enger Zusammenhang zwischen Vision und Dogma, daß man sagen kann, die Geschichte der christlichen Visionen in ihrem Gesamtablauf sei eine Art Bilderbuch der Dogmengeschichte; ebenso kann man sagen, daß die Visionen jeder bestimmten Epoche der Kirchengeschichte ein charakteristisches Bilderbuch der spezifisch dogmatischen Anschauungen dieses Zeitabschnittes bilden, soweit die betreffenden Visionäre nicht ihre Offenbarungen gegen die Kirchenlehre ausspielen und damit eine neu Epoche der Dogmenbildung einleiten." Ernst Benz, *Die Vision: Erfahrungsformen und Bilderwelt* (Stuttgart: Klett, 1969), 481.

86. Karl Rahner and Karl Lehmann, "Geschichtlichkeit der Vermittlung," in *Die Grundlagen heilsgeschichtlicher Dogmatik* (Einsiedeln: Benziger, 1965), 756 and 28.88. "Das Problem der Dogmenentwicklung besteht im Grunde in der Aufgabe, die Selbigkeit der späteren, 'entfalteten' Glaubensvorlage mit der in Christus ergangenen apostolischen Vorlage der Offenbarung als grundsätzlich möglich und in den einzelnen Fällen als wirklich identisch nachzuweisen." Ibid., 728.

87. Volken, *Visions, Revelations and the Church*, 252.

88. Anselm of Canterbury, *Miraculum de Conceptione Sanctae Mariae*, ref. in George H. Tavard, *The Thousand Faces of the Virgin Mary* (Collegeville: Liturgical Press, 1996) 90–91.

89. Volken, *Visions, Revelations and the Church*, 253.

90. Owen Chadwick, *A History of the Popes, 1830–1914* (Oxford: Oxford University Press, 1998), 120.

91. Frederic W. Baue, *The Spiritual Society: What Lurks beyond Postmodernism?* (Wheaton: Crossway Books, 2001), 173.

92. Charlene Spretnak, *Missing Mary: The Queen of Heaven and Her Re-emergence in the Modern Church* (New York: Palgrave Macmillan, 2004), 63.

93. Richard P. McBrien, *Catholicism* (San Francisco: HarperSanFrancisco, 1994), 1088.

94. Nancy Bradley Warren, *Spiritual Economies: Female Monasticism in Later Medieval England* (Philadelphia: University of Pennsylvania Press, 2001), 47 and 205, n. 73.

95. Col 1:24.

96. Paul Maria Sigl, *Die Frau aller Völker* (Amsterdam: Pro Deo et Fratribus, 1998), 21f.

97. Ibid., 104f.

98. Ibid., 121.

99. Pius XII, *Fulgens Corona*, Catholic Community Forum/Liturgical Publications of St. Louis, available from http://www.catholic-forum.com/saints/bvm00016.htm.

100. Ann Ball and Neil J. Roy, *Encyclopedia of Catholic Devotions and Practices* (Huntington: Our Sunday Visitor, 2003), 123.

101. Ibid., 318.

102. Ibid., 121.

103. Ibid.

104. Ibid., 273.

105. Ibid., 120f, 318, 499.

106. Karl Rahner, *Saggi di Cristologia e di Mariologia*, 2nd ed. (Cinisello Balsamo: Edizioni San Paolo, 1967), 289–90. See also Ann Ball and Neil J. Roy, *Encyclopedia of Catholic Devotions and Practices* (Huntington: Our Sunday Visitor, 2003), 498f.

107. Erminio Lora and Rita Simionati, eds., *Enchiridion delle Encicliche: Edizione Bilingue*, 8 vols. (Bologna: Edizioni Dehoniane Bologna, 1994), 5:240.

108. Ball and Roy, *Encyclopedia of Catholic Devotions and Practices*, 200.

109. Ibid., 513.

110. Ibid., 80.

111. Ibid., 619.

112. Ibid., 639.

113. Ibid., 200.

114. Ibid., 217.

115. Ibid., 209.

116. Ibid., 394.

117. Ibid., 209.

118. Ibid., 201.

119. Ibid., 239.

120. Paul Maria Sigl, *Die Frau aller Völker* (Amsterdam: Pro Deo et Fratribus, 1998).

121. Ball and Ann Roy, *Encyclopedia of Catholic Devotions and Practices*, 273–74.

122. See section 3.3.15 and Saudreau, *L'État Mystique*, 221.

123. Alois Stenzel, "Liturgie als Theologischer Ort," in Feiner and Löhrer, *Die Grundlagen heilsgeschichtlicher Dogmatik*, 620.

124. Johannes Feiner, "Die Vergegenwärtigung der Offenbarung durch die Kirche," in Feiner and Löhrer, *Die Grundlagen heilsgeschichtlicher Dogmatik*.

125. Saudreau, *L'État Mystique*, 219.

CHAPTER 7

1. Magnus Löhrer, "Träger der Vermittlung," in *Die Grundlagen heilsgeschichtlicher Dogmatik*, edited by Johannes Feiner and Magnus Löhrer (Einsiedeln: Benziger, 1965), 545.

2. Matthias Joseph Scheeben, *Theologische Erkenntnislehre* (Freiburg: Herder, 1903), 160f.

3. Jl 3:1.

4. Rino Fisichella, "Prophecy," in *Dictionary of Fundamental Theology*, edited by René Latourelle and Rino Fisichella (New York: Crossroad, 1995), 795. For more on the interpretation of Joel and the concept of the prophethood of all believers, see Roger Stronstad, *The Prophethood of All Believers: A Study in Luke's Charismatic Theology* (Sheffield: Sheffield Academic Press, 1999). The notion is taken furthest in Unitarianism's "radical laicism"; James Luther Adams and George K. Beach, *The Prophethood of All Believers* (Boston: Beacon Press, 1986).

5. Augustinus Suh, *Le Rivelazioni Private nella Vita della Chiesa* (Bologna: Dehoniane, 2000), 167f.

6. Victor Witter Turner, *From Ritual to Theatre: The Human Seriousness of Play* (New York City: Performing Arts Journal, 1982), 29.

7. Alessandro Toniolo, "Il Tema 'Liminalità' in Victor Turner. Un Contributo Antropologico-Culturale alla Riflessione sulle Forme di Iniziazione Religiosa," *Rivista Liturgica* 79 (1992).

8. Alessandro Toniolo, "Il Catecumenato: Periodo Liminale?" *Rivista Liturgica* 79 (1992).

9. Alessandro Toniolo, "Nostalgia delle Origini: Profezia o Anarchia Celebrativa?" *Rivista Liturgica* 84 (1997).

10. "La comunità nella celebrazione rituale, anche se si tratta di una comunità solamente 'simbolica' o 'giuridica' anziché di un gruppo spontaneo scopre che 'la struttura sociale' è tutta una montatura, una 'bugia,' nobile o ignobile, 'una costruzione sociale artefatta della realtà.' La vera realtà è l'antistruttura." Victor Witter Turner, "La Religione nell'Antropologia Culturale," *Concilium* 16 (1980): 143.

11. Victor Witter Turner, *Dramas, Fields, and Metaphors: Symbolic Action in Human Society* (Ithaca: Cornell University Press, 1974), 272.

12. Martin Buber, *Between Man and Man* (London: Collins, 1961), 51.

13. Toniolo, "Il Catecumenato: Periodo Liminale?" 249–52.

14. John 15:18–19.

15. Acts 2:44–45.

16. Acts 4:32.

17. Frère Ephraïm, *Marthe: Une ou deux Choses que je sais d'Elle* (Paris: Lion de Juda, 1990), 145f and 63f.

18. Victor Witter Turner, *The Ritual Process: Structure and Anti-Structure* (New York: de Gruyter, 1995), 128.

19. "La funzione del capo carismatico è importante perché essa riassume il momento etico fondamentale della *communitas* in quanto i membri in tale contingenza non si sentono sudditi nella misura in cui riescono a far coincidere atti di massima dipendenza—vista come pura forma di oblatività—con atti di assoluta libertà. D'altro lato, il capo carismatico si presenta con segni tangibili di autorità: la profezia, la rivelazione, la visione che corrobora la sua funzione e gli crea intorno un alone di mistero. In questo contesto alla persona del capo fa riferimento tutta la *communitas* che ritrova in esso il centro propulsore, la forza per difendersi all'esterno e per aver coesione all'interno." Aldo Natale Terrin, *Religioni, Esperienza, Verità: Saggi di Fenomenologia della Religione* (Urbino: Quattro Venti, 1986), 204.

20. "In uno stato particolare di essere esterno alla struttura sociale ma nel contempo di esercitare per la struttura sociale un particolare ruolo. Caratteristica fondamentale degli *outsiders* è quella di risultare in una data situazione di anormalità rispetto al comune vivere sociale, ma nello stesso tempo di venire considerati solo un modo diverso di vivere una situazione particolare del sistema stesso." Toniolo, "Il Tema 'Liminalità' in Victor Turner," 96–97.

21. Mircea Eliade, *Myth and Reality* (London: Allen and Unwin, 1964), 50.

22. "È un paradiso che è stato perduto, è un periodo di beatitudine che è stato smarrito, è un momento estatico profondo e inequivocabilmente affascinante che si vuole ripristinare, che, a volte, si cerca e non si riesce a far riemergere dalla realtà storica o dal profondo del proprio io." Toniolo, "Nostalgia delle Origini," 794.

23. Eliade, *Myth and Reality*, 51.

24. Toniolo, "Il Tema 'Liminalità' in Victor Turner," 88.

25. Mircea Eliade, *Myth and Reality*, 51–52.

26. Ibid., 68.

27. "Si associa al tema degli inizi e non può essere diversamente all'interno del paradigma della nostalgia delle origini che stiamo tratteggiando." Toniolo, "Nostalgia delle Origini," 795.

28. Mircea Eliade, *Myth and Reality* (London: Allen and Unwin, 1964), 78.

29. "Prolungano e completano il mito cosmogonico; raccontano come il mondo è stato modificato, arricchito o impoverito." Mircea Eliade, *Mito e Realtà* (Rome: Borla Editore, 1985), 45.

30. "La ricapitolazione è insieme una commemorazione e una riattualizzazione rituale, per mezzo dei canti e della danza, degli avvenimenti mitici essenziali che sono accaduti dopo la creazione." Ibid., 47.

31. "Non si ha una semplice riparazione, un rattoppo, ma una vera e propria ricreazione. Non si ha la guarigione dalla malattia o il superamento della situazione critica, ma un ritorno alle origini, un ripristino della perfezione degli inizi." Toniolo, "Nostalgia delle Origini," *Rivista Liturgica* 84 (1997): 796.

32. "il mito cosmogonico sia il racconto mitico servono per superare la storia: essa è contingente e rovinatrice della bellezza iniziale e deve quindi essere annullata. Essa inoltre fa dimenticare le origini con la sua incrostazione, che deve essere tolta per far splendere il vaso nella sua pregnanza cromatica." Ibid.

33. Eliade, *Myth and Reality*, 34.

34. "Attraverso apparizioni o visioni che superano il ricordo e la storia, perché in questo modo il ricordo delle origini è chiaro, voluto da Dio; ripristinando l'ordine iniziale e abbattendo qualsiasi interpretazione sorta nel momento intermedio; ricercando in se stessi, nel proprio spirito, nella propria anima, nella propria mente il senso delle cose perché liberandosi della mortalità, affinando lo spirito si entra in diretto contatto con chi o con che cosa può rivelarci il senso intimo e profondo della realtà." Toniolo, "Nostalgia delle Origini," 797.

35. "Memoria perfetta, che può realizzarsi solo attraverso un cammino interiore o la rivelazione divina." Ibid.

36. "Non c'è da meravigliarsi, quindi, se a volte accade che studiosi, siano essi teologi, filosofi o scienziati, rimangano affascinati da chi si presenta come colui che è chiamato ad avere—attraverso rivelazioni o visioni—la memoria perfetta. La conoscenza dell'origine delle cose e della loro storia conferisce un magico dominio sulle stesse. Chi è capace di ricordarsi dispone di una forza magico-religiosa più preziosa di ogni altra forma di sapere." Ibid.

37. Turner, *Dramas, Fields, and Metaphors*, 273.

38. Turner, *The Ritual Process*, 94–95.

39. Ibid., 193.

40. Ibid.

41. Ibid.

42. "In una società industrializzata sia la marginalità come la liminalità, che trovano nel sacro la anti-struttura, hanno la necessità di costruire un luogo, un forte, una città per circoscriversi." Toniolo, "Nostalgia delle Origini," 806.

43. "Abbisogna per rientrare nella cosiddetta struttura sociale normale di un processo di rieducazione" Ibid.

44. "Chi invece è vissuto nella liminalità è considerato pienamente iniziato alla struttura sociale nella quale dovrà inserirsi." Ibid.

45. "La *liminalità* tende verso forme momentanee di separazione per la piena integrazione sociale della persona, mentre la marginalità si orienta verso di esse per configurarsi come antistruttura permanente." Ibid.

46. "L'impedimento allo scambio sociale e all'uscita verso il mondo esterno, spesso concretamente fondato nelle stesse strutture fisiche dell'istituzione." Erving Goffman, *Asylums: Le Istituzioni Totali: La Condizione Sociale dei Malati di Mente e di Altri Internati* (Turin: Giulio Einaudi editore, 1968), 34f.

47. "I meccanismi di esclusione non sono superabili e non hanno alcuna finalità se non quella di identificare in modo permanente l'individuo come strutturalmente inferiore." "Si impegnino per acquisire una piena identificazione sociale e quindi lo stato di inferiorità strutturale divine finalizzato e funzionale al momento post-liminale." Toniolo, "Il Tema 'Liminalità' in Victor Turner," 100.

48. "Chi sta sulla soglia di casa sa di occupare una posizione di attesa ben precisa: il limitare è il luogo necessario al passaggio per potere entrare. Chi invece sta ai margini di una stanza o di una casa, si trova nella posizione di chi sa di occupare uno *status* e di esercitare dei ruoli di inferiorità, ormai per lui caratterizzati e determinati." Ibid., 101.

49. "Antistrutturale all'interno della struttura stessa, voluta e finalizzata dalla struttura, un'anti-struttura della struttura e per la struttura." Ibid., 102.

50. Turner, *From Ritual to Theatre: The Human Seriousness of Play*, 46–47.

51. Turner, *The Forest of Symbols: Aspects of Ndembu Ritual* (Ithaca: Cornell University Press, 1967), 97.

52. Turner, *From Ritual to Theatre*, 47.

53. Witter, *The Ritual Process*, 128–29.

54. Ibid., 133.

55. Ibid., 129.

56. Turner, *From Ritual to Theatre*, 28.

57. Ibid.

58. "Perde le caratteristiche tipiche della spontaneità e della autogestione, cost-ringendo l'antistruttura a sorgere sotto forme marginali che, per difendersi, dovranno divenire a loro volta istituzioni." Toniolo, "Il Tema 'Liminalità' in Victor Turner," 104.

59. Ibid., 104.

60. "Non solo il momento che riporta le forme religiose allo statu nascente ma lo spazio capace di creare forme nuove che consentono l'adattamento continuo della religiosità al mutare dei sistemi culturali." Ibid., 103.

61. "Anche le grandi forme di religione istituzionalizzata, Chiesa cattolica in-clusa, devono possedere un proprio momento di liminalità." Ibid., 103.

62. "Data da un lato dall'incontro dell'individuo con il nucleo integro originario e dall'altro dalla successiva rielaborazione prodotta nel momento di adattamento dovuto al rientro nella struttura sociale." Ibid., 104.

63. "Il momento di incontro fra presente e passato, fra le origini, la tradizione e il mutamento." Toniolo, "Nostalgia delle Origini," 810.

64. "Appartiene alla struttura stessa che vuole mutarsi, come l'altra faccia della medaglia." "Cercare di comprendere le situazioni di liminalità, distinguendole con discernimento pastorale dalle situazioni di marginalità, per essere sospinte verso un continuo rinnovamento." Ibid., 812.

65. Ratzinger, "Christianity Always Carries within It a Structure of Hope."

CHAPTER 8

1. I.e. Magnus Löhrer, "Träger der Vermittlung," in *Die Grundlagen heils-geschichtlicher Dogmatik*, edited by Johannes Feiner and Magnus Löhrer (Einsiedeln: Benziger, 1965), 562f.

2. See the elaborations on the matter in Augustinus Suh, *Le Rivelazioni Private nella Vita della Chiesa* (Bologna: Dehoniane, 2000).

3. John Paul II, *Apostolic Letter of His Holiness Pope John Paul II on Reserving Priestly Ordination to Men Alone* (Washington, D.C.: Office for Publishing and Promotion Services, United States Catholic Conference, 1994). Response by CDF is in Joseph Ratzinger, Tarcisio Bertone, and Congregatio Pro Doctrina Fidei, "Responsum ad dubium circa doctrinam in Epist. Ap. 'Ordinatio Sacerdotalis' traditam," *AAS* 87 (1995), available from http://web.infinito.it/utenti/i/interface/Ordinatio.html.

4. John Paul II, *Ad tuendam fidem: Apostolic Letter Motu Proprio of Pope John Paul II: By Which Certain Norms Are Inserted into the Code of Canon Law and into the Code of Canons of the Eastern Churches* (Boston: Pauline Books and Media, 1998).

5. Joseph Ratzinger, "Doctrinal Commentary on the Concluding Formula of the Professio Fidei," *Adoremus Bulletin* 4, no. 6 (1998).

6. Ibid., par. 5.

7. "Gibt die Kirche ein unfehlbares Urteil über eine Wahrheit ab, die nicht in den Quellen der Offenbarung enthalten, aber mit einer Offenbarungslehre innerlich verknüpft ist, so muß diese Wahrheit (nach der besser begründeten Ansicht) von allen Christen *fide ecclesiastica* angenommen werden, weil die unfehlbare Kirche sie festgestellt (definiert) hat. Und dieser Glaube ist zugleich eine *fides mediate divina*, weil die Unfehlbarkeit der Kirche als formelle Offenbarungswahrheit durch Gott selbst verbürgt wird." Franz Diekamp, *Katholische Dogmatik nach den Grundsätzen des heiligen Thomas* (Münster Westfalen: Aschendorff, 1958), 14.

8. "Fehlt... die propositio Ecclesiae, so tritt für den einzelnen Christen, falls er auf anderem Wege, etwa durch Forschung in der Hl. Schrift oder durch eine Privatoffenbarung, zur Gewißheit gelangt ist, daß Gott eine bestimmte Lehre unmittelbar geoffenbart hat, die Pflicht der *fides immediate divina* ein, da *Gott* die Wahrheit einer solchen Lehre nach der festen Überzeugung des Betreffenden unmittelbar verbürgt." Ibid.

9. "Ob es eine fides divina (im Sinn des Glaubens an die öffentliche, allgemeine Offenbarung, nicht an Privatoffenbarungen) geben könne, die nicht in irgendeiner Weise auch fides catholica ist, ist umstritten. Die Auffassung scheint richtiger zu sein, daß jeder (theologische) Glaube doch in irgendeiner Form an die kirchliche Gemeinschaft gebunden ist."

10. Karl Rahner, "Les Révélations Privées: Quelques Remarques Theologiques," *Revue d'Ascétique et Mystique* 25 (1949).

11. "Dans le premier cas (fides catholica) la révélation est proposée par l'Église, dans le second (foi théologale) par Dieu d'une manière directe. Mais le motif de l'assentiment est le même de part et d'autre: l'autorité de Dieu révélant." Pierre Adnès, "Révélations Privées," in *Dictionnaire de Spiritualité Ascétique et Mystique: Doctrine et Histoire*, ed. M. Viller et al. (Paris: Beauchesne, 1987), 487.

12. Giuseppe Alberigo, *Conciliorum Oecumenicorum Decreta*, 3rd ed. (Bologna: Istituto per le scienze religiose, 1973), 613/30.

13. Ibid., 173.

14. Benedict XIV, *Benedicti papae XIV doctrina de servorum Dei beatificatione et beatorum canonizatione in synopsim redacta ab emm. de Azevedo* (Brussels: Typis Societatis belgicae de propagandis bonis libris, 1840).

15. Prospero Lambertini, *Doctrina de servorum Dei beatificatione et canonizatione in synopsim redacta* (Rome, 1749), 175–76.

16. Ibid.

17. Pius X, *Actes de Pie X: Encycliques, Motu Proprio, Brefs, Allocutions, Actes des Dicastères, etc.* (Paris: Maison de la Bonne Presse, 1920), 175.

18. "Lorsqu'il y a approbation, il s'agit habituellement d'une approbation au sens large. Le magistère intervient à titre prudentiel pour permettre la divulgation de récits de révélations où rien n'a été trouvé qui soit répréhensible ou inopportun. On n'est pas pour autant obligé d'y croire. Cela résulte des déclarations mêmes du magistère." Adnès, "Révélations Privées," 488.

19. Henri Holstein, "Les Apparitions Mariales," *Maria* 5 (1955): 774.

20. "Il semble . . . qu'on puisse qualifier l'adhésion requise ici comme un acte de foi humaine impérée par l'obéissance, elle même sous l'influence des vertus de piété et d''observance.'Cette adhésion de foi humaine est ici donnée non en conclusion d'une étude critique de crédibilité, mais pour ce motif propre qu'est l'obéissance due à l'autorité ecclésiastique dans les limites de sa compétence." Yves Congar, "La Crédibilité des Révélations Privées," in *Sainte église: Études et approches ecclésiologiques*, edited by Yves Congar (Paris: Editions du Cerf, 1963), 375–92. See also Yves Congar, "La Crédibilité des Révélations Privées," *Supplément de la Vie Spirituelle* 53 (1937).

21. See Eric W. Kemp, *Canonization and Authority in the Western Church* (London: Oxford University Press, 1948), 151f. James Tunstead Burtchaell, "Community Experience as a Source of Christian Ethics," in *From Christ to the world: Introductory Readings in Christian Ethics*, edited by Wayne G. Boulton, Allen Verhey, and Thomas D. Kennedy (Grand Rapids: Eerdmans, 1994), 69. For an ecumenical discussion of the infallibility of canonizations see Jeffrey Gros and Joseph A. Burgess, *Building Unity: Ecumenical Dialogues with Roman Catholic Participation in the United States* (New York: Paulist Press, 1989), 193, with references to Catholic statements that support the belief at 214, n. 107.

22. Eugenio Valentini, "Rivelazioni Private e Fatti Dogmatici," *Maria et Ecclesia* (1962): 10.

23. "[Ce] qu'elle seule peut connaître: Son être, son opération." F. Roy, "Le Fait de Lourdes devant le Magistère," in *Maria et Ecclesia: Acta congressus mariologici-mariani in civitate Lourdes anno 1958 celebrati* (1962), 11–56.

24. Karel Balic, "De Auctoritate Ecclesiae circa apparitiones seu revelationes. Adnotationes ad encyclicam 'Pascendi' occasione primi centenari apparitionum Lourdensium," *Divinitas* 2 (1956).

25. Karl Rahner, *Visions and Prophecies* (London: Burns and Oats, 1963), 25–26.

26. Rahner, "Les Révélations Privées," 507.

27. "La différence de valeur établie entre les canonisations et les reconnaissances d'apparitions ne relève pas des critères de discernement, mais des problèmes politiques de gouvernement. Une des préoccupations congénitales de tout pouvoir, c'est de contrôler les influences qui risquent de soulever des mouvements populaires et de déborder l'autorité. Ainsi a-t-on favorisé la mystique de contemplation 'pure, ineffable et sans image,' qui donne lieu à des expériences incommunicables, et dévalué le prophétisme . . . à cause de son retentissement spontané dans la vie de l'Église." René Laurentin, "Fonction et Statut des Apparitions," in *Vraies et Fausses Apparitions dans l'Église: Exposés*, edited by Bernard Billet (Paris: Bellarmin, 1976), 187.

CHAPTER 9

1. Tadeusz Czakanski, "The Christian Prophets and the Charism of Prophecy in the New Testament and the Origins of the Church" (Ph.D. diss., Rome: Università Lateranense, 1987), 189.

2. Morton T. Kelsey, *Discernment: A Study in Ecstasy and Evil* (New York: Paulist Press, 1978), 3.

3. Robert Wuthnow, *After Heaven: Spirituality in America since the 1950s* (Berkeley: University of California Press, 1998), 123.

4. James Dunn, *Jesus and the Spirit: A Study of the Religious and Charismatic Experience of Jesus and the First Christians as Reflected in the New Testament* (Grand Rapids: Eerdmans, 1997), 301.

5. See the discussion of true and false prophecy with reference to other works on the issue in Marvin A. Sweeney, "The Truth in True and False Prophecy," in *Truth: Interdisciplinary Dialogues in a Pluralistic Age*, edited by Kristin De Troyer, Katie Goetz, and Christine Helmer (Louvain: Peeters, 2003), 11.

6. On the discernment of Christian prophecy see Wendy Love Anderson, "Free Spirits, Presumptuous Women, and False Prophets" (Ph.D. diss., University of Chicago, 2002); Ann Ball and Neil J. Roy, *Encyclopedia of Catholic Devotions and Practices* (Huntington: Our Sunday Visitor, 2003), 54–55; Bernard Billet, ed., *Vraies et Fausses Apparitions dans l'Église*, 2nd ed. (Paris: Bellarmin, 1976); Nancy Caciola, *Discerning Spirits: Divine and Demonic Possession in the Middle Ages* (Ithaca: Cornell University Press, 2003); Dyan Elliott, *Proving Woman: Female Spirituality and Inquisitional Culture in the Later Middle Ages* (Princeton: Princeton University Press, 2004), chap. 7; and "Seeing Double: John Gerson, the Discernment of Spirits, and Joan of Arc," *American Historical Review* 107, no. 1 (2002); Deborah A. Fraioli, *Joan of Arc: The Early Debate* (Woodbridge, England: Boydell Press, 2000); Morton T. Kelsey, *Discernment: A Study in Ecstasy and Evil* (New York: Paulist Press, 1978); Adel Theodor Khoury and Dirk Grothues, *Zur Unterscheidung der Geister* (Altenberge: Oros, 1994); Mark Allen McIntosh, *Discernment and Truth: The Spirituality and Theology of Knowledge* (New York: Crossroad, 2004); Giandomenico Mucci, "Le Apparizioni. Teologia e Discernimento," *Civiltà Cattolica*, no. 4 (1989); Mucci, *Rivelazioni Private e Apparizioni* (Rome: Civiltà Cattolica, 2000); Auguste Poulain, *Revelations and Visions: Discerning the True and the Certain from the False or the Doubtful* (New York: Alba House, 1998); Karl Rahner, *Visions and Prophecies* (London: Burns and Oats, 1963), chap. 3; Leo Scheffczyk, *Die theologischen Grundlagen von Erscheinungen und Prophezeiungen* (: Johannes-Verlag, 1982), chap. 2; Marianne Schlosser, *Lucerna in caliginoso loco: Aspekte des Prophetie-Begriffes in der scholastischen Theologie* (Paderborn: Schöningh, 2000), chap. 5; Lisa J. Schwebel, *Apparitions, Healings, and Weeping Madonnas: Christianity and the Paranormal* (New York: Paulist Press, 2004), chap. 5; Augustinus Suh, *Le Rivelazioni Private nella Vita della Chiesa* (Bologna: Dehoniane, 2000); Laurent Volken, *Visions, Revelations and the Church* (New York: Kenedy, 1963), chaps. 5–7.

7. Mt 7:15–16.

8. Volken, *Visions, Revelations and the Church*, 153.

9. Ibid., 156.

10. See Maria Paraklyta Pieller, *Deutsche Frauenmystik im XIII. Jahrhundert* (Vienna, 1928); and Joseph Otto Plassmann, *Vom göttlichen Reichtum der Seele. Altflämische Frauenmystik.* (Düsseldorf: Diederichs, 1951).

11. See also Rosalynn Voaden and Stephanie Volf, "Visions of My Youth: Representations of the Childhood of Medieval Visionaries," *Gender and History* 12, no. 3 (2000).

12. Volken, *Visions, Revelations and the Church*, 158.

13. Ibid., 160.

14. Mt 18:3: "I tell you the truth, unless you change and become like little children, you will never enter the kingdom of heaven."

15. Bernard McGinn, " 'Trumpets of the Mysteries of God': Prophetesses in Late Medieval Christianity," in *Propheten und Prophezeiungen Prophets and Prophecies*, edited by Tilo Schabert and Matthias Riedl (Würzburg: Königshausen und Neumann, 2005), 127.

16. Ibid.

17. Ibid.

18. Volken, *Visions, Revelations and the Church*, 160.

19. Ibid., 162.

20. Lisa J. Schwebel, *Apparitions, Healings, and Weeping Madonnas: Christianity and the Paranormal* (New York: Paulist Press, 2004), 126.

21. "Ist eine Seele noch nicht zur mystischen Verlobung gelangt, hat sie also noch nie in Ekstase die mystische Liebesvereinigung auch nur vorübergehend genossen, so ist alles, was sie an Visionen und Offenbarungen vorbringt, als Täuschung anzusehen." Konrad Hock, "Johannes vom Kreuz und die Nebenerscheinungen der Mystik," *Theologisch-Praktische Quartalschrift* 78 (1925): 703.

22. Gertrude the Great of Helfta, *The Herald of God's Loving Kindness*, translated by Alexandra Barratt (Kalamazoo, Mich.: Cistercian Publications, 1999), L. II, xxiif.

23. Volken, *Visions, Revelations and the Church*, 164.

24. Ibid.

25. Faustina Kowalska, *Divine Mercy in My Soul* (Stockbridge: Marian Press, 1987), 16.

26. "Une révélation met son sujet—le prophète ou le voyant—dans un état d'exception et par là, nécessairement, en opposition à la vie ordinaire, et à une mentalité qui s'installe dans l'ordinaire et qui y ramène, comme la loi de la pesanteur, tout ce qui le dépasse." (Shortcomings in published English translation). Laurent Volken, *Les Révélations dans l'Église* (Mulhouse: Salvator, 1961), 169.

27. Léon-Joseph-Marie Cros, *Histoire de Notre-Dame de Lourdes, d'après les Documents et les Témoins*, (Paris: Beauchesne, 1925): 310.

28. Randall Sullivan, *The Miracle Detective: An Investigation of Holy Visions* (New York: Atlantic Monthly Press, 2004), 103.

29. For Lourdes, see Suzanne K. Kaufman, *Consuming Visions: Mass Culture and the Lourdes Shrine* (Ithaca: Cornell University Press, 2005), 104f; Rosemary Mahoney, *The Singular Pilgrim: Travels on Sacred Ground* (Boston: Houghton Mifflin, 2003), 63. For Medjugorie, see Sullivan, *The Miracle Detective*, 217f.

30. René Laurentin, *The Apparitions of the Blessed Virgin Mary Today* (Dublin: Veritas, 1990), 53.

31. Pio Bello Ricardo Bishop of Los Teques, Pastoral *Instruction on the Apparitions of the Blessed Virgin Mary in Finca Betania,*, November 21, 1987, Los Teques, 12. Available from http://www.catholicculture.org/docs/doc_view.cfm?recnum=5245.

32. Laurentin, *The Apparitions of the Blessed Virgin Mary Today*, 86.

33. Ibid., 84.

34. Ingvar Fogelqvist, *Apostasy and Reform in the revelations of St. Birgitta* (Stockholm: Almqvist & Wiksell International, 1993), 32.

35. *AAS 12* (1920) 113.

36. *AAS 43* (1951) 561.

37. *AAS 26* (1934) 433.

38. J. C. Tierney and Michael P. Duricy, *Marian Apparitions of the Twentieth Century*, available from http://www.udayton.edu/mary/resources/aprtable.html.

39. See Kenneth L. Woodward, *Making Saints: How the Catholic Church Determines Who Becomes a Saint, Who Doesn't, and Why* (New York: Simon and Schuster, 1990).

40. Bonnie S. Anderson and Judith P. Zinsser, *A History of Their Own: Women in Europe from Prehistory to the Present*, rev. ed. (Oxford: Oxford University Press, 2000), 188.

41. Anna Silvas, *Jutta and Hildegard: The Biographical Sources* (University Park: Pennsylvania State University Press, 1999), 253.

42. F. J. Baumgartner, "'I Will Observe Absolute and Perpetual Secrecy': The Historical Background of the Rigid Secrecy Found in Papal Elections," *Catholic Historical Review* 89, no. 2 (2003): 169.

43. Fogelqvist, *Apostasy and Reform in the Revelations of St. Birgitta*, 246.

44. Ibid., 169.

45. Volken, *Visions, Revelations and the Church*, 85.

46. "Nulle ne les a plus combattues que Jean Gerson." Pierre Adnès, "Visions," in *Dictionnaire de Spiritualité Ascétique et Mystique: Doctrine et Histoire*, edited by M. Viller et al. (Paris: Beauchesne, 1993), 980. For Gerson's theology of discernment, see Elliott, "Seeing Double." *American Historical Review* 107, no. 1 (2002).

47. Joseph Schumacher, *Der apostolische Abschluss der Offenbarung Gottes* (Freiburg: Herder, 1979), 73.

48. 1 Thes 5:19–21.

49. "Aujourd'hui, Vatican II, qui a revalorisé le peuple de Dieu, son initiative, sa participation, sa coresponsabilité, invite à réaliser le discernement de manière collective, éducative et pastorale. Que le peuple concerné soit associé autant que possible, à l'exercice du discernement et du jugement critique." René Laurentin, "Fonction et Statut des Apparitions," in *Vraies et Fausses Apparitions dans l'Église: Exposés*, edited by Bernard Billet (Paris: Bellarmin, 1976), 197.

50. Hill, *New Testament Prophecy*, 192.

51. *Adv. Haer.* 3.9.9. An English translation is *St. Irenaeus of Lyons Against the Heresies*, translated by Dominic J. Unger (New York: Paulist Press, 1992).

52. Karl Rahner, "Les Révélations Privées: Quelques Remarques Théologiques," *Revue d'Ascétique et Mystique* 25 (1949): 507; Rahner, *Visions and Prophecies*, 20.

53. Rahner, "Les Révélations Privées," 507; Rahner, *Visions and Prophecies*, 20.

54. Lk 13:34 and Mt 23:37–39.

55. 1 Thes 5:19–21.

CHAPTER 10

1. Lk 2:34.

2. 1 Cor 14:1.

3. 1 Cor 12:7.

4. 1 Cor 14:3–4.

5. Rino Fisichella, "Prophecy," in *Dictionary of Fundamental Theology*, edited by René Latourelle and Rino Fisichella (New York: Crossroad, 1995), 788.

6. 1 John 4:1.

7. Jared Wicks, "Loci Theologici," in Latourelle and Fisichella, *Dictionary of Fundamental Theology*, 606.

8. Christian Pesch, "De Legato Divino," in *Compendium Theologiae dogmaticae* (Freiburg, 1913), 54.

9. John 16:5–15.

References

Adam, A. K. M. *Postmodern Interpretations of the Bible: A Reader.* St. Louis: Chalice Press, 2001.

———. *What Is Postmodern Biblical Criticism?* (Guides to Biblical Scholarship. New Testament Series). Minneapolis: Fortress Press, 1995.

Adams, James Luther, and George K. Beach. *The Prophethood of all Believers.* Boston: Beacon Press, 1986.

Adnès, Pierre. "Révélations Privées." In *Dictionnaire de Spiritualité Ascétique et Mystique: Doctrine et Histoire,* edited by M. Viller, F. Cavallera, J. de Guibert, A. Rayaz, A. Derville, P. Lamarche, and A. Solignac. Paris: Beauchesne, 1987, 13: 482–92.

———. "Visions." In *Dictionnaire de Spiritualité Ascétique et Mystique: Doctrine et Histoire,* edited by M. Viller, F. Cavallera, J. de Guibert, A. Rayaz, A. Derville, P. Lamarche, and A. Solignac. Paris: Beauchesne, 1993, 16: 949–1002.

Alberigo, Giuseppe. *Conciliorum Oecumenicorum Decreta.* 3rd ed. Bologna: Istituto per le scienze religiose, 1973.

Albright, Judith M. *Our Lady at Garabandal.* Milford: Faith Publications, 1992.

Alkier, Stefan. *Wunder und Wirklichkeit in den Briefen des Apostels Paulus: Ein Beitrag zu einem Wunderverständnis jenseits von Entmythologisierung und Rehistorisierung.* (Wissenschaftliche Untersuchungen zum Neuen Testament; 134). Tübingen: Mohr, 2001.

Althaus, Paul. *Die christliche Wahrheit: Lehrbuch der Dogmatik.* 5th ed. Gütersloh: Gütersloher Verlagshaus Gerd Mohn, 1959.

Anderson, Bonnie S., and Judith P. Zinsser. *A History of Their Own: Women in Europe from Prehistory to the Present.* Rev. ed. Oxford: Oxford University Press, 2000.

Anderson, Wendy Love. "Free Spirits, Presumptuous Women, and False Prophets." Ph.D. diss., University of Chicago, 2002.

Andersson, Aron. *Boken om Birgitta, Helgon och Profet*. Vadstena: Birgittasystrarna i Rom, 1977.

Andersson, Lotten. *Europe's Patron Saint Brings Separated Churches Together*. Available from http://www.svenskakyrkan.se/tcrot/press/eng/99/Heliga_Birgitta.htm. 1999 [accessed 13 July 2005].

Andrés Martín, Melquiades. *La Teología Española en el Siglo XVI*. Madrid: La Editorial Católica, 1976.

Annales Fuldenses. Monumenta Germaniae Historica Scriptores 1, 847.

Annales Palidenses. Monumenta Germaniae Historica Scriptores 16, 1158.

Anselm of Canterbury. *Miraculum de Conceptione Sanctae Mariae*. Edited by J. P. Migne. In *Patrologia Latina: The Full Text Database*, 221 vols. Chadwyck-Healey, 1996.

Apolito, Paolo. *The Internet and the Madonna: Religious Visionary Experience on the Web*. (Religion and Postmodernism). Chicago: University of Chicago Press, 2005.

Augrain, Charles, and Theodore A. Koehler, eds. *Kecharitoméne: Mélanges Rene Laurentin*. Paris: Desclee, 1990.

Aune, David Edward. *Prophecy in Early Christianity and the Ancient Mediterranean World*. Grand Rapids: Eerdmans, 1983.

———. *Revelation 1–5*. (Word Biblical Commentary 52a). Nashville: Nelson, 1997.

———. *Revelation 6–16*. (Word Biblical Commentary 52b). Nashville: Nelson, 1998.

———. *Revelation 17–22*. (Word Biblical Commentary 52c). Nashville: Nelson, 1998.

Baldermann, Ingo, Ernst Dassmann, and Ottmar Fuchs, eds. *Prophetie und Charisma*. (Jahrbuch für biblische Theologie 14). Neukirchen-Vluyn: Neukirchener Verlag, 1999.

Baldwin, Anne B. *Catherine of Siena: A Biography*. Huntington: Our Sunday Visitor, 1987.

Balic, Karel. "De Auctoritate Ecclesiae circa apparitiones seu Revelationes: Adnotationes ad encyclicam 'Pascendi' occasione primi centenari apparitionum Lourdensium." *Divinitas* 2 (1956): 85–103.

Ball, Ann, and Neil J. Roy. *Encyclopedia of Catholic Devotions and Practices*. Huntington: Our Sunday Visitor, 2003.

Balthasar, Hans Urs von. "La vita, la Missione Teologica e l'opera di Adrienne von Speyr." *Mistica oggettiva*, no. 35 (1989): 11–65.

———. *Pneuma und Institution*. (Skizzen zur Theologie 4). Einsiedeln: Johannes Verlag, 1967.

———. *Thomas und die Charismatik: Kommentar zu Thomas von Aquin, Summa Theologica Quaestiones II II 171–182*. Einsiedeln: Johannes Verlag, 1996.

———. *Verbum caro*. (Skizzen zur Theologie 1). Einsiedeln: Johannes Verlag, 1960.

Barackman, Floyd H. *Practical Christian Theology: Examining the Great Doctrines of the Faith*. 4th ed. Grand Rapids: Kregel, 2001.

Barth, Karl. *Ad Limina Apostolorum*. Zurich: EVZ-Verlag, 1967.

———. *Church Dogmatics*. Translated by Geoffrey William Bromiley. 2nd ed. Edinburgh: Clark, 1975.

Bauckham, Richard. *The Theology of the Book of Revelation*. (New Testament Theology Series). Cambridge: Cambridge University Press, 1993.

Baue, Frederic W. *The Spiritual Society: What Lurks beyond Postmodernism?* Wheaton: Crossway Books, 2001.

Baumgartner, F. J. "'I Will Observe Absolute and Perpetual Secrecy': The Historical Background of the Rigid Secrecy Found in Papal Elections." *Catholic Historical Review* 89, no. 2 (2003): 165–81.

Beinert, Wolfgang. "Depositum Fidei." In *Lexikon für Theologie und Kirche*, edited by Michael Buchberger, Heinrich Suso Brechter, Karl Rahner, and Josef Höfer. 3rd ed. Freiburg: Herder, 1995, 3: 99–102.

Benedict XIV. *Benedicti papae XIV doctrina de servorum Dei beatificatione et beatorum canonizatione in synopsim redacta ab emm. de Azevedo*. Brussels: Typis Societatis belgicae de propagandis bonis libris, 1840.

Benoit, Pierre, and Paul Synave. *Prophecy and Inspiration: A Commentary on the Summa Theologica II-II, Questions 171–178*. New York: Desclee, 1961.

Benz, Ernst. *Die Vision: Erfahrungsformen und Bilderwelt*. Stuttgart: Klett, 1969.

Bertetto, Domenico. *Acta Mariana Joannis PP. XXIII*. (Bibliotheca Theologica Salesiana 2, 1). Zurich: PAS-Verlag, 1964

Bianchi, Enzo, ed. *La Profezia*. Bologna: Dehoniane, 2000.

Billet, Bernard, ed. *Vraies et Fausses Apparitions dans l'Église*. 2nd ed. Paris, Montréal: P. Lethielleux, Bellarmin, 1976.

Blanco, M. Martin del. *Visiones místicas en Santa Teresa de Jesús*. Burgos, 1969.

Blenkinsopp, Joseph. *Prophecy and Canon: A Contribution to the Study of Jewish Origins*. Notre Dame: University of Notre Dame Press, 1977.

Blount, Brian K. *Cultural Interpretation: Reorienting New Testament Criticism*. Minneapolis: Fortress Press, 1995.

Blum, Georg Günter. *Offenbarung und Überlieferung: Die dogmatische Konstitution Dei Verbum des II. Vaticanums im Lichte altkirchlicher und moderner Theologie*. (Forschungen zur systematischen und ökumenischen Theologie 28). Göttingen: Vandenhoeck and Ruprecht, 1971.

Bonaventure. *Itinerarium mentis in Deum*. Translated by Zachary Hayes. Edited by Philotheus Boehner. Rev. and expanded ed. Saint Bonaventure: Franciscan Institute Publications, Saint Bonaventure University, 2002.

Bondi, Roberta C., and Linda Kulzer. *Benedict in the World: Portraits of Monastic Oblates*. Collegeville: Liturgical Press, 2002.

Bord, André, ed. *Mémoire et Espérance chez Jean de la Croix*. (Bibliothèque de Spiritualité 8). Paris: Beauchesne, 1971.

Boring, Eugene. *The Continuing Voice of Jesus: Christian Prophecy and the Gospel Tradition*. Louisville: Westminster, 1991.

———. *Sayings of the Risen Jesus: Christian Prophecy in the Synoptic Tradition*. (Society for New Testament Studies 46). Cambridge: Cambridge University Press, 1982.

———. "What Are We Looking For? Toward a Definition of the Term 'Christian Prophet.'" *Society of Biblical Literature 1973 Seminar Papers 2* (1973): 135–54.

Børresen, Kari Elisabeth. "Birgitta's Godlanguage: Exemplary Intention, Inapplicable Content." In *Birgitta: Hendes værk og hendes klostre i Norden*, edited by Tore Nyberg. Odense: Odense University Press, 1991, 21–72.

Bouflet, Joaquim. *Faussaires de Dieu*. Paris: Presses de la Renaissance, 2000.

Brasher, Brenda E. *Give Me That Online Religion*. San Francisco: Jossey-Bass, 2001.

Bromiley, Geoffrey William, Erwin Fahlbusch, Jan Milic Lochman, John Mbiti, Jaroslav Pelikan, and Lukas Vischer, eds. *The Encyclopedia of Christianity*. Vol. 3. Grand Rapids, Mich.: Eerdmans, 2003.

Brown, Peter Robert Lamont. *The Body and Society: Men, Women, and Sexual Renunciation in Early Christianity*. (Lectures on the History of Religions; New Ser., no. 13). New York: Columbia University Press, 1988.

Brunner, Emil. *Dogmatics: The Christian Doctrine of the Church, Faith and the Consummation*. 3 vols. Vol. 3. Cambridge: Clarke, 2001.

Buber, Martin. *Between Man and Man*. London: Collins, 1961.

Bulst, Werner. *Offenbarung: Biblischer und theologischer Begriff*. 1st ed. Düsseldorf: Patmos-Verlag, 1960.

———. *Revelation*. New York: Sheed and Ward, 1965.

Bunt, Gary. *The Good Web Guide: World Religions*. London: Good Web Guide, 2001.

———. *Virtually Islamic: Computer-Mediated Communication and Cyber Islamic Environments*. Cardiff: University of Wales Press, 2000.

Burtchaell, James Tunstead. "Community Experience as a Source of Christian Ethics." In *From Christ to the World: Introductory Readings in Christian Ethics*, edited by Wayne G. Boulton, Allen Verhey, and Thomas D. Kennedy. Grand Rapids: Eerdmans, 1994, 64–78.

Butler, Alban, ed. *Butler's Lives of the Saints*. Edited by Michael J. Walsh. Concise ed. San Francisco: Harper and Row, 1985.

Butler, Edward Cuthbert. *Western Mysticism: The Teaching of Augustine, Gregory and Bernard on Contemplation and Contemplative Life*. 3rd ed. London: Constable, 1967.

Buttiglione, Rocco. *Karol Wojtyla: The Thought of the Man Who Became Pope John Paul II*. Grand Rapids: Eerdmans, 1997.

Caciola, Nancy. *Discerning Spirits: Divine and Demonic Possession in the Middle Ages*. (Conjunctions of Religion & Power in the Medieval Past). Ithaca: Cornell University Press, 2003.

Calabrese, Gianfranco, ed. *Chiesa e Profezia*. Rome: Edizioni dehoniane, 1996.

Campenhausen, Hans von. *Ecclesiastical Authority and Spiritual Power in the Church of the First Three Centuries*. Translated by John Austin Baker. London: Black, 1969.

Caniato, Riccardo, and Vincenzo Sansonetti. *Maria, Alba del Terzo Millennio: Il Dono di Medjugorje*. 6th ed. Milan: Ares, 2002.

Cano, Francisco Melchior. *Opera*. Rome, 1890.

Cantoni, Pietro. "Lo 'Status' Teologico del Messaggio di Fatima." *Cristianità* 313 (2002).

Caputo, John D. *The Prayers and Tears of Jacques Derrida: Religion without Religion*. (The Indiana Series in the Philosophy of Religion). Bloomington: Indiana University Press, 1997.

Carruthers, Mary. *The Craft of Thought: Meditation, Rhetoric, and the Making of Images, 400–1200.* (Cambridge Studies in Medieval Literature 34). Cambridge: Cambridge University Press, 1998.

Cartledge, Mark. "Charismatic Theology: Approaches and Themes." *Journal of Beliefs and Values* 25, no. 2 (2004): 177–90.

Castellano Cervera, Jesús. "The Church in the Life and in the Thought of Saint Bridget." In *Saint Bridget: Prophetess of New Ages, Proceedings of the International Study Meeting, Rome, October 3–7, 1991.* Rome: Casa Generalizia Suore Santa Brigida, 1993, 241–66.

Congregation for the Doctrine of Faith. *The Message of Fatima.* Vatican City: Libreria Editrice Vaticana, 2000.

Congregation for the Doctrine of Faith and Pontifical Biblical Commission. *Instruction Concerning the Historical Truth of the Gospels.* Edited by Benjamin N. Wambacq. Available at http://catholic-resources.org/ChurchDocs/PBC_Interp-FullText.htm.

Congregation for the Doctrine of Faith and Pontifical Biblical Commission. *The Interpretation of the Bible in the Church.* Vatican City: Libreria Editrice Vaticana, 1993.

Chadwick, Henry. *The Early Church.* (The Pelican History of the Church). Harmondsworth: Penguin, 1967.

Chadwick, Owen. *A History of the Popes, 1830–1914.* (Oxford History of the Christian Church). Oxford: Oxford University Press, 1998.

Chasle, Louis. *Schwester Maria vom göttlichem Herzen Droste zu Vischering.* Freiburg: Herder, 1929

Chenu, Bruno. *L'Urgence Prophétique: Dieu au Défi de l'Histoire.* 2nd ed. Paris: Bayard Editions, 1997.

Chiron, Yves. *Enquête sur les Apparitions de la Vierge.* Paris: Perrin-Mame, 1995.

Collins, John Joseph. *The Apocalyptic Vision of the Book of Daniel.* (Harvard Semitic Monograph Series 16). Missoula: Scholars Press, 1977.

Congar, Yves. "La Crédibilité des Révélations Privées." *Supplément de la Vie Spirituelle* 53 (1937): 29–48.

———. "La Crédibilité des Révélations Privées." In *Sainte église: Études et approches ecclésiologiques,* edited by Yves Congar. (Unam Sanctam 41). Paris: Editions du Cerf, 1963, 375–92.

———. *Tradition and Traditions: An Historical and a Theological Essay.* Translated by Michael Naseby and Thomas Rainborough. New York: Macmillan, 1967.

Conley, John J., and Joseph W. Koterski. *Prophecy and Diplomacy: The Moral Doctrine of John Paul II: A Jesuit Symposium.* Bronx: Fordham University Press, 1999.

Copray, Norbert. *Kommunikation und Offenbarung: Philosophische und theologische Auseinandersetzungen auf dem Weg zu einer Fundamentaltheorie der menschlichen Kommunikation.* (Themen und Thesen der Theologie 8). Düsseldorf: Patmos, 1983.

Cothenet, Edouard. "Les Prophètes Chrétiens comme Exégètes charismatiques de l'Écriture." In *Prophetic Vocation in the New Testament and Today,* edited by J. Panagopoulos. (New Testament Studies 45). Leiden: Brill, 1977, 77–102.

————. "Prophétisme dans le Nouveau Testament." In *Dictionnaire de la Bible, Supplement,* edited by Louis Pirot. Vol. 8. Paris: Letouzey et Ané, 1972, 1222–337.

Courcelle, Pierre. *Les Confessions de Saint Augustin dans la Tradition Littéraire.* Paris: Études Augustiniennes, 1963.

Crane, Sidney D. "The Gift of Prophecy in the New Testament: An Inductive Study in the Exercise and Meaning of the Prophetic." Ph.D. diss., Princeton University, 1962.

Crone, Theodore. M. *Early Christian Prophecy: A Study of Its Origin and Function.* Baltimore: St. Mary's University Press, 1973.

Cros, Léon-Joseph-Marie. *Histoire de Notre-Dame de Lourdes, d'après les Documents et les Témoins.* 3 vols. Paris: Beauchesne, 1925

Crowe, Jerome. *From Jerusalem to Antioch: The Gospel across Cultures.* Collegeville: Liturgical Press, 1997.

Cullmann, Oscar. *Salvation in History.* New York: Harper and Row, 1967.

Czakanski, Tadeusz. "The Christian Prophets and the Charism of Prophecy in the New Testament and the Origins of the Church." Ph.D. diss., Rome: Università Lateranense, 1987.

Damaskinos, Métropolite. "Intervention du Métropolite Damaskinos." *Choisir* 2 (1996): 11–14.

Dautzenberg, Gerhard. "Prophetie bei Paulus." In *Prophetie und Charisma,* edited by Ingo Baldermann, Ernst Dassmann, and Ottmar Fuchs. (Jahrbuch für biblische Theologie 14). Neukirchen-Vluyn: Neukirchener Verlag, 1999, 55–70.

————. *Urchristliche Prophetie: Ihre Erforschung, ihre Voraussetzungen im Judentum und ihre Struktur im ersten Korintherbrief.* (Beiträge zur Wissenschaft vom Alten und Neuen Testament 6, 4). Stuttgart: Kohlhammer, 1975.

Dawson, Lorne L., and Douglas E. Cowan, eds. *Religion Online: Finding Faith on the Internet.* New York: Routledge, 2004.

Denzinger, Heinrich, and Adolf Schönmetzer. *Enchiridion symbolorum, definitionum et declarationum de rebus fidei et morum.* 33rd ed. Barcinone: Herder, 1965.

Dermine, François-Marie. *Mistici, Veggenti e Medium.* Vatican City: Libreria Editrice Vaticana, 2002.

————. *Vassula Ryden: Indagine Critica.* Turin: Ediz. Elle Di Ci, Leumann, 1995.

Dervilles, André. "Paroles Intérieures." In *Dictionnaire de Spiritualité Ascétique et Mystique: Doctrine et Histoire,* edited by M. Viller, F. Cavallera, J. de Guibert, A. Rayaz, A. Derville, P. Lamarche, and A. Solignac. Paris: Beauchesne, 1982, 11:252–57.

Dhanis, E. "Sguardo su Fatima e Bilancio di una Discussione." *La Civiltà Cattolica* 104, no. 2 (1953): 392–406.

Diekamp, Franz. *Katholische Dogmatik nach den Grundsätzen des heiligen Thomas.* Münster Westfalen: Aschendorff, 1958.

Dierkens, Alain. *Apparitions et Miracles.* (Problèmes d'histoire des religions 2). Brussels: Editions de l'Universite de Bruxelles, 1991.

Dinzelbacher, Peter. *Mittelalterliche Visionsliteratur: Eine Anthologie.* Darmstadt: Wissenschaftliche Buchgesellschaft, 1989.

————. *"Revelationes."* (Typologie des Sources du Moyen Age Occidental 57). Turnhout: Brepols, 1991.

—. "Saint Bridget and Mysticism of Her Time." In *Saint Bridget: Prophetess of New Ages. Proceedings of the International Study Meeting, Rome, October 3–7, 1991.* Rome: Casa Generalizia Suore Santa Brigida, 1993, 338–72.

—. *Vision und Visionsliteratur im Mittelalter.* (Monographien zur Geschichte des Mittelalters 23). Stuttgart: Hiersemann, 1981.

Dinzelbacher, Peter, and Dieter R. Bauer, eds. *Frauenmystik im Mittelalter.* Ostfildern bei Stuttgart: Schwabenverlag, 1985.

—, eds. *Religiöse Frauenbewegungen und mystische Frömmigkeit im Mittelalter.* Vienna: Böhlau, 1988.

Dodds, Eric Robertson. *Pagan and Christian in an Age of Anxiety: Some Aspects of Religious Experience from Marcus Aurelius to Constantine.* (Wiles Lectures 1963). Cambridge: Cambridge University Press, 1991.

Dore, Michael. *Rome et Vassula.* Hauteville: Parvis, 1996.

Doronzo, Emmanuel. *Theologia Dogmatica.* Washington, D.C: Catholic University of America, 1966.

Dublanchy, E. "Dépot de la Foi." In *Dictionnaire de Théologie Catholique.* Paris, 1951.

Dulles, Avery Robert. *The Assurance of Things Hoped For: A Theology of Christian Faith.* Oxford: Oxford University Press, 1994.

—. *Models of Revelation.* Garden City: Doubleday, 1983.

Dunn, James. *Jesus and the Spirit: A Study of the Religious and Charismatic Experience of Jesus and the First Christians as Reflected in the New Testament.* Grand Rapids: Eerdmans, 1997.

Dunn, James D. G. *Jesus Remembered.* Grand Rapids: Eerdmans, 2003.

Echeverria, Eduardo J. "The Gospel of Redemptive Suffering: Reflections on John Paul II's *Salvifici Doloris.*" In *Christian Faith and the Problem of Evil*, edited by Peter Van Inwagen. Grand Rapids, Mich.: Eerdmans, 2004, 111–47.

Edwards, Richard Alan. *A Theology of Q: Eschatology, Prophecy, and Wisdom.* Philadelphia: Fortress Press, 1976.

Ehrman, Bart D. *The Apostolic Fathers.* Cambridge: Harvard University Press, 2003.

—. *Jesus: Apocalyptic Prophet of the New Millennium.* Oxford: Oxford University Press, 1999.

—. *The New Testament: A Historical Introduction to the Early Christian Writings.* 3rd ed. Oxford: Oxford University Press, 2004.

Eliade, Mircea. *Mito e Realtà.* Roma: Borla Editore, 1985.

—. *Myth and Reality.* London: Allen and Unwin, 1964.

Elliott, Dyan. *Proving Woman: Female Spirituality and Inquisitional Culture in the Later Middle Ages.* Princeton: Princeton University Press, 2004.

—. "Seeing Double: John Gerson, the Discernment of Spirits, and Joan of Arc." *American Historical Review* 107, no. 1 (2002): 26–54.

Ellis, E. Earle. *Prophecy and Hermeneutic in Early Christianity: New Testament Essays.* (Wissenschaftliche Untersuchungen zum Neuen Testament 18). Tübingen: Mohr, 1978.

Ellis, Roger. "The Swedish Woman, the Widow, the Pilgrim and the Prophetess: Images of St. Bridget in the Canonization Sermon of Pope Boniface IX." In *Saint*

Bridget: Prophetess of New Ages, Proceedings of the International Study Meeting, Rome, October 3–7, 1991. Rome: Casa Generalizia Suore Santa Brigida, 1993, 93–120.

Engelbert, Pius. "Christusmystik in der Autobiographie des Rupert von Deutz." In *Mysterium Christi: Symbolgegenwart und theologische Bedeutung (Festschrift für Basil Studer)*, edited by M. Löhrer and E. Salmann. (Studia Anselmiana 116). Rome: Pontificio Ateneo S. Anselmo, 1995, 259–87.

Ephraïm, Frère. *Marthe: Une ou deux Choses que je sais d'Elle.* Paris: Lion de Juda, 1990.

Espinel, José Luis. *Profetismo Cristiano: Una Espiritualidad Evangélica.* (Glosas 13). Salamanca: Editorial San Esteban, 1990.

Essen, Georg. "Privatoffenbarungen." In *Lexikon für Theologie und Kirche*, edited by Michael Buchberger, Heinrich Suso Brechter, Karl Rahner, and Josef Höfer. Freiburg, 1999, 8: 603–4.

Eusebius. *Historia Ecclesiastica.* Available from http://www.ccel.org/fathers2/NPNF2-01/ Npnf2-01-10.htm#TopOfPage [accessed December 2005].

———. *Life of Constantine.* Translated by Averil Cameron and Stuart G. Hall. (Clarendon Ancient History Series). Oxford: Oxford University Press, 1999.

Evans, Craig A. "Paul as Prophet." In *Dictionary of Paul and His Letters*, edited by Gerald F. Hawthorne, Ralph P. Martin, and Daniel G. Reid. Downers Grove: Intervarsity Press, 1993, 762–65.

Evans, Michael. *Jesus, Fads, and the Media: The Passion and Popular Culture.* (Religion and Modern Culture). Philadelphia: Mason Crest, 2006.

Fanning, Steven. *Mystics of the Christian Tradition.* New York: Routledge, 2001.

Fascher, Erich. *Prophetes: Eine sprach- und religionsgeschichtliche Untersuchung.* Giessen: Töpelmann, 1927.

Fee, Gordon D. *God's Empowering Presence: The Holy Spirit in the Letters of Paul.* Peabody: Hendrickson, 1994.

Feiner, Johannes. "Die Vergegenwärtigung der Offenbarung durch die Kirche." In *Die Grundlagen heilsgeschichtlicher Dogmatik*, edited by Johannes Feiner and Magnus Löhrer. (Mysterium Salutis 1). Einsiedeln: Benziger, 1965, 497–544.

———. "Offenbarung und Kirche der Offenbarung." In *Die Grundlagen heils- geschichtlicher Dogmatik*, edited by Johannes Feiner and Magnus Löhrer. (Mysterium Salutis 1). Einsiedeln: Benziger, 1965, 497–544.

Finkenzeller, Josef. *Offenbarung und Theologie nach der Lehre des Johannes Duns Skotus: Eine historische und systematische Untersuchung.* (Beiträge zur Geschichte der Philosophie des Mittelalters 38). Münster: Aschendorff, 1961.

Fisichella, Rino. *Gesù di Nazaret: Profezia del Padre.* (Saggistica Paoline 1). Milan: Paoline, 2000.

———. "La profezia come segno della credibilità della Rivelazione." In *Gesù Rivelatore*, edited by Rino Fisichella. Casale Monferrato: Piemme, 1988, 208–26.

———. *La Rivelazione: Evento e Credibilità: Saggio di Teologia Fondamentale.* (Corso di Teologia Sistematica 2). Bologna: Edizioni Dehoniane Bologna, 1985.

———. "Prefazione." In *Le Rivelazioni Private nella Vita della Chiesa*, edited by Augustinus Suh. Bologna: Dehoniane, 2000.

———. "Prophecy." In *Dictionary of Fundamental Theology*, edited by René Latourelle and Rino Fisichella. New York: Crossroad, 1995, 788–98.

Flanders, Henry Jackson, David A. Smith, and Robert W. Crapps. *People of the Covenant: An Introduction to the Hebrew Bible*. 4th ed. Oxford: Oxford University Press, 1996.

Fogelqvist, Ingvar. *Apostasy and Reform in the Revelations of St. Birgitta*. (Bibliotheca theologiae practicae 51). Stockholm: Almqvist and Wiksell International, 1993.

Forbes, Christopher. *Prophecy and Inspired Speech in Early Christianity and its Hellenistic Environment*. Tübingen: Mohr, 1995.

Fraioli, Deborah A. *Joan of Arc: The Early Debate*. Woodbridge, Suffolk: Boydell Press, 2000.

Friedrich, Gerhard. "Prophets and Prophecies in the New Testament." In *Theological Dictionary of the New Testament*. Grand Rapids: Eerdmans, 1969, 6: 828–61.

Fries, Heinrich. "Die Offenbarung." In *Die Grundlagen heilsgeschichtlicher Dogmatik*, edited by Johannes Feiner and Magnus Loehrer. (Mysterium Salutis 1). Einsiedeln: Benziger, 1965, 159–238.

Gabriel, Karl, and Dietrich Wiederkehr. *Wie geschieht Tradition? Überlieferung im Lebensprozess der Kirche*. (Quaestiones Disputatae 133). Freiburg: Herder, 1991.

Gaffin, Richard B., Jr. "A Cessationist View." In *Are Miraculous Gifts for Today? Four Views*, edited by Wayne A. Grudem. Grand Rapids: Zondervan, 1996, 25–64.

Gaillardetz, Richard R. *By What Authority? A Primer on Scripture, the Magisterium, and the Sense of the Faithful*. Collegeville: Liturgical Press, 2003.

———. *Teaching with Authority: A Theology of the Magisterium in the Church*. (Theology and Life Series 41). Collegeville: Liturgical Press, 1997.

Galot, Jean. "Le Apparizioni Private nella Vita della Chiesa." *Civiltà Cattolica* 136, no. 2 (1985): 19–33.

Garvey, Mark. *Searching for Mary: An Exploration of Marian Apparitions across the United States*. New York: Plume, 1998.

Gassmann, Günther, ed. *Documentary History of Faith and Order, 1963–1993*. Geneva: WCC, 1993.

Gavrilyuk, Paul L. *The Suffering of the Impassible God: The Dialectics of Patristic Thought*. (Oxford Early Christian Studies). Oxford: Oxford University Press, 2004.

Geiselmann, Joseph Rupert. "Das Konzil von Trient über das Verhältnis der Heiligen Schrift und der nichtgeschriebenen Tradition." In *Die Mündliche Überlieferung: Beiträge zum Begriff der Tradition*, edited by Josef Rupert Geiselmann, Michael Schmaus, Heinrich Fries, and Heinrich Bacht. Munich: Heuber, 1957, 123–206.

Gentili, Antonio. *Profezie per il Terzo Millennio*. Milan: Àncora Editrice, 2000.

Gentry, Kenneth L. *The Charismatic Gift of Prophecy: A Reformed Response to Wayne Grudem*. Lakeland: Whitefiled Seminary Press, 1986.

Gertrude the Great of Helfta. *The Herald of God's Loving Kindness*. Translated by Alexandra Barratt. (Cistercian Fathers Series 63). Kalamazoo: Cistercian, 1999.

Gillespie, Thomas W. *The First Theologians: A Study in Early Christian Prophecy*. Grand Rapids: Eerdmans, 1994.

Goffman, Erving. *Asylums: Le Istituzioni Totali: La Condizione Sociale dei Malati di Mente e di Altri Internati*. Turin: Giulio Einaudi Editore, 1968.

Gössmann, Elisabeth. *Hildegard von Bingen: Versuche einer Annäherung*. Munich: Iudicium Verlag, 1995.

Goubert, Joseph. *Apparitions et Messages de la Sainte Vierge, de 1830 à nos Jours*. Paris: La Colombe, 1954.

Grabbe, Lester L. *Priests, Prophets, Diviners, Sages: A Socio-Historical Study of Religious Specialists in Ancient Israel*. Valley Forge: Trinity Press International, 1995.

Graf, Friedrich Wilhelm. "Vom Munus Propheticum Christi zum prophetischen Wachteramt der Kirche: Erwägungen zum Verhaltnis von Christologie und Ekklesiologie." *Zeitschrift für evangelische Ethik* 32, no. 2 (1988): 88–106.

Greeven, Heinrich. "Propheten, Lehrer, Vorsteher bei Paulus." *Zeitschrift für die neutestamentliche Wissenschaft* 44 (1952): 1–29.

———. "Propheten, Lehrer, Vorsteher bei Paulus: Zur Frage der 'Ämter' im Urchristentum." *Zeitschrift für die neutestamentliche Wissenschaft und die Kunde des Urchristentums* 44, no. 1–2 (1952–53): 1–43.

Gregory. *Life and Miracles of St. Benedict*. Collegeville: St. John's University Press, 1995.

Greinacher, Norbert. "Apostel, Propheten und Lehrer: Damals und Heute." *Theologische Quartalsschrift* 171 (1991): 49–63.

Gros, Jeffrey, and Joseph A. Burgess. *Building Unity: Ecumenical Dialogues with Roman Catholic Participation in the United States*. (Ecumenical Documents 4). New York: Paulist Press, 1989.

Grudem, Wayne A. *The Gift of Prophecy in the New Testament and Today*. Westchester: Crossway Books, 2000.

———. "A Response to Gerhard Dautzenberg." *Biblische Zeitschrift* 28 (1978): 253–70.

Gutiérrez, Gustavo. *Teología de la Liberación: Perspectivas*. Salamanca: Ediciones Sígueme, 1972.

Guy, Harold A. *New Testament Prophecy: Its Origin and Significance*. London: Epworth Press, 1947.

Hahn, Ferdinand. *The Titles of Jesus in Christology: Their History in Early Christianity*. London: Lutterworth, 1969.

Hallbäck, Geert. "The Earthly Jesus, the Gospel Genre and Types of Authority." In *The New Testament in Its Hellenistic Context*, edited by Gunnlaugur A. Jonsson. (Studia Theologica Islandica 10). Reykjavik: Gudfraedistofnun—Skalholtsutgafan, 1996, 135–45.

Hanson, Paul D. *The Dawn of Apocalyptic: The Historical and Sociological Roots of Jewish Apocalyptic Eschatology*. Rev. ed. Philadelphia: Fortress Press, 1979.

Häring, Bernhard. "Prophètes." In *Dictionnaire de la vie Chrétienne*. Paris, 1983, 905–12.

Harnack, Adolf von. *Die Mission und Ausbreitung des Christentums in den ersten drei Jahrhunderten*. 4th ed. 4 vols. Vol. 1. Leipzig: VMA-Verlag, 1924.

Hasenhüttel, Gotthold. *Charisma: Ordnungsprinzip der Kirche*. (Ökumenische Forschungen 5). Freiburg: Herder, 1969.

Heil, Christoph, ed. *Q 12:8–12: Confessing or Denying.* (Documenta Q). Louvain: Peeters, 1997.

———. *Q 22:28, 30: You Will Judge the Twelve Tribes of Israel.* (Documenta Q). Louvain: Peeters, 1998.

Heintz, Peter. *A Guide to Apparitions of Our Blessed Virgin Mary.* Sacramento: Gabriel Press, 1995.

Helland, Christopher. "Online Religion Religion Online and Virtual Communitas." In *Religion on the Internet: Research Prospects and Promises*, edited by J. K. Hadden and Douglas E. Cowan. London: JAI Press, 2000, 205–23.

Herrera, Robert A. *Silent Music: The Life, Work, and Thought of St. John of the Cross.* Grand Rapids: Eerdmans, 2004.

Hierzenberger, Gottfried, and Otto Nedomansky. *Erscheinungen und Botschaften der Gottesmutter Maria: Vollständige Dokumentation durch zwei Jahrtausende.* Augsburg: Bechtermünz Verlag, 1993.

Hildegard, Columba Hart, and Jane Bishop. *Scivias.* (Classics of Western spirituality). New York: Paulist Press, 1990.

Hill, Clifford. *Prophecy Past and Present: An Exploration of the Prophetic Ministry in the Bible and the Church Today.* Guildford: Eagle, 1995.

Hill, David. *New Testament Prophecy.* (New Foundations Theological Library). Atlanta: John Knox Press, 1979.

———. "On the Evidence for the Creative Role of Christian Prophets." *New Testament Studies* 20 (1973): 262–74.

———. "Prophecy and Prophets in the Revelation." *New Testament Studies* 18 (1971): 401–18.

Höcht, Johannes Maria. *Träger der Wundmale Christi: Eine Geschichte der bedeutendsten Stigmatisierten von Franziskus bis zur Gegenwart.* Wiesbaden: Credo-Verlag, 1952.

Hock, Konrad. "Johannes vom Kreuz und die Nebenerscheinungen der Mystik." *Theol. und prakt. Quartalschrift* 78 (1925): 506–19; 698–705.

Holstein, Henri. "Les Apparitions Mariales." *Maria* 5 (1955): 757–78.

Holtz, Traugott. "Zum Selbstverständnis des Apostels Paulus." *Theologische Literaturzeitung* 91 (1966): 321–30.

Hooker, Morna Dorothy. *The Signs of a Prophet: The Prophetic Actions of Jesus.* Harrisburg: Trinity Press International, 1997.

Houston, Walter. "New Testament Prophecy and the Gospel Tradition." Ph.D. diss., Mansfield College, Oxford University, 1973.

Hurtado, Larry W. *Lord Jesus Christ: Devotion to Jesus in Earliest Christianity.* Grand Rapids: Eerdmans, 2003.

Hvidt, Niels Christian. "Christian Prophecy: Actualizing Revelation." In *Pax in virtute*, edited by Francesco Lepore and Donato D'Agostino. Rome: Libreria Editrice Vaticana, 2003, 177–96.

———. "Christian Prophecy and Birgitta of Vadstena." *Birgittiana* 16 (2003): 139–59.

———. "De l'Ancien Testament à l'Eglise." In *La Voix des Prophètes*. Paris: Famille Chrétienne, 2000, 40–55.

———. "Les Critères de Discernement." In *La Voix des Prophètes*. Paris: Famille Chrétienne, 2000, 84–93.

———. "Profeti og Åbenbaring." Ph.D. diss., University of Copenhagen, 1997.

———. "Prophecy and Revelation: A Theological Survey on the Problem of Christian Prophecy." *Studia Theologica* 52, no. 2 (1998): 147–61.

———. "Så siger Herren!" *Teol-information* (winter 1998).

———. "Vassula: A Contemporary Christian Prophet?" *Scriptorium* 5 (1998): 19–21.

Irenaeus. *St. Irenaeus of Lyons Against the Heresies*. Translated by Dominic J. Unger. (Ancient Christian Writers 55). New York: Paulist Press, 1992.

Isichei, Elizabeth Allo. *A History of Christianity in Africa: From Antiquity to the Present*. Grand Rapids, Mich.: Eerdmans, 1995.

Jenkins, Philip. "After the Next Christendom." *International Bulletin of Missionary Research* 28, no. 1 (2004): 20–22.

———. *The Next Christendom: The Rise of Global Christianity*. New York: Oxford University Press, 2002.

———. "The Next Christianity." *Atlantic Monthly* 290, no. 3 (2002): 53–68.

Jewett, Paul King. *Emil Brunner's Concept of Revelation*. London: Clarke, 1954.

John, C. J. "Report of Vassula Rydén's Meetings in India, Sri Lanka, and Bangladesh 2002." *TLIG Forum*. Available from www.tlig.info/forum/forum507.html.2002 [accessed 22 May 2005].

John of the Cross. *The Collected Works of Saint John of the Cross*. Translated by Kieran Kavanaugh and Otilio Rodriguez. Washington, D.C.: Institute of Carmelite Studies, 1991.

John Paul II. *Ad tuendam fidem: Apostolic Letter Motu proprio of Pope John Paul II: By Which Certain Norms Are Inserted into the Code of Canon Law and into the Code of Canons of the Eastern Churches*. Boston: Pauline Books and Media, 1998.

———. *Apostolic Letter, Issued Motu Proprio, Proclaiming Saint Bridget of Sweden, Saint Catherine of Siena and Saint Teresa Benedicta of the Cross Co-Patronesses of Europe*. Available from www.vatican.va/holy_father/john_paul_ii/motu_proprio/ documents/hf_jp-ii_motu-proprio_01101999_co-patronesses-europe_en.html [accessed May 2006].

———. *Apostolic Letter of His Holiness Pope John Paul II on Reserving Priestly Ordination to Men Alone*. Washington, D.C.: Office for Publishing and Promotion Services, United States Catholic Conference, 1994.

———. *Encyclical Letter Redemptoris Missio of the Supreme Pontiff John Paul II on the Permanent Validity of the Church's Missionary Mandate*. Washington, D.C.: United States Catholic Conference, 1990.

———. "Message of the Holy Father for the Thirty-sixth World Communications Day. Theme: Internet: A New Forum for Proclaiming the Gospel." In *Pontifical Council for Social Communications*. Available from http://www.vatican.va/holy_ father/john_paul_ii/messages/communications/documents/hf_jp-ii_mes_ 20020122_world-communications-day_en.html. 2002 [accessed 9 July 2005].

———. *Sources of Renewal: The Implementation of the Second Vatican Council*. San Francisco: Harper and Row, 1980.

Justin Martyr. "Writings of Justin Martyr." In *Ante-Nicene Fathers 1*. New Advent. Available from http://www.newadvent.org/fathers/1885 [accessed 16 June 2005].

Kahl, Werner. "Überlegungen zu einer Interkulturellen Verständigung über Neutestamentliche Wunder." *Zeitschrift für Missionswissenschaft und Religionswissenschaft* 82, no. 2 (1998): 98–107.

Käsemann, Ernst. "An Apologia for Primitive Christian Eschatology." In *Essays on New Testament Themes*. (Studies in Biblical Theology 42). Naperville: Allenson, 1964.

Kaufman, Suzanne K. *Consuming Visions: Mass Culture and the Lourdes Shrine*. Ithaca: Cornell University Press, 2005.

Kelber, Werner H. *The Oral and the Written Gospel: The Hermeneutics of Speaking and Writing in the Synoptic Tradition, Mark, Paul, and Q*. Philadelphia: Fortress Press, 1983.

Kelsey, Morton T. *Discernment: A Study in Ecstasy and Evil*. New York: Paulist Press, 1978.

———. *God, Dreams, and Revelation: A Christian Interpretation of Dreams*. Rev. and expanded ed. Minneapolis: Augsburg, 1991.

Kemp, Eric W. *Canonization and Authority in the Western Church*. London: Oxford University Press, 1948.

Kerby-Fulton, K. "Prophet and Reformer: Smoke in the Vineyard." In *Voice of the Living Light: Hildegard of Bingen and Her World*, edited by Barbara Newman. Berkeley: University of California Press, 1998, 70–90.

Kerby-Fulton, Kathryn. *Reformist Apocalypticism and Piers Plowman*. (Cambridge Studies in Medieval Literature 7). Cambridge: Cambridge University Press, 1990.

Kerkhofs, Louis Joseph. *Notre-Dame de Banneux: Études et Documents*. 2nd ed. Tournai: Casterman, 1954.

Kern, Walter, Hermann Josef Pottmeyer, and Max Seckler, eds. *Handbuch der Fundamentaltheologie*. Freiburg: Herder, 1985.

Kezel, Albert Ryle, ed. *Birgitta of Sweden: Life and Selected Revelations*. (The Classics of Western Spirituality). New York: Paulist Press, 1990.

Khoury, Adel Theodore, and Dirk Grothues. *Zur Unterscheidung der Geister*. Altenberge: Oros, 1994.

Kierkegaard, Søren. *Philosophical Fragments, Johannes Climacus*. Princeton: Princeton University Press, 1985.

King, Karen L. "Prophetic Power and Women's Authority: The Case of the *Gospel of Mary (Magdalene)*." In *Women Preachers and Prophets through Two Millennia of Christianity*, edited by Pamela J. Walker and Beverly Mayne Kienzle. Berkeley: University of California Press, 1998, 21–41.

King-Lenzmeier, Anne H. *Hildegard of Bingen: An Integrated Vision*. Collegeville: Liturgical Press, 2001.

Klanac, Daria. *Medjugorje: Réponses aux Objections*. Paris: Sarment, 2001.

Koch, Klaus. "Propheten/Prophetie II." In *Theologische Realenzyklopädie*, edited by Gerhard Möller and Gerhard Krause. Berlin: de Gruyter, 1997, 27:473–99.

Kolb, (Texts and Studies in Reformation and Post-Reformation Thought). Robert. *Martin Luther as Prophet, Teacher, Hero: Images of the Reformer, 1520–1620.* Grand Rapids: Baker Books, 1999.

Körner, Bernhard. "Melchior Cano." In *Lexikon für Theologie und Kirche,* edited by Michael Buchberger, Heinrich Suso Brechter, Karl Rahner, and Josef Höfer. Vol. 2. Freiburg, 1994, 924–25.

———, ed. *Melchior Cano, De locis theologicis: Ein Beitrag zur theologischen Erkenntnislehre.* Graz: Styria Medienservice Verlag Ulrich Moser, 1994.

Kowalska, Faustina. *Divine Mercy in My Soul.* Stockbridge: Marian Press, 1987.

Kraft, Heinrich. "Vom Ende der urchristlichen Prophetie." In *Prophetic Vocation in the New Testament and Today,* edited by J. Panagopoulos. (Supplements to Novum Testamentum 45). Leiden: Brill, 1977, 162–85.

Labriolle, Pierre Champagne de. *Les Sources de l'Histoire du Montanisme: Textes Grecs, Latins, Syriaques.* Paris: Ernest Leroux, 1913.

Ladd, George Eldon. *A Commentary on the Revelation of John.* Grand Rapids: Eerdmans, 1972.

Lambertini, Prospero. *Doctrina de servorum Dei beatificatione et canonizatione in synopsim redacta.* Rome, 1749.

Latourelle, René. *Théologie de la Révélation.* (Recherches de Philosophie et de Theologie Publiees par les Facultes S. J. de Montreal 15). Brussels: Desclee de Brouwer, 1969.

———. *Theology of Revelation, Including a Commentary on the Constitution "Dei verbum" of Vatican II.* 2nd ed. Staten Island: Alba House, 1967.

Laurentin, René. *The Apparitions of the Blessed Virgin Mary Today.* Dublin: Veritas, 1990.

———. "Fonction et Statut des Apparitions." In *Vraies et Fausses Apparitions dans l'Église: Exposés,* edited by Bernard Billet. 2nd ed. Paris / Montréal: P. Lethielleux / Bellarmin, 1976, 153–207.

———. *La Vierge Apparaît-Elle à Medjugorje?* 5th ed. Paris: de Guibert, 2002.

———. *Le Apparizioni della Vergine si Moltiplicano.* Casale Monferrato: Piemme, 1989.

———. *When God Gives a Sign.* Independence, Mo.: Trinitas, 1993.

LeGates, Marlene. *In Their Time: A History of Feminism in Western Society.* New York: Routledge, 2001.

Lennerz, Heinrich. "Scriptura Sola?" *Gregoriana* 40 (1959): 38–53.

———. "Sine Scripto Traditiones." *Gregoriana* 40 (1959): 624–35.

Leo XIII. *Encyclical "Annum Sacrum" of Twenty-fifth May 1899.* (Leonis XIII P. M. Acta 19). Rome, 1900.

Lewis, C. S. *Transposition, and Other Addresses.* London: G. Bles, 1949.

Liber divinorum operum. (Corpus Christianorum, Continuato Mediaevalis 92)

Lindblom, Johannes. *Gesichte und Offenbarungen. Vorstellungen von göttlichen Weisungen und übernatürlichen Erscheinungen im ältesten Christentum.* (Acta Reg. Societatis Humaniorum Litterarum Lundensis 65). Lund: Gleerup, 1968.

———. *Prophecy in Ancient Israel.* Oxford: Blackwell, 1962.

Lohmeyer, Ernst. *Grundlagen paulinischer Theologie.* (Beiträge zur historischen Theologie 1). Tübingen: Mohr, 1929.

Löhrer, Magnus. "Träger der Vermittlung." In *Die Grundlagen heilsgeschichtlicher Dogmatik*, edited by Johannes Feiner and Magnus Löhrer. (Mysterium Salutis 1). Einsiedeln: Benziger, 1965, 544–86.

Löhrer, Magnus, and Johannes Feiner. *Die Grundlagen heilsgeschichtlicher Dogmatik.* (Mysterium salutis 1: Grundriss heilsgeschichtlicher Dogmatik). Einsiedeln: Benziger, 1965.

Loisy, Alfred Firmin. *Autour d'un Petit Livre.* Paris: Picard, 1903.

———. *The Gospel and the Church.* Philadelphia: Fortress Press, 1976.

———. *L'Évangile et l'Église.* Paris: Picard, 1902.

Lora, Erminio, and Rita Simionati, eds. *Enchiridion delle Encicliche: Edizione Bilingue.* 8 vols. Bologna: Edizioni Dehoniane Bologna, 1994.

Loron, Philippe. *J'Ai Vu Écrire Vassula: Analyse Scientifique de la Vraie Vie en Dieu.* Paris: de Guibert, 1994.

Losel, Steffen. "Unapocalyptic Theology: History and Eschatology in Balthasar's Theo-Drama." *Modern Theology* 17, no. 2 (2001): 201–25.

Lossky, Vladimir. *Orthodox Theology.* Crestwood: St. Vladimir's Press, 1958.

Louth, Andrew. *The Origins of the Christian Mystical Tradition from Plato to Denys.* Oxford: Oxford University Press, 1981.

Lubac, Henri de. *Credo: Gestalt und Lebendigkeit unseres Glaubensbekenntnisses.* (Theologia Romanica 6). Einsiedeln: Johannes, 1975.

Lundskow, George N., ed. *Religious Innovation in a Global Age: Essays on the Construction of Spirituality.* Jefferson: McFarland, 2005.

Luther, Martin. *Dr. Martin Luthers Werke.* 67 vols. Vol. 46. Erlangen: Heyder, 1912.

———. *Works.* Edited by Jaroslav Jan Pelikan and Daniel E. Poellot. 55 vols. Vol. 24. Saint Louis: Concordia, 1961.

Mack, Burton L. *The Lost Gospel: The Book of Q and Christian Origins.* San Francisco: HarperCollins, 1994.

Madsen, Richard. *China's Catholics: Tragedy and Hope in an Emerging Civil Society.* (Comparative Studies in Religion and Society 12). Berkeley: University of California Press, 1998.

Mahoney, Rosemary. *The Singular Pilgrim: Travels on Sacred Ground.* Boston: Houghton Mifflin, 2003.

Malley, Francois. "*Las Casas* et les Théologies de la Libération." *La Vie Spirituelle* 139 (1985).

Mariotti, P. "Contestation Prophétique." In *Dictionnaire de la Vie Chrétienne.* Paris, 1983, 188–96.

Marriage, Sophia, and Jolyon P. Mitchell, eds. *Mediating Religion: Conversations in Media, Religion and Culture.* London: Clark, 2003.

Martin, Angela K., and Sandra Kryst. "Encountering Mary: Ritualization and Place Contagion in Postmodernity." In *Places through the Body*, edited by Heidi Nast and Steve Pile. London: Routledge, 1998, 207–29.

Martin, James. *Awake My Soul: Contemporary Catholics on Traditional Devotions.* Chicago: Loyola Press, 2004.

McBrien, Richard P. *Catholicism.* San Francisco: HarperSanFrancisco, 1994.

————. *The HarperCollins Encyclopedia of Catholicism.* San Francisco: HarperSan-Francisco, 1995.

McDonnell, Kilian, and George T. Montague. *Christian Initiation and Baptism in the Holy Spirit: Evidence from the First Eight Centuries.* Collegeville: Liturgical Press, 1991.

McGarvey, John W. *Short Essays in Biblical Criticism, Reprinted from the Christian Standard, 1893–1904.* Cincinnati: Standard, 1910.

McGinn, Bernard. "Apocalypticism and Church Reform (1100–1500)." In *The Encyclopedia of Apocalypticism,* edited by Bernard McGinn, John Joseph Collins, and Stephen J. Stein. Vol. 2. New York: Continuum, 1998, 74–109.

————. " 'To the Scandal of Men, Women Are Prophesying': Female Seers of the High Middle Ages." In *Fearful Hope: Approaching the New Millennium,* edited by Christopher Kleinhenz and Fannie LeMoine. Madison: University of Wisconsin Press, 1999, 59–85.

————. " 'Trumpets of the Mysteries of God': Prophetesses in Late Medieval Christianity." In *Propheten und Prophezeiungen/Prophets and Prophecies,* edited by Tilo Schabert and Matthias Riedl. Vol. 12. Würzburg: Königshausen und Neumann, 2005, 125–42.

McGrath, Alister E. *The Blackwell Encyclopedia of Modern Christian Thought.* Oxford: Blackwell, 1999.

McIntosh, Mark Allen. *Discernment and Truth: The Spirituality and Theology of Knowledge.* New York: Crossroad, 2004.

McKim, Donald K. *The Cambridge Companion to Martin Luther.* (Cambridge Companions to Religion). Cambridge: Cambridge University Press, 2003.

Meier-Staubach, Christel. "Ildegarde di Bingen: Profezia ed esistenza letteraria." In *Lo Statuto della Profezia nel Medioevo,* edited by G. L. Potestà and R. Rusconi. Bologna: Dehoniane, 1996, 2:271–303.

Melançon, Ovila. *Jesus Appelle sa Messagère.* Paris: de Guibert, 1994.

Messori, Vittorio. "Presentazione." In *Profezie per il Terzo Millennio,* edited by Antonio Gentili. Milan: Áncora, 2000.

Meter, David C. Van. "Apparitions." In *Marian Apparitions and Catholic Apocalypticism.* Available from http://members.aol.com/UticaCW/Mary-App.html. 2005 [accessed 21 July 2005].

————. "A Marian Bibliography." In *Marian Apparitions and Catholic Apocalypticism.* Available from http://members.aol.com/UticaCW/Mar-bibl.html. 2005 [accessed 21 July 2005].

Meyer, Christian. "Von der 'Privatoffenbarung' zur öffentlichen Lehrbefugnis: Legitimationsstufen des Prophetentums bei Rupert von Deutz, Hildegard von Bingen, und Elisabeth von Schönau." In *Das Öffentliche und Private in der Vormoderne,* edited by Peter von Moos und Gert Melville. Köln: Böhlau, 1998, 97–123.

Meyer, Rudolf. "Prophecy and Prophets in the Judaism of the Hellenistic-Roman Period." In *Theological Dictionary of the New Testament,* edited by Gerhard Kittel, Gerhard Friedrich, and Geoffrey William Bromiley. Grand Rapids: Eerdmans, 1969, 6:812–28.

Michel, Otto. *Prophet und Märtyrer*. (Beiträge zur Förderung christlicher Theologie 37, 2). Gütersloh, 1932.

Mommaers, Paul. *The Riddle of Christian Mystical Experience: The Role of the Humanity of Jesus*. (Louvain Theological & Pastoral Monographs 29). Louvain: Peeters Press, 2003.

Monin, Arthur. *Notre-Dame de Beauraing: Origines et Développements de Son Culte*. 2nd ed. Bruges: Pro Maria, Desclée de Brouwer, 1952.

Montague, George T. *The Spirit and His Gifts: The Biblical Background of Spirit-Baptism, Tongue-Speaking, and Prophecy*. New York: Paulist Press, 1974.

Montoya, Fernando Umaña. *Vassula: Un Charisme Oecuménique pour notre Temps*. Hauteville: Éditions du Parvis, 1995.

Mucci, Giandomenico. "Le Apparizioni: Teologia e Discernimento." *Civiltà Cattolica*, no. 4 (1989): 424–33.

———. *Rivelazioni Private e Apparizioni*. Rome: Civiltà Cattolica, 2000.

Myers, Jacob M., and Edwin D. Freed. "Is Paul Also Among the Prophets?" *Interpretation* 20 (1966): 40–53.

Nabhan-Warren, Kristy. *The Virgin of el Barrio: Marian Apparitions, Catholic Evangelizing, and Mexican American Activism*. (Qualitative Studies in Religion). New York: New York University Press, 2005.

The New Jerusalem Bible. Garden City: Doubleday, 1985.

Newman, Barbara. *God and the Goddesses: Vision, Poetry, and Belief in the Middle Ages*. Philadelphia: University of Pennsylvania Press, 2003.

———. "Hildegard and Her Hagiographers: The Remaking of Female Sainthood." In *Gendered Voices: Medieval Saints and Their Interpreters*, edited by Catherine M. Mooney. (Middle Ages series). Philadelphia: University Pennsylvania Press, 1999, 16–34.

Niederwimmer, Kurt, and Harold W. Attridge. *The Didache: A Commentary*. (Hermeneia—A Critical and Historical Commentary on the Bible). Minneapolis: Fortress Press, 1998.

Norelli, Enrico. "I Profeti nella Communità Cristiana." In *La Profezia*, edited by Enzo Bianchi. (Parola, Spirito e Vita 41). Bologna: Dehoniane, 2000, 147–72.

Nørgaard-Højen, Peder. "Einig in der Rechtfertigungslehre." *Ökumenische Rundschau* 1 (1996): 6–23.

Nyberg, Tore. "St. Bridget's Charism and Prophecy for Our Time." In *Saint Bridget: Prophetess of New Ages, Proceedings of the International Study Meeting, Rome, October 3–7, 1991*, edited by Tore Nyberg. Rome: Casa Generalizia Suore Santa Brigida, 1993, 404–16.

———, ed. *Saint Bridget: Prophetess of New Ages, Proceedings of the International Study Meeting, Rome, October 3–7, 1991*. Rome: Casa Generalizia Suore Santa Brigida, 1993.

O'Carroll, Michael. *Vassula of the Sacred Heart's Passion*. Belfast: J.M.J., 1993.

O'Collins, Gerald. "The Deposit of Faith." In *A New Dictionary of Christian Theology*, edited by Alan Richardson and John Bowden. London: SCM Press, 1983, 152–53.

———. *Fundamental Theology*. New York: Paulist Press, 1981.

————. *Retrieving Fundamental Theology: The Three Styles of Contemporary Theology.*
New York: Paulist Press, 1993.

O'Collins, Gerald, and Mario Farrugia. *Catholicism: The Story of Catholic Christianity.*
Oxford: Oxford University Press, 2003.

O'Connor, Edward. *Vassula and the CDF.* (Touched by the Spirit of God 2). Independence, Mo.: Trinitas, 1998.

O'Grady, John F. *Catholic Beliefs and Traditions: Ancient and Ever New.* New York:
Paulist Press, 2001.

O'Meara, Thomas F. *Theology of Ministry.* Rev. ed. New York: Paulist Press, 1999.

Oakes, Edward T., and David Moss. *The Cambridge Companion to Hans Urs von
Balthasar.* (Cambridge Companions to Religion). Cambridge: Cambridge University Press, 2004.

Odell, Catherine. *Those Who Saw Her: Apparitions of Mary.* Rev. ed. Huntington: Our
Sunday Visitor, 1995.

Öhler, Markus. "Jesus as Prophet: Remarks on Terminology." In *Jesus, Mark and Q:
The Teaching of Jesus and Its Earliest Records,* edited by Michael Labahn and
Andreas Schmidt. (Journal for the study of the New Testament. Supplement
series 214). Sheffield: Sheffield Academic Press, 2001, 125–42.

Omara, Robert. "Spiritual Gifts in the Church: A Study of 1 Corinthians 12:1–11."
Ph.D. diss., Lateran University, 1997.

Oraison, Marc. "Le Point de Vue du Médecin Psychiatre Clinicien sur les Apparitions." In *Vraies et Fausses Apparitions dans l'Église,* edited by Bernard Billet. 2nd
ed. (Sociéte française d'études mariales). Paris: Lethielleux, 1976, 127–52.

Packer, James I. *A Quest for Godliness: The Puritan Vision of the Christian Life.*
Wheaton: Crossway Books, 1990.

Pagliaroli, Jessy C. "Kodak Catholicism: Miraculous Photography and Its Significance
at a Post-conciliar Marian Apparition Site in Canada." *Canadian Catholic
Historical Association* 70 (2004): 71–93.

Panagopoulos, Johannes, ed. *Prophetic Vocation in the New Testament and Today.*
(Supplements to Novum Testamentum 45). Leiden: Brill, 1977.

Panakal, Justin. *Intimacy with God: Praying with St. Teresa of Avila.* Rome: Pontifical
Institute, 1993; reprint, 1997.

Pannenberg, Wolfhart. *Revelation as History.* New York: Macmillan, 1968.

Pannenberg, Wolfhart, and Theodor Schneider. *Verbindliches Zeugnis.* (Dialog der
Kirchen 7, 9, 10). Freiburg: Herder, 1992.

Paul VI. "Dogmatic Constitution on Divine Revelation Dei Verbum." In *Documents
from Vatican II.* Available from http://www.vatican.va/archive/hist_councils/
ii_vatican_council/documents/vat-ii_const_19651118_dei-verbum_en.html 1965
[accessed 1 November 2005].

————. *Dogmatic Constitution on the Church: Lumen Gentium.* Boston: St. Paul
Editions, 1965.

Perica, Vjekoslav. *Balkan Idols: Religion and Nationalism in Yugoslav States.* (Religion
and global politics). Oxford: Oxford University Press, 2002.

Perrone, Juan. *Praelectiones theologicae.* Vol. 21. 1866.

Pesch, Christian. "De Legato Divino." In *Compendium Theologiae dogmaticae.* Freiburg, 1913.

Petrides, Michael W. "Discernment and Scientific Study of the Visionairies in Medjugorje." *Catholic Transcript,* September 10, 1993.

Peyret, Raymond. *Marthe Robin: The Cross and the Joy.* New York: Alba House, 1983.

Pieller, Maria Paraklyta. *Deutsche Frauenmystik im XIII. Jahrhundert.* Vienna, 1928.

Piltz, Anders. "Inspiration, vision, profetia: Birgitta och teorierna om uppenbarelserna." In *Heliga Birgitta: Budskabet och förebilden. Föredrag vid jubileumssymposiet i Vadstena 3.–7. oktober 1991,* edited by Alf Härdelin and Mereth Lindgren. Västervik, 1993, 67–88.

———. "Uppenbarelserna och uppenbarelsen: Birgittas förhållande til Bibeln." In *Birgitta, hendes Værk og hendes Klostre i Norden,* edited by Tore Nyberg. Odense: Odense University Press, 1991, 447–69.

Pius X. *Actes de Pie X: Encycliques, Motu Proprio, Brefs, Allocutions, Actes des Dicastères, etc.* Paris: Maison de la Bonne Presse, 1920.

Pius XII. *Fulgens Corona.* Catholic Community Forum/Liturgical Publications of St. Louis. Available from http://www.catholic-forum.com/saints/bvm00016.htm .1954 [accessed 22 June 2005].

Plassmann, Joseph Otto. *Vom göttlichen Reichtum der Seele. Altflämische Frauenmystik.* Düsseldorf: Diederichs, 1951.

Pottmeyer, Hermann J. "Tradition." In *Dictionary of Fundamental Theology,* edited by René Latourelle and Rino Fisichella. New York: Crossroad, 1995, 1119–26.

Poulain, Auguste. *Revelations and Visions: Discerning the True and the Certain from the False or the Doubtful.* New York: Alba House, 1998.

Pseudo-Dionysius. *Pseudo-Dionysius: The Complete Works.* Translated by Colm Luibheid. (Classics of Western spirituality). New York: Paulist Press, 1987.

Purdy, W. A. "St. Birgitta, Her Times and Ours." In *Brigida: Una Santa Svedese. Birgitta: A Swedish Saint.* Rome: Bulzoni Editore, 1973, 61–100.

Rad, Gerhard von. *Old Testament Theology.* 2 vols. Vol. 2. Louisville: Westminster John Knox, 2001.

Rahner, Karl. "Der Tod Jesu und die Abgeschlossenheit der Offenbarung." In *Pluralisme et Oecuménisme en Recherches Théologiques: Mélanges offerts au R. P. Dockx OP,* edited by Yves Congar and R. P. Hoeckmann. Gembloux: Duculot, 1976, 263–72.

———. *The Dynamic Element in the Church.* Freiburg: Herder, 1964.

———. "Les Révélations Privées: Quelques Remarques Theologiques." *Revue d'Ascétique et Mystique* 25 (1949): 506–14.

———. "Private Revelations. Some Theological Observations (Translation of "Les révélations privées"). CatholicCulture.org. Available from http://www .catholicculture.org/docs/doc_view.cfm?recnum=202. 1949 [accessed December 2005].

———. "Privatoffenbarung." In *Herders Theologisches Taschenlexikon.* Freiburg, 1975, 80–82.

——. "Privatoffenbarung." In *Lexikon für Theologie und Kirche*, edited by Josef Höfer, Michael Buchberger, and Karl Rahner. Freiburg: Herder, 1963, 8:772–73.

——. *Saggi di Cristologia e di Mariologia*. 2nd ed. Cinisello Balsamo (MI): Edizioni San Paolo, 1967.

——. *Theological Investigations*. Baltimore: Helicon Press, 2001.

——. "Über Privatoffenbarungen." *Münchener katholische Kirchenzeitung* 40, no. 49 (1947): 352ff.

——. *Visionen und Prophezeiungen*. 2nd ed. (Quaestiones Disputatae 4). Freiburg: Herder, 1958.

——. *Visions and Prophecies*. London: Burns and Oats, 1963.

Rahner, Karl, and Paul Imhof. *Schriften zur Theologie*. Einsiedeln: Benziger, 2001.

Rahner, Karl, and Karl Lehmann. "Geschichtlichkeit der Vermittlung." In *Die Grundlagen heilsgeschichtlicher Dogmatik*. Einsiedeln: Benziger, 1965, 727–87.

Rahner, Karl, and Joseph Ratzinger. *Revelation and Tradition*. Freiburg: Herder, 1966.

Ranft, Patricia. *Women and the Religious Life in Premodern Europe*. New York: St. Martin's Press, 1996.

Ratzinger, Joseph. "Besprechungen zu W. Schachten, *Intellectus Verbi, Die Erkenntnis im Mitvollzug des Wortes nach Bonaventura*." *Theologische Revue* 75 (1975): 328–31.

——. "Christianity Always Carries within It a Structure of Hope: The Problem of Christian Prophecy." *Thirty Days*, January 1999, 72–83.

——. "Das Problem der Christlichen Prophetie: Niels Christian Hvidt im Gespräch mit Joseph Kardinal Ratzinger." *Communio* 2 (1999): 177–88.

——. *Das Problem der Dogmengeschichte in der Sicht der katholischen Theologie*. (Arbeitsgemeinschaft für Forschung des Landes Nordrhein-Westfalen, Geistes-wissenschaften 139). Köln: Westdeutscher Verlag, 1966.

——. "Doctrinal Commentary on the Concluding Formula of the Professio fidei." *Adoremus Bulletin* 4, no. 6 (1998).

——. "Ein Versuch zur Frage des Traditionsbegriffs." In *Offenbarung und Über-lieferung*, edited by Karl Rahner and Joseph Ratzinger. (Quaestiones Disputatae 25). Freiburg: Herder, 1965, 25–49.

——. "Letter Regarding Mrs. Vassula Rydén." In *True Life in God: Clarifications with the Congregation for the Doctrine of Faith*. Amsterdam: True Life in God NL, 2004, 8.

——. "Offenbarung-Schrift-Überlieferung: Ein Text des hl. Bonaventura." *Trierer Theologische Zeitschrift* 67 (1958): 13–27.

Ratzinger, Joseph, Tarcisio Bertone, and Congregatio Pro Doctrina Fidei. "Respon-sum ad dubium circa doctrinam in Epist. Ap. 'Ordinatio Sacerdotalis' traditam." *AAS* 87 (1995): 1114. Available from http://web.infinito.it/utenti/i/interface/ Ordinatio.html. 1995 [accessed December, 2005].

——. "Responsum ad dubium circa doctrinam in Epist. Ap. «Ordinatio Sacerdotalis» traditam." *AAS* 87 (1995): 1114.

Reiling, J. "Holy Spirit." In *Dictionary of Deities and Demons in the Bible*, edited by Karel Van Der Toorn, Pieter W. Van Der Horst, and Bob Becking. Grand Rapids: Eerdmans, 1999, 424.

Renczes, Philipp Gabriel. *Agir de Dieu et Liberté de l'Homme: Recherches sur l'Anthropologie Théologique de Saint Maxime le Confesseur.* Paris: Cerf, 2003.

Reymond, Robert L. *"What about Continuing Revelations and Miracles in the Presbyterian Church Today?" A Study of the Doctrine of the Sufficiency of Scripture.* Nutley: Presbyterian and Reformed, 1977.

Rickenmann, Abbé Agnell. "Letter of February Twenty-Third." In *The Catholic Church's Position Regarding TLIG*, edited by Maria Laura Pio. Available from http://mypage.bluewin.ch/cafarus/tligchurchposition.htm. 2005 [accessed 12 May 2005].

Ricoeur, Paul. *Dal Testo all'Azione.* Milan: Jaca Book, 1994.

Root, Michael. "The Development of Doctrine: A Lutheran Understanding and Its Ecumenical Application." *Ecclesiology* 2, no. 1 (2005): 35–51.

Roy, F. "Le Fait de Lourdes devant le Magistère." In *Maria et Ecclesia: Acta congressus mariologici-mariani in civitate Lourdes anno 1958 celebrati.* (Pontificia Academia Mariana Internationalis 12), 1962, 11–56.

Ruffin, Bernard. *Padre Pio: The True Story.* Rev. and expanded ed. Huntington: Our Sunday Visitor, 1991.

Ruthven, Jon. "Answering the Cessationists' Case against Continuing Spiritual Gifts." *Pneuma Review 3, no. 2*, available from http://www.pneumafoundation.com/resources/articles/answers02.pdf. 2000 [accessed December 2005].

———. "On the Cessation of the Charismata: The Protestant Polemic of Benjamin B. Warfield." *Pneuma* 12 (1990): 14–31.

———. *On the Cessation of the Charismata: The Protestant Polemic on Postbiblical Miracles.* Sheffield: Sheffield Academic Press, 1993.

Rutten, René. *Histoire Critique des Apparitions de Banneux.* Namur: Mouvement Eucharistique et Missionnaire, 1985.

Rydén, Vassula. *True Life in God.* 12 vols. Independence: Trinitas, 1991–2003.

Sahlin, Claire L. *Birgitta of Sweden and the Voice of Prophecy.* (Studies in Medieval Mysticism 3). Woodbridge: Boydell Press, 2001.

———. "Gender and Prophetic Authority in Birgitta of Sweden's Revelations." In *Gender and Text in the Later Middle Ages*, edited by Jane Chance. Gainesville: University Press of Florida, 1996, 69–95.

———. "Preaching and Prophesying: The Public Proclamation of Birgitta of Sweden's Revelations." In *Performance and Transformation: New Approaches to Late Medieaval Spirituality*, edited by Mary A. Suydam and Joanna E. Ziegler. New York: St. Martin's Press, 1999, 69–97.

———. "The Prophetess as Preacher: Birgitta of Sweden and the Voice of Prophecy." *Medieval Sermon Studies* 40 (1997): 29–44.

Saint-Joseph, Lucien-Marie de. "Jean de la Croix." In *Dictionnaire de Spiritualité Ascétique et Mystique: Doctrine et Histoire*, edited by M. Viller, F. Cavallera, J. de Guibert, A. Rayaz, A. Derville, P. Lamarche, and A. Solignac. Paris: Beauchesne, 1974, 8:408–47.

Sainte-Marie-Madeleine, Gabriel de. *Visions et Vie Mystique.* Paris, 1955.

Salmann, Elmar. *Der geteilte Logos: Zum offenen Prozess von neuzeitlichem Denken und Theologie.* (Studia Anselmiana 111). Rome: Edizioni Abbazia S. Paolo, 1992.

Sánchez-Ventura, and Pascual Francisco. *The Apparitions of Garabandal.* Pasadena: St. Michael's Garabandal Center, 1997.

Sanders, E. P. *The Historical Figure of Jesus.* London: Penguin Press, 1993.

Sandmel, Samuel. *Judaism and Christian Beginnings.* Oxford: Oxford University Press, 1978.

Sandnes, Karl Olav. *Paul, One of the Prophets? A Contribution to the Apostle's Self-Understanding.* (Wissenschaftliche Untersuchungen zum Neuen Testament 2d Series 43). Tübingen: Mohr, 1991.

Sato, Migaku. *Q und Prophetie: Studien zur Gattungs- und Traditionsgeschichte der Quelle Q.* (Wissenschaftliche Untersuchungen zum Neuen Testament 29). Tübingen: Mohr, 1988.

Saudreau, Auguste. *L'État Mystique, sa Nature, ses Phases et les Faits Extraordinaires de la Vie Spirituelle.* 2nd ed. Paris, 1921.

Schäfer, Peter. *Die Vorstellung vom heiligen Geist in der rabbinischen Literatur.* (Studien zum Alten und Neuen Testament 28). Munich: Kösel-Verlag, 1972.

Scheeben, Matthias Joseph. *Handbuch der katholischen Dogmatik.* Vol. 1. Freiburg: Herder, 1878.

———. *Theologische Erkenntnislehre.* Freiburg: Herder, 1903.

Scheffczyk, Leo. *Die theologischen Grundlagen von Erscheinungen und Prophezeiungen.* Leutesdorf: Johannes-Verlag, 1982.

———. "Prophetin (Prophetissa)." In *Marienlexikon,* edited by Remigius Bäumer and Leo Scheffczyk. St. Ottilien: EOS Verlag, 1988, 5:324–25.

Schlosser, Marianne. *Lucerna in caliginoso loco:Aspekte des Prophetie-Begriffes in der scholastischen Theologie.* (Veröffentlichungen des Grabmann-Institutes 43). Paderborn: Schöningh, 2000.

Schmaus, Michael. *Handbuch der Dogmengeschichte.* Freiburg: Herder, 1956.

Schmeller, Thomas. *Das Recht der Anderen: Befreiungstheologische Lektüre des Neuen Testaments in Lateinamerika.* (Neutestamentliche Abhandlungen; n.F., 27). Münster: Aschendorff, 1994.

Schmitz, Josef. "Das Christentum als Offenbarungsreligion im kirchlichen Bekenntnis." In *Handbuch der Fundamentaltheologie,* edited by Walter Kern, Hermann Josef Pottmeyer, and Max Seckler. Freiburg: Herder, 1985, 2:15–28.

Schöllgen, Georg. "The Didache as a Church Order: An Examination of the Purpose for the Composition of the Didache and Its Consequences for Its Interpretation." In *The Didache in Modern Research,* edited by Jonathan A. Draper. (Arbeiten zur Geschichte des antiken Judentums und des Urchristentums 37). Leiden: Brill, 1996, 43–71.

Schönborn, Christoph von. "Offenbarung und Privatoffenbarung." *Katechesen 1999/2000,* available from http://www.kirchenweb.at/schoenborn/. 1999 [accessed 18 June 2005].

Schumacher, Joseph. *Der apostolische Abschluss der Offenbarung Gottes.* (Freiburger theologische Studien 114). Freiburg: Herder, 1979.

Schüssler Fiorenza, Elisabeth. "Apokalypsis and Propheteia: The Book of Revelation in the Context of Early Christian Prophecy." In *L'Apocalopyse Johannique et l'Apocalyptique dans le Nouveau Testament*, edited by J. Lambrecht. Louvain: Duculot, 1980, 105–28.

———. *The Book of Revelation: Justice and Judgment*. Philadelphia: Fortress Press, 1985.

Schwebel, Lisa J. *Apparitions, Healings, and Weeping Madonnas: Christianity and the Paranormal*. New York: Paulist Press, 2004.

Seckler, Max. "Der Begriff der Offenbarung." In *Handbuch der Fundamentaltheologie*, edited by Walter Kern, Hermann Josef Pottmeyer, and Max Seckler. Freiburg: Herder, 1985, 2:60–84.

———. "Die ekklesiologische Bedeutung des Systems der 'Loci theologici.'" In *Weisheit Gottes, Weisheit der Welt: Festschrift für Joseph Kardinal Ratzinger zum 60. Geburtstag*, edited by Walter Baier. St. Ottilien: EOS Verlag, 1987, 1:37–65.

Serre, Jacques, and Béatrice Caux. *Garabandal: Apparitions Prophétiques de Marie*. Paris: de Guibert, 1999.

Shogren, Gary-Steven. "Christian Prophecy and Canon in the Second Century: A Response to Benjamin B. Warfield." *Journal of the Evangelical Theological Society* 40 (1997): 609–26.

Siebers, Tobin, ed. *Religion and the Authority of the Past*. Ann Arbor: University of Michigan Press, 1993.

Sigl, Paul Maria. *Die Frau aller Völker*. Amsterdam: Pro Deo et Fratribus, 1998.

Silvas, Anna. *Jutta and Hildegard: The Biographical Sources*. (Brepols Medieval Women Series). University Park: Pennsylvania State University Press, 1999.

Smith, Morton. *Jesus the Magician*. San Francisco: Harper and Row, 1981.

Söll, Georg. *Dogma und Dogmenentwicklung*. (Handbuch der Dogmengeschichte 1, 5). Freiburg: Herder, 1971.

Sommer, Benjamin D. "Did Prophecy Cease? Evaluating a Reevaluation." *Journal of Biblical Literature* 115 (1996): 31–47.

Spretnak, Charlene. *Missing Mary: the Queen of Heaven and Her Re-emergence in the Modern Church*. New York: Palgrave Macmillan, 2004.

Stenico, Tommaso, and Francis A. Arinze. *Il Concilio Vaticano II: Carisma e Profezia*. Vatican City: Libreria Editrice Vaticana, 1997.

Stenzel, Alois. "Liturgie als Theologischer Ort." In *Die Grundlagen heilsgeschichtlicher Dogmatik*, edited by Johannes Feiner and Magnus Löhrer. (Mysterium Salutis 1). Einsiedeln: Benziger, 1965, 608–21.

Stockmeier, Peter. "Offenbarung in der Kirche." In *Die Offenbarung, Von der Schrift bis zum Ausgang der Scholastik: Handbuch der Dogmengeschichte*, edited by Ed. M. Seybold. Freiburg: Herder, 1971, 1:27–87.

Stolpe, Sven. *Birgitta i Rom*. 5th ed. Stockholm: Askild & Kärnekull, 1980.

Streeter, Burnett Hillman. *The Primitive Church, Studied with Special Reference to the Origins of the Christian Ministry*. London: Macmillan, 1929.

Stronstad, Roger. *The Prophethood of All Believers: A Study in Luke's Charismatic Theology*. (Journal of Pentecostal Theology. Supplement Series 16). Sheffield: Sheffield Academic Press, 1999.

Studer, Basil. "Träger der Vermittlung." In *Die Grundlagen heilsgeschichtlicher Dogmatik*, edited by Johannes Feiner and Magnus Löhrer. (Mysterium Salutis 1). Einsiedeln: Benziger, 1965, 588–605.

Stull, Andrew T. *Religion on the Internet 1999–2000: A Prentice Hall Guide*. Upper Saddle River: Prentice Hall, 2000.

Suh, Augustinus. *Le Rivelazioni Private nella Vita della Chiesa*. Bologna: Dehoniane, 2000.

Sullivan, Randall. *The Miracle Detective: An Investigation of Holy Visions*. New York: Atlantic Monthly Press, 2004.

Sweeney, Marvin A. "The Truth in True and False Prophecy." In *Truth: Interdisciplinary Dialogues in a Pluralistic Age*, edited by Kristin De Troyer, Katie Goetz, and Christine Helmer. (Studies in Philosophical Theology 22). Louvain: Peeters, 2003, 9–26.

Talbert, Charles H. *Reading Corinthians: A Literary and Theological Commentary on 1 and 2 Corinthians*. New York: Crossroad, 1987.

Tampere, G. "Revelatio privata: Revelatio privata et progressus dogmaticus." Ph.D. diss., 1954.

Tavard, George H. *The Thousand Faces of the Virgin Mary*. Collegeville: Liturgical Press, 1996.

Teresa of Avila. *The Collected Works of St. Teresa of Avila*. Translated by Kieran Kavanaugh and Otilio Rodriguez. 5 vols. Washington: Institute of Carmelite Studies, 1976.

Terrin, Aldo Natale. *Religioni, Esperienza, Verità. Saggi di Fenomenologia della Religione*. Urbino: Quattro Venti, 1986.

Thiel, John E. *Senses of Tradition: Continuity and Development in Catholic Faith*. Oxford: Oxford University Press, 2000.

Thomas Aquinas. "Summa Theologica." In *The Collected Works of St. Thomas Aquinas*. Available from http://eresources.library.nd.edu/databases/aquinas. 1993 [accessed 1 July 2005].

Tierney, J. C., and Michael P. Duricy. *Marian Apparitions of the Twentieth Century*. Available from http://www.udayton.edu/mary/resources/aprtable.html. 2005 [accessed 21 July 2005].

Tjørhom, Ola. *Visible Church, Visible Unity: Ecumenical Ecclesiology and "The Great Tradition of the Church."* (Unitas Books 3). Collegeville: Liturgical Press, 2004.

Toniolo, Alessandro. "Il Catecumenato: Periodo Liminale?" *Rivista Liturgica* 79 (1992): 249–68.

———. "Il Tema 'Liminalità' in Victor Turner: Un Contributo Antropologico-Culturale alla Riflessione sulle Forme di Iniziazione Religiosa." *Rivista Liturgica* 79 (1992): 86–105.

———. "Nostalgia delle Origini: Profezia o Anarchia Celebrativa?" *Rivista Liturgica* 84 (1997): 787–812.

Tonquédec, Joseph de. "Apparitions." In *Dictionnaire de Spiritualité Ascétique et Mystique: Doctrine et Histoire*, edited by M. Viller, F. Cavallera, J. de Guibert,

A. Rayaz, A. Derville, P. Lamarche, and A. Solignac. Paris: Beauchesne, 1993, 16:801–9.

Torrell, Jean-Pierre. *Recherches sur la Théorie de la Prophétie au Moyen Âge, XIIe–XIVe Siècles: Études et Textes.* (Dokimion 13). Fribourg: Éditions Universitaires Fribourg Suisse, 1992.

Toussaint, Fernand, and Camille J. Joset. *Beauraing: 1932–1982.* Paris: Desclée De Brouwer, 1981.

Tugwell, Simon, ed. *Albert and Thomas: Selected Writings.* Translated by Simon Tugwell. (Classics of Western Spirituality). New York: Paulist Press, 1988.

Turner, Max. *The Holy Spirit and Spiritual Gifts: In the New Testament Church and Today.* Rev. ed. Peabody: Hendrickson, 1998.

———. "Spiritual Gifts Then and Now." *Vox Evangelica* 15 (1985): 7–64.

Turner, Victor Witter. *Dramas, Fields, and Metaphors: Symbolic Action in Human Society.* (Symbol, Myth, and Ritual Series). Ithaca: Cornell University Press, 1974.

———. *The Forest of Symbols: Aspects of Ndembu Ritual.* Ithaca: Cornell University Press, 1967.

———. *From Ritual to Theatre: The Human Seriousness of Play.* (Performance Studies Series 1). New York City: Performing Arts Journal, 1982.

———. "La Religione nell'Antropologia Culturale." *Concilium* 16 (1980): 143ff.

———. *The Ritual Process: Structure and Anti-Structure.* (The Lewis Henry Morgan Lectures). New York: de Gruyter, 1995.

Turner, Victor Witter, and Edith L. B. Turner. *Image and Pilgrimage in Christian Culture: Anthropological Perspectives.* (Lectures on the History of Religions 11). New York: Columbia University Press, 1978.

Underhill, Evelyn. *The Essentials of Mysticism and Other Essays.* London: Dent, 1920.

Valentini, Eugenio. "Rivelazioni Private e Fatti Dogmatici." *Maria et Ecclesia* (1962): 1–9.

Van Erp, Stephan, Hille Haker, and Erik Borgman, eds. *Cyberspace-Cyberethics-Cybertheology.* London: SCM Press, 2005.

Vergote, Antoine. "Visions et Apparitions, Approche Psychologique." *Revue Théologique de Louvain* 22 (1991): 202–25.

Voaden, Rosalynn, and Stephanie Volf. "Visions of My Youth: Representations of the Childhood of Medieval Visionaries." *Gender and History* 12, no. 3 (2000): 665–84.

Volken, Laurent. *Les Révélations dans l'Église.* Mulhouse, France: Salvator, 1961.

———. "Um die theologische Bedeutung der Privatoffenbarungen: Zu einem Buch von Karl Rahner." *Freiburger Zeitschrift für Philosophie und Theologie* 6 (1959): 431–39.

———. *Visions, Revelations and the Church.* New York: Kenedy, 1963.

Vooght, Paul de. *Les Sources de la Doctrine Chrétienne d'après les Théologiens du XIVe Siècle et Début du XV.* Bruges: Desclée De Brouwer, 1954.

Warfield, Benjamin Breckinridge. *Miracles, Yesterday and Today, True and False.* Grand Rapids: Eerdmans, 1953.

Warner, Marina. *Joan of Arc: The Image of Female Heroism.* New York: Knopf, 1981.

Warren, Nancy Bradley. *Spiritual Economies: Female Monasticism in Later Medieval England.* (Middle Ages Series). Philadelphia: University of Pennsylvania Press, 2001.

Watt, Diane. *Secretaries of God: Women Prophets in Late Medieval and Early Modern England*. Woodbridge: Brewer, 1997.

Weber, Hans-Ruedi. "Prophecy in the Ecumenical Movement." In *Prophetic Vocation in the New Testament and Today 45*, edited by J. Panagopoulos. (Supplements to Novum Testamentum). Leiden: Brill, 1977, 218ff.

Weible, Wayne. *The Final Harvest: Medjugorje at the End of the Century*. Brewster: Paraclete Press, 1999.

Wicks, Jared. "*Dei Verbum* Developing: Vatican II's Revelation Doctrine 1963–1964." In *The Convergence of Theology: A Festschrift Honoring Gerald O'Collins, S.J*, edited by Stephen T. Davis and Daniel Kendall. New York: Paulist Press, 2001, 109–25.

———. *La Divina Rivelazione e la sua Trasmissione. Manuale di Studio*. 2nd ed. Rome: Pontificia Università Gregoriana, 1996.

———. "Loci Theologici." In *Dictionary of Fundamental Theology*, edited by René Latourelle and Rino Fisichella. New York: Crossroad, 1995, 605–7.

Williams, Janet P. "Pseudo-Dionysius and Maximus the Confessor." In *The First Christian Theologians: An Introduction to Theology in the Early Church*, edited by G. R. Evans. (The Great Theologians). Malden: Blackwell, 2004, 186–200.

Witherington, Ben. *Jesus the Seer: The Progress of Prophecy*. Peabody: Hendrickson, 1999.

Wolfson, Harry Austryn. *Philo: Foundations of Religious Philosophy in Judaism, Christianity, and Islam*. (Structure and Growth of Philosophic Systems from Plato to Spinoza 2). Cambridge: Harvard University Press, 1947.

Woods, Richard. *Mysticism and Prophecy: The Dominican Tradition*. (Traditions of Christian Spirituality). London: Darton, Longman and Todd, 1998.

Woodward, Kenneth L. *Making Saints: How the Catholic Church Determines Who Becomes a Saint, Who Doesn't, and Why*. New York: Simon and Schuster, 1990.

Wright, George Ernest. *God Who Acts: Biblical Theology as Recital*. (Studies in Biblical Theology 8). London: SCM Press, 1952.

Wuthnow, Robert. *After Heaven: Spirituality in America since the 1950s*. Berkeley: University of California Press, 1998.

Young, Glenn. "Reading and Praying Online: The Continuity of Religion Online and Online Religion in Internet Christianity." In *Religion Online: Finding Faith on the Internet*, edited by Lorne L. Dawson and Douglas E. Cowan. New York: Routledge, 2004, 93–105.

Zaleski, Jeffrey P. *The Soul of Cyberspace: How New Technology Is Changing Our Spiritual Lives*. San Francisco: HarperEdge, 1997.

Zenit. "Pope Consecrates Third Millenium to Our Lady of Fatima." In *Vatican Dossier*. Available from http://zenit.org/english/archive/0003/ZE000322.html#item5. 2000 [accessed 16 July 2005].

Zimdars-Swartz, Sandra. *Encountering Mary: From La Salette to Medjugorje*. Princeton: Princeton University Press, 1991.

Zizioulas, Metropolitan John of Pergamon. "Apostolic Continuity of the Church and Apostolic Succession in the First Five Centuries." *Louvain Studies* 21 (1996): 153–68.

Index